WHEN GOD BECAME HUMAN

Owen Crouch

When God Became Human

COLLEGE PRESS PUBLISHING COMPANY
Joplin, Missouri

International Standard Book Number: 0-89900-374-5

TO

My family which always has been supportive:

Lucille, wife whose loyal devotion has lifted the spirit through the firey trials of life;

James Edwin, son whose pursuit of excellence in every venture has left its imprint on many, not least of whom is his father;

Lorna Jeanne, daughter whose insight and intensity of faith are an inspiration to others, including her father!

PREFACE

This book is a part of an ongoing series of works which include diagrams of the Greek and English text of the New Testament. The College Press of Joplin, Missouri published Hebrews and Revelation. Romans (Not Guilty) was published privately by the author.

These works contain five features: A translation, outline, exposition of each paragraph. Also a diagram of every sentence in both Greek and English with grammatical notes to assist the student to work through the diagrams.

The present volume follows the format of Romans being divided into Book I and Book II. Book II contains the diagrams accompanied by grammatical notes. Book I displays the outlines and expositions. The present volume has eliminated translations to shorten the work.

In the series this is the first of the four Gospels to appear. Though the Gospel writers drew on similar sources each author states his own view of the Christ, his nature and mission. It has been my constant effort to uncover Luke's particular emphasis as he unfolds the living Lord. It's been a joy to discover Luke's skillful portrayal of Jesus as God's human revelation of his divine nature. "To sin is human" is not the whole truth. Man, God's human creation, became sinful, He wasn't created in order to be sinful. He was created in the "image" of God, morally pure, spiritual in quality, ethically righteous and mature. Thus it is the human point at which God could enter his creation at the creature's level without sacrificing any of his divine nature. Luke grasped this idea of the humanity of God in Jesus. That is a bold large line in Luke's sketch of the "Word" become flesh.

Growing out of that same creation of divine nature appearing as human nature is its essential universality. That which is human is universally human in any age, time, culture, race or nation. That which is human is universal and what is universal is human! Luke also saw and struck that chord. Sometimes in a minor, sometimes major, this double stress is noted in the expositions of Luke's view of the Christ.

This is not a commentary in the usual sense of the word. But it does include some attention to every sentence, particularly in the diagrams. And no paragraph is neglected in the outlines or expositions. It goes forth with the hope and prayer that God may make good use of it to His glory and man's redemption!

202 University Parkway 24E
Johnson City, Tennessee 37604
January 1991

CONTENTS

BOOK I

Outlines - Expositions

AN OUTLINE OF LUKE

Prologue: Statement of literary purpose! 1:1-4
I. THE ADVENT OF GOD AS MAN. 1:5-4:13
Luke displays the origin, development, and preparation of
Jesus as a complete man for work as saviour of mankind.
1. The origin, birth, revealing to men. 1:5-2:20
   A. Earliest announcements of his advent. 1:5-56
     (a)To Zacharias of the forerunner. 1:5-25
     (b)To Mary: her song to Elizabeth. 1:26-56
   B. The forerunner's birth; song of Zacharias. 1:57-80
   C. His birth; angels' song to shepherds. 2:1-20
2. Jesus develops perfect human nature under law, human
   and divine. 2:21-52
   A. In the Temple at Jerusalem. 2:21-40
     (a) His circumcision and presentation. 2:21-24
     (b) Songs of Simeon and Anna. 2:25-38
     (c) Childhood growth in Nazareth. 2:39-40
   B. Visit to Jerusalem at 12 years of age. 2:41-52
3. Special preparation for his work as saviour. 3:1-4:13
   A. The forerunner's work until Jesus' baptism. 3:1-22
   B. Genealogy traced to Adam, son of God. 3:23-38
   C. Temptation in the wilderness. 4:1-13
II. WORK OF THE HUMAN GOD FOR THE JEW. 4:14-9:50
1. Teaching in Galilean synagogues. 4:14-6:11
   A. Nazareth. Universal gospel rejected. 4:14-30
   B. Capernaum: dead raised, sin forgiven, lordship
     asserted. Rejected by leaders. 4:31-6:11
2. Constitution & development of kingdom of God. 6:12-9:50
   A. The constitution. 6:12-8:3
     (a)Call of the 12; Sermon on the plain. 6:12-49
     (b)Human faith(centurion); divine mercy(widow's
     son). 7:1-15
     (c)Embraces all classes: people, publicans, penitent
     woman,"ministering women."Excludes pride.7:16-8:3
   B. Development of the kingdom. 8:4-56
     (a)From seed of truth(sower). 8:4-18
     (b)By obedience to the word(his family). 8:19-21
     (c)By faith in the power of Jesus: displayed in
     four signs: storm, demoniacs & swine, daughter
     of Jairus, woman with issue of blood. 8:22-56
   C. Kingdom claims pressed on Galilean Jews and his
     disciples. 9:1-50
     (a)Mission of 12:fame, withdrawal, miracles.9:1-17
     (b)Peter's confession. Prediction of his death
     and their cross. 9:18-27
     (c)Transfiguration confirms the cross. Epileptic
     in the valley, a cross of service. 9:28-43
     (d)2nd teaching of death;ambition rebuked.9:43-50
III.WORK OF THE HUMAN GOD FOR THE GENTILE WORLD. 9:51-18:30
In Perea the universal man reveals God's grace
1. Last trip to Jerusalem; Gospel goes to Gentiles.9:51-11:13

1

A. Envoys to Samaria refused: The 70 sent. 9:51-10:24
B. Mankind is one family; one thing needed; the
   Holy Spirit the one way to get it. 10:25-11:13
2.Condemnation of religious of the age. 11:14-13:21
A. Rejection by hypocritical Pharisees contrasted to
   humility.(Dumb demoniac; unwashen hands).11:14-12:12
B. Covetous Jew contrasted to faithful steward.12:13-53
C. Impending judgment(barren fig tree). Mercy and God's
   kingdom(Sabbath healing). Kingdom's expansion and
   transforming growth(mustard seed & leaven).12:54-13:21
3. God's grace: universal for sinners. 13:22-15:32
A. Question: "Are few saved?" Answer:"Strive to enter."
   Jew "shutout." Gentile received. Revealed by series
   of parables. 13:22-14:24
B. Cost of kingdom citizenship. 14:25-34
C. God's kingdom is for sinners. 15:1-32
4. Life in the kingdom of God. 16:1-18:30
A. Life of faithful stewardship(unjust steward; rich
   man and Lazarus) 16:1-31
B. Life of forgiveness, humility(master and servant),
   gratitude(Samaritan leper), patient waiting. 17:1-37
C. Life of prayer(unjust judge; Pharisee & publican),
   obedient self-denial(rich young ruler). 18:1-30
IV. SACRIFICE OF THE HUMAN GOD FOR EVERY MAN. 18:31-23:49
1. Preparation for sacrificial offering. 18:31-22:38
A. Prediction of death; approach to Jerusalem;
   the public royal entry. 18:31-19:46
B. Verifying Messiahship in the temple. 19:47-21:4
C. 2nd coming; Jews rejected; Gentiles received.21:5-36
D. Passover week; conspiracy advances. 21:37-22:38
2. Jesus yields self as sacrificial offering. 22:39-23:49
A. Gethsemane, betrayal, arrest, trials, sentence and
   delivery to executioners. 22:39-23:25
B. The crucifixion. Prayer for executioners, word to
   dying thief, centurion's testimony. 23:26-49
V. THE HUMAN GOD, SAVIOUR OF ALL PEOPLE. 23:50-24:53
1. Burial: common to all men. 23:50-56
2. Resurrection: fulfillment of prophecy about himself as
   son of man and a pledge for all mankind. 24:1-12
3. God's plan has always been for repentance and forgiveness for all peoples. 24:13-53

1:1-4	1:5-4:13	4:14-9:50	9:51-19:27	19:28-23:56	24:1-53
Introduction	30 years preparation	2½ years of Galilean Ministry	6 months Ministry "to Jerusalem."	8 days Jerusalem Ministry	50 days Ministry after Resurrection

2

AN OUTLINE OF LUKE 1:1-4

Firm Footings For Faith!

The literature of the Bible sprang from mortal lacks and the compulsion of human crises. Apostle, poet, prophet, historian, psalmist labored under divine constraint to answer felt needs. Some one or some situation cried out because of hurt. Such was true of the Luke-Acts salvation history. Luke wrote to give assurance to a friend in need.

I. THE NEED OF THEOPHILUS.
    1. His racial cultural level.
    2. Prior instruction left him lacking.
    3. Needed more knowledge for greater assurance.
II. THE NEED OF LUKE, THE AUTHOR
    1. To express faith: "it seemed good to me."
    2. For a more comprehensive account.
III. NEED FOR RESEARCH AND WRITING.
    1. Reliable sources: "eye-witnesses."
    2. Method: An orderly connected account.

Luke's narrative is more than an accumulation of historical facts. He must explain the meaning of the facts in relation to the whole salvation history. His is the story of God's entrance into human affairs in the person of Jesus of Nazareth. It's the record of God's activity among and for humanity. It began in the heart of God, came through the virgin's womb, climaxed at Calvary and the open tomb. It advanced through every inhibiting barrier until the story of salvation got to Rome, center and heart of world empire.

FIRM FOOTINGS FOR FAITH!

Half informed is not well informed. It's not that which one knows that weakens faith. It's what one doesn't know! "For lack of knowledge the people perish." If anything is worse than ignorance, it is half knowledge. Garbled information beclouds vision, fosters failure, assures disaster. Truth builds faith!

If his incipient faith was to rest on sound footing, Luke's friend, Theophilus, must gain more knowledge than he thus far had. Full facts faithfully reported form a foundation for firm faith. Moreover the significance of those facts must be clearly explained. The story of Jesus ought be told from beginning to end, from its earliest origins to its ultimate goal. Anything short of that would leave faith vulnerable to degrading defeat in the crisis of life.

"Many Wrote!"

It would hardly be possible for people who witnessed the ministry and miracles of Jesus not to tell others. And had they come from afar they would write to tell others. If five thousand experienced the feeding from the five barley loaves and two fish, that means that other thousands heard about it from those who were present.

"Inasmuch as many attempted to arrange a connected account of the events..." By "connected account" Luke means something

3

other than isolated fragmentary stories. Some wrote extended narratives. And a few of these narratives grew into full length "lives" of Jesus. Such "lives" used sources from eye witnesses of the events about which they wrote. They were logical, well arranged narratives describing that which Jesus said and did.

Some of these eye-witnesses became "ministers of the word." They included the twelve who "from the beginning" faced daily dealings with Jesus. They were men of integrity who saw plainly, thought clearly, and reported accurately. They sealed their testimony with their blood. A fact is established as a fact when testified to by a plurality of honest, intelligent, eye witnesses. Thus faith in Christ rests on the best evidence available in human affairs. Firm foundations rest on research into the testimony of those whose eyes, ears, taste and touch witness to the truth of that to which they testify. "That which we have heard...seen...and hands handled"(I Jn.1:1)form the firm footing on which Christian belief rests.

The Need for Writing!
Theophilus was a Gentile, a Greek of noble quality. He had garnered some instruction in Christian thought. At least he had been informed about this faith, fast spreading through the Gentile world. Was it sectarianism with a Jewish flavor? Was it religious racism sheltered by a universalism with Mosaic cultural norms? Was it a fanatic cult? Or could it be God's redemptive approach to humanity?

As a Greek Theophilus would hold to the human longing for reason, order and beauty. Ethics, philosphy, art and science reflect the Greek search for truth, goodness and virtue. That which was human appealed to sensitive Greek spirits. Theophilus was just such a man. He was typical of the vast Gentile world of men. The needs of Theophilus were those of mankind.

Many had already written. In justifying his own writing Luke asserts, "To me it seemed good also." He was a physician. In his professional practice he became familiar with many forms of human pain. Orphans, widows, social outcast, soldier and saint were objects of his medical concern. From the sensitivity, both as to manner and content, with which he wrote we conclude that he was involved with humanity without regard to race, color, creed, or social status. He saw men as people, not classes, races, or fragments. His Christ was divine in nature but one who came to, for and with any or all human beings. If Matthew presented Jesus as "son of David, son of Abraham," and Mark revealed him as mighty "son of God," Luke unveiled him as "son of man." Luke's Christ came "to seek and to save" him who was lost whoever that might be. Theophilus needed to know for certain that God's son was that kind of a Christ. Moreover, for his own good, Luke needed to tell the whole story. It was proper that such a sensitive author write to that kind of Gentile a complete account of that kind of saviour. Thus, "...to me it seemed good also..."

The Full Account
Luke does not fault the many who preceeded him. In fact, he obviously read some of them. From them he found personal power

4

as well as material for his own story. But he did sense a lack. They did not tell enough, at least not enough for his Greek friend. What they tell is good but something vital is wanting. If the story is to be complete, thorough and in a sequence to build conviction then some author must supply the lack. Luke responds to that need. He aims to write a full account reaching from the heart of God through Bethlehem's manger, the cross and open tomb even to Rome, the world capital of the human race.

If Luke did not learn the gospel from Paul he was greatly influenced by the apostle's grasp of the universal goal of the gospel. It was Paul who turned the tide of gospel history from narrow Jewish sectarianism into a broad stream of universal redemption. Not law but grace, not race but humanity, not out ward conformity but inner heart was the central factor in the gospel as Paul preached it. The secret of the ages, now "made known," was that the "Gentiles are fellow-heirs, members of the same body, and partakers of the promise..."(Eph.3:6) From Paul Luke drank deeply of the wine of this truth. His Greek temperament was rich soil for such seed.

Salvation history which Luke authored(Luke-Acts)accents two aspects of the gospel: (1)God's world-wide, age-long universal love for all men and (2)redemption through the free grace of God revealed in Jesus Christ. By choice of episodes, subtle touches in style, Luke shows the divine Christ as a most human saviour. Luke's Christ reached to all kinds of outcasts--women, children, unclean (ceremonial & otherwise), publican, prodigal, Samaritan, shepherd, thief, prostitute. No level of society is denied his refining, redeeming touch. Matthew sees Jesus as Messianic king of God's Israel. Mark paints Jesus as God's powerful son. John reveals the eternal cosmic Christ in the laboratory of time subject to the scrutiny of ear, eye and hand of men. It is given to Luke alone to show God's son as man among men. No point of man's pain is neglected by the feel of his human hand. All three synoptics draw on Isaiah 40 to show John the Baptist preaching the preparatory message. But it is peculiar to Luke to include in the reference, "And all flesh shall see the salvation of God."(Lk.3:6) And all three of these writers make mention of a leper whom Jesus healed. But it's only Luke who enlivens the picture with the detail, "he was full of leprosy." Jesus felt the depth of man's misery. All men in the deepest needs were the object of salvation to Luke's Christ. Using some of the same stories Luke's emphasis rests on God's universal love and his incredible grace.

Nor is Luke's account complete with the crucifixion and resurrection. In chapter 24 Luke reports Christ as saying, "Thus it is written, that the Christ should suffer and the third day rise from the dead and that repentance and remission of sins should be preached...to all nations."(24:45f) That which Jesus "began" appears in the first treatise. That which he continued is told in Luke's second treatise, the Acts. Until God's universal grace gets out to the whole world Luke's story is not complete. Acts continues the ever-widening advance of the Christ and his gospel. Luke follows the gospel's victory as it surmounts each hindering barrier, racial, religious, social, human, and governmental, until it reaches Rome, its inevitable goal. When it gets to this hub of all that's human the story stops. Though obstacles restrain nothing can halt God's ever forward outreaching to his lost prodigals. What is implicit in other gospel writers is explicit in Luke. He tells the entire story. His narrative is thorough, accurate, orderly, complete. It furnished Theophilus a certainty for faith that fits every demand of any human heart for assurance.

* * * * * *

AN OUTLINE OF LUKE 1:5-25

Some Human Roots!

Theophilus had some information about Jesus as the Christ of God. He was not without reports of the <u>divine</u> nature of Jesus. But as a Greek he needed to apprehend the genuine <u>human</u> quality of the origins of Christ. That the Christ's roots were acutely human needed buttressing.

    I.   A PERSONAL PROBLEM. 1:5-7
        1. When - "in the days of Herod king of Judea."
        2. Who - A priest, Zacharias and wife Elizabeth.
        3. Who - Childless, a cultural stigma.

    II.   A PROMISED SOLUTION. 1:8-22
        1. The situation: Sensitive to the promise. 1:8-10
        2. The promise received. 1:11-22
           (a)Angelic announcement. 1:11-17
           (b)Zacharias' response and results. 1:18-20
           (c)Consequences on the people. 1:21-22

    III. THE PRAXIS OF THE PROMISE. 1:23-25
        1. The return home. 1:23
        2. Elizabeth and the new situation. 1:24-25

Without overlooking the divine it is the <u>human</u> nature of the Christ's origin that Luke underscores as the sure foundation for the faith of Theophilus.

SOME HUMAN ROOTS
Luke 1:5-25

The Greek temperament could envison gods as glorified men more easily than they could conceive God being human. To a pagan Greek gods were uncontaminated with material bodies. For a man to be divine was acceptable; but for god to be a man was impossible. In fact, most any conception of gods was the glorification of the human; never the incarnation of the deity! Hence, "Christ crucified...to Gentiles foolishness."(I Cor.1:23

Luke begins at the beginning. The virgin's near kinswoman, Elizabeth, was of a poor priestly family from the rugged region of Judea west of the Dead Sea. But it wasn't poverty of things but absence of children that left body and soul withered and barren. Her priest husband shared her heavy burden, her social shame, the cutting stares, unspoken questions of near neighbors and close relatives. Why had God passed them by and left them childless? Their purity and piety offered no substitute for a child's laughter or youthful tears. It wasn't lack of love or faulty desire . No! The plain fact was "Elizabeth was sterile."

This life-long burden of these pious people furnished the subject of their daily prayer. Ancient Hannah never prayed more earnestly for a child than did this righteous couple. Passing years increased the intensity of their prayer. Advancing age made their praying practically hopeless. Though no longer might they expect their own son they could still pray for Israel as their son, their hope, their future.

Such were the people and this the situation with which Luke begins his story of the Christ. "Having followed everything from the beginning..." is Luke's justification for this opening episode about Zacharias and Elizabeth's life-long frustration. This is the earthy soil from which the tale of Christ sprouts its first bud. "Not many mighty" form the first roots which fed the human origin of Jesus, the Christ of God.

When Zacharias was "chosen by lot" to serve in the sacred Holy Place it raised him to a lofty position in the eyes of his neighbors and relatives. A rare honor, it was the fulfillment of a dream that could come only once in a lifetime. It couldn't heal, but it eased the pain and salved the sore of their daily heartache. It softened the sharp barbs of well-meaning friends. It might even put the lie to the idea their life's lack came by divine displeasure. Zacharias' moment at the sacred altar of incense was a solemn point in the life of this pious pair.

Looking back and recapturing this hour in his memory became for Zacharias, not to say his wife, the day for which all his previous years had prepared. All of life had conditioned him for this time! A moment, an hour, a day, is not to be measured by its length but by its quality. A human spirit, mentally and emotionally ready, can live more in one moment than others do in years. Such was this day for this righteous couple. The long bleak days of a silent deity, the oft-repeated prayers, seemingly so useless and unheeded by a brazen heaven, those years of public loss of face, this mortifying odium, all had their place in shaping this man for this day. God is never idle when dealing with his own.

But the significance of this day does not lie in how God lifted their burden so much as in what the lifting did in the story of redemption. Salvation for <u>all</u> humanity is Luke's real theme, the ultimate point in salvation history. The son of Zacharias was vitally tied with spiritual bonds to the Christ, the saviour of the <u>world</u>. The faithfulness of Zacharias and Elizabeth was to touch the whole of humanity. This is the glory and reward of their patient piety. Indeed such is every man's glory who knows his life is the fulfilling of a part in God's eternal plan. Though I didn't lay the brick, I mixed the mortar for building the temple of God.

Solving the Problem

Angels are "ministering spirits" with which redeemed men are surrounded. But conditions in this life are such as to require special sensitivity to appreciate their presence. Zacharias was in a solemn place, performing a sacred service. He had been foiled by personal frustration. In this holy hour, not to say providential, the people were praying for him, this pious priest in the sanctuary. If a man is to "see" spiritual things and be impelled by spiritual beings, he must be upgraded in spiritual perceptions. Zacharias was clearly conditioned, finely tuned, spiritually sensitized to an appearance of the "angel of the Lord." The world desperately needed a word from God. Zacharias, shaped by the obscurity of the Judean wilderness, chiselled by family disappointment, sharpened by his priestly heritage was God's prepared instrument to begin this new stage in redemption history.

Too frequently faith is academic rather than vital, proxy instead of personal, creedal more than living, starched not spirited. We pray for rain but don't take an umbrella. An angel of the Lord announced to this pious priest that the burden of his prayer had been heard by heaven. But heaven's answer proved too incredible for Zacharias to grasp. Prayer for a son during the child-bearing years seemed sensible. But at this late day it simply was not logical. God's "Yes" to a prayer is not necessarily, "Yes, right now." In fact, God must answer in such a way and at such a time that men may become aware that the "yes" is from God, not just "naturally" inevitable. It must be <u>God's</u> answer, not man's demand. The son of Zacharias must be seen as God's gift, not man's necessity. Thus it happened that this priest's rare opportunity became the occasion for God's angel to announce God's answer to the life-long prayer of this ancient couple. But it was more than just an answer to <u>their</u> petitions. It involved <u>God's</u> eternal redemptive purposes. <u>Their</u> son was to be a link in the chain of man's salvation. <u>That</u> was the importance of this angelic announcement.

So the angel divulged the consequences of the coming child. He would bring "joy and exhaltation" to a whole generation of Israel not to mention the parents. "Many shall rejoice at his presence..." This son would not need artificial stimulants to inspire and guide his service. No "wine or strong drink" but "even within his mother's womb he shall be filled with God's holy spirit." His service to humanity shall include preparing

8

a people, equipped to serve the coming Lord. And he himself shall "go before" that Lord as a herald announces the coming of an earthly potentate. No prophet of ancient Israel shall prove more important in the divine program than this son about to be born of Elizabeth. God's answers to man's prayers go far beyond the pigmy form of self-interest that prompts the prayer. The divine answer doesn't always fit man's form. We pray that weakness be eliminated; we get power to surmount the weakness. Elizabeth prayed for a son to remove <u>her</u> "reproach among men." She got a son who removed a nation's reproach before God.

The Response of Zacharias!

Instead of belief the priest responded with doubt! He whose life was a pattern of faith became an example of disbelief. He said, "According to what standard shall I <u>know</u>? Trust was not enough; he demanded absolute knowledge. The <u>word</u> of God's angel wasn't adequate. The angelic message did not dispel doubt. The burden of his prayer through the years was for a son. How strange that the tidings that he was to have a son furnished the occasion for skepticism. The "facts" of his life stacked against the facts of faith became his stumbling block. "I am old, and my wife well advanced in day." Verities such as these were too formidable for faith.

Disbelief of God is self-distructive. Man, made in the image of God, is made to trust. God trusted man with awesome freedom. "You may freely eat of every tree..but of the tree of knowledge of good and evil you shall not eat."(Gen2:16f) Though he warned of the deadly result of that tree, he trusted man to regard the divine will. The sequal involving man's failure shows that God did not <u>force</u> man to leave it alone. Man does not <u>have</u> to heed God's word. And Zacharias didn't! He demanded a sign that he might <u>know</u>. Trusting was not enough. So God granted such a sign that fitted the doubt.

Even the irreligious take joy at the promise of a child. How much more men of piety praise with speech the pleasure of being parent. Not so with Zacharias! A sign he demanded. A sign he got! Immediately he became deaf and dumb(1:62). Whatever joy was his could not be expressed in speech. He would be repressed by dumbness for nine months. Punishment began on the spot!

His dialogue with the angel prolonged his stay in the sacred room far past the usual time. Outside the praying people became restive, uneasy, unsettled. Times were charged with expectant hope for the long-awaited Messiah. Besides, resentment against Rome aggravated tension. With the delay of the priest anxious concern overflowed. When Zacharias finally did appear it didn't quiet the crowd. His expected blessing was not forthcoming. His wild gestures and muted gutterals were hardly more than animal grunts. It became clear that Zacharias had seen some vision within the temple. What did this mean? That question with the excitement of this day would follow the people far into the night. Some, even 30 years later, would recall this scene. A generation hence the son of Zacharias in the wilderness would herald Jesus as Messiah. These were the roots which would bear fruit in Israel's redeemer.

The Promise Fulfilled!

When the week's work was completed Zacharias returned to his wilderness home and his aging wife. Life stirred in her barren womb. Despite their age both felt the ardent joy of approaching parenthood. Luke reports: "His wife conceived." New life in the womb brought new hope in the home. Yet a special anxiety arose. If the absence of a child was a reproach what would a <u>claim</u> of pregnancy be? If Elizabeth alleged pregnancy before it was manifest her humiliation would be compounded. So she took care to hide herself five months.

It was not doubt that prompted such caution. No! Zacharias had his dumbness! That was sufficient assurance even to the most doubtful. But let events run their course. In five months people could observe that she was to be a mother in Israel. They could themselves behold what "the Lord has done...to take away my reproach." God answers doubts by deeds, not claims. Whatever doubts men have about the ongoing purposes of God, <u>events</u> best answer.

Why?

Why does Luke begin with this simple story of an unrenowned couple hidden in the Judean wilderness? Someone said, "God must have loved common people! He made so many of them." The saviour of the world was "introduced" by one who sprang from common soil; from pious people not immune to pain, the common lot of man as man. If the Christ is to save <u>all</u> he must be able to save <u>any</u>. His earliest roots identify <u>him</u> with <u>all</u>. This is Luke's theme until the gospel gets to Jerusalem. And in his second treatise, even unto Rome.

Why does Luke begin with this story? Why does a mansion have a porch? It's where the visitor initially meets the family. The porch doesn't reveal the glories of the inside. But it is a first point of acquaintance, a place to meet the man of the house, his family, traditions, ambitions, dreams and purpose. This is Luke's introduction to "the Christ of God," mankind's saviour.

AN OUTLINE OF LUKE 1:26-38
The Son!

The focus of Luke 1:26-38 is on none of the actors, neither the angel or Mary. The "son" captures the spotlight. But whose son is he? The virgin's? Is he of man or of God? Who is his father? What is his nature?

I. ANNOUNCEMENT TO THE VIRGIN. 1:26-33
1. You shall:(a)conceive,(b)bear a son, (c)name him.
2. His nature:(a)"great" (b)"son of Most High."
3. His work:(a)heir to David's throne, (b)endless reign.

II. HOW CAN SUCH THINGS BE? 1:34-38
1. The Holy Spirit "shall come..."
2. The "power of the Most High shall overshadow."
3. Any word "from God" is not "impossible."
4. Example: Elizabeth's child in her old age.

By this story Luke introduces Theophilus to this remarkable son, who he is, his nature and work, even from the mother's womb. He is "born of woman" thoroughly human, yet "son of God."

* * * * * * *

THE SON!

When the angel Gabriel appeared to the virgin Mary she was "troubled." And well she might be. To her eyes this angelic messenger was a man. Men, strangers or otherwise, just did not talk to women in public or private. A tradition of the rabbis was that men offer "a woman no greeting at all." Thus for this strange man suddenly to show up in the privacy of her home was enough to shake her cool. Remember too that this young virgin was engaged to marry. In that day and place engagement was equivalent to marriage.

Besides, being a man approaching her in the privacy of her home, the news he brought was enough to disquiet a sensitive maiden innocent of romantic contact with a man.

None of the main characters in this dramatic episode enjoy the prime focus of the author. Neither the angel nor the virgin occupy the spotlight. Nor does God or his Holy Spirit appear as the center of attention. Rather it's the son, unborn, as yet unconceived. The story converges on him as heart and core. The unconceived, unborn "son" is the focal point on the stage. He's the star! The others are supporting cast.

Who is this son? Is he the virgin's? Is he human or divine? Neither or both at the same time? What's his origin? Why's he here? What's his destiny?

Announcement to the Virgin!

It was the "sixth month" after God generated a minor miracle for the aged Elizabeth. Linked to that marvel was this present scene displaying a much mightier miracle of creative life. Mary was greeted as "one having been graced." Such "grace" proved that "The Lord is with you." Such a greeting agitated the virgin. Not only a man, but from whence came this word? What could it mean? It was enough to strike awesome fear into her young heart.

11

Gabriel must allay her fears, quiet her emotions, clarify her mind that she may discern what she's about to hear. "Quit being afraid! You have found grace with God." This grace disclosed itself by placing on her a three-fold task. "You shall conceive." Her lack of sexual activity will be no barrier to new life spawned in her womb. The wonder of creation is to be repeated and "You, Mary, are the agent through whom this second Adam is to be produced."

Moreover, "You shall bear a son." The pregnancy shall come to full term. The joy of Jewish women was, not only to birth a child, but a son! This pure maiden was to know the pride of mothering a son. True, giving birth before marriage would create heavy burdens. Reproach and shame would be her lot. Yet that wouldn't destroy the joy of mothering a son.

"You shall call his name _Jesus_." The name "Jesus" means "God helps." To give this name was part of the task of birthing this son. Men must learn that "God helps!"

The Nature and Work of the Son!

Who is this son? Obviously he was Mary's. That being so, he was definitely human. Nine months of fragile life in the womb stamped this son as being _man_, dependent, weak, limited. As other human beings he had "to learn by the things which he suffered." If he stubbed his toe, it hurt. If he cut his hand, it bled. This son must pass through each stage of human growth. Luke later affirms, "Jesus was growing in wisdom and stature and grace with God and man."

The angel declares another important detail about the son: "He shall be great." The word "great" is always qualified when used of human beings. But in keeping with Old Testament usage the absolute use of the term "great" is reserved for God alone. "_Great_ is the Lord, and greatly to be praised, his greatness is unsearchable."(Ps.145:31) Thus this son is to bear the divine label "Great." And as if to confirm this the angel adds, "He shall be called son of the Most High." Yes! This son of the virgin is to be strictly human but will bear divine epithets. He will be man with God's name, human with God's nature.

The role which this unborn son is to perform is now set forth to Mary's wonder-struck mind. He is to be a king! In fact God has assigned him to sit on David's throne with all its hallowed memories. And the most marvelous fact was the eternal nature of his reign: "of his kingdom there shall be no end." All patriarchal promises, all prophetical visions, all divine plans and purposes shall be perfected in this son. "All the families of the earth" was the goal of God's unfolding purpose through the Old Testament era. God's redemptive love was to be consummated in the virgin's son. The nature of his rule made it eternal. Of his reign there shall be "no end."

How Shall This Be?

Had Mary already married the question still would be: "How shall this be?" Her logic was faultless:"..._since_ a man I know not?" Her virginity precluded her having a child. She was engaged, bound by pledge to her espoused and she wasn't about to violate that commitment. And it should be noted that Mary's question sprang from her faith, not doubt. In effect she was declaring, "I'll accept all this as true but tell me please, How shall it be possible? I've had no relations with a man, and I certainly won't until my marriage to Joseph."

The angel responded in all seriousness to the question of her heart. "The Holy Spirit shall come upon you and the power of the Most High shall overshadow you." In a word, God is involved! He will take charge. The breath of God shall generate the life. And his omnipotence shall be a protecting shield to ward off danger or damage from man or nature. Luke is concerned that his friend, Theophilus, should know for certain that this son is not only the woman's son but also God's. This son is Redeemer! Saviour! God's promised Messiah! This son came through God's initiative, not man's. He would "help" man from his lostness!

As for this unusual method of bringing a son into the world let it be known: "every word of God shall not be impossible." If all creation flowed from the hand of God what's so odd about the producing of this son? Even the usual begetting and conceiving of a child is wonder beyond comprehension. Since God has ordained that new life and personality should come by the union of male and female is it such a marvel that _he_ should bring a child by an altered method? If evolution can invent its mutations, cannot God have his _mutation_?

If we reach back into history we find a Sarah, a Hagar, or a Hannah to testify that God could and would supervise the birth of a child under extraordinary circumstances. In fact, _anything_ "from God is not impossible." The most recent example of divine intrusion of the "normal" is seen in Elizabeth having a child long past her child-bearing years. And to this "kinswoman" Mary is cited for confirmation that a similar thing will happen to her. After years of sterility aged Elizabeth is already six months along with life stirring in her womb. In the solitude of the rugged recesses of Judea Mary may confirm the truth of this startling announcement that will ever alter her life.

So far as human penetration of the past is possible Luke has begun at the beginning. One cannot go further than begetting and conceiving of life. So Theophilus now perceives the origin and nature of the hero of Luke's story. This "son" is God's gift yet "born of woman." In nature he is thoroughly human _and_ divine. He is universal son of man!

13

AN OUTLINE OF LUKE 1:39-56
Two Women!
God's ways with man are shown in his dealing with two women,
Elizabeth and Mary. This exemplify God's ways with man.
I.   THE TWO WOMEN VISIT. 1:39-45
    1. Mary's journey and salutation. 39-40
    2. Elizabeth's response:
       (a)The babe in the womb. 41a
       (b)Elizabeth's praise of Mary. 41b-42
       (c)The honor accorded Elizabeth. 43-44
       (d)Happy is she who "believed." 45
II. MARY'S MAGNIFICAT. 1:46-56
    1. Mary "magnifies" the Lord. 47
    2. The underlying cause. 48-50
    3. God's ways with men. 51-54
    4. God's promise to the patriarchs fulfilled. 55
    In this scene involving two women critical to the beginning
of his story, Luke shows Theophilus how God has, does and will
work with men in his unfolding revelation to humanity.

* * * * * * *

TWO WOMEN!
    God's ways with man are exhibited in the way he dealt with
two women, Elizabeth and Mary. In getting his son into the
world, identified with the human race, so situated in a social
setting suitable for his redemptive purposes, God had to use
women. At least he did use women.
    Though Elizabeth and Mary were "kinswomen" we have no record
of their visiting one another before or after this. Now they
were together "about three months." And except for the first
half hour we know nothing of what they said or did. So that was
of primary import in what Luke wanted Theophilus to know.
The Visit of the Women!
    After the angel's announcement it didn't take Mary long to
get up and go to her elder kinswoman. Not that she needed any
confirmation to bolster faith faltering faith. Not at all! She had
yielded in humility, "Behold! the maiden slave of the Lord; may
it become according to your word." And in this very visit Mary
would be praised for her astounding trust: "Happy the one who
believed that a completion of the things having been spoken to
her from the Lord shall happen." But it is perfectly normal for
anyone to thrill when faith find's endorsment in fact. To see a
woman of Elizabeth's age, six months pregnant, would stir
Mary's emotions, already riding the clouds because of the
angel's word. No doubt the virgin welcomed any confirmation of
such an improbable promise that a virgin would give birth. But
it was also the joy of support from an aged woman already
feeling new life in her womb. This is more than confirmation.
It's the thrill of participation, the serenity of sharing with
a like-minded soul. More than proof, Mary claimed the bliss of
faith. At any rate Mary "arose and went with haste ...and
entered the house of Zacharias and she saluted Elizabeth."

14

What were the feelings of Mary when she entered the home of Elizabeth? Pain and shame of being an unwed mother would come later. For the present only the reality of being chosen for the privilege of being mother to the Lord flooded her thoughts. Whatever she voiced at the moment of her salutation must remain a secret between the women. Did Mary have to tell of Gabriel's announcement? Or did the same Holy Spirit who generated life in Elizabeth's womb covey the marvel of the virgin's womb? However the initial response came not from Elizabeth but from the babe in her womb: "when the voice of your salutation came unto my ears, the babe leaped in joy..."

Luke assures us that "out of his mother's womb" Elizabeth's babe "was filled with the Holy Spirit." If this lies beyond human cognition so be it. What or who is man that he limit God on how or what He does in history. Thus from the womb of his mother came John the Baptist's initial testimony to him "the strap of whose sandal" he was "not fit to unfasten."

The "breath"(spirit)of God animates every living thing. It was the spirit of God who stimulated life in Elizabeth's womb. The same spirit generated life in the virgin's womb. And the same spirit prompted the babe in one woman's womb to hail the new life in the other woman's womb. Thus Luke's gospel takes his reader back to the "beginning" of the "Christ of God" in his sojourn as man among men. The life of God as man has its roots in the birth process of two women. God works so closely allied with the "human" processes that he merges into the human. Theophilus could not miss the point. Jesus was true human.

But Elizabeth added her voice of praise for how God invaded human joys with his divine presence. She too was "filled with the Holy Spirit" and cried out, "You are blessed among women." From the outset God has loved men, all men. But to reach all men with his love he has consistently elected to work through individuals. When leaven is inserted into dough it must be imbedded at one point. It isn't instilled en mass. In history God initiated his redemptive movement in a single individual, Abraham. It wasn't that he loved Abraham more and other men less. On the contrary, it was because he had "all the families of the earth" in mind that he called one man. To inject his son into humanity as a human, God must choose someone through whom the son becomes man. Mary was "blessed among women" because she was God's selection for the task. Furthermore, as Elizabeth added, "blessed is the fruit of your womb." From this principle of selection Mary's offspring was "blessed" because he was selected to be the instrument of God for man's redemption. Elizabeth was overwhelmed with God's gracious way in selecting such humble people as his agents for action. "Whence this to me, that the mother of my Lord should come to me?" The wisdom of men selects men of talent, fame and fortune for the important jobs in society. God's ways are not man's. He selects the poor in spirit. "The foolishness of God is wiser than men and the weakness of God is mightier than men."(I Cor.1:25)

Mary's Magnificat!

In surpassing beauty Mary's Magnificat sings exalted praise to God for his ways with men. "My soul magnifies the Lord and my spirit rejoiced upon God my saviour." Looking back on the shock of Gabriel's tidings of her conception, her fears could now subside. She can only exult in praise to God. In fact, in retrospect she said, "My spirit rejoiced" when God "my saviour" informed me that I would mother the son of God. Joy of being thus selected outweighed any fear of human censor. Mary's magnifying of God lay in his passing over more prominent women and selecting her. Mary sang, "Because he looked upon the humbling of his maiden-slave, for behold, from now all generations shall bless me." Mary was of "the house of David," of royal descent. But over the centuries her family was brought low. The process of humanizing royal blood found a prize sample in this virgin of Nazareth. Her real royalty lay in the honor of her person, not the blue blood of her heritage. Pure in mind, virtuous in spirit, unassuming in disposition, responsible in deeds, these were the qualities which God sought in the mother of his earth born son. Through the ages this is the kind of person God has chosen as servant. Integrity of character, not "success" in position, is his standard of value.

When Mary declared that "all generations shall bless me" she was not basking in self-glory. She was underscoring the divine method of always seeking the humble, the poor in spirit, the meek to "inherit the earth" as his servants. Every generation shall acknowledge God's wisdom in choosing such a humble young girl as vital to his redeeming love.

Divine Qualities!

Three qualities led God to use these methods for selecting servants: his power, his purity, his mercy. Mary declared, "The powerful one did great things to me." It was the power of God as Creator that enabled him to forge new life in the virgin's womb. He repeated that which he did "in the beginning" when he said, "let us make man." Here he said, "let us remake man!" For such profound power Mary praised her "Potentate."

God's holiness furnished another basis of praise. Mary said, "Holy is his name." A name reflects the essential person of him who bears it. God's power doesn't crush; it lifts, supports, works in keeping with his holiness. His power works in purity. His omnipotence flows through the channels of holiness. God can not lie because his power operates in harmony with truth. Mary experienced God's holiness by the manner in which he aroused new life in her womb. God respected her holiness because it reflected his holiness.

A third attribute of God is that of mercy. Sang Mary, "...and his mercy is unto generations and generations." To a human being God's power and holiness are formidable, awesome, overwhelming. They suggest an appalling distance between God and man. But mercy spans the chasm. Shakespeare has Portia say, "Mercy is above the scepter'd sway,--it is enthroned in the heart of kings, it is an attribute of God himself." It's this divine mercy that breaks all barriers between man and God. It's

16

mercy that bridges the gap, binds the warring parties, tempers the chains with pardon and seals human redemption in the loving hands of the divine Father. Mercy puts power and purity within man's reach and directs both into saving grace.

With the next stanza Mary states some specific ways in which her "potentate" Lord uses his incredible strength. In language suitable to human thought patterns she proclaims, "He executed strength in his arm." As one who "feared" him her own selection to be the mother of the Christ was a sample of the execution of his "strength." However, she specifies ways in which God has continuously managed his majestic power. "He scattered haughty, the arrogant in the understanding of their hearts." Disdainful philosphers, self-esteeming scientists, proud bloated doubters, arrogant emporers, kings and governors--all these haughty human greats, "in the understanding of their hearts" God "scattered." In their precocious life-style they lived under the illusion of their own greatness. Yet, without exception, in good time, he who rules human destiny "scattered" them. All Napoleons end up on their Elbas! The sands of time bury all Pharoahs! History is a continuing demonstration of how "from thrones he cast down potentates." And at the same time "he exalted those who are humble." Even Napoleon was corporal before being emporer. How much more a humble, unheralded virgin be exalted to motherhood of Messiah! That's the normal way God works in history. Don't measure God's method by the time he takes but by integrity of character. Over the long haul "those who hunger he filled with good and he sent away the rich empty." Moreover, "those who hunger" are not just those whose stomachs are empty. They include those who hunger for righteousness, justice, peace and fulness of spirit. "God works all things for good"--moral and spiritual good.

God's dealing with Israel exemplifies his unerring way of turning weakness into strength. He covenanted with Abraham. He delivered enslaved Israel from Egyptian power. He disciplined his people by Babylonian power and then "remembered" to return them to the land of their heritage. But more than these time measured remembrances, by putting life in the virgin's womb he "remembered mercy, even as he spoke to our fathers, to Abraham and his seed forever."

Through the centuries God was refining Israel's knowledge of his goal for his people. "All the families of the earth" were his predetermined goal. Taken from the loins of David one would always be available to sit on the throne of the kingdom. Said the prophet, "I have given you as covenant to the people, light to Gentiles."(Is.42:6b) "All families," David's throne, the "people" and "Gentiles" signify progressive, ongoing, ever upward movement of God's self-revelation to and through Israel. The time must come when men learn that "he is not a Jew who is one outwardly" and that "real circumcision is a matter of the heart, spiritual and not literal."(Rom.2:28f) The "people of God" concept must graduate from being national to universal, from being "Hebrew" to being "human."

17

And thus Mary voiced her "magnifying" of the Lord and his ways with men. In spite of what appears to be injustices, reverses, a forgetfulness on God's part, he is ever attending to his unfolding, developing program for human redemption. "God having spoken hath spoken!" He remembered his long-pledged word by placing in the virgin's womb the "son of the Most High." He announced the astonishing birth to unacceptable, unknown, unnamed, shepherds. Kings and thrones God "scattered." The virgin and shepherds he "filled with good." This is God's way! This is the divine method of involving himself with men and history.

He who has ears to hear, let him hear! He who has eyes to see, let him see! He who has heart to understand, let him understand. God made known his ways to the virgin of Nazareth. In her Magnificat, she sang of some of these ways of God with men.

* * * * * * *

AN OUTLINE OF LUKE 1:57-80

God Is Gracious!
The name "John" signifies: "God has shown grace."

I.   THE BIRTH OF JOHN. 1:57-66
     1. The baby's birth propels the people's praise.
     2. The baby's name reflects his role.

II. PROPHETIC PRAISE. 1:67-80
     1. Because God "visited" his people.
     2. Because of John's role in salvation history.

John was God's advance public relations man. Even his name carried in it the graciousness of God in his redemptive visit!

18

GOD IS GRACIOUS!
Luke 1:57-80

In keeping with the angel's mandate Elizabeth and Zacharias insisted on naming the new-born babe, John. That name signified "God has shown grace." And everything about the baby's birth, not to say, his later ministry, exhibited God as gracious. The birth and naming was a foregleam of him whom John announced to Israel and for whom he was the final preparatory prophetic voice. Besides, that divinely given name was one more striking example of the grace of God ever manifested to man since he first voiced, "let us make man in our image."

The Birth of John

Two factors about John's birth certify its value in God's ongoing revelation. First is the birth itself.

If the biblical teaching be true that this universe is a creation of God, then nothing of itself is of a so-called "nature." Since God created, nothing is "natural." All is supernatural! It arose from something other than, outside of, and above "nature." Nature itself is a creation of God. The processes of "nature" are merely methods by which God engineers the life of the universe.

The birth of any baby is an amazing event. We are so familiar with the normal way babies come into the world that we overlook that God is quite present in the process. The birth of a baby is a divine event. The fact that we ignore, deny, or forget God's involvement doesn't lessen his presence in the event. If he withdrew his active part in the birthing there would be no babies. No generation of humans would again appear on the earth. "In him we live and move and have our being."

That Elizabeth birthed a son was only unusual because of her advanced age when the baby was conceived. Both parents "were well advanced in days." Though for years they had prayed for a child the time had long since passed when they might expect a child's laughter to grace their home. And though the angel had told Zacharias, "your prayer was heard," we conclude he refers to the prayers offered through the normal child-bearing years. Like other factors in their married experience those prayers were a matter of the past. Now, in old age, she and her neighbors viewed her barrenness as God's unpleasant will. Thus it was exciting beyond measure when aged Elizabeth gave birth to a son. "Her neighbors and kin heard that the Lord had magnified his mercy in fellowship with her. And they were rejoicing with her." What a time of joy! Making merry was the passion of the moment in the hill country of Judea. Even in his birth John performed the function of forerunner. He excited all the vales and hills of Judea!

But the birth was not all. His naming prompted a serious precursory question, "What, then, shall this child be? For the Lord's hand was with him!"

Eight days from birth the day of circumcision came. Such was the time for formally conferring a name. Under the claims of custom friends and relatives began to call the baby after his father. Were they ever surprised at the vigor with which the mother objected, "No, not so! He shall be called, John." When they failed to persuade her with the argument, "No one of your kin is called by this name" they began gesturing to the father what he "might wish the child to be called." To this Zacharias scrawled on a writing slate, "His name is John." Both parents were incredibly firm. No hesitation! No maybes! No "his name ought to be." It was a settled fact, His name is John." His name was already fixed by heaven; earth shall not change it.

In the history of revelation names have played an important part. A name may reveal a salient point of character. It may declare the role one plays on the stage of history. God's name "I AM" divulged something of the divine character and intent toward enslaved Israel. It was no accident that Jacob became Israel after the "deceiver" fought with God at Jabbok's brook. Thus "John" was living testimony that "God is gracious" in that he was "visiting" his people with his redemptive presence.

The very circumstances surrounding John's birth and naming made clear his appointed lot in redemptive history. John became the herald who prepared the hearts of God's people for Messiah, now just over the horizon. Though but a week old baby he was already performing his role. Ravines, plateaus, mountain tops were aflame with talk of the remarkable birth to Elizabeth. The insistence on the name John provoked the question, "What, then, shall this child be?" In a word, the minds of the countryside were aroused to think about approaching events. The hearts of God's people in the hills and valleys of Judea were stirred to recognize that God was at work in current affairs. In fact, John's birth reminded that God is always at work in the affairs of men. God never abandoned man in the "silent" years after Malachi. On the contrary, all along he had been transplanting, weeding, cultivating, grafting. John's birth was announcing that harvest time was near. The time for fruitage is at hand. "God is gracious." Another revealing of that grace is being displayed.

Prophetic Praise!

Times come in human life when the spirit rises to an ecstacy of inspiration when one must sing, speak, or in some dramatic way demonstrate his deepest feelings of gratitude. If this be so in general, how much more of those near the first upbubbling of the water of life? It was inevitable that John's father sing prophetic praises.

Godly people in ancient times, while the world was ever with them, were not disturbed by invasions of radio, TV, and other distracting gadgets. Furthermore, pious people like Zacharias and his wife spent devoted lives in the seclusion of the Judean hills. Their reading consisted largely of the sacred scripture. As Mary had done, so Zacharias poured forth his praise quite literally in the words of the Old Testament. "Blessed is the Lord God of Israel, because he visited and executed salvation for his people."

It had been years, even centuries, since God had "visited" his people. At least not so specific and direct as in the case

20

of his "visit" in the person of John. This "visit" would change
the destiny of the nation, yea, even the world. Bound up with
the arrival of John was the future of man.

When a three-ring circus arranges to visit an American town
it sends in advance public relations people to herald coming
tigers, clowns, and high wire performers. By every means they
seek to arouse the interest and whet the appetite of the whole
community. They are to prepare for the coming show. Preparation
involves stirring the imagination of the people and urging full
participation in the shows. Advance publicity is to provide a
preview of all that is to come.

John was the advance publicity man. Within his person and
ministry lay the potential of all to follow in the coming
Christ. Thus Zacharias could sing in the past tense: "he (God)
visited and executed salvation for his people." So certain was
the "visit" that Zacharias sang as though salvation were a past
fact. The birth of John was God's pledge of his visit.

Besides, that visit was in terms of redemption. "He executed
redemption for his people." God was to "raise up a horn of salvation in the house of his servant David." That is to say, no
bull of Bashan or wild ox of Gilead would equal the strength of
God's Redeemer for his people. And that redemption would come
through the dynasty of David. The golden age of the past could
not equal that of the future. Moreover, the promised salvation
would expand far broader than mere political freedom from
tyrannical despots. Its roots would plumb far deeper than
economic liberation. Enemies from which God swore deliverance
to the patriarchs involved moral, religious, spiritual service
to God in "holiness and righteousness before him all our days."
Liberation from the chains of a tyrant or from pressing poverty
is not genuine freedom. No man is really free until delivered
from sin, that which creates tyrants and causes poverty. It is
"holiness" that undergirds any abiding political liberty. It is
"righteousness" that assures stability to economic freedom. For
without "holiness and righteousness" the political and economic
revolutions are but turns in the highway from one slavery to
another. Cuba was set free from the despotism of a Baptista to
the tyranny of a Castro.

* * * * * * *

AN OUTLINE OF LUKE 2:1-20
A Child Is Born!

How human can God get?   Or can he get to be human?
I.   THE PROVIDENTIAL SETTING! 2:1-5
     1. God moves in history.
     2. Joseph and Mary journey to Bethlehem.
II. THE BIRTH OF THE CHILD. 2:6-7
     1. The birth.   2. Signs and symbols.
III. THE BIRTH ANNOUNCED. 2:8-20
     1. By an army of angels to shepherds.
     2. To Mary and Joseph.
     3. The human response.
God cannot become any more human than being human!

21

A CHILD IS BORN!
Luke 2:1-20

How human can God get? Or is it that God become human be
beyond the possible? Such questions find an answer in Luke's
tale of Jesus' birth in Bethlehem. That birth, its time,
place and people demonstrate in fact, not only that He became
human but it also declares how!

The Providential Setting!

God does not manipulate but he does move in history.
Arrogant emperors or inconstant kings may ignore or deny God
but they cannot eliminate him. He guides history. In fact,
history is "his story." Thus Caesar Augustus issued a "decree
that all the world should get itself registered." And though
Caesar may have ignored God in his decree, God did not ignore
Caesar. Silently, unrecognized, almost, as it were, secretly,
God is at work in men. Hates, joys, failures, successes,
acts, deeds, motivations are as much the means by which God
works as so-called "laws of nature" are the expression of his
ruling will in creation. If a sparrow can not fall without
God's concern an emperor does not issue a decree apart from
God's involvement. That man doesn't recognize God's place in
the process does not mean that He's absent from the event.
Augustus may have acted without concern for God but he could
not issue his drecee without God's use of that edict. Though
Augustus was not a puppet manipulated by a divine puppeteer,
he was a channel through which God worked his divine purpose
in His ongoing, eternal will for man's redemption. Though men
claim "God is nowhere" believers affirm, "God is now here!"
To the believer God's invisible silence testifies to his
method, not his presence or absence.

On the human level Caesar's edict set the world in motion.
"All were going to get themselves registered, each unto his
own city." Joseph and his espoused had their problems without
the burden of a tiresome journey in response to the government's decree. The virgin and her proposed husband were
weighted with a load of shame. Who could believe their story
of Mary's loss of virginity? Added to the heart ache of
public disapproval came the physical inconvenience of a three-
day journey on crowded roads to the ancestral home of Bethlehem.

These were anxious days. Yet not without hope! The very
circumstances of Mary's pregnancy made it possible that they
perceive a divine purpose in going to the city of David. Had
not the ancient prophet said, "And you, O Bethlehem, in the
land of Judah, are by no means least among the ones ruling
Judah, for from you shall come a ruler who will shepherd my
people Israel." To a thoughtful, trusting couple such as
these it's at least possible, if not probable, that they
recognize that they were tools in the hand of God for
bringing God's Messiah to Israel. Incredible? Yes! But who
could deny the providence of the circumstances?

22

Whether at the moment Mary and Joseph perceived the divine purpose, the birth of the babe was of human significance. Roman peace, of which Augustus was guardian, was not man's greatest need. Humanity hungered for divine peace in God's Christ. Human salvation lay, not in the boast of Rome, but in the babe of Bethlehem. By power of the sword Rome enforced peace. Mary's son would plant the seed. In due time humanity could harvest the fruit of peace. Caesar's edict reached all the "inhabited world," the extent of Rome's power. The babe's peace was for all men, everywhere, any time, who bore the scarred image of the Creator. Rome's salvation was political; Messiah's was from the corruption of sin. Augustus displayed the majesty and renown of Roman rule. God's babe in Bethlehem honored the low, the poor, the humble, the pious in heart. It was not at the sword's point but at the point of the spirit for which the babe was born. Not the empire but the human was God's concern.

The Birth!

So "the days that she should deliver were fulfilled and she birthed her son, the first-born, and wrapped him in swaddling cloths and was laying him in a manger because there was not for them a place in the Inn." Such are the facts of the birth. But in these facts lay serious signs and symbols. When the angel announced the babe's birth to the shepherds he said that the confirmatory sign would be "swaddling cloths" and a "manger." What signs are these? Aren't new-born babes wrapped in cloths? And though a manger may not be normal it's surely quite logical if one can't find lodging at such a time. To lay a baby in a warm, secure, private place away from tumult or push of crowds is sensible. Besides, Jewish literature speaks of swaddling cloths and mangers with significant import. Isaiah said (1:3) "An ox knows his owner, and an ass his master's manger." And the apocryphal Wisdom of Solomon describes the birth of the wise king as "cared for with cloth bands and concern another king ever had..." As David's wise son was "wrapped in swaddling cloths" so was his greater son. And as the prophet saw the manger as the feeding trough for God's people so it was appropriate that God's Messiah should be laid where people might come and feed. It was significant(a "sign")that David's son be born in David's city and that he be found, not in a public lodge, but in the privacy, warmth and protection of what a simple family with human limitations could provide. He was swaddled like a king; he would nourish the hearts of human beings. Thus the Davidic Messiah was born sovereign of souls, not a political potentate or military liberator.

The Birth Announced

The first announcement of the birth of this saviour-child was not to kings or conquerors, but to lowly shepherds whose social standing matched the wretched odor of their labor. The smell of the flock measured the level of their life. What a contrast with birth announcements of nobility among men! Even the shepherd's life of David's youth could not lend repute to a shepherd's status in first century Judea. The angelic report to such as shepherds were, itself betokened God's redemptive concern for men as humans, not as classes.

Moreover, the content of the angel's announcement fortifies this view of God's interest in the human condition. Three terms about the baby the shepherds heard: Saviour, Christ, and Lord. The import of these titles was confirmed by the heavenly host who sang, "Glory in the highest to God and on earth peace among men..." Peace in all relations between God and man as well as man and man was the mission of him who was born that night.

And what was the human response to the angelic message? On the part of the shepherds it was, "Let's go see..." They sought to experience personally God's gift to man. The word of God must be real in their lives. Saviour, Christ and Lord combine in an objective Person but he must become an inward experience for all who hear, handle and see.

The shepherds took the angelic message to those around the manger, particularly Mary. They became evangels of God's good news about the person and mission of the baby. Those at the manger "marvelled at the things spoken by the shepherds." When faith in fulfillment and hope for the future become real in experience it breeds amazement. That which is credible to believe is incredible when encountered. So "they marvelled." "But Mary was keeping all these matters, pondering them in her heart." From Gabriel's word about this babe to the tidings of the shepherds the pieces of the puzzle were taking shape. The plan of redemption would eventually fully form as Mary pondered on all she endured. Angels of the highest and shepherds from the lowest combined in manifesting who and what this child should be. He at once joined the divine and human. He held meaning for heaven and earth, God and man. Such was the pondering of the mother of the child!

How Human Can God Get?

Can God be more human than sharing the living experiences of a human? From the crisis and dependency of birth through the formative years of youth, the pain of hunger, scorch of thirst, misunderstanding, loneliness, rejection, betrayal, all these and more are the common lot of human kind. God in Christ tasted them all. How more human can one be than this? In fact, HE became the first genuine human being this side of Adam. He alone is the one man in all history that was all that God created man to be. How human can God get? Just as human as God created men to be! He was "tempted" in all points..." His humanness reached around the world and identified with the whole of humanity.

At this stage in his story that is what Luke sought Theophilus to recognize and feel.

AN OUTLINE OF LUKE 2:21-40
Who Is This Child?
Men are born to decisive destiny implied in the idea of Creator.
I. THIS CHILD! 2:21-24
     1. His name, community-family.
     2. His personal family and presentation to God.
II. TESTIMONY ABOUT THE CHILD. 2:25-38
     1. From Simeon, the sentinel.
     2. Anna, the prophet.
The child grows in body, mind, and spirit toward his destiny.

WHO IS THIS CHILD?
Luke 2:21-40

Every human being is born to a significant destiny. This is inherent in the concept of a Creator. God created man "in his own image." He made man to think, choose, deliberate, imagine, act with creative purpose. Moreover, God makes each human to achieve particular goals.

Who is this child so marvelously born of a virgin? What could Mary possibly think? or Joseph? or the shepherds? or any to whom this birth was reported? Who is this child?

This Child!

What is more helpless than a baby? He cannot feed himself, clean himself, name himself. He can't even choose to be born. Someone else makes that decision.

A baby needs a name. It identifies him as an individual person. So this child "was called Jesus," a name of divine origin before he was conceived in the virgin's womb.

In that time and place names carried more weight than just a means of distinguishing one person from another. They signified personal traits, experiences and such like. Eliab means, "God is father," or Elizabeth, "God is majesty." The name "Jesus" means, "Yaweh saves," a clear indication of his role in history. Who is this child? His name is Jesus!

Moreover, this child became identified with a distinct community, a national culture, a family of people. On the eighth day after birth he was circumcised, a time-honored ritual that formally ushered each child into the community of the people of God. This child was not an isolated being floating on a vast sea of humanity unattached to a social unit. His circumcision joined him as a link in a chain, a grain of sand on a beach, a tree in a forest, a person in a social group contributing to a divine purpose in history. Who is this child? He identified as a part of the people of God.

But he became even more. He held a place in a very personal human family, not just a nation but a child with a mother, father, and siblings. True, he was a "first-born." But brothers and sisters of the same mother arrived in due time. And though Jospeh did not beget him Jesus was "obedient to them"(Lk.3:51). Obedience to Joseph as a human father was included. He would experience the inter-action of the small family unit. His human adventure was to be that of all such households. He became human "in all points."

As in other such family units Mary his mother must go through the ritual of purification after his birth. "When the days of their purification were fulfilled according to the law of Moses" Mary cleansed herself by the ritual sacrifice required by Levitical law, "a pair of doves or two young pigeons." Even the symbolism of sin must be wiped from her. No taint can cloud the home in which this child grew. Who is this child? He's the child of a holy human family. Such was his environment!

Testimony about "this" child!

Two Godly saints, divinely designated, bear witness about this child. Simeon testifies to the arrival in the child of the means of God's saving man. The prophet Anna evangelizes the news of the advent of the child.

When the Greeks fought for Troy it was a trying time in the homeland for the mothers of youthful Greek soldiers. Atop the sentinel's tower Agamemnon peered across the Aegean looking for the fire that would signal the taking of Troy and victory for the Greeks. When at last the expected flames arose he sang at once the song of victory and included in it release from his long vigil. Something such as this was the feeling of Simeon. He had been set as a sentinel to watch for the fire of God's salvation. "To him it had been revealed by the holy spirit that he should not see death before he should see the Lord's Christ." Along with other sensitive souls he was eagerly expecting "the consolation of Israel." So when Mary and Joseph brought the child to the temple the ancient saint cradled the babe in his arms and sang his song of liberation. "Now, Despot, relieve your slave, according to your word, in peace." At long last the weary vigil was over. In the person of this child the divine means of man's salvation had arrived. It was time for death to relieve the sovereign's slave.

But Simeon had more to say. He testified to the ministry and destiny of this child. So he spoke of God's "saving...prepared before all the peoples..." The word "peoples" is plural of the term usually reserved for reference to God's people. Thus Simeon implies the Gentile nations must be involved as "God's people." And the aged servant makes that more pointed by specifically saying, that this child shall be "Light for revealing to Gentiles." Simeon was reflecting that which Old Testament prophets had declared to be the real purpose of God throughout all history: "He will bring justice

26

to the nations...light for the Gentiles."(Is.42:1,6) Mental blindness, moral stupidity, sinful ignorance and death were all to wilt and disappear when God's servant came to man. In addition Simeon said that this child should be "Glory for your people Israel." By means of this child Israel should finally reach the glory promised to their father Abraham, "in you shall all families of the earth be blessed." In its long history how often Israel failed to measure up to its promise. Israel had been a leaky channel through which the water of life flowed. But this child would be a well of water bubbling up to give life to the world.

It is no accident that Simeon placed the Gentiles before the Jews in the order of the child's ministry. "Light to the Gentiles" precedes "Glory for Israel." Simeon declares that Israel would realize its true glory only after light came to the Gentiles. Furthermore, the enlightenment of Gentiles would be the means by which Jews would be persuaded to conversion to their promised Christ. Thus they would reach their "glory." Marvelous are the ways of God with men!!

Simeon says more. "Behold, this one is set for falling and rising of many in Isarel and for a sign spoken against...that reasonings of many hearts shall be revealed." As God's Messiah this child in his personal ministry will incite hostility toward God. Since the dawn of history man has been hostile to God. But he has veiled this enmity with the veneer of formal ritual and moral conformity. He's hidden his hostility from himself. Piety can't remove, it only hides pollution. The purity of Jesus aroused the opposition of man's impurity. His goodness revealed man's badness and stimulated hatred. This opposition to this child, her son, was a sword piercing Mary's heart. He became the occasion for the "falling" of many.

But he also became the occasion for the "rising" of many. God never wills evil. Nevertheless, when evil is present in a man God wills that the evil become manifest to the man. Only by recognizing his evil as evil can a man be healed from the sickness of his sin. Confession of guilt is the way for a "rising" to salvation. Christ's presence makes this rising possible. Many have found salvation in him. "Thoughts of many hearts" are revealed because of "this child."

An Evangel for "this child."

Simeon saw, and sought release from life. Anna, lived and gave ongoing testimony to "all those expecting Jerusalem's redeeming." Anna's spirit was sensitized by a century of living among the sacred signs and symbols of the temple. She "never left the temple, serving in fastings and prayers night and day." She was a fine-tunned instrument in harmony with all who awaited "the consolation of Israel." She was a landmark in the city, prophetic person among dry bones of formalism. In God's providence the paths of the two saints interlaced. Simeon saw! Anna announced! At "that very hour" when Simeon saw the Lord's salvation Anna approached and "was

27

thanking God" and began "speaking about him to all those expecting Jerusalem's redeeming." Anna became the first evangel of God's grace in this child.

In Judean society what did people expect in Messiah? Pharisees looked for a political leader, a military conqueror to "save." Those of Sadducean hopes preferred the status quo. Leave us alone in our protected positions. But there were the hurting multitudes who longed for spiritual renewal, a rebirth of soul, a consummation of Israel's prophetic promise of redemption from sin and death. To these Anna, the prophet, published Simeon's word about this child. "Salvation...prepared before all the peoples."

The conclusion of the matter!

"This child" must endure those growing pains that fall to every child. "The child was increasing and growing, being filled with wisdom; and God's grace was upon him." The child was fully human. In body he expanded, in intellect he enlarged; in soul he developed; in spirit he was saturated with God's spirit. His wasn't the usual but his was the normal growth of what a human being might experience.

AN OUTLINE OF LUKE 2:41-52
An Obedient Boy!

Luke has stressed obedience to and respect for Mosaic law and tradition. Filial obedience is included. In this episode the boy Jesus reveals respect for his Father. That doesn't void obedience to Mary and Joseph though it may transcend it.

I. THE SETTING: PASSOVER IN JERUSALEM. 2:41-42
   1. Regular journeys to Passover festival.
   2. The twelfth year of Jesus.
II. THE MISSING BOY. 2:43-45
   1. Jesus remained in Jerusalem.
   2. The searching.
   3. Found "among the teachers."
III."YOUR FATHER" AND "MY FATHER." 2:49-50
   1. Mary's rebuke.
   2. Jesus' pronouncement.
   3. "They did not understand."
   4. The boy's obedience.

The first recorded words of Jesus reflect his awareness of his relationship to God. That is followed by human failure to understand.

* * * * * * * *

AN OBEDIENT BOY!

In the pagan world the goddess Minerva fell full grown from the head of Zeus. Not with Jesus. "Though he was son, he learned..."(Heb.5:8)   As a fetus the Lord's Christ grew in a woman's womb. As a baby he had to grow through the diaper stage and "learn" to keep himself clean. At twelve years of age he encountered the rituals of religion in Jerusalem at Passover. He sat "among the teachers" of the law to ask and answer questions. In such sacred environment he became more completely aware of his personal relationship to his heavenly father. "You knew didn't you that I must be about my father's affairs?" Luke presents Jesus as divine, God being the Father who begot him. But he is at pains to show Jesus as thoroughly human in "all points." Jesus "grew in wisdom and stature..."
The Passover in Jerusalem!

"His parents were going year by year to Jerusalem to the feast of the Passover." Other Jewish lads between 12 and 13 "learned" the meaning of Passover ritual. He too must hear the story of Jewish origins and the thrilling tales of Moses, Samson, Jephtha, David and Solomon. If Jesus be true human he "learned." Festival, ritual and sacred days have little or no meaning except as they find meaning in personal experience. Passover had its historical origins in the Exodus from Egypt. To a Jewish lad of twelve it took on flesh by the ritual of Passover week in Jerusalem. It was the year in which boys became men.

The text says, "having completed the days."   "Completing the days" means more than just spending a week of sight

29

seeing in the historic holy city. It included sacrifices, family gatherings, learned discussions, ideas new to the mind of a growing boy, the stirring of imagination in the recollection of centuries of Jewish history. All these matters were avenues through which the boy, Jesus, "learned." But at some point the lad "learned" with new insight his own personal relation to God. In the very first recorded words of Jesus he spoke of "my father's affairs." If he did not have a sense of his peculiar relationship to the heavenly Father before this he certainly had it here. At some point before or during this 12-year-old experience he became aware, he learned, of his unique and peculiar relationship to God.

The Missing Boy!

When Mary and Joseph began their return to the Narareth home Jesus "remained in Jerusalem." Conscious of his heavenly father, exhilarated by sharing in "my father's affairs," confident that his mother would perceive with sympathy his need for this divine fellowship he "remained" in Jerusalem. The purity of his heart, sensitivity of his mind, innocence of his emotions, honesty of his motives and sinlessness of his soul gave insight beyond his years to his perceptions into God's redemptive truth. He stayed in Jerusalem by choice.

Jesus in Jerusalem, especially in the temple environed by signs and symbols of his heavenly father, was a new awakening exposure. He learned with new depth his rapport with the God of heaven. It was exhilarating to his spirit, refreshing to his soul. He wanted more! So he chose to stay in Jerusalem to become more involved in his "father's affairs." Such a choice left Mary and Joseph in a disturbing position. "They, having supposed him to be in the caravan, went a day's journey" before they missed him. When they did not find him "among their kinsmen and friends" they "returned unto Jerusalem seeking him." With growing concern they searched along the way back and throughout the city. On the third day they located him "in the temple sitting among the teachers hearing and questioning them."

Nothing in his sitting with "the teachers" implies that he did the teaching. We are told: "all were amazed at his understanding and answers." He was a learner, howbeit an apt one. Part of his human experience was learning to submit to the human situation.(vs.51) Exactly what these teachers taught Jesus, if anything, is a matter of speculation. But that he learned is not. If nothing more he learned how obtuse is the human spirit in its failure to grasp with clarity God's truth. This is why they "were amazed at his understanding."

"My Father's Affairs!"

When his parents discovered Jesus they were "shocked." Not so much at what he was doing among the teachers but that which he had done to them. Mary voiced their feelings by saying, "Why did you do thus to us." Wasn't this tantamount to disobedience? At least carelessness in not informing the parents of his purpose to stay in Jerusalem. And Mary enforced her feeling by relating their anxiety. "Being distressed, your father and I were seeking you." Though you may have been lax in your filial responsibility to us, on our part we have not left a stone unturned in our parental searching for you. It was at once a rebuke and defense on Mary's part. Jesus should have asked permission to stay behind; she didn't make sure he was in the caravan before they left the city.

The answer of Jesus to Mary reveals several vital facts. First, it shows what difficulty Mary herself had in learning who this son really was. Besides the angel Gabriel's pre-natal announcment she had the word of the shepherds, the witness of Anna not to mention the ancient Simeon. As far as facts went Mary knew enough to draw valid conclusions about his divine nature and what his relation to God might be! But it takes more than an intellectual perception of facts to know. One must not only see; he must feel in order to know.

Futhermore, in view of what Jesus had now "learned" about his relationship to God he was under other obligations than those to his earth-bound parents. Jesus was not disclaiming his God-endorsed obligation to obey parents. That role he "learned" during these first twelve years. But of all people Mary should have known his relation to God. "You knew didn't you, that I must be about my father's affairs?"

Jesus' answer to Mary's rebuke has two items of particular import. First, in speaking to Jesus Mary did not address him as "son" or "child." Her word was τέκνον. That word involves the notion of a naturally conceived child borne by a mother.

Mary also used the quite pointed expression, "Your father and I..." This too stressed the mutual bond between child and parent. Family ties were strong in Israel; no less so in this family. In fact, in this family stronger. Regardless of who was to blame for this disurbance in family relations, from Mary's point of view it was a painful disruption of family trust. It must be corrected at once.

But from this entire visit to Jerusalem Jesus had "learned" a great deal about a deeper, far more transcendent relation than even the bonds of the human family. He did not deny nor repudiate his filial obligation to Mary or Joseph as his later behaviour proves. But he did point out that he had now learned of a commitment at a loftier level than that to his Jewish parents. "Why were you seeking me?" said Jesus. Through all these twelve years you have had information about me and my origin that even I have had to learn. Of all people involved, you know that Joseph isn't my father. God is my father. And the first law of the family is that one ought pursue his own father's affairs. And the way in which Jesus framed his question shows that he knew that Mary knew who his real father was. The text says: "You were knowing were you not, that I must be involved in the affairs of my father?" I really shouldn't be all that hard to find. Any son, worthy of the name, will be involved in his father's business.

31

These are the first reported public words of Jesus since he was born. And they are a recognition of his peculiar relationship as son to the supreme God. He is deity and that relationship transcends all other. The rest of his earthly career will be an unfolding of that essential commitment.

The very first pattern of behaviour in that commitment is noted in the text: "And he went down with them unto Nazareth and was submitting himself to them." The next eighteen years his obedience to the heavenly Father meant voluntary submission to his human parents. The time will come when the sword that pierces Mary's heart will sever his ties to his human family to release him to the whole family of man. But until then obedience to God meant submission to Mary and Joseph.

The roles reverse: "They didn't understand the word which he spoke to them." Mary and Joseph now were faced with the task of "learning" that which Jesus had just learned. Namely, who he really was; and what that meant for them and the world. "And his mother was keeping all these things in her heart." It was to be a life of learning.

In the meantime, "Jesus was advancing." He had to keep on growing both inward ("wisdom") and outward ("stature"). And such growing brought to Jesus "favor with both God and man." Unlike Minerva Jesus "learned." As deity he was a son of man!

32

AN OUTLINE OF LUKE 3:1-20
The Preparation!
To fail to prepare is to prepare to fail.
I.   WHEN? IN TIME. 3:1-2
II. THE MAN: John the Baptist. 3:3-6
III. THE MESSAGE: "Baptism of repentance." 3:7-14
IV. THE SIFTING: Chaff and wheat. 3:15-20
This was a moral preparing for a spiritual king and kingdom.

* * * * * * *

THE PREPARATION

To fail to prepare is to prepare to fail! This is true in the affairs of men. With God it is true in the sense that He prepare men in his approaches to man. God's grace lies too far beyond man's present limits not to need to prepare them for new advances for His kingdom.

Even among the Hebrew people, among those who dwelt in the "land of promise, among those in Judea-Jerusalem, steeped in traditional lore, hope of prophetic promise had taken the form of political freedom, economic independence, and ritual visible comformity to divine law. If God were ever to get through to the human race, he must find some change in the Hebrew race. The mold must be broken, the pattern changed, the callous must feel, the hard become soft, the closed be opened. God must get the attention of his people if he would claim the mind of all peoples. He must prepare men if He would win man! This is why "the word of God came upon John the son of Zacharias." It came "in the desert" at that particular time with that message for that people! It was a moral preparing for the coming of a spiritual king.
When!
He who lives in eternity, unlimited by space, must deal with man at a point in time and a place in space. He who has no beginning deals with those who, by virtue of being creatures, have to begin sometime and somewhere! God came into this world in his Son at a point of time. It was in the "fifteenth year of the sovereignty of Tiberias Caesar, Pontius Pilate being governor of Judea." Rome was at its height and the Roman pax was present.

At this point in time David's kingdom was but a shadow of its ancient glory. It presently was severed into quarters administered, not by "kings" but by "tetrarchs." The kingdom of God's people needed a new quality of king not to mention a new kind of kingdom. Even the ancient priesthood had fallen from its sacred pinnacle of purity. Luke speaks of the priesthood(singular)of "Annas and Caiaphas"(plural), living testimony of the low estate of religious leadership in the Israel of this point in time. The times demanded an introduction of a kingdom of the heart, a rule of the spirit. Providence was calling for fulfilling the ancient idea of

Davidic kingdom with a new kind of kingship in a new kind of kingdom. Old ideas needed a new mold! Such was the moment when "in the desert, the word of God came upon John, the son of Zacharaias."

The Man!

And who was this man "upon" whom the "word of God came"? Luke does not describe his appearance or life-style; only his name and that of his father, Zacharias. His name "John" means "God is gracious." Apparently Luke feels that the man's work and word is more to the point than his dress, diet or life-style. He is a "voice." His pulpit is "the desert."

John the Baptist describes himself as a voice crying in the desert surrounding the Jordan." As one called of God he was to "prepare the way of the Lord." The imagery of John was taken from the custom of an oriental sovereign sending a courier to announce to all to prepare the road by which he would enter the land. The king was coming to the people. The people must be aroused to do their part in preparing his coming. No hindrance is to thwart him. Eliminate curves, fill up potholes, make level rock-strewn hills. Resurface the highway for the king's entrance.

The Baptist painted the need for a moral change on this imaged backdrop. His word is summed up in Luke's report that John "came preaching baptism of repentance unto remission of sins." The "desert" was the moral wilderness in which Israel was bogged down. The potholes which needed filling were the spiritual lacks of the people. Pharisaical pride needed to be levelled. Sadducean arrogance needed removal; self-satisfaction needed the surgeon's scalpel. The word "repentance" means a "change of mind." A radical change in men's minds would give meaning to the ritual of baptism. John preached preparation by a commitment in baptism made meaningful by a change of mind toward one's guilt. Such were the "crooked places made staight." A moral change was the aim of John's work. When the people accepted this moral message then "all flesh shall see the glory of the Lord." God would disclose himself as king.

John's "baptism of repentance" involved specific "fruits." A change of mind is exhibited by a change in life. It's not blood relationship but an altered life-style that demonstrates repentance. God's understanding of "Abraham's children" was different than that of the Jews. God has more ways of creating "children" than by ancestral birth. Those who rely on blue-blood pedigree will be axed from the orchard. They must make way for a new kind of child of Abraham, one of moral-spiritual fiber. That which cumbers the ground producing no fruit is pruned or cut down.

Such preaching shook the multitudes. So John got down to specifics. The crowds were asking, "What shall we do?" To repent, answers John, is to share what you have with those who have not. "The one having two cloaks give to the one not

34

having and the one having several loaves share with him who has none." Repentance is an inward trait producing fruit.

And how may public servants demonstrate repentance? the publican? the mercenary? The fruit of repentance relates to the vocation of the person. The publican must not collect "more than has been authorized." Don't manipulate, coerce, extort, or violate the person. The soldier is not "to intimidate" by threats, or "falsely accuse." Furthermore, he shall "be content with his pay" for services rendered. In a word, repentance means to share, be honest, be content in your calling! John's preaching got the national attention away from a political fulfillment to a moral kingdom of the spirit.

The Sifting!

John's announcement of such a revolutionary message proved to be divisive as harvest separates chaff from wheat. Jesus, his life, ministry, death and resurrection became a judgmental divisive factor in history. And John in his preparatory word made this plain. "But as the people were expecting and all were reasoning in their hearts about John whether he might be the Christ." To this he responded, "I on my part in water baptize you, but the one mightier than I, of whom I am not worthy to loose the strap of his sandals, he on his part shall baptize you in the Holy Spirit and fire." My business, says John, is to shake the nation out of its complacency, to get the people to think in terms of moral integrity and spiritual reality. I am but a menial slave compared to him. He, by his coming, will divide the wheat from the chaff, the kingdom's citizens from its rebels. Even now the winnowing "fan is in his hand to clean his threshing floor, even to store the grain into his barn and the chaff he will burn with unquenchable fire." Later Luke would confirm this divisive ministry of Jesus, "Think you that I come to give peace in the earth? No! but division...father against son,..son against father."(12:51ff)

From that announcement by John until this day the history of Christ has been just that. He has become the dividing marker! He reveals men for what they are. HE becomes the standard by which men are judged "good" or "evil." To those who turn to him for mercy he gives his Holy Spirit to thereby change from bad to good. To those who cling to their evil he burns with the fires of eternal conscience. He consumes men with purity or desolates them with the flames of conscience. "So, with many other exhortations he was evangelizing.

Verses 19-20 are transitional in Luke's scheme for his message to Theophilus. He now gets the reader ready for the full ministry of Jesus. But he also hereby seals the truth that Jesus divides. Herod cannot stand to face his own adulterous life. Jesus in the person of John the Baptist sets the conscience of Herod afire with guilt. Since he can't get rid of the guilt he gets rid of the mirror who reflects the guilt. He "adds this" in that he "locked up John in prison." Thus the history of John becomes the history of the Christ and of his people. The sifting goes on!

35

AN OUTLINE OF LUKE 3:21-22
A Voice Out of Heaven!
"No man has ever seen God" is the testimony of scripture and
the experience of humanity.
 I.   HEAVEN WAS OPENED.
        1. At the baptism of Jesus.
        2. The point and act of commitment.
        3. God made himself visible in bodily form.
 II.   THE HOLY SPIRIT CAME DOWN.
        1. To defeat the spirit of evil.
        2. Bodily: to give assurance of his presence.
        3. To infuse divine power.
        4. Given to all who welcome him.
 III. A VOICE CAME!
        1. The voice said: "You are my son."
        2. The gospel; not rules but the person of Christ.
Christ's power to cure people has been displayed through 2000
years. The revelation finds meaning in the person of Christ.

* * * * * * *

A VOICE OUT OF HEAVEN

"No man has ever seen God." This is the testimony of the
scripture. This is the experience of humanity. "No man has ever
seen God."
    To the woman at the well Jesus affirmed, "God is spirit."
That's the nature of God. HE is "spirit." Therefore he can not
be seen, touched, handled or investigated by the physical
sciences. God can't be fingered, carressed, palmed, poked,
weighed, or measured by yardstick or scales. In the upper room
after his resurrection Jesus reassured the doubting disciples.
He said, "Handle me and see,...a spirit does not have flesh and
blood..." It remains a fact, "God is spirit." So it is true, "no
man has ever seen God."
    Who can unlock the secret of man's existence? Has there ever
lived a philosopher who has penetrated the mystery of man's
nature? Has any thinker ever pierced the veil of heaven to
uncover the secret of God's essence, His relationship to
creation, His planned future for man? Have the pundits, poets,
or preachers punctured the cryptic puzzle of divine-human
quality. What theologian has ever explained the enigma of human
pain? Why do the righteous suffer while the wicked prosper? Why
storm, earthquake, famine, disease and death? It's enough to
make a strong man weep. In fact, when John was invited into the
halls of heaven and there saw a "book written on the inside and
outside" he erupted into violent tears because no one "in heaven
or upon earth" could break the seven seals to explain what was
in the book. To view human history and not be able to unveil its
meaning, its pain, misery and death breaks the human heart!
    It is at this acute point that the story of the baptism of
Jesus draws back the veil and begins to unmask the mystery.

36

HEAVEN OPENED

The text says, "When all the people were baptized, Jesus also having been baptized and praying, the heaven was opened." That which philosopher, theologian, poet or prince could not do heaven did. Heaven itself "opened" its doors and revealed itself, its hopes, plans and purposes for human kind. What man cannot discover for himself heaven openly discloses for man's reception. For those who will to see light, the darkness has become light. At a particular point in time, when all the people were stirred by the apocalyptic preaching of John the Baptist, and "were baptized, Jesus also having been baptized," that is to say, at the point when Jesus in the commitment of baptism identified himself with the people, at that point "heaven was opened." Heaven was throwing wide its doors for human understanding of God's redemptive plan and hope for man.

Baptism is the point and act of commitment. In his baptism Jesus made his openly public commitment to his God-given task of human redemption. He was baptized "for the remission of sin." Not his own. He had no sin! But in his baptism Jesus was making his commitment to the forgiveness of man's sin. It was Christ's way of submitting to God's plan for human redemption. "Moses, the prophets and the Psalms" had written about him. The baptism was the event in ongoing history when God threw open the doors of heaven to declare, "Redemption is ready!" God, who is spirit and cannot be seen, is ready to make himself available in visible form. He would share human life, identify with mortal flesh, be a man among men that men might partake of the divine image. In the beginning God said, "Let us make man in our image, in our likeness..." Now deity would become man that man might become deity. "Heaven opened" that the inconceivable might become believable on the plane of human history.

THE HOLY SPIRIT CAME DOWN!

The text states: "the heaven opened." But it also reports: "the Holy Spirit came down." When we consider the cesspool of corruption into which man has turned this garden of God it is crucial that God's Holy Spirit come down to underwrite the redemptive program of Christ. If purity is to prevail the defiled must dissolve the sin within them. The spirit of God must confront, counteract and defeat the spirit of evil. To that end the Holy Spirit "came down" at the baptism of Jesus.

Furthermore, God's Spirit "descended in bodily form as a dove." In a material, wicked world such as this Jesus needed the assurance of the presence of God's Spirit. Not only that, he needed the presence of that spirit to nullify the forces of evil that daily would attack him. The devil's temptations must be resisted by the power of the Spirit of God. That the Christ himself maintained his personal purity by the power of the divine Spirit is documented by scripture. Luke says (4:1) "Jesus, full of the Holy Spirit...was led by the Spirit in the desert." By the Spirit of God he resisted prostituting his divine power to satisfy selfish desires. And visions of capturing the world by bowing to Satan's methods rather than

37

God's cross would have been fatal apart from God's Spirit working within. Peter, in the home of Cornelius declared, "how God anointed Jesus...with the Holy Spirit,...and he went about doing good and healing all who were under the power of the devil, because God was with him."(Acts 10:38)

If Jesus could not maintain his purity without the presence of God's Spirit how much more is that presence needed in every man's life. It is at the baptism of Jesus that we are reassured that God's Holy Spirit is available to every man who responds to the open door of heaven. The apostle Paul reminds us that God's Spirit is for all when he says, "God has poured out his love into our hearts by the Holy Spirit, whom he has given to us."(Rom.5:5) Again he declares: "He saved us through the washing of rebirth and renewal by the Holy Spirit, whom he poured out on us generously through Jesus Christ our Savior."(Titus 3:5) It was at the baptism of Jesus when heaven revealed that God's Holy Spirit was openly available to any who welcome Him. No man can sustain holiness apart from the presence of God's Holy Spirit.

A VOICE CAME!

The text makes yet a third vital statement: "A voice out of heaven came." And that voice said, "You are my son, the beloved; in you I thought well!" It's the voice of God speaking to Jesus as he rose up out of the waters of baptism. As God looked on Christ rising from the Jordan he recognized him and so declared him to be his Son. And he affirmed that such a commitment to human redemption pleased him; "in you I got good thoughts." In other words, "it pleases me that you dedicate yourself to my redemptive will."

The essence of the gospel is not the written word. Nor is it orthodox doctrine. Neither can it be the outward forms of conformity to righteousness. Nor should we think that the church as an institution is the substance of the gospel. The good news of the gospel is not a book, a doctrine, nor a ritual nor an institution. It is a Person! The news that is good is that God has trod this earth in the person of Jesus of Nazareth. That he "went about doing good," that "he died according to the scriptures, that he was buried, and that he has been raised the third day according to the scriptures."

The bottom line of our redemption is the person of Jesus Christ and our personal relationship to Him. The Bible teaches about him but the power of redemption is not the Bible but the person of the Saviour whom the Bible reveals. My sin is against God, not a book. My rebellion is against God, not a doctrine. It is a person who must forgive me, not the New Testament, nor any ritual taught in it. The teachings enlighten my mind. The rituals offer objective forms by which I identify in forgiveness with him against whom I have sinned. But the bottom line for me is my faith in, love for, and dedication to the living person of him of whom God said, "This is my Son."

38

What makes a ball team win? It's not the rules of the game nor the rule book. It's not even the superior talent of the players as important as that may be. But it's the person of the leader be it coach, player, or an idol as a role model. It is people who lift people, not institutions, doctrines, programs, or methods. Remove Christ and all the doctrines of the past 2000 years of history would be vain and useless; remove Christ and the church would be an empty shell, a powerless paradox. It is the reality of the person of the living Christ that propels the gospel power. Without the person there is no good news, no power.

Heaven's open door and the descent of the Holy Spirit find meaning in who Jesus is. The voice of God has declared:"This is my son." And the centuries verify the power of the person. In changed, redeemed lives history has demonstrated Christ's power to cure people.

* * * * * * *

AN OUTLINE OF LUKE 3:23-38
The Genealogy and Jesus!
A genealogy is a way of showing one's relationship to family, clan, nation, or, as in Luke, to humanity. In Luke's genealogy Jesus is equally kin to all mankind and God.
I. NEW TESTAMENT GENEALOGIES.
    1. Matthew: "Son of David son of Abraham."
    2. Luke: the son of Mary and "son of God."
II. THE GENEALOGY OF LUKE
    1. Negative: Not son of Joseph, "as was supposed."
    2. Positive: (a)From Adam as son hence human.
              (b)From God, hence divine.
When we consider the theme of Luke in his Gospel rather than being "incredible" it is logical, natural and quite "credible" that he present the genealogy of Mary, the mother of Christ.

* * * * * * *

THE GENEALOGY AND JESUS!
Above all else Luke desires Theophilus to see Jesus as God's son completely and totally identified with humanity. One way to do this is to trace his origins to both human and divine sources. Thus he traces the family tree back to the man, Adam, and to the creator, God. Thus Theophilus can see Jesus as related to both the human and divine.

Luke's first reader probably had never read Matthew's Gospel with its genealogy. Matthew, writing to a Jewish audience, wished only to establish the Christ's relationship to David, the king and Abraham the patriarch. For Messiah, in order to inherit David's throne must be a legitimate and legal son of David. And to be heir to the divine promises to Abraham he must relate to the patriarch. These Gospel writers were not concerned with "problems" of harmoney that occupy the energies of modern scholars. Gospel authors went to the core of the matter to create impressions. They wanted their reader to "see" points of fact. Hence Luke gives the actual, the real, the human ancestry of Jesus. Matthew gives the legal. It's the human that Luke wants his Greek reader to see in Jesus. As a Greek the legal would make less impression. Its the fact that God became human, an earth-born man, that would startle and impress the Gentile Greek mind.

The Negative

Luke makes clear at the outset that Mary's son was not the son of Joseph by natural begetting. He has gone to great lengths to insure Theophilus that Jesus had a virgin mother. The story of Gabriel's announcement to Mary, the virgin, was enough to establish the fact that Joseph was not the natural father. Only twentieth century scholars seem troubled with duplications, omissions, and other such "problems." To Luke it was the strong effect of the Christ's universal relations that proved important.

The Positive

Besides his having already made plain that God begot the baby Jesus Luke's method of introducing Joseph makes plain that he was not the real father. The text says: "Jesus...being, as was supposed, the son of Joseph." The verb translated "was supposed" is imperfect which indicates the supposition was continuous through the years. He was really the "son of God" and the son of Mary. But he was "supposed" by the public to be the son of Joseph.

Furthermore, the definite article appears with each member of the genealogy from Heli to Adam except that of Joseph. Luke thus sets Joseph apart from the list of ancestors.

That Jesus was kin to the entire human race through Mary is the very point of Luke's genealogy. It supports the over-all theme of his entire Gospel. Mary was a mother! And mothers are those who carry the lives of any and all human beings from the moment of conception until birth. Moreover, from the beginning of time babies have nursed at the mother's breast. The warmth of life's food is dependent on the mother. That the baby Jesus thus nursed identifies him with humanity as no other thing could. He was totally human. This is the point of the entire Gospel of Luke.

But that Jesus was of divine origin is not neglected by Luke. Not only the nativity stories but this genealogy traces Jesus back to the ultimate source, "Adam, the son of God."

AN OUTLINE: LUKE 4:1-13
The Temptation!
Trials are universal to all human kind. To be mortal is to endure trial. To be human is to suffer temptation. In a world of moral and ethical values in which "wrong" contests "right" temptation is inevitable.
I. THREE ACCOUNTS.
  1. The temptation as by Mark. 1:12-13
     (a)"The spirit drives him forth..."
     (b)He is "in the wilderness."
     (c)"forty days being tempted."
     (d)"the angels were ministering to him."
  2. The temptation as by Matthew. 4:1-11
     (a)The inevitable event: "Was led."
     (b)The agent: "By the spirit."
     (c)Purpose: "to be tempted."
  3. The Temptation as by Luke. 4:1-13
     (a)The ongoing event: "was being led..."
     (b)Environment:"in the spirit...in the wilderness."
     (c)A constant trial; "being tempted."
II. THREE TEMPTATIONS. 4:1-13
  1. Stone to bread: appeal to material need.
  2. Kingdoms of inhabited earth: desire for dominion.
  3. Temple pinnacle: celebrity status.
III.LUKE'S ORDER TO IMPRESS HIS GREEK GENTILE READER.
  1. Matthew's order: (a)Stone (b)Pinnacle (c)the World.
  2. Luke's: (a)Bread (b)inhabited earth (c)pinnacle.
These temptations exhaust the kinds of trials to which man is subject. They are the temptations "in all points" to which Christ and all men are subject. They are the most innocent of man's needs. The temptation lies in the perversion of the "need" from service to indulgence. The goals are good; the means corrupt the good!

* * * * * * *

THE TEMPTATION!
Trials are the universal legacy of human kind. In the physical realm no man escapes pain. From birth to the choking gurgle of death man is heir to suffering. When we move to the moral world of conscience a similar ordeal of pain prevails. All are guilty! To be mortal is to endure trial. To be human is to suffer temptation. If Christ be truly human he will suffer pain, he must encounter temptation. Trial is inevitable!
If there be a "right" there must be a "wrong." It is the part of man to weigh the difference and make his choice. It's this "weighing the difference" that produces the moral struggle, creates the inner tensions, and leads to the eventual outward commitment to one or the other. Diabolic force pulls one way; divine power draws the other. It becomes war in the trenches for the souls of men. The devil versus God are competing for human beings. No one escapes temptation in the spiritual cosmos which surrounds us.

41

Three Accounts!

Three accounts of the temptation of Christ appear in the New Testament. Though our concern is with Luke's particular story it is of value to compare and contrast some features of Luke with Mark and Matthew. That Theophilus never read Mark or Matthew is a reasonable assumption. It is probable that Luke did consult them. He refers to "many having taken in hand to draw up a narrative..." If he consulted the "many" Luke surely would not overlook these two apostolic witnesses. One reason why he would alter details about the temptation torture would be to create a particular impression on the mind of Theophilus. In other words, the peculiar need of his reader determined the particular emphasis in Luke's use of the material of his Gospel. By placing the three accounts side by side we may arrive at Luke's special perception of the Christ.

All three synoptists place Christ's great moral struggle immediately after his commitment of baptism. In obedience to his heavenly calling Jesus was baptized "to fulfill all righteousness." Once committed immediately that commitment is challenged. Luke says, "But Jesus, full of the Holy Spirit, returned from the Jordan and was being led in the spirit in the desert forty days being (continuously) tempted by the devil." The time of the devil's approach to any man is that moment when his thought turns upward, his will resolves to commit to God's task, his emotions rise toward the light of truth. Even Christ, yes, especially Christ, cannot seek to rise but Satan attempts his fall. A human cannot even want to do good but evil tries to empower him to do bad. All three synoptics show the tempter at work straightway after the baptism. Furthermore, they agree that it happened "in the wilderness." Alone, in the solitude of wilderness wastelands. Mark adds that wild beasts were his companions.

The three differ somewhat as to how he got there. Mark states: "The spirit drives him forth." Jesus was "hurled" out into the desert. But Matthew indicates that Jesus "was led by the spirit." And he reports the purpose was "to be tempted." Matthew focuses on the fact that a tempting took place.

Luke gives more emphasis to the continuous nature of the days spent in the wilderness and the constant ongoing struggle as enduring over the entire forty days. Jesus "was being (continuously) led." He was "in the spirit" while he was in the struggle. Although the three climactic trials came when "he hungered," the trial was constant without any let-up during the entire forty-day onslought.

The Three Temptations

Mark does not specify any particular temptations. He is satisfied to present the reality and victory of God's son when confronted with an invitation to sin.

Though they are the same details of the temptations differ in Matthew and Luke. Regardless of details, order or form sin is sin and temptation is temptation. The reason for differences in the report of them is the particular impression each author wants to make on his reader.

42

Consider the three climactic temptations regardless of the differences in the manner in which they are reported. Matthew and Luke place the "turn this stone into bread" as the first. At the outset we must note that <u>none</u> of these trials deal with <u>anything</u> that in itself is sinful. Nothing is more needful to human life than food. Bread is the "staff of life" in a very real sense. Hunger is a physical need as pure and innocent as soil, sunshine and rain. The babe in the womb <u>needs</u> food and unless the mother nurses him after birth he dies before he's conscious of himself as human. To be hungry and to get bread is in itself not temptation. But to prostitute one's bread-getting ability for selfish indulgence rather than as a way of serving the needs of others of God's children <u>is</u> wrong. Money is not of itself evil. But acquiring money for self-gratification becomes bread baked in a different oven. It is the corruption of the very meaning of human life. The first and most fundamental of all temptations is the appeal to the material. Bread (money) as a means of security for self is sin; money as a means of service to God's people is a blessing.

At creation God told our first parents that part of their purpose for living in such a world was "to have dominion." Man in his nature as made "in the image" of God has been created to "have dominion." When the devil took Jesus to the high mountain and offered the "kingdoms of the world" it was an appeal to a God-given divine element in his nature. Here again nothing is more innocent than the power to rule. But to abuse the instinct to "have dominion" by becoming tyrannical over other men is to degrade and defile that divine quality in man. To bake bread or "have dominion" for selfish ends perverts the "good" into the "bad." To rule is divine; to dictate is to destroy the divine.

As Luke records it the third temptation took Jesus to the "pinnacle of the temple." There Satan said, "If (since) you are the son of God, cast yourself down." And he fortified his invitation to sin by quoting from the Psalm to plead his diabolical cause. This is an invitation to gain the attention of people in order to win their quick approval. Jesus came to win the people of the world. He needed to capture their hearts, draw popular support and sway the multitudes. This was the devil's appeal to gain the plaudets of the crowd by becoming an instant celebrity. Use your personality to diffuse the truth rather than the power of truth to persuade. It's the gaudy, sensational display of self rather than the revelation of God's will. Make a show rather than a teaching of truth!

Details of Luke's Report!

Certain details in Luke's record of the temptations show his special thesis of the universality of Christ and his gospel. In the first temptation Luke has the devil say, "Speak to this stone that it become (a) loaf of bread." In contrast Matthew reports, "Tell these stones that they become loaves." Luke has the singular instead of Matthew's plural. Luke reduces every appeal to the sensuous to <u>one</u> basic attraction. Though infinite in variety the bottom <u>line</u> is bread for the stomach. The universal desire for food represents man's craving for material things.

43

A second noteworthy detail. When the devil took Jesus to "an exceeding high mountain" Matthew relates that Satan "shows him all the kingdoms of the world (κόσμου) and their glory." But in Luke Satan showed "all the kingdoms of the world (οἰκουμένης) in a moment of time." The two authors use different words for "world." To Matthew the devil offered Jesus the political power and economic muscle of society. But in Luke the world offered was the inhabited, civilized culture of humanity with all its nuances of subtle beauty, art and science. Luke's was the world of refinement of mind, thought and philosophy. A noble Greek would be tempted more by that appeal than the power of politics or the sword. Luke also adds a detail: "having completed every temptation, the devil left him for a season." Luke wanted Theophilus to realize that temptation would not be exhausted in one session with Satan. To human beings trial would be life long. The devil returns again and again through all of life.

The prime difference of Luke is the reversed order of the last two temptations. Luke has Jesus on "the pinnacle of the temple" as the final supreme temptation. Matthew has the vision of the "kingdoms of the world" as the last and climactic trial. To the Jew the supreme question was, What kind of king is Messiah? What's the nature of the kingdom over which he is to rule? Is the sceptre to be the sword or the spirit of truth? Is it the cross or compromise?

But to the Greek the greatest temptation was to substitute the bizarre, the brilliant, the dazzling gawdy prestigeous for God's normal providence and slow but sure triumph of truth. Take matters into your own hands. Shall it be human display or God's presence and providence, that governs one's life? He who could resist this temptation could resist any! At least so felt the cultured Greek. The center in Luke's narrative-is people. But people are not to be manipulated by popular, ornate display but by solid, down-to-earth realities of the truth of God revealed in the person of Christ.

The temptations of Christ are objective events in history. They happened to Him at a point in time and a place on the earth. They run the gantlet of all temptations to which man is subject. They are realities regardless of how they are reported or conceived in men's minds. However, the manner in which they are told does affect our reactions. The report can affect our perception of God's identifying with us as human beings. If HE experienced them on the same terms as we do, then we know that he understands our struggle, sympathizes with us at our level. He identifies! This is the value of Luke's record of the temptations of the Christ. He was "tempted in all points as we are." He knows our frailties!

AN OUTLINE OF LUKE 4:14-30
The Year of the Jubilee!

God's Holy Spirit was present at the baptism and temptations of Jesus. In Luke the next sequence is: "Jesus returned in the power of the spirit unto Galilee." Committal and trial is followed by inauguration of the task. Jesus begins in Nazareth where he grew to manhood.

I.   THE JUBILEE - WHAT IS IT? 4:14-20
1. Old Testament background of Jubilee.
2. Reading the Jubilee passage of Isaiah.
3. "The eyes of all fastened on him."

II.   WORDS OF GRACE. 4:21-22
1. "He began to say, Today this scripture fulfilled."
2. They marvelled "at the words of grace."
3. The paradox: "This is the son of Joseph isn't it?"

III.   THE CHALLEGE AND RESPONSE. 4:23-27
1. Do here what you've done elsewhere!
2. "No prophet is acceptable in his own town."
3. Old Testament examples of Jubilee beyond Israel.
4. Violent rejection.

This first synagogue message and experience set the tone and direction of his Galilean ministry. God's year of Jubilee is fulfilled in Jesus. But it has always been in God's intent to include the Gentiles beyond Israel.

✦ ✳ ✳ ✦ ✳ ✳ ✦

THE YEAR OF JUBILEE!

Jubilee! Sounding of trumpets! Fresh beginning! Bound to baptismal commitment and temptation is the start of Christ's Galilean ministry. The Spirit descended and God claimed, "You are my son..." Forthwith Jesus "full of the Holy Spirit...was being led in the spirit.." Now "Jesus returned in the power of the Spirit unto Galilee." His baptism was commitment to the ministry of reconciliation. Temptation was testing God's methods of ministry. At Nazareth Jesus begins the task.

The Year of Jubilee - What is it?

"You shall count...forty nine years. Then you shall send abroad the trumpet throughout all your land. You shall hallow the fiftieth year, and proclaim liberty throughout the land to all...it shall be a jubilee for you, when each shall return to his property and each shall return to his family."(Lev.25:8ff) As revealed from God by Moses, land, houses, life are all sacred trusts. "The land shall not be sold in perpetuity, for the land is mine; you are strangers and sojourners with me."(Lev.25:28) If a Hebrew "sold" a farm; if one mismanaged life so as to sell himself into slavery; should one be imprisoned for crime; should anyone keep and farm his land for 49 years, the year of Jubilee was the gracious provision of God for a new start. Prisoners were released, land lay idle, "sold" property was returned to family heirs. The Jubilee year was a periodical social restoration for Israel.

When he came to Nazareth Jesus "began to teach in their

synagogues, being glorified by all." And "fame(report)went out concerning him through the surrounding country." John's Gospel reveals that Jesus had turned water into wine at Cana. And he had ministered six months or more in Judea, long enough to gain some _fame_. With such publicity he entered his home town synagogue to begin unfolding the _meaning_ of the Old Testament prophetic message relative to Messiah. He starts with Isaiah 61:1-2: "Spirit of the Lord is upon me, because he anointed me to annouce good news to poor, he has sent me to herald release to captives and (clear) sight to endungeoned, to send off, healed, ones having been wounded, to herald the acceptable year of the Lord." True, Isaiah had in mind the returnees from Babylon. But his words reflect the joy of Jubilee!

In the prophet's mind the message of Messiah encompasses five elements. (1)To bring hope to the poor. Poverty has its rewards, if not material, then moral wealth of redemption. (2)He's to proclaim "release to captives." This release goes beyond imprisoned criminals. It includes setting free ones chained in their own moral jails. (3)"Sight to blind" refers to the clearing of vision after long imprisonment in dark dungeons where eyes, seeing nothing, became useless. Messiah is to give light of truth in terms that the morally blind and spiritually sightless could see and perceive. (4)"To sent off those wounded in healing." To be healed of mortal wounds of moral sin is greater than to heal the body pierced by the sword. Salving sin heals the heart! (5)"To herald the acceptable year of the Lord" refers to the Jubilee year of Leviticus tradition. Jubilee was God's special giving of grace.

This was the "text" of the Christ's sermon on the Sabbath in his home town. The text, his "fame" and his person captured the rapt attention of the people. "The eyes of all in the synagogue were fixed on _him_." The text, person, and circumstances combined to arouse excited expectation. What might this _carpenter_ say to this people on this text?

His Words of Grace!

"He began to say, Today this scripture has been fulfilled in your ears." He "_began_" implies that he explained at length. He taught word by word. He went behind the image of "poor" to show who were and what real "poverty" meant. Moral captivity and spiritual blindness was worse than the outward. He revealed Messiah to be redeemer of the souls of men, the saviour of the minds, hearts, and spirits of humanity. Such explanation of the prophet startled people and priest out of mental ruts which long years had channelled. He was breaking new ground with the scriptures. They "were testifying to" and "marvelling at the words of grace coming out of his mouth." Can a carpenter, specially _this_ one, have such insight? "This is Joseph's son isn't it?" He's man among men; our neighbor!

If God dwells in his heaven he's so far over and beyond us that we doubt he can sympathize or understand us. Yet when he becomes human, lives next door, we doubt that it's he! This is the paradox of incarnation. Can God be human? A carpenter?

46

The Challenge and Response!

The questioning doubt of his fellow-citizens prompted them to challenge him as to who he really was. They knew, at least they thought they knew, that he was "the son of Joseph." Yet they could not deny their ears. They had just witnessed "the words of grace" flowing from his lips. His piercing the depths of Isaiah's image of Messiah's ministry was persuasive. But he had no more schooling than they. Whence this wisdom? They'd heard of Cana's miracle. Reports came of similar Capernaum wonders! Could he support his views by miracles?

Jesus reflected their challenge, "Physician, heal yourself. Whatever happened in Capernaum, do here in your home town!"

The response of Jesus began with a proverbial note. "No prophet is acceptable in his own country!" Familiarity breeds contempt and feeds doubt, pride, envy and jealousy. But in the face of such roadblocks Jesus met the challenge head on. He proposed the basic theme of their scriptures. From the first God has targeted "all the families" of the earth as objects of his redemptive purpose. Jesus said, "Upon truth I say to you, Many widows were in Israel in the days of Elijah, when the heaven was locked up three years and six months, when a great famine came upon all the land, and Elijah was sent to none of them except to Serepta of Sidon to a woman, a widow." God gave witness of his concern for people other than Israel often enough to remind that he was the God of all men. And in this instance he helped a Gentile woman, the most helpless, a widow. Mercy includes women!

A second sample, a male, was Syrian, traditional enemy of Israel. "Many lepers were in Israel at the time of Elisha the prophet, and no one of them was cleansed except Naaman the Syrian." God's merciful purposes encompasses enemies.

Jesus selected these examples by deliberate choice. God has never loved one person more than another. It's difficult for men to recognize or accept the immensity of his love and the extensiveness of his grace. Jubilee for Israel was a visible symbol of God's desire for Jubilee for all men. It's not Jew or Gentile but poor, captive, blind, and wounded who receive God's universal redemptive Jubilee. It's not a race, nation, class or clan that gets God's Jubilee. It's a human of any place, time, need or condition. God's grace is for sinner and the saint who sins! "By grace you have been saved through faith...God's gift...we are his work, having been created in Christ Jesus for good works."(Eph.2:8ff)

Violent Rejection!

Thirty years of genteel life in Nazareth did not soften explosive anger. "All were filled with wrath when they heard these things." To admit that God made no distinction between Israelite and Syrian was proof of heresy beyond endurance. Hatred cannot erupt unless it's already in the heart. Their arrogant view of the limits of God's purpose was the festering sore that burst its scab when he recalled facts from their own history. God's Messiah must reflect God's grace. Men judge themselves by response to that grace.

47

It is important to note that the violence which erupted at
his teaching turned against him. It's not doctrines, false or
true, that experience rejection, it's people. The citizens of
Nazareth may have thought they were protecting the truth of the
scripture. But their hatred vented itself against the person of
the Christ. When you cannot answer facts you can always attack
him who expresses the facts. Thus these Nazarenes "rose up and
hurled him out of the city, and brought him to a ridge of the
mountain on which their city had been built so as to cast him
down." Hatred in the heart finds fruit in outward murder. So
they proceeded to harvest the fruit of their hate. But it's the
person of Jesus who felt the brunt of their murderous
rejection.

That which Luke wrote to Theophilus in this episode was a
clear indication of the thesis of his entire book. God's grace
includes Israel. In fact it came to these Nazareth Jews first.
But the message at Nazareth demonstrated in word and deed that
it reached beyond Israel to Sidonian and Syrian. Theophilus
could hardly miss the point: God's grace is for the Greek also!

* * * * * * *

AN OUTLINE OF LUKE 4:31-37
When Evil Confronts God!
When the "spirit of an unclean demon" faced him in the
Capernaum synagogue Jesus ordered, "You shut up and you come
out from him." By "you" and "him" Christ treated the "spirit"
as an objective creature. Christ dealt with demons as personal.
If one prefers to think of "forces of evil" the result is the
same. The man in the synagogue was "possessed" to the extent
that he was not free to use his own will. He was wholly
ensnared. Jesus set him free from that captivity!
  I.   AUTHORITATIVE TEACHING. 4:31-32
       1. Astounded "at his teaching."
       2. Because: "his word was in authority."
  II. AUTHORITATIVE CLEANSING. 4:33-35
       1. Evil confronts good(God).
       2. The Cleansing: "Shut up and come out of him."
  III. THE AUTHORITATIVE MESSAGE. 4:36-37
       1. The Marvel: "What is this word?"
       2. He "commands and the evil spirit comes out."
       3. "Report went out concerning him.
If Jesus in the Nazareth synagogue showed the breadth of
redemptive love, in the Capernaum synagogue he reveals the
depth of his cleansing power. He's victor over ultimate evil!

WHEN EVIL CONFRONTS GOD!

Jesus viewed evil as personal. He addressed demons as real creatures. In the Capernaum synagogue he commanded the spirit of an unclean demon, "<u>You</u> shut up and <u>you</u> come out from <u>him</u>." To Jesus two personalities were involved, the "unclean <u>demon</u>" and the "<u>man</u> having (a) spirit of unclean demon." If he knew there was no such entity as a "demon" yet accommodated his teaching and practice to the ignorant level of the populace, he was a fraud and hypocrit. That is inadmissable in view of his lofty moral life and spiritual integrity. He treated demons as real for the simple reason that they were real.

However, if one prefers to look on evil as impersonal force the consequences in humanity are the same. When evil arrives at the point of dominating a man until he no longer can exercise his own will, he is captured, possessed, enslaved, a prisoner of "the forces of evil." What's the difference? Don't confuse the issue by juggling the terms. Whether a diabolical person nudges men to set their wills against God or whether a man generates the corruption in his own heart the results are identical in fact. Men are slaves to sin when they cannot do with freedom what they wish to do. Scientific or psychological jargon does not change realty.

Moreover, evil becomes so utterly nauseating in human beings that it's difficult to think a <u>human</u> could conceive it without some outside person or force enticing him as bait lures a fish.

When Jesus returned to Galilee to begin his public ministry "he began teaching in their synagogues." In Nazareth he was violently rejected because he declared that God's redemption reached beyond Israel to Gentiles. In his appearance in Capernaum he showed that God's grace stretched to the depth of human depravity, even to a man completely controlled by demonic power. Man is created to be "in the image of God." That fact implies that he is capable of becoming "the image" of the devil. If he can be truly <u>good</u>" he can be equally <u>evil</u>. And when he becomes so thoroughly addicted to evil he has transformed into a slave of Satan or the forces of evil. However the slavery is defined he is "possessed."

Authoritative Teaching!

The worshippers "were being astonished at his teaching because his word was in authority." "Was being astonished" is a strong word signifying repeated action. They were "shocked" and showed the impact of their agitation by a ceaseless buzz of exchange about his doctrine. What he taught certainly included that which he voiced at Nazareth. God's gracious purpose was not confined to Israel. But the universal reach of the message goes further and deeper. It extends to the depth of human depravity. No sin or sinner falls so low that God's redeeming grace cannot touch him. "All have sinned" but all are objects of God's eternal purpose.

The most amazing fact about his teaching was its <u>authority</u>. ἐξουσία derives from ἐκ εἰμί "to be." It's the "authority" inherent in truth. It's not power of position, office, skill, or anything other than the nature of truth itself. An ear of corn, full-grained, growing on a stalk in an open field doesn't get that way by someone gluing the grains on the cob. No! Life inherent in the seed corn, intrinsic to such plant life, the essence of the biolological stuff of corn, that produces corn. The grain is not artificially stuck on; it grows from the life within. Such was the "teaching" of the Christ in Capernaum. It sprang out of the nature of him who did the teaching. He spoke with the authority of truth. Christ did not disect dry quotes from learned Rabbis. He drew on the vast reservoir of knowledge that flowed within him as one of whom it is said "in him was life, and the life was the light of men."(Jn.1:4) He told truth which carried within it its own evidence. He did not quote the scholars to substantiate his teaching. HE was truth, therefore he spoke truth. He wasn't a lawyer interpreting the law. He was the legislator who made the law. The tone, manner and substance of what he taught had the impact and power of the authentic. It was pure water of the mountain stream, not cistern water which had been gathered by others. His doctrine was not artificially imposed; it blossomed from the seed. To the people it was refreshingly different. It sounded true, it felt true, it responded to their experience. It came across as reasonable, sensible, real. Of course, they were absolutely "astonished" because he spoke with "authority."

The Authoritative Cleansing!

Doctrine without deed is deadening. Teaching with no example is ineffective. Thus the cleansing of the demon possessed man demonstrated with a deed Christ's doctrine of redemption. Christ came to cleanse humanity of its corruption, to wash us from our sin, to purify man from his pollution. To do this he must involve himself in the long slow process of teaching, of enlightening man to the need for cleansing. If a man does not know he is sick he won't call for a physician. So man must become aware of his dirt before he will call for a cleansing or accept a washing. Authoritative teaching comes first. But the bottom line is the actual removal of the dirt. Demonstration must come in fact, not just in doctrine.

In the Capernaum synagogue that Sabbath came a perfect opportunity to exhibit a sample of redemptive cleansing. "In the synagogue was a man having spirit of unclean demon, and he cried out in a loud voice, Aha! What's between us, Jesus Nazarene? You came to destroy us! I know you, who you are, the Holy One of God!" This is a prime example of what happens when evil faces good, the devil confronts God. In any form, at any place, at any time, sin feels threatened by righteousness. By nature the lawless fears the lawful, an athiest shrinks facing faith, guilt cringes before innocence, sin grabs the nearest fig leaf to cover its nakedness from God. When the demonic spirit cried, "What do we have in common" he knew they had nothing in common. By nature they were inveterate opposites. Wrong cannot face right without antagonism to the death of one or the other.

Furthermore, evil always recognizes righteousness. "I know you who you are, the Holy One of God." With the instinct of

50

reality sin recognizes the quality of purity and recoils from it. Sin knows that right can eventually destroy wrong, hence it immediately challenges the right. Satan senses that to tolerate God is to guarantee his own abandonment to perdition. For its own existence evil cannot tolerate the presence of good. To survive it must repudiate and destroy God and all for which he stands and all who stand with him.

Christ did not need or want the testimony of evil. With peremptory command he charged the "spirit of the unclean demon, Shut up and come out of him." To set the man free from his evil captor it took the authoritative power of God's grace, "Come out!" No matter how much a man may be enslaved to sin God can liberate him from his chains. At the word of Christ the unclean demon came out.

But he didn't depart without a final violent attack to maintain his control over the man. He ripped, tore, and struggled with the man until he "hurled him into the midst" of the synagogue crowd. The man appeared dead though in reality he left the man "not having injured him." It is a terrifying struggle for a man to give up his addiction to sin in any form. The final fight has its own peculiar pain. But the end result is healing. The man was left "uninjured." The cleansing was complete; the freedom from evil was real.

The Authoritative Message!

The immediate reaction of the people was "What is this message? For in authority and power he commands and the unclean spirits are coming out!" They recognized a relationship between the teaching and him who taught. The authority and power came from him who did the teaching. It was not abstract doctrine or theological dogmas but the influence of the teacher who fulfilled his teaching by demonstrating its meaning.

And this idea of the Person having the power to exemplify his teaching by deed scattered throughout the region. "The report ($\mathring{\eta}\chi o \varsigma$ = echo) was going out through every place in the surrounding countryside concerning him." It was he about whom they were talking. He was the exemplar of his teaching. And he cleansed a man who was enslaved to the most abject sin, a man "possessed" of evil, handcuffed to an "unclean spirit." If this man could be cleansed from his bondage to filth any man could have hope in him! The power of the person of Christ is the power of the gospel. He is the fulfillment of the truth in his teaching!

Why did Luke include this story in his narrative to Theophilus? With their worship of Bacchus and Venus, deities to wine and women and revelry, the Greeks were as much in need of moral cleansing as the worshippers of Astarte and the Baals of Canaan. God's Christ, born of woman, is able to descend to the depths where sin does its ultimate destruction. The Gospel is for all men and every man. None fall below his outstretched arm of redemption.

AN OUTLINE OF LUKE 4:38-44
In Home and Market Place!
Disease and its suffering were not in God's purpose at
creation. That came later as a consequence of sin. Sickness is
not sin though its presence in human experience has come as a
sequel to sin.
Evil in its milder forms may appear as a pin prick rather
than a death wound. But even so it must be "rebuked" and
healed.
I.   THE HOME OF SIMON PETER. 4:38-39
      1. The Hostess "sick of a fever."
      2. The cure: (a)Requested.
                   (b)His human touch.
                   (c)He "rebuked" the fever.
II.   THE STREETS OF CAPERNAUM. 4:40-41
      1. The sick sought him: He touched them.
      2. "Many" demoniacs cried, "You are God's son..."
         He rebuked them.
III. THE CROWDS PRESSURED HIM. 4:42-44
      1. They disturbed his search for solitude.
      2. They sought to control him for their own ends.
      3. His purpose: The kingdom for "other cities."
    If the Christ is for those abandoned to sin he also came for
those whose sin flourishes among the refined citizens of the
community. The pin-prick of sin must be "rebuked" while it is
still a pin-prick. The kingdom of God is "for other cities" and
is open to all. And the "all" includes those conforming to
standards of human conduct in home and market.

* * * * * * *

IN HOME AND MARKET PLACE!
    Sin in the depths is dramatic. It shocks the human sense of
what is morally proper. He who is "possessed" of sin placards
his evil before the public without shame or concern. But most
"respectable" people cover sin with a veneer of cultured
conformity to "decent" behaviour. Such sin lies just below the
surface as it tries to justify itself by quack substitutes. Our
"good" done here salves the conscience for "bad" done there! Men
attempt to drown their evil by outward display of benevolence.
    Distortion of the conscience through compromising moral
integrity will eventually show up in various forms of physical
pain, even illness. This is not to say or imply that every cold
or cancer comes directly as a result of one's sin. But neither
can we forget that some relationship between sin and suffering
does exist. "In pain you shall bring forth children" (Gen.3:16)
is closely related to sin. And here in 4:39 Luke states that
Jesus "rebuked the fever" as he had the demon in the synagogue.
He treated disease as though it were a person rather than a
thing! Though disease may not be a consequence of my sin, in
human experience it came as a result of sin. It is sin in
social history that has left its effect on humanity in the form
of sickness.

52

In the Home of Simon Peter!

"Having risen up, he entered into the house of Simon." But upon arrival a problem presented itself, embarrassing to Peter and family. His mother-in-law was "being held down in a great fever." The situation was serious. Guests unexpected are enough distress but when the hostess is on fire with fever it's more than embarrassment, it becomes a family crisis. So they "asked him concerning her." They hoped he would understand the situation; maybe even a cure might be expected. But it is not necessarily implied that they asked to heal her. At any rate Jesus bent over her bed, looked deeply into her eyes, and enlisted her soul's cooperation. The text says, "he rebuked the fever and it left her."

In human relationships touch is important. Matthew tells us that he touched her hand. Mark even states that "having grasped her hand he lifted her up." But Luke confines his description to the eye to eye, soul to soul trust. He wanted her to feel his sympathy, to know that he understood. And thus his power of healing drove the fever out; she became completely cured on the spot. "Immediately, having arisen, she began serving them."

It takes some time, even days, to regain full strength after a "great" burning fever. Weakness hangs on, legs are wobbly, hands are unsteady, muscles are slow to respond. But in the case of Peter's-mother-in law the cure was instant and full. Immediately she went about her hosting her guests with full strength. Her healing was complete.

The Streets of Capernaum!

As soon as the Sabbath sun set crowds of people streamed to the house of Peter. Events of the day's synagogue worship excited the villages round about. "The sun having set, they brought to him all howevermany were being weak with various diseases." In spite of the incredible numbers , "having put his hands on each one, he healed them." He did not neglect a single person. He took care to touch; he cured every one. His healing was for all but he touched each. Every person in need was made to feel his own particular worth. God doesn't cure crowds. He redeems individuals.

But a different group of people mingled in the streets of Capernaum that Sabbath evening. "Also demons were coming out from many crying and saying, You are the son of God." Jesus touched the sick; the demons he "rebuked." Moreover, "he was not permitting them to go on speaking." Jesus did not need nor want recommendations from demons even though their testimony was accurate. God doesn't need sin to testify to his purity. Nor does he want it. He wants to attract people but not through the influence of diabolical forces. That kind of testimony confuses the issue. He saves men from demons, not by them!

The Pressure of the Crowds!

"Day having come, he went out to a deserted place." After an exhausting Sabbath day and night Jesus needed his batteries recharged. For that he sought solitude. People drained him; a vigil with God would refresh his spirit and renew his power.

But it was not to be. He who gave himself for others was besieged by people who would get for themselves. They were not concerned about his need, but about getting. Thus they hunted him down, invaded his privacy, "were restraining him so he would not go from them." Once they recognized the power of his person they weren't about to let him escape their control. They would keep him for their own advantage. As so often we, as human beings, seek to manipulate the gospel for our salvation with little or no consideration for others in the same plight. We attempt to wall him in while the same wall keeps others out. We imprison him within institutions and partisan doctrines which rob him of the full redemptive power that flows from his life, death, and resurrection.

But God, and therefore Christ, cannot be manipulated by short-sighted men for their own ends. Jesus cited to them his divine mission. God's goal was his goal and no man, certainly no self-centered man, would turn him from those for whom he "was sent." Jesus "said to them, Even for me to announce the kingdom of God in other cities is necessary, because upon this mission was I sent."

The message of the kingdom of God is unique in concept. Kingdoms of men have "subjects" over which kings, dictators, emperors hold tyranny. But the kingdom of God has no subjects, just believers who share sovereignty with him who is "King of kings." Christians are the "kings" with whom he reigns.

So he must go to "other cities" to find other kings who will share his rule. "And he was preaching in the synagogues of Judea." It is startling to read "Judea" here. Yet, if this text be correct, it signifies that Jesus will not be manipulated or restrained from carrying out his mission to the entire land. The verb "was preaching" strongly affirms continued repeated action. He kept on preaching throughout the whole land. The announcing of the kingdom of God is to go on being repeated again and again throughout the whole world! Until he comes it's his mission as he works in his reigning kings.

What is Luke saying to his first reader in this episode? The Christ has come for those whose sin is veneered by the refinements of civilization. Those who are crippled by the burning fever, the heritage of a sin-sick society, are also to receive his healing. Their sin may be but a pin-prick compared to the outcast demon possessed. But it must be faced and "rebuked" while still only a pin-prick.

Theophilus must also realize that God's gospel cannot be manipulated or controlled by redeemed men. His mission includes "other cities," other peoples, other cultures, other countries, other clans. He's not to be walled in but taken out to the "uttermost part" of the land!

AN OUTLINE OF LUKE 5:1-11
How to Succeed as Fishers of Men!
When Simon Peter first followed Jesus he knew nothing about
how to win and influence people. He didn't even know the
gospel! But shortly he got a prime lesson on how to be
successful at fishing - for men!
I.   SEASIDE AT GENNESARET. 5:1-3
     1. Standing on the seashore.
     2. Boats & fishermen.
     3. A floating pulpit.
II. A LESSON TO FISHERMEN ABOUT FISHING. 5:4-7
     1. The place and time for a proposed catch.
     2. Simon Peter's protest:
        (a)A night's fishing caught nothing.
        (b)But "at your word!"
        (c)The huge catch and how handled.
III. THE RESULTS OF THE FISHING EXPERIENCE.
     1. Spiritual results.
     2. Effective results:
        (a)"You shall catch men alive."
        (b)"They followed him."
The disciples were each called "to be fishers of men." The
world is so immense, the task so overwhelming, the means so
limited that success depends upon "thy word."

* * * * * * *

HOW TO SUCCEED AS FISHERS OF MEN!
As he walked along the shore of the sea of Galilee Jesus
called four fishermen. Matthew and Mark have him inviting,
"Come after me, and I will make you fishers of men." No crowds
were present. Two were "casting a net in the sea." Two others
were "mending their nets."
The portrayal in Luke 5:1-11 is decidedly different. Crowds
were pressing Jesus as he was "standing by the lake." He "saw
two boats...standing by the lake, but the fisherman had gone
out...and were washing the nets." Matthew-Mark tell of a call
to discipleship. Luke narrates a story that happened shortly
after the "call" of the four. It displays discipleship on a
background of the trials of fishermen. The experience is a
teaching tool in a form to make an indelible impression of who
Jesus is, and when, where, and how to fish for men.
Seaside at Gennesaret
By now Jesus' fame was widespread in Galilee. Crowds packed
the seashore jostling and shouldering each other and pressing
Jesus into the water. The swarming people were impatient and
dangerously near to pressing on each other to their own harm.
Jesus eyed two boats standing ashore nearby. One belonged to
Peter, recently called to be a follower. So, he asked Peter to
row out a short way from the shoreline that he might use the
boat as a floating pulpit. He thereby relieved pressure in the
crowd. He also gained for himself a better position to be seen
and heard by the people. Then he began to teach the multitude.

A Lesson to Fishermen About Fishing!

These fisher disciples were men of the sea, not the soil. Of their waking hours they spent as much time on sea and shore as on street or farmland. They were proud of their skills of their trade. They were acknowledged professionals knowing the best time, places, and ways to fish. On the sea of Galilee they knew that night was the best time, the shoals the best places. They were aware that in their vocation no substitute for experience existed. As fishermen they were confident of their abilities; assured by their success. Others might be their equal but none their superior as skilled fishermen. Such were the men whom Jesus called as his first disciples.

What Jesus taught that day is not reported by Luke. Without doubt it covered similar themes as in Nazareth and Capernaum synagogues. In this episode it was not the vital feature. This story's main point surfaces when Jesus said, "Sail out into the deep and lower your nets for a catch." Jesus is about to dramatize a lesson on how, in their discipleship, to fish for men. For fishermen the lesson could best be couched in images and terms from their life's vocation.

They had fished all night without a catch to reward their labor. The choicest shoals had been barren of fish that night. So when Jesus told Peter to "sail out into the deep and lower the nets for a catch" years of experience at fishing protested, "Master, having toiled the whole night we took nothing." By trade Jesus was a carpenter, not a fisherman. His home was in the highlands, not the seashore. He had become an itinerant teacher, more relaxed in school room or rabbinical seat than a fishing boat. Peter's protest was respectful but it hardly veiled his feeling of superior knowledge as a fisherman. Who was Jesus that he should instruct an old salt such as Peter as to where, when and how to catch fish?

These disciples were recently called. Knowledge of the true nature of Jesus was just beginning to unfold in their unlettered minds. If he was ignorant of fishing were they not as lacking in experience in spiritual matters, especially about his person? Thus Peter yielded to Jesus as "Master" and said, "But upon your word I will lower the nets." I will overlook the fact that it is daytime, not night. We will forget that it is the deep waters rather than the shoals. And we will disregard that we just spent the entire night fruitlessly. But "I will respect you as Master. I will follow your request and obey your order."

Contrary to Peter's experience; opposed to his expectation, the results proved to be absolutely incredible to this seaman. "They enclosed a great multitude of fish." So large was the catch that their nets could not bear the weight. "Their nets were beginning to rip." Peter had no time at the moment to show shock. He gestured wildly to his partners to come quickly to help lest they lose fish and boats. And even with this added help both boats were more than filled and "began to sink."

Peter was overwhelmed with awe, not by the catch but by him

56

who engineerd it. The catch was a rarity in more ways than one. It had positive results, spiritual and practical. First is that which grows out of Peter's protest before the catch. His experience taught Peter that to go fishing with any real hope for success one should adhere to sound principles of the trade: night is more productive than day. The shallow shoals offer better opportunity for a catch than the "deep" to which Jesus ordered them. Jesus was ignoring the experience of all the experts. Yet in the face of such odds Peter voiced one of the basics of service to God: "Having toiled all night we took nothing, but at your word I will lower the nets."

Results of the Fishing Experience!

Christ's mission, message, and person run counter to the flow of this world's standard of values. "My kingdom is not of this world." The way he measures "success" clashes with the experience of the world. Yet success in winning men to his kingdom must be "at your word." It is complete trust in the word of Christ that makes men good "fishers of men." If men are not won to genuine commitment to God's Christ by God's methods we have reason to question whether they are truly won. On the other hand "my word shall not return to me void." When we yield to this word of faith: "Upon your word" we may be confident of the catch. In catching men for God there's no substitute for obedience. "Upon your word I will labor!"

This catch under such circumstances brought to focus the person of Jesus and the human situation of Peter. Whoever this Jesus might be he far outdistanced Peter in moral, spiritual, and practical qualities. "All have sinned!" But men manage to keep personal sin adequately buried so as to live without noticeable vexation from conscience. But the presence of Jesus, especially when he invades me and my way of life, brings to the fore the realities of my moral limitations. The contrast can be crushing. My real worth at the side of him leaves me nowhere to hide.

But the presence of Jesus not only makes me aware of my moral problem, it also offers the solution. Jesus said, "Quit being afraid. From now you shall catch men, alive!" He offers two remedies: (1)You have no need to fear your standing or relationship to me. God's grace is sufficient to cover your disturbed conscience. (2)You have a task to which you are to devote yourself. "You are to catch men." Constructive redeeming work will turn your attention away from former self serving sin. This is a practical way of establishing and keeping right and wholesome relationships in the kingdom of God; accept God's grace and fish for God's catch.

One revolutionary result of this fishing excursion was a radical change in vocation for Peter and his partners. Discipleship became their calling. From fishermen for fish they became fishers for men! There can be no "part-time" devotion to the work of Christ's kingdom. It's all or nothing. The very nature of God requires total commitment. How can one believe half way? So the text says:"Having left all they followed him."

57

That they had already answered the call of Jesus is true. It is also true that their discipleship had been spasmodic, broken by intermittant return to their vocation as fishermen. But this present colossal catch at "the word" of Jesus removed any doubt as to where their future lay. From this day Jesus, his person, his mission would be their life calling. Henceforth they would do more than make a living, they must make a life! Fishing as honorable as it was, could no longer match the appeal to service to the Christ's desire to catch men. His call was to be their calling! From now on fishing for men would have their entire time and talent. It was now final: "They followed him!"

What was Luke trying to say to "noble Theophilus" by recording this fishing adventure? What contribution does it make to his developing thesis as to the universal outreach of the divine redemptive purpose? And how does this incident contribute to Luke's insistence on the humanity of God? Does the eternal God lower himself to become involved in the labors of fishermen?

The answer to such questions lies implied without being stated in this story. Yes, God rubs elbows with the sweat of honest laboring men. Yes, he uses men and depends on men as instruments through whom he catches men.

But there is much more than this! God's purpose and program is so vast in its world-wide age-long reach that the skill, intelligence, and administrative talent of man alone cannot accomplish it. It's the presence of the divine <u>word</u> that gives hope and confidence of victory. And that in the <u>face</u> of man's failure, "having fished all night and taken nothing." The world is too immense, the task so overwhelming, and the means so limited that success only comes "upon your word." On the other hand, in trusting obedience to the word of God success of the venture is assured. Though the Christ's mission runs counter to human experience, Theophilus, should he commit to Christ, would not be **joining a** failing cause. God's goal is assured by the "word" of Christ. Furthermore, should Theophilus himself "follow" Jesus he too could catch men "at your word."

AN OUTLINE OF LUKE 5:12-16
Healing a Social Outcast!
If demon possession depicts the depth of sin leprosy traces
the utmost social effects.
I.   THE LEPER: HIS PROBLEM. 5:12
     1. He was full of leprosy.
     2. Though able, is Christ willing to heal?
II. THE CHRIST'S RESPONSE. 5:13-14
     1. "I will."
        (a)"Grasped" him.
        (b)The leprosy left him.
     2. The exhortation:
        (a)Tell no one.
        (b)Show the priests for "testimony."
III. THE RESULTS. 5:1415-16
     1. Word about Jesus spread abroad.
     2. Multitudes sought to "hear and be healed."
     3. He withdrew for solitude and prayer.
The social outcast included in the "will" of Jesus. And he was
in need of solitude and prayer to renew his moral and spiritual
resources.

* * * * * * *

HEALING A SOCIAL OUTCAST!
To be human but separated from social relations with other
men is devastating to mental, moral and spiritual health.
Hospitals are crowded with people who suffer from social
exclusion. Whether we choose it or by physical or mental causes
are forced into separation makes little difference.   To be
socially ostracized leads to maladjustment at the least; a
ravaged wrecked soul at worst. Even for scientific research to
study the effects of isolation from human contact, results on
the individual are disturbing. Men are made as social beings.
When isolated we live abnormally strained lives. We depend on
each other for support in every area of existence.
In ancient society leprosy was the ultimate in social
isolation. The disease was unnerving without the terrifying
effects of isolation from society, even from one's own family.
Emotionally a leper was at the bottom looking up without hope.
His only social fellowship was in the community of lepers.
Within normal society he constantly called the cry of despair
"Unclean!" This is the context of Luke 5:12-16.
The Leper's Problem!
One word in Luke's account not only adds color but reflects
Luke's point of view. He says the man was "full of leprosy."
That's a physician's observation. The disease was far advanced!
Months of physical pain and social separation lay behind. The
fame of Jesus offered a glimmer of light on an otherwise dark
horizon. The leper had heard of Christ's cures. He had become
convinced the power for healing was present. But from past
personal experience as an outcast he was unsure that Christ
would be willing to bridge the social gap.   The anxious concern

of this leper is revealed by the way he approached Jesus: "If
you are willing you are able to cleanse me!" The way he states
the conditional part of the sentence leaves open whether Christ
will or will not cleanse. On the other hand the concluding part
clearly affirms the man's faith in Christ's power to heal. His
problem involved faith in the power; doubt as to willingness.
When faith and doubt face each other in the same heart conflict
occurs until one or the other is overcome. The issue is clear.
The man believes in Jesus to the extent that he recognizes he
is in control of divine power. But his experience of rejection
by men feeds his doubt whether <u>this</u> <u>man</u> will use that power on
one who is cast out by man!

The Christ's Response!

Demonstration removes doubt! Jesus, "having stretched forth
his hand grasped him saying, I will, be cleansed." Of the three
terms for "touch" the word used by Luke is the strongest. It is
more than to "feel in search of something." It is more than to
"touch" lightly. Jesus "grasped" him firmly. By his firm hold
Jesus instilled confidence in the leper even as the healing was
taking place. "<u>At once</u>" the leprosy went off from him." Jesus
did more than just heal the man of leprosy. He responded so
quickly, so thoroughly, and in a manner that turned the man's
attention to the <u>person</u> who did the healing. Jesus was all man,
completely human, thoroughly mortal. But he was also God as
man. It was important that men see the divine nature in him.
That "the leprosy left him" did more than rid the man of his
pain, humiliation and social stigma. It introduced him to God
as a human. As dimly as he may have realized, it demonstrated
in a living experience that God was walking among men.
Jesus "charged him to tell no one." What the healed leper
saw in Jesus wasn't clearly perceived by the populace. Truth
must not be twisted by false forms of popular views. Ignorance
and preconceived ideas do not provide fertile fields for growth
of truth about God's Messiah. So! 'Tell no one!"
Nevertheless, the witness of this cure with its revelation
about the person of the Christ must be preserved. "Go, show
yourself to the priest and offer concerning your cleansing just
as Moses commanded, for a <u>testimony</u> to them." The priestly and
public files must contain a record of this healing.

Results of the Cleansing!

To keep quiet about the healing of a leper is well beyond
expectation of human beings. Luke does not report that the
cured leper began to publish abroad his healing. Matthew does
that. But by that ommission Luke concentrates on Christ's
withdrawal in his search for solitude and prayer. Crowds came
to "hear and be healed." Jesus, being thoroughly human, is
subject to physical, nervous, spiritual exhaustion. As do all
men, he must renew his spirit. He is as much dependent, if not
more so, on God as any other man. No man can work God's work
apart from constant inflow of divine power. He began the
Galilean ministry "in the power of the Spirit." He does not
neglect keeping open that divine source.

In considering results it must not be overlooked that the leprous man was healed. His body was rid of the putred rotting flesh. His mind was enlightened with new insight about Jesus, who he was, his mission, message and purpose. A constructive unit in society was restored to the man. These factors tell a lot about Jesus. And that's why he came, to reveal the grace and will of God for man.

Even the failure of the cured leper to "tell no one" was used by Jesus as a blessing. Jesus came to call people, to win multitudes, to save humans from sin, disease, and destruction. The whole countryside was stirred by the leper being healed. By the hundreds suffering individuals came "to hear" what Jesus taught. They came "to be healed" of their infirmities. In so doing Jesus was given an open door to the hearts of the multitudes. Though he wished that the healed leper should "tell this to no one" yet without rebuking the man for his disobedience Jesus turned it to his own advantage. And beyond that, as already observed, it led him to seek desert places where he could, by seclusion and prayer, keep alive his constant touch with his heavenly Father. God "works all things together for good."

And what might Theophilus gain from this story? What does this thread furnish to the fabric Luke is weaving for his noble Greek friend?

The burden that sin has placed on the human race is infinite in its variety of forms. Great fevers burn us all at one time or another. At some point in each man demons get control, evil "possesses" us. Each man is subject to the temptation to resent God's being shared with "other cities," races, peoples. And we all in one form or another are alone, isolated, in our own little personal world, separated from our fellow creatures. Who has not felt the loneliness of social ostracism? The story of Christ's cure of the leper is God's answer to the universal experience of social isolation. Christ came to make known that God is the "friend of sinners," the companion of people, the lover of the lonely and the redeemer of the lost! Such is the God who identifies with all men and each man. Though many may refuse, no man is beyond the intent of God's redeeming grace. In Jesus, the man, God made this known to man!

AN OUTLINE OF LUKE 5:17-26

Who Can Forgive Sin?

He against whom sin is committed is the one capable of forgiving the sin. If sin is the free exercise of a man's will against God's then God is the one who forgives. The scribes were right in challenging, "Who is able to forgive sins except God?"(5:21)

I. THE OCCASION FOR CONFLICT. 5:17-19
   1. Spies from Judea.
     (a)Pharisees and lawyers.
     (b)Jesus "teaching" and power "for healing."
   2. Friends with paralytic seek Jesus.
     (a)The crowds hinder.
     (b)Faith overcoming obstacles.
II. FORGIVENESS OF SIN DEMONSTRATED. 5:20-26
   1. Forgiveness of sin declared.
     (a)The friends' faith! What they sought.
     (b)"Your sins forgiven." What the paralytic needed!
   2. The question raised: "Who can forgive sins?"
   3. The question answered.
     (a)By dilemma proposed.
     (b)By deed the dilemma resolved.

The reaction of the people was: "Amazement took hold of all and they were glorifying God." Yet not without awesome fear. "We have seen gloriously strange things today."

* * * * * * *

WHO CAN FORGIVE SIN?

In the incident of the paralytic the key question is:"Who is able to forgive sins?" In the story Jesus refers to himself as "the son of man." The lawyers and Jesus did not differ on God's capacity to forgive sin. The issue was, "Is anyone except God able to forgive sin?" Can or does God delegate to a man, even him who is "the son of man," representative man, him who is God as man, does he have authority(ἐξουσία)inherent in himself to represent God in what is obviously God's prerogative as God? This is the most important point of the narrative.

But the occasion which prompted the question has within it other important points of vital interest. That which motivated the friends contrasts with that which burdened the paralytic. That difference is loaded with lessons for life. If no need for forgiveness exists why be concerned about who can forgive?

Furthermore, what does this conflict between Jewish critics and Jesus say to a Greek Gentile who is considering the claims of Christianity? In what way does Luke here depict his thesis of the humanity of God in Jesus? And what, if anything, does Luke present of the universality of God's grace for every man?

The Occasion for the Conflict!

The fame of Jesus was spreading; the crowds he was attracting aroused the critical attention of Jewish leaders in the Galilean cities and stretching to Judea, even unto the hierarchy at Jerusalem. Pharisees with their expert lawyers

had gathered together to investigate the deeds and doctrines of
Jesus. His growing popularity had raised serious questions
about who he was and especially about the nature of the
"kingdom" which he apparently was promoting. He appeared to
strike at the heart of their power as teachers of Israel. He
seemed to threaten their authority as leaders. In a word, they
surrounded him in order to spy. When anyone sets out to find
fault, if he is patient enough, he can detect that for which he
searches. The bait on a trap must always be covered with lure
that is lucious to the one being trapped.

The text says that the "Lord's power was upon him to heal."
That indicates that such healing powers as had been so
captivating to the people were even greater as his reputation
grew. As the peoples' needs expanded so his ability to respond
increased. In the present instance crowds were so pressing that
the house where he was teaching was cut off from anyone else
entering. Thus when friends of a paralytic came carrying on a
pallet their sick companion they found no way to penetrate the
press of people. They were frustrated; the sick man was
discouraged over the failure to get to Jesus.

But to faith obstacles are but stepping stones to success.
Hindrances spur effort; faith builds on barriers. They set out
to find a way to get to Jesus. They refused to fail! Having
lifted the pallet with its burden up the outside stairway
leading to the tiled roof, they ripped off the tiles and
lowered the paralytic into the presence of Jesus.

Forgiveness Demonstrated!

The response of Jesus was immediate and positive. "Having
seen their faith, he said, Man your sins have been forgiven."
What an unexpected thing to say! Surprising to the four
friends, startling to the crowd, shocking to the Pharisees.
Forgiveness of sins was not what the four companions sought
from Jesus. They had brought their friend to be healed of his
paralysis. Bodily ailment looms large when we suffer from
sickness. Pain is the immediate need. Men don't go to a
physician to be relieved of the pangs of conscience; we want
rescue from stabs of pain. The most immediate need is strength
to rise from the sick bed. Moral and spiritual ailments may be
taken care of later, if at all.

The first remark of Jesus uncovers a basic difference
between what the four friends sought and what the paralytic
felt. Jesus said, "Man, your sins have been forgiven." These
words reveal three factors. First, Jesus addresses the
paralytic as "Man!" The other synoptists have Jesus adressing
him, "Son." By saying "Man" Jesus recognizes the humanity of
the paralytic. He views him as a human. The paralysis in no way
depreciated the man as a human being. A man who is sick is
still a man! Paralysis may hinder from functioning as God
designed but it cannot destroy his basic human nature. Jesus
approached each person as a human. Whatever his problem, be it
sickness or sin, he looked on each as man, God's image caught
in the down draft of sin and its consequences.

63

A second element in the word of Christ rises from the form of the verb "has been forgiven." It denotes a point at which guilt for sin is dissolved and following which it holds no power to convict. Sin has been "sent away" and it is permanently gone as a factor that can condemn. When God forgives it is permanent. Jesus is saying, "Your sins have been forgiven and henceforth are gone. You are in a state of forgiveness." This is important. As human creatures we are constantly tempted to recognize the doctrine of divine forgiveness but in our feelings we don't forgive ourselves! God's grace lies so far beyond our comprehension that we accept his forgiveness as biblical teaching but reject it in our subjective soul. Jesus is saying to the paralytic, "Since God has taken away your sin don't you hold onto it. If God has dissolved it don't you keep on resurrecting it. Let go of it; God has!"

A third point is the felt need of the paralytic in contrast to that which his friends sought. They wanted their comrade healed from his paralysis. Judged by the words of Jesus the man's burden was more moral than physical. Jesus addressed the felt need of the sick man. He removed the spiritual burden before he addressed the secondary sickness.

All men carry the weight of guilt. None escape! The core of the human situation is guilt for moral transgression. It pervades the spirit of mankind sapping moral, spiritual and physical strength. It eats at the vitals of the soul like termites. And in the face of this unseen gnawing of the spiritual vitals men keep trying to cover the guilt with quack nostrums. Surgery is what is needed, not quick cover that merely hides without destroying the root germs.

Whether this man's paralysis sprouted from his own sin is not stated or necessarily implied. But that he was weighted down with guilt is clear from the fact that Jesus spoke to this problem immediately. When a physician treats a heart condition he doesn't work as though setting broken bones. No! He deals with the disease causing the trouble. The man was under some deep sense of sin. Jesus gives what the man needs, not what his friends want. Jesus came to "seek and to save that which was lost." Social sins are caused by individuals who sin. To change society the individuals who constitute society must be healed of their guilt.

Who Can Forgive Sins?

The word of Jesus announcing that the paralytic's sin "has been forgiven" became for the Pharisees a point of attack. Their fundamental assumption was: "only God can forgive sin! It is blasphemous for a man to assume that which alone belongs to God. Either Jesus assumes to be deity or he blasphemes.

That Jesus was God in the flesh was the cornerstone of Luke's faith at the time he was writing his Gospel. But at the time of this conflict not even the disciples were clearly aware of the true nature of Jesus. Jesus was their "Teacher" and "Master" but as yet none had acknowledged him as the "Christ of

64

God." To the Pharisees this was the snare for which they were looking. Certainly to them Jesus was but a man, unauthorized to teach and one who in their presence had uttered unquestionable blasphemy. As they "began to reason" with each other their conclusion satisfied them that Jesus was a fraud; certainly "one who speaks blasphemy." They had found that for which they came. Jesus had entrapped himself.

The Question Answered!

The critics of Christ celebrated their catch prematurely. Jesus takes up their question and provides an unexpected answer. "When Jesus knew their thoughts, having answered he said, What are you reasoning in your hearts? Which is easier to say, Your sins have been forgiven? or to say, Rise up and walk?" To claim to forgive sins may be challenged. A stated claim consists of words easily voiced. Objective evidence is needed to verify the right to such a claim. Jesus proceeds to offer a deed to vindicate his word of forgiveness.

As the son of God no doubt Jesus possessed the power to forgive sin. However, as yet he was not acknowledged as God's son even by his followers, much less his critics. Thus in his response he adopts the title "son of man." "That you may know (εἰδῆτε) that the son of man has inherent authority (ἐξουσιαν) on earth to forgive sins,--he said to the paralytic, To you I say, Rise up and having lifted up your pallet go unto your house." The power to heal verifies the right to forgive. Health to the sick flesh assures health in the sick soul! From the divine point of view healing the physical affliction, the consequence of sin, proves the power to heal the heart.

Paralysis, unlike leprosy, was not so much a social handicap as it severed one's ability to contribute constructively in society. It thwarted opportunity to use talent or time in service to self or others. It destroyed dreams of doing great deeds, shattered visions of rendering great service, withered ambition to fulfill life's goal. It was a dying while living! It is symbolic of the universal frustration of human kind to rise to the potential resident in each baby at birth. Certainly it was sufficiently prevalent in all races to symbolize man's general failure to attain the heights of divine purpose in creation.

Two words clue us in on Luke's intent in this story for Theophilus. The first is: "Man, your sins have been forgiven." To this may be added Jesus' testimony about himself, "the son of man." The "son of man" came that "man" might know that his sins "have been forgiven." His authority in word has ample confirmation in his work!

AN OUTLINE OF LUKE 5:27-32
The Physician's Patients!

Hospitals are for the sick; medical schools train Doctors!
If nobody became ill, there would be no physicians. The medical
profession exists for unhealthy people.

I. THE PUBLICAN. 5:27-28
   1. The "publicans" of the New Testament.
   2. Matthew Levi: the Capernaum toll house.
   3. Jesus "beheld" Levi "before the place of toll."
   4. Christ's call and Levi's response.
II. THE RECEPTION AT LEVI'S HOUSE. 5:29
   1. Levi's first act of "following" Jesus.
      (a)A "great banquet."(b)"In his house."(c)For "him."
   2. The guests:(a)Publicans. (b)"Others."
III. THE CRITICS. 5:30
   1. They faulted him to his disciples.
   2. Justify Why "You eat with publicans and sinners!"
IV. THE COMMUNITY OF THE PENITENT. 5:31-32
   1. The sick, not the well, need a Doctor.
   2. "I have come to call sinners to repentance!"

The Saviour-Physician has come to disinfect any who will use
his healing power! His kingdom consists of called sinners in
the process of being purified!

* * * * * * *

THE PHYSICIAN'S PATIENTS!

The law of supply and demand operates in realms other than
economic. With the advent of tractor and automobile need for
the work horse has well nigh disappeared. Where there is no
need no provision will be forthcoming. If nobody became ill
physicians would be of no value. There'd be none! The entire
profession of the healing arts would disappear. The medical
profession exists for unhealthy people.

It's also true that if there were no sin there'd be no need
of a Saviour. Jesus says, "I have come to call sinners to
repentance." Since "all have sinned" all need redemption!

Matthew Levi, the Publican!

In every age, in any kind of government the tax collector is
a woeful necessity. The "publican" of the New Testament fared
even worse ill repute than many such tax collectors in ancient
times. In Judea were poll-taxes, custom duties, road tax, land
tax, and many others. Publicans were the agents who collected
these monies. From time immemorial Jews felt they should pay no
money taxes except to temple and priest. But in New Testament
times at every turn the publicans intruded distastefully into
the life of the people as they exacted these various taxes. It
was particularly galling because it reminded them of their
subjection to Rome. Besides, the publicans were Jews who
served as agents of Roman tyranny. Because they extracted money
from their own people they became even more despised than if
they had been Romans or Canaanites. Pharisaic legalists felt
the traitor's profession marked them contemptible sinners.

Levi, Aramaic name of the "son of Alphaeus," who, in Hebrew, was "a man called Matthew." He was "sitting before the toll house" in Capernaum. It was an important center for caravan and boat traffic. The lines of commerce stretched from the coastal cities of the Mediterranean to Damascus in Syria. Quite probably Levi collected custom duties of the wealthy trade between West and East. He was a man of business acumen and of broad experience in dealing with a wide range of men. He could be an effective disciple in Christ's growing band of followers. Would he respond if the call came?

The text states that Jesus "beheld" Levi "sitting before the place of toll." The word translated "beheld" signifies more than "he saw." It designates fixing the eyes with "careful and deliberate vision which interprets."(Abbott-Smith ,Lex.,pg.203) Jesus studied the publican, contemplated his being one of his close and trusted followers. Apparently Jesus had to use his judgment as a man in selecting the twelve. The resources of God were available to Jesus. But so they are to any man who will call upon God and use the resources. Jesus as man must use the divine resources in making his human judgments. He "beheld" Levi, evaluated the publican in view of his own need for a band of faithful followers. And then he called accordingly.

No doubt Levi had, in the past, some contact with Jesus. He had observed with interest not only his teaching and behaviour but also had witnessed that Jesus was gathering a group of disciples who were committed to "following" him. Had he, Levi, envisioned the possibility of being a part of such a band? At any rate, this day Jesus "beheld" him and issued a call: "Be following me." The imperative of Jesus signified a constant companionship, a permanent decisive discipleship, a total abandonment to a new vocation in life.

To Levi the call of Christ involved no small financial loss. It entailed quite some change in social relationships, maybe for the better, but none the less a radical change. But Levi's response was immediate, thorough, and final. "Having left behind all, he got up and began following him." The publican's reaction was resolute. The narrative seems to suggest that he didn't even go back into his office. Immediately he turned his back upon all and completely committed himself to Jesus.

A Reception at Levi's House!

The publican didn't tarry long in putting into effect his commitment. "Levi made a great reception for him (Jesus) in his house. And a large crowd of publicans and others were reclining with them." Having suffered for years the odium of rejection, it was refreshing to be accepted by so famous a teacher. He wanted all his former vocational associates to meet his new Master. He wished his colleagues to learn from his newly found Teacher; to know the thrill of being accepted by a true peer. The first mission field for a new idea, cause, project or person is one's immediate family and friends. The community of publicans was numerous in the province. And "others" of like repute were in the city.

67

It was a "great banquet." Levi was a man of wealth. Nothing in the story intimates whether his wealth came ill-gotten or honestly. It is important that he was a man of means. If he were successful as a publican, becoming a follower of Jesus did not diminish his capacity for grand vision. He combed the country for fellow-publicans. Collectors of every conceivable kind of tax got a pressing invitation to his grand party.

No expense was spared. The best chefs, the richest viands, professional decorators, the finest artists, in both music and dance promised a delicate background for entertainment. His new Master, the guest of honor, himself would challenge thought and stimulate conversation. Levi withheld nothing to make this "great" feast the most noteworthy Capernaum had ever known.

The reception was "in his house" and it was "for him." The house of Levi became the platform on which this erstwhile tax collector honored his new-found Master. And he provided Jesus with a ready introduction to a host of potential learners, all conveniently assembled at one place on one evening. Levi's was a remarkable missionary strategy.

It should not be overlooked that besides publicans "others" were guests that swelled the crowd at this "great" banquet. Who these "others" were is noted in the criticism of the Pharisees, "Why with publicans and sinners do you eat and drink?" From the standpoint of acceptable society this was a kaleidoscopic group of "sinners" gathered at Levi's home. Not a single person in the lot would be tolerated in the "best" Capernaum society! To the man they were offenders against the current social and religious values of orthodox Israel.

The Criticism of the Critics!

To attack at the weakest point is practical and prudent. It is a first-class way to win a war and the safest way to remain unscathed by the carnage of the conflict. So the critics cornered the disciples outside the house, "Give us reasons why you eat and drink with publicans and sinners!"

Though the attack thrust at the weakest point the defense came from the strongest. Eating together in all societies is the sign and symbol of the most intimate friendship. When Jesus accepted the invitation to be guest of honor at such a gathering he was straining far beyond the limits of social propriety. "Birds of a feather flock together" and Jesus was eating on most intimate terms with the social rejects of the community. If these were rejects it was for just such rejects that he came. When they honored him they honored his mission, his kingdom, his God and Father. In attacking his disciples the Pharisees were attacking him and his purpose in the world. It wasn't the weakest point but the very strength of the whole kingdom of God. They really were assaulting their own biblical heritage. He shattered their self-sufficiency. Said he: "The healthy are not having need of a physician but rather the ones who are desperately sick. I have not come to call righteous but sinners to repentance." It's the sick, not the well, who need a doctor! What could be more obvious? They themselves judged these as "sinners." They themselves, being healthy, ought be

68

healing the sick. The fact they define the "others" as sinners is the most conclusive answer to their criticism!

Called to Repentance!

Two factors in Christ's answer to his critics set him apart. First, is the verb form "I have come." It is John's Gospel that shows Christ as pre-existent. "In the beginning was the Word, the Word was with God, and the Word was God...the Word became flesh."(1.1,14) That's the cosmic Christ. But Luke deals with Jesus as man in this world. But when he has Jesus saying, "I have come..." the very form of the word implies more than his being born as other men. Luke has already clearly displayed he was "born of woman" as all men are born of women. Others were "born" human, but he, though born, "became" human. There is a difference. Others are born as new creations; he ""has come" into the world on an assigned mission. In the words of the text he came "to call sinners unto repentance." Luke is aware of something below the surface in him of whom he writes. Jesus is extraterrestrial in origin yet thoroughly human in nature and mission.

Luke, unlike the other synoptics, adds "unto repentance." It is a significant phrase. Jesus did more than "call sinners." He came identifying with the poor, the prostitute, the outcast, the weak and wayward. None lay outside his mission of love, grace and redemption. He felt comfortable in the presence of "publicans and sinners" of all stripes. Humanity in its lost condition was his field of association. He saved by association rather than separation. But though he mixed and mingled with the pervert he rejected the perversion. He will die for the sinner but reject the sinner's sin. Indeed, Jesus "called the sinner." But he called him to something other than his immoral practice. The word "repent" means "to change." To repent means to change from this to that; from one pattern of thought to a different one, from one lifestyle to an altered one. One can't respond to Jesus and remain unchanged. He who follows Jesus becomes an integral part of the community the penitent, the fellowship of the changed. Jesus welcomed any and all sinners. But he tolerated no compromise with sin.

And what does this say to Theophilus? What advance can take place in the reader's mind and heart?

Truth is universal; what is universal is true. The infinite varieties in which reality appears does not alter its reality. He who knew not sin "has come" to call those who sinned to a change of mind, a change of moral behaviour. In the call of the publican Jesus demonstrates man's capacity to respond to right and wrong. That which is universal in all men is the sense of what is moral. Christ's kingdom is one of righteousness. It is an appeal to that which is universal in human beings and separates them from the animal. The "son of man" shows what any man can become when "called to repentance." Anyone who is a "sinner" is capable of becoming a saint. Jesus did not come to make the old man better; he came to make new men!

69

AN OUTLINE OF LUKE 5:33-39
Patched Pants and Broken Bottles!
Fasting or feasting! Which shall it be? Which is appropriate
for the citizen of the kingdom of God? "The disciples of John
are fasting often...but yours are eating and drinking!" Is one
more proper than the other?
I.   TWO CRITERIA FOR FASTING. 5:33-35
     1. The law.
        (a)Moses and Fasting.
        (b)The Pharisaical legal system.
     2. Jesus and fasting.
II. THREE PARABLES ILLUMINATING JESUS' PRINCIPLE. 5:36-39
     1. New cloth patched on old garment.
     2. New wine in old wine-skin bottles.
     3. Dealing with those who like the taste of the Old!
     The life of God in Christ grows from within out rather than
from without in. Life cannot be forced into fixed forms. It
creates its own forms for its peculiar personal expression as
demanded by each stage in its growth.

* * * * * * *

PATCHED PANTS AND BROKEN BOTTLES!
     The aftermath of the feast at Levi's house produced a
question about feasting and fasting. Some of his critics raised
the question with Christ. "The disciples of John are fasting
often and are making prayers, also those of the Pharisees, but
yours are eating and drinking." Their objection to his eating
with "publicans and sinners" had boomeranged. Agreed! The
"publicans" and the "others" are "sinners." So, by their own
assumed health the critics should be healing, not hurting them.
     This time their criticism is less direct, more implied than
stated. They adopted a more cautious approach. In effect they
queried, "Your practice about fasting is different from ours,
or even from your forerunner John's. Which is correct? Should
we feast or fast?"
                    Two Criteria for Fasting!
     The question posed is legitimate. Though their motives may
be doubted, the problem of feasting or fasting is valid. Moses'
law had provided for only one regular periodical fast. That was
annual, the day of atonement. "And it shall be a statute
forever that in the seventh month on the tenth day of the
month, you shall afflict (fast) your souls..."(Lev.16:29) In
the course of time other fasts arose prompted by transgression
or calamities. Also individuals were aroused to fast because of
some personal grief. But the one regularly repeated legal fast
was that of the annual day of atonement.
     After the Captivity regular periodic fasts appeared. They
were memorials of periods of bitter humiliation which the
nation endured. By the time of our text fasts had grown to the
point that sincerely devout persons would fast twice each week,
Mondays and Fridays. Such regular fasts became so traditional

that they obtained the force of law. They were Pharisaical mechanisms devised as a "hedge about the law" by which these formalists sought to maintain their legal system.

Jesus and Fasting!

From the nuptial ceremonial customs Jesus pictures the real reason for fasting. The Old Testament had characterized Messiah coming under the figure of a wedding feast. Jesus had already used this figure of himself: "He who has the bride is the bridegroom...(Jn.3:29) Bridal festivities are times for joy, not for self flagellagtion. By its very nature it's a time of feasting, not fasting. On the face of it one need only ask the question to appreciate the folly of fasting at such a time. "You are not able are you to make a fast for the sons of the bride chamber while the bridegroom is with them?" Of course not! Fasting is not for joyous occasions. Fun, fete, feast and frolicking are befitting joy. For such occasions fasting would be incompatible.

On the other hand, fasting can be most suitable, even becoming. When a man is suddenly apprised that he has a deadly disease in its advanced stages, that he should immediately inform his family, arrange for final rites and put his personal house in order to face his Maker; this is a time for sober thought, sincere prayer and fasting. Certainly it does not call for partying.

There are appropriate times for fasting; there are fitting times for feasting. It's the situation, the circumstances, the mood that determine which is more suitable. Outward features may create the conditions. It's the inward man that responds in appropriate fashion. This determines whether to feast or fast. It's not a rule, law, regulation or tradition that coerces the kingdom man's behaviour. A tree grows from within out, not from from without in. Indeed, every living thing senses that which best suits the particulars. This is precisely what Jesus meant when he declared, "Days shall indeed come whenever the bridegroom shall be snatched from them, then they shall fast in those days." In this early vision of his violent death he intimates that his disciples will fast. The somber days of doubt, frustration, disbelief and dispair will create a set of circumstances that will make fasting quite seemly. Christ's principle is: Fasting must not be done because of a rule; it is a choice of the heart responding to an appropriate occasion.

Three Parables Illuminate Jesus' View!

First is the image of a patch cut from a new cloth to be sewn onto trousers grown threadbare by long use. "No one having ripped a patch from a new garment casts it upon an old garment." But if anyone should do such an unheard of thing he generates a double danger. If and when the garment is laundered shrinkage of "the new will rip also the old." Besides that "the old patch will not harmonize with the new" in texture or color, even should it not tear through shrinkage. Matching the two is not only impossible the attempt will form an ugly contrast. To apply the force of law to a free spirit won't work. He who does

71

"right" only because of peer pressure or due to society's laws or even divine moral law has missed the entire spirit and meaning of redemption in Christ. "You shall love God with all your mind...heart..." The rich young ruler kept God's laws but he failed to find God. David didn't murder Uriah. He conformed to the commandment but violated its meaning and spirit. "God is spirit and he who worships him must worship in spirit." To patch God's Spirit onto formal regulations is to quench the Spirit. To obey because one is forced destroys the "fruit of the spirit." It removes "love, joy, peace, etc..." Against those who have God's spirit "there is no law." He who lives by the spirit does not need to be conscripted. He volunteers to fulfill the meaning, spirit, and letter of the law. Coercion has no place in the life of the spirit. It is an ugly patch! Jesus did not come to patch up the law. Nor did he come to reform people broken by their own sin. He came to make men new! New men don't obey because they are forced to but because their new spirit within prompts them to fulfill life's highest moral and spiritual goals. Jesus does not patch the old; he clothes with new garments!

A second parable springs from the Oriental practice of retaining water or other liquids in goatskin bottles. The fermentation of fresh wine in old skins bursts the skins which of course is disastrous to both skin and wine. In the parable Jesus likens his redemptive doctrine to new wine. Sinners are given a new clean start. His redemptive mission is available to each man who opens himself to the incoming of the Spirit. This fresh new life is induced from within by the urging of the Spirit, not exacted from without by force of law.

But to put this new spirit of truth in the hands of the old legalists would pervert truth and turn these formalists into confused dissembling vessels. Christ's new gospel demands a new kind of vessel, new persons. In order for the gospel to be preserved as gospel it must have clean new containers to carry it. The calling of fishermen, publicans and "others" of that type is justified by the inability of the "old" ritualists to appreciate the principle of freedom of truth to find its own forms. The new wine of the gospel needs fresh souls whose merit is their humility and receptivity to the changes which truth brings. Fresh wine needs fresh bottles! Truth needs bottles that won't burst.

The difficulty of the legal system to be patched onto the new, the impossibility of the old bottle to retain the new does not mean that the old can be discarded without some human concern. A third parable addresses this fact. "And noone drinking old (wine) wishes new, for he says, The old is good," Two truths lie buried in this brief statement. First, to pass from a system of religious behaviour imbedded from childhood and sanctioned by long tradition is difficult. Men must be given time to absorb new truth, to familiarize themselves with new principles and practices. To keep the regular ritual of fasting holds no inherent wrong. And that leads to the second

72

factor in this parable. If one likes the "taste" of the old
ritual because "the old is good" then practice it. The old
ought not be rejected merely because it is old. Nor should the
new be accepted only because it is new. However, the new must
be practiced because it is true, because the essential needs of
human life demand it. One must welcome the Spirit of God within
to make the form vital. God's Holy Spirit can transform the
person, therefore can restyle any form to express the spirit's
life. The indwelling spirit is the vitalizing agent, the
ingredient that makes a formal ritual right. Baptism is not
just immersion in water. If that's all that is involved then it
is a poor substitute for a good bath. But when preceded by
personal faith, genuine repentance, and generated by the spirit
of God it becomes the commitment of a living soul to the living
Christ. Jesus never taught that it was wrong or inappropriate
to drink old wine. He did insist that if not performed by the
power of the Spirit it would be a "dead" work. The old wine is
"good." But life responds best when we taste the new!

Theophilus could well appreciate the teaching of this
paragraph in Luke's letter. The Greeks weren't accustomed to
the old wine of Pharisaical formalism. Philosophically they
were in a position to accept the fresh new wine of the gospel.
They had enough of their own old cultural traditions with which
they might be tempted to "patch" the new gospel truth.
Nevertheless, Theophilus, as a noble-hearted Greek, could sense
the universal appeal of this "new wine."
That which is universal is true; and the truth is universal!

* * * * * * *

AN OUTLINE OF LUKE 6:1-5
The Lord of the Sabbath!
Man was not created for the sake of laws. On the contrary
laws were made to help educate man as to how human life can
best be lived. When a law fails to assist man it must be
discarded for something that can. Especially ritual law!
I.   THE DEED. 6:1
    1. Travellers on the Sabbath day.
    2. Passing "through the grains."
    3. Plucking and rubbing: Harvesting and winnowing.
II. THE DOUBT. 6:2
    1. "Certain Pharisees" object.
    2. You "are doing" that which is unlawful.
    3. On "the Sabbath."
III. THE DEFENSE. 6:3-5
    1. Liturgy and life?
       Illustrated in the case of David.
    2. "The son of man is Lord of the Sabbath."
Liturgy, ritual, ceremony are servants of human beings, who
are made to be God's "image." Men are not slaves of ceremony.
On the contrary, ceremonies are made to serve man's need.

73

THE LORD OF THE SABBATH!

In this world "things" can't compete in value with "humans." Birds, bees, animals, and trees are as much creatures of God as are people. But man has the distinct difference of being in "the image and likeness" of God. The "heavens declare the glory of God, and the firmament shows his handiwork." (Ps.19:1) But "what is man...? You have made him little less than God,...You have given him dominion over the works of your hands, and put all __things__ under his feet." (Ps.8:4-6) No "thing" can compare in value to the least of men. Whether good or bad is not the point. It's that man, the worst or best, has within him the God-like capacity, the divine "image."

Rules, regulations, commands, laws, institutions, traditions have all developed that man might grow into the image for which he has been created. Man is God's masterpiece. Institutions or laws, though they may be his gracious creation, are not his grand design. They are supporting staff but not the reason why man was made. They form frame and background but are not the picture. Only man, even fallen man, has more deity than any other __thing__ that has come from God's hand.

The Deed!

"And it happened on a Sabbath that he was going through the grain fields. And his disciples were plucking and eating the grains, rubbing them in their hands." For travellers to be strolling along narrow pathways between fields of growing grain was common occurance. That wayfarers pick grains to satisfy hunger was normal. In fact, Moses made specific provision for this very thing. "When you go into your neighbor's standing grain, you may pluck the ears with your hand, but you shall not put a sickle to your neighbor's standing grain."(Deut.23:25) Thus providence supplied the wayfarer and the stranger. It was not picking and eating grain belonging to a "neighbor" that was the issue. Doing it on the Sabbath was that which disturbed "certain Pharisees." They were upset over such flagrant disregard for the law of the Sabbath.

Man is so constituted, the soil is so "cursed" as to make the "sweat of his brow" require a periodic rest from toil. If there were no Sabbath law, in order to guard against burn out man would invent one. In fact, atheistic societies have found it necessary to legalize a periodic day for workmen to be given relief from the daily drive of the assembly line. Need for rest and a change of pace are built into the nature of man.

But how could serious students of the scriptures ever conclude that action so innocuous as satisfying basic hunger be __sinful__? The fourth command says:"Remember the sabbath day, to keep it holy...in it you shall not do any work..."(Ex.20:8ff) This is simply and clearly stated. Yet in a noble but vain effort to guarantee absolute obedience the Rabbis began to build a "hedge about the law" by __interpreting__ it. What is meant by "work" "burden" "house" "place" and such terms were defined in specific and minute detail. In the days of Jesus the "hedge" had grown to such height, firmness, and details that it became too heavy a weight even for the scribes and Pharisees. The minutia proscribed were not forbidden by scripture. They were interpretative fancies of Pharisees. For example, it was "unlawful" for a tailor to go out with his needle or a scribe to pick up his pen on the sabbath. If anyone tossed an object into the air with his left hand and caught it in the left it was a sin. But if he caught it in his right hand it was open to doubt whether it be sinful. However should he catch it in his mouth it would not be sin. These legalists had 39 "fathers of work" that included such items as sowing, ploughing, reaping, binding, threshing, winnowing, sifting, kneading, baking, shearing, dyeing, spinning, weaving two threads, separating two threads, making a knot, undoing a knot, sewing two stitches, tearing to sew two stitches, and other similar piddling provisions. Such unspiritual trivia dominated the religious environment when Jesus and his disciples plucked grain, rubbed it in their hands and ate. Though it did no violence to Moses' law it transgressed the sabbath traditions. It furnished the Pharisees the opportunity to trap Jesus by which they might bring him to public condemnation. Their shock, real or feigned, is voiced in their horrified question, "Why are you doing on the sabbath that which is not lawful?" The very form of "are doing" shows that this was just one instance of such brazen sabbath behaviour. This is not to be tolerated! It stamped Jesus as false!

The Defense!

The attack was launched against the disciples, "Why are you (plural) doing that which is not lawful..." Jesus provided the defense. His preliminary answer came from their scripture. He framed a question expecting "yes" for an answer. "You have read haven't you what David did when he hungered, and those being with him? How he entered into the house of God and when he had taken the loaves of the setting forth, he ate and gave to those with him, that which is not lawful to eat except only the priests?" In other words, can you not make a distinction between liturgical ritual and the needs of life? Ritual law is not an end in itself; it is a servant to higher ends. And there are situations that arise in which life is served by stepping beyond the legal restriction to the goal for which the law was really designed.

When life's true needs conflict with forms of law, choose life! People are sacred, not law! Sanctity is found in human life, not law! Laws are carved on stone or written on paper. Life is experienced by living persons. All creations of God or man, including laws, serve the ends of making men what God intended them to be. Each human situation offers its own particular application of law to life.

He who serves God revealed in Christ is not free to do as he pleases, he is not given license to disregard law. But he is free to do whatever it takes to serve Christ in meeting human needs. God loves mercy, not legal sacrifices. Sacrifice to God is service rendered to Christ and his people.

75

In verse six Luke has Jesus rise to the higher, general view which governs the whole question. "And he was saying to them, The son of man is lord of the sabbath." Even if the twelve had ignored Moses' sabbath law they would not have sinned by plucking, rubbing, winnowing and eating the grain. Jesus, as representative Man, as example of everything man was designed to be, was master not only of the sabbath but all law. Laws are under his control, at his service, subject to his purposes. The sabbath was given as an educational means for moral ends. The goal of the sabbath is rest for men. Real rest, abiding rest, eternal rest comes to man through the "Lord of the sabbath." When he brings redemption to human beings they enter into his rest. The sabbath was a means to an end. When the end is attained the means has no further use. It is set aside! As "son of mankind" Jesus is "even Lord of the sabbath."

In the physical demands of life in this world the seventh day sabbath filled a definite need. But that rest is not to be mistaken for the "rest" into which God entered upon completing his six days of creative work.(Gen.2:2) The redemptive rest that comes because of Christ is "God's rest." And "We who have believed enter that rest...There remains a sabbath rest for the people of God; for whoever enters God's rest also ceases from his labors as God did from his.(Heb.4:3,9f)

At this stage in the ministry of Jesus such a claim that he be "lord of the sabbath" may not have been convincing to his critics. But it does certify that Jesus was clearly aware of his own Person, who he was, why he had come, and what his destiny in history was to be. This early in his ministry he was fully conscious of himself as the "Lord of the sabbath." And if of the sabbath, then Lord of all of God's laws, purposes and intents. This sabbath conflict displays the growing intensity of the enemies of Jesus. The cross may be over the horizon but it is there and the Christ is aware of it.

In trying to evaluate the impact of each episode of Luke's gospel it is possible to overstate its contribution. Without question, at least in Luke's mind, each paragraph advanced some point in his overall thesis. Yet we must keep in mind that there is a cumulative effect as each section leaves its deposit on the mind and heart of Theophilus. Being involved in such human struggles with prejudices of man-made traditions is a part of life in any culture. Luke's story is a record of the Christ being "tempted in all points just as we are." His reader is increasingly aware that God in Jesus is so human!

AN OUTLINE OF LUKE 6:6-11
Is It Wrong To Do Right?

A surgeon hurts to heal else he cannot heal the hurt! It is not whether to cut or not to cut but whether to heal or not to heal. Healing is the problem, not the method or manner.

On the plucking of grain Jesus established himself as "Lord of the Sabbath." On this "other" sabbath he confirmed the right to do what is right on the sabbath.

I.   THE OCCASION: A SYNAGOGUE SERVICE. 6:6-7
   1. Jesus teaching in a synagogue.
   2. A man "with his hand withered."
   3. The Pharisees:
      (a)Purpose: "Does he heal on the sabbath."
      (b)Motive: "that they might accuse him."
II. JESUS RAISES THE QUESTION. 6:8-9
   1. He was "knowing their thoughts."
   2. To the man: "Rise and stand in the midst."
   3. Question:"Is it lawful on sabbath to do good...?"
III. THE QUESTION ANSWERED BY AN EXHIBITION. 6:10-11
   1. To the man: "Stretch out your hand."
   2. The results:
      (a)"The hand was restored."
      (b)Pharisees "were filled with insane madness."
      (c)"Whatever might we do to this Jesus?"

Is it wrong to do right on the sabbath? Since creation God's goal has been to recreate man into the image scarred by sin. To heal man is the supreme end of all laws, institutions, symbols and ceremonies. To heal is the supreme "right."

* * * * * * *

IS IT WRONG TO DO RIGHT?

To heal is the ultimate right! If it's a broken bone, an ill body or a sick soul the most decisive need is healing. The soul of man is strickened by sin. The soul craves health more than anything else. The human race is sick in spirit. Sin against God has ravaged from within out. It has deranged man's mind, diseased his body, twisted his soul, and perverted his spirit until he cannot recognize who he is, why he's in his present painful condition. It has destroyed his sense of direction and blinded him to any meaning in life. Man's great want is healing!

Luke has placed two sabbath day episodes together to create a specific impression. In the first, the plucking of the grain, he affirmed himself to be "Lord of the Sabbath." A second was that of a synagogue service in which a "man with his hand withered" became the central figure. Jesus displayed his doctrine by demonstration. One must seize each opportunity to do that which is right in restoring paralyzed man back to his original health. That is the true purpose and meaning of the law of the sabbath. The right to healing in mind, body, soul and spirit is the universal need. It is also the primary purpose of every institution or law of God!

77

A Synagogue Service!

"And it happened on a different sabbath that he entered into the synagogue and he began to teach." Though what he taught is not specified no doubt he continued the thesis he gave in his beginning message at Nazareth(5:25-27). God's gracious purpose reaches beyond Israel to all men. This typified his mission and message. It also aroused powerful opposition.

Two centers of interest in the audience this sabbath provided Jesus with an opportunity and danger. A man "with his hand withered" was present. Nothing so unusual about afflicted people in such gatherings. But the presence of a particular group of other men made this man of special note. "The scribes and the Pharisees" were also there that sabbath day. Enough time had passed in the ministry of Jesus for his fame as a wonder worker to have aroused the enmity of the Jewish leaders. The purpose and motive for their being there gave special importance to their presence. They were there for the purpose of "watching" as spies. Their concern was: "Does he heal on the sabbath?" No doubt they were aware of his plucking, winnowing and eating on an earlier sabbath. Today their motive was: "that they might accuse him."

The Pharisaical view of sabbath behaviour excluded any "work" of healing. No bandage designed to heal a wound should be worn on a sabbath. That would be work! A bandage could be used if its object was to prevent the wound from getting worse. If someone had a sore in his ear to which a soft wad of cloth or cotton was applied he might go about on a sabbath with that wadding only if it had been placed there before the sabbath began. It could not be put on any time during the sabbath day itself. Nor could it be replaced should it fall out. Nothing should be initiated on the sabbath designed for healing! It was by such unspiritual legal fictions that the Pharisees sought to preserve the sanctity of the sabbath. No healing "work" should spoil that holy day!

It was just such a non-spiritual environment that made for tension between Christ and the Pharisees in the presence of the man "with his hand withered."

Jesus Raises the Question!

The text says of Jesus that "he was knowing their thoughts." Not only did he know their immediate desire to ensnare him but he knew the perverted theological concept of righteousness upon which their malicious enmity rested. The rabbinical view about the sabbath was: "Shall I do or not do this? According to Jesus that was not the proper issue to be decided. Rather it should be: "Shall I show mercy or not on the sabbath?" "Shall I do right or withhold that which is right?"

On this particular occasion Jesus demonstrated his teaching. To the man "with the hand withered" he said, "Get up and stand in the midst." And the man "having gotten up stood!" In a direct confrontation Jesus said to "them" the Pharisees, "I ask you personally, Is it lawful (right) to do good on the sabbath or to do evil, to save life or to destroy it?" He thus focused

on the rightness, not the what was done or not done. To do or
not do is not the question. The real issue is: "Is it merciful?
Does it renew, refresh, restore health and life?" The form in
which Christ stated the question showed the falseness of the
Pharisees and placed them in an embarrassing light. It also made
crystal clear the divine purpose of the sabbath, the renewal of
life!

The Question Answered!

Jesus had asked: "Is it lawful on the sabbath to do good or
to do evil, to save a soul or to destroy?" Having proposed the
problem he demonstrated the answer by a deed.

First, he gave the Pharisaical critics their opportunity to
answer. They held their peace! Not a word broke the hushed
stillness! You could "hear" the silence! It "spoke" more than
words!

Then Jesus broke the silence with a calm quiet of his own!
"When he looked upon them all..." His piercing eyes revealed
withering contempt on any who would withhold help from fellow
human beings when in their power to help. One does not have to
give poison to kill. He only needs to withhold the healing
medicine. That's murder as much as the overt act. The Pharisees
missed the whole point of the sabbath. They had backed
themselves into the impossible moral corner: "It's wrong to do
right on the sabbath."

Jesus said to the man, "Stretch out your hand." What a
challenge to the man! And what a demonstration to the critics!
The man's hand was paralyzed. How could he "stretch out" his
hand? But the text tells us, "That one did (stretch out his
hand) and the hand was restored."

It is important to note that Jesus did nothing on this
sabbath. He said something but he did not one thing. He
"taught" the people. He ordered the man to "stretch out" his
hand. But Jesus carefully avoided doing any deed that could be
interpreted as healing! He did not set a bone or apply a
bandage; he did not even touch the man. He just said, "Stretch
out your hand" to a man whose hand had lain limp in his lap for
years. He demonstrated in an objective form the meaning of the
sabbath. It is not wrong to do right on the sabbath!

The Results!

The most immediate result was the healing of the man with
the hand withered." That said a lot as to the nature of this
man Jesus! Divine power plainly was at work in him. But in this
immediate situation it was an objective lesson on God's intent
in giving Moses the sabbath law. God's "rest" involved more
than just doing or not doing. It was for renewing and redeeming
the human spirit.

The Pharisees "were filled with insane rage and they were
discussing among themselves, What may we do to (kill) this
Jesus?" They became crazed in their wrath. Anger consumed
them! They to whom to heal on the sabbath was mortal sin did
not hesitate to plot how to murder this Jesus, even if it were
the sabbath! To them to do mercy was evil; to plot murder was
good!

What enraged these Pharisees? Why were they so insanely mad? When the light of truth comes in such clear form from such a genteel source, in a worship designed to glorify God one would suppose men would welcome it with open minds. But one of strange paradoxes of the human heart is its inane tendency to protect the ego. It takes moral honesty, humility of spirit, and a clear recognition of one's sinful situation to welcome the surgeon's knife that cuts the moral cancer from the heart. The Pharisees were hardly in this kind of spiritual condition. Furthermore, their minds were calloused over by the thick skin of their own theological prepossessions. In addition to that, their hypocrisy was exposed to open shame in a public forum. The whole situation left the ego shattered. It became too personal. Rather than face their real selves in the mirror of truth which Jesus held up they exploded; rather than wash away their blemishes they insanely plotted to brake the mirror. It is self-destructive to resist the light. It is redemptive to face with honesty the shadows of one's ego in the light of truth about oneself. The same sun that softens the mud hardens the clay. It's the soil, not the sun, that determines the results. The Pharisees plotted Christ's death. Though they knew it not, in reality they were planning their own destruction. If law does not serve life it will destroy life.

Theophilus would be hard put not to recognize what Jesus did in that which Luke reports here. Man is the reason for any law, tradition or institution. Laws are means to an end. If they fail to serve the ends for which they are made they are to be disregarded and changed. If men misuse or abuse law they will be destroyed by those very same laws.

Men are sacred, not laws. Man made in God's image is divine. Laws are to protect, renew, restore that image. If laws are perverted to other ends than that for which they were designed they are to be transcended by fulfilling their original intent.

When the man Jesus, "the Lord of the Sabbath," the ideal, representative, universal man meets a(any)man "with his hand withered" healing brings to fulfillment God's purpose in law(s)! Laws find their meaning in him who is "Lord of law!"

AN OUTLINE OF LUKE 6:12-16
The Selection of Twelve Apostles!
In any social group structure is imperative. Coordination of
differing personalities requires some kind of framework. Thus
Jesus "appointed" twelve as "apostles" to lead in formulating
the new people of God.
    I.   A NIGHT IN PRAYER. 6:12
          1. Jesus "went out to pray."
           (a)His need to pray!
           (b)The energy and urgency of his praying.
           (c)"Prayer to God," a mutual conversation.
   II. SELECTION AND APPOINTMENT. 6:13-16
          1. He "summoned his disciples."
          2. He "selected twelve."
          3. He "named them apostles."
          4. The list in quarterions.
The diversity of the twelve found unity in the Person of him
who was the master of each. Their diversity manifested the
unity in diversity of the new humanity, the new people of God
which He came to establish.

* * * * * * *

THE SELECTION OF THE TWELVE!
To channel the choices of free individuals until they become
a caring family unit is the challenge of leadership. It demands
wisdom beyond the usual, patience beyond normal, tolerance beyond ordinary and dedication beyond average. Without leadership
no group can function as a social unit. For any society to act
as a responsible fellowship some structuring must take place.
That requires leaders! To coordinate differing personalities
into a fellowship that functions as a people takes those who
can rise above personal preferences for the good of the whole.
The time had come in the ministry of Jesus when responsible
leadership must be chosen. Disciples had increased in numbers
until they now were "crowds." Enemies too were increasing in
ardor and numbers. His own challenges to their deadening
formalism was more bold. A coming crisis was increasingly
apparent. Jesus must not delay choosing leaders for his growing
movement. Thus it is he "selected" twelve men and "named them
apostles." They would become leaders who would formulate the
new people of God which it was his mission to establish.
A Night in Prayer!
"It came to pass in those days that he went out into the
mountain to pray." That Jesus needed to pray is quite a
revealing fact. Was he not uniquely son of God? Was he not God
"become flesh?" Yes! He was all this. But he was not God and
man; he was God as man! And if a man, as such he needed to talk
matters over with his father. The fact that Jesus felt the need
to pray at this time of choosing leaders is a dramatic
demonstration of his humanity.
That God be a living God, the archetype of human beings
implies that he wants to be recognized for who he is. People do

not like to be ignored. As persons they value being recognized, talked to, consulted and respected. Since man has been created "in the image" of God, we conclude that God shares these same personal qualities. He desires to be recognized, appreciated, valued as a Person.

Furthermore, Jesus, being thoroughly human, quite naturally sought to talk important decisions over with Him who is the source of all wisdom. The kingdom he came to establish is God's. So Jesus felt the burden of making wise choices for the the kingdom. His need for prayer demonstrates his humanity as deity. Jesus did not have a dual nature, God and man. No! He was God as man! The divine nature came as human because the human was created "in the image and likeness" of the divine. He needed to talk to Him he knew as Father.

Luke is the sole writer of the Gospels who relates that Jesus went "unto the mountain" in order "to pray." In addition the form of expression "he was spending the night" discloses the continuous energy and urgency that he spent all through the night. Even the expression "in prayer to God" is distinctive. It intimates not only that God was the object of prayer but that He, God, responded with equal urgency. It was not a one way series of requests; it was a two-way conversation. These grammatical notes reveal the "persevering energy of this vigil" as well as "the rapt contemplation of God's presence,..arising out of the most profound communion with him."(Godet, Luke, pg.190) Nothing is lacking in Luke's language to make clear the seriousness of this crisis to Jesus. He needed all the insight, intelligence, wisdom to make right choices for leadership in the kingdom program. All night was not too long to be "in prayer to (with) God" when such crucial choices had to be made!

The Selection and Appointment!

Having canvassed the whole problem in prayer, having come to definite decisions, Jesus came down the mountain to a "level place." There he "summoned his disciples." Many hundreds had attached themselves to him as committed disciples. Now he must choose some whose commitment would allow them to enter an intensive involvement in teaching and leading. From this band of loyal followers he "selected twelve." The number twelve indicates that the old Israel of God was to be superseded by a new, a new people of God. The new Israel would consist of believers from all nations, peoples, and cultures.

But the new Israel needed enough structuring so as to be more than a mob of individuals. To assure stability it needed some framework. Hence the twelve "he named apostles." The word means ones "sent on a mission." They were authoritative ambassadors, specified representatives of the kingdom!

The List in Quarterions!

During the lengthy session of prayer without question Jesus reviewed each selection one by one with God his Father. He sought the Father's approval. Then he decided on the twelve.

The four times these leaders are listed in the New Testament they appear in three groups of four each. Peter, Philip, and

82

James (son) of Alphaeus head each quarternion. This suggests that even among the twelve these three developed qualities of unusal leadership. But why these three? For that matter, why these twelve? Doubtless leadership qualities were present in a goodly number out of the "crowds" of disciples who by now were constant followers of Jesus. So why these twelve?

That question can only be answered by taking a hard look at the basic nature of man as God created him "in the beginning." The mankind which God originally conceived in mind and made in fact had within him the imprint of the deity himself. Such is implicit in God's description of his human creature as his "image and likeness." So sacred and inviolable is this quality in man that God himself would not nor will he diminish, modify, or change under any circumstances the least iota. Even the vilest of men retains this "image" of his original divine nature. And what is this image? It is the inherent responsibility to evaluate moral action and choose. No man can avoid making choices! This is what in every man is "like" God himself.

But we need to know that making right choices carries with it the possibility of making wrong choices. The moment one is forced to do that which is right, at that moment it ceases to be right. For any decision to be right or wrong there must unincumbered free choice. It must be within the framework of moral responsibility of choosing that we see Christ's concern about his appointing specific disciples to be "apostles" of the new people of God.

Of the twelve we know very little. But enough is recorded to indicate that the wide variety of personal traits included weak and strong points common to all men. Weaknesses did not keep Peter, John or Judas from sharing in the apostolic company. Peter's impulsive quickness to act made him a natural leader. The name "Rock" which Jesus gave him testifies to his staunch character that he became. Yet he was weak and unstable enough under pressure to deny with curses that he ever knew Christ! It has been said of John that he was, above the others, the closest as a friend to Jesus. John kept in his heart the words of Jesus that revealed Christ's inner consciousness of himself. On the other hand, John inherited the epithet "son of thunder." It reflected his impatient ardor, his quick zeal to call down fire from heaven on those who would not readily receive the Lord.

And as for Judas, "the betrayer!" Why would Jesus select one whose destiny was to be so false? In the first place we must remember that even if (which is not a necessity) Jesus foreknew the end from the beginning, that does not imply that Judas had to betray his Lord. I may see a wreck take place without having anything to do with making it happen. Foreknowledge and foreordination are distinct matters.

The answer to the problem of the selection of Judas lies in the fact Judas was a man. He had good qualities, as did all the twelve. He also had weak and questionable qualities as did all the others. But God himself must allow every man "in his image" to make his own moral decisions. When Judas Iscariot initially heard and accepted the call of Jesus, "Follow me" he responded with as fullness of faith as that to which he was capable. He had weaknesses different but no greater than the others. But he was a man and, as such, opportunities to grow in grace were as open to him as to any of the others. He will not be denied his opportunities to rise or fall in choosing faithful service or self-serving betrayal. He was not forced to be false to trust. He freely chose his course. He made his own decision.

But it was for that very reason that Jesus had to struggle through a whole night of prayer before he made his final choice of which twelve to appoint as apostles. Christ must weigh all possibilities; the weak points, the strong traits in each man. One by one he "talked" them over with his heavenly Father and the decisions were made. Publican, Zealot, Thomas the doubter! How would each respond under the pressures yet undreamed of by them? What would the end result be in their personal lives? And what contribution could each make in the coming kingdom? These were the factors with which Jesus, as a man, wrestled in prayer through that night.

And it should be said that without exception every choice contributed to the total result intended by the choices Christ made. Even Judas "the betrayer" fulfilled his function when he cried "I have betrayed the innocent blood." It is its own unique testimony to the Person of the Christ. So far as results are concerned that word of Judas is as real in positive preaching as Peter on Pentecost or the blood of James, the first martyr. "God works all things for good!"

Two facts find a focus in this brief paragraph on the selection of the twelve. First is the humanity of our Lord as it is laid bare in his all night struggle in prayer. If he needed prayer before making such important decisions, we surely do. In the moral, ethical, and spiritual decisions we must make in God's kingdom work we must talk with our Father and seek his counsel.

A second truth is that each man, leader or not, in the kingdom of God will not be denied his place of service merely because he has weak traits of character. As a human being he will be granted equal opportunities to choose his response. God will use all who choose to be used!

AN OUTLINE OF LUKE 6:17-49
The Sermon on the Mount!
For whom is the kingdom prepared? Who comprise its citizens?
What are the guidelines of conduct in the kingdom? On what moral
principles does it operate? Who administers its judicial power?
Such questions are answered in Jesus' message given following
his naming of the twelve.
  I. PERSONS OF THE KINGDOM. 6:17-26
      The positive versus the negative:
      1. The "poor"   ---   The "rich."
      2. The "hungry" ---   Those "having been filled."
      3. Those "weeping" --- Those "laughing(rejoicing)."
      4. The "hated"   ---   The "reputable."
 II. PRINCIPLES OF THE KINGDOM. 6:27-45
      1. Statement of the new principle. 6:27-30
         (a)Love in its active form.
         (b)Love in its passive resistance.
      2. A capsule description. 31
      3. Its singular quality, disinterested love. 32-35a
      4. Pattern and source of such love. 35b-36
      5. Love, guiding source of all moral good. 37-45
III. JUDICIAL POWER IN THE KINGDOM. 6:46-49
      1. Christ's claim of Lordship. 46.
      2. In the wisdom of obedience; folly of disobedience.
The "natural" man acts with selfish interest to protect his
ego. He lives to preserve his rights. One may even rise to
respect a neighbor's rights. But Jesus describes the man of the
kingdom as one who, through disinterested love, disclaims his
rights for the sake of the rights of others, even enemies! Love
is unlimited self-sacrifice!

* * * * * * *

THE SERMON ON THE MOUNT!
"Having come down with them he stood on a level place." On
the mountain plateau Jesus revealed the basics of the kingdom
of God, the constitution for the people of God. He revealed for
whom it was designed, the pattern of its lifestyle, and its
power of enforcement. The concept of the kingdom is more
radical than anything this world has ever seen.
The Persons of the Kingdom!
Citizenship in the kingdom is for four kinds of people: the
"poor," the "hungry," the "weeping," and the "hated."
"Blessed are the poor, for the kingdom of God is yours." No
virtue is attached to poverty as such. People are not virtuous
because they lack material means. The word πτωχός derives from
the verb πτώσσω = to cower, crouch, cringe. It is more kin to
humiliation, self abasement, than lack of money. The poor in
material means can appreciate acceptance among the people of
God. Poverty isn't virtue but it opens the door to dependence.
The kingdom is for "you" the humble! It is for the dependent.

85

"Woe to you, the rich, for you are being paid your comfort now in full." As poverty is no virtue, wealth is no sin. But it does indicate a lack of privation. The rich are those who become socially prominent, politically powerful, economically independent. Nothing they wish is denied them! Such as these have no privilege in the kingdom of God. That is for the lean, the empty, the forlorn!

Two more types whom the kingdom welcomes are "the hungry" and "those weeping." Jesus is not suggesting that lack of food or the presence of grief in themselves reflect nobility of character. Nothing morally good is inherent in being hungry or sad! But here again he is designating those believers in his audience who were then experiencing temporal privations. He was pointing out that God's kingdom consists of just such suffering people. God's new society was inaugurated for this kind of poor, those who not only hungered for meat and potatoes but for the nourishment of the word of God. And also for those who needed the joy and consolation of heaven's blessing.

On the other hand "Woe to those who have been filled (with food) now, for they shall hunger (for the food of the spirit hereafter)." And for "those who are laughing (partying) now shall experience what it is to be hungry"(after the lights are out and the party is over).

A fourth class of citizens for whom the kingdom holds special meaning bears the brunt of "hate" from this world's society. "Blessed are you whenever men shall hate you, separate you off...cast out your name as evil on account of the son of man..." In the immediate social context Jesus is alluding to the names of his followers being erased from the synagogue rolls. If one experiences excommunication from his "church" "on account of the name" of Christ it is time to "skip for joy." The kingdom of God provides a security for just such persons. "Behold, your reward is great in heaven." The Kingdom of God offers ample compensation for that kind of personal sacrifice. And by so suffering that one enters into God's list of martyrs. "Their fathers were doing the same to the prophets!" Whenever good confronts evil in a wicked world some kind of loss is the lot of the good. However, the kingdom of God furnishes its compensations for people who endure destitution.

By the same token, whenever "all men speak well of you, woe to you!" A false world will praise the false. If worldly men endorse you that's a prime sign you are one of their kind.

<u>Principles of the Kingdom</u>!

A succinct summary of kingdom principles is: "Love your enemies." All that Luke has to say to Theophilus about God's guidelines for life are embedded in the concept of "love."

Jesus sets forth love in three active effects: (1)"Be <u>doing</u> good to ones hating you." (2)"Be <u>blessing</u> ones cursing you." (3)"Be <u>praying</u> for ones abusing you." <u>Do</u>, <u>say</u>, and <u>pray</u> for those who <u>hate</u>, <u>curse</u>, and <u>abuse</u>! Now <u>that</u> is radical! It is behaviour unheard of in this world! That's the "wisdom from above...pure...peaceable...gentle...reasonable." The highest to which the natural heart can rise is the justice of "an eye for and eye..." Does not fairness deserve rights? Yet here Jesus says the kingdom man ignores his "rights" in order to sacrifice himself for healing of another. Love puts no limit on itself.

Love is boundless! "To the one slugging you on the jaw, be supplying to him the other also." To hit back may be "justice" but its effect increases rancor. To absorb the blow by turning the other cheek confuses and disarms an enemy. And it opens a door for reconciliation. He who has strength of character to take physical abuse displays love. He shall be recognized as son of "the most high." He has attributes of God himself. "From the one demanding your outer cloak don't withold your inner coat. Be giving to everyone demanding." The only limit love sets is that which rises from within its own nature. "God is love" and love in the kingdom man is as infinite as God.

When Jesus said: "Love your enemies" he wasn't exhorting men to _feel_ nice about enemies. "Feeling good" is not love. He was urging that men _act_ properly toward an enemy. To act right one must use his will even when feeling runs counter to his will. "Just as you are wishing that men _do_ to you, you be _doing_ to them." Doing to enemies is the measure of love. Doing to friends is to be expected. "If you love those loving you, what kind of grace is that? For even sinners are loving those loving them...and if you lend to those from whom you are hoping to get back, what kind of thanks is that to you?" Love, to be love, is unmindful of what it gets. It is gratuitous. It is not created or determined by the beauty or blemish in the object. It holds within itself its own cause. It is disinterested. Thus it's able to embrace him who is its moral opposite, an enemy! It can and does "do good to enemies and lends, hoping for nothing" in return. Love's standard is: "Just as you will that men be doing to you, you be doing to them in like manner."

Men in the new society are to surpass in lifestyle men of the old. They are to _love_ expecting nothing in return. But their behaviour rises even higher. "You be merciful just as your father is merciful." God is the pattern and source of your lifestyle. God is "kind" to men. God's people are to be "kind" to their fellows. The "reward" of heaven is not _pay_ but the inevitable result of such a lifestyle. Love bears fruit in more love! Goodness breeds goodness as its own reward "in heaven." God is the pattern, source, and strength for such a life.

Love is the guiding source of all moral good. Love refuses to set itself as the judge of the moral worth of another. Love condemns immoral acts but not him who does the deed. "Do not be condemning and you won't be condemned." Love tries to find ways of accepting the person without condoning the sin. Love in men gives as love in God gives, "good measure having been pressed, having been shaken together, running over, shall they give into your bosom." The reward of loving another returns in exact measure as the love given. He who gives sacrificial love can never lose for it comes back to him in exact measure. "With what measure you measure it shall be measured to you."

87

If love permeates the inner heart it manifests itself in positive, constructive, healing ways in its outward effects. For example it instinctively wishes to teach, instruct, guide a neighbor into higher moral ways of life. Only love can do that! "He who is blind cannot make a way for him who is blind. Will they both not fall into(a)pit?" Love keeps one from such folly!

Love leads a disciple to rise to perfect imitation of his teacher. "A disciple does not go beyond his teacher. But having been completely equipped by his teacher (having graduated), he shall be as his teacher." Thus the teacher's precept realizes its power in the embodied example of that which he teaches. He doesn't follow the foolish pattern of trying to remove a speck of husk out of a friend's eye when his own vision is blocked by a large log. Ridiculous! First, remove your own saw-log! Then you can see clearly to remove a speck from your friend's eye. This is the way of love. It exercises strict self discipline before it teaches or corrects another.

Outward instruction gains its power to transform from the power of purity in the heart. "A good tree does not produce rotten fruit, nor does a rotten tree produce good fruit....A good man out of the good treasure of his heart bears the good, and the evil (man) bears the evil from the evil (heart). Out of the abundance of the heart the mouth speaks." It is the heart that produces words. It is the heart that gives form and power to the teaching of the mouth. If a disciple wishes to transform others by the word of teaching he must transform himself. Then his teaching can transform others. Christ's word had power because he was the perfect man. Doctrine, life, relationships are all shaped and determined by the presence or absence of love in the heart. Out of the heart the mouth speaks! Love in the heart produces redemptive power for others.

Judicial Power in the Kingdom!

What or who is the arbiter? Who enforces the rule of love as the undergirding principle of the kingdom of God?

So far as a person is concerned Jesus states who is Lord. "Why do you call me Lord, Lord and do not do that which I say?" If you acknowledge me as King, the teacher of the law of the kingdom, why not obey? Don't, as the Pharisees, spend your time discussing love, do love! Perform the deeds of love. Obey the law of love because I am the Lord of love. The disciple is to love as the Teacher loves!

But nothing is arbitrary in the administration of the law. Sanction, judgment, enforcement lie within the law of love itself. Reward and punishment do not force the Lord's will. It is rather inherent, inbred, innate in the nature of love. The Lord does not stand as a tyrant spying lest one break the law. Violation of the law carries its own judgment.

Jesus enforces this idea with the vivid parable of the wise and foolish builders. "Everyone coming to me and hearing my words and doing them, I will show you whom he is like. He is like a man building (a) house, who dug deep and put (the) foundation upon the rock. But a flood having come the river dashed against that house, and did not shake it because he built it properly." Love deposits its own reward. When the kingdom man builds his life on love he can conquer the floods of corruption, sensualism, and materialism. This strength lies inherent in obedience to the Lord and law of love. Discipline and punishment is not inflicted from without. Neither is reward given from without. Both punishment or reward rise from within the deed of hate or love.

It is true for him who builds his house on the sands of selfish hate. The same floods that strengthen the good man demolish him who hates. Innate in selfishness is the seed of its own undoing. The power of enforcement lies in the presence or absence of love in the heart.

Luke's distinctive message to Theophilus is sharply defined when contrasted to Matthew's report of the sermon on the mount. Matthew sets Jesus' fulfillment of the intent of the law in contrast to the Pharisaical conformity to legal minutia. "You have heard it said of old time, but I say to you..." The inward meaning and spirit of the law was defeated by Pharisaical explanations of the letter of the law. But Christ's fulfillment comes in realizing in experience the meaning and intent of the law. The letter kills; the spirit gives life! It fulfills!

Luke's presentation largely ignored the old, as contrasted to the now. He preferred to present the law of love as the foundation principle governing the kingdom of God. Nothing is more universal than love. In its very nature love surpasses all other systems, old or new. Love embraces and encompasses any good in every system. No principle of life can outstrip love in its power to purify the springs of human behaviour. It is at once universal and human.

Amazing Faith!

Jesus never showed surprise at man's abusing him. He wasn't
shocked at the dullness of disciples. He wasn't startled at
denial or betrayal by friends. But at a Centurion's faith Jesus
was thoroughly amazed!

I. THE PROBLEM. 7:1-2
1. A "certain centurion."
2. A dying house-slave.
3. Dearly loved by his master, the centurion.
II. A STRATEGY FOR SOLVING. 7:3-5
1. The near presence of Jesus.
2. A Delegation of Jewish elders.
3. Earnest exhortation: "he is worthy."
III. THE SOLVING INTERRUPTED. 7:6-8
1. "Jesus was going..."
2. Second delegation: "I am not worthy...!"
(a)You "to enter my house."
(b)That "I come to you."
3. "But say (a) word..." I understand authority!
IV. AMAZING FAITH! 7:9-10
1. Jesus "marvelled at him."
2. Unmatched faith: (a)in quality (b)in whom found!
3. Problem solved without a word.

Sin has separated man from God to the point that doubt has
become more normal than faith. When faith is found in its
simplicity, purity, and power results come without a word!

* * * * * * *

AMAZING FAITH!
God created man capable of trust. But when man violated the
trust doubt became a way of life. Doubt misplaced faith until
it became the usual, the normal, the natural. As doubt became
the way to perdition, faith became the way of redemption. But
faith is something human not national or cultural. Faith is not
restricted to Hebrews. It has the same redeeming effect in the
heart of a Gentile. In this story a Roman's faith startled
Jesus. He contrasted it with faith found in Israel!

The Problem!
"After he finished all these words in the hearing of the
people, he entered into Capernaum." From the mountain plateau
where he taught the kingdom constitution, Jesus returned to his
nearby home city. Here he soon found opportunity to display the
love about which he taught. "A slave of a certain centurion was
desperately ill. He was about to die." The last stages of
disease had already marked him for death. Many a Roman soldier,
acquainted with pain and death by profession, would not be too
concerned about a slave's death. But here was a difference! "He
was precious to him." This slave was a house-hold favorite. By
faithful labor and winsome ways he had become more than a
slave. He had won a warm place in the heart of the family.

As the tale develops it becomes clear that this centurion plays the role of a respected part of the community. He stands high in the estimate of the city elders. Though a Gentile, he was greatly influenced by the religious convictions of the citizenry. In fact, the local elders were proud to testify that "he built for us our synagogue." It may have been for practical considerations, nevertheless, this particular Roman captain was well thought of in Capernaum. The fact that he held his house servant with such close personal affection is in keeping with the warmth of relationship between community and captain. He certainly was one who knew how to interrelate with people.

When he learned of the presence of Jesus in the city and remembered his growing fame, he immediately decided to approach the teacher in behalf of his beloved servant. On two counts, however, he felt unworthy to make direct advances to so exalted a Rabbi. He was a Gentile, a Roman, a representative of an alien government, considered oppressive. His feeling also sprang from an uneasy sense of guilt that always rises in the presence of genuine moral purity. But affection for his servant surmounted any insecurity of his own person. Life for the servant outweighed personal unworthiness.

Strategy for Solving the Problem!

The centurion devised a strategy that would nullify any lack in himself. He decided to call upon fellow Jews of Jesus as intermediaries. What he himself lacked they would have. Jesus and the city elders were of the same race, heritage, and tradition. He quickly called them together, laid before them the desperate situation, and delegated them to approach Jesus with his plea: "Come, save my servant from death!"

Luke reports three particulars about the work of the elders. First, "When they came to Jesus they were exhorting him earnestly." Each of the elders in turn repeatedly urged upon Jesus that he honor the request of their benefactor. And they did so with fervor. Furthermore, their uniform apology was, "He is worthy that you do this." Their plea was based more on the centurion's worth than on the sick servant's need. One wonders whether theirs was not economic and political manipulation more than compassion for a human being!

For proof of his "worth" they argued, "He built for us our synagogue." His economic investment in their community proved, not his love, but his worth—not his economic worth, but his practical asset in the life of the city. It is quite possible that, consciously or unconsciously, they imputed worth of character in one so liberal with his money.

An Interruption to the Strategy!

In the narrative Luke does not relate a single word, if any, of Jesus' response to the elders. The record states, "He (Jesus) was going with them." If Jesus said anything we aren't told. The impression given is that Jesus immediately dropped whatever he was doing and without a word started walking in the direction of the centurion's home. While Jesus was approaching and yet was "not far" from his house the centurion suddenly changed his mind. Jesus was a Jew currently of wide reputation. It would cause a Jew to become unclean to enter a Gentile's house. The illness of the servant had so disturbed the centurion that he apparently had overlooked this breach of taboo before he sent the elders. Or he had hardly expected such a positive ready response by Jesus. At any rate when he saw or was told that Jesus was nearing his house he hastily sent a second group of "friends" with the message, "Quit troubling yourself, for I am not sufficient (clean) that you should come under my roof." He realized his standing as a Gentile in a Jewish community. His gratitude for Christ's coming so readily brought him to realize what a great social stain he had inadvertently placed on Jesus. He even added, "Wherefore I even deemed myself unworthy personally to come to you." He was overjoyed, yet humbled by the willingness of Jesus to heal his servant in the face of Jewish scruples.

It is striking to note the contrast between the elders' evaluation of the centurion and his own about himself. They said, "He is worthy that you do this..." He said, "I am not sufficient...nor do I deem myself worthy to come to you." They viewed him as an economic, social asset to the city. He viewed himself as a man in desperate need and as such with nothing to plead but the need. What makes a man valuable in the sight of God? That which we bring to God? Or that which God has invested in his creature? Is it worth or need that prompts God's healing grace? Or both? At any rate the centurion had a firm grasp and a clear vision of his relationship as a needy man and Christ as the giver of life. Even his experience as a military officer gave him insight as to who Jesus was. It clarified his faith. "But speak (a) word and my house servant shall be healed. For I am a man subjecting myself under authority, having soldiers under me, and I say to this one 'Go' and he goes. And to another 'Come' and he comes." In other words, this centurion saw the relationship between authority, possession of power, and the fulfilling of a task. In his position of authority he exercised his power to get his will done. So, he perceived, Jesus could as authority over the forces of life fulfill his purpose in giving health and life.

Amazing Faith!

At this point Jesus displayed unfeigned amazement at the centurion's faith. The text tells, "And having heard this, Jesus marvelled at him. And having turned to the crowd following him, he said, 'I say to you, Not even in Israel did I find such great faith.'" The fact that Jesus "marvelled" is itself a marvel. It wasn't the man's wealth, profession, race, social position, lifestyle that amazed the Lord. It was the man's faith, the greatness of it!

And why was it great? It was great because none of these other things upon which men place such value distracted him from seeing the heart of the issue. That is, who Jesus was in relation to the creative forces of life. It was great because he never forgot why he approached Jesus in the first place, to

92

effect a healing for a beloved servant-friend. It was great because he surmounted religious, racial and cultural barriers to get to Jesus. It was great because he recognized the chief characters in the whole episode were Jesus and the servant, not himself. He was the channel of faith but not the source of healing power. It was great because of the self-effacing humility of him who believed. It was great because of the intellectual purity and simplicity of his trust in Jesus the object of his faith.

Jesus "marvelled" at the centurion's faith! The reader, Theophilus, had to be amazed at the clear distinctness of Jesus' response to the soldier's faith. When the elders came with the centurion's initial request Jesus asked no questions, raised no objections, set aside present matters, immediately turned toward the household where lay the sick servant. Not a word was spoken! When the second delegation of "friends" arrived with the centurion's discount of his worth joined with the man's logical insight into the nature of Christ's authority Jesus still said not a word. He addressed the crowd about the "great faith" of the Roman soldier. At no point in the entire story did Jesus say a word to, about, or for the young man who was sick. In fact, were it not for Matthew's record (and Theophilus did not have Matthew) we would not know that Jesus ever saw or talked to the centurion. Not only did Jesus not say a word but we have no record that anything such as a gesture, a sign, a visible object, <u>nothing</u> appears in the story to indicate that anyone <u>knew</u> that the sick young man was made well. It was only when "the ones having been sent, when having returned to the house, they <u>found</u> the servant healed." What an unusual story, an amazing feat! The whole affair took place without Jesus saying, doing, signaling anything! It's as though Jesus was in a vacuum of silence while all around was the talking, acting, maneuvering of all the other characters. The man's faith is the "hero" of the narrative. Jesus' redeeming power for healing is released by faith, not a word, symbol, or deed.

And what would Theophilus think when he read this story? That such "great faith" appeared in a non-Jew would make its impression. And that Jesus "marvelled" at and praised such faith would also be impressive to a Gentile reader. The fact that faith is a universal, a non-sectarian, non-racial, quality would impress. Then too, that Jesus identified so easily and readily with such a human situation would speak volumes as to his human nature. To <u>be</u> as well as to say or do has its own testimony.

Luke's genius as an author is so manifest. He gets so much harmony out of a variety of instruments. God's <u>universal</u> reach within the limits of one <u>man's</u> ministry could not help but make an indelible impression on a sensitive Greek reader.

AN OUTLINE OF LUKE 7:11-17
A Visit From God!

The tenderness of Jesus is nowhere better portrayed than in the details of the raising of the widow's son at Nain. In this story a solemn procession to the cemetary meets a joyful crowd journeying with the Lord of life. The result turned death into life! The people declared: "God visited his people!"

I. THE MEETING OF TWO PROCESSIONS. 7:10-12
    1. The procession to Nain from Capernaum.
    2. The procession to the cemetary of Nain.
II. THE MIRACLE AT THE MEETING. 7:13-15
    1. Jesus was "moved with compassion."
       (a)The circumstances which moved him.
       (b)"Stop weeping!"
    2. Jesus "took hold of the bier."
    3. Jesus said: "To you I say, 'Arise!'"
    4. Jesus "gave him to his mother."
III. RESULTS OF THE MEETING. 7:16-17
    1. Both processions:
       (a)Felt fear(awe).
       (b)"Were glorifying God."
    2. Increasing understanding of the nature of Jesus.
    (a)Prophet of the first order.
    (b)God visited his people.
    (c)"This word went out..."

This story features two factors. (1)The tenderness of Jesus. (2)A growing appreciation of the nature of Jesus!

* * * * * * *

A VISIT FROM GOD!

Does God, dwelling in celestial seclusion from earthiness, really have feelings such as we human beings have? How can one who is never subject to human tears really know the heartbreak of tears? How can he who is Life and who never has experienced death ever know the feeling of one who suffers death? And all the emptiness, separation, brokenness that envelopes a parent who has buried a beloved one! How can anyone, man or God, enter into the "feeling" of anyone if he has never been subjected to the "feeling?"

Is this not the reason why "the Word became flesh?" Whether in an abstract theoretical way God can "feel" we do not know. But we have been told on good evidence that God "became flesh" and thus entered into human experiences. It has also been witnessed that he was "tempted in all points" as are we. The purpose of the incarnation may have been other than to be able to feel as man feels but that is one of its effects. The report of Jesus confronting the breaking heart of a widow at Nain reveals God experiencing human feelings. And more than that, it shows God voiding those feelings by rescinding the cause of the breaking heart. He terminates the sadness by giving gladness. He replaces death with life!

94

The Meeting of Two Processions!

"And it came to pass that on the next day he was going unto a city called Nain. And his disciples and a great crowd were journeying with him." A number of factors raised the level of excitement among the followers of Jesus. Designating twelve as special apostles, developing the law of love as foundational to his new kingdom, healing the house servant of the centurion all contributed to growing expectations.

The next day Jesus began another circuit of Galilean cities. Nain was scarcely a day's journey up into the hills west of Capernaum. "Crowds" of disciples along with the twelve walked with him as he journeyed westward toward Nain. Why would so many follow on such a prolonged excursion if they weren't conscious of new insights and fresh opportunities? Exchange about recent events animated the conversation as they walked the road to Nain. It was an aroused procession of people!

The crowd of disciples approaching Nain weren't the only procession travelling the highway. "As he (and his disciples) neared the gate of the city, behold also an only son of his mother, and she a widow, having died, was being carried in an open bier. And a large crowd from the city was with her."

The processions which met on the highway near the gate of the city offer comparison and contrast. Each is described by the term "crowd." Each was sympathetic to the one who occasioned the crowd to be formed. That from Capernaum was filled with hope and expectation. The one from Nain was filled with sadness and sorrow. It was united in sincere sympathy for an esteemed citizen of the city, a widow. The enthusiasm of life contrasted with the despair of death. The one represented man's unquenchable hope for better days. The other depicted the prematurely cutting off of hope for all days.

The Miracle at the Meeting!

The two processions were moving toward an inevitable meeting. Each would have to note the other to make way for passing. The procession from Nain was headed for the cemetary. The grief of the mother was underscored by her uncontrolled sobbing. Her friends from Nain shared her sorrow. By tears and sobs they openly embraced her grief. Jesus, having halted his group out of respect, stood silently observing the scene. The text states, "And the Lord, having seen, was moved with compassion over her." Nothing is more revealing of the true humanity of Jesus than his tears over a human corpse. Later at the tomb of Lazarus, knowing full well that he would raise Lazarus, he could not hold back tears of sympathy; "Jesus wept!" So perfectly is the heart of Jesus identified with the sadness of human kind that he "was moved with compassion." The fact that health lies beyond sickness and that life lies beyond death does not lessen the pain of present suffering. A violin in perfect tune with another instrument manifests its accord only when the strings are plucked or stroked! That God in the flesh was "moved with compassion" was only seen when Jesus saw the suffering of the widow at the death of her only son. If men are to "know" God as they see Him in the ministry of Jesus then this scene opens a window for a view into the heart of God.

But Jesus did more than be "moved with compassion." He stepped to the widow and gently said, "Stop weeping!" In other words, he spoke with reassurance in a voice of compassion. Urging her to "quit crying" he turned to the bier and clutched it firmly with his hand. His seizing the bier esserted authority! "The ones who carried (it) stood still." His urging the woman and his fixed grip on the bier stopped the whole procession. Then Jesus moved to deal with the dead son. He turned and said, "Young man, to _you_ I say, 'Rise up.'" How remarkable! That Jesus expected him to hear who no longer could hear! Yet he clearly anticipated a dutiful response.

The most amazing thing was yet to come. "The dead sat up and he started talking..." He who had been prematurely cut off from sights, sounds, and speech once again enjoyed all three. For the moment he became quite garrulous. He not only "began to talk" but he "kept on talking." He may have been so shocked at the presence of so many friends; or he may have had a lot to tell; or he may have been so surprised to be alive that he could not contain himself. But whatever he was saying Jesus interrupted. Above all there was one person with whom the young man needed to talk. The text tells us that Jesus "gave him to his mother." What an emotional reunion; a son, returned from the dead, embracing his mother!

Results of the Meeting!

The immediate result of the meeting of processions was, "Fear came upon all." It was fear inspired by wonder, surprise, reverence and awe. A sense of bewilderment took hold of the people of both groups.

Moreover, such fear found expression in their "glorifying God." The verb form designates that they all "kept on glorifying." It was a stupendous wonder: a _man_ renewing _life_ to a young son. And their "glorifying God" took the _form_ of attempts to explain the person of Jesus. Some said, "A great prophet has arisen among us." This was a higher estimate than the Pharisees had accorded Jesus. And the people said he was not just a prophet but a "_great_ prophet" of the highest order!

Others declared "God visited his people!" This was a real advance in the perception of Jesus. Not yet did they see him as "Son of God." But they recognized that God by the presence of Jesus had "visited" their community. He provided renewed life for a beloved young man. At least in the minds of these citizens Christ's presence represented a brief but powerful "visitation" from God's representative.

"And _this word_ went out in the whole of Judea concerning him and in all the surrounding countryside." "This word" means more than just a report of the marvelous miracle of raising the dead. It included the people's judgment that Jesus was a "great prophet" and that "God visited his people." These views about Jesus were widely circulated as a result of Nain's experience with him. Little did they know that God _had_ "visited" that day.

96

The fact that Luke alone records this narrative of the confrontation of life with death at Nain shows its importance to his theme. It forcefully sketches for Theophilus the tender humanity of Jesus as God in the flesh. Indeed, God is _so_ human that when he "visits" his people in the trauma of daily affairs men don't recognize him as being present. God is visiting his people in the midst of daily routines as well as all tragedies.

In addition the impact of this story stresses the growing appreciation of the real nature of Jesus. Bit by bit, that Jesus, the man, was the divine Man was beginning to penetrate the consciousness of the people, especially the disciples.

* * * * * * *

AN OUTLINE OF LUKE 7:18-35
Shall We Look for Another?
Conversion to Christ as Lord brings joy, hope, enthusiasm! Often experiencing life as a Christian brings disenchantment. The world resists; doubts arise; unanswered questions persist. Distrust of leadership dampens confidence. Uncertainty chills faith. Eventually the inevitable question rises: Have I been mistaken? In Christ the answer? Shall I expect another?
I.   JOHN THE BAPTIST'S QUESTION. 7:18-20
      1. Report to John about Jesus.
      2. The question proposed.
II.   THE ANSWER OF JESUS. 7:21-23
      1. His deeds speak for the Christ.
      2. "Blessed be whoever shall not be tripped over me."
III. THE DISCOURSE ABOUT JOHN. 7:24-30
      1. The expectations in John!
         (a)Instability?
         (b)A Soft, indulgent man!
         (c)A prophet?
      2. What you found in John!
         (a)The promised forerunner.
         (b)The "greatest born of women."
IV.   THE RESPONSE TO GOD'S MESSENGERS. 7:31-35
      1. The people and publicans.
      2. The Pharisees and lawyers.
      3. The "men of this generation."
"Wisdom is justified from all her children." Results count! Christ's deeds answer John's questioning. Results in response to John's message and ministry "justify" God's sending John to "this generation." Results also count in the message and ministry of the "son of Man."

97

SHALL WE LOOK FOR ANOTHER?

Conversion to Christ brings joy, hope, enthusiasm; it lifts the load of guilt. Christians are given power **over** the world but we are not taken **from** the world. The world around us won't go away. It's standard of values is directly opposed to that of God's Christ. The world resists the Christian. Not only do one's personal struggles shatter early hopes but inconstancy in other believers leads to disillusion. Practical experience invites disenchantment. Why do these evil thoughts, deeds, tensions, confrontations continue? Thus added to the down-drag of sensuous pressures is the chilling doubt that threatens to sweep away faith. Why is heaven so silent? Where is the power? Am I misled in Christ? Shall I look elsewhere?

The Question of John the Baptist!

The questions of the struggling Christian are not unlike those which crossed the mind of John, languishing in the fortress of Machaerus. When John had been free, roaming the hills of the Judean wilds, he had no misgivings about Jesus. As the forerunner he said of Jesus: "He will baptize you with the Holy Spirit and with fire. His winnowing fork is in his hand, to clear his threshing floor, and to gather the wheat into his granary, but the chaff he will burn with unquenchable fire." He had heard God say of Jesus, "You are my beloved Son, with you I am well pleased." No doubt arose in John's preaching about Jesus as God's promised Christ. But now the rugged free-hearted spirit of John the Baptist had been cut down by Herod. John had traded the open skies and weathered craggs of Judean mountains for the damp gloom of Machaerus' dungeon. Days had dragged into months. Did he never wonder about Messiah to whom he had given such sure testimony? What had become of that ministry? Had God forgotten John?

John's thought was interrupted by the arrival of disciples from Nain. They gave eye-witness account of how Jesus "was moved with compassion" over the tragic loss of a widow's son. And they brought other tales of the ministry of mercy carried on by Jesus. Such reports assured John that Jesus as the Christ was indeed at work. His influence was spreading throughout Galilee and even into Judea.

John did not doubt that Jesus was Messiah. His problem was whether "another" Messiah with a different message was to be expected? The ministry of Jesus was one of "compassion." He was healing the hurt of people. Where was judgment? John had testified that the Christ would "baptize...with the Holy Spirit and fire." John was hearing about the Christ's giving the "Holy Spirit." But the "fire," where was it? Why was God's judgment not being exhibited? Not once did John doubt that Jesus was Messiah. It was the **kind** of Messiah about which he was wondering! That's his problem. He delegated two disciples to go directly to Jesus with the carefully phrased question: "**You**, are you the one coming? Or is there another (of a different kind)?" The scriptures had set forth two images of God's anointed! Mercy and judgment! Were there two Christ's?

98

The Answer of Jesus!

When John's disciples came to Jesus "in that hour he healed many from diseases and plagues and unclean spirits, and to many blind he graciously gave sight." Whether they interrupted Jesus in order to present John's query or waited for a pause in Christ's ministry of mercy it appears that Jesus went right on with his healing. If we imagine John's disciples standing uneasily waiting an opportunity to present their question they could hardly miss the implication of the Lord's miracles. Deeds speak louder than words; yea! even instead of words!

But while they watched, Jesus turned and "having answered said to them, 'When you go, declare to John the things which you saw and heard; blind are seeing, lame are walking, lepers are being cleansed, dumb are hearing, dead are being raised, poor are being given good news.'" No logic surpasses deeds in communicating ideas. Just tell John what I do. Mercy brings its own judgment to those who reject mercy! Be patient! In due time judgment will come. Then Jesus added a brief negative word of warning: "Blessed is he whoever shall not be snared in me." The power of what Jesus did in merciful service to the physically handicapped, even to the dead, demonstrated better than argument who he was. Moreover, it left the ministry of judgment to John's faith. In the meantime John must not bite the bait of what Jesus did not do to trap him into failing to grasp that which Jesus did do. "Tell John what you saw and heard!" Let his faith in who I am rest in what I do! The absence of judgmental works must not blind John to the glory of the works now being done. I am who my deeds declare me to be! Don't be trapped by that which I don't do.

The Discourse About John!

"The messengers of John having gone off, he began to speak to the crowds about John." The question of John was really an expression of his faith. John believed in Jesus else he would not have asked him to deal with his doubt! He knew where to get answers! Raising the question did not mean lack of trust. It gave opportunity to show trust. It brought a clarifying of his faith; a purifying of his insight. At any rate Jesus took the opportunity of pressing home to the people the greatness of the testimony of John to his own ministry.

What did you expect when you went into the Judean wilderness to hear John? "What did you go out into the desert to behold? A reed shaken by wind?" An unstable, fanatical, rabid, hysterical, frenzied man? Was John unbalanced? "Yea! What did you go out to see? One clothed in rich raiment? luxurious garments? Behold! those garbed in rich luxury are living among the royalty!" John partook of the stability of the mountains among which he was born and to which he drew the multitudes to hear his message of reform.

"But what did you go out to see? A prophet? Yea! I say to you, even more than a prophet! This is concerning whom it stands written in Malachi, 'Behold, I send my messenger before your face, who shall prepare your way before you.' I say to

99

No one born of women is greater than John." That which people expected when they went out to the wilderness to hear him was not always that which they found. But that which they found was twofold: (1)The forerunner of the promised Messiah. (2)But more, they found the "greatest born of women."

Is Jesus saying that John was greater in faith than the faithful Abraham? Or the lawgiver Moses? Or Elijah the fountainhead of prophecy who stemmed the flood of Jezebel's Baalism? Or greater than Isaiah, prince of prophets whose vision of the coming Christ dominates the scriptures? Hardly! Each of God's roll call of "greats" has his unique place in the unfolding divine purpose. It was not in personal faith or character that John was the "greatest." It lay in his position in relation to Messiah. His inward life or his personal worth may have been equal to but did not surpass that of any of the Old Testament "greats." But his position in relation to the appearance and person of the Christ was the highest yet established. It was John's privilege as servant to introduce the Christ to Israel.

That John's greatness lay in his relationship to the Christ is indicated by Jesus when he said, "the least in the kingdom of God is greater than he(John)." The new kingdom which Jesus came to inaugurate surpasses the old so much that even the weakest citizen has more spiritual assets than any of the old. The least believer is united with Jesus as God's Son more than any servant of the old. The believer may not prove more faithful than John or any others of the old. But he is heir of higher privileges in Christ than all who went before. It's the quality of opportunity more than personal character that makes the least believer greater.

<u>Response to God's Messengers!</u>

Since John was so "great" his reception should be equal to his greatness, should it not? How was he actually received by people and priest?

"All the people and the publicans justified God, having been baptized by the baptism of John." Jesus goes out of his way to distinguish "the people" from "the publicans." Not only the public mass of people but in particular the most rejected of them, "the publicans" stamped God as being right in sending John. To "justify" basically means to declare "not guilty." By accepting John's word about the forerunner, and by dedicating themselves in the commitment of baptism they agreed that God was "not guilty" in demanding repentance. According to the people including the publicans God's message and ministry through John was "justified."

On the other hand, "the Pharisees and the lawyers rejected God's counsel, <u>not</u> having been baptized by him." Rejection of John's baptism was in reality a rejection of God and his promised Messiah. That which one does by accepting or rejecting God's messenger shows one's respect (or lack of it) for God. One "justifies" God by obedience or disobedience! The Pharisees and lawyers refused God's call to repentance.

100

It really isn't John who is fickle and unstable. It's the "men of this generation." You don't really know what you want or need. You are "like children sitting in the market place and calling to one another, "We piped and you didn't dance; we played funeral and you didn't weep." John's person and message was austere, ascetic, withdrawn from a socializing lifestyle. The son of man practiced a lifestyle that involved "eating and drinking" in normal social behaviour. Yet neither of these men of God found approval from the "men of this generation."

It is appropriate to fast; it is appropriate to feast depending on circumstances. Neither is "right" or "wrong" in itself. The "men of this generation" must relate to the person of God or his messenger. Thus enjoying proper personal relationship one may fast or feast as need demands. "Wisdom is justified from all her children." In other words, results count! It may be wise to repent; it may be wise to rejoice! It may be wise to speak of judgment to come; or to formulate a ministry of mercy.

The fact that Luke is the only synoptist that tells of raising the widow's son at Nain followed immediately by the Baptist's question to Jesus reveals that he felt an important relationship between the two narratives. At Nain Jesus was "moved with compassion" over a human experience with universal overtones. Death, an only son, a bereaved widow, sympathetic townspeople. John a preacher of righteousness in a sinful society, unjustly imprisoned by political, religious, and social pressures, left alone, apparently abandoned, doubts arising over him who was Messiah yet ignoring John's prediction of judgment. Justice, mercy, Messianic assurances, these are matters of universal human concern. And Jesus, as he moved among the people, dealt with all these issues. He acted as a man among men teaching, rebuking, healing, judging, ministering to every conceivable human situation. Judgment is universal; mercy is universal. He reached out to each man and every need be it man or woman, Jew or Gentile, rich or poor, belief or unbelief, living or dead!

This is Luke's ever recurring message to Theophilus!

AN OUTLINE OF LUKE 7:36-50
The Measure of Faith!
This is a story about a "woman in the city, sinner;" a self
righteous Pharisee; and Jesus, saviour of both. It's a perfect
example of "wisdom justified from all her children."
I.   THE WOMAN, "SINNER."
     1. She was "woman."
     2. She was "in the city."
     3. She was "sinner."
     4. Her behaviour at the feast.
II. THE PHARISEE.
     1. He "was inviting" Jesus to a banquet.
     2. His observation:
        (a)Of the woman's behaviour.
        (b)Of Jesus' response to her.
III. THE ACTION OF JESUS!
     1. Acceptance of the woman.
     2. His "word" (parable) "to Simon."
     3. Application of the parable.
     4. Final assurance: "Go into peace!"
Faith is the means of salvation. Love is the measure of faith!

* * * * * * *

THE MEASURE OF FAITH!
"Wisdom is justified from all her children." Thus Jesus
explained the public's reaction to the message of John the
Baptist. Now Luke describes an encounter of Jesus with a
Pharisee and a woman sinner as a prime portrait of "wisdom
justified." Each in his and her own way displayed the wisdom
of God in dealing with human beings.
The Woman, "in the city, sinner."
In the first place she was "woman." In that time and place
she was definitely second class. Human! Yes, yet something
less than human. A chattel to be used, even abused. But not on
the social level with men.
The description "in the city" indicates something special
about this woman. And the added descriptive "sinner" defines
precisely what was peculiarly discernible. True, "all have
sinned." But this woman had sinned in such a manner that she
had become a focal point of prominence. She was not a sinner;
she was sinner. Many assume that she was a prostitute. That
may be! But it's true that when a woman of above average
wealth, education, and social standing fell into an "affair"
she would be branded as "sinner" with more shock and disdain
than an ordinary prostitute. More likely this woman was not a
professional prostitute. She plunged into shame through some
discrepancy that had become public information. To the depths
she was crushed; life had flayed her. She held no hope! Then
she met Jesus and all was changed. The present story doesn't
report the circumstances that relieved her burden of sin. But
that Jesus did it no doubt is left. The outpouring of her
love exhibited the measure of her faith.

102

This woman was "in the city." She was a resident. But more, she was prominent, identifiable and, until her "affair," quite acceptable. But when her "sin" became public she bcame the subject of community gossip. She gained a new label, that of "sinner." But her access to the home of a prominent Pharisee remained open. And when she learned that Jesus dined in the Pharisee's house she sought his company to express her thanks for his gracious forgiveness. To be accepted by such a prominent public teacher as Jesus restored her self image. It gave her a sense of well being not known since her shame. Thus it was that she stood over the feet of Jesus as he reclined at table. And though Simon had neglected the common courtesies of host, with the instinct of love, she supplied them. "Having stood behind his feet, weeping, with her tears she began to wet his feet, and with the hairs of her head she wiped, and was kissing his feet and was anointing with the perfume."

The cleansing of a human conscience is a gift above price. No monetary value can be placed on such a bounty. Relief from guilt of moral wrong lifts a weight too heavy for any human to bear without permanent scars. At some point in the recent past Jesus had assured her of God's grace in forgiveness. She placed her confidence in Christ's word. What could she do other than let her gratitude pour out in unrestrained love by giving what she could? She had been "forgiven much." She gave "much." Her faith is validated by her display of love.

The person and behaviour of the Pharisee offers a contrast. She was "sinner" while he was of those who took pride in "righteousness," howbeit self-righteousness! And though this Pharisee fitted that category, he had traits that set him off. First, "He was inviting him (Jesus) that he dine with him." The form "was inviting" describes a continuing inviting. He was persistent. It took more than one invitation to get Jesus to his home. Not that Jesus was unwilling. Far from it! Jesus came to "seek and save" all who were lost, even the selfrighteous. But circumstances of a busy ministry had to be adjusted to the time schedule of the Pharisee. At any rate the repetition reveals persistence. Many who comment see in this "certain Pharisee" a hostile person. That may be true of Pharisees in general but exceptions occur such as Nicodemus and Joseph of Arimathea. This Pharisee wavered between belief and unbelief! If we take Jesus' parable "to Simon" at face value this Simon had experienced God's grace in forgiveness, even though so "little."(vs.47) Apparently he wanted to be friendly but as yet felt insecure in abandoning himself to his incipient faith. He wished to "test" Jesus.

Simon's behaviour also reflects his uncertain stance. His neglect of the usual courtesies in receiving Jesus suggests unwillingness to break with his Pharisaical friends. He didn't want to lose face before them. Then too observing Jesus' acceptance of the woman left a negative impression. "If this one were prophet, he would know who and what sort of woman which holds onto him, that she is sinner!" For Jesus to allow such familiarity did not commend him as prophet, much less as Messiah! This woman did more than touch Jesus, she "held onto him" with obvious affection and resolve. To the selfrighteous, any kind of fellowship with the unrighteous was taboo.

The Response of Jesus!

The reaction of Jesus both to the woman and Simon is quite revealing. To the woman it confirms her forgiveness and Christ as God's representative. To the Pharisee it reveals the Lord's capacity to forgive sin. That in turn shows him to be God's Messiah of promise. It exposes Simon's need as greater than the woman's. Besides, it exhibits God's grace available to Simon or others whose sin is selfrighteousness.

With the insight of heaven Jesus read the mind and heart of Simon and he said to him, "Simon, to you I have something to say." Then, with Simon's permission, Jesus dramatized in a parable Simon's real condition before God. "Two debtors were to a certain moneylender. The one owed five hundred pieces of silver, but the other fifty. Not having anything with which to pay, he freely forgave them both. Which then of them will love him more?"

Judged by how Simon phrased his response it seems that he was reluctant to acknowledge the obvious. Simon declared, "I suppose, him to whom he forgave the most." His "suppose" reveals his hesitation. The parable was a mirror reflecting Simon's selfish concern, his wavering weakness -- and that in the presence of his Pharisaical peers. He knew that he had answered correctly but he was timid before his guests. Like a storm rising over the horizon, he saw the meaning of the story. So he sought to soften the blow.

But Jesus refused to allow Simon to hide behind a "suppose." He proceeded to sharpen the point by describing Simon's failure as a host, not to mention his hesitating faith. Jesus concurred, "You answered rightly!" And then, having turned to the woman, Jesus reminded Simon of his specific lacks in common courtesy. Then, having turned to the woman, he said to Simon: "You see this woman? I entered your house. For me water for my feet you did not give. But she, with her tears, washed my feet and with her hairs wiped (them). A kiss (of greeting) you did not give me. But she, from which time she entered, did not quit kissing my feet. With oil my head you did not anoint. But she, with perfume, anointed my feet." Thus Jesus sharply reviewed point by point Simon's disregard for the social graces given to other guests. It was callous if not calculated misbehaviour!

As though the point were not clear Jesus pressed home the crux of the matter. "I say to you, her sins, the many of them, have been forgiven." Her slate has been wiped clean. She lives in a fixed state of absolution. And on what evidence? "Because she loved much."

The underlying eternal principle is: "He to whom little is forgiven, loves little." This is firing at close range with a double barrel! By this remark Jesus recognized the "sinner's"

104

purity of heart. At the same time, though granting God's grace in forgiveness of the Pharisee, Jesus pointed to the lack of love as evidence of his anemic faith. Whatever forgiveness he had experienced he had not yet plumbed the depths of personal shame. To rid the soul of the comfort of conformity is more difficult than to reach the heart of an outcast, the "publican and sinner." In the analogy of the parable this woman "sinner" was morally indebted to God up to at least a measure of 500 silver coins; the Pharisee by only 50, one tenth of her debt. Yet she was at peace with herself and God. But he was still struggling because of the weakness of his faith. He needed to know the experience of grace to a greater degree than yet experienced. He needed an __honest__ self evaluation followed by a severe dose of humilty! The failure to convey to Jesus the courtesies of welcome into his home revealed his failure in faith. That accounted for his lack of love. "He to whom little is forgiven, loves little." If Simon would enjoy great love, he must face the enormity of his own sin! The woman's sin was her problem, not Simon's. He must face the reality of __his own__ guilt, little or much as it might be.

Jesus was now ready to clinch the point before the whole gathering. He turned to the woman and said to her, "Your sins have been forgiven." The shocked audience of dinner guests raised the question, "Who is this, who indeed forgives sins?" That is the crux of the whole matter! Who is this Jesus? His pronouncement of forgiveness was the occasion. But the basic point at issue is "Who is this man Jesus?" Is he mere man or more than man? And if more, then who and what is he? The woman had settled that issue for herself.

To the woman Jesus added two points. First, "Your faith has saved you." Confidence in Jesus as God's representative is the avenue that releases power to dissolve guilt of sin. "Without faith it is impossible to please God." Men "are saved by grace through faith." To abandon oneself to God in Christ, from the human standpoint, provides the power of salvation.

His second point is: "Be going (linear action) __into__ faith." The present tense "be going" urges continued action of a process going on. And the preposition (εἰς) "into" after a verb of motion underscores that "peace" from guilt is a process going on, not just a fixed state. The woman already enjoyed peace. Jesus urges her to "continue moving forward deeper into the exposure to peace."

How could Theophilus miss the point of this episode? A "woman," a "sinner," a "Pharisee" struggling between doubt and faith, disinclined to face the guilt of his own self righteousness! Surely "wisdom is justified by her children." God's love for __all__ is certainly justified in this profound narrative of a "woman," a "Pharisee," and Jesus, he who __is__ "able to forgive sins!"

AN OUTLINE OF LUKE 8:1-3
Certain Women!
In the sequence of events in the ministry of the Christ the
time had now come when the kingdom must expand. So Jesus not
only "was journeying" but he gave on the job training to "the
twelve" and to "certain women."
I. WHAT OCCURRED "NEXT" IN KINGDOM WORK!
1. He "was journeying..."
2. The twelve & certain women...with him."
3. "Heralding & evangelizing" as they journeyed.
II. WHO THE "CERTAIN WOMEN" WERE!
1. Women "who had been healed..."
2. Joanna, wife of Chuza, Herod's steward."
3. Susanna and "many others..."
III. WHAT THESE WOMEN FURNISHED TO THE CAMPAIGN!
1. "Were ministering to them!"
2. "Of their possessions."
The present scene depicts the "next" vital sequence in the
unfolding drama of the kingdom of God on earth. Expansion into
each "city and village" by a troup of several dozen people is
expensive. It takes money, organization, and equipment. A few
women whose lives Jesus had touched provided the financial and
organizational undergirding for the program. Humanly speaking
the ministry of Jesus could not have expanded without this
group of "certain women."

* * * * * * *

CERTAIN WOMEN!
The word "soon afterward" of 8:1 is the same word as in
Luke 1:3 "an orderly account." In the N.E.B. it is rendered
"connected narrative." The word ($\kappa\alpha\vartheta\varepsilon\xi\tilde{\eta}\varsigma$) suggests "vital
sequence." One thing follows another in a logical, orderly
succession. Each episode builds upon that which precedes and
prepares for what follows. Here in 8:1 nothing joins the term
"next" to indicate what "next" is meant. Was it the "next day"
or "week" or just whatever? In the absence of any such
specific the idea would seem to be "the next thing of vital
sequence" which moves the story along!
Luke has carried the developing story up to a point at
which expansion is the "next" matter of import. The virgin
born Lord has grown to manhood, initiated his public ministry
in his home town. He has set the pattern and tone of his
message and ministry. He has designated twelve men dedicated
to him and his work. His group of followers has enlarged
beyond numbering. The "next seqence" is the systematic
spreading of the kingdom message into every city and village
throughout the countryside of Galilee. To that end Luke
relates the movement of Jesus through city by city and village
by village. And journeying with him were "the twelve and
certain women who had been healed from evil spirits and
frailties..."

106

So, that which occurred "next" is "he was travelling..."
The good news of the kingdom won't be extended by sitting in
one spot and hoping people will come to learn of it. One must
go to where the people are. Kingdom growth entails travelling!
To be at anchor in the harbor may be safe for the ship but to
reach a distant port the crew must lift anchor and sail beyond
the safe confines of the sheltered port. Jesus did not come
into the world to preserve his safety. He came to seek after
the lost. The shepherd doesn't rescue the wandering sheep by
staying at the fold.

Furthermore, he went "city by city and village by village."
No hamlet was omitted; no home was neglected; no one was
denied his opportunity to hear the kingdom message. Jesus was
going "heralding and evangelizing..." The message must be
delivered! The announcement of the kingdom must be told,
talked about, explained, communicated by word of mouth. No
substitute has been found for personal testimony. In Acts 1:1
Luke speaks of that which Jesus "began to do and teach." Jesus
did more than just tell about the kingdom. He demonstrated the
kingdom life style. What he did gave meaning to what he
taught. But he did not fail to teach. He "announced and
evangelized." He "preached the word!"

But Jesus did not travel alone. The text states: "And the
twelve were with him and certain women (were with him)..." The
twelve we have already met in Luke's narrative. Jesus had
"appointed" these as apostles. He would develop them into the
agents of the new kingdom, leaders whose message and lives
would furnish the standard for doctrine and behaviour. But in
this text we note for the first time the mention of "certain
women." While women find a place in the other Gospel writers
it is only in Luke that women are displayed as vital to the
life and ministry of Jesus. In our text three of these are
referred to by name. Then Luke adds "many others" as
supporting cast in the ongoing drama of Jesus' life.

This mention of "certain women" poses a question of signal
importance. Without this band of "certain women" the ministry
of Jesus would have been greatly weakened if not defeated. In
spite of his unusual divine power and his access to heaven's
undiminishing resources Jesus depended on these women for
material provision. Throughout history God has invariably
worked in and through human beings. He has used "natural"
resources. Thus in his public work on earth God worked
through this group of devoted women. Jesus and his men could
not have "travelled" had not "certain women...ministered to
them of their substance." Without their finances the men
couldn't have evangelized.

Who Were These Women?

But it wasn't a group of women as women. It was "certain
women who had been healed." Something radical had taken place
in the lives of these women. So basic was it that the whole
current of life was changed for each of them. They "had been
healed from evil spirits and illnesses."

That each woman "had been healed" furnished the basis for her uninhibited dedication to the Lord Christ. The person who "has been healed" from some life-despoiling disease needs no other incentive to self-effacing service. As women, who in that culture had been denied the privilege of "preaching" (κηρύσσων), they turned to what they could to nurture the evangelizing project. They funded the "travelling," equipped "the twelve," and otherwise provided the material means for all those who were "travelling with him." That was quite an undertaking for any group of bankers, much less "certain women." But the point is, it was those who "had been healed" who, without complaint, "were serving from their substance." Jesus had touched their lives with his healing power. He had graced their souls by cleansing their hearts. They needed no coercion to travel "with him" or to provide every material and financial need. True service springs from gratitude for healing of mind, body, soul and spirit. It's the criminal, rescued from a life of crime, who finds motivation to save other criminals. It's the poor, having found riches, who knows how and is willing to guide the poor into riches. It's the sick who has been made well who points others who are sick to the physician who healed. The fact they "had been healed" gave unspoken assurance that these women would serve him wherever they could fulfill a need.

Furthermore, Luke specifies by name three of these women. That is significant! The first is "Mary, the one being called Magdalene from whom he had cast out seven demons." What evil chained this woman's life and character is symbolized by seven. She had been completely captivated by sin in all its seductive sensual variety. She was a slave to sin! But Jesus had set her free. She became her own person, liberated from evil. Such an example of redemption guarantees that no one is beyond the redemptive power of the Christ. Anyone and all may experience the saving power of Jesus!

The second woman named is "Chuza, Herod's steward." What her need was in terms of sin is not specified. But the fact that she partook of the upper crust in society testifies that such levels find relief from their socially imposed chains. Even those captured by the harsh taskmaster of government beaurocracy can find freedom in Christ.

By adding "Suzanna and many others" Luke underscores the universal breadth of the healing ministry of the Christ. Who this Suzanna was we are not told. But the fact her name is given indicates that she was of some reputation. She was typical! The "others" in the expression "many others" indicates "others of a different kind." In other words, No area of sickness is beyond the healing power of Jesus.

To his first reader this was as pointed as Luke could get in writing. The "most noble Theophilus" had to be impressed with the breadth of Jesus' power for healing! Chuza was of the "noble" class and the "many others" encompassed all "other kinds" of human beings.

A note on Luke's presentation of women!

The immediate context demands that the "many others" refers to many other kinds of women. In principle it properly extends to "many other kinds" of human beings, male or female. Jesus came to save humans be they men or women. Human nature is the same regardless of gender. The second class inferior status of women through the centuries is the result of the fall into sin on the part of our first parents in the Garden of Eden. That woman be subjected to the domination of man was not the original intent of God at creation. God's curse in Gen.3:13,17 was on the serpent and on the ground, not on the woman or man. That which God said "to the woman" in Gen 3:16 was to inform her as to the result of her disobedience, not his will in creation. "Your desire shall be for your husband, and he shall rule over you."(Gen.3:16) is the consequence of her sin, not God's intent in creating her. By throwing off her submission to her real Lord she lost her equal standing with her male companion. All human beings were made to "have dominion." Thus when the woman disobeyed God and thereby rejected his dominion the male took advantage and began his dominion over her. The consequence of her sin was to relinquish God as Lord and substitute Adam as her lord. She lost her equal standing with her male companion!

Christ came into this world to restore that which was forfeited in Eden. He came to restore the broken fellowship between God and man as well as between man and man. One area in which his saving grace is manifest is his restoration of God's original creative intent of the relationship between man and woman. That which the woman lost in Eden is restored in Christ. She is no longer to be "ruled" by a subordinate male "lord." She has been restored to her intended Lord, the God who created her. A man, her husband, is her companion, not her lord!

Luke's attention to the place of women in Christ's redemptive program is the initial revelation that women were restored to the place God intended at creation. She's a helpmeet, not a subordinate. She's equally human!

109

AN OUTLINE OF LUKE 8:4-15
Parable of the Four Soils!

His teaching in parables depicts an abrupt change of method by Jesus. He had reached a critical point in his kingdom teaching. His initial preaching had been to cast the fishing net broadside into the waters. Now a selection, a distinction between good and bad must be made. The parable furnishes the ideal method of such a selection.

I.   THE FOUR SOILS. 8:4-8
   1. "Great crowds" prompt Christ's first parable.
   2. Four kinds of soil.
      (a) The "wayside" soil.
      (b) The "rocky" soil.
      (c) The thorn-possessed soil.
      (d) The "good" soil.
II. INQUIRY AND ANSWER! 8:9-10
   1. The question: "What might this parable be?"
   2. The answer: Double purpose--to reveal _and_ conceal.
III. THE PARABLE EXPLAINED. 8:11-15
   1. The wayside: those impervious to faith.
   2. Rocky ground: those without depth.
   3. Thorny ground: those with divided hearts.
   4. Good soil: those who "hear" and "hold" the word.

For the human heart open to truth the parable is the perfect vehicle for enlightening the mind. It also darkens him who is callous, shallow or prepossessed. "Take heed how you hear!"

* * * * * * *

PARABLE OF THE FOUR SOILS!

He who declares the word does not determine fruitfulness! It is he who hears! It's not the sower but the soil which decrees results in terms of fruitage. The teacher must be well prepared. His message must be thoughtful and studied out in careful detail. His enthusiasm and style must be contagious and winsome. But in the last analysis it's not the teacher but the student who decides the outcome. It is urgent to "take heed _how_ you hear." How you hear conditions what you do.

Though Jesus had given some parables before it is at this point that he adopts the parable as his usual method of teaching "the kingdom of God." So noticeable was his change that the disciples took note and inquired as to why parables! Jesus had reached a crisis in his kingdom work. At first he had cast broadside his net into the social waters around him. But now he must begin making a selection between the useful and useless fish in the crowds. How was he to do that without being harshly direct and personal? The parable was his choice of method. It could reveal truth in an easy to remember form. At the same time it would repel any who were idle, curious, or callous. It made it possible for the hearer to determine for himself whether he was worth being "caught" in the net of the kingdom.

110

"A great crowd being with him of those travelling city by city with him, he spoke through a parable." As he journeyed the cities of Galilee emptied of the people until the crowds grew beyond measure. Rich and poor, begger and thief, refined and dissolute, the idly curious and the eager seeker for truth. These and many others made up the multitudes. By what test is such a mixed multitude to be screened? There was need to identify the serious from the senseless, the true from the false, the sincere from the vagrant? Jesus painted a picture identifying four kinds of hearers. To some his story would appear as fanciful babbling. To others it would indelibly impress the fact that each hearer was classifying himself as a certain kind of listener. On the hillsides behind Jesus could see the four kinds of soil that furnished material for his story. He detected in the faces of the vast throng each of the four kinds of people sketched in his parable.

"The sower went out to sow his seed. And as he was sowing some fell along the roadway and it was trampled down and the birds of the heaven devoured it." The roadways of Galilee were hardened with the trample of centuries of travellers. They were harder than concrete. Any seed falling on them bounced futilely on the surface or into the ditch. With no possibility of taking root it was immediately pounced upon by voracious birds who devoured every grain. To sow seed on the roadway was as profitless as dumping it into the garbage.

"And other fell upon the rocky soil and having taken root it withered because it did not get moisture." This soil was rich but so shallow that it couldn't give depth to roots. Furthermore, moisture was so scarce it was hard to generate roots at all. It became difficult to hold what little moisture was available. Without depth of root the dry hot air withered the newly generated sprouts. No depth of root means no length of life for primitive plants.

"And other fell amid thorns and the thorns, growing, choked the seedlings." If soil is preoccupied with nourishing a hardier thorn bush it has little left to encourage growth to new seedlings. Too much competition ensures death to new life. One must cut out the old things if new life is to enjoy opportunity for fruitful growth. At least there must be constant pruning of the old to make possible growth of fresh life in newly planted seed.

Last, "other seed fell upon the good earth and, having sprouted, it produced fruit a hundred fold." Rich soil of good depth and unpreoccupied is guarantee of bountiful harvest.

At this point Jesus, "Called in an uplifted shout, The one having ears is to be hearing!" Jesus shouted so the most distant in the crowd could hear his charge. He who has ears has responsibility to hear. None can blame God or others who will not hear. This is more than an idle story to entertain for the moment. It contains a measuring rod of self judgment. Hence, if you are able to hear you are obligated to hear! "Take heed how you hear."

A Question Answered!

The twelve were perplexed! Such a huge crowd offered a great opportunity. Why adopt story telling as a method? The more direct presentation had proved attractive to many people. Why change now? Was he now performing rather than teaching? Was he to be an entertainer? At any rate "His disciples were inquiring, What this parable might be?" Apparently their curiosity extended beyond this one story to parables as a mode. The answer which Jesus gave to their question suggests this broader aspect.

Jesus said, "To you it has been given to know the secrets of the kingdom of God, but to the rest in parables, in order that seeing they may not see and hearing they may not perceive." To speak in parables is a form of chastisement, discipline, reproof, or punishment. It has the effect of identifying the chaff and separating it from the wheat. If the human heart fails to open to the first glimmer of truth, later brighter rays will be less likely to enlighten the mind. What you don't use you lose. The truth to which you fail to respond will dull your heart to any further truth. That which enlightens the open mind dulls the closed. To him who shuts his eyes the brighter the light the greater the darkness. The brilliance of the light leads him to close his eyes ever more tightly. Punishment is built into the rejection of truth. Such is God's way of judging those who will not hear!

When Pharoah refused to submit to God's initial signs through Moses the later signs only served to harden him the more. Thus is it at this juncture in the ministry of Jesus. As a people Israel was rejecting God's light which shone in Jesus. So the light veiled itself under the form of parables. The veil became the divine means of separating the wheat and chaff. "To you it has been given to know the secrets of the kingdom of God." The light which you have welcomed shall increase more and more. The truth you have received shall generate ever more capacity for more truth.

But to "the rest" I speak in parables with this purpose in mind, "that seeing they shall not see and hearing they shall not understand." He who hears the truth and refuses to embody it will be unable to receive later truth. Securing truth is accomplished only by means of, and in proportion to, that which has been already obtained. Truth begets more truth; rejection of truth not only makes one **ignorant** of the truth rejected but compounds the ignorance until one becomes incapable of perceiving truth. He who stays for years in a dungeon eventually won't be able to see even when released into the sunlight. To choose not to see ultimately leads to inability to see. Darkness by choice begets blindness in fact.

The time had come in the unfolding ministry of Jesus when a separation must be made between those who wanted God's kingdom and those who preferred the husks of this world. The parable became the divine means of separation.

112

Explanation of the Parable of the Four Soils!

Having warned of the judgmental trait of the parable Jesus proceeded to explain its application to his kingdom message. "The seed is the word of God." Though soils may be different the seed is constant; it is consistently the same. Whether it be Old Testament history, psalm, or prophet; or whether it be New Testament apostolic message of the Christ; or whether it be the personal incarnate Word living before that generation God's word generates life! No seed cast by any farmer into any soil has more life generating power than the word of God in any of its forms. When or where the seed of the word is sown, life springs up. It may not last long. That is contingent on the soil. But it's the nature of the word to spark life!

"The ones alongside the way are those who heard, then the devil comes and lifts the word from their heart lest, having believed, they shall be saved." Jesus wasn't giving advice on farming to farmers. He was preaching "the kingdom of God." And this was a pointed warning on how not to listen to God's word. Be not a cold, hardened, insensitive listener!

"Those upon the rock, whenever they hear receive the word with joy, and these do not have root, who believe for a time but in a season of trial fall away." Thoughtless, flippant, shallow, careless, listening breeds superficial faith. It has no depth, no discernment, no range or breadth of insight. Its faith is tentative for it has nothing to hold it stable in time of stress. It has not thought out what it believes. It withers under fire and falls in its own ashes.

"And that having fallen into (among) the thorns are those who heard, and under the cares and wealth and pleasures of this world's life are choking themselves and do not come to maturity." The human mind striving for "success" in terms of money, position or pleasure has a hard time retaining what it hears of the word of God. It hears, it believes, but rushing after business, social, and material goals squeezes out genuine interest in the "kingdom of God."

"But that in the good earth are those who in noble and good heart, having heard, are holding fast to the word and in patience are bearing fruit." It is well to note that each of the four heard the word. Also note the prepositions used in connection with each kind of soil: "along the way," "upon the rock," "into(among) the thorns," and "in the good earth." The manner in which one hears the word affects the out come. Is it casual, light-hearted, divided, or attentive? How one hears determines what one hears and thus determines destiny!

Luke wishes Theophilus to know that all kinds of soils "hear" the word. No one is left out. The opportunity for the birth of new life is open to every kind and class of human beings. It behooves Theophilus to classify himself as of "the good earth."

AN OUTLINE OF LUKE 8:16-18
The Go-Getter!
The text reflects a piercing principle in the moral realm.
"Whoever gets, to him shall be given; whoever does not get
even what he seems to have shall be taken away."
I.   THE PURPOSE OF LAMPS. 8:16-17
     1. Negative: Not to hide.
     2. Positive: To illuminate all, the clean and dirty.
     3. The hidden made manifest.
II. THE LAW OF GETTING AND LOSING. 8:18
     1. To him who gets more shall be given.
     2. From him who does not get, shall be taken away.
Be a go-getter and that which you got shall increase!

* * * * * * *

BACKGROUND GRAMMATICAL NOTE!
     In the exposition of 8:16-18 it is important to get this
brief note on Aktionsart. If the reader will be patient and
"take heed how you hear" you will be richly rewarded as the
exposition develops.
     First, the term Aktionsart, so far as I am aware, does not
appear in any English dictionary. It is an Anglicised German
word. Aktionsart is the kind of action native to the naked
root of a word.
     The Greeks did not view verb tense as primarily conveying
the notion of time. Their view of tense was kind of action,
not time of action. Basically they considered two kinds of
action, linear and punctiliar. Linear action views action in
progress, repeated, descriptive of a process, or distributed
over several individuals. Punctiliar action views any action
as concentrated to a point. Even though it might be continuing
in fact, repetitive, or distributive, any of these actions
might be arbitrarily presented as a focused point.
     Aktionsart went behind tense to the basic root idea
inherent in the nature of the action. For example, the
Aktionsart of the verb "live" is linear. The very nature of
the idea of "live" is continuation over a period of time. If
one lives five months or fifty years it is an extended
process. By tense the Greeks could impose on this linear
notion a sense of point action, such as "he lived 50 years."
     In contrast the words "grab" and "get" are in their
AKTIONSART punctiliar. The native quality of the action is
essentially a point. The Greeks could impose on a point the
linear idea by showing it as repeated, or distributively. They
even describe a point by using a phrase "he was getting."
     In 8:18 verb have(ἔχω)appears three times, twice present
active subjunctive, once with μὴ "not," once present active
infinitive ἔχειν. The lexicon meaning given to ἔχω is "have,"
"hold," an obvious linear idea. But the Aktionsart is
punctilar "get," not "have." Thus when the present tense
appears the idea is a series of "gettings," not a static
possessing.

114

THE GO-GETTER!

The affinity of 8:16-18 to the parable of the four soils seems obvious. Some students view this text as the application by Jesus of that parable. It very well could be. But we give it separate attention simply because of its clear statement of the principle of _loss_ or _learning_. The parable implies it; this text explicitly states it. Originally it may have been part of the parable. Nevertheless, it's worthy of distinct discussion.

The Purpose of Lamps!

When darkness descends, men need light. If business or social affairs are necessary or even just the task of preparing for a night's rest, light becomes important if not essential. In the ancient orient a "lamp" was a saucer filled with oil into which a wick was inserted. When not in use during the day it was put under a divan or under a bushel measure. But come night the darkness must be diffused. To that end lamps were brought from their cover and located on lampstands. They were prudently placed so as to give the broadest dispersal of light. "No one having lighted a lamp covers it with a vessel or puts it under a divan." Covering a lamp was only done during the day. At night it is lit and strategically stationed so as to diffuse most darkness.

The truth of God's kingdom had been long buried under centuries of the theological debris of rabbinical legalism. In Jesus light had come. "As long as I am in the world, I am the light of the world."(Jn.9:5) The time was at hand to put the lamp of God's truth on the lampstand where it could dispel the darkness of human sin. Light is to reveal truth, not to shadow it. Light hides neither itself nor the objects on which it falls. It is to make clear the obscure, to illuminate the dirt so it may be cleaned out, to eradicate the darkness from the corners and drive out the vermin from the cracks and crevices.

But light can be resisted, covered up, diverted and otherwise rejected. In truth and falsehood the human _will_ is involved. Men live in the darkness and have come to love the darkness more than light. Being accustomed to the dark, light blinds them. To disguise their own moral dirt they blow out the light, at least they cover it. Adam tried fig leaves; modern man attempts more subtle cover-ups. We "interpret" the light so that it becomes darkness. We divert attention to other issues so as to get the mind off _our_ guilt. We protest that our _human rights_ are being violated. Thus we change the moral climate so that evil becomes right and right becomes evil. If necessary we simply murder him who advocates the righteousness of God's moral climate. _We_ determine moral right and thus escape our sense of wrong.

However, the word of Jesus still stands, "I am the light of the world." The fact remains that light is for the purpose of eradicating darkness. Truth is in the world to eliminate the false.

The Hidden Made Manifest!

"Not anything is hidden which shall not become manifest." In this immediate context the "anything" of verse 17 refers to the truth of the kingdom. Jesus has just uncovered some of that truth in the parable of the four soils. By explaining the parable he had placed the truth on a lampstand that it might be light as well as give light.

By stating that "anything hidden shall be manifest" Christ is pronouncing a principle that encompasses more than just the immediate message. His view of "the kingdom" is far broader than the current context. That "anything hidden" will sooner or later come into the open light is a universal principle.

At creation God made man to live honestly, openly, in the brilliant light of complete display of himself. But when man fell into the sinful state immediately he began to "cover himself" and to hide from God and man; especially from himself. Human history has been a long night of fleeing from the truth. We dare not appear naked before God or man, physically or morally. Our sense of guilt presses too heavily upon each of us. We do not live in bare unprotected honesty.

Within such a framework of hiding from the truth we compound our tragic dishonesty with deliberate attempts to cheat on one another, not to mention God. Headline news daily reports of men who manipulate financial markets for selfish profits at the expense of unsuspecting fellow men. The gossip columns are filled with stories of husbands or wives cheating on spouses in unfaithful "affairs." Our attempts to excuse and rationalize misbehaviour are but samples of this ever present attempt to hide the truth about ourselves from ourselves. Yet it is all to no avail for "anything that is hidden will come into the open," if not here before men then hereafter before the universe and God. At creation God built into the nature of the moral world basic honesty. That means that everything shall eventually come to the open light. Nothing shall remain hidden. This is an honest universe. And part of Christ's redemptive work is to restore this innate honesty. Nothing shall remain hidden!

By coming into this world as "the light of the world" Christ has uncovered the "lamp" and placed it on the lampstand where it may give light to all who enter into the room. To those who open their eyes life becomes clear, including their own guilt. And is that not the reason for the coming of light? To reveal dirt so as to eliminate it?

The Law of Getting and Losing!

Thus far Christ has prepared a solid foundation for the brilliant ray of light in verse 18. "Watch out how you are hearing, for whoever is getting, it shall be given to him, and whoever is not getting, even that which he supposes he has shall be taken from him."

The standard English versions translate present tense ἔχῃ as "have." That does not recognize the Aktionsart of the verb. At bottom it means "get," not "have."(See note above) This

116

verse placards a principle so transparently universal that men look through it without seeing it. It's like looking through a clean transparent glass without realizing it's there. But here Jesus places it on the lampstand that all may be aware of the law of getting and losing and the light it sheds on "the sovereign rule of God." As humans "enter into God's house" what they "get" leads to more "getting." "Get by get," that is, gradually all about God and his rule becomes clear. As long as they keep "getting," more and more of God becomes theirs. God's knowledge, moral power, mental insight, and spiritual strength become the possession of each believer. Personal living fellowship with God comes in the same way!

Our son with his family sailed for Germany in early November 1961. The responsibility to which he was called was to serve as pulpit preacher for the local Christian church in the University city of Tubingen. When he left America he had no knowledge of German. Upon arrival in Tubingen he started immediately to "get" a mastery of the language. He was determined to "get" a speaking grasp of German enough so as to preach for German nationals. He delivered his first public message to the congregation on the last Sunday of January 1962. One has to do a lot of "getting" to speak fluent German within three months. But it really wasn't a miracle. It was steady and determined application of this law of getting: "Take heed how you hear; for whoever continues getting, it shall be given to him."

That which is true about learning a language is true about anything over which God reigns. So you want to be a master pianist! "Take heed how you hear" the teacher's first day's instruction. Pay attention; practice faithfully on the first assignment and the second lesson on the next day will fill you with "more" music. Be a go-getter day by day and eventually you will become a concert pianist. Nothing can keep you from it unless you fail to keep on getting.

The opposite side of the law of getting is the law of losing. The moment one stops being a go-getter he begins losing even that which he has. Paderewski said: "If I fail to practice one day I can notice it. If I do not practice for two days the director can notice it. If I don't practice for three days the public can tell it. He was merely confirming the obverse side of Christ's law of getting and losing, "whoever does not keep on getting even that which he thinks he got shall be taken away." That was true before Jesus said it. And Jesus said it because it is true, universally true. He placed it on the lampstand so that "all who enter the house" might see. This is why Jesus exhorted his disciples to hear with the greatest of care. He who would get God must "take heed" that he hears, what he hears and how he hears. The Holy Spirit of God makes clear only that which has been obediently kept. "He who has my commandments and keeps them...I will love him and and will manifest myself to him."(Jn.14:21) For one to hear and not keep is to "get" nothing and thereby lose what he "got."

If God be God and He be the only God, and He be the living God then He is universally real and present in all creation. Nothing exists without his involvement. Grass, flower, fish, bird, and so called "laws" of nature including those governing mind, body and soul of human beings are but expressions of his vital presence. Cut the universe at any point and God is there in some significant way. This is one cosmic universe. That's why "nothing is hidden which shall not be made manifest." That God became a man is possible because God created the man in his "image" and after his "likeness."

These two strands thread their way through Luke's Gospel, the universality and humanity of God's gospel revealed in the Christ. These ideas form the substrata in Luke 8:16-18. They underlie the message in this paragraph to Theophilus.

* * * * * * *

AN OUTLINE OF LUKE 8:19-21
Brotherhood in Christ!

The sense of family brotherhood is a strong bond present in all history. Family furnishes emotional strength in times of stress. The sense of family is among the foremost of human values. But is blood the strongest bond?
I.   BLOOD RELATIONSHIP - THE HUMAN FAMILY. 8:19-20
1. "His mother and brothers arrived near him."
2. The "crowd" kept them from him.
II. SPRITUAL RELATIONSHIP - THE DIVINE FAMILY. 8:21
1. A family bond greater than blood.
2. Parents beget and conceive new life.
3. Siblings sustain and support in crises.

God is the father "from whom every family in heaven and on earth is named...(Eph.3:15) The very idea of "family" arises from God as Father of all. Earth's family is a miniature of the family of God in Christ.

* * * * * * *

BROTHERHOOD IN CHRIST

So strong is the sense of family brotherhood that man has mirrored it in business, social, educational ventures. Labor and trade unions are imitations of the ties that bind families together as a group. Fraternal orders, sororities, service clubs, college alumni associations all echo the concept of the family. The sense of brotherhood is among the foremost of human values. The very idea of family is native to man as the creation of God. Paul speaks of God as "the father from whom every family in heaven and on earth is named..."(Eph.3:15) These human institutions are subconscious expressions of the basic family bonds.

118

Blood Relationship!

The kinship of blood forms fast ties. By its very nature those whose kinship is based in blood are closely bonded. Such bonds can transcend that which is "right." In fact, blood brotherhood often determines the "right." At least it makes a determination of the "right" from the standpoint of brothers. When you attack my father or mother you attack me! And if you attack me you attack my family for they rush to my defense. "God sets the solitary (lonely) in families." (Ps.68:6) He who is desolate can find his refuge in his family. It's both human and divine to find the family as a fortress.

Luke reports: "His mother and his brothers came to him." Why they came he does not say. In Mark's account we are told that his family had concluded that Jesus was "mad," "beside himself," at least "burned out" and needed family pressure to force him to get some rest. But even though Luke may have had Mark's record before him, his reader, Theophilus did not. The fact Luke omits the reason for the family concern is itself testimony that Luke's point was not why the family came but that they came. That the brothers felt that Jesus was overworked or unbalanced, or just needed an encouraging emotional lift isn't Luke's concern. It's the fact of family solidarity, family support, family unity that is the stress of Luke to Theophilus. Jesus was an important part in a human family. When God became human he became all human, subject to the blessings and limitations of the bond of blood relationship. His "mother and brothers came to him..."

The efforts of the family were diverted. "They weren't able to get to him on account of the crowd." The very success of Jesus, his popularity as a teacher thwarted the family from functioning as it would. It has always been true that those around Jesus frequently hinder his getting the kind of human support he could use. But even so, that doesn't take away from the fact that the family was there. And the knowledge of that is itself encouraging support.

It was from out of that crowd that someone said to Jesus, "Your mother and brothers are standing outside wishing to see you." The crowd that hinders is also the crowd that helps. And Jesus is informed that his family is seeking him.

The Divine Family - Spiritual Relationships!

Is blood relationship the strongest bond? Does the human family represent the ultimate in the family idea? Is there a stronger, deeper, a divine family bond? Judging by the word of Christ there is.

When he answered he said, "My mother and my brothers are these, the ones hearing and doing the word of God." Nothing is more binding than that instituted by God at creation. "In the beginning God created...so God created man in his own image, in the image of God created he him; male and female created he them."(Gen.1:26f.) Man was to be one family of children of the one Father, God. The very concept of family was rooted in the nature of God as Father and human beings as his children.

119

Sin disrupted the trust between the divine Father and the creature, children. Adolescent rebellion has been the pattern ever since. Involved in the purpose of Christ's coming was the restoration of the broken family relationship. He indicated the prior and higher bond of the divine-human family when he said, "My mother and my brothers are these, the ones hearing and doing the word of God." The spiritual bond of man to God is firmer, more sure, more basic than any earthly tie. Hearing the word of God and doing it revives the original family pact between man and God.

The human family based in blood kinship will break at some point. Family feuds devastate the bonds. Economic exploitation and sexual perversion shatter family ties. But, if not these, death destroys the closest family links. If there is no union greater than the earthly family, life of necessity is a dead end. "When my father and mother forsook me, the Lord took me up."(Ps.27:10) No matter how strong the tie death dissolves the union of parents and children. In the resurrection they "neither marry or are given in marriage...they are sons of God being sons of the resurrection." (Lk.21:34,36) Death destroys the possibility of father and mother not forsaking me! And "in the resurrection" there is no blood family, only the original, renewed in Christ.

Parents beget and conceive new life. As the bride of Christ the church daily is bringing to birth new sons and daughters of God. Its the part of siblings in concert with parents to sustain and support one another in all crises. This is the task of the church family. In performing its family function it provides food, shelter and clothing for the widow and orphan. For its wayward it restores; for the wounded it heals; for the hurting it comforts; for the weak it strengthens; for the guilty it forgives.

In spite of the church's falling short of its own ideals it has rendered Christ's saving ministries through the centuries. Halting, inconsistent, even hypocritical at times, still those of the church who practice the "hearing and doing the word of God" have given the emotional, financial and spiritual support to its sons and daughters in need. The misguided zeal of a youthful father shattered the life of his wife and baby when he abandoned them to "obey" Jesus' word to "deny all and follow me" in preaching the kingdom. It was the church that surrounded her with the love and support of a family. And there's the seventeen year old girl whose suicide father and whose mother died at 43 leaving her alone without family support. It's the responsibility of those within the church who are "hearing and doing the word of God" to surround her and be her family. Only eternity can reveal how much the divine family has functioned in supporting its children.

If Theophilus hadn't appreciated the universal human love of God in Christ at this point surely now it would be clear. Christ makes real genuine universality and reveals God to be so undeniably always human.

AN OUTLINE OF LUKE 8:22-25
"Who Is This?"

"Who then is this, that even the winds are subject, (to him) and the water, and they are obeying him?" This is the first time that the twelve saw their master clash with the forces of "nature." It prompted the problem: "Who then is this?"

I. THE SCENE AT SEA. 8:22-24
1. Purpose of the journey. vs.22
2. The sleeping Lord. vs.23a
3. The storm. vs.23b
4. The panic of the disciples. vs.24a
5. Confronting the storm; the great calm. vs.24b

II. THE CHALLENGE TO FAITH! 8:25
1. "Where is your faith?"
2. "Who then is this?"

The Master of disease and death is the Master of the forces of creation! He is in control of both storm and calm.

* * * * * * *

WHO IS THIS?

Two terms which appear in a dictionary definition of <u>natural</u> or <u>nature</u> are <u>innate</u> and <u>inherent</u>. When one looks on "nature" as that which exists from <u>innate</u> forces <u>inherent</u> within apart from any outside force exerting itself we may rightly speak of "nature " and "natural." But if we start with the assumption of faith, that is, GOD, then nothing is natural. All is created! This is a created, not a natural order. "Things" do not work of themselves; God "works all things." It is more in keeping with the biblical view to say that this is the first time the twelve saw their master clash with the forces of creation.

The Scene at Sea!

In the plan of Jesus to journey to and preach in "city by city and village by village" (8:1) he, on "one of those days" got "into a boat" with his disciples and said, "Let's go to the other side of the lake." His purpose was to include the cities of the eastern shores of Galilee in his preaching of "the kingdom." The "other side of the sea" was influenced more by a gentile population. None must be omitted from hearing the good news. Thus "they launched" the ship toward the East.

But "as they were sailing, he slept." So tired was the Master, so overwhelmed with the weariness of labor he succumbed to the demands of the body. He was too human to advance to new labors without the renewal of sleep. He who moments later would confront and control the wildest forces of God's creation was himself so much a creature that he must sleep. How human can one get than to sleep when tired?

But, as so often in human experience, the relaxation of sleep was interrupted by the disturbing destructive storms of the world around us. "A storm of wind, a tornado, came down into the lake, and they were being flooded and being in danger." The Sea of Galilee lies 682 feet below sea level, some

121

2200 feet below the surrounding hills. The hot winds from the east joining the cool sea beezes from the west meeting over this depression often created sudden and violent squalls, tornado-like storms. It was this kind of storm that hit the little band of evangel sailors. Even to storm-tested sailors it became more than their experience could handle. They panicked and rushed to the sleeping Jesus. In their terror they cried, "Master, Master, we are perishing!" The cry of the unnerved disciples grew from their very knowledge of the ways of sea and storm. In their clamor they did not plead that they might perish. They exclaimed, "We are perishing." In reporting this scene Matthew adds "Save, Lord; we are perishing." And Mark mentions a mild rebuke, "Is it not a concern to you that we are perishing?" It appears that Matthew felt that even yet Jesus could do something to save them from this desperate situation. Was Mark reflecting the feeling of Peter in implying that Jesus, instead of sleeping, might have been awake to guide and help the hard laboring men? But Luke's emphasis suggests that any saving was now too late. He has the disciples saying, "Master, Master, we are perishing!" Luke has them making a statement of fact, not an exhortation to help. Even Luke's word for "Master" means "Commander" or "Chief." It's too late now to give commands. Just be aware of our impending doom!

Such a description of the mental and psychological condition of the twelve prepares the reader for that which Jesus does upon being thus aroused. "But that one, having been aroused, rebuked the wind and the surge of water. And they ceased! And a calm came!" What a startling turn of events! It was more than the disciples could comprehend. The turmoil of one moment became the peaceful calm of the next. The tranquil serenity of the stilled waters and gentle breeze was more shocking to the twelve than the passion of the winds and waves. The fear of death was replaced by the awesome fear of the forces of life!

Challenge to their faith!

Amidst the calmness of the moment Jesus addressed the disciples, "Where is your trust?" The twelve had been through a number of critical events with him before. They had been present in synagogues when he silenced his enemies. They had seen the raising of dead persons, the healing of paralytics, the casting out of demons and the repelling of fevers. Though they had never before witnessed his power over such violent physical forces of creation they had confidence in his person as one in touch with divine resources. What had become of this confidence? That's his immediate challenge to them. If they witnessed his handling of disease and death, was this violent storm enough to make them forget the power of his person?

The answer is: "Yes, it was!" We must not forget that these men were just that, mere men. Experienced fishermen, acquainted with the sudden tempests of the Sea of Galilee. But no matter how many storms one has experienced each has its own dangers, each must be dealt with under whatever circumstances arise. Each such experience is always new. Their very knowledge and experience as sailors gave them the means by which to measure the desperate situation of this storm. They concluded, "We are perishing!" That which amazed them was the way Jesus handled wind and wave. Their faith could cover desperate sickness, demons, and death. But a tornado! A wall of surging water! Apparently they never even thought to call upon faith.

Yet Jesus expected them to relate their faith in him to these violent forces of creation. This ordeal opened up a new area for faith. The very point of the story rises in their hearts and pours out of their lips. "Who then is this, that even the winds are subject to him, and the water, and they are obeying him?"

The word "even" (καί) is of special note. More often it is a simple coordinate conjunction "and." But here it is used adverbially with the ascensive notion. One shouldn't be startled that the Christ dealt with death, demons and sickness. But that he should deal with "even the winds and waves..!" That is a little too much to be expected! And just think! "They obey him!" It certainly offered a new dimension to their view of Jesus. It was a challenge to their faith in him. It broadened the horizon of faith.

"Who then is this?" What relation does this man, Jesus, have not only to life and death but to the entire creation? If the body, demons, death and even the laws governing creation are subject to him what does this all say about Who Jesus is? HE is related to wind and wave, sun, moon, and stars, the flower of the field and birds of heaven. If he's involved in all these there's nothing in creation with which he is not involved? He did not talk about "high pressures" or "low pressures." Nor did he mention anything about "jet streams." And we never read of his making weather predictions as modern meteorologists do. In fact, he never dealt with wind or wave academically. He just "rebuked" the wind and "commanded" the wave and "they obeyed" him. He was in a living vital relationship with these forces.

Then, Who is he? This is God's world, God's universe! And though the term "Son of God" is not used in this story, HE, Jesus, is in control of all God's creation. He at least is the revealer of the invisible God, the Creator of all! What other conclusion is there?

It seems that the first reader, the noble Theophilus, would be driven to the same conclusion. No area in God's vast order of things lies outside the province of the Christ's control. He's God's son or at least the supreme revealer of the God whose face is hidden within his creation. HE is universal. HE appeared on this earth as a man!

123

AN OUTLINE OF LUKE 8:26-39
A Gerasene Demoniac--Another Storm Stilled!

The stilling of the storm at sea permitted the boat with its disciple band to come quickly to the eastern shore. There they confronted a different kind of storm. A many-demoned man met Jesus as he stepped on land. Can or will he still this tempest as he had the one at mid-sea?

I. THE CONFRONTATION. 8:26-36
1. Sailed to the land of the Gerasenes. 26
2. A Gerasene demoniac confronts Jesus. 27
3. The demoniac's defiance. 28
   (a)"What do we have in common?"
   (b)"Don't torment me!"

II. THE CURE. 8:27-32
1. The demon's identify: "What's your name?" 30
2. The demon's destiny. 32
   (a)The "abyss."
   (b)An inferior bodily form (swine).

III. THE CONSEQUENCES. 8:33-39
1. On swine: "rushed down precipice and choked." 33
2. On herdsmen: Eyewitnesses to the countryside. 34
3. Gerasene populace urged Jesus to depart. 37
   Property or People.
4. The man from whom the demon was cast. 35,38-40

Jesus stills storms whether of creation or human! But his relation to either is for redemptive purposes. He demonstrates power, not for the sake of showing power, but for the redemption of people. Divine power is not an end in itself. It is for serving and saving human beings!

* * * * * * *

A GERASENE STORM STILLED!

"He even subjects the winds, and the water, and they obey him." But is that different or greater than subjecting the tormenting tornadoes of demons? Is a life threatening storm at sea more destructive to human life than addiction to and absorption by demoniacal evil? Jesus controls either! It's not "either or" but "all." Christ came to remove the "curse" from "the ground" (creation) as well as the death sentence on man. He stills all storms.

The Confrontation!

"They sailed unto the land of the Gerasenes which is over against Galilee." The stilling of the storm at sea delayed but did not alter the destiny or purpose of Christ. He would evangelize Gerasa and its environs. But the awe of the stilled storm scarcely subsided before the equally dangerous encounter with embodied evil faced the evangel band. "A certain man of the city having demons met him when he came onto the shore." This was more than an ordinary case of demon possession. "For a long time he went unclothed, and he was not living in a house but was staying among the tombs...many times it (the demon)

124

seized him, and being guarded, he was being bound with chains
and fetters, but snapping the bonds, he was driven by the
demons into the desert." This is an extreme case of total
domination by evil. The man is no longer able to make free
choices. And yet enough self-recognition and assertion was
present for him to seek silence and privacy by living in a
cemetery. Uncleanness of the dead guaranteed solitude. His
violence toward society led to his being chained with fetters.
But even these weren't able to control his violence for he
"snapped them" on each recurring attempt to tame him.

The demon's melancholic maniacal hysteria rose to new
heights at the appearance of Jesus. "When he saw Jesus, having
cried out, he fell before him and shouted in a loud voice, What
to me and to you, Jesus, son of the Most High God.?" With the
instinct of Evil in the presence of supreme Good, the demons in
the man came to the core of the ever-present moral conflict. In
effect he said, "We have nothing in common. At no point do we
have any personal affinity. Nothing in you appeals to me and
I'm aware that nothing in me attracts you."(See pgs.48-51) By
its nature evil cannot and will not patronize with good, nor
good with evil! So, why bother? Why go through the motion?
Evil, with the instinct of the real issues involved, wants
nothing to do with the Lord of righteousness. Evil cannot
tolerate good if it expects to survive! The demons within the
man took note that Jesus "was commanding the unclean spirit to
come out of the man." Jesus was in the process of ordering the
cleansing(inchoative imperfect). So the demon rushed to say,
"I beg you, don't even start to torment me." Leave us alone!
The possessed man identifies himself with the demons who hold
him in their power. The torment which they fear most is that of
being sent to "the abyss"(vs.31). To be deprived of the power
over a human being through whom he might express his evil is
like a paroled prisoner being cast unceremoniously back behind
bars. Unembodied spirits had only the "abyss" as a habitation;
no means with which to exhibit their evil.

This confrontation of Evil with the Christ was no attempt to
invade the Person of Jesus so as to control Him. It was a
defensive ploy to avoid being disembodied and thus forced to
return to the "abyss." Evil gets desperate in the personal
presence of God. "Don't torment me!" was a death cry of the
demons.

The Cure!

The first verbal response of Jesus was to focus on the
identity of the demons and the man. So he said, "What is your
name?" Even now the man could not answer for himself. The demon
exclaimed, "My name is Legion." This he declared "because many
demons had entered into him." The man had become totally and
completely captured by Evil. Later he was his own man again for
he "was sitting at the feet of Jesus, clothed and in his right
mind."(vs.35) But for the moment he was so ensnared that only
the demon answered. "Our name is Legion. We are in complete
control."

It was true. The demons were in control. For Jesus to set the man free he must deal with the demons. The text has said that Jesus "was commanding the unclean spirit to come out of the man." And this, Jesus was determined to do. No demon can withstand God's resolute purpose to redeem. Yet the demons resisted abandonment to nihilism. They "were exhorting him that he should not command them to go off into the abyss." However futile they grabbed at any hope to keep from falling below some form of bodily expression. "There was a herd of many hogs feeding in the hill. And they exhorted him that he permit them to enter into those. And he permitted them." For spirit, good or evil, not to have a body through which to verbalize and otherwise manifest itself is worse than prison; in effect it is death. The word "spirit" (πνεῦμα) means "breath." To be denied "breath" is death, oblivion, extinction, nihility. An unembodied spirit is as though it were non-existent. It has no being in terms we in this world can understand. Obviously these demons shrank from being without any material form. Anything was better than nihilism. They would exist in pigs rather no body at all. In swine at least they could maintain some means of self expression.

Their very request was a subconscious recognition of the authority of the Christ. They asked that "he permit that they go into the swine." In other words, they recognized that he held ultimate control of their existence, not to mention that of the possessed man. Christ is the son of God whether or no! Men's opinions and demons' opposition cannot alter or modify facts, especially the fact as to who Jesus is! In the final analysis the claim of the demons, "We are in control" was not true. The ultimate authority is God, and that in the Person of his Christ.

The Consequences!

The initial result of the confrontation of Jesus with Legion was that the demons be embodied in the hillside swine. That precipitated their rushing down the steep and "choking themselves" in the sea. Why permit such destruction of property of great economic value? Was it not thoughtless? Was Jesus unsympathetic to the prosperity of the people?

Jesus had sailed to this region to declare the good news of God's sovereign rule. On stepping ashore he was confronted with a concrete example of why good news was needed. Here was a prominent example of how subject man had become to the demonical forces of Satan. Evil had become a fact of human life. It cannot be ignored. Jesus was confronted with a great opportunity of exemplifying his redemptive power over evil.

A part of Jesus' revelation was to dramatize that people are more important than property. The community needed a demonstration of how tightly their attachment to economic prosperity contaminated their lives. The saving of this one man was more important than a hog. In fact, the redeeming of any human being exceeds in value all hogs. "What will a man give in exchange for his soul?"

126

For a herd of 2000 swine to be suddenly snatched away from a farmer, or from an enterprising combine of business men was no small loss to the economy. This large a loss at one swing of the pendulum adversely affected banking and employment in the entire community. When the employees, the herdsmen who cared for the herd, fled into the countryside they reported the terrible loss. They were eye-witnesses of this threat to their community. If Jesus were to invade their country with that kind of destruction, they wanted none of him. And though "they found the man from whom the demons went out, sitting, clothed and sober-minded at the feet of Jesus, they became terrified." The sooner they could thrust him out would not be too soon.

Is money of more value than life? Property more to be protected than people? Do hogs or health rate higher in the scale of values? Are hogs or heaven that for which men are created? The issue Jesus presented to the people was health and saving of one man versus a considerable loss of wealth. What is the meaning of life? Which shall we save, man or money? If the purpose of human life is success in the acquirement of material prosperity then we may sacrifice the salvation of any number of men. The real issue is human character or a cash crop? Which is higher in the scale of moral values?

A word should be said concerning the basic need for money. This story is not to downgrade or suggest that money is not an important, even essential, to life as we must live it in this world. The issue is it's relative importance when the redemption of character is at stake. When the pursuit of money becomes an end in itself it becomes destructive to moral values. Men become pawns to be exploited rather than people "in the image of God." Under the pressure of this sudden upheaval of their economy "all the crowds of the country of Gerasa asked him to depart from them, for they were gripped by a great fear." Fear of the loss of income blinded them to the value of a criminal restored to constructive citizenship.

But Jesus was not through with Gerasa. He had come to this eastern shore to evangelize. He had only this one meeting with this one single demented demonized violent man. And though Jesus "having gotten into the boat, returned," he intended to get done what he came to do. He would see to it that Gerasa got a true view of him and his ministry of redemption.

"The man from whom the demons had gone out was begging that he be with" him. But Jesus departed saying, "You return to your house, and keep declaring how many things God did for you." That which was denied to Jesus this redeemed man was privileged to perform, namely, to declare his personal experience when God met him among the tombs. He was not to argue the doctrines of the kingdom. He didn't know any of them! He was simply to keep telling that which God did in his personal life. No greater voice can be heard than that of personal witness to the cleansing that God has done in a life soiled by sin. To be enthusiastic about what God has restored in my life brings greater results than a library full of theological theories.

127

It is worth more than passing interest to note that Christ exhorted the man to, "be declaring all whatsoever <u>God</u> did for you." But the man "went off through the whole city heralding whatsoever <u>Jesus</u> did for him." Theological speculations about a "trinity" would have been bewildering to the man. And just how the God of heaven was related to this man, Jesus, lay beyond his present concern. But in his experience to tell what Jesus <u>did</u> was to tell what God did. His grasp of God was identified with his encounter with Jesus. Regardless of the theological distinctions in the "Godhead" to him Jesus was God and God was Jesus. To tell the story of the one was to reveal the other. And after all is that not precisely why Jesus came, that is, to reveal the reality and nature of God? And Jesus, a <u>man</u>, did just that. Thus verse 39 would be quite significant for Theophilus and his understanding of the humanity of the Christ.

* * * * * * *

AN OUTLINE OF LUKE 8:40-56
The "Sleep" of Death!

When those in Jairus' home heard Jesus say, "She didn't die" "they laughed him down." They "<u>knew</u> that she <u>did</u> die." It was their experience versus his word! "<u>We</u> know; <u>you</u> ignore the fact!

I.   THE SITUATION - THE DYING DAUGHTER. 8:40-42
     1. A waiting expectant crowd. 40
     2. The petition of Jairus. 41-42
        (a) A synagogue ruler (Capernaum)!
        (b) At the feet of Jesus!
        (c) His only daughter "was dying."
II. AN INTERRUPTION. 8:43-48
     1. Woman with "flow of blood." 43a
     2. Failure of physicians for 12 years. 43b
     3. "Grabbed the hem of his garment." 44
     4. Jesus, "Who grabbed me?" 45-46
     5. The woman's acknowledgement! 47
     6. "Your faith has saved you." 48
III. AWAKENING THE DAUGHTER. 8:49-56
     1. Bad news: "Your daughter has died." 49
     2. "Stop fearing, only trust." 50
     3. A select few to witness the awakening. 51
     4. Contrasting views of the daughter's death. 52-53
        (a) "Weeping & mourning...laughed him down."
        (b) "Stop weeping...she didn't die!"
     5. The awakening. 54
     6. The aftermath!
        (a) "Give her to eat."   (b) "Tell no one!"

The reevaluation of death is the point of the story. Death is not annihilation; it is "sleep" from which an awakening is assured.

THE "SLEEP" OF DEATH!

The tragedy above all tragedies in human existence is death. We camouflage it, disguise it, cover it, hide it, cloak it, and deny it. But we cannot escape it. Each human succumbs to it. We euphemize death with soothing terms such as "rest," "peace," and "sleep." But when we face the facts of corpse, coffin, and cemetery neither words or fantasies can deceive us. In this world of sense and sound death is a fact of life, the ultimate fact we face as human beings.

But when, before Jairus and friends, Jesus said, "she did not die, but is sleeping" he was doing more than using a figure of speech. By his term "sleep" he gave a new meaning to "death." From his point of view, though a tragedy, "death" was not the final act. It was in fact a "sleep" from which God is preparing an awakening. In human experience death is the final note in a bad musical. To Jesus it was a "rest" before the last crescendo of a divine drama. Death was never intended to be. In the beginning it was foreign to the eternal purpose of God. It is sand in the machinery, a detour on the highway of history, an interruption in God's unchanging and unchangable purpose. He who was created "in the image of God" was not made to die. At worst death is only a "sleep" before awakening to a refreshing eternal fellowship. In stating about Jairus' daughter "she is sleeping" Jesus was placing a true evaluation on death. New and revealing but nevertheless, real!

The Dying Daughter!

"When Jesus was returning (from Gerasa) the crowd welcomed him, for all were expecting him." Work in Galilee had been left unfinished. The multitude expectantly awaited his return.

Two of the crowd typify the unfinished task. "A man whose name was Jairus..his only daughter of twelve years was dying." A father with an only child, and she not yet in her teens struggling on her death bed with life's last gasp. How sad! Yet how human! Does anything tear at a human heart more than to watch an only child slowly slip away in death before she has an opportunity to live life to its full? What is "fair" about life? How does one control resentment, bitterness, even hatred against "whatever gods there be?" Besides, this father was a "ruler of the synagogue." His life was committed to the God of the Hebrews who "created the heavens and the earth." He was a prominent leader in the community, a man of wealth, culture, education and highly respected.

Was he the "ruler" in that synagogue of Capernaum built by the Roman centurion whose house servant had been healed by this same Jesus? And was not this father one of those "elders" through whom the centurion had pled so effectively? And was this the "ruler" over the same synagogue in which a man with a withered hand had been healed in front of the carping critics who plotted the death of Jesus? Possibly! Yet whatever barriers may have stood between this father and Jesus the danger of death for his twelve-year old overcame them all. He worshipped "at the feet of Jesus" and poured out his exhortation. He repeatedly pressed on Jesus his plea, "that he enter into his house" because "his only daughter was dying." She was at this moment entering into her death struggle. Barriers of party and theological differences, racial and cultural enmities come down when the reality of death overtakes us. The life of a twelve year old only daughter took precedence over all such artificial walls. Life is more important than partisan bias!

An Interruption!

"But while he was going the crowds were pressing together (against) him." In this multitude, jostling against Jesus, was a woman "in a flowing of blood." She had endured this malady for twelve years" and had exhausted every avenue of healing without any results. But in Jesus hope was renewed that where others failed he would heal.

Her "unclean" condition (Lev.15:25ff) left her vulnerable to public humiliation. She would avoid publicity. She sought secretly to gain her goal! Approaching Jesus from "behind" and being forced along by the press of the crowd she "grabbed hold" of the tassle of scarlet wool attached to his outer robe. She did more than touch, she "grabbed" with firm grip. The result amazed even the woman. "Immediately the flowing of her blood stopped!" Twelve years of living death muzzled in a moment of time.

Her agony was gone but her secret must be discovered! Jesus, realizing that healing power had gone from him, asked "Who grabbed me?" When those immediately around denied having touched him, Peter pointed out that the crowd, pushing against him made possible that "many" touched him. But there's a difference between multitudes who carelessly press and one who with intelligent purpose and personal faith "takes hold." Multitudes give God a passing nod. Even with oaths they backhandedly acknowledge him. But it is he who with intelligent faith enjoys conscious gifts from God's hand. So it was that Jesus rejected Peter's point and repeated, "Who grabbed me? For I know that power has gone out from me!" God is infinite in power but he does not dispense it vainly, carelessly or secretly. It is always with the purpose of his glory and man's good. The woman, by being a living witness to her healing, has her part to play in bringing God in Christ the glory.

"The woman, having recognized that she was not hidden, declared before all the people why she grabbed him and how she was immediately healed." God's gifts are open for all. They witness to his redemptive interest in man. They bless the recipient but they are to glorify God who gives.

Then Jesus turned to the woman to confirm and reassure her trembling faith. He said, "Daughter, your faith has saved you. Go into peace!" Three matters are to be observed in this remark. First, however weak, immature, and misdirected it might be "faith" opens the door for entrance into God's presence and power. "Without trust it is impossible to be pleasing to God." But with faith all God's resources are available. He stands ready to shower his power upon any who trust him to do so.

130

Second, Jesus called her "Daughter!" This is one among several links that binds this interruption to the ongoing story of Jairus and his "daughter" who also was in a continuing struggle with death. The shattering of an agonizing father over his dying daughter was but an island tip of the depths of humanity's suffering below the surface of the sea. We are all "daughters" in the process of dying. God's Christ has come to stop the flow of death immediately. Behind the sickness is health; beyond the "sleep" is awakening!

Third, "Go into peace." The preposition "in" after a verb of motion signifies "into." Peace is more than a state, it's a process "into" which the healed are going. Peace ever increases in tranquil quietness and steadfastness of soul. It is not just something we get." It's that into which we increasingly go!

Awakening the daughter!

With torturing anguish the suffering father could only view this stopping of Jesus as fatal to his daughter's life. There was no time for delay! And it befell as he feared. A messenger from his house confirmed the fatal news. "While he (Jesus) was yet speaking ("Go into peace") a certain one came from the ruler of the synagogue's (house) saying, 'Your daughter has died. Quit bothering the Teacher.'" The worst had befallen! He was too late, and that because the Teacher had stopped to find out "who grabbed" his garment! The healing of one daughter brought on the death of his daughter. It was not only enough to crush faith. It offered the seed of bitter resentment. At least such possibility was present.

The text states, "But when Jesus heard..." Heard what?? When Jesus heard, "Your daughter has died!" Knowing full well what was testing the father's heart, Jesus "answered" the rising doubt. He urged Jairus, "Stop being afraid. Only trust and she shall be saved." Don't turn loose of your faith. Grip it even tighter in the face of this disappointing news. When the night is darkest, remember the dawn is coming. In a crisis hold onto your faith; don't drop it! When hope fades faith revives it. To give up faith now is to surrender all hope. So hold steady that which you have. It's your anchor in the storm. Hence Jesus constrained Jairus, "Only believe and she shall be saved."

Upon arrival at the home of Jairus Jesus found that "All were weeping and mourning her." With professional mourners already rending the air with their wails of grief Jesus determined to take only a select few into the death chamber. The parents and a favored three of his disciples were enough as witnesses to the awakening. And even these would be sworn to silence. This boisterous lament of the mourners, though well intended, gave a false meaning to death. After all, if death be but "sleep" then it cannot be the finality it seems.

To the sobbing crowd Jesus declared, "Quit weeping; she didn't die but is sleeping." That turned the mourning into ridiculing laughter. "They were laughing him down." How absurd! They were "knowing that she did die!"

131

This contrast of attitudes toward the death of the daughter of Jairus mirrors the divergence between the human and divine views of man's destiny. "All (the people) were weeping and bewailing her." That is normal behaviour. We as humans look on death as the "natural" end. Judged by its universality death is surely normal as the end.

But in contrast the remark of Jesus, "She did not die but is sleeping" rejects that death is "natural." It is "sleep" the prelude to larger life. Death may be "normal" but it is not natural. And it should not be considered final. If "sleep" is "natural" then death may be conceived as "natural" but only in a figure of speech. Death suspends life as sleep suspends a day's activity. But it does not destroy life. It merely holds it in abeyance awaiting an awakening. In the beginning man was created with the eternity of God as its pattern. The "image of God" includes "eternity" as an essential part of human existence. Death came as an interruption, a foul ball in the game of life as designed by God. That which now seems natural is in fact contrary to creation. God in Christ came to restore the original intent. Hence seeing man from the lofty peak of God's eternity Jesus could say, "She didn't die. But she is sleeping!" This is God's view of death!

The Awakening!

Having taken the parents and three disciples into the death room Jesus turned to the task of awakening the little daughter. "He, having taken hold of her hand, called saying, 'Child, Arise!' And her spirit (breath) returned, and immediately she arose. And he commanded to give her something to eat." That the little girl had died Jesus never doubted. But he used the fact of her death to reveal the divine view of what death really is. The behaviour of Jesus was so relaxed and unhurried that it hardly seems to be a "miracle." And from his point of sight it wasn't. It was a restoration of life to its "normal" place of growing up and becoming "the image and likeness of God." Like a good parent awakens a child for the new day's tasks, Jesus, called saying, "Child, get up!" Having had your rest, it's time to rise and eat!

A remarkable order of Jesus brings this story to a close. After he presented the daughter, live and healthy, to her parents, "He strictly charged that they tell no one that which had taken place." When the Gerasenes asked him to leave their land Jesus instructed the purified demoniac to go everywhere and tell everyone "what God did for you." Yet here he emphatically told everybody to tell nobody anything about the awakening of the little girl. The awakening of the little daughter was not done to get revenge on those who "laughed him down." It was an awakening that could stand on its own merit. It proclaimed its own message. It needed no human enhancement. Besides, it was the awakening of an innocent little girl. At Gerasa it was the purifying of an evil possesed adult. Others weren't exhorted to tell his story; he was! And that as a preparation for Christ's return to resume his message of the kingdom of God. An awakening from "sleep" is to be expected!

132

Two Points of Emphasis!

In Luke's Gospel two strands have threaded through the story casting their strength and color to the whole narrative. As each episode unfolds we expect the <u>universality</u> of God's good news to appear in some form. And this good news is embodied in each detail of the life of the <u>man</u> Jesus. As God's Christ, Jesus does not betray any bias for the sectarian, partisan culture of the Jewish people. Though born and reared a Jew his vision, message and labor was to bring the kingdom of God to people as people rather than to Jew, Gentile or any national or cultural limitation. Luke uses all the literary skill at his command to weave these threads into the fabric of his story. As an intelligent reader Theophilus by now would be expecting these ideas to surface as each episode unfolds.

In 8:40-56 the agony of death has played a prominent part. That coupled with the insistence of Jesus on death as a "sleep" relates to the two threads of emphasis. In human life nothing is more universal than death. And, as one enduring ridicule from fellow-men, the <u>man</u> Jesus interprets death as "sleep." Even the interruption of the woman with the "flow" of blood sounds the note of universality. Not only her own illness is typical of human experience but her thrusting herself in so as to delay Christ's movement toward relieving Jairus' anxiety serves as a foil against which the awakening from death is painted.

Each of Luke's episodes adds its own details. But there is an accumulative effect as we approach the halfway mark in the Gospel. God in the person of the man Jesus is so human!

* * * * * * *

SPECIAL NOTE ON LUKE 8:40-56!

This passage contains a story within a story. Jairus and his daughter are central characters with Jesus giving a creative view of death as the highlight of the incident.

The sudden appearance of the woman with the flowing of blood, while presenting a "lesson" of its own, nevertheless is an integral part of the story of Jairus. Her "interruption" provides a ready foil reflecting more sharply the encounter of Jairus with Jesus.

Besides, a number of ideas link the two stories. The term "daughter" is used of both the girl and the woman. "Twelve years" concerns each of these daughters. No description of the affliction of Jairus' daughter is given, only that she "was dying." The woman had a "flowing of blood." Since "life is in the blood" we conclude she was enduring a living death. Both are typical of what every human being faces, namely "death." Though not God's original intent, man <u>now</u> is born to die. At best life is a parenthesis before death. These two "daughters" typify each human being's experience.

For these reasons we feel the two stories should be treated as one. They are too closely related both in literary form and in what they epitomize to deal with them separately.

133

AN OUTLINE OF LUKE 9:1-9
The Kingdom of God!
In this section Jesus assigns the 12 a mission of training. Their message was to announce "the kingdom of God." Their work was "to heal."
The effect of their mission typified by their government in the person of Herod the tetrarch: "Who is this?
I. THE MISSION OF THE TWELVE. 9:1-6
1. Final appeal to Galilee; mission of the twelve.
2. He gave equipment for their task. vs.1
(a)"Power." (b)"Authority." (c)"To heal."
3. He commissioned them. vs.2
(a)To announce: "the kingdom of God."
(b)To cure illness.
4. Instructed as to methods. vss.3-5
(a)For setting out,(b)for remaining,(c)for exiting.
5. Their effective labors. vs.6
II. THE FEARS OF HEROD. 9:7-9
1. Attention of populace aroused. vss.7-8
(a)"John risen from the dead."
(b)"Elijah appeared."
(c)"One of the prophets of old."
2. Herod's fears. vs.9
(a)"I beheaded John."
(b)"Who is this?"
(c)"He was seeking to see him!"
In this, Christ's final appeal to Galilee, the twelve get their apprenticeship discipline for future evangelizing. While the instruction has local limited application it entails also some universals. The "kingdom of God" as the message is timeless. The "healings" take other forms but the gospel still "heals." Herod's reactions are reflected in all societies.

* * * * * * *

THE KINGDOM OF GOD!
Luke has traced the publication of the kingdom of God by Jesus personally visiting cities, towns and hamlets of Galilee. He even ventured East into the Decapolis. Before setting his face toward Jerusalem once again he would give Galilee a final opportunity to respond to the "kingdom of God." This time through the twelve! This would afford an opportunity for schooling the twelve in the skills of evangelizing. More important than teaching is the developing of teachers.
The Mission!
Time was of the essence. His rendezvous with destiny at Jerusalem was on the horizon. Methods of speeding up a last appeal to Galilee included the sending of the twelve with his kingdom message. Hence "having called together the twelve" he "gave them power, and authority over all demons," and "to heal diseases." These three gifts were not the goal of their going. They were the means by which he undergirded their mission. The goal was to reveal "the kingdom of God."

134

In dispatching the twelve on such a crucial mission Jesus "gave" them necessary equipment. Three specific items mentioned are: "power" (δύναμιν) to perform miracles, "authority" (ἐξουσίαν) to make decisions "upon all the demons," and "to heal diseases." Such powers, authority, and healing are dramatic, visible, and capable of stirring the imagination. But they were only supportive of the main mission. Their purpose was not to exhibit power, exercise authority or to heal. But accompanying such graphic displays they should be about the chief point, namely, "to be announcing the kingdom of God." That is why he "sent them!" While they were healing they were to be preaching "the kingdom of God."

Even their method of movement into, during and out of each city, town and village was to subserve this main purpose, "to herald the kingdom of God." He charged, "Be taking nothing into the way, neither staff, money bag, bread, silver, neither to have two cloaks." In other words don't go hampered by a lot of luggage. Look to God to guide and provide.

Furthermore, after you get to a community and you enter a home receptive to you and your message "remain there during your stay in that town." Don't misuse time or create trouble by moving from house to house. That makes for problems rather than solving them.

In addition, when you leave a city, demonstrate by the usual cultural symbol your moral responsibility (and theirs) as to the "kingdom of God." "However many do not receive you, as you exit from that city, shake the dust off your feet for a witness against them." You are not to manipulate people into the kingdom of God. You are to "announce" it, portray its values, illustrate its moral qualities and even persuade people to enter. But for the kingdom to be God's each must participate by his free choice. God forces himself nor his sovereign rule on no human being. The mission was "to declare, announce, proclaim, publicize the kingdom of God." But never are they to force or manipulate anyone into it.

The Fears of Herod!

The text testifies, "Going out they were journeying village by village evangelizing and healing everywhere." Though no specifics are given as to the results of their preaching expedition, Herod's reaction furnishes clues. The entire province of Galilee was aroused! Variety of opinions were being circulated. Not only were people talking about "the kingdom of God" but more particularly about this Jesus as to who he might be!! Some were affirming that Jesus was none other than "John (the Baptist) risen from among the dead." That pricked the conscience of Herod to the core for he said, "I beheaded John!" His very use of the emphatic personal pronoun "I" is a certain sign that his beheading of John weighed on his conscience. Herod, like all who abuse a privileged position, must go on living with the guilt of wrong doing. Thus the mission of the twelve reached into the highest courts of government.

As a result of this Galilean preaching mission some people confusedly claimed that in Jesus "Elijah appeared again!" Though they thought of a literal appearance, this opinion does reflect that Jesus was identified with Old Testament expectations. He _was_ Elijah in spirit and power. Though in shadowy forms distorted by cultural expectations, the message was getting through. We note "others" thought "that a certain prophet of old had risen." Without saying as much these opinions flirted with the idea that Jesus was the fulfillment of Old Testament foregleams of Messiah. Thus the mission of the twelve stirred the Galilean countryside. Though confused in their grasp of the reality, they were talking and thinking in terms of God's kingdom.

In this also Herod gives a clue to the people's feelings. He said, "John _I_ beheaded. But who is this concerning whom I hear these things?" The people, as well as Herod, were raising the question, "Who is this?" That was good! It is important to an understanding of the kingdom to determine, "Who is this Jesus concerning whom I am hearing these things!" Where and what the kingdom is hangs on the answer to that question.

Another of Herod's reactions is of import: "And he was seeking to see him." Herod's motive is questionable. He wished to see Jesus perform some magic as though he were some entertainer. The depth of Herod's concern was ego centered. Nevertheless, it represents a true need. I must "seek to see him" if I am to discover the kingdom of God, its nature and how to share in it. If one wants to participate in the kingdom he should meet and know the king!

The central idea of this text is "the kingdom of God." But where and what it is never is specifically defined. Luke, along with the other synoptists, assumes the reader grasps the kingdom idea. It is a question that requires defining.

The Anglo-Saxon suffix -_dom_ signifies "dominion." Thus "kingdom" is the realm or sphere in which a king has dominion. His domain may be geographical, political, legal, military or cultural. The kingdom of God may touch any or all of such realms but it is not identified with any of them.

In the kingdom of God the king is God. Since the biblical God is the Creator of "the heavens and the earth and all that in them is" there can be no limit to his geographical rule. He is universal in the physical extent of his authority. The same is true of the extent of his human sovereignty. No race, nation, tribe or clan is outside his royal reign. He may not be recognized as king, nevertheless he rules over all peoples.

But if these things be true why send out heralds to teach "the kingdom of God" and to exhort people to enter? The "kingdom of God," as used in our text, is more restricted than such a broad general idea of sovereignty of God by virtue of his Creation. After all, he created man "after his image" and in his "likeness." That implies that to each human being he has given the right and responsibility to choose. Each one must freely decide the realm to which he subjects himself. Man is more than the flower of the field or the beast of the wild. He is "moral" as God is "moral." He makes decisions as God makes decisions. And God wants man to choose Him, God, as moral sovereign, spiritual monarch! The kingdom of God consists of any and all human beings of any and all races, cultures, nations, tribes and clans who "choose" God to be king!

Such a view of the kingdom of God implies that the kingdom is not limited to any particular dispensation of time, any geographical area, any national or political entity. It is truly universal in outreach and scope. The _form_ it takes has varied but the idea of God as sovereign is present in all stages and every era. Wherever God has been or is in fact recognized and accepted as king, _there_ the kingdom of God is! He rules in the moral and spiritual realm by the power of love. His subjects form a united fellowship by reason of their common choice of God as supreme potentate.

The divine kingdom, from this point of view, stretches back into patriarchal, even pre-patrarchal times. In the Old Testament Melchisedec appears as "priest of God Most High." Abraham, exemplar of faith, looked to the same God Most High as his supreme Lord of heaven. His descendents, the Hebrew people, became God's "chosen," His kingdom, at least in type. And the apostle Paul says that "he (God) has put all things under his (Christ's) feet and has made him the head over all things for the church, which is his body, the fullness of him who fills all in all."(Eph.1:22f) God's sovereign dominion reaches into the remote past and extends through all time and is to be consummated in eternity to come. It is a present reality wherever men yield allegience to the God who "is over all, through all, and in all."

This is not to say that the twelve on their mission through Galilee presented such a theological explanation of "the kingdom of God." They simply preached God as sovereign in Jesus the Christ. But in any preaching of "the kingdom of God" more lies in the message than any single messenger comprehends. In its extent, breadth, and depth God's thought far surpasses any man's comprehension of that kingdom. But underlying all God's revelation to man is this crucial fact, _God reigns as supreme king_! In this text Luke attempts to convey that idea to Theophilus. Nothing is more _universal_ than the "kingdom of God." And for that reason nothing is more _human_!

AN OUTLINE OF LUKE 9:10-17
Food for the Famishing!
Food anywhere, anytime is vital for human existence. In the
desert it is crucial for survival. For a crowd, if without
food for any length of time, it can be hazardous to its
stability. Peace is fragile for a mob without food.
I.   THE OCCASION - SOLITUDE SOUGHT! 9:10-11
     1. The report of the twelve. 10a
     2. Seeking solitude near Bethsaida Julius. 10b
     3. The multitude "followed him." 11a
     4. He "received them" and taught "the kingdom..." 11b
II. THE CRISIS: FAILURE OF FOOD. 9:12-13
     1. Alarm as the "day began to decline." 12
     2. "You give them to eat." 13a
        (a)Christ's directive.
        (b)Disciples' despairing response.
III. THE CRISIS RESOLVED. 9:14-17
     1. The crowd seated orderly. 14-15
     2. The available food blessed. 16-17
        (a)Word of blessing.
        (b)Food distributed.
     3. Surplus food after all are fed.
God may not supply all human beings want. But, even in a
desert, he supplies all people need!

* * * * * * *

FOOD FOR THE FAMISHING!
     The vision of people perishing without food is familiar to
modern viewers of Television. Drouth coupled with selfish
political programs have displayed in every living room millions
of starving people in Ethiopia and such third world countries.
Indeed, food is vital for human subsistence. In drouth ridden
desert lands food is imperative for survival. And for the mob
to be without food or the prospect of finding any is dangerous
to the stability of society.
                         The Occasion!
     Upon the return of the twelve from their Galilean preaching
mission, "the apostles recounted to him how many things they
did." Accompanied by "healing everywhere" their message had
been "the kingdom of God." Though they were not yet aware of
the centrality of the Christ's death at the hands of the
"elders and high priests and scribes" Jesus was quite conscious
of his Jerusalem destiny. That preyed on his mind! Besides, the
disciples needed some rest and solitude in which he might begin
to instruct them about his approaching suffering. Thus "he took
them and withdrew apart alone into a city being called
Bethsaida" just east of Capernaum. The fact that he was seeking
solitude apart from crowds suggests it was Bethsaida Julius on
the northeastern shores of the Lake. He was trying to avoid
crowds and would not seek solitude in a city. The word
"Bethsaida" is best taken here in its literal sense "fishing

138

place." It was not the city but an inhabited countryside carrying the name "Bethsaida." That it was desert country is confirmed by the disciples, "we are here in this desert place."(vs.12) Such desert country extended down the northeastern shore of the sea of Galilee. Jesus and his band were crossing by sea from the western shore. But when the multitude saw him depart and recognized where he was headed they "followed him" on foot around the north end of the sea. Many outran him, arriving at the "fishing place" before he did.

The crowd thwarted the plan of Jesus to withdraw and be alone with the twelve. Luke does not state whether Jesus was disappointed. Nor does he give any trace of irritation or frustration on the part of the Lord. The text states, "Having received them he began speaking concerning the kingdom of God." This was burdening his heart. It was the same subject he had assigned to the twelve to herald throughout Galilee. Moreover, the text significantly adds, "and the ones having need of healing he was curing." The kingdom involves "curing." And at bottom there could be no "curing" of any kind unless, at the cross, he fulfilled the divine prescription for redemption! Immediately following this feeding in the desert Luke presents Peter's confession of faith. That in turn is followed by Jesus' first formal instruction about his coming cross. Thus it seems obvious that "the kingdom of God" is the burden of Jesus' thought, message, and action in this desert narrative. Even the developing need for food and how it was supplied makes its peculiar contribution to the kingdom theme.

When Jesus stepped ashore and the multitude began gathering the text indicates "he gladly welcomed" them. Whatever his burden was or his disciples' needs nothing could dampen his joy of an opportunity to feed the people the truth of God. Limited only by their capacity to grasp that truth he unveiled the kingdom principles throughout the day.

The Failure of Food!

Jesus seemed completely absorbed in the opportunity for teaching. The hours slipped away until "the day began to decline." As the sun sank behind Galilee's western hills the disciples became concerned. What food the people brought had been consumed. Shadows were lengthening; cooling breezes of the evening warned of the coming night. There was precious little food. In view of the size of the crowd and the desert place practically no food! So "the twelve, having approached, said to him, 'Send the crowd away, that having gone into the surrounding villages and fields they might get lodging and find food. For we are here in this desert place.'" To the disciples the situation had the makings of a first class crisis. Jesus had a measure of responsibility for this huge crowd being in this desert environment. At best they had thousands of hungry people on their hands. At worst it could become an ugly rabble. At any rate they suggested that Jesus dismiss the people so they might find food and lodging for the night.

Were the twelve ever surprised? More than surprised! They

were shocked when Jesus directed them, "You give them to eat!"
How did he expect twelve men to scour that desert countryside
and search out enough food to feed even for one meal over 5000
people? It would be much more logical to dismiss the people so
they might ferret out food for themselves. The meager supply of
"five loaves and two fish" was proof of the predicament in
which they found themselves. What was this among so many?

The Crisis Resolved!

To be logical one must have all the facts. The twelve failed
to take into consideration the prime source of food. It's not
nature but God who feeds the birds and nourishes the flowers.
Neither is it people who grow the crops from which food comes.
True, men plow, plant, cultivate. But it's God who gives the
increase. People are the agents; but God is the source. And men
must always recognize God as the source. In times of need men
must appeal to God from whom the blessing of food comes. Thus
Jesus disregarded the "logic" of the twelve and urged them to
"seat them in groups of about fifty each."

The disciples abandoned their logic for obedience to his
instruction. "And they did thus and seated all." It was the
spring of the year; the grass was green.(Mk.6:39) It was
Passover time.(Jn.6:4) The crowd numbered 5000 men "besides
women and children."(Matt.14:21) One hundred groups of fifty in
a group would be 5000. So at least fifty groups, probably more,
dotted the green hillside. God likes beauty and order! The
people were expectant. The disciples anxious. Obvious to all
something was in the offing. They watched his every move!

In view of the whole multitude Jesus took the available food
of "five loaves and two fish" and deliberately directed
attention to Him who is the ultimate source of all food.
"Having looked up unto the heaven he blessed them..." The sin
of man is not so much denying God as ignoring him. Men fail to
recognize or acknowledge God's presence in their affairs. This
is the basic wrong men inflict on God. No person likes to be
ignored, particularly if he is concerned in that which is going
on. Thus God, being personal, likes to be invited to share in
human experiences in which he is so involved. It was no
accident that Jesus, "having looked up unto heaven, blessed
them."

After Jesus recognized heaven as the giver of the food the
text reports that "he broke and was giving to the disciples to
deposit before the multitude." The verb "was giving" is vividly
descriptive. Each of the twelve received broken pieces of food
from the hand of Jesus and went from group to group depositing
enough food for each person's need. Four or more groups to each
disciple would cover the entire crowd until all were satisifed.
"They all ate and were filled." Bread and fish may not be all
men might want but it's everything a man needs in terms of one
meal. And that is all God has promised. Manna in the wilderness
of Sinai came one day's supply at a time. And here in the
"desert place" nothing was wasted. After "all ate and were
filled, of the overabundance of broken pieces left over twelve

140

large wicker baskets were taken up." That more food was on hand
than before they began eating suggests abundance of God's gifts
to human needs. But the point of the story does not depend on
the overabundance but rather on the source and how it came. God
is the author of life. God sustains life. Jesus is the agent
through whom God gives and sustains life. In turn each disciple
becomes an agent of God. No human need lies outside God's
capacity or willingness.

* * * * * * *

Note on the four accounts of the Feeding the 5000!

Aside from the crucifixion and resurrection the feeding of
the 5000 alone is recorded by all four Gospels. Each of the
authors established at the outset his distinctive approach to
the story. Matthew presents Jesus as "the Christ the son of the
living God." Jesus, "son of David, son of Abraham" is he who
fulfills Old Testament shadows.

Mark, following the tradition of Peter, gives "the beginning
(elemental ABC's)of the gospel of Jesus Christ(son of God)." He
portrays one who does powerful deeds, a man of action.

Luke fills in a picture of a sympathizing, compassionate son
of man, an intensely human Christ who knows no boundary to his
universal reach toward all disadvantaged.

John, written a generation later, tesitifies to the cosmic
Christ who steps out of eternity into the world of flesh and
time.

The first readers of these Gospels had just the one, not
four, to read. Even if the authors had before them the other
records, their readers did not. Each author was writing to
create an impression suitable to his distinctive theme. That
which he included or left out was designed to help make this
impression.

In studying these four records we seek for the author's
impression. Matthew: "son of David, son of Abraham" Mark:
"Jesus, son of God." John, "the Word became flesh (human)."
Luke: Jesus, the "son of man."

In this narrative Luke tells how Jesus "gladly welcomes" the
crowds that interrupt his wish to be alone with his disciples.
He alludes to the burden bothering Jesus, namely, "the kingdom
of God" in view of the approaching suffering at Jerusalem. He
"was healing" those needing healing. He demonstrated God as the
ultimate source of food. Using what was available he showed
God's infinite supply for human need.

We look for the impression of the episode in the light of
the whole gospel story. The people's hunger is seen in Christ
"gladly receiving" them, "teaching the kingdom of God," and
"healing them." Then that which followed, multiplying the
little available food to demonstrate God's ample supply.
Christ's identifying with the hunger of the people and
supplying their need is the emphasis of Luke's account.

141

AN OUTLINE OF LUKE 9:18-27
The Christ and the Cross!
None of the gospels give a "Life of Christ." Each portrays
the death of the Christ to which is appended a sketch of his
resurrection from the grave.

The brief earlier portion of each gospel narrative gives
only enough to verify what the author thought necessary to
identify who was crucified. Each author added that which he
felt was needed about Christ's struggle to prepare his chosen
twelve for the rejection, suffering, and death.
  I.   THE CONFESSION! 9:18-20
       1. "While he was praying apart." 18a
       2. Popular opinions about Jesus. 18b-19
       3. "Whom are you saying me to be?" 20a
       4. Peter's answer: "The Christ of God." 20b
  II. THE CROSS. 9:21-22
       1. Urgent charge: "Say this to no one." 21
       2. "It's necessary that the son suffer." 22a
       3. He is to be "be rejected by the leaders." 22b
       4. "And be killed." 22c
       5. "And be raised on the third day." 22d
  III. THE CROSS IS UNIVERSAL. 9:23-27
       1. Commitment involves the cross. 23
       2. The paradox of discipleship. 24
       3. The logic of the disciples' cross. 25
       4. Consequence of disciples' cross. 26
The kingdom of God with its demand of the cross is in the
immediate future. "Some of those standing here shall not taste
of death until they see the kingdom of God."

* * * * * * *

THE CHRIST AND THE CROSS!
Most material in each of the four Gospels deals with the
death of Jesus including the events which led to that death.
That which gives special significance to the death is the
bodily resurrection which followed. So every gospel author
appends some description of his resurrection. Thus "Christ and
him crucified" is the essence of all four of the Gospels.

The authors introduce Jesus in different ways. Their earlier
material fits the distinctive emphasis of each. But in general
the introductory material draws a picture of who it was that
came to such suffering, rejection, and death. Mark's abrupt
beginning and earliest descriptions suit his portrayal of
"Jesus Christ, son of God." Matthew's early chapters sketch
Jesus, "son of David, son of Abraham" who fulfills Old
Testament outlines. Luke penetrates to the human origins as
they link to Christ's divine begetting. Then he proceeds to
demonstrate his human touch in the face of ever growing
hostility from the nation's official leaders. Each of these
Gospel authors gives that which he felt was needed to identify
who it was that was thus rejected and crucified. But the major

142

portion of Luke's narrative (as also the others) is confined to Christ's death. Beginning with this text of 9:18-27 everything relates to the coming death and its sequel the resurrection.

The Confession of Peter!

The confession of Peter is a highwater mark in the unfolding revelation of the person of Christ and his relationship to the kingdom of God. It was evoked by Jesus. And that confession verbalizes the impact on them of his life and ministry. It also summarizes the conviction of the entire twelve. Peter voiced it but they all believed it!

As told by Luke the circumstances surrounding the confession differ from Mark and Matthew. All three place it following the Galilean preaching mission and after the feeding of the 5000. But Mark and Matthew tell of a trip to Caesarea Philippi, the topography and history of which suit the remarks of Jesus after the confession. But Luke prefers to relate the moral situation which drew forth the confession. "And it came to pass as he was praying..." Which says the spiritual and moral need drew forth the confession as much or more than the geographical location. The kingdom of God, and particularly his suffering for it, was burdening the heart of the Christ. What the twelve thought in personal conviction as to his person was crucial to their stability as believers in him and his mission. What did they really think about him? This question must be answered before he reveals the nature of the kingdom and the necessity of his rejection and death.

To reveal to them, not him, Jesus inquired as to the current popular opinions. On their recent preaching circuit of Galilee they had picked up all kinds of opinions about him. So he asked, "Whom are the crowds saying me to be?" such a question served as a mirror on which could be reflected, not just popular opinions, but also the contrast between their opinion and that of the public. The answers given of course are the same as had filtered back to Herod (Lk.9:7-9). They included, "John the Baptist," "Elijah," or "one of the prophets." Without exception these opinions reflected an exalted view of Jesus. The prophets, Elijah or John all were high in the esteem of the people. These were not degrading. But they did not represent the truth as to who he was nor his place in God's promised kingdom. Thus it was decisive that they formulate their opinion about him. "Whom are you saying me to be?" Jesus placed an unusual emphasis on the pronoun "you." Whatever the opinions of men may be, good or bad, they do not determine truth. Majority vote doesn't decide fact. Besides, my personal conviction is pivotal so far as my behaviour is concerned. Therefore, "what do you believe" was the decisive point!

The brevity and form of Luke's report of Peter's confession is distinctive. "The Christ of God!" Matthew's report, "You are the Christ, the son of the living God" suits the Hebrew concept of God as "living." Mark's "You are the Christ" fits the factual, abrupt, to-the-point character of the Roman. Luke agrees with the others by using the term "Christ" (anointed)

143

but affixes the subjective possessive idea "of God." Jewish tradition expected a special "anointed one." But he is not restricted to Jews; he is "<u>God's</u> Christ," hence universal.

The Cross of Christ!

Peter's confession is a mountainpeak in the progressive revelation of Jesus. These men did not understand all the implications of what they had just confessed. But they held much different views of Jesus than the general populace. His personal presence, their immediate sharing with him, his words and influence have had their impact on them. Their's was superior than the opinion of the people. For them it was a determinative conviction. It must be strong enough to withstand coming storms. In fact, Christ's immediate teaching following the confession was a shock to their declared faith in him.

He firmly ordered them to keep quiet as to his being Messiah. This startled them for had not the Christ come for the purpose of disclosing himself as God's anointed? Yet "having strictly charged them he commanded that they tell this to no one." That he was the Christ must be withheld from the people. The public notion of the kind of Christ to be expected must be radically changed before he should be announced as God's Christ. His was no political panacea. Nor would he lead a rebellion against Rome.

The underlying reason why they should "tell no one" lay in the nature of him as Christ as well as the nature of the kingdom he came to establish. So, as painful as it would be to the twelve, Jesus was impelled to begin the troublesome task of prying open their minds to the necessity of his ordeal of suffering just ahead at Jerusalem. So he said, "It is necessary that the son of man suffer much and be rejected after being tested by the elders and chief priests and scribes, and that he be killed, and on the third day arise." What could be more shocking, disastrous, or disturbing than that "the Christ of <u>God</u>" be subjected to such humiliation. To them it seemed so utterly unreasonable and therefore impossible. No way could human logic reconcile a humiliating death to the fact of his being "the Christ of God." To say the least, this was a severe testing of their recent confession.

The Universality of the Cross!

Luke does not report the horrified, almost profane reaction of the twelve to this, Christ's first clear declaration of his death. Rather than dwell on that which upset the disciples Luke preferred that Theophilus learn forthwith the lesson of the cross in its <u>universal</u> bearing. Thus Luke at once discloses Jesus' words, "If <u>anyone</u> wishes to be coming after me he is to deny himself and take up his cross daily, and be following me." The cross as instrument of death is not only a necessity for me but it holds the secret of a successful life for "anyone" who would find redemption in the kingdom of God. By its very nature truth is universal. And nothing is more true than that one deny self, take up the cross and die daily. That's what "follow me" means says the Lord of the kingdom. Commitment involves a cross.

144

But what does "cross" mean? If the cross be the instrument of capital punishment and one dies as a result, how can one die "daily"? The twelve were shocked to hear Jesus say that he, the Christ, would be put to death as a common criminal. But even more shocking was it to learn that the Christ's death was only the supreme example of what is the "normal" result of a righteous life in an evil world.

The cross as a principle of life has been woven into the fabric of human life as it must be lived in this wicked world. Jesus stated as much when he declared, "for whosoever wishes to save his soul, shall lose it, but whosoever shall lose his soul for my sake, this one shall save it." This is the paradox of discipleship. To do right is to die to the world's standard of success. To live successfully, as the world measures success, one is called upon to compromise right and choose the wrong. The Christ came as a human being. As such he daily did "right." As a consequence the world rejected and murdered him. Yet by so doing he conquered death in his resurrection. He thus saved both himself and those who commit themselves to him, that is to say, those who "deny self, and take up the cross." The pattern of a godly life is a daily cross!

The cross makes sense to him who looks below the surface. It is logic of the highest order. "For what does it profit a man, if he gain the whole world but he lose or forfeit his own self?" Money kept is lost; it's gone! Only when it is spent does it generate life. To "spend" one's self in the service of the Christ is to save one's soul. But to conserve one's self instead of giving one's self to the needs of others is to lose one's self. That isn't good logic!

Thus it is that identification with the Christ, his person, his teachings, his cross, his kingdom is the key to a man's eternal destiny. "For whosoever shall be ashamed of me and my words, of this one the son of man shall be ashamed whenever he shall come in his glory and of the Father and his holy angels." Relationship to the Christ is determined by my acceptance or rejection of the cross. That determines my destiny, here and hereafter!

The cross, as experienced and defined by Christ, is the most universal of his revelations. It is the most all-embracing fact of discipleship to Christ. If one would follow Jesus there's no way to escape the cross. This is the crux of the matter of being Christian.

Luke places it squarely before Theophilus. And he pointedly says, "What does it profit a man if he gain the whole world..."

AN OUTLINE OF LUKE 9:28-36
Christ Transfigured!
To replenish the vision of Christ's glory and the purpose of
his suffering God gave the mountainside transfiguration. It was
also to confirm the word of Jesus to the disciples about his
approaching death. In this prayer session they got a glimpse of
"glory," that of the cross, his and theirs!
- I.   THE CHRIST TRANSFIGURED! 9:28-29
    1. Occasion:"He went up into the mountain to pray."
    2. "While praying his appearance became other."
- II. CONVERSATION WITH MOSES AND ELIJAH. 9:30-32
    1. "Two men" appeared "in glory." 30-31a
    2. The subject of the conversation; "his exodus." 31b
    3. The response of the three disciples. 32
       (a)"Weighted down with sleep."
       (b)Aroused, they "kept awake."
- III. THE VOICE OF GOD. 9:33-36
    1. Three tabernacles proposed by Peter. 33
    2. The overshadowing cloud. 34
    3. Voice of God out of the cloud. 35
    4. Jesus only.
God insisted that they "hear him and none other." Listen to
what he says - about the cross! Moses and Elijah disappeared.
Jesus alone was left. He alone is the one to whom to listen.
They determined that what they had seen and heard was too
subject to misunderstanding. So "they kept silent and told no
one in those days anything of that which they had seen."

* * * * * * *

CHRIST TRANSFIGURED!
The resurrection of Christ is essential to evaluating the
meaning of his death. Without the resurrection Jesus is just
one more tragic miscarriage of justice in the long history of
man's injustice to man. But by the resurrection he is displayed
before all history as God's anointed, man's redeemer. But not
even the resurrection compares with the transfiguration in its
capability of revealing Christ's "glory."
The word translated glory ($\delta\acute{o}\xi\alpha$) means "essential nature" or
"honor" "repute" "splendor" etc. The two meanings are not
totally unrelated. That which is one's "essential nature"
often gives the reputation, the honorific status among peers.
This transfiguration revealed to the three disciples, and all
posterity, the essence of Christ's nature, his "glory."
The Christ Transfigured!
That Christ "went up into the mountain to pray" is quite
significant. This tranfiguration experience followed by "about
eight days" after Peter's confession and Christ's teaching that
"it is necessary that the son of man suffer...be rejected...and
be murdered...and be raised.." The shock of that created a
valley of depression through which the disciples must be guided
and out of which they must be lifted. As so often in crises

146

Jesus sought strength in prayer. And so "about eight days after these sayings, having taken Peter and John and James, he went up into the mountain to pray." This relates the mountain praying to the need for his rejection and death. However disquieting to Jesus such a prospect might be, he accepted it as necessary to his mission. But to the disciples it was totally depressing. Jesus must lift them from such emotional paralysis. He must also get them to accept the need for his dying. Luke reports that he wished to pray with them.

Jesus' felt it best to bathe the mind and recover the heart in the silence of a mountain retreat. So he took the three for a renewal of faith, a clarifying vision of his nature and purpose. "It came to pass while he was praying the appearance of his face became other and his garment glistening white." The praying of Jesus led to this cryptic event. His devotion, dedication, and harmony of spirit with that of God illumined Christ's face. He didn't see "glory" he was "glory." His innate character broke through the veil of flesh.

Luke describes: "the appearance of his face became other!" The word "other" indicates "other of a different kind." It was the stuff, the fabric of the soul's future majesty. Heaven's grandure descended to earth. This radiance dazzled Jesus with such intensity that "his garments were glistening white." This was a transfiguration, an unveiling of the "glory" of Christ, a revealing of his "essential nature." As a growing human being this was the apex beyond which there was no growth. In his inward development he was mature, perfect, fully developed.

Where can perfection go? Nowhere is there to push forward! He will allow no reversal, no retreat to less than where and what he is! The limitations of flesh are too cramped for perfect personality. In this life of flesh only death lies ahead. But he is sinless! For such the darkness of the grave cannot be a final destiny. At worst death can only be an open door for a glorious transformation! As a human this mountain adventure has led Jesus into an immediate experience of eternity. It was a preview of timeless glory! The change wrought was such as took place at the ascension after his resurrection. For the disciples it could not but restore faith, shaken by the teaching of his coming death. This was part of the purpose of this mountain retirement. It not only reestabished faith it opened up vast areas of vision lying far beyond ordinary human conceptions of man's infinite destiny.

Conversation with Moses and Elijah!
Yet more amazing things were in store. "Behold, two men were speaking with him." Heaven came to have fellowship with earth! The two "who by nature were no other than Moses and Elijah..." They were the most effective and revered of the Old Testament covenant people; one, giver of the law; the other, spearhead of the prophets. Besides, each of them ended his earthly life differently than normal. Moses just walked off and disappeared. No one ever found his body! Elijah ascended in a chariot of fire without the disrobing of death! From hindsight the closing

of their careers sent a signal about death. Actually death is a great deceiver. It isn't all that bad! It's really an exit out of a trying situation; an entrance into a fabulous future! Death is a "sting" but only a sting. It isn't annihilation after a brief consciousness "full of sound and fury."

The subject of the conversation of Jesus with these "two men" was enlightening in view of their career ending and that facing Jesus as God's anointed. Luke is the only one who tells explicitly that about which they conversed: "having appeared in glory, they were talking about his exodus which he was about to fulfill in Jerusalem." If the living disciples were confused, frustrated and depressed over his approacing rejection and death, both the law and the prophets certainly understood, encouraged and strengthened him for the ordeal. While Moses and Elijah served on earth they had foreshadowed Messiah's death. In their own departure from earth they had unveiled death's deceitful sham. This was an encouragement to Jesus in view of the disturbing dullness of the disciples. Not that Moses or Elijah could instruct Jesus about life or death. But they did understand and could encourage. After all, they did not die. He must! The topic of the conversation was what he was to "accomplish" in and by that death. He was teaching Moses and Elijah how his death was to "fulfill" their shadowy outlines given to ancient Israel. His instruction to these ancients were for the ears of the disciples. Jesus was not to be "translated" as Elijah. Nor was he to disappear as did Moses. He was to accomplish a task, do an assignment, fulfill a prescribed outline. His was a job to be done, not a death merely to be endured. In his death he would not be abandoning men to their sin. On the contrary he would be redeeming them from it. This was the meaning of his "exodus" in Jerusalem. It was this about which they talked!

How much of this conversation the three disciples heard is a question. The text states, "Peter and those with him had been weighted down with sleep." They surely failed to hear some of it. But on the other hand when they aroused themselves and observed what was going on "having kept alert, they saw his glory and the two men standing with him." So heavy had been their sleep, they were groggy. With difficulty they revived. But once fully awake they "kept" alert! They heard enough that they wanted to hear more. "It came to pass as they (the two men) were departing, Peter said to Jesus, 'Master, it is good that we are here. Let us make three shelters, one for you and one for Moses and one for Elijah.'" Peter would hold onto this miraculous moment no matter what he might say. The words rushed out without consideration for the suffering people in the valley below. Peter was "not knowing what he was saying." His idea was to preserve this joy! Repudiate suffering, sadness and death! Obviously Peter had much to learn. We can only wonder how much of the discussion he heard or having heard how much he absorbed about Christ's "exodus which he was about to accomplish at Jerusalem!"

148

The Voice of God!

Peter didn't have to wait for a much needed lesson. "While he was saying this a cloud was overshadowing them but they feared as they entered into the cloud." Why would seamen fear a cloud? This was an unusual cloud. In the wilderness Moses went up to Sinai and God "called...out of the cloud."(Ex.24:16) At the dedication of Solomon's temple, "the priests could not...minister because of the cloud; the glory of the Lord filled the house."(I Kings 8:11) When God visits earth on special occasions he invests himself with an overshadowing cloud. Hence it was not the cloud but God who stunned the disciples with fear. And the voice of God justified their fear: "This is my son, the one having been selected, you hear him!"

By some devices of grammer God shows the folly of Peter's desire to prolong the mountain top thrill. He also defines Jesus as authoritative Teacher. When God uses demonstrative pronoun "this one" he spotlights Jesus as Teacher. Perfect tense "having been selected" indicates a fixed, decisive appointment. At some point God had chosen "this one" to be his Christ among men. He was no afterthought or accident but a premeditated selection. The present imperative "be hearing" suggests repeated action: "keep on hearing" each time he speaks. Genitive after verbs of sense (hear) expresses "this and not that" "this and no other," which is to say: "Listen to him, not Moses, Elijah, or any one else." Thus both the circumstances and the form of expression make God's words sharply emphatic. Then as if to give further force, "After the voice came, Jesus was found alone." Jesus was the only one left to whom they could listen. The episode isolated Jesus as the sole revealer of truth.

How does an author depict God as human? Such a task is difficult if possible. Thus far Luke has traced God's human ordeal through the virgin's womb and early childhood. He has "grown" to manhood, assumed his public service on God's mission. His "call" was confirmed at his baptism followed by a volley of temptations common to all men. He has introduced the kingdom of God and aroused opposition from the leaders of Israel. All the episodes have fused the divine and human in the one person in a remarkable way. Without lessening the deity Luke has underscored the humanity of Christ. And he highlighted the universality of God's purpose.

The transfiguration reaches a highpoint in this unfolding revelation. That God and man, heaven and earth, deity and flesh appear as one is skillfully depicted. The impact on Theophilus can only be imagined. Though it is a scene "out of this world" it keeps the story moving forward as on this earth. Without doubt it encouraged Jesus to keep going on his movement toward Jerusalem and its redemptive suffering. But it was primarily to lift the disciples to a loftier view of Christ's approaching death. It was to enlighten and encourage them to "be hearing him." The story would help Theophilus "hear him."

AN OUTLINE OF LUKE 9:37-43
Christ in the Valley!
Jesus went from the tranquility of heaven on the mountain to the pain of humanity in the valley. The cross meets human need in the valley where men suffer.

I. THE TIME, PLACE, AND PEOPLE. 9:37-38a
   1. Time: "The next day..."
   2. Place: "having come down..."
   3. People: "A crowd met him."
   4. "A man from the crowd."

II. THE HUMAN NEED. 9:38b-40
   1. The father's plea: "Look on my son!"
     (a)My "only begotten."
     (b)"Spirit" possesses him!
   2. Disciples "unable" to cast it out.

III. THE RESPONSE OF JESUS. 9:41-42
   1. Christ's lament of disappointment.
   2. "Bring your son here."
   3. The son saved.
     (a)"Rebuked the unclean spirit."
     (b)"Healed the son."
     (c)"Gave him to the father."

The ease with which Jesus healed the father's son after the repeated failure of the nine disciples completely "struck the people out of themselves," which is to say, "they went on being astounded, dumbfounded, dazzled at the majesty of God!" God's restoring of health displays his grandeur more than anything.

* * * * * * *

CHRIST IN THE VALLEY!
Without question Christ was lifted in spirit by his heavenly tryst. But at that rendezvous Moses, Elijah and Christ (the law, prophets, and gospel) agreed that displacing heaven's peace and choosing a painful, ignominious scandal of a cross would gain the greater glory! Dying to save man would harvest greater rewards than to have heaven without the fellowship of creatures cast in the "image of God." The cross would be less painful than a heaven that has abandoned man to the judgmental wrath of God. If one can see through and beyond the shadow of the valley of suffering there is a light of greater glory in rejection and death. With this in mind Jesus descended into the valley to deal with the pain of humanity. He met it head on in the person of a father's only son, sick with an unclean spirit.

The Time, Place, and People
"It came to pass on the next day" states Luke. Apparently the mountain transfiguration was a night time adventure. But dawn had arrived by the time Jesus and the three got to the valley. The turmoil they met contrasted with the tranquility of the night before. The chaos on earth is a perpetual contrast to the harmony of heaven. It's the difference between hate and love, sin and salvation, war and peace!

150

The text continues: "they having come down from the mountain a large crowd met him." From the inspiration and vision on the mountainside they "came down to humanity's harsh realities in the valley. The "valley" is where the "crowd" lives, labors, does business, suffers and dies. Even those who live high above the shadows have to come down to the level of the common man to get and give the necessities of life. Sickness and death drive even the high and mighty into the common lot of human heartaches. It's down in the valley where men face sin, suffering, and death. When Jesus came down from the night's mountain vigil the first thing he confronted was a "great crowd." But crowds are made up of individuals each with his own particular physical, mental, emotional, spiritual pain. All humans hurt! Sin and suffering is the common denominator that threads its way through humanity.

"And behold! A man from out of the crowd..." It's as though by design a "man from out of the crowd" in his desperation typified the entire crowd. Luke's story focuses on a specific man's pain and thereby exemplifies every man's need. If Christ can conquer this man's pain he can control any man's need.

A Father's Plea!

The man cried out saying, "Teacher, I'm begging you to look upon my son,..." If the God of heaven be "living," Creator of all creation, he has much to occupy his attention. How can he "look upon" one single, simple, soul? And even in the time span of the one life and ministry of Jesus as God's representative how can he give detailed attention to one individual demon possessed lunatic? Yet the father entreated, "Lord, take time to look upon my son!"

Then the father fortified his plea with a very personal reason. "He is my only begotten." He has no brother, no sister. He is our sole joy, our only hope to perpetuate the family.

So the problem the father lays out in detail. "A spirit grabs him, and suddenly he cries out and seizes him with foam. And when he departs he goes with difficulty, crushing him terribly." Luke describes him as an "unclean spirit." This was an instance of demon possession. But it was unusual in that the "spirit" had taken control while the lad was young. The seizures had wracked the lad's life from childhood. It was out of hopeless despair that the father came. His last hope was the famed Teacher of Galilee. But alas, the Teacher was on the mountainside. In his desperation the man approached the nine disciples left in the valley. But "I begged your disciples to cast it out and they were not able."

This is what Jesus faced when he descended from the mountain. To him it was a confrontation of the cross about which he conversed with Moses and Elijah. It was an opportunity to demonstrate what the cross means in the affairs of a day. Shall I shun or bare the pain of another? Shall I subserve my desires to the suffering of another. Shall I save myself or give myself to the needs of another? In the valley of suffering this is the meaning of the transfiguration.

151

The Lament of Disappointment!

When Jesus heard the father's cry, "I begged your disciples that they cast it out and they weren't able," he burst out with a deep lament, "O faithless and perverse generation, how long shall I be with you and endure you?" Indeed, how human can God get? If man is "in the image of God" then God _is_ the prototype of man. He is the model on which he created human kind. God is the model-man, if you please! God possesses in ideal measure every trait found in man. That, in the person of Jesus, includes impatience, frustration, disappointment. No "feeling" to which any man is capable lay beyond the range of the human Jesus. Hence, here Jesus let his feeling of impatient disappointment break through the veil of flesh. After the storm not many days before he had exclaimed, "Where is your faith?" They had witnessed the cleansing of the Gerasene demon possessed, the feeding of 5000, and had themselves confessed him "the Christ of God!" Even on their Galilean preaching mission they had healed and cast out demons. Why now should they fail to heal this lad through lack of faith?

We note that faith can fail. Jesus had more in mind than just the disciples when he sounded off, "How long shall I tolerate you?" When faith bathes in an environment of doubt it is hard to hold onto faith. As a sponge soaks up water faith can absorb doubt. When Jesus spoke of "faithless generation" he was referring to that "generation." Israel as the household of faith was compromised by doubt. It was not doubt as to the existence of God. They were "without faith" in the practical sense of "trust" in the God whom they believed to be objectively real. I may not doubt God's existence. But to "believe" he exists and then not "trust" him or heed him is to be "faithless," "without faith." Even the father recognized this dichotomy for Mark has him crying, "I believe; help thou my unbelief." The panic of the present can dilute the force of faith by inserting doubts.

The word "perverse" means "having been thoroughly turned around." It's possible that "faith," confronted by the reality of material fact, gets "turned completely around." It thus loses power to channel God's healing power. When faith floats in a sea of doubt it may end up faithless. That was true in the current case. "Your disciples were unable to cast it out!"

But the lack of faith on the part of the nine did not lessen the power of faith to heal. So Jesus, full of faith fortified by the transfiguration called, "Bring here your son!" All God needs is a channel unsullied by doubt. The demoniacal forces of evil will not give up to God without a struggle, however desperate. The Legion of Gerasa had sought final refuge in a herd of hogs. In the present instance the unclean spirit exploded in a final frenzied effort to destroy the lad. "The demon ripped him (to shreds) and crushed him (as in a vice)." It would seem that the Evil that dominated this young man, knowing that his control was at an end, would do as much harm as possible. He left the lad lacerated, bruised, limp as death.

The Son Saved!

In the process of saving the son Jesus did three deeds. He first "rebuked the unclean spirit." Then he "healed the child." After that he "gave him to his father." While closely related each conveys its own message.

Once again we note Jesus dealing with an "unclean spirit" as a distinct entity. The "spirit" has his own personality, separate from the boy. He is personal and can be addressed, talked to, "rebuked." Apparently the constitutional nature of "demons" is personal! That is the biblical view of the demonic world of spirits. The devil has his "angels" to do his bidding.

But besides dealing with the spirit Jesus had something further to do for the boy. "He healed the child." Evil disfigures everyone it touches. It bruises the body, distorts the mind, smirches the soul, stains the spirit. Thus though an "unclean spirit" is rebuked and repelled it leaves a sick body, mind, soul and spirit. The scars which the spirit has left need healing. The "spirit" is gone. But if the house isn't swept and kept clean, the spirit may return and do more damage than at the first. Jesus rid the lad of his epilepsy, gave him a clean mind, a strong body, and a purified spirit. The young man got a new beginning in life. He was now a "whole" person!

Nevertheless, he is still a young lad. He needs gentle guidance, firm discipline, and the affectionate support from a loving family. So Jesus "gave him to his father." Luke felt something important was involved in this act. The father, older, experienced, responsible, must do his part in providing an environment in which the young son can grow to mature into "the image of God" for which he was created.

These three saving elements are a pattern for the ministry of the church. The church is the "body of Christ," the "family of God." It provides the gospel power to drive out evil, heal the afflicted, and give the warmth of family support. This is the primary business of the church in the world.

The ease with which Jesus healed the father's son after the failure of the nine completely amazed the multitude. Our versions struggle to translate the descriptive imperfect ἐξεπλήσσοντο. They try, "were amazed," "astonished," "struck with awe," "utterly astounded." The word literally means "struck out of themselves." The imperfect suggests continued repeated action distributed over the entire crowd.

They were astonished at the "majesty" of God. The most exalted aspect that overwhelms man is the largeness of soul, the unpretentious dignity, the unceasing kindness, the infinite patience of God in his relationship to men in all their infirmities. God, in Christ, may be human enough to be disappointed and frustrated with the poverty of our faith but still he helps, heals, lifts, cleanses and restores us to his divine family. This is God's "majesty."

Cannot Theophilus clearly detect the human in Jesus in this story? And surely he feels the "majesty" of the divine Jesus?

AN OUTLINE OF LUKE 9:43b-50
Three Lesson on the Cross!
The cross casts its ominous shadow on all done and said from
this point on until Jesus is nailed to it. Christ is consumed
by it; the disciples are increasingly averse to it!
I.   EXHORTATION: LISTEN TO THE LESSON. 9:43b-45
      1. Excitement of the moment. 43b
      2. Warning: "Put these things in your ears." 44a
      3. "The son of man is about to be delivered up." 44b
      4. Dullness of the disciples. 45a
      5. Failure to "ask concerning" the lesson. 45b
II.   A CONSEQUENCE OF NOT LEARNING THE LESSON. 9:46-48
      1. A Disputation: "Who is greatest?" 46
      2. Jesus demonstrates the answer. 47-48
      (a)Placed a child at his side. 47
      (b)A measure that determines the greatest! 48
      3. Lesson of the cross throws light on who is great!
III. THE UNAFFILIATED DISCIPLE.9:49-50
      1. A different disciple observed. 49
      2. "Quit forbidding him." 50
      3. Lesson of the cross shows why.
The cross in the human history of Jesus climaxed his service
to man. But it also demonstrated the foundational principle of
God's program for men in a godless world.

* * * * * * *

THREE LESSONS ON THE CROSS!
From this point on all that Luke records he views as related
to the cross to be endured at Jerusalem. Both deed and teaching
articulate something relative to the cross in fact or in
principle. The cross in Christ's teaching will not become clear
to his followers until after he endures it in reality. But
everything reveals something about the cross. While the cross
consumes his attention, it is an unwelcome subject to the
disciples. They are callous to the idea of the Christ being
humiliated by suffering and death.
An Exhortation!
When Christ came down from the mountain the situation was
tense. For their failure to heal the demon-possessed boy the
nine disciples were warding off sneers of Jewish leaders. They
were in a confused state of mind over that failure. They were
feeling the emotional distress of the lad's father. Tensions
were running high and unity in their own ranks was stretched to
the breaking point.
The excitement aroused by Jesus' healing the epileptic
prompted a surge of emotion that was leading to the opposite
extreme. Christ's success erased the failure of the nine. The
ripple of animation kindled by the cure was furmenting feelings
dangerous to the stability of the disciples. Popular concepts
of political power were generating false hopes. Jesus must do
something immediately to curb the mistaken notions of kingdom
power.

154

After Peter's confession, "The Christ of God," Jesus taught his first open lesson that it was "necessary that the son of man suffer...be killed and rise on the third day." But that fell on deaf ears and hard hearts. They rejected such a possibility. Since then the transfiguration had come with its confirmation of the cross by Moses and Elijah. Yet the disciples were being carried away with the popular ideas of the kingdom's being a sovereignty of political power and its king ruling in Jerusalem. Somehow, someway, Jesus must arrest this false idea. In most solemn and forceful terms, he invited the undivided attention of the twelve, "You put these words into your ears.." By use of the personal pronoun "You" he not only gives special emphasis but he implies, "You of all people should understand that which I'm saying!" In other words, "There is no excuse for your not grasping that which I am teaching." Get your ears open and keep them open; let nothing distract you from hearing! In this, his second distinct lesson on the cross, Jesus omitted any reference to his resurrection lest even that distract their minds from the reality of what he was putting in their ears. If Jesus were living in our 20th century with its technology he would be saying this on TV in prime time followed by full page adds in national publications. "Let this sink into your ears." Don't let popular opinions distract you from the truth! He could be no more forceful.

The lesson, simply put, is this: "The son of man is about to be delivered into the hands of men." That's the simple truth, that's the reality which I, therefore you, must face. If I, as "son of man," son of righteousness, live in a sinful order then there can be no other end than to accept rejection by men who are controlled by sin's standards. "Put this in your ears, the son of man is about to be delivered into the hands of men."

Luke reports the reactions of the twelve to this counsel. "But they were remaining ignorant of this." The inability of the twelve to comprehend the announcement of his death baffles our ability to understand their inability. Of course we must remember that we look back on the events, an advantage which the first disciples did not have. In fact, after the death, and after the forty-day teaching period following the resurrection when they could no longer deny the fact, they faithfully taught the necessity and meaning of the death of the Christ.

But for the present they refused to accept the possibility of God's Christ as having to be subject to death. They were too steeped in the Old Testament and prevailing opinion that God's kingdom was to be patterned after every other kingdom with which they were familiar. Power of rule was invested in kings and governors and enforced by power of military and police action. And the kingdom of the Jews was to dominate "all the families of the earth." This, coupled with the immediate excitement of the people, was proving too much for the disciples. The necessity of the Christ's rejection and death could not take root in that kind of soil. "They were remaining ignorant of this matter, and it had been veiled from them so

155

they might not perceive it."

Besides all this, "they were fearing to ask him concerning this matter." When a student in a schoolroom is afraid to ask the teacher to resolve a problem he, the sudent, forfeits the opportunity to learn. He remains ignorant. Or if by reason of fear of his peers he fails to ask he also loses his opportunity to gain knowledge. The twelve were content to be blind. By staying spiritually illiterate they could cling to their political concept of the kingdom.

A Consequence of their not learning!

The cross of Christ took place at a point in history at a specific place in Jerusalem. But the cross of Christ was the outcropping of a universal principle that obtains in human existence in this sin-cursed world. Jesus had already told the twelve, "if anyone wishes to come after me...he is to take his cross daily..."(9:23) In ancient times capital punishment was the sole purpose of a cross. Literally and figuratively it was both in fact and symbol a reminder of the shame of death, a criminal's death! The death of the cross is an experience every follower of Jesus must endure; and that daily!

That which followed the disciples' failure to "put in their ears" the lesson of the cross they had to learn the hard way. They had to confront their cross in the fires of a dispute amongst their own group. "A reasoning (dispute) entered in among them, that is, Who might be greatest among them." Such a sharp personal argument could never have arisen had each been willing to "deny himself" and "suffer" the humiliation of treating the other as "better than himself." They could not see the necessity of Jesus' cross at Jerusalem. Therefore they failed to recognize the cross in their "daily" relationships with each other.

Little would it have helped had Jesus begun to point out this "dispute" as an example of their cross. If they could not comprehend his cross they certainly would be unable to perceive the necessity of their cross. Jesus decided to demonstrate in an object lesson what "taking up the cross daily" meant. Jesus "having taken a child, stood him alongside himself, and he said to them, Whoever shall receive this child in my name, receives me. And whoever receives me, receives the one who sent me. For the one existing as least among you, this one is greatest!" According to this standard the greatness of a man is not found in his position of political power or his physical prowess or his financial clout or social eminence. On the contrary, it's his ability to identify with the simplicity of spirit found in a little child. Innocence, meekness, desire to learn, and receptivity to such who have these virtues is the measure of a man's greatness. This is the "cross" in daily life.

And why should such a standard be a marvel? Is it not this very willingness of God to bend low to the need of the least that reveals his majesty? Men are most like God when they yield their selfish interest to that of another, even such a one as an unloveable brother.

156

A Third Lesson on the Cross!

Luke inserts another example of the disciples' failure to grasp the meaning of Christ's cross in their daily affairs. "John, having answered said, Master, we saw a certain one casting out demons in your name, and we repeatedly were forbidding him, because he does not follow with us." Here was a man who had never formally joined the band of disciples who "followed" Jesus in his public ministry. He's unaffiliated with "us" said John. That this man was "casting out demons" and accomplishing God's purifying among the people seemed to be of no value since he was not of "us." That implies that the virtue in the healing is in the "group" who does the healing deed rather than in the deed. When a man's doctrinal belief gets entangled with his cultural bias and academic ignorance, does that invalidate the faith of a sinner whom he leads to obedient faith in Jesus? What is the issue? Salvation for the lost or the one through whom the redemption is channelled?

Here again is the cross in human relationships. If my motive is to gain credit for "me" or "my group" then I avoid the cross. The goal of Christ and his redemption program is defeated. But if the goal is to redeem the lost and save the enemies of the kingdom, then the cross in me becomes the means of redemption.

Christ confirms that redemption is his goal, not partisan pride. Jesus said to John, "Quit forbidding him! For he who is not against us is for us." In other words, "healing is the goal, not the glory of him who does the healing!" If "he" casts out a demon that's one less demon that needs casting out. Inasmuch as that is what we came to do he's doing "our" work for us. He's on "our" side even though not "one of us."

"Every good and perfect gift....comes down from the Father..."(Jas.1:17) If an atheist has discovered the laws of the God whom he denies yet conforms to those laws in healing some mentally deranged human, praise God for the healing in spite of whom God used in the process. God is for health at every level, physical, mental, moral, spiritual. And if health comes through some group other than God's people then praise God for his grace. He values the healing more than the agent through whom he worked.

Like the cross of Christ at Jerusalem; like any cross, this is difficult to grasp, and having grasped it, more difficult to accept. Nevertheless, this is the cross in "daily" life.

In the light of what Luke sets forth in these lessons what is more universal than the cross? The cross is the supreme revelation to man of the nature of God.

Furthermore, what can be more human than for God's Christ to humble himself by yielding to the suffering of the cross? Theophilus could hardly miss the point!

AN OUTLINE OF LUKE 9:51-56
The Set Face!

"He <u>also</u> set his face to go to Jerusalem!" Nothing of worth in life is accomplished without a goal. To hit a bull's eye one must aim at the bull's eye. Jesus came on a specific mission. To do "right" in a world addicted to "wrong" he had to make hard choices. In Jerusalem rejection, suffering, and death were awaiting him. Yet with fixed determination he "set his face to go to Jerusalem." This was his goal. He "set his face" come what may! He "also" determined on this destiny.

I. THE SET FACE. 9:51
   1. During "the days of his being taken up." 51a
   2. "He set his face to go to Jerusalem." 51b
II. ON THE WAY REJECTION IN SAMARIA. 9:52-53
   1. Messengers to a "village of Samaria." 52
   2. The messengers rejected. 53
III. THE REACTION. 9:54-56
   1. Resentment of James and John. 54
   2. The Christ's reaction. 55-56
   (a)Rebuked James and John.
   (b)Went unto a "different village."

The "set face" fixes the goal. Obstacles delay but do not alter the goal. They simply drive us to different methods of reaching the goal. Life is not determined by chance but by providence. It is goal oriented!

* * * * * * *

THE SET FACE!

The text states: "...he (Jesus) <u>also</u> set his face to go to Jerusalem..." The word "<u>also</u>" intimates that someone before Jesus had determined that he "go to Jerusalem." Jesus was quite aware that at Jersualem he would meet a humiliating death. But when Luke recorded, "he <u>also</u> set his face" he is making clear to Theophilus that Jesus was himself "choosing" that which God before him had "set" for him.

Paul mentions that God, "selected...before the foundation of the world..."(Eph.1:4). He also says, "we have our redemption through his blood, the forgiveness of our trespasses."(Eph.1:7) The redemption of which Paul speaks occurred in Jerusalem through the death of which our text says, "he <u>also</u> set his face." So Jesus, in keeping with God's eternal choice, "also" freely chose to set out on the final lap of his mission!

The Set Face!

Luke 9:51 reflects some noteworthy ideas. "While the days of his being taken up were being fulfilled..." The phrase "were being fulfilled" means "the gradual filling up of a series of days which form a complete period, and extend to a goal determined beforehand."(Godet, Luke, pg.288) The present tense denotes a <u>continuous fulfilling</u> of the days involved. The form of the verb (ἐν τῷ and infinitive) indicates a temporal idea "<u>while</u> the days were being fulfilled."

158

The phrase "of his being taken up" depicts a word compounded of ἀνά "up" and verb λαμβάνω "take." It is a Genitive action noun, "of the taking up." The noun is difficult to render in English. The versions resort to participle "taking up" or finite passive "being taken up." But it's a noun pointing to Christ's ascension including his death. Genitive case is adjectival in force describing "the days." "The days of his being taken up" represent the period beginning with his descent through the virgin's womb, his growth to manhood, his public ministry including his trial, death, resurrection and ascension back to the glory from whence he came.

Another point of emphasis which Luke uses in this verse is the personal pronoun αὐτός "he on his part set his face..." While these days of his being taken up" were moving toward completion "he also set his face to go to Jerusalem." This is a crucial point as he turns his face for the final trek to his divine destiny. It represents his determination against all opposition to see his task through to the end.

Rejection in Samaria!

The shortest distance between Galilee and Jerusalem is straight south through Samaria. Besides, Jesus wished to preach "the kingdom of God" to these traditional enemies of the Jews. For his large entourage Jesus must arrange lodging. So "he sent two messengers before his face. And they having gone ahead, entered into a village of the Samaritans so as to prepare for him." In ancient times clean safe public lodging was difficult if not impossible to obtain. Travellers were dependent on relatives, friends, or business associates for such accomodations. For Jews passing through Samaritan country it was doubly difficult due to the historic enmity between the peoples. Samaritans did not forbid Jews travelling through their land. But hospitality was another matter.

An added feature fuelled the fires of hostility. "They received him not because his face was journeying to Jerusalem." Ample evidence is available that people, including Jews, going south from north to Jerusalem travelled through Samaria. But something in his face generated resentment to the point of intolerance. They would not approve his presence even for one night.

Commentators struggle in attempts to explain this cause for the Samaritans' rejection. To what does Luke refer by "because he set his face to go to Jerusalem!" We need not look to any gruff abusive approach on the part of the two messengers as causing this abrupt rejection. With notable emphasis the text states, "He set his face..." And it adds, "...because his face was going..." The term "face" may be rendered "person." Something about his person made them reluctant to receive him. When Jesus turned his "face" toward Jerusalem he stiffened his resolve, he firmed up his feelings, he radiated a holy enthusiasm. His whole personality diffused the light that flamed in his soul. He knew what lay ahead; the disciples, though they don't know, have a foreboding of danger ahead!

159

Beginning at the point of Peter's confession, "The Christ of God" Jesus taught often and plainly the necesity of his death. And though he exhorted them to "tell no man" that he was the "Christ of God" he obviously accepted the confession as true. He was indeed the "Christ of God." And as the "Christ of God" his kingship involved a frightful miscarriage of justice about to be imposed in Jerusalem. Something about his face, his person, radiated that destiny. This "village of the Samaritans" did not want to be a part of that scenario. Their rejection of Jesus had to do with his Christhood, his spiritual kingdom. They would wash their hands of him and his kingdom.

But it is impossible to wash one's hands of the Christ. He and his kingdom are so innately and universally human that none can escape him. The rejection by this Samaritan village presaged Jerusalem's rejection of Jesus. The world did not and does not want Jesus as king. His view of God as sovereign king over men's souls, as expecting and demanding upright moral character, was and is unacceptable to humanity. Man rebels against such autocratic authority over his spirit. The Samaritans foreshadowed what would happen at Jerusalem and what would repeat itself throughout human history. The God of the Bible as revealed by Jesus Christ is not welcome in the villages of the world.

The Reaction!

When James and John, observed the rejection of their Master, they were outraged! With frantic anger they exploded to Jesus, "Lord, are you wishing that we call fire down from heaven and destroy them?" They had good Old Testament precedent for a prophet of God to destroy such ememies by an all consuming fire from on high. Elijah, recently again on earth at the transfiguration, called fire down to destroy the prophets of Baal. Certainly these Samaritans deserved as much!

How little does the mind of man grasp the infinite grace and loving purpose of God toward all men including those who curse and reject God. Do not we even yet wonder why God does not rain destruction on men and nations who violate every law of divine decency? As the Samaritans' rejection of a night's lodging reflects humanity's rejection, so the livid wish for flaming revenge typifies mankind's rash reaction for those who reject God's moral sovereignty.

But the reaction of Jesus to their reaction brings into focus the right reaction. "Having turned he rebuked them!" The rash anger voiced by the two disciples got strong censure. Such an attitude does not reflect the redemptive purposes for which Christ came into the world. It got prompt correction. It must not become a standard for behaviour. Such an attitude toward God's enemies is alien to God's nature or purposes.

Something divinely eloquent appears in the next reaction of Jesus. He did not rebuke the Samaritans. Having rebuked the disciples "they went to another village." The word translated "another" means "another of a different kind." Jesus had no quarrel with the Samaritan villagers who refused him. Jesus

160

offered himself as a guest to the Samaritans but he would not
impose himself on them. They must be willing or he will just
turn to "another village" that will receive him.

Life as Jesus viewed it is not determined by chance, luck,
or the dice throw of men. It is governed by the providence of
God. That means that God is guiding through the maze of this
rebellious and rebelling world of evil. God fixed a goal for
Jesus. As our Lord walked through his earthly career he "set
his face" to fulfill that goal. When people, villages,
cultures, and civilizations, thwart and block him on his
journey toward his chosen goal he simply uses a different
method to reach his appointed destiny. He goes to a "different
kind" of village. But he never changes his purpose for that is
fixed. Thus with determined resolve he "sets his face to go to
Jerusalem!"

The awe that surrounded Jesus when he "set his face to go to
Jerusalem" is embedded in Luke 9:51. Christ's enthusiasm for
fulfilling God's purpose breathes in this verse. It cannot be
stifled in the words. It hides while it reveals! It declares
more than it says! There is something dramatically universal
and human in "he stiffened his face to go to Jerusalem."

It still remains true: "if anyone would come after me, let
him deny himself, and take up his cross daily and follow me."
Each man must find his own Jerusalem and "set his face to go!"

* * * * * * *

AN OUTLINE OF LUKE 9:57-62
Three Candidates for the Kingdom!

Jesus came to gain followers! But he would take only those
who appreciate the cost involved. Three candidates exemplify
the cost!
   I.   THE CROSS! 9:57-58
        1. A Volunteer:"I will follow wherever you go."
        2. "The son does not have where he may lay his head."
   II. THE PRIMACY OF THE KINGDOM. 9:59-60
        1. An Invitation: "Be following me!"
        2. "Permit me first to bury my father!"
        3. "Let the dead bury the dead."
   III. LEARN TO PLOW AHEAD! 9:61-62
        1. A Volunteer: "Permit me to say goodbye!"
        2. To plow straight keep your eye on the goal.

One must pay a high price to follow Jesus "wherever he
goes." The cost includes giving oneself up to a cross, making
kingdom interest of primary concern, and keeping your eye on
the kingdom goal regardless of temptations to deviate!

THREE CANDIDATES FOR THE KINGDOM!

When Luke mentions these three immediately after Jesus "set his face to go to Jerusalem" he is making clear to Theophilus the cost of discipleship. Redemption cost Jesus his life. But it also costs, in one form or another, the life of anyone who would "follow" Jesus. The underlying theme in each case is the necessity of the cross!

Self Confidence and the Cross!

Jesus has "set his face to go to Jerusalem" the last time. "And as they were going in the way a certain one said to him, 'I will follow you wherever you go.'" This, to say the least, shows an inflated confidence in his own reliability. Self confidence is not necessarily a bad trait. But it must be viewed as God's gift, not self achievement. Without some confidence we would take little if any initiative to do great things for God. But when this man asserted with such unmodified selfconfidence, "I will follow you wherever you go," he was not aware of where Jesus was going. This young would-be candidate ought to know that Jesus had just "set his face to go to Jerusalem." And he wasn't headed on a sight-seeing tour; he was headed for a cross of shame! Thus in the light of where Jesus was going this young volunteer must examine himself. Does he wish to go to a cross with Jesus? Jesus came into this world to gain disciples. But he would invite only those who knew the cost and would freely take the cross as their calling.

So it is that Jesus gives this particular young man a rather enigmatic answer. "The foxes have holes and the birds of the heaven nesting places, but the son of man does not have where he may lay his head." When men go fox-hunting they sit by an open fire while the dogs chase the foxes. The fox, growing up in any given countryside, knows where all the caverns are, the hollow logs, and all such places of refuge. He can cross and criss-cross his own trail in order to throw the hounds off his trail. Jesus is saying that though the foxes have places of refuge when the dogs are after them, "I have no such place to hide." Certainly Jesus had numerous homes throughout the land in which he would be a welcome guest. He wasn't saying that he had no places of rest available. What he was saying was that the Pharisaic hounds were after him and he had no place where he could lay his head and they not find him. In other words, "I want you to follow me but know for sure you cannot follow me where I'm going and escape a cross."

The Primacy of the Kingdom!

The first potential recruit was a volunteer. To the second Jesus extended an invitation. "He said to another (of a different kind), 'Be following me!'" Jesus was relentless in seeking out disciples. Even though he was on his final journey to his Jerusalem death he still sought to gain new disciples. In fact, the shadow which the cross cast over his life intensified his desire for more disciples. After all, the cross was the heart of his redemptive message, the central core of the kingdom he came to proclaim. The sooner a prospective candidate faced the cross the better disciple he would be.

162

The second prospect did not show self-confidence. On the contrary, he needed encouragement, an urging to overcome hindrances. So Jesus worded his invitation with care. "You be my constant continuing follower." Jesus wanted undivided dedication that could cut loose from all other obligations.

The answer of this second candidate does not show unwillingness. It does reveal a certain hesitation rooted in customs of the current culture. "But that one said, 'Permit me first, having gone off, to bury my father.'" What could be more reasonable? A funeral would take at most a few days. Then he would be free to indulge his desire to follow Jesus. No question of where was raised. We assume his hesitation was not because he would face a cross. That's not the issue.

Here is an instance in which the custom of first century Jewish Palestine is at variance with 20th century western social custom. This man's father was not dead; it was not a corpse needing to be put in a sepulchre that hindered the young man.

Modern social security systems were never dreamed of in that place or those days. Their social system, if it be called that, was formed around the family clan. The head of the clan was the patriarch and matriarch. The father led the destiny of the entire clan. He made final decisions and directed the interests of the clan. And this clan consisted of more than a father and mother and a child or two. Besides the old parents it embraced numerous grown children with offsprings, servants, cattle and possessions. When the patriarch became too old and feeble to direct the business of the clan he would give way, usually to the eldest son. As long as he, the older patriarch, lived it was the responsibility of the younger leader to care for his father and mother until they died and were buried. Thus it is that when this young man was invited to "follow" Jesus full time, in effect he said, "I want to follow but I have a prior social obligation. I must care for my father as long as he lives. Then I will be free for more personal ambitions." The choice faced was between two possibilities: the kingdom of God or society's demand to care for an aging father.

The answer of Jesus was, "You allow the dead to bury their own dead, but you, when you've gone off, declare the kingdom of God." Jesus was not forbidding the young man to attend his father's funeral. In effect he was saying that others who had not caught the vision of the kingdom could discharge the pressing social obligations. But "you who have caught the vision of who I am and why I have come and where I am going, your primary obligation is to proclaim the kingdom of God." Others in the clan who do not, at least have not, caught the primacy of God's kingdom, they are to discharge the social obligations of life. But "you publish abroad the kingdom of God." This is the primary obligation, (even for society) of a kingdom candidate. Nothing in the cultures of this world transcends the kingdom man's obligation to God's kingdom! "Seek you first the kingdom of God."

163

Plowing Straight Ahead!

Once again a volunteer offers himself: "I will follow you, Lord. But first permit me to bid adieu to those of my house." He wanted to turn back before he trudged forward! He was diverted by the emotional pull of his family ties before he would unreservedly attach himself to the disciple band. He did not shrink from the severity of the cross. It was more a distraction from concentration on the cross. He wished for a final goodbye before losing himself in the cause of Christ!

In his response Jesus employed a figure common to farmers of all ages and every land. "No one having put his hand upon a plow and looking back is suited for the kingdom of God." In order to plow a straight furrow a plowman must keep his eye on a fixed object across the field. I recall a grizzled East Tennesse hill farmhand telling of an unusual experience of plowing. When he started a new row he fixed his eye on an enlarged hump at the top of a fencepost across the field. He carefully kept his eye on the fence top. Behold! When he reached the other side the "hump" was a small rooster. It had slowly moved down the fence. The furrow he had plowed formed a half moon curve. He applied the correct principle of concentration but had picked a moving object.

But the point of Jesus was: "If you do not know how to keep an undivided mind on your plowing you can't farm in my field." The common experience of plowmen supports the need for keeping the eye on a fixed object. If the plowman looks back to see if he is plowing straight, at the point where he turned to look a jog in the furrow will appear. Moreover the Palestinian plowman had an added incentive to keep his concentration. He struggled with rock infested fields. He had only sharply shaped wooden plowshares with which to turn the unyielding soil.

To this candidate Jesus is insisting that an undivided mind is absolutely essential for a disciple of his. No double vision is possible. No half work is acceptable. Discipleship cannot be a first this and then that journey. No man can farm for Jesus if he is not decisive in his commitment.

What does the story of these three say to Theophilus? They increase the sense of the humanity of Jesus. His feet are on solid ground of human experience. He knows when evil huntsmen pursue good men, unlike birds, they can not lose themselves in the foliage of the trees. Good can't escape the cross that evil raises. This is not only human it is universal to men of all ages, cultures, and places. Theophilus learns that kingdom demands bridge all divisions of humanity. The primacy of the kingdom is laid on men as men, not on fragments of the human race. Moreover, if Theophilus is considering discipleship he is aware that there is no looking back. It's Christ or nothing! Anything that is universal is true and that which is true is universal. Truth belongs to humans as humans!

AN OUTLINE OF LUKE 10:1-24
"I Saw Satan Falling!"

Christ came to destroy evil. Human evil is rooted in unseen spiritual forces which from the biblical viewpoint reside in the person and power of Satan. He must fall before man can rise from his evil. This episode gives a snapshot of the method by which Satan falls.

I. THE MISSION OF THE SEVENTY. 10:1-16
  1. Jesus "sent them two by two." 1
  2. Reason for the mission:"the harvest is great." 2
  3. Conduct on the mission. 3-12
     (a)Travel light and in haste.
     (b)Giving and withholding "your peace."
     (c)Securing food, drink,and material support.
  4. Warnings on three cities. 13-16
     (a)On Chorazin and Bethsaida. 13-14
     (b)On Capernaum. 15
     (c)Rejections in terms of the persons heard.
II. RESULTS OF THE MISSION. 10:17-24
  1. Rejoicing of the seventy. 17
  2. The joy of Jesus: 18-21
     (a)"I was seeing Satan falling!" 18
     (b)Promise of protection in dangers. 19
     (c)Where to find true joy. 20
     (d)Thanksgiving for revealing to "babes."
  3. Reciprocal knowledge: Disciples, Son, Father. 22
  4. Blessing pronounced on the disciples. 23-24
God in Christ has decreed that Satan "falls" by declaring the "kingdom of God." His Word brings down evil in high places.

* * * * * * *

"I SAW SATAN FALLING!"

The whole purpose of Christ's invasion of this world was to eradicate evil at its source. Sin manifests itself outwardly in an infinite variety of forms. But at bottom it is a spiritual problem rooted in the spirit and heart. According to the biblical account of the origin of evil it springs from the personal presence and power of Satan. By lie and guile he led man into doubt and distrust of God. Once man had set himself against the will of God the sordid evil of man has made a hell out of the beauty of the world. Christ came to restore the pristine "image of God" in man. He must eliminate evil!

The Mission of the Seventy!

Rejected by a "village of the Samaritans," Jesus "went unto a different village." Whether it was another Samaritan village or one along the southern borders of Galilee is not stated. Maybe he journeyed along both travelling east toward the Decapolis east of the Jordan. But the "harvest was great" and he had limited time and few workers. So he planned another sweeping preaching mission, this time he "appointed and sent them two by two before his face unto every city and place where he was about to go."

Two is better than twice one! In life's tasks men working alone inevitably fall into periods of deep depression, dark discouragement and defeat. But working in twos the gifts of one support and sustain the other. This is especially true in the teaching of truth in a world darkened by falsehood. At creation God said, "It is not good for man to be alone." So it was that Jesus strengthened the message of the kingdom by deputizing the heralds "two by two." Indeed "two" is more than twice one!

The need for such a preaching mission at this late point in the redemptive work of the Christ was pressing. "The harvest is great; the workers are few." No human being is without infinite moral value. Each is a grain which contains seed for potential harvest beyond imagination. Not only can he grow in personal moral development but he can germinate into a vast field of like grains.

But "the laborers are few!" In a world saturated with sin workers with vision of the unharvested grain fields are so inadequate in numbers. The enormity of the harvest disheartens the few available workers. In view of the need for laborers should workers take off from their harvesting to recruit other workers? Christ's answer is, "Pray the Lord of the harvest that <u>he</u> cast (new) workers out unto his harvest." Send petitions to the owner of the farm that he get more farm hands. Petitions, even complaints, have often been helpful in improving working conditions, not to mention production results. Use that same principle in relationship to God. "Be praying that the Master of the harvest be **aggressive** in sending more laborers into <u>his</u> harvest." God is <u>person</u>! Thus he can be influenced by <u>the</u> workers' concern about <u>his</u> harvest. The nature of his "grain" field is such that he wants the worker to have a personal concern about getting the harvest into the barns. Persons respond to personal interests. Therefore, "<u>You</u> be praying..."

Conduct on the mission!

Instructions to the seventy for their immediate mission had its local, temporary limits. But it contains timeless lessons for harvesters of all ages. Jesus laid down three timeless truths about harvesting for God's kingdom. Travel light and be in haste on your mission. Give and withold your "peace" determined by acceptance or rejection of the message. The "worker is worthy of his pay!"

"Haste makes waste" is proverbial. But to be loitering while on such a critical mission is self defeating. The urgency of life and death involved in the kingdom message allows for no sluggish foot-dragging. "The harvest is great!" So the work demands complete concentration without distraction. Don't stop to admire the beauty of the grain field; harvest it!

You carry a message of redemption and hope. Be it one household or an entire city leave your blessing of "peace" where it is welcomed. But if unwelcome in home or city "let your peace return upon you" and go on and find the next one who will welcome it. It's a critical message and a critical time. Don't hesitate; give peace to those who want it; press on when rejected!

166

Travelling in the Graeco-Roman world lodging was a problem. Safe clean housing was almost non existant. Relatives, friends or acquaintances furnished the best housing along the Roman road system. In Palestine, with its heavy Jewish population, the sense of kinship may have been stronger. Movement toward the annual religious feasts inspired opening the homes to those enroute to the Holy City. Jesus encouraged his disciples to stay in "whichever house you enter...eating and drinking that which is placed before you." Material support was clothed in the custom of the times. But the abiding principle is, "the worker is worthy of his pay." The harvester of grain grows grain to feed the needs of many people. But he feeds his own family out of that which he produces for others. A factory worker labors to supply products essential to a wider public. But in so providing he gains a living for himself and his family. Such mutual benefit finds a place in supporting the preacher of the kingdom of God. Out of serving salvation to others the harbinger of truth makes gain for himself. No matter what the economic system "the worker is worthy of his pay!"

Warning on three cities!

Privilege always brings responsibility! To him who receives much, much shall be required. This includes opportunities to receive the king and the kingdom of God. In his instructions to his disciples Jesus included a warning of judgment. "Woe to you, Chorazin, woe to you Bethsaida! for if in Tyre and Sidon the mighty powers, the ones which came among you, sitting in sackcloth and ashes, long ago they would have repented. But for Tyre and Sidon it would've been more tolerable in the judgment than for you." No question that the cultural centers of pagan idolatry should find destruction "in the judgment." But more so for Chorazin and Bethsaida because of greater opportunity in witnessing the personal presence of the living God incarnate.

Even among contemporaries does this principle adhere. Look at Capernaum! This city by the sea became the earthly home of him who came from heaven to man. Not even Jerusalem had so great an honored privilege. The "daily" life plus innumerable special works of the Christ were spread before the eyes of Capernaum's citizens. Indeed, these people were privileged to peer into the halls of heaven. They remained profoundly blind.

"You, Capernaum! you won't be exalted to heaven will you? You shall be cast down to Hades!" If Chorazin, Bethsaida, and Capernaum were so privileged how much more those who have two milleniums of history to bear witness to the redeeming power of the son of Man? Where the light shines there responsibility falls heaviest! If one curses the darkness where the sun is shining it can only mean that his eyes he has closed.

Rejection of him who bears the light is really rejection of him who is the light! "The one hearing you hears me, and the one rejecting you rejects me! And the one rejecting me rejects the one who sent me." When men reject the message of the kingdom it isn't the message but the king who is rejected. It's the person of the Christ, the person of God who is being set at naught.

167

In giving instructions to the seventy Jesus repeated, "Upon you the kingdom of God has drawn near!" It was to be pronounced by his disciples as they left every city whether it accepted or rejected the message. In a word, each town is to recognize its own responsibility in receiving or repudiating the kingdom of God. Where God makes himself known there can be no shunning of responsibility. The presence or absence of light determines guilt. Each must be told, "The kingdom of God has drawn near."

Results of the Mission!

At an appointed time and place the seventy returned to Jesus to report the outcome of their preaching. "They returned with joy." Their elation was unbounded! They were electrified that "even the demons are subject to us in your name." They had been authorized by Jesus to "heal the sick" as proof "the kingdom of God has drawn near." So effective were their labors that even Satan's vassal agents were driven from their human captives. Their success exceeded expectations. To heal bodies they expected; but to drive out the controlling power of evil from the hearts of men was beyond their rational hopes.

The joy of the seventy sparked an outburst of joy from Jesus. Nowhere in scripture does Jesus better demonstrate the deep emotions of a human being than here. His feelings erupt in an outpouring of praise. First comes his joy over the fallen power of God's great adversary. "I was seeing Satan like lightning fallen from heaven." The old serpent, Satan, had thwarted God's eternal purpose at creation. He scarred the "image of God" in man. And while he had disrupted and delayed he could not destroy God's purpose. God simply set in motion his plan of redemption. In the triumph of the seventy Jesus caught a lightning-like vision of the fall of Satan. No longer would Satan be able to keep his vice-like grip on mankind. In driving disease and demons out of men the fall of Satan was confirmed. As Christ had defeated the Adversary in the wilderness so now his disciples drove out the same Satan from his hold on men. Jesus burst out in feelings of exultation that marked him as completely human. When Jesus sees Satan defeated by the seventy, his feelings reveal the depths of his humanity. The righteous rejoice at the defeat of the wicked!

But the "feelings" of Jesus on the success of the seventy did not blind him to the joy that they, the seventy, had already felt in the redeeming power of God's revelation. This too was part of Christ's vision of Satan's fall. "Behold! I have given to you the power to tread upon serpents and scorpions and upon every power of the enemy, and nothing shall harm you!" Being a disciple of Jesus will not release men from the pain and death common to all men. But it does assure of protection through such mortal ordeals. Christ's men cannot be "harmed" by such distress. In fact adversity is a tool in God's hands by which he shapes his own into what he wants them to be. These seventy had just tread on arrogant Pharisaical "serpents" and learned scribal "scorpions." After such conflicts they had returned unharmed by such poisonous opponents.

168

Seeing hearts set free from the captivity to Satan's minions has no joy compared to that of one's own heart set free from sin. Jesus reminded of this. "But in this be not rejoicing that the spirits are subject to you, but rejoice that your names have been written in heaven." Defeating Satan in another's life is satisfying. But it is of no personal value unless one's own heart is rid of its evil. Exhilarating ecstasy that is personal comes from one's own salvation. It's not enough to say, "Lord, Lord, did we not prophecy and cast out demons in your name?" Preaching without purity may save others but personal salvation is the basis for genuine joy! Saving others fails to justify one's own failure in faith! God catalogues people! Hence, "Rejoice that your names have been registered in God's divine journal." Nothing can substitute for the validity of personal redemption!

The Divine Method of Revealing!

"In that very hour Jesus exulted in the spirit and said, 'I praise you, Father, Lord of heaven and earth, that you hid these things from wise and shrewd and revealed them to babes. Yea, Father, it seemed good before you.'" God's methods of educating people in his redemptive truth is foreign to man's ways. When men would "sell" something to vast numbers they seek endorsement from celebrities, the high and mighty, the "wise and sagacious." Not so God! "Not many wise...not many mighty...not many noble." God uses the "low and despised..." God prefers not to mix the alloy of human scientific learning with the pure truth of divine wisdom. In God's methods the "great" are humbled to find out that they aren't needed for God to succeed in his redemption project. The fact God uses "babes," the simple minded, childlike spirit of the least powerful shows that salvation comes only from his person and power. Even when God takes a learned man of the world, such as a Paul, before calling him God first must break him by the foolishness of his own folly. Paul had to learn, "It is no longer I who live, but Christ who lives in me."(Gal.2:20)

Jesus praised his heavenly Father for using instruments who had no wisdom other than that given from above. Pride of knowledge destroys a man's usefulness in kingdom work. Simple rustics, unlearned fishermen, the mean and lowly became channels through which the water of life streamed. By the lowliest of instruments God accomplished the greatest of works. The prize of the highest God gets through the humility of the lowest! For this wisdom Jesus "adores with an overflowing heart." For this contrarian method Jesus poured out his admiring praise. "Babes" are safer with truth than those who are inflated with their own importance!

The halo of praise generates joys of eternal relations! "All things were deposited with me by my father. And no one knows who is the son except the father and who is the father except the son, and he to whom the son wills to reveal him." The rock bottom foundation for all life, human and divine, is the interlinking of mind, heart, soul of divine persons and human persons "to whom the son wills to reveal him."

169

Knowledge of Son, Father and Disciple!

How do we share in divine power without which the fall of Satan cannot be realized? The answer lies buried in the words, "All was committed to me by my father. And no one knows who (what)the son is except the father and who(what)the father is except the son and he to whom the son wills to reveal him." Before "the foundation of the world" in eternity past "all was committed" to the Word(λόγος)which "became flesh" in time. But this "all" became realized progressively in the human Jesus as everything human must gradually grow to maturity. The "Word" was subject to birth. Then he must grow, enter his public ministry, die, rise, ascend to glory. As a man Jesus had to "learn."(Heb.5:8) So he progressed through every stage of human development. He learned, "all was given" to him for salvation and/or judgment. Furthermore, he learned that the conquest of Satan depended on his personal relationship to (knowledge of) God as his eternal father. "All" this was "given" in eternity past but, becoming human, even though it was always true, he had to learn it as man.

The truth just expounded rested on the reciprocal knowledge between him as son and God as father. "No one knows who (what) the son is except the father and who(what)the father is except the son..." The knowledge of which Jesus speaks is not knowing about the father. It rather indicates knowing the father, what it means to be "son" of the father.

The reverse is equally true. "No one knows the son (what it means to be son) except the father." Of all men Jesus alone "knows" (experiences) all that God is as father because he, Jesus, is son. And God "knows" all that Jesus is as son because he, God, is father. Jesus "feels" the fatherhood of God and God "feels" the sonship of Jesus. Because of their community of nature each understands the paternal filial relationship. It's this knowledge of God that bestows the power of the kingdom on those who experience it. The believer is included in this knowledge of God. Jesus said, "...and to him whom the son wills to reveal him." Though such experiential knowledge of God is the private privilege of the Son it becomes open to those who trust that son. It is the believer to whom the son "wills to reveal it." By participation in Jesus the Christ we share in the power of the kingdom. Men become conscious of sonship to God through faith in Jesus who reveals and bestows the power of knowledge. Everything that God is to Jesus is available to any man who commits himself in trust to Jesus. It's intuitive, experiential knowledge, the knowledge given to "babes" to whom "the son wills to reveal." Such knowledge can never be to the self-sufficient pseudo-wise of Jerusalem.

Though they were subjects of the kingdom and open to such incredible knowledge of God even the disciples could not yet appreciate their privileged place. "And having turned to his disciples, privately he said, 'Blessed the eyes, the ones seeing which things you are seeing. For I say to you that many prophets and kings wished to see what you see and didn't see, and to be hearing what you hear and did not hear.'"

170

Recently at the transfiguration Elijah the prophet and Moses the lawgiver had discussed with Jesus the "exodus which he was about to fulfill in Jerusalem." These eminent leaders in Israel had themselves seen in shadowy outline the coming of a "prophet like unto me." These and other "kings and prophets" led Israel to expect "one coming" who should lead them to "bless all the families" of the earth. But they knew little if anything of the nature of the one promised; and less as to the kind of kingdom he would bring. These are the ideas which formed the topic of conversation at the Transfiguration. To Moses and Elijah Jesus sketched in that which they and all "kings and prophets" had prefigured. He enlightened the deeper meaning of even that which Moses and Elijah had outlined.

Now the promised Christ had come in the person of Jesus. And "kings and prophets" had longed to see and hear that which he was revealing. Jesus would open the eyes and ears of his disciples to the greatness of his revelation and to the privilege of their being his agents.

It scarcely needs to be said that if they were so privileged, how much more those who have two milleniums of witness to the redeeming power of the gospel of God? Satan "falls" when the word of God is proclaimed. The message of the kingdom brings down evil in high places!

What could Theophilus make of all this? The deity of the Christ is matched by the reality of his humanity. It had all been "committed to him" in eternity but he had "learned" in a growing, developing human experience as a mortal man. If Jesus rejoiced and marvelled at the wisdom of God in revealing it through "babes" it certainly would challenge a noble Greek to marvel at the inscrutable providence of God!

AN OUTLINE OF LUKE 10:25-37
Three Questions and an Answer!

To desire continued life at any level is universal. Fitness clubs, aerobic exercises, and health centers testify to man's hunger for physical life. All religions witness to the longing for life beyond life. Death opposes all instincts of the heart!

I. QUESTION: WHAT WORK, HAVING BEEN DONE, SAVES? 10:25-28
   1. Who asked the question? 25
   2. His motive for asking! 25
   3. The answer to which Jesus led him. 26-27a
   4. Praise of Jesus for the answer. 28

II. A SECOND QUESTION. 10:29-35
   1. "Who is my neighbor?" 29b
   2. Motive for the question. 29a
   3. The answer dramatized. 30-35
      (a)"A certain man fell among robbers."
      (b)Priest & Levite "passed by on the other side."
      (c)A Samaritan "cared for him."

III. A THIRD QUESTION. 10:36-37
   1. "Which of these three became neighbor?" 36
   2. "The one having made mercy." 37a
   3. "Go and do likewise."

The original question finds no answer in abstract truth or religious orthodoxy. It comes in practiced love; in becoming neighbor. That is the gift of grace.

* * * * * * *

THREE QUESTIONS AND AN ANSWER!

Humbolt cried, "O for another 100 years!" It's the cry of man as he turns from the grief of the grave. But given a hundred more years the cry would be, "O for a thousand more years." Thirst for life is insatiable. Time and its tyranny of minutes, months, and milleniums still limits life. Life is voracious, ravenous, craving to continue without ceasing. It is an aspect of the divine "image" making man kin to God. Longing for life was a persistent problem in the time of Jesus.

The Question Asked!

"And behold, a certain lawyer stood up testing him saying, Teacher, what, having done, shall I inherit eternal life?" He who asked possessed the finest education. Learned in law, disciplined in mind, conscientious in heart, though guilty, he wasn't calloused. His question was popular with scholar and layman reflecting universal concern.

The lawyer was "testing" one not "recognized" by the rabbis. Though unordained Jesus appealed to the people. Was he orthodox? Was he skillful in intellectual, theological debate? These may have motivated the lawyer to "test" Jesus. But his incentive may have been less noble. He was of that class whose enmity was thoroughly aroused. He may have tried to trap Jesus. A combination of all these reasons might have stimulated him.

By his question the lawyer adopted the view that God would

not grant eternal life without demanding some specific deed that would merit such a reward. He was obviously a man of good repute, one who merited the good will of his fellow citizens. He was respectable, upright, law-abidng, socially sensitive, a responsible community leader. These very virtues underlay his inquiring of such a popular teacher as Jesus. Quite possibly he already had his idea as to the answer to his own question. But he would "test" to see how Jesus' answer might measure at the side of his own. Such a test could determine whether Jesus was worthy of his popular acclaim or even whether he as a prominent scribe should reject or accept him as Teacher!

Jesus did not give a direct answer. He answered the question with a question. He challenged the man to use his knowledge of the law. He turned the question back upon the lawyer. "In the law, what stands written? How are you reading?" In this double question Jesus focused on two factors. One, What does your law say about your question? Two, How do you interpret what it says? That is, What does it mean by what it says?

Language is the best means men have for communication but it has limitations. We not only must know what language says but also what it means by what it says. Words in a context may mean, on occasion, the very opposite of what they, out of a context, seem to say. "The horse is fast..." may mean he is tied fast to a post. Or it can mean that he runs fast in a race. Context determines meaning. So Jesus asked, "What does the law say in relation to your question?" And "How do you read the meaning of what it says?"

Thus answering by a double question Jesus placed the "test" squarely on the lawyer. The lawyer is now himself on trial! And yet Jesus did answer the lawyer's question. He challenged the man's thinking until he himself discovered the answer. One learns better by working out a problem than by being handed an answer. Without hesitation the lawyer responded to Jesus' challenge, "You shall love the Lord your God out of your whole heart and in your whole soul and in your whole strength and in your whole mind and your neighbor as yourself." The first part of this answer appears in Deut.6:5, the second part from Lev.19:18. The Jews practiced repeating this each day, morning and evening. Thus the lawyer had this ingrained within since youth. It contained the essence of the law. It is also the essence of the gospel. The law and the gospel have the same goal. They differ in method and the power to perform. In his life, death and resurrection Jesus exemplified love for God and every man in his need. Small wonder that Jesus gave the lawyer high marks for his answer. Jesus could himself identify with the lawyer's judgment. The "work" which the lawyer sought was not a "work" but a disposition of heart, a complete, absolute, unmarred love for God from (ἐκ) the heart. And if a man so love God there's no way he can with-hold love for his neighbor. "By this we know love, that he laid down his life for us; we ought to lay down our lives for the brethren."(I Jn.3:16) Jesus revealed what love is; the believer is impelled to meet the brother's need; "lay down our lives for the brethren." So Jesus extolled the lawyer's answer, "You answered correctly. This <u>be</u> <u>doing</u> and you shall get life." The Lord signified that love <u>is</u> something to <u>do</u>. It's more than a warm-hearted feeling or an emotional reaction! Love is intelligent good <u>will</u>. It is to <u>will</u> the highest good whether the object of the love is lovable or not.

A Second Question!

The lawyer found himself completely disarmed. If his motives were of the lower nature he felt defeated and embarrassed. If his motives were of the higher order his guilt was deepened. He manifestly was disconcerted and sought to cover himself with a rational defense. The text reports: "That one, wishing to justify himself, said to Jesus, 'And who is my neighbor?'" For Jews "neighbor" encompassed only fellow Jews. Gentiles could not be neighbors. This lawyer never considered any Gentile as a possible neighbor. His guilt sprang from lack of demonstrated love toward fellow Jews or he was trying to justify his Jewish prejudice against Gentiles.

At any rate Jesus dramatizes his answer by encasing it in an oft-repeated experience of the Jerusalem-Jericho road. Jesus, having picked up the man's question said, "A certain man was going down from Jerusalem to Jericho, and he fell among robbers, who also having stripped him of his clothes and having flogged him, they went off, having left him half dead."

Jesus described a man whose desperate need no one could question. Here was a Jew returning from a business trip to the capital city who was hurrying home to the warmth of his family at Jericho. As often happened on this robber-infested road he "fell among thieves" who having plundered his goods, flayed him to within an inch of his life.

The capacity of human beings to respond to human misfortune is a remarkable trait of human nature. Members of a labor union on strike risked their own lives for "scabs" and strike breakers trapped in coal mines as they labored. Incredibly these men who one moment threatened to kill the hated "scabs" the next hour hazarded their lives to save the very same men they just cursed. Amazing expression of the divine "image" buried in man's heart and soul.

Surely this universal human trait would appear in Jewish hearts! Their entire history was one in which the living God revealed his love and redemptive purposes. Their laws and traditions inspired them to help the poor and pain-ridden. On the other hand that very human quality of free choice makes it possible to muzzle the heart against a wounded man's extremity. In his story Jesus shows two temple servants of God deliberately choosing not to bind the wounds of a broken piece of humanity; and a fellow Jew at that! "But by coincidence a certain priest was going down that way, and having seen him he came along opposite on the other side. And likewise also a Levite, having come down along the place, when he saw he went by opposite on the other side." Two functionaries of the living God having just engaged in service at the temple in behalf of sinful man, now by choice stepped to the other side of the road

174

rather than contaminate themselves with the blood of a brother Jew. With evidence of violent robbers being in the vicinity they would not risk delaying their journey. For whatever reason they suppressed any impulse toward compassion. Here were two whose calling as God's servants was to serve the needs of fellow men yet they failed the opportunity that by "coincidence" was thrust on them! They did not see this abused Jew as "neighbor."

The story continues. "But a certain Samaritan, as he was travelling, came down to him and having seen, was moved with compassion. And having come to him he bound his wounds supplying oil and wine. And having put him on his own donkey, he brought him unto an Inn and cared for him." This man, by virtue of being a Samaritan, was hated by Jews. Yet the common bond of being <u>human</u> stirred him to reach out to the <u>need</u>. His humanity transcended racial and national differences.

But he went beyond the immediate hurt. He used his own donkey as an ambulance and brought him to the nearest public Inn. Then "on the morrow he gave the innkeeper" enough money for two months care. This Samaritan apparently travelled this way regularly. He told the innkeeper, "Whatever you may spend <u>I</u> on my return will repay you." His "care" for the hapless Jew, a human, went beyond the usual. It extended over weeks until the fallen man was firmly on his feet again.

A Third Question!

The crucial question comes at the close of the parable. Jesus proposes to the lawyer, "Who of these three does it appear to you to have become neighbor to the one who fell among the robbers?" Jesus reverses the question! The lawyer had asked, "Who is my neighbor?" Jesus answered, "To whom are <u>you</u> a neighbor?" A neighbor is not determined by geography, culture, race or any other bond that is not inherent in man as man. A neighbor is that <u>human</u> being, whoever he may be, to whom providence leads to meet a <u>need</u>! The question ought to be, "To whom may I <u>be</u> neighbor?"

Questions normally are asked to be answered. The lawyer confronts a dilemma he did not anticipate. The obvious answer choked in his throat. He would not say, "The Samaritan!" With restraint he forced out, "The one who made mercy with him." The word translated "made" carries the idea of producing a <u>deed</u>. So in the final response of Jesus he picked up that same word: "You go and <u>be doing</u> likewise." Jesus urged him to make such action a life practice, "be doing."

All this is not to say that being a neighbor is the basis on which eternal life is granted as pay for deeds done. On the contrary, the ability to love springs from the nature of Him who is love. "Love is from God, and everyone loving has been begotten from God..."(I Jn.4:7) Life here and hereafter is the gift of grace. The capacity, willingness, and determination to <u>be</u> a neighbor springs of God's grace. And love is not only the essence of God's nature, it is the most universal of human capabilities.

175

AN OUTLINE OF LUKE 10:38-42
The One Necessity!

The Jerusalem-Jericho road is the location of the episodes
of Luke 10:25-37 and 10:38-42. And the point of each section is
not unrelated. What one thing is essential to life?

I.   THE SETTING: JESUS AS GUEST. 10:38-39
     1. "He entered a certain village." 38
        (a)Bethany, village of Mary & Martha.
        (b)Jesus "received" into their home.
     2. Mary, "sat at his feet...hearing his word."
II. MARTHA'S COMPLAINT. 10:40
     1. "Distracted by much serving."
     2. "You care don't you that my sister left me alone?"
     3. "Tell her to take her part of the load with me."
III. THE ANSWER: ONE NECESSITY! 10:41-42
     1. "Martha, you are divided about many things."
     2. "Only one" is the supreme necessity!
     3. "Mary selected the good portion."

The lawyer asked, "What, having done, shall I inherit life?"
Mary sought and found that one necessity for genuine life. And
because she made it her priority it would not be denied her.

* * * * * * *

THE ONE NECESSITY!

Everything after Luke 9:51 when Jesus "set his face to go to
Jerusalem" relates to that final movement toward his cross,
burial, and resurrection. The narrative is not chronological.
Nor does it follow a geographical sequence. But the events do
have a significant moral psychological order. How to get life
is the theme linking the episodes of verses 21-37 and 38-42.
What is the one thing necessary?

From John 10:22ff we know that Jesus visited Bethany near
Jerusalem at the Feast of Tabernacles in winter before his
crucifixion. Luke does not tell Theophilus of that visit nor of
the intimate friendship of Jesus with Martha and Mary. Nor does
Luke report that they had a brother Lazarus whom Jesus raised
from the dead. These facts, while important for John's readers,
are not vital to the main point of Luke's present episode. They
do help fill in as to why Jesus was in Bethany just now, but
they aren't crucial for understanding the "one necessity," the
point of this story.

As far as the movement of Jesus is concerned he must have
made a quick journey to Bethany while the seventy were on their
preaching mission. He went to help prepare Martha and Mary for
their brother's crisis of death. But Luke's point in the story
is not Lazarus (he isn't even mentioned) but Mary's finding the
"one necessity" for life-fulfilling purpose.

The Setting: Jesus as Guest!

Luke introduces this story by alluding to the general
movement toward Jerusalem. "While they were journeying he
entered into a certain village." Emphatic pronoun subject "he"

contrasts to _they_ and implies that "he" alone became guest in the home. Their friendship of long standing excited Martha to "welcome him under her roof." As was her want Martha wished to shower her finest hospitality for their dear friend. She set about preparing a lavish meal demanding "much serving." Jesus did not object to her wish for a fine meal. But from his point of view food was secondary to his present purpose. He had come to serve more than to be served.

To Martha there "was a sister being called Mary, who having sat at the feet of the Lord, was hearing his word." "To sit at the feet" signifies "to be a pupil." We are not to suppose that Mary ignored her role as hostess. She "left" helping her sister and made deliberate choice to "sit at the feet of the Lord."(note vs.9 "left") But something Jesus said or something in his manner or tone of voice gave a cue to Mary that Jesus had something special on his mind. So the moment Jesus hinted that he had something to confide she became pupil rather than hostess. She "sat at his feet" and gave undivided attention to "hearing his word." To "listen" to Jesus' teaching with receptive ready heart deserves total concentration. He who would find the springs of eternal life must give complete commitment to sit "at the feet of the Lord hearing his word." To close the heart, deafen the ear, distract the mind, for whatever reason, is fatal to life. It cuts off the stream of life! Martha loved Jesus as a mother loves a son. Furthermore, she believed him to be "the Christ the son of God."(Jn.11:27) She could profit as much as Mary if she had leisure to "sit at his feet and be hearing his word."

Martha's Complaint!

It did not take long for Martha to feel the heavier load with sister Mary sitting listening to the Lord. No doubt Martha would enjoy that same luxury. But if the planned meal was to be served she needed Mary's renewed help. It wasn't long before Martha became "distracted with much serving." Martha and family had been acquainted with Jesus long and intimately. She felt confident enough that she could enlist their guest to join her in getting Mary to renew her help in the work of getting the meal ready. But both Jesus and Mary appeared completely absorbed in their conversation. Her divided mind and frayed emotions soon prompted Martha to approach Jesus and say, "It is a concern of yours isn't it that my sister quit helping and left me alone to do the serving?" It didn't occur to Martha that Jesus would think otherwise. She framed her question in such a way as to indicate that she expected "Yes" for an answer. In other words, "You want Mary to help me get this meal ready to serve don't you?"

So sure was Martha that Jesus sympathized with her point of view she was emboldened to urge on him his help in arousing Mary to get to work. "Speak, therefore, that she take hold of her end of the load together with me!" This was a family task. Each must share the load of hosting a beloved guest. Jesus was close enough to all to feel part of the family. As friend he could spur Mary on to renew her share as a family member.

The Answer of Jesus!

To Martha's outburst Jesus said, "Martha, Martha, you are divided and troubled about many things; there is need of but one! Mary selected the good portion, which by its nature shall not be taken from her." This is the heart of the story, the reason why Luke recorded this incident. It was vital that Theophilus confront this fact.

Consider the double naming, "Martha, Martha!" It reveals the tender tone and affectionate feeling of Jesus for Martha in her divided troubled condition. It's design was to return her firmly though gently to a peaceful heart and soothed soul. It would prepare her emotionally to receive the gentle rebuke Jesus was about to offer. Surprised as it seemed, Martha was the one who chose the lesser "portion," not Mary.

Said Jesus, "You are divided and troubled" because "many things" are absorbing your attention and draining your energy. Now there's nothing amiss in getting a sumptuous meal ready. Indeed the banker must work at his job, the farmer must labor on his farm, the business man must toil at his business, the miner must mine his coal, the sailor must sail his ship. Each responsible person must discharge that which his craft demands. These "secular" vocations are important to life in this world. It is wrong to neglect them. But it's also wrong to do them when the one necessity, having appeared, goes unheeded.

There comes a time in each person's career when the supreme purpose of life becomes clear and presents its demands. At some critical point God offers himself to every human. And when he comes, God comes to serve, not to be served; to give, not to receive. Martha loved Jesus and would offer him the very best hospitality at her command. She felt that Mary was letting her down by neglecting her part of the load. It did not occur to her that Mary's choice of "hearing the word" at such a time was the right choice. Nor did she think that she, Martha, was making a wrong choice! When God in Christ speaks it's time to stop all else and "be hearing his word."

To say the least Martha was surprised to hear Jesus declare, "There is but one necessity" that gives meaning and purpose to life. Mary has latched onto that one necessity; "she selected that good portion." In addition, since she has found it, chosen it, determined to get it, "because of its nature it shall not be taken away from her."

Just what did Mary find? What did she choose that Martha missed? Basically the answer lies in the words, "having sat at the feet of the Lord, she was hearing his word." To discover the word of God and to listen to it not only brings life's greatest joy but unlocks the secret of a successful human life! We do not mean that hearing sermons or lectures are sufficient. But to find Him who is life is necessary. To hear and to focus one's thought and energies on Him who is truth is to unravel the tangled mystery of life.

Martha's problem was not being divided by too many tasks in entertaining a guest. It was being divided between serving a guest and the one necessity of listening to God when he speaks.

178

"There is only one necessity!" And _that_ Martha did not have. Furthermore, in the present instance she failed to sense that the "one necessity" was now being offered to her. Mary saw and grasped the opportunity. Martha allowed the getting of a meal to distract her from listening to God. When exercising life's vocation not hearing God when he speaks leaves one distracted and troubled. But to hear God when he desires to be heard relieves life's tensions. Finding the "one necessity" eliminates professional work as a distraction or a divisive force. "Come unto me...and you shall rest for your soul." Mary found rest from a divided mind, peace from a distracted soul, and this prepared Mary for dealing with the "many things" that divided Martha. The only thing in the entire story that Mary does is to _sit_ at the feet of Jesus and _hear_ what he has to say. Martha busies herself flustering about the house doing all those little and big chores it takes to entertain a guest. Jesus commended Mary as having "chosen the good portion." By saying to Martha that Mary "chose the good portion" Jesus is gently urging Martha to sit down and do the "one necessity" that can bring peace to her divided heart. This is the whole point of the incident.

If there is only "one necessity" in life it is the same any place, any time, any where, for any people, in every culture and at any level within a culture. Nothing is more _universal_ than the "one necessary thing."

The lawyer asked, "What, having done, shall I inherit eternal life?" "Hearing the word at the feet of Jesus" Mary found that about which the lawyer inquired. The one all inclusive necessity from birth to death is to "be listening to the word of God" when he speaks! That brings unity and calm to a frustrated divided soul.

179

AN OUTLINE OF LUKE 11:1-13
Teach Us to Pray!
For persons to talk to each other is as normal as breathing, particularly when they <u>know</u> one another. Intimacy of friendship encourages talk. And what is prayer but a man talking to the <u>living</u> God? Yet strained relations have left a barrier. Man has become self-conscious, ill at ease, insecure when attempting to talk to God. Hence, the disciple's request: "Lord, teach us to pray, even as John taught his disciples."

I.   THE CONTENT OF PRAYER. 11:2-4
    1. Concerns of God as Father and King. 2
    2. For human needs. 3-4
    (a)Daily bread.
    (b)Forgiveness of sin.
    (c)Guidance through trials.
II. PERSISTENCE IN PRAYER. 11:5-10
    1. Parable exemplifying persistence. 5-8
    2. Exhortations with promises. 9-10
    (a)"Ask - it shall be given."
    (b)"Seek - you shall find."
    (c)"Knock - it shall be opened."
III. THE LOGIC OF PRAYER. 11:11-13
    1. Requests are honored in human relationships. 11-12
    2. How much more in divine-human relationships. 13

Prayer rests on the unity of nature between God and man. God made man in his "image" and after his "likeness." That implies personal, living, intelligent, moral, spiritual similarities. Such beings must inevitably talk with one another.

* * * * * * *

TEACH US TO PRAY!
Human beings cannot live in complete isolation. Even hermits on occasion must speak to other persons. Man is a social being. He must and will confer with familiar friends. It's as normal as breathing, as natural as flowers stretching to the sun. The intimacy of friendship provokes communication. Why should there not be constant conversation between men and God?

But "by man came sin" and since that day man has been running from God and hiding his sinful soul from fellowship with Him against whom he violated friendship. Yet in spite of that fatal break God initiated renewed talk when he challenged man's conscience, "Where art thou?" And He has ever provided for inter-communication between himself and his human creatures. Prayer is the essence of man's relationship to God. And for that reason it is something that man must <u>learn</u> again. It's no marvel that those closest to Jesus asked, "Lord, teach us to pray." Prayer is something that can be <u>taught</u>; something that can be <u>learned</u>. As Luke presents Christ's lesson on prayer he stresses three elements: The content, What shall I pray? The need for persistence in prayer; keep on praying. And third, the reasonableness of prayer.

The disciple who asked, "Teach us to pray" without question heard Jesus praying. So different from the "vain repetitions" with which he was familiar was it that it inflamed his desire for vital prayer with God. He had enough of memorized prayers mechanically recited and slavishly given by rote. He felt no warmth of spirit, no stimulation of heart, no sense of personal exchange from the incessant replays of ceremonial mumblings. He wanted to talk to God with the same sparkle as he spoke with Jesus, friend to friend. To this voiced hunger Jesus responded.

The Content of Genuine Prayer!

The opening word of any prayer sets its tone! "Father!" Genuine prayer is based on the filial relationship. It is communion between parent and child; the heavenly Father and his earth bound child. It gives to prayer warmth of feeling, earnest emotion, friendly attitude. It won't allow formalism to erode the personal touch of true talk.

From that filial beginning Jesus divided vital prayer into two general phases: the concerns of God and the needs of man. A true child's concern is the parent. As long as there are sons or daughters the primary claim should be that of the parent. Hence the first petition of a good prayer is, "Father, Hallowed be your name."

The word "name" expresses the real person of him who bears the name. In the case of God his name represents what he is in his essential being; his character, his purity, holiness, his untainted moral quality. To Moses God said, "I send an angel before you...Give heed to him...for my name is in him." (Ex.23:20f) In this immediate instruction on prayer "name" means the concept which the term "God" holds in the heart of the one praying. This "name" is to be held in ever increasing reverent holiness. And that not just in the prayer's heart but in other hearts. The first and prime concern in any true prayer is that the holy character of God be revered, hallowed, kept holy in the minds and hearts of men. If God's pure nature can be revered in an ever widening circle of men then idolatry, formalism, sham, hypocrisy will cease. Righteousness will return to the earth! My first petition is that I and all others may hold the Father as "holy, holy, holy!"

A second petition in a good prayer is kin to the first: "Your kingdom come!" Here the term "kingdom" does not refer so much to an organized government, an institution of dictatorial power as it does to the sovereign will of a gracious Father. The burden of every subject's soul is that the righteous and just will of the heavenly Father-King extend to its furthest breadth, height, and depth. If and when the sovereign will of God is universally acknowledged and accepted then will come universal piety, peace, and prosperity for which the ages have longed. In order for God to reign over men he only needs to be well known by men. This petition expresses the hunger of the child of the king to be a worthy subject of the divine king. Moreover, it expresses the longing for the hearts of men to be subject to the just laws (will) of a holy Father who is also sovereign king.

Prayer for Human Needs!

Having established God's glory as the primary concern of any and all prayer the next essential is to consider human need. If one is to bring glory to God, he must live. In order to revere the name of God we need to maintain health and strength. That requires food in constant supply. In a material world man cannot exist without bread, sample and symbol of all man's material needs. The next petition lays this need before God: "Be giving to us day by day the bread of our existence." Food and clothing for the body are essentials in order to carry on one's labor and to contribute to society's wants. Housing to protect from thieves and elements of weather are included in "bread." These are proper subjects of prayer. At the same time such petitions imply that God providentially provides in the ongoing of human life in this world. Thus in good praying we recognize God's sustaining place in material affairs.

But note that God's providence gives "day by day the bread for existence." Jesus doesn't teach that we ask for surplus; only that which is sufficient for every day's existence. The manna in the wilderness came one day at a time. It's necessary that our sense of dependence on God's providence be a daily experience. Accumulation of abundance, though not innately wrong, does tempt to independence of God. In teaching this plea Jesus, by present imperative urges, "Be giving..." That is, "Constantly continue giving day after day after day." There is no day in which man is not dependent on the provision of providence. So, "keep on giving daily!" At every point man's life depends on God's attention to our needs.

But after bread no need of man is greater than that posed by a guilty conscience. Some men hide from their guilt by covering themselves with the fig leaves of fame and/or fortune. Others run from guilt by denying its existence, comparing one's own sin to others of greater blame. Some seek escape by denial that God exists. If there is no God there is no absolute moral standard. But this petition recognizes and accepts guilt. It seeks forgiveness as the only real relief.

Forgiveness implies grace! Once I've stolen, lied, murdered nothing can change the fact of my guilt. Though I cease completely from all future wrong doing the stark fact remains that I once did steal. Even grace in forgiveness can't change that fact of my past wrong. Grace changes the effective consequence but the fact remains a fact. Therefore the plea, "forgive us our sins" rests on God's grace in his eternal plan of redemption. Paul speaks of the "beloved, in whom we have the redemption through his blood, the forgiveness of our trespasses according to the wealth of his grace."(Eph.1:7) Thus in this petition we cast ourselves on the mercy of God's grace: "Forgive us our sins."

The change in my character due to his forgiveness leads me to offer my forgiveness to him who has wronged me. Hence I pray, "For we ourselves are forgiving everyone indebted to us." Grace begets grace; forgiveness begets forgiveness. And that fact blends into a good prayer. Thanks for grace given; thanks for grace to forgive!

There is yet another petition concerning man's need. "Don't lead us into temptation." Again, this recognizes God's guidance by providence. We recognize God's leading in all the tangled affairs of life. Many of them are threatening. We need wisdom and strength beyond human. Jesus teaches that we ask for the guidance of God to stear clear of <u>temptation</u>. Temptation, be it physical attack from without or moral allurement from within, is painful. We would avoid the hurt. And for this reason it is a legitimate request that God guide us away from the agony of trial. This in spite of the moral good that may and often does come from temptations.(Cf.Jas.1:2-4) If temptations come, well and good; we'll "rejoice" in them and make the most of them. Guide us; but don't guide us into them!

<u>Persistence in Prayer</u>!

A weakness of man is his lack of persistence in all that he attempts, prayer included. Results come largely from "keeping on keeping on." This is particularly true of praying. There are so many reasons not to persist. God loves and knows our needs before we ask. Why bother him? We have asked once; doesn't he listen? does he need more information? I am a responsible man, why shift my responsibility to God?

In spite of all such reasons Jesus took the pains to draw a picture to engrave in our minds the need of perseverance in prayer. In the story a man has a "friend" who comes at midnight to borrow "three loaves of bread" with which to feed an unexpected late arriving guest. But from within the father has already bundled his children into the pallets on the floor before the front door. He would not disturb his family's rest. But when the banging on the door continues, just to stop the noise he arises and meets the desperate need.

The reader of the parable should not conclude that God is like the reluctant father. It is not God who needs us to persist. The point is: How badly do <u>we</u> want that for which we pray? Do we really need? Do we really want? God is willing and gracious and wants to give to us our needs. But we must deeply feel the need and so persevere in asking for them.

Furthermore, it must not be forgotten that the underlying wish of <u>all</u> prayer requests lie in the first two petitons, "Hallowed be thy name, thy sovereign reign come!" In asking for <u>our</u> needs we ask for those things which enable us to fulfill those first two basics of a good prayer. If I pray for more "food" it is because I need to <u>give</u> more food to increase God's holy name, His sovereign rule!

For these reasons Jesus enforces the need for preservering persistence in prayer. He gives three exhortations coupled with three promises. "Continue to ask and it shall be given to you. Continue to seek and you shall find. Go on knocking and it shall be opened to you."

The form of the verbs in these exhortations stresses repetition. God acknowledges the resolute, persistent, repeated

petition. Repeating a request demonstrates not only that I am
earnest about that for which I pray but it also purges my plea.
As I restate my request it takes sharper shape in my mind. I
may ask for money. But as I pray it takes the form of $1000
for helping one of God's children survive surgery. As I "keep
on asking" one plea molds another.

The admonition to "keep on seeking" is really a prayer that
God help me fulfill my own prayer. The man of the parable faced
a personal crisis of friendship. He needed bread at midnight.
He "asked", but more, he "sought" by walking to a neighbor's
house and knocking on the door. As a man of God he could "ask"
God for bread. But he on his part did what he could to find
them. He must "be seeking!" As God's children we ought always
to pray, and that "without ceasing." But then we must do our
share to bring to realization that for which we pray!

"Keep on knocking and it shall be given to you." During
World War II building material was quite scarce for private
home construction. Yet one builder of a development project
never seemed to lack nails, lumber, metal and such like. When
asked how he managed to find such scarce things he replied. "I
keep knocking on doors until someone tells me where I can find
what I need for the task at hand." There's no substitute for
consistent, persistent knocking. In fact, at bottom, all three
exhortations are but three ways of saying the same thing, "keep
on keeping on."

The Logic of Prayer!

The final point in this lesson of Jesus argues for the
reasonableness of prayer. Since prayer is basically an exchange
between persons there ought be no marvel that any two persons
who are amicable should confide their wants to one another.
Through the centuries God has revealed himself and his eternal
purpose of reclaiming his lost confused creature. On his part
man has responded in various ways as he has found his place in
God's program. This involves good communication. And there is
no basic difference between how man talks to man and how man
talks to God. If, in response to a man's need, man meets man's
needs isn't it reasonable to conclude that God, the Creator and
supreme Sovereign should meet his creatures' needs? So Jesus
said, "Which father of you whose son shall ask for a fish, he
won't give to him a serpent will he? Or should he request an
egg, he won't give him a scorpion will he? Jesus framed the
question to indicate that he expected "No!" as an answer. The
answer is so obvious. The family bond would make such a thing
unthinkable for a father. Hence Jesus proceeds with the
logical application of his analogy. "If then you, being evil,
know to give good gifts to your children, how much more shall
your father, the one from heaven, give the Holy Spirit to the
ones asking him?"

Nothing sectarian, cultural or racial is in this clear
simple teaching about prayer. It's universality undergirds its
power. Greek or Jew can embrace such a natural expression of
relationship between son and Father.

184

AN OUTLINE OF LUKE 11:14-27
A Lesson on Housecleaning!

Housecleaning is as old as men's living in houses. A clean house signals a civilized, organized, well-ordered life.

Moral house cleaning is as important, or more so, as washing windows, cleaning rugs, cleansing clothes or dusting furniture. In fact, the sense of moral cleanliness may very well show up in a clean well-orderd home.

I. THE SITUATION: CLEANSING A MAN POSSESSED. 11:14
1. Jesus cleansed a demon-man who was dumb. 14a
2. The effect on the crowd. 14b

II. ACCUSATION:"HE WORKS BY PRINCE OF DEMONS." 11:15-16
1. Low level of the charge! 15
2. Challenged to give a "sign from heaven." 16

III. CHRIST'S DEFENSE: 11:17-23
1. A "kingdom divided makes itself desolate." 17
2. Principle applied to Satan's kingdom. 18
3. Similar effects come from similar causes. 19-20
4. Parable: "Stronger" defeats the "strong." 21-22
5. Application of the parable. 23

IV. KEEPING THE HOUSE CLEAN. 11:24-26
1. Evil needs means in which to express its evil. 24
2. Empty house is no sign of freedom from evil. 25-26
3. The Spirit of God must dwell within or Evil will!

A "certain woman" from the crowd, hearing Jesus answer his critics, praises the mother who bore such a son. Jesus spoke to her indicating whom one ought to praise!

* * * * * * *

A LESSON ON HOUSECLEANING!

Housecleaning is traditional for announcing that winter is over and open air living can be renewed. It notifies that dust accumulated through house-bound wintry days is to disappear. Housecleaning marks a well-ordered family home.

As in the physical realm so, at least once in a lifetime, must come a moral, spiritual cleansing of the soul. Accumulated moral trash with which evil has possessed the spirit of man needs casting out. "All have sinned" means that all are bound with chains too strong for man to break. Every man has become imprisoned in and by his own depravity. Guilt is the common denominator of human kind. Universal guilt is itself another strand of evil that wraps itself around each human being. Were it not for the grace in God's Christ no one could escape the stifling bondage of sin.

But man needs not only God's grace in forgiveness he also must have release from the ongoing power of sin to handcuff his free moral action. True, the power of past guilt has to be broken. But of equal importance to man's freedom is that the power of present evil habit must be nullified. Freedom from guilt and freedom from sinning are two sides of the same coin of man's moral need.

185

Curing a Demon-Possessed!
Demon possession was the acceptable term in biblical times in referring to Satan's complete domination of a man. In modern western culture the terminology is outmoded but the fact is as real as tomorrow. Men **need** God's help to secure spiritual and moral freedom from the bondage of Evil. We may not refer to it as "demon possession" but it shows the same symptoms and finds its roots in the same personal impulses as those of the first century. Changing names does not change that which lies back of moral evil. If Satan existed in the first century, referring to him by a scientific term doesn't alter objective reality. Evil is evil is evil by whatever name and in whatever culture.

The text describes the situation as follows: "He was casting out a demon and he was dumb. And it happened, the demon having gone out, the dumb spoke; and the crowds marvelled." The special effect of the demon's domination over this man was that he strangled the man's speech. In other words, the man was "dumb." The effect of the evil control of Satan was not violence. The possessed man harmed no one nor did he damage property. The man could think clearly and act responsibly. He just could not speak! A sad situation! It made life doubly burdensome for the man, his family, and his friends.

Nothing in the record tells who initiated the cure. That Jesus defeated the demon in this unusual case is the focus of attention. Jesus, with obvious ease, "cast out the demon." Then the "dumb spoke!" It was an incident in which the "strong" was defeated by the "stronger." So startling was the cure that it had an immediate effect on the people: "The crowds marvelled!" The forces of the Evil one could not withstand the healing power of this Jesus. The popularity of Jesus was growing, his influence was increasing.

The Accusation!
From the standpoint of the leaders in Israel something radical had to be done to check the growing influence of Jesus. The opposition against Jesus had been steadily deepening. It now reached a new low when the leaders claimed, "In league with Beelzebul, the ruler of the demons, is he casting out the demons." The opposition was developing such intense malice that it became desperate. To accuse a man's good deeds as empowered by the King of Evil marks a new level of depravity. It also reveals the desperation of their hatred against Jesus. For evil men to claim that God does his work by being in league with Satan shows how malignant men can become.

But other critics of a different mold "trying him, were seeking from him a sign out of heaven." Their motives were equally vicious but their approach was different. They proposed that he show a "sign from heaven." They believed that no mere man could demonstrate a sign manifestly unearthly in origin. Such a sign must be untouched by magic. It should be a sign not dealing with earthly need but entirely of an other worldly order! An imposter could not perform such a sign. They believed he could not produce such a sign. He would thus be discredited with the people.

186

Christ's Defense!

Christ, hearing these accusations, laid hold of them as a basis not only for defense but as a springboard from which to launch an offense. First, the defense! "Every kingdom being divided against itself makes of itself a barren desert." The absurdity of the accusation is patent. Kings have armies to defend against and invade enemies, not to war against friends. The indictment is thus reduced to its obvious absurdity. The fact that Jesus was doing good works of healing, enlightening, strengthening the sick in mind, body and soul, puts the lie to the accusers and their flimsy reproach. The accusation falls of its own weight for a "house against a house falls!"

From this withering defense Jesus turns to another. "If Satan is divided against himself, how shall his kingdom stand?" That's a conditional sentence which assumes the premise to be true: Satan is divided..." It withers the opposition with its flawless logic. But Jesus follows through by reminding them that they prompted this war of words, "...because you say that "in Beelzebul I am casting out the demons!"

But Jesus doesn't rest on one defensive statement. He attacks! "If I on my part by Beelzebul am casting out the demons (and we assume your claim as true), then in whom are your sons casting them out?" Your sons and disciples infest the land with claims of conquering evil by casting out demons. On the basis of your assumption that I use evil to cast out evil, where does that leave you and your miracle working sign salesmen? Your own logic self destructs. Based on your own presuppositions, "You yourselves shall be your own judges."

By his incisive logic Jesus has undercut the force of his critics' attack. If they cast out demons that leaves the door open that he casts out demons, not by alliance with the Devil but by the power of God. So he presses on with the attack: "If in the finger of God I am casting out the demons (and let's assume that I do)," then the unavoidable conclusion is that in me "the kingdom of God has arrived upon you." Thus that which was meant to be an embarrassment to Jesus became a sword in his hand to defeat those Jews who would destroy him. He has turned their attack into his offense.

But Jesus doesn't leave the matter there. He moves to clinch his point by an objective example. "Whenever a strong man guards his own court, his goods remain secure. But whenever a stronger arrives, he overcomes him and takes away his panoply on which he has trusted and he distributes his spoils." By this simple logical syllogism Jesus thwarts his critics. Only total victory permits total pludering. Jesus freely fleeces Satan. Therefore, Jesus and his kingdom of truth enjoys total victory over the banditry of the Evil one. And Jesus underscores the fact that there is no middle ground in the warfare between the kingdom of God and the dominion of Evil. "The one not being (in fellowship) with me is (militant) against me! And the one not gathering with me is scattering." The issue is clear: truth versus error; right versus wrong!

Keeping the House Clean!

Spirit seeks expression! The Greek πνεῦμα may be translated by "wind," "breath," or "spirit." Apparently to the Greeks "breath" "spirit" "wind" most closely describe the immaterial, psychical, incorporeal, airy. But whatever is its substance, if any, spirit seeks some way to express itself in a material world. Thus "whenever the unclean spirit goes out of the man he goes through waterless places seeking rest, and not finding it he says, 'I will return to my house whence I came out.'" To assert his nature, good or bad, disembodied spirit (breath, wind) __must__ externalize himself. Bodiless spirit exists in "waterless places," that is, lifeless barren desert with no one in whom or to whom he may express himself. To exist in an infinite spacial universe __alone__ is the worst of hells.

To avoid such suffering the "unclean spirit" mused to himself, "I will return to my house from whence I came. And having come, he finds it swept and set in order." Note that the unclean spirit refers to the "dumb" man as "__my__" house. What is another's is __mine__ is the arrogant conceit of evil. Evil has no regard for the property or person other than himself. "He" is the center of his universe and all in it exists for the gratification of __his__ self-serving desires.

Furthermore, upon his return to "his" house he finds it "having been swept and having been decorated" in good order and beautiful taste. He had left it undone, unkempt, filthy and in rotting disorder. Now it was ready and waiting to be occupied.

No man (house) has ever been created to be vacant. Bodies are "houses" in which a spirit is to live. A man has been created to be in God's "image" and "likeness" in quality and character. Houses must be filled with the furniture of pure thoughts, good deeds, unselfish service to others of similar nature. A house left empty invites vandals to deface its character and beauty. A "saved" man must fill the house of his spirit with divine furniture. A mind or heart will not remain vacant. An "unclean spirit" will move in if the house stays empty. The light of Christ must illuminate the mind; trust in God as Father must fill the soul in divine fellowship; the breath of the Holy Spirit must animate the human. If these are left out, the "unclean spirit" will occupy the house. Nor will he return alone. "He goes and takes seven other spirits more evil than himself, and having entered they lodge there." Then they will destroy the divine and leave little but disordered rotting immoralities. "The last (stages) of that man are worse than the first." An empty soul invites unclean renters. A God filled spirit is armed against all evil!

The text ends with two beatitudes. "It happened that while he was saying these things, having lifted up her voice, a certain woman of the crowd said to him, 'Blessed the womb the one that bore you and the breasts at which you nursed.'" Jesus did not rebuke the woman for her praise of his mother. But he did indicate a greater blessing. "Blessed are the ones hearing the word of God and who are __keeping__ it." The finest praise is obedience!

188

The Sign from Heaven!
Some critics of Jesus, demanding a "sign from heaven," had questionable motives. Yet God realizes a need for evidence to support his Word, personal or written. Thus he offers a sign. But a "sign shall not be given except the sign of Jonah."
- I. THE SIGN OF JONAH. 11:29-32
  1. "Sign such as demanded shall not be given." 29
  2. The "sign of Jonah" suits the demand. 30-32
     (a)The Queen of the South.
     (b)The men of Ninevah.
- II. CONDITION ON WHICH SIGNS SIGNIFY. 11:33-34
  1. The purpose of lamps! 33
  2. The "lamp of the body is the eye." 34a
  3. Condition of the lamp's serving its purpose. 34b
- III. EXHORTATION: "KEEP WATCHING." 11:35-36
  1. "Watch the lamp(heart)in the body(soul). 35
  2. Consequences of careful continuous watching. 36

A clear "eye"(heart)results in the whole man being "wholly bright as when the lamp illuminates by its shining flash." An "evil eye"(heart)brings an increasing gloom of darkness.

* * * * * * *

THE SIGN FROM HEAVEN!
To ask for evidence is as normal as facing a problem in which choice between alternatives is demanded. It's as necessary as deciding which way to turn when facing a fork in the road. Why, then, is this an "evil generation" because it seeks signs?

Jesus did not object to "this generation" wanting a sign. His concern was with the fact that "this generation" was blind to the sign offered. "This generation" demanded a sign from out of this world, beyond what this world could give. When facing and rejecting such signs as were suitable to the canons of evidence in such a world as this, they demanded signs "from heaven." Their demands sprang, not from evidence suitable for disputes in "this world" but signs entirely unrelated to "this world." They must display some erie other-worldliness. In fact their demand sprang from unbelief. It sprang from moral differences more than canons of evidence.

The Sign of Jonah!
"And as the crowds were thronging together, he began to say, 'This generation is an evil generation.'" The term "evil" indicates "active evil." It is not only evil in itself, that is, in its ideas, practices and deeds but it cannot rest until it has infused its evil into others. Jesus is asserting that "this generation" is so evil it won't rest until it has saturated all society around it with its own corruption of sin. It is so evil it won't tolerate anything righteous around it. Evil is its standard of "right."

Jesus had come offering himself as God's son among men. HE was God's "sign" among and for men! Moreover, HE was the only sign needed for faith. Yet "this generation" was accusing Jesus as being in league with Satan claiming, "in Beelzebul, the ruler of demons, he casts out demons." Jesus came teaching a lofty standard of righteousness, doing deeds of personal virtue. Yet their plea was that he present a "sign from heaven," a sign unrelated to the accepted standards of evidence. He must either defy the laws of nature such as "cast yourself down" from the pinnacle of the temple, or he must transport himself to a heavenly experience totally beyond the realm of this world.

The demands of these sign seekers expressed doubt, not faith. They did not <u>believe</u> he could do such a sign. They failed to see that <u>he</u> <u>was</u> the "sign from heaven." In addition, he pointed out that a "sign (such as you are demanding) shall <u>not</u> be given..." Yet, "if you have the eyes with which to see, such a sign has been and will be given. Just as Jonah became a sign to the Ninevites, <u>thus</u> the son of man <u>shall</u> <u>be</u> to the men of this generation." Upon the preaching of Jonah the men of Ninevah repented. But it was not the preaching that was the "sign." It was <u>Jonah</u> and that which happened to him. That was the sign! Jonah presented himself to the Ninevites as one who amazingly had escaped the clutches of death. <u>That</u> was the sign on which his call to repentance was based. And, said Jesus, that's the kind of sign which shall be offered to "this generation" on the basis of which it shall be called to repentance.

The "queen of the South" came "from the ends of the earth to hear the wisdom of Solomon." But it wasn't anything <u>she</u> brought that became a "sign." It was that which Solomon was and taught that made her marvel. Solomon was the "sign" not the queen! And now a "greater than Solomon" was present. And a "greater than Jonah" was here. <u>HE</u> and he alone would be the "sign from heaven." Furthermore, if the "men of Ninevah" and the "queen of the South" are to be judged by their response to the "sign" given them, how much more those of "this generation" shall be condemned because the sign given them is "greater" than that vouchsafed to the earlier generations? As Jonah escaped from certain death so Jesus, risen from the dead, offers salvation to those who trust him. <u>HE</u>, Jesus, is the "sign from heaven!" The question remains as to how "this" generation will receive this sign!

Condition on which Signs Signify!

"No one having lit a lamp puts it in a crypt, neither under a measure." Lights are not lit to be hidden. It would be a waste of time, fuel and money. Such misuse would encourage confusion rather than order. Lamps are positioned on lampstands in prominent places "that the ones entering may see the light." The obvious purpose of light is to illuminate dark areas that men may live without stumbling. To put a lamp in a crypt destroys its function!

Jesus Christ is the "light of the world" given by God to illuminate moral and spiritual darkness. Christ is the "sign from heaven" the light of whose truth God intends to radiate over the world. Nor does God propose that it should be replaced by the darkness.

190

"The lamp of the body is the eye." The eye is the physical instrument that allows the light to enter so a man may function in society. But when Jesus uses the singular "eye" he is suggesting that he's not referring to the physical eye. He is speaking in figurative language. When there is a lamp which shines outside the body there must be an organ inside that's equipped to receive the light from without. The same is true of the soul. If there is the Light from without (Christ) there must be an organ _within_ a man that can receive spiritual and moral light. That organ is the _heart_, that with which a man thinks, feels, and wills. Thus Jesus is saying, "If the _heart_ is single, without folds or pleats that cover, obscure, or blur the light from without then a man is entirely filled with the light of truth. The whole inner life of a man is determined by the condition of his moral heart. A man's entire understanding, his essential being, his power of will, his ideas and emotions are determined by the healthy (or sick) condition of his moral heart. When his "eye" (heart) is single, no wrinkles, over folds, twists, or other such blemishes, _then_ the man is completely illuminated with the light which is Christ. A man is enlightened by as much light as his heart will admit.

On the other hand, "whenever his eye (heart) be aggressively evil, then his body will be full of darkness." A corrupt heart is a diseased organ, twisted, deformed and thus allowing darkness to appear as light and light darkness. It's like a man who has ridden a bicycle with crooked handlebars. Having thus ridden for so long, when the handlebars are straightened he can't ride in a direct line. He is used to crooked handlebars. To him straight has become crooked and crooked straight. When man's heart is contorted for so long then the contortion seems virtuous and virtue appears warped. Unless the heart allows the lamp's light to penetrate into the darkness of the soul then it's not performing its function. Had the critics of Jesus had true hearts, without over-folds which hid their evil motives they would have seen in Jesus the "sign" for which they asked. But their inner organ of the heart was perverse. So the light shines outside but they remain dark inside. They were worse than the Ninevites; less in moral quality than the queen of the South.

Keep On Watching!

It's a true proverb that says, "Guard your heart with all diligence; for from it flow the springs of life." Hence Jesus' exhortation was an urging that "this generation" not fail in keeping its moral vision clear and unclouded. "Be watching therefore lest the light in you be darkness."

Consider two factors. First, don't allow moral distinctions to become blurred. Morality is not determined by popular vote but by the moral nature of God. Light is light and darkness is darkness. These are absolutes, not relative qualities. Anything in between these antithetical opposites represents the soul in transit. We are either moving upward toward the light or sinking toward the darkness. The paradox is that light may appear as dark and dark as light.

191

Salvation from this paradoxical dilemma is "Go on watching!" There is no substitute for continual, regular, ceaseless, day-in and day-out watching! In fact, the nature of darkness is such the moment the light of truth is compromised darkness will elbow its way in to take possession of the soul. Light redeems man's soul but it must keep on shining in the heart without ceasing. The entire spiritual nature of a man is informed and guided by the divine light which the heart accepts. With each admission of righteousness light is diffused into the spirit of man. Hence, if the heart be "single," that is, clean, uncorrupted, healthy, patterned after Him in whose image it was created, the whole man is illuminated by the light of truth.

Had the critics of Jesus enjoyed singleness of heart ("eye) they could have perceived the divine "sign" before their eyes. They could at least have "seen" as quickly as the queen of the South "saw" in front of her. Or the Ninevites "saw" in their day! Therefore, to these Jews of Jesus day the light without them did not become the light within them. They died in their darkness!

The consequence of careful watching is manifest. "If then your body is entirely light, not having any part dark, it shall be entirely light as when the lamp enlightens you with its shining brilliance." As darkness brings more darkness so light issues in more light. If a man continuously lets more truth in yet more truth will follow to illuminate the inner soul. In the infinite growth of the soul more begets more! "We all, with unveiled face, beholding the glory of the Lord, are being changed into his likeness from glory unto glory." (II Cor.3:18)

Why did Luke include this episode in his story? What insight could Theophilus gain from this incident? Aside from the fact this paragraph continues the conflict with the "Jews" over demands for a sign from heaven, Luke clearly plays the same chord of Christ's universal humanity! That which is human is universal. And that which is universal is human! Light is the same wherever it appears. Truth is the truth whether found in Jew or Gentile, Ninevite or African! Neither gender or race can change the nature of the light of truth.

AN OUTLINE OF LUKE 11:37-12:12
Fake or Fact?

Like much in life one can fake faith. Can faith in Christ introduce one to the reality of fact. Or does faith fake man into the cruelest of unsubstantial fancy? Is faith fake or fact?

I. WHAT DETERMINES MORAL CLEANLINESS? 11:37-41
1. The Occasion: Breakfast in a Pharisee's house. 37-38
2. The Pharisees' method. 39a
   (a)Clean the outside; a half-measure.
   (b)The inside remains dirty.

II. PATTERNS OF HYPOCRICY. 11:42-54
1. Pharisaical examples. 42-54
   (a)Tithing versus justice & love to God. 42
   (b)Pride of recognition. 43f
2. The lawyers: Interpret but do not keep law. 45-54
   (a)They "burden others" but avoid obedience. 45-46
   (b)Build prophets' tombs; practice their fathers' behaviour. 47-51
   (c)Take the "key of knowledge" but abuse it. 52-54

III. GUARDING AGAINST HYPOCRICY. 12:1-12
1. Warning Against Hypocrisy. 1-3
2. Motive Against Hypocrisy. 4-7
3. Following the Holy Spirit in Confessing Christ! 8-12

Open rebellion of him who is committed to sin avoids the sham of hypocricy. It does not confuse the issue. Hypocricy blurs the vision, and corrupts the soul under the pretense of purity. It's the most deadly of sins. An antidote is "give as merciful gratuity the things within, and behold all is pure for you."

* * * * * * *

FAKE OR FACT?

So far down the scale of moral purity has man fallen that he can present the pretense of right while practicing the blackest of sins. He has turned the sublime spirit into the lowest devil. He twists right into wrong and wrong into right.

What Determines Moral Cleanliness?

Jesus accepted the hospitality of a Pharisee. "As he spoke a Pharisee invited him to breakfast with him. And when he entered he reclined." When the Pharisee observed that Jesus "reclined" at the table without first "washing" before breakfast he "was amazed." The failure to wash was not washing to get filth off the hands. It was solely for ceremonial purposes. The issue was symbolic of dirt on the soul, not the hands.

Apparently "amazement" was displayed on the Pharisee's face or in his actions. Jesus attacked the Pharisee's shallow false "cleanliness." Bluntly he said, "You, the Pharisees, are cleaning the outside the cup and the plate but your inside (heart) is full of thievery and gnawing evil." They practiced half measures! Who, washing dishes, would go to the trouble of washing the outside while leaving the inner part full of drying decaying food?

193

But Jesus was not referring to washing dishes. He was using a figure of speech for explaining the proper basis of moral cleanliness. In matters of morals it is proper that the outside be kept clean but the place to start is not the outside. "The one who made the outside is also the one who made the inside is he not?" When dealing with a human soul, not a dish, cleaning must start with the inside. Hence, "Give the things within as a gracious grant, and behold, all things are pure." In other words, if one commits his thoughts, emotions, motives, purposes to pure and holy ends then that which he does in his outward life shall be clean in its effects. Think clean and the results will be clean! But if one does a good deed with malicious motives his good turns sour and becomes bitter in his soul. To feed the poor, not for the sake of the poor but to gain his support for an evil deed destroys the moral quality of feeding the poor. It's the motive that makes the deed good or bad. "Keep the heart with all diligence, for out of it are the issues of life."(Prov.4:23) To clean up the outside first get the inside clean!

Patterns of Hypocricy!

Teaching gets results if enforced by example. The Pharisees offered samples of hypocricy. "But woe to you, the Pharisees, because you tithe the mint and the rue and every green herb, and you pass by the judgment and the love to God." Jesus in no way denied tithing as a method of giving to God. He insisted, "it was necessary to do "these things..." But he assured that they should "not pass by those other things, "justice and love to God." It was not a matter of "this" or "that" but priorities! Justice and love give to tithing any virtue it may have.

Pharisaical examples of hypocricy were prolific. Jesus cited another. "But woe to you the Pharisees, because you love the chief seat in the synagogues and the salutations in the market places." Their worship of God was mutilated by their seeking to be the center of attention. That the assembled people recognize them was of greater importance to them than that the people worship God. Their proposed worship became self-destructive. Because their inner heart held evil motives their worship became vile.

In reality these Pharisees who prided themselves on keeping themselves "clean" were the very ones who, without realizing it, contaminated society with their filth. To touch the dead or the graves where the dead lay was considered "unclean." By ceremonially cleansing the outside but leaving their "inside" corrupt they became "dead" in fact and thus "unclean" in fact. People who "touched" them in daily affairs were touching the "dead" as it were. They were "as the tombs, invisible" because of overgrowth of vegetation. People walked over such graves without realizing it and so became "unclean." Hence men who associated with those who were wicked within but formally clean without were morally and spiritually dead. The Pharisees, thus, became a source of spreading moral filth. Their hypocricy was a source of making a generation corrupt.

194

"Lawyers" were a professional class amongst the Pharisees. They specialized in interpreting the law of Moses. It was theirs to relate the Mosaic commands to the daily affairs of practical living. Moses said, "Remember the Sabbath day to keep it holy." But in a given situation how is one to "keep the Sabbath?" Through the centuries, notably after the Babylonian captivity, traditional dogmas began to carry more weight than the law itself. The "traditions" became more authoritative than Moses because they "explained" what Moses meant in specific settings.

Two examples of such "traditions" about Moses' Sabbath law include, "If a poor man stood outside and the householder inside, and the poor man stretched his hand inside and put aught into the householder's hand, and took aught from it and brought it out, the poor man is culpable and the householder is not."

"The men of Tiberias once passed a tube of cold water through a spring of hot water. The sages said: If this is done on the Sabbath it is like water heated on the Sabbath and is forbidden both for washing and drinking; and if it is done on a Festival day it is like water heated on a Festival day and is forbidden for washing, but permitted for drinking." (The Mishna, Danby, pgs.100, 103) These illustrate the trivia that consumed the attention of scholars of the law. In this way they expounded how to "remember the Sabbath day" to "keep it holy."

It was from one of these "experts" in traditional law that Jesus was severely reproached. "Teacher! Saying these things, you are insulting us!" Jesus responded with an attack against the hypocricy of these lawyers. "Woe also to you lawyers because you are burdening on men burdens heavy to carry and you yourselves do not touch with one of your fingers the burdens." Hypocricy is pretending to be something you are not, while at the same time it hides that which you are! This precisely defines the lawyer who complained to Jesus. By their tradition they "bound" the simple hearted to rules of Sabbath, cleanness, tithes, flux, vows, first-fruits, etc. While some they "bound" to these "traditions" they "loosed" themselves from submission to such trivial "laws." They fell into the error of thinking that truth seen is truth fulfilled. They omitted obedience to their own "teachings." They laid traditions on the people instead of "loosing" them from such thin routine.

Besides, the very interpretations failed to get at the inner heart of the law they sought to interpret. Had the people obeyed all the traditions they still would have missed the meaning of the original law of Moses. The "unclean" still would have retained their filth!

"Woe to you because you build the tombs of the prophets, though your fathers killed them." When Stephen was martyred (Acts 7:58) "they put their garments at the feet of a young man named Saul." That is to say Saul thus entered into the guilt of those who cast the stones. In "building the tombs" of the prophets the sons thereby approved the deeds of their fathers. The accumulated sins of the past became the guilt of the sons in the present generation. "Because of this," that is, because of

195

the "wisdom of God" which leaves sin to bear the fruit of its own judgment in its own time. God's judgment against sin doesn't reach its full end in the lifetime of the one sinning. God allows sin to ripen until present sin reaps the full results of past sinning. At the proper time judgment strikes. The sin of the fathers unites with the sin of the sons. The sin of the sons accords with the sin of the fathers. Thus the sons are accomplices with the fathers. So the sons become responsible for the accumulated guilt.

Jesus pronounced judgment on these "sons." "I send prophets and apostles to them, some of whom they will kill and persecute, that the blood of the prophets, shed from the foundation of the world, may be required of this generation, from the blood of Abel to the blood of Zechariah, who perished between the altar and the sanctuary. Yea, it shall be required of this generation." These lawyers, by imposing the "traditions," were foisting upon the people a corruption of Mosaic law. They thus "took the key of knowledge and you didn't enter and you hindered those entering." The original reason for the law was defeated by those whose profession it was to guard it. This was the ultimate of hypocritical pretense. Jesus sharply condemned such dissembling.

What might Jesus expect from such a confrontation? Humanly speaking, the gauntlet was cast. From this moment "the scribes and the Pharisees, lying in wait to snare something out of his mouth, began to belittle him fiercely and to catechize (him) about more things." Facing increasing hostility Jesus moved among the people as he turned toward Jerusalem.

On Guarding Against Hypocricy!

Turning from rebuking the Phariees Jesus began to warn his disciples of hypocricy. "While the thousands of the crowd were mingling so as to trample one another, he began first to say to his disciples, 'Take heed that you keep yourselves from the Pharisees' leaven, which is hypocricy!'" No disciple of Jesus is ever free from the temptation to pretend. And every disciple needs constant warning and encouragement. Thus Jesus gives three words of encouragement!

First, he points to human life, in spite of appearances, as really a book open for universal reading. From the sin in Eden man has sought to hide his guilt and his actual moral condition. But God created human life to be open and honest. So the truth is, "Nothing has been covered which shall not be uncovered and (nothing) is hidden which shall not be made known." This is an urging to live not only an open honest life but also to teach the truth candidly no matter whether popular or persecuted. Truth will out; if not immediately, eventually! Truth shall not forever be on the scaffold. It's the nature of reality to be exposed by a world governed by God. Faith in God demands faith in God's truth. Therefore, give it the greatest publicity no matter the personal cost. "Whatever you said in darkness shall be heard in the light, and that which you spoke in the ears in secret places shall be heralded from the rooftops!" This is not a threat. It is kin to a promise. It is a statement testifying that human life is to be lived openly, honestly, consistent with truth. In the course of time and/or eternity everything thought, said, or done shall be displayed on the screen of the universe. Both God and man shall view the "truth," the "reality" of each human being. Therefore, one should not recoil from commitment to truth. It will be openly displayed before the universe! Truth is destined for universal public exposure. Give yourself to it!

A second incentive to avoid the pretense of hypocricy is in the assurance that God guides. "Don't be afraid!" Those "after killing the body have nothing more they can do, are not the ones to fear!" The physical body is important as an __instrument__ through which the inner man, the real spirit, operates. But the body is only an __instrument__. Those who destroy the instrument but can't hurt the spirit are not to be feared. Said Jesus, "I'll show you whom you shall fear. Fear him who after killing has power to cast into Gehenna. Verily, I say to you, Fear this one!" Not man nor Satan controls the moral laws governing human life; only God! So, "I say to you, Fear this one!" Let the conduct of your lives be determined, not by men who threaten life and limb. On the contrary, be governed by Him who infuses moral principles and human relationships.

So involved is God in human destiny and relationships that even the minutia of life is his concern. "Are not five sparrows sold for two pennies? And not one of them has been forgotten before God! Yea! Even the hairs of your head have been numbered. Quit being afraid! You are worth more than many sparrows!" When Jesus spoke these words he did not address his disciples as disciples. He called them, "My __friends__!" It was not just as "Teacher" and "disciple" but as __human__ being that Jesus felt for them. He knew, personally and in principle, that which integrity of soul demanded in a world which honored pretense. Be faithful, for God is concerned over the details of your life. How much more the great issues of morality and truth. As diciples they may fall under the hatred of evil men but should they fall it won't be without the knowledge, consent, and sustaining hand of a heavenly Father!

Yet one more encouragement Jesus offered. "Whoever shall confess in me before men also the son of man shall confess in him before the angels of God." That which confronts faithful disciples of Jesus is painful rejection of the Christ they herald not to mention personal attack in mental and moral abuse. If the world crucifies the Christ it will crucify those who faithfully proclaim him. But as long as this proclamation is done "__in__ him" He assures that __He__ will confess his presence "__in__ them" on the final accounting before the angels of God. The moral, spiritual kinship between Jesus as God's only begotten Son and disciples as God's adopted sons cannot be broken by rejection, persecution, or banishment.

It holds more than passing interest to note that Jesus does not say __he__ will deny those who deny him. On the contrary, he declares, "The one having denied me before men __shall be denied__

(passive) before the angels of God." Innate in reviling of
Christ "before men" is the guarantee of the humiliation and
expulsion of the self "before the angels of God." We reap
hereafter that which we sow here! In the coming age Christ
honors those who honored him. And they who betray their trust
in this age "shall be denied" by their own failure!

This confessing or denying the Son has eternal consequences.
But whether the result is fatal or not is determined by whether
a man reviles the holy Spirit of God or "speaks a word against
the son of God." Some accused Jesus of casting out demons "in
Beelzebul, the prince of demons." It was more than Jesus they
scorned. It was the very spirit of holiness that worked within
him that they ridiculed. They ascribed his holy deeds to unholy
sources. At bottom it wasn't so much hatred of him as hatred of
goodness in him that they manifested. Theirs was not the sin of
ignorance, prejudice, or bias. It was pernicious malice that
motivated them. They despised the holy! Their hearts were
bathed in cancerous evil that would not rest until it painted
goodness as evil. The very nature of the sin left it without
pardon. In the face of that kind of sin grace is barred from
being gracious; love is thwarted in reaching out to redeem. Sin
against holiness is sin against God's Holy Spirit, hence is
unpardonable. It is fatal! Sin against the son of God may not be
malicious. But that against the fact of holiness is malicious,
willful, determined. It wills to oppose God's holy will. Nothing
remains but to abandon it to its eternal destiny!

But Christ's aim is to encourage his disciples to be faithful
witnesses. Even his warning about the sin against the Holy
Spirit is to encourage them to be faithful witnesses to Him and
his word. The Holy Spirit, which some revile, shall be their
support in their hour of need. "Whenever they shall bring you
before the synagogues (Jewish religious rulers) and the
governors (Gentiles) and (any other kinds of) authorities, don't
(even begin to) be anxious how you shall defend or what you
shall say. The Holy Spirit shall teach you in that very hour the
things which it is necessary to speak." That very Spirit of
holiness which they deny and revile shall be your ever ready
Teacher to guide you in defense and supply your word of triumph
in your hour of trial. The Holy Spirit will do His work through
them. Disciples are to make themselves open and available to
the Spirit. Then they shall be the mouthpiece of God's Spirit!

Nothing is more universal, less sectarian than holiness! God
is spirit! God is holy! What is more universal than the Spirit
which is holy?

Hypocricy demeans, denies, contradicts the holy humanity of
man. Christ came to remake men "in His image." He was to make
the formal fakes they had become into the "likeness" of the Holy
God after whom they had been molded. The conflict between
hypocricy and holiness is that which Jesus came to resolve. "The
light shines in the darkness, and the darkness did not overcome
it."(Jn.1:5)

198

AN OUTLINE OF LUKE 12:13-21
The Ownership of Property!

It would seem obvious that I own my property! If I don't, who does? I have legal title to certain properties, bank accounts, cars, clothing, furniture! What is my relationship to properties registered in my name?

I.   THE OCCASION: A CLAIM OF OWNERSHIP. 12:13-14
    1. A Complaint: "Divide with me the inheritance!"
    2. Jesus disclaims being a civil authority! 14

II. COVETOUSNESS AND OWNERSHIP OF PROPERTY. 12:15
    1. Warning against greed. 15a
    2. Ownership and "Life." 15b

III. ILLUSTRATIVE PARABLE: A RICH FOOL! 12:16-21
    1. A Successful Farmer. 16-18
      (a)A bumper crop. 16
      (b)Material prosperity brings a problem. 17
      (c)Solution to the problem. 18
    2. Conclusions drawn. 19-21
      (a)The farmer's conclusion. 19
      (b)God's conclusion. 20

Who owns "my" property? If I don't, who does? What is my relationship to property registered in my name? If this world and all in it is God's creation then He is sole owner. That which he sends through my hands is a trust given. I hold His properties in trust for Him. That includes me, my soul! For all "things" I am accountable to Him.

* * * * * * *

THE OWNERSHIP OF PROPERTY!

When we start with God as creator that determines who I am and my relationship to all His creation. Creation is his property. That which I have I control as trustee; He owns. Nothing is absolutely mine. God delegates to me as his creature obligations of management in his behalf. This is the biblical view of ownership of property.

A Claim of Ownership!

"A certain one from the crowd spoke to him, 'Teacher! Tell my brother to divide with me the inheritance.'" In the story of the prodigal son (Luke 15) we become aware that an "elder" son felt certain obligations not burdening the younger. The older was responsible to furnish care to all in the family in case of the father's death. The older must support his mother and sisters; other sons too if they chose to remain at home until of age. But the younger could ask for his portion of "the inheritance" if he decided to leave home.

Apparently in the present instance a younger son was having difficulty in getting his "elder" brother to release the inheritance. We are not sure why tension existed between the brothers. But we are aware that there was a tension. And the young man took advantage of Jesus' public stature and manifest wisdom to put unexpected pressure on the elder brother to "divide the inheritance with me!"

Jesus held no office, religious or civil. He spoke with the authority of truth, not of office. He had no synagogue save the mountainside; no pulpit except the barren rock, fallen log or stump of tree. The grace of his person lent power to his word. It was person to person rather than ruler to subject that gave strength to his service to people. Thus when the young man sought help as though Jesus were a civil servant he spoke with pointed sharpness, "Who made me a judge or arbiter over you?" Jesus disclaimed being an arbiter of differences which normally courts of law performed. It was the business of judge to decide points of law; the "divider" saw that sentences were properly executed.

By this disclaimer Jesus made clear that he was more than a civil servant or a social reformer. His teaching would recast society like leaven in dough. But his doctrine was for the mind and heart struggling to release itself from the bondage of sin. Redeemed men can and will create inevitable social changes. But his task was not to be "judge" or "divider" in the entanglements of men. Such seems to be the force of his disclaimer to this young man.

Covetousness and Ownership!

Jesus did use the complaint to reveal man's relationship to property. First he addressed the people. He began with a warning exhortation, "Watch and be guarding yourselves from covetousness."

Man has an uncanny confidence in the possession of material goods of the world. Property and money are assumed to guarantee security, fulfillment, contentment, and a joyful peace. Of themselves "things" are presumed to engender utopia! This instinctive view treats man as animal without a spiritual base! When his stomach is full he is supposed to have the ultimate in buoyant delight. So says the gross materialist.

The word translated "covetousness" indicates more than protecting that which one possesses. It is an inordinate desire to keep getting more than one needs. It's greed that feeds on avaricious getting more and more. It takes pleasure in the power of property. Hence Jesus begins by a solemn warning of the destructive power of greedy getting!

But that which one acquires in abundance beyond what he needs is itself conditional upon something that lies beyond the material. Though a man possesses more than he needs, even a glut of "things" cannot profit him unless he has life! Property is not to be equated with life. So Jesus states: "To the one having an over abundance, his life is not in the goods existing to him!" If one doesn't dwell among the living what does title to property mean? At the lowest, most natural definition of "life" how much "breath" a man has is more significant than how much "property" he possesses. If I hold title to millions of acres but lie in bed suffocating with pneumonia what joy is there in that? Greed casts a cloud over the vision of reality; it distorts the sharp outline of values; it reverses moral distinctions and blinds one to the potholes on the highway of life!

200

Parable of The Rich Fool!

To cast a living image in the form of a story makes clear a truth while it engraves it in the soul. Jesus embedded his truth about man and property in a lucid story. "The land of a certain rich man bore well." The man is unnamed. It's not who he is but what he has that is his mark of eminence. In the societies of this world wealth more than character defines who is "great." Its absence declares who is "little." One is good or bad, strong or weak, success or failure by whether his land bears well! Investments that "bear well" make a man rich in money and marks his station in life. It's his property that gives him a name remembered. The dictionary describes Croesus as a "Lydian king, noted for his wealth;...any very wealthy man." The name of the man crept into our language. Wealth is what the world remembers about him, not who he was or what he did. That's a reflection of how the world esteems riches!

But there's nothing in Christ's parable that indicates that this "certain rich man" got his wealth by fraud or deceit. He simply had bumper crops. And for a farmer there's nothing wrong in having productive land. Indeed, scripture does not hint that having wealth in itself makes a sinner. In so far as morality is concerned wealth is neutral. This farmer labored long hours in the field, regularly paid on his mortgage, honored his debts, clothed and housed his family. He was simply skilled at farming and had fields that "bore well."

Success in acquiring and using property created problems. What is to be done with the acquired property? How shall it be used? He must turn the crops into cash. To do that he must care for the crops until they can be marketed. They couldn't be left in the field to rot. So he "was reasoning in himself saying, 'What shall I do, because I do not have where I may gather my fruits?'" Unless he can manage the produce, having it is a burden rather than a blessing. The more he pondered his problem the clearer the solution became. Suddenly he got a bright idea, "I will tear down my barns and I will build larger ones." This wasn't so easy as we might think. Our barns are constructed of lumber and built above ground. Their barns were dug into the ground and walled with stones. Solution to his problem entailed much outlay of capital and hours of hard labor. It was the lesser of evils but it seemed the wisest choice if he was to preserve his wealth.

That which reassured him of the wisdom of his decision was the long range sense of security and personal pleasure he could get from his prosperity. "I will gather there my grain and all my goods, and I will say to my soul, 'Soul! You have many goods laid up for many years; relax, eat, drink, be cheerful!'" Note how often the first personal pronoun "I" and "my" appeared in his meditation. He even addressed his own "soul" as though he owned it. This reflects a universal assumption that what I possess is mine by ownership.

For a farmer to have land that bears well creates an illusion of ownership. It can blind us to the fact that "in the beginning

God created the heavens and the earth..." He, God, is the owner! He is the landlord who has loaned in trust his property to men. We are trustees who are to render an account as to how we use his property.

We must give this "certain man" whose field "bore well" the benefit of any doubt as to his integrity. That he was honest is to be stressed. He was not a cheat, fraud, or criminal. He was simply overwhelmed with the mass of money at his command and the fearsome decisions he had to make as to how to get the money to produce even greater dividends. His mind was so preoccupied with the amount of money he controlled; he was so concerned with weighing alternative choices; so completely absorbed by the immediate decisions that he forgot, overlooked, or selfishly ignored, God's ownership. He lived with the problem so much that he began to feel that it really was his property! Is that not the way most human beings react to God's material blessings? Our attention is so absorbed in acquiring, managing, protecting property that we fall into the illusion that it is ours! It so occupies our attention that we consider it ours! The fact is that it is ours to manage and use for him!

The man of the parable received the shock of his life the very day his newly constructed barns were completed and his grain safely stored. The last sheaf stashed away, he walked wearily from the barn to the house and plopped down into an easy chair and mused, "Soul! you have many things laid up for many years. Take a long rest; eat, drink, be cheerful, merry, gay and light-hearted." He had plans for a lighter work load, frequent vacations, foreign travel, and some home town partying! Those were his plans!

Man makes plans; God governs human affairs. God has his plan. He includes each human being in his over-arching purpose. He entrusts to each man material means with which to contribute to His goal. But when we take his property entrusted to us and divert it to our personal private indulgence eventually his ownership will come to bear. If I have used his property as though it were mine judgement is at hand. God said, "Fool! This night they are requiring your soul!" The man mentioned "many years." God said, "Tonight!" The man claimed, "I have many goods!" God reminded, "Fool! they require your soul!" Even my soul is not mine. It is subject to God's determination.

On this globe sea and land furnish man's stage of operation. From these elements he gains his practical means of "making a living." But it is God who created both sea and land and to whom it all belongs by right of creation. Furthermore, "in him was life" which indicates that man's life is the gift of God. That means man's very "soul" belongs to God. By God's grace all is given for man's benefit. We hold both self and property in trust. And for it we are to give account. Both property and life (soul) is the universal responsibility of all men. None can escape the use or misuse of property and life! This is the impact on the mind and heart of Theophilus of the story of this "certain man."

202

AN OUTLINE OF LUKE 12:22-40
Breaching the Power of Property!
Man's addiction to greed is a fact of life. Covetousness is
a universal sickness of the soul. How may it be broken?
  I.   CONFIDENCE IN THE GOODNESS OF GOD! 12:22-28
       1. Negative: even necessities are not to distract. 22
          (a)Food or clothing. 22-23
          (b)God's care of birds and flowers. 24-27
       2. Positive: the logical inference. 28
  II. CONCENTRATE ON AFFAIRS OF THE SPIRIT. 12:29-34
       1. Don't focus on getting the necessities. 29-30
          (a)The "nations" are not the pattern. 29
          (b)The heavenly Father knows your need. 30
       2. Concentrate on his kingdom. 31-34
          (a)His kingdom the foremost priority. 31a
          (b)Kingdom work includes the necessities. 31b
          (c)The Father's strategy. 32-34
  III. THE CERTAIN RETURN OF THE MASTER. 12:35-40
       1. Be prepared for Master's return from wedding. 35-36
       2. Be ready for returning Master to banquet them. 37f
       3. Be primed as householders watch against robbers. 39
     When a believer trusts God's grace, he won't permit pursuit
of money to distract. If the kingdom absorbs his attention
property won't divert him. If he's alert to and watches for the
Master's swift return, he won't turn to amass money.

                    * * * * * * *

              BREACHING THE POWER OF PROPERTY!
     In the parable of the Rich Fool Jesus pointed his teaching to
men in general. He ended:"the things which you prepared, whose
shall they be? Thus (is) the one treasuring for himself and not
being rich to God." This he taught all men.
     Then he "said to his disciples!" That which he now teaches is
aimed at believers. To be his follower the vice-like clutch
with which material wealth encases every human must be broken.
How may this be done?
              Confidence in the Goodness of God!
     Jesus said, "On account of this (universal covetousness) I
say to you, 'Don't divide your soul as to what you shall eat,
neither your body, how you shall clothe yourselves.'" The most
immediate need in sustaining life is food; a close second is
clothing! These are elemental necessities! This is a highly
competitive world. If one must spend his waking hours fighting
for food and clothing, there's none or little room for any
higher cultural or spiritual exposure. To be distracted with
filling of the stomach and covering up one's nakedness pilfers
enlightenment from the mind and spirit.
     Jesus reminds his disciples that "the soul is more (greater)
than the food and the body more than its clothing." The
relative importance of the soul (and body) demands more time and
attention be given to the greater soul than the lesser food.

                         203

Twice in the text(24,27)Jesus exhorts, "Consider the ravens," "consider the lilies." The word literally means "put your mind down on ravens...lilies!" Ravens, least attractive, most useless of birds, are not able to plan, plant, or reap. The rich fool at least could think, plan, plant, harvest, make barns, and store the fruit of his labor. Ravens couldn't do that. Yet, in his scheme of things, God provided food and plumage for such creatures. Would he deny planning food for a creature "in his image"? And when you "hold your mind on the lilies that neither spin nor weave" what beauty can compare? "Not even Solomon in all his glory could clothe himself as one of these." Solomon commanded weavers and seamstresses by the dozen. Artists and designers served him on call. But results couldn't match the delicate color of a single orchid! Since provision is made in God's world for the flora and fauna surely he has a plan for providing for the highest order of his creatures.

Between these two examples of God's care Christ inserts an idea about the folly of a divided mind. "Who of you, being distracted in mind, (worrying), is able to add one measure to his stature (or length of life)? If, then, you cannot control the length of your life, why worry about the rest of things?" The rich fool died surrounded by overabundance. God is safer warrant than a warehouse full of "things" or money in a bank!

Faith Focuses on the Kingdom!

The "nations" of the Gentile world are not a pattern for faith. They spend their time and energy getting, accumulating, protecting, and spending! It's their's to get and their's to spend. If God plays any part in the process, it is to be maneuvered by the magic of ritual. God must be manipulated to serve them, not they him.

Jesus taught a different approach. "But you, don't you be seeking what you shall eat or what you shall drink; and quit having a distracted divided mind." In other words, "Don't be worrying about food and clothing." On first thought such teaching seems impractical if not irresponsible. Shall I not sow, cultivate, harvest, build barns? Shall I neglect spinning, weaving, and sewing garments? As a mature man shall I not provide necessities for my family? This is my "first thought!"

Jesus clearly says, "Your father knows that you need these." God is not ignorant of man's condition in this material world of his creation. Furthermore, he has a plan for providing these necessities; a plan that lifts the human heart above self. "Be seeking his kingdom!" Make the kingdom of God top priority. Do that first; focus on God's sovereign will for humanity, then "all these (necessities) shall be added to you."

Of course one must plant, cultivate and harvest. Of course man must invest time and energy in productive labor which will feed and clothe society. But why? What's the basic purpose for such labor? Why must I make money? Is it for self or God and his family? On the answer to this question hinges the right or wrong of my relationship to material things and ultimately my relationship to God!

If and when a believer has eliminated all distractions from his single-hearted devotion to the kingdom then he knows that food and clothing will come as surely as the morning sun or as fruit on the vine. First, the sovereign will of God, then the necessities needed to discharge his will. God will not lay on me responsibility in his kingdom and not furnish me all essentials, material or spiritual, to fulfill that task.

God the Father has a definite strategy for getting his will fulfilled on earth. His kingdom advances, not by cunning or trickery, but with purpose, plan, and calculated plot. "Quit being afraid, little flock!" Why? "Because your father deemed it well to give to you the kingdom!"

In what sense has the father "given the kingdom to you?" From the divine point of view in that he, as sovereign, has revealed his will! From the human, the subject's point of view (the citizen's) the revelation gives the vision, the principles of righteousness, and the charge to do that will, personally; that is, to incorporate God's righteous will into my own life. And no less, to persuade others to accept that will into their lives. It means to use every legitimate device, talent and energy that God has "given" to propel forward his will, his righteousness throughout society.

One specific way to "seek first the kingdom of God" is "Sell your possessions and give alms!" By doing that you "Make for yourselves purses that don't age." And you also "lay up treasure in heaven where a thief does not draw near, nor does moth consume." In saying "sell your possessions" and give "alms" Jesus is not teaching that possession of material means is wrong. To give all possessions away would place each believer in need of alms rather than the giver of alms. On the contrary, Jesus is simply calling upon his followers to apply his teaching on the possession of property. The money you make is not yours to own, but yours in trust from God. Where any need in God's family arises "give an alms." The believer is commissioned to make money in order to have money to give to the kingdom cause. Thus we are "to seek first the kingdom of God!" Doing that, necessities inevitably follow!

If a man makes money with the purpose of piling it up for himself he has failed to "seek first the kingdom of God." If a man makes money in order to give it in service to the kingdom and its citizens he is seeking first the kingdom. If a man makes money and buys necessities for himself and his family he is seeking first the kingdom. Is he not a kingdom man himself? God's strategy involves breaking the control that material possessions have. Keep matters of the kingdom in balance with the need for material things! "Seek first the kingdom of God and all these things shall be added!" The essence of God's strategy is found in the words of Jesus, "where your treasure is there also your heart will be!" Life's treasure lies in that on which the heart is fixed! "Keep your heart with all vigilance; for from it flow the springs of life!"(Prov.4:23) "Seek you first the kingdom of God!"

The Master's Certain Return!

Included in God's strategy in breaking the clutch of material possessions is the certainty of Christ's return! To enforce this idea Jesus depicts a marriage festival to which a "Master" of servants had been invited. His slaves were to "be watching" for his return. "Blessed are those slaves, whom, the master, having come, shall find watching." The basic task assigned to these servants was "watch." They must keep themselves ready to receive their returning master at a moment's notice. "Your loins are to be girded and your lamps burning." The servant is waiting over night for the homecoming. He's to keep himself alert so that though there be a delay, even until early morning, he will not collapse under exhaustion. Slaves must persist in watching.

It must be kept in mind that his exhortation to "be watching" is set in the context of the believer's relationship to money, material possessions. The servant must always "be watching!" To take even an hour off to pursue private interests a servant could fail to be before the door when the master knocks for entrance. A servant's primary business is to serve the master's need, not his own. The very delay of the master is the servant's opportunity of displaying his loyalty; it becomes a test of his faithfulness! It strengthens him in character. It keeps his heart fixed on the master, not amassing or arranging his possessions. It requires him to "seek first" the master's will! The servant's most important assignment is to "watch!"

The climax of the parable of the returning Master introduces an unexpected surprise. "Verily I say to you that he will gird himself and he shall have them recline at table and having come he shall serve them!" How amazing! Servants served by the Master! The Master's relationship to his servants is not one of tyranny. It is rather one of respect, grace and love. The Pharisaical notion of superior inferior status is brushed aside. At another time Jesus said, "I have called you friends." Because they were faithful in "watching" he rewarded them by giving his affection; he reversed positions. He served them!

The importance of "watching" is underscored again by the addition of the figure of a thief's unexpected break-in. "You know that if the householder was knowing what (kind of) hour the thief comes, he wouldn't have allowed his house to be robbed." The point is not the thief but his abrupt invasion! With that kind of quick entrance shall the Master come. Watch! Be prepared! Don't be hoarding! The moral of Christ's teaching is: "You on your part, be prepared, because in an hour you think not the son of man comes!"

So much in the world tempts to distract from "watching." Nothing in the New Testament is emphasized more than "Be alert" to his coming. "If you will not watch, I will come like a thief, and you will not know what hour I come"(Rev.3:3) In an hour you think not...!" Our lack of knowledge of that unknowable hour is incentive to labor "seeking first the kingdom."

AN OUTLINE OF LUKE 12:41-48
The Faithful Prudent Manager!
   Moving steadily "toward Jerusalem" Jesus teaches the twelve,
"disciples," and "crowds." From the complaint, "Bid my brother
divide the inheritance"(12:13) the theme has been colored by the
idea of man's relationship to property. At 12:41-48 Jesus turns
attention to managing someone else's estate with its domestics.
He highlights responsible management.
   I.   THE FAITHFUL, PRUDENT STEWARD. 12:41-44
        1. Peter's Question: To whom do you speak?
        2. A Manager's delegated responsibility. 42-43
        3. Added trust to the faithful, prudent manager! 44
  II.   THE FAITHLESS, IMPRUDENT STEWARD. 12:45-46
        1. What he says "in his heart!" 45a
        2. How he manages his Master's trust. 45b
        3. Consequences: punishment "with the unfaithful." 46
 III.   PRINCIPLES OF MANAGEMENT UNIVERSAL! 12:47-48
        1. Unfaithful servant receives "many stripes." 47
        2. Imprudent servant receives "few stripes." 48a
        3. The universal principle: Consequences measured
           by the trust bestowed. 48b
   Life is the Lord's capital bestowed in trust. Both material
and spiritual is to be invested looking for an increase to be
returned to the Lord. The Master expects an accounting at his
coming. To "everyone to whom much is given, much shall be
sought, and to whom they deposited much, they shall ask much."

                    * * * * * * *

                THE FAITHFUL PRUDENT MANAGER!
   Though all property is at bottom God's we as men have legal
title to certain properties during our lifetime. How we manage
our "own" reveals the quality of our faith and relationship to
God. But managing someone else's property and their domestic
servants says much more about one's depth of character. To
manage "things" is one level of liability; to manage people is
another, especially when the "people" belong to someone else!
"Who then is the faithful, prudent, steward whom the Master
shall set over his domestics?"
                The Faithful Prudent Steward!
   Before "myriads of crowds"(1:1) Jesus "began to speak to his
disciples first." And 12:22 states, "He said to his disciples."
In 12:32 he addressed them as "little flock" to whom the father
"gave the kingdom." The responsibility attached to money seemed
awesome! Peter could not restrain himself. "Lord, to us do you
speak this parable or to all?" Jesus never belittled the
material "things" of this world. Money, property, possessions
contain no inherent evil. On the contrary such "things" not only
measure a man's character they contribute greatly in shaping
character for good or ill. But once the true value of "things"
is seen the burden presses heavily on the conscience. Peter
wanted the Lord to define exactly to whom he was pointing his
teaching!

                          207

The answer of Jesus to Peter is not so direct as Peter may have wanted. But it instilled a principle upon which Peter could discern for himself. "Who then is the faithful, the wise, steward whom the Master will establish over his domestics." When an ancient landowner went on an extended business trip he would select from his slaves one as caretaker. This slave, now manager, must manage affairs of the estate so as to direct daily duties of all the plantation. That included planning the crops, delegating labor, storing and distributing grains, discipling mavericks, rewarding good servants, providing daily food for the laborers. It was an awesome yet a distinct honor to be selected for such a wide-ranging responsibility. Obviously the servant whom the Master chose must be faithful; but he must be prudent, wise in the ways of men. Managing human beings demands far more wisdom than managing money! It takes knowledge of human nature!

Peter asked Jesus, "Are you speaking to us, the twelve? Or are you speaking to all, disciples and crowds?" Jesus did not give Peter any names of individuals. Nor did he specify a select group. But he did indicate that anyone who bore these traits of character was the one of whom he spoke. In effect Jesus said, "I speak to anyone who prudently bears the responsibility of the station to which he is appointed in the Master's kingdom!"

But Christ's answer does not rest there. To any faithful, prudent servant there comes additional honor with increased distinction. Faithfulness in a trust is rewarded by greater trust coupled with greater homage. "Blessed that servant, whom, the Master having come, shall find doing thus (faithfully managing the estate). Truly, I say to you that he shall appoint him over all his possessions." It's a law of God; trust is rewarded with more trust. No human being has been left without some talent, task, or trust that is unique to him. He's not responsible for that which he does not have. But he and he alone is answerable as to how he uses that with which he is entrusted! As he invests what he has he shall gain or forfeit his status with the Master. Let each one look to the service assigned to him in his Master's estate!

The Faithless, Imprudent Steward!

Unfortunately it is a fact of life that many prove to be unfaithful. Too many play the part of the foolish imprudent manager of God's trust. "If that slave shall say in his heart, 'My Master delays coming.'" Storms don't arise in a moment. First a speck on the horizon, a gentle shift in the breeze. But from such small beginning the winds increase, clouds darken, lightning flashes, thunder roars, sun and stars are blotted out, the whole earth trembles under the power of the raging heavens. This is the history of an untrustworthy steward. First his mind dwells on, "The Master delays his return!" That takes possession "of his heart!" He is the one who faces the daily problems of the domestics. He makes the decisions. It's his to manage. The Master is absent; he fails to return. To all practical purposes it's mine! So says the steward "in his heart."

208

Beginning "in the heart" the manager changes his method of managing. He begins "to beat the men and maid servants, and to eat and drink and get drunk..." The change of viewpoint "in his heart" alters a change in the way he administers his trust. And this is especially true in his personal relations with the young men and maidservants. Younger people are more aggressive, more independent, more rebellious than older servants. Besides, his need to make decisions, his inward feeling of ownership put him on the defensive when confrontations arose. It's quicker, easier to "beat" than to reason with people. To escape his sense of guilt he drowned himself in wine. Drunkenness blotted from his mind all consequences of his faithless behaviour. Besides, it made his imprudent lifestyle appear prudent. Getting drunk makes a fool appear (to himself) wise and a wise man a fool! Thus it was that he who in the beginning had the confidence of the land lord lost his self-respect, his hold over the servants, and in the end the trust of his Master. Such is the difference between how the steward _ought_ to have managed and how he _did_ manage.

Faithless or faithful, imprudent or prudent a steward is still a steward. A day for accounting must come; the Master, though he tarry, will come. "The master of that slave will come in a day in which he doesn't expect and in an hour of which he is unaware, and he will cut him in two and will appoint his portion with the unfaithful." This is the issue of any trustee in God's kingdom who fails to "keep on watching" for the Lord's return. He forfeits his trust not to mention his personal place in the kingdom. He is as though he were an "unbeliever" and is given a "portion with the ones unbelieving."

Inherent within the God-given trust of leadership over the people (domestics) of God's family lie both punishments or rewards. "That servant, the one who got to know his master's will and did not prepare or do according to his will, shall be flogged with many stripes. But the one not having known, but having done that worthy of floggings shall receive few stripes." Punishment does not stem from personal revenge on the part of the master. It springs out of the nature and degree of imprudent unfaithfulness of oversight. To the degree of our neglect to "watch" over the souls entrusted to us, so shall punishment be! The unfaithful receives "many floggings." The imprudent receives "few floggings." The divine principle is: consequences are measured by (1)the trust bestowed and (2)by knowledge of the master's will on the part of the steward. "To everyone to whom much is given, much shall be asked of him; and to him with whom much is deposited, they shall ask more (of) him."

Peter's question has been answered! Jesus was speaking to anyone who accepted a responsibility of trust over the souls of men. "Watch" over their welfare while the Master tarries! "Watch" and teach them to "watch" for the certain coming of the Master! Enlighten their minds; cleanse their hearts, fortify their wills, "watch" over their souls until the Master comes! This is the _universal_ trust deposited with any or all who have come to "know his will."

AN OUTLINE OF LUKE 12:49-53
An Unearthly Fire on Earth!
As the Bible speaks so God speaks! More important than what
he says is what he means by what he says. Luke 12:51 declares,
"Are you supposing that I came to give peace on the earth? Not
at all; but I came to give division!" In 12:49 Luke reports
Jesus as saying, "I came to cast fire upon the earth, and how I
wish it were already kindled!" What does he mean?
I. PURPOSE: "TO CAST FIRE ON THE EARTH!" 12:49-51
    1. The purpose stated. 49a
    2. Christ's feeling that it "be already kindled." 49b
    3. His personal baptism of fire. 50
II. THE BAPTISM OF SUFFERING(FIRE). 12:51-53
    1. Supposition versus fact. 51
    2. Specific divisions created. 52-53
       (a)Family against family.
       (b)In-laws against in-laws.
Reconciling the apparent conflict lies in discerning between
purpose and result, design and effect.

* * * * * * *

AN UNEARTHLY FIRE ON EARTH!
"I have come to cast fire on the earth!" So said Jesus as he
contemplated the effect of his "coming" into the world.
    In the Old Testament "fire" was used as a figure for
purification, discernment, judgment. In the words of John the
Baptist the coming of Messiah was to effect a separation. He
"will gather the wheat into his granary, but the chaff he will
burn with unquenchable fire."(Lk.3:17) Fire was purifying and
thus redemptive. He came to bring an unearthly fire to the
earth! In the process the fire became judgmental and divisive.
Why Did Christ Come?
    The text seems clear in stating why Christ came into the
world. "I came to cast fire upon the earth." And the entire
text makes plain that this "fire" involved suffering, both his
own and that of those who heard him.
    The expression "I came..." implies his pre-existence. Jesus
was conscious that he "came" into this world from "out" of this
world! And he "came" with design, a determined objective. It
was "to cast fire on the earth!" The fire of suffering,
purification, redemption! It would discriminate and divide. It
would separate "wheat from chaff" and cleave between believer
and unbeliever.
    As he spoke of this fire the human nature of Jesus erupted.
It may equal but nothing in Luke surpasses this expression of
the humanity of the man Jesus. "How I wish that it (fire) were
already kindled!" Feelings are as much a part of human nature
as the capacity to think or do. Man is a rational creature; he
also must act. But he would never do what he thinks if he never
felt! Feelings generate action. To think draws a blueprint; the
will decides to act on the thought. But the emotions impel to
act. Feeling is the motor which drives the man to do what he
210

thinks. Feelings are human; they constrain, press, persuade, urge, spur, prod, prick. They disclose joy, hate, wonder, sorrow, rapture. To _feel_ is to be human! When Jesus burst out with "I came to cast fire upon the earth" he let go with unrestrained fervor: "How I wish it were already kindled!" These words were spoken on this, his final journey to Jerusalem at the end of which was the cross. And though the cross was the heart of the reason why he came nevertheless it was a painful, ugly, humiliating experience. Even the thought of it provoked his feelings to white heat. God in Christ was so _human_!

This "firebrand" which had "come" from heaven to earth had already ignited a fire that was destined to spread throughout the whole world. But, though kindled, it waited a condition that only _he_, the Christ could consummate at Calvary. It weighed on _his_ heart, filled his mind, awakened his emotions. In his outburst he used the figure of a baptism. "A baptism I have with which to be baptized, and how I am being pressed together until when it shall be brought to completion!" To baptize is to submerge! His own personal "fire" included the overwhelming of the cross. He daily envisioned the oncoming injustice to be wrought on him. Its reproach, disgrace, and shame inundated his sensitive spirit. The image of the coming cross filled his supersensitive soul. The necessity of the cross, his willingness to endure it, his commitment to it did not lessen its pain and shame! Without the cross the conflagration enflamed by the coming of Jesus would die not even leaving smouldering ashes. _He_ must embrace this engulfing torture that the fire of redemption might ignite the world. So vivid to his imagination was his "baptism" of suffering that the reality of it submerged him in emotional turmoil.

The word translated "straightened," "constrained" in our English versions literally means, "hold together, grip, press close." It's a strong word that indicates that Jesus was completely, totally controlled by this coming "baptism." Jesus would not have been "human" had he not unleashed his feelings. And the fact he did discloses how truly human he really was. While welcoming the cross he shrank from it! His feelings revealed how much he was inundated by it!

The Fire of His Suffering Spreads!

The baptism of suffering into which Jesus plunges shall set the whole world aflame! Gethsemane and Calvary must needs be reproduced in the life of every human being who would escape eternity's fire of condemnation. "Do you suppose that I came to give peace on the earth? No! No! But rather division" (did I bring). The word translated "suppose" is the most subjective of all words for "think." It is a thoughtless thought, a shallow opinion, that Jesus as "Prince of peace" came to bring peace. By its nature corruption must oppose incorruption. Darkness will contradict light! Sin will war against righteousness. Sons of Satan are committed to war against sons of God! In a corrupt sin-cursed, wicked world to introduce righteousness creates strong tensions that only ferment strife and conflict.

211

The supposition that Christ came to bring peace contradicts the fact that he came to bring division and strife. Yet how can this be? Does not the scripture in its most golden text say, "God so loved the world that he gave his only begotten son that whosoever believes might not perish!" And "God sent the son into the world, not to condemn...but that the world might be saved through him." Our text seems to indicate the opposite: "I came to cast fire...I came to give division!" How may his stated purpose of saving versus division be reconciled? Does not redemption and conflict come from the same Lord!

Jesus leaves no doubt that division falls within his design. He specifies certain divisions he introduces within the warmest most intimate of human relationships, the family. The bond of human ties is strongest, most affectionate, most lasting in the parent child, brother sister rapport than any other alliance known among men. Even the bond that makes the people of God one is pictured under the image of the family. Yet the division which Jesus brings to the world penetrates into the deep-seated warmth of the family. "From now five shall be divided in one house, three against two and two against three;...father against son and son against father, mother against daughter and daughter against mother." If Christ's coming would divide such wholesome attachments as these what bond known to man can escape such a divisive force? These passages seem to suggest that Jesus came to destroy, not to save! And as if to enforce the idea he says that the normal tension existing between "in-laws" shall be made firm by the division which he "gives." "Mother-in-law against daughter-in-law" shall add to the warring confusion which his appearance on earth shall bring!

To reconcile his redemptive versus his divisive purposes lies in the nature of man as created "in the image of God." The most singular quality in man as God's "image" is his responsibility to weigh alternatives and choose one and reject the other. This is profoundly true in choosing moral alternatives. This being true God would not force morality onto man. To be moral man must freely choose that which is right. The ten commandments were not given to legislate morality. They describe it. But by its very nature law cannot force obedience. Law is light in a dark room, it reveals moral standards; it's a blueprint of what moral conduct ought to be; it's a textbook teaching what a spiritual life can be. It proposes but it doesn't compel. Law reveals a design but it can't bulldoze a result; it can enlighten a mind but it won't browbeat a soul.

In the light of such facts God must persuade, not force men to righteousness. He must win rather than coerce. He wants humans, not robots. Men must choose him and reject evil. They must will the good and refuse the wicked. Thus God "so loved...that he gave his only son...not to condemn but to save..." God placed squarely in front of men the epitome of righteous law in the living person of Jesus. And since "all have sinned" and "none are righteous" by his grace in Christ God removed the barrier of sin that men might be reconciled to him.

The marrow of the matter is to distinguish between the intended purpose and the effective result of Christ's coming. True, "God so loved...that whoever believed might not perish.. but he who does not believe is condemned!" "Light has come...men loved darkness rather than the light...everyone who does evil hates the light..."(Jn.3:18f) God's purpose is to remove sin, bring harmony, peace, redemption. But he does not, nor will he, invade the human will. He leaves man to choose his offer of peace and redemption. If man chooses to reject the gracious will of God then the effect of Christ's coming is disharmony, conflict, war. From that point of view it can be honestly said, "I came to bring, not peace, but division."

It remains true as it was when Jesus first spoke the words: "I came to cast fire on the earth...from now there shall be in one house five divided, three against two and two against three..." Whether it be in an unnamed obscure American family or a great nation officially committed to atheism, throughout the centuries Jesus Christ has been a dividing factor in human relationships. Faith in the Person of Christ and commitment to his moral values have turned father against son, brother against brother, wife against husband and king against peasant. This is what Jesus means by what he says, "I came to cast fire upon the earth!"

Two themes have threaded their way through Luke's Gospel thus far. They form the pith and marrow from which stems Luke's masterful story of Jesus. Sometimes one dominates; sometimes the other. Together they form the truth with which he seeks to penetrate the mind and heart of his reader, the "most noble Theophilus!" In this text it's the humanity of the Lord that rises to a mountain peak. The humanity of Jesus breaks forth in all its fervor and reality. No man has been more man than Jesus as displayed in this passage. And it's because he is shown to be so filled with human emotions that we are able to recognize his humanity. These feelings are so universal it isn't hard to see him as human in their display.

That which is human is universal. It is present everywhere, in all people, in any age and any time. He who sees the deity in Jesus' humanity and rejects that may expect the fire of judgment. He who responds in faith may look forward to, in this life, the fire of painful purification and in eternity the fire of fellowship with him who, having become human, is eternal Saviour!

AN OUTLINE OF LUKE 12:54-59
Reading Signs of the Times!
Forecasting weather has been reduced to about 80% accuracy!
But it has always intrigued man. In forcasting he can plan in
the light of his prediction. If we know whether we will have
sun or showers, cold or heat, it will affect how we invest our
time and money.

   I. READING THE SIGNS. 12:54-56
      1. Matters over which men have no control.
        (a)To whom spoken.
        (b)"Acts of God," social movements, investments.
      2. Those affecting higher moral matters. 56
        (a)Those lacking, not insight, but the will to do!
        (b)God-given opportunity, "this season."
  II. APPLICATION: JUDGING THE RIGHT THING. 12:57-59
      1. The Question Raised. 57
      2. A Practical Example. 58-59
        (a)Be reconciled with adversary "while going."
        (b)Avoid the consequences.

If a man journeying with an "adversary" on the way can and
will induct a reconciliation he rids himself of embarrassment,
pain and cost of court room justice. If one can rightly read the
"signs" of his moral relationships, he can resolve them if he
will before they destroy him.

* * * * * * *

READING THE SIGNS OF THE TIMES!
Someone has said, "Life is too short to be small." How true!
Personal differences, harmful entanglements, warring conflicts
fracture peace of mind; shatter the tranquil heart and serene
soul. Aberrations of moral rectitude, deviations from spiritual
integrity destroy friendships, families, partnerships. They can
even rupture entire societies. Economic order, governmental
agencies, religous groups, family units, are held together by
ethical, moral and spiritual values. This is true even in an
atheistic, amoral society. Moral bonds are not as visible as
sun, storm, or volcano. But their presence or absence is as
vital to the course of human life as any physical force.
Morality is the cement of society, the bond of unity without
which humanity disintegrates into a vast array of individuals,
unattached sparks; not a cohesive unity.
On Reading Signs!
The most familiar incidence of sign-reading is forecasting
weather. It's an ancient practice. Moreover, it affects human
conduct, both individuals and society at large. Our weather
prophets influence our plans. Whether I venture out or stay at
home may be determined by what the weather man says.

Technology has raised forecasting almost to a science. High
and/or low pressures, jet streams, barometric changes all
contribute to the news reports. And these affect our decision
making for the next day's activities in business or pleasure.

214

That Jesus addressed the words of 12:54-59 "to the crowds" is suggestive. It isn't that he did not want his disciples to be alert to reading the "signs of the times." But they already had read aright the vital signs of "this season." And though it was important that they keep current and alert to reading the signs constantly before them, his present message pointed toward "the crowds" who not yet had responded to the moral and spiritual signal so prominently placarded before them. "The crowds" consisted of common people; landowners, tenants, laborers, farmers, sheep-herders, housewives, servants both man and maid. City people and country rustic, rich and poor, learned and ignorant all were ingredients in "the crowds" to whom Jesus appealed in this warning to read aright the "signs."

The signs of which he spoke divide into two kinds. One was those over which men had no control, or little, if any. The hot sirocco scorchers from the desert southeast definitely signaled a torrid, broiling day of heat. In contrast, when dark clouds assembled over the Mediterranean in the west any weatherwise Palestinian knew that drenching showers were not far off. They could predict the weather with such success.

And we take this sign-reading of the weather to be typical of "acts of God" which lie beyond man's ability to control, or in some cases even to predict. Storm and flood, drouth and famine, volcano and earthquake lie beyond man's ability to regulate.

Not too different in nature to these "acts of God" are economic, social, governmental and business upheavals. Men may affect and influence such revolutionary turbulance in such matters. And yet as single individuals men often feel helpless. Men ride them out as chips of wood awash in a stormy sea. But to the acute observer even such violent social upheavals give "signs" in advance. Those who have gained the wisdom of years can read social, economic, moral "signs of the times" and prepare for the coming distress.

Jesus uses harsh language in describing men who can read such "signs" yet seem so blind to signs that signal coming moral spiritual disasters. He says, "Hypocrites! The face of the earth and the heaven you know to test. But this season you do not know how to test!" His use of demonstrative "this" is strong indication that he has in mind a special, particular "sign" now in front of them. They were "pretenders," "play actors," toying with signals of matters much more important than weather. It was something they saw every day yet ignored its implications. John the Baptist had come and shaken their nation out of its moral lethargy. He shattered their callous hearts! He said to "the crowds," "the axe lies at the root of the trees; every tree that does not bear good fruit is cut down and thrown into the fire." Jesus had been with them for several years preaching and demonstrating the kingdom of God. The righteousness of God was embodied before their very eyes. Yet they pretended not to read the sign of God. Jesus described their reaction by, "Hypocrites!" They possessed eyes to see but not the will to accept! Their reaction was but a pretense!

In his reference, "You do nor know how to test this season" (vs.56) Jesus referred to their lack of will to see in him the obvious moral and spiritual implications. When from the dungeon prison John the Baptist asked, "Are you the one coming?" Jesus responded, "Declare to John that which you saw and heard; blind are seeing, lame are walking, lepers are cleansed..." To those disposed to see their moral import, the person, character and mission of Jesus was demonstrated in his life and deeds. If men had the heart to perceive, it was clear that Jesus cast out demons by "the finger of God." Yet "the crowds" professed not to recognize the meaning of the sign before them. As hypocrites they resolved not to see the spiritual stature or moral claims of "this epoch of time" in which they lived. They lacked the moral will, the spiritual sensitivity to the presence of God in Jesus as the Christ. Isaiah had said, "Behold your God!"(40:9). "The crowds" were living in "this season" of fulfillment, yet refused to read the "signs of their times."

Judging the Right!

Jesus enforced the moral dullness of "the crowds" with a parable. First came a rhetorical question, "Why are you not from yourselves judging what is the right?" In other words, you have in your hands the capacity to judge what is the right thing to do in a situation. When you know the fatal consequences of failure why do you fail to make right moral judgments?

Along life's way come many relationships. Some develop into heart-warming friendships. Others evolve into bitter enmities. Marriage bonds fracture and create vitriolic rivals. Business conflicts produce hostile adversaries. Professional partners often betray one another and become harsh enemies. Religious fellowships turn into warring camps destroying each other in their dissensions. And in all such shattered relationships a common denominator is the unwillingness to read moral signs that clearly point to sure self-destruction. Calamities do not come without warning. Even a death-dealing earthquake gives advance rumbles which announce the threat of destruction and death. So the right thing to do is to heed the warning signs, correct the moral deviations that give rise to the signs, and thus rid yourself of the disastrous consequences.

"As you journey with your adversary to appear before a ruler, give diligence to settle with him while you are in the way lest he drag you before the judge, and the judge deliver you to the executor, and the executor throw you into jail...you won't come out thence until you have paid the last little coin!" Background details give color and reality but the lesson in a parable is seen in the main point of the story. We are not here concerned with who the adversary, judge, executor are or what the jail represents. The point of the parable is: interpret the signs which produce adversarial differences. Do something "while in the way" to correct them no matter how humiliating the cost. If you do this now before the fruit of wrong doing has time to bear its ill fruit then you can be rid of any ugly consequences. If you can read the signs of the weather, you surely should be able to

216

note abnormal ethical behaviour, sure sign of moral collapse. If detected and confronted with honest change, such deviations in conduct can be corrected. The point of the parable is: Read the signs, alter your behaviour, align yourself with God-given principles of right; get rid of the cancer of sin gnawing at your vital spiritual essentials. Take advantage of "this season" of grace in your life. Thus you will avoid the rotting of the moral fiber of your soul throughout eternity.

Weather and weather forecasting are not the major concerns of human life in this world. Such are peripheral! Yet they reflect underlying forces in all creation about us. And they illuminate moral, ethical, spiritual norms as fundamental to spiritual health. These norms are as basic to spiritual wholeness as physical laws are to the material world. They are underlined_universally_ present in every _human_ being. When violated they destroy both the plush and the _poor_, king and commoner, Jew and Gentile, male and female, rich and rustic, educated and ignorant, slave and free; in a word, _all_ strata of human kind. These divine criteria for human behaviour serve as sure "signs" by which men may evaluate their moral and spiritual condition. They are road markers, guidelines to help us drive the highways of life. It is the part of wisdom periodically to take stock and evaluate just how we are reading and heeding the "signs of our times."

In every paragraph in his unfolding story Luke sketches the universality and humanity of Jesus the Christ. Theophilus could scarcely escape the impression of these two dominate features in the Christ's rvelation of the nature of God.

AN OUTLINE OF LUKE 13:1-9
Fruitbearing and Judgment!
The word of God says, "It is given to men once to die and
after this, judgment."(Heb.9:27) Without moral responsibility
the world would be a chaos, not a cosmos. There would be no
ultimate of any kind, good or bad. Judgment is inevitable in a
moral universe.
I. TRAGEDY AND JUDGMENT! 13:1-5
    1. The unjust violence of Pilate. 2-3
    2. The fall of the tower of Siloam
    3. The call to repentance is universal.
II. JUDGMENT ON A FRUITLESS FIG TREE. 13:6-9
    1. Three years without bearing fruit. 6
    2. Decision by the Master of the Orchard. 7
    3. One more opportunity before judgment. 8f
The inevitable consequence of sin is judgment. Inexorable
judgment provides the neccessity of repentance.

* * * * * * *

FRUITBEARING AND JUDGMENT!
Why should there be judgment? Why have the Judgment? Paul
says, "there is no distinction; since all have sinned and fall
short of the glory of God, they are justified by his grace as a
gift."(Rom.3:23) Since God justifies "by his grace" why have any
judgment? Why not graciously forgive everybody? Does he not
limit his grace by granting it to those who "believe" and
witholding it from those who don't? When we view the inequities
in life, are we, as thinking men, not warranted in questioning
God's administration of justice? Some die in their youth
through some "act of God" over which men have no control? Some
die at birth; others live to the full "three score and ten."
"Little people pay taxes!" She who made such an inhuman
observation, Leona Helmsley, went her merry way untouched by the
scandal of refined thievery! If God runs this universe with a
modicum of justice why do such abuses abound?
    We may not know why God allows such lechery but we are
assured that he who imposes this kind of foul play is to be held
accountable. "It is given to men once to die and after this,
judgment."(Heb.9:27)
Tragedy and Judgment!
    The absolute standard of right and wrong is not determined by
democratic vote. It stems rather from the eternal nature of
God. He is righteous! Therefore "right" springs from his will
and his moral nature. Righteous laws are the expressions of
himself in stated forms. With instinct of spirit men, even in
the breach, recognize and respond to his laws as like responds
to like. Men are drawn to his laws as metal responds to magnet.
We are "in his image" hence recognize in God the mold from which
we have been created. The sense of guilt in the violation of law
testifies to the intrinsic "rightness" of God's statutes, his
written descriptions of that which is "right."

218

Man, with limited vision and darkened, distorted mind, often has imposed on tragedy this innate sense of justice. "Why did this happen to me?" Why do the innocent suffer in accidents that seem so capricious? If God is in control and watches over his own, why must 37 innocent die in a church bus because some drunken driver, crossing the median, plunged head on into their church bus? Does God "send" earthquake, fire and storm to render havoc on his human creatures?

Throughout time tragedies have come and men have concluded that God is sending judgment on the victims because of the victims' secret sin! In 13:1-5 Luke reports two such incidents. "Some were present at that very season who spoke to him of the Galileans whose blood Pilate mingled with their sacrifices." Pilate exercised Rome's rule over Judea with a cruel brutal hand. Among the many displays of his violent force this example agitated theological debates of the times. Where was the justice of God when his chosen were in the act of sacrificial worship yet were murdered by Pilate's police? Why did God allow it? Or did God use Pilate to send judgment on his people because of _their_ sin? Since God does punish wrong-doers does every tragic occurrence imply some hidden sin is being punished?

Jesus introduced a tragic accident of recent history that reinforced the problem to his hearers. "Or those eighteen upon whom the tower of Siloam fell and killed them, are you supposing that they became debtors beyond all the men, the ones dwelling in Jerusalem?" This disaster to which Jesus alluded brought to mind a violent incident not caused by man's brutality to man. It was, at least it seemed, an "act of God." Why did this particular group of eighteen men "happen" to be in that tower just at the moment it's foundations gave way and its walls crumbled? Were they hiding secret sin? Was God bringing just punishment?

If Jesus answered the question Luke does not report. But he does use the question as an occasion to show the necessity of repentance on the part of those who asked. When they raised the question about the justice (or its lack) of worshippers being killed by the governor they apparently were asking what God should be doing about it! Or should they, as God's people, force justice by protesting to Rome; even return violence for violence and themselves forcefully remove Pilate?

Jesus ignores or looks beyond God's involvement. He turns to _their_ coming judgment, _their_ need of repentance! In effect Jesus said, "It's not the Galileans whose blood Pilate mingled (wrongfully) with the sacrifices that need your attention. It is _your_ sin with which you must deal lest judgment fall upon _you!_ "Except you repent, all you shall perish" (even as those worshippers and as those on whom Siloam's tower fell!)

Judgment is not imposed by the _amount_ of sin. It comes as a consequence of the _fact_ of sin. "All" have sinned. "All" have played havoc with moral law! "All" must bear the consequences. Cancer augers death! But the nature of cancer, not its size or stage, heralds death! Sin brings judgment no matter its bulk!

219

Since "sin brings judgment no matter its bulk" and since "it is given to men once to die and after this, judgment" then it is imperative that everyone face the reality of his own plight. Judgment hangs over man's head like a Damocles sword. Nothing is more important to _every_ human than the change of mind and lifestyle entailed in repentance.

Men try to avoid responsibility for their own wrong doing. They refuse to repent as long as they can shift blame to some other one or thing. By fixing attention on those whom Pilate killed during the worship the questioners of Jesus avoided facing their own guilt. It was a subtle way of rejecting repentance. It was as foolish as one dying of cancer reproaching a friend for not seeking the healing services of a physician, yet he himself refuses to go to the doctor. To attend to his own healing is the most important thing a person with a deadly disease can do. Then he may be able to help others suffering with the same sickness. So when "some present spoke to him about the Galileans whose blood Pilate shed," Jesus ignored their theological ploy to assault _their_ need for repentance. "Except you repent, you all shall perish!" Face up to the fact of your own desperate disease of sin with its guilt. _You_ are the ones who face judgment. Don't squander energy guessing other peoples' guilt or God's management of justice. Before the judgment bar of God _my_ guilt is the most pressing demand on _me_! The fall of Siloam's tower or the violence of Pilate need not be my concern. What happened to others is history and nothing I do can affect them. But while I am living I _can_ change my present condition and alter my future. While change can be made, _that_ must be the focus of my attention.

Judgment on a Fruitless Fig Tree!

Jesus embedded in a parable the possibility of changing a fruitless into a fruitful life! He declared the imperative of repentance. Change now and a lost life can become lush! "A man was having a fig tree planted in his vineyard." Soil in a vineyard proved quite fertile for fig trees. Three years is enough for even a newly planted tree to bear fruit. So the master said to the vinedresser "Behold! three years it has been from which time I am coming seeking fruit on this fig tree and I don't find any. Cut it out that it not encumber the ground." A tree that doesn't produce fruit not only is useless but it takes the soil in which another could bear fruit. It is unprofitable to permit a fruitless tree to be a financial liability.

But the master meets with an aggressive vinedresser who hesitates to waste what _could_ be a fruitful tree. So he pleads, "Leave it alone also this year and I'll dig around it and throw manure on it, if indeed it may make fruit. But if not, you shall cut it out." In the light of the context the point of the parable is: God gives ample opportunity for repentance. God's grace never falters. But man's response in repentance has limits. At some point man must "repent" or be "cut out" and cast on the rubbish heap of history. Call upon God "before the dust returns to the ground...and the spirit returns to God who gave it."

AN OUTLINE OF LUKE 13:10-17
The Role of Religious Ritual!
Religions use ritual. But ritual in itself is not religion.
What vital function does ritual perform in religion, if any?
The text suggests an answer
I. JESUS DEMONSTRATES THE ROLE OF RITUAL. 13:1-13
   1. Teaching in the synagogue the occasion. 10
   2. A crippled woman in the worship. 11
   3. Jesus chose to heal on the sabbath. 12-13a
   4. Results: Healed, she "began glorifying God." 13b
II. RULER OF SYNAGOGUE CHALLENGES JESUS' ACTION. 13:14
   1. The "indignant" ruler. 14a
   2. Addressed "the crowd," not Jesus. 14b
   3. Pharisaic philosophy as to purpose of sabbath. 14c
III.CHRIST'S RESPONSE. 13:15-16
   1. Christ's answer to him. 15a
   2. Inconsistent Pharisaic practice. 15b
   3. Healing humans the intent of the sabbath! 16
IV. CONTRASTING EFFECTS! 13:17
   1. His adversaries "were put to shame." 17a
   2. The crowd was "praising God." 17b
Ritual is not an end in itself. When it does not serve the
purpose of renewal to God it hinders rather than helps!

* * * * * * *

THE ROLE OF RELIGIOUS RITUAL!

Ritual is defined as: "Prescribed form or method for the
performance of solemn ceremony." In a general sense Sabbath
observance may be classed as ritual. It was a "method" of
periodic resting that man might renew his fellowship with God,
refresh his body with energy, stimulate his jaded emotions, and
renovate relationships with family and friends. It's original
design included healing!

Christ demonstrates the Sabbath role!

As he journeyed steadily toward his destiny at Jerusalem
Jesus never missed an opportunity to teach. "In one of the
synagogues he was teaching on the Sabbath." Teaching was like
planting seed. If the soil was barren, if rains delayed and
drought came, if vandals destroyed the budding crop the farmer's
labor became fruitless. But if the soil was rich, sun and rain
descended, if the laborer cultivated and monitored the crop then
the barns burst with new grain and the household prospered.
Though death lay before him Jesus didn't neglect to plant the
seed of truth. After his death this seed would bear fruit.

But he did more than deliver lectures. He demonstrated his
doctrine. "Behold, a woman having a spirit of weakness eighteen
years. And she was bent together and was not able to straighten
up entirely." It was a sabbath. And that which his critics
later observed was true. There were six days other than a
sabbath in which he could have healed the woman. But the fact
that he didn't suggests that he with deliberation chose to heal

221

her on the sabbath. He would objectify his teaching before he verbalized it. To exhibit doctrine in concrete deed is the best kind of teaching method. It not only attracts attention but it assists memory. The fact that he was challenged multiplied the effect of his words. Thus it was that when Jesus saw her he called and said to her, "Woman! you have been released from your infirmity. And he put his hands on her! And immediately she was made straight and began glorifying God."

Three facts about this woman are to be noted. One, she was a woman and hence, in that society, second class, subordinate human being. Second her "infirmity" is described as "spirit of weakness." In some way her affliction was related to, maybe even caused by, a "spirit." Physically speaking, diseases may be related to "allergies," "germs" and such scientific physical causes. These have been thoroughly established by modern scientific research. But no one has penetrated, at least with equal thoroughness, the relationship of moral and spiritual factors to the "weaknesses" that afflict human kind. This woman was plagued with a "spirit" characterized by a "weakness." Third, she had endured this harsh torment for eighteen years. Her bones were so rigidly fused together that she was not "able to straighten up entirely." It had been a long ordeal. We observe also that she was here in a synagogue at worship. Whatever her spiritual condition may have been, for the present she sought whatever relief worship might offer. Thanksgiving, confession, inspiration contributed to her present feelings. If God is to be found he must be sought!

As noted above Jesus designedly chose to heal this woman on the sabbath. Having seen her at worship and beholding her condition, he could just as well have waited until another day to give the cure. But her healing was not the main point; it was the sabbath day on which it was done that was the issue. The sabbath in the scheme of God had long been buried under the rubbish of human efforts to "interpret" it. It had been hedged about with so many rules of human opinion that it's original divine purpose had long since been lost. Thus it was Christ gave relief to this mortal flesh as a demonstration of the true meaning of sabbath!

When Jesus said, "You have been released from your infirmity" the verb form suggests the permanacy of her cure. Christ's cure was immediate, complete, clear-cut and permanent. Any crutch she may have used could be thrown away permanently. There would be no relapse.

Furthermore, "he placed on her his hands." Jesus appreciated the need for touching the afflicted one. Nothing makes God in Christ more human than his touching the afflicted. That he identified with her suffering, that God "felt" with the weakness of a woman was displayed by the touch of his hands.

And "immediately she began glorifying God." The pain of the past, her humiliation in the present all completely faded in the presence of God in Christ. The damned up emotions long buried under her physical and social pain exploded. "She began and kept on praising God."

222

A challenge to the action of Jesus!

"The ruler of the synagogue answered..." Whom or what did he answer? Jesus had spoken to the woman, not the ruler! It was the crowd, not Jesus, that he answered. He became "indignant" at the open disregard by Jesus of sabbath traditions. The ruler's view of sabbath observance was typical of the whole Pharisaical community. Consciously or unconciously they had altered the design of the sabbath. In God's intent the sabbath was a means to an end, not an end in itself. It was made "for man" not man for it! To reinvigorate man in his relation to God, man and himself was its purpose. The Pharisees had reduced it to law for the sake of law.

Laws are guidelines for behaviour, not chains to hamper, restrict or imprison freedom of action. The law restricting speed to 55 miles per hour on U.S. interstates was intended to protect lives, not to restrict freedom. In fact that purpose, in certain situations, can only be achieved by ignoring the 55 mile limit. When an ambulance rushes to the scene of an accident it must push aside the 55 speed limit not to mention traffic lights, road crossings and such like. And we note that more than 20 miles per hour is unsafe in some situations such as funerals etc. It is life, not law, that needs protection. And the same can be said of the biblical sabbath law. Life was the point of concern, not law. The law was to govern the normal, not the abnormal situation.

The indignant ruler "answered" the sabbath behaviour of Jesus by speaking to "the crowd." Jesus was too popular with the people to attack him personally. The charge was made under the guise of protecting the sabbath law. The hypocrisy lay in the pretense of defending the law when in fact it was the person of Christ that was the issue. "He was saying to the crowd that there are six days in which it is necessary to be working. So, coming in these days, you are to get yourselves cured and not on the sabbath." The ruler did not question that Jesus healed. But he disregarded the miracle as evidence that Jesus had the right to heal on the sabbath. The Pharisees had a mind set to kill Jesus; his practice of sabbath observance was merely the means by which they would entrap him.

The response of Jesus!

The ruler of the synagogue delivered his criticism to "the crowd." Since the assault was against Jesus in fact, Jesus took up the challenge and answered him who made the attack. The substance of his answer was that the Pharisaic practice was inconsistent with their doctrine. "Hypocrites! Does not each of you on the sabbath release his ox or ass from the manger and, leading it off, does he not water it?" You protect the life of your animals on which your livelihood is based. But "this one" in whom you have no financial interest and who, is a "daughter of Abraham," one of your faith and family, and one "whom Satan bound eighteen years," whose long period of painful suffering ought excite brotherly sympathy--was it not a logical necessity that she be released from her bondage on this, the sabbath day?"

The point of Jesus' reply was that in removing the painful torture of the woman he was in fact fulfilling the real purpose of the sabbath law. After all, the healing of human beings was God's intent in the giving of the sabbath law. It's not law but people who are sacred. Jesus did not break the law; he fulfilled it. In answering the need of the woman Christ honored God; and especially so since it was the sabbath on which he did it!

Jesus achieved two objectives by this sabbath miracle. First and foremost he renewed life and bestowed hope on this suffering woman. That was enough to justify any violation of Pharisaic tradition. But second, he made clear the double standard of the Pharisees in their view of God's law. To them theory and practice had ceased to be related; dogma and deed were severed from each other; what they said and what they did were divorced in life so far as their lifestyle was concerned. Their care for the sabbath law could be bent if they needed to "work" to provide food and water for their beasts of burden. But law (tradition) was more important than giving life to a fellow human being! Such theory coupled with such practice represented the essence of hypocrisy. And Jesus so named them, "Hypocrites!" They were play actors, imitators, caricatures of the real thing. They parroted words while ignoring human hurt.

Contrasting effects!

Reaction to the sabbath healing was two-fold. The adversaries of Jesus were humilated before the very public they sought to capture. The text testifies that they "were put to shame." The making public of their selfish concern over their animals in contrast to their callous disregard for human need ruined their image in the popular mind. They either must alter their enmity to Jesus and convert to him or compound their hypocrisy by redoubling their efforts to kill him. That was enough to make them crimson with shame.

On the other hand the crowd "was rejoicing at the glorious things which were being done by him." In spite of the weight of sin, the fickle inconstancy of the crowd, people do respond to the light of truth and the display of hypocrisy. If and when their own self-centered interest is held in abeyance, people naturally and quite instinctively respond to truth. At any rate this crowd "rejoiced at all the glorious things" which Jesus did, especially the cure of this woman and the Pharisaic hypocrisy which it uncovered.

Thus Jesus openly publicized, that in some situations, to obey the sabbath ritual may actually defeat its purpose. Ritual as such is not an end in itself. It does not have life in itself. It is a tool, an instrument, a conduit through which God may channel the power of his life to human life. The ritual is not the power; it is the channel! When the ritual does not renew life it defeats its purpose! It becomes worse than no ritual. But in God's hands and used as he designed, ritual becomes a practical means to a divine end.

AN OUTLINE OF LUKE 13:18-21
What Is the Kingdom of God Like?

"Kingdom" is that area, realm, or condition in which a king exercises rule. Where or over what does God rule? To what may his sovereignty be likened?

I. THE QUESTIONED RAISED. 13:18
1. There is an analogy in creation to the kingdom. 18a
2. Jesus is he who must unveil the likeness. 18b
II. THE LIKENESS PROPOSED. 13:19-21
1. The mustard seed. 19
(a)Small beginning.
(b)Large expansion.
2. Like leaven in a loaf. 20-21
(a)Kingdom embodied in one person.
(b)It will penetrate the whole!

God is sovereign. He rules over people, not territories. He enters the world of people in unexpected, insignificant ways. His rule grows beyond measure. His sovereign power penetrates the whole of humanity.

* * * * * * *

WHAT IS THE KINGDOM OF GOD LIKE?

The word "kingdom" is a compound consisting of the noun king and the Anglo-Saxon suffix -dom. And -dom indicates "quality," "dominion," or "condition." "Wisdom" is the quality of being "wise." Hence, "kingdom" is that realm, state, or condition in which a king exercises authority. How then are we to liken the sovereign rule of God? Where and over what does he reign? Is there an analogy by which the kingdom of God may be compared?

The question raised!

In the narrative just related (13:10-17) Luke has shown the power of God to redeem a particularly pain-wracked woman. The people praised him. His adversaries were shamed and their mouths shut by him. This is a validation of God's sovereign power. What then is the sovereign power of God like? Where does it appear in the misery of human existence? Can some comparison be found by which it may be clearly seen? Jesus himself raised that very question. "To what is the kingdom of God like and to what shall I liken it?"

A glance below the surface reveals that to be a question involving two valid points of emphasis. "To what is the kingdom...like" implies that analogies, emblems, comparisons do exist that can make clear what and where the kingdom of God may be understood with clarity. A second point is, "To what shall "I" liken it?" In other words, "It is up to me to discover and lay out the comparison so that you may perceive the nature and domain of the kingdom of God."

In the creation around us there is a unity that pervades the whole. The law of gravity does not vary between Washington, Berlin, Moscow or Tokyo. There is one God! There is one set of principles that operate through the entire universe! If this be so then each part of creation is analogous to other entities and organisms. If I uncover the secret of how the physical creation works, that throws light on how the moral, spiritual forces operate. The question Jesus raised is: What in the natural creation throws light on the nature of the kingdom of God? What image, emblem, or symbol can I use to enlighten human minds so they may grasp the moral power of God as it works throughout humanity? The principles governing the physical universe find similar principles governing the spiritual, moral, and ethical universe. Each illuminates the other! Hence Jesus asked, "To what is the kingdom of God like?" There _is_ a suitable analogy!

The likeness proposed!

Jesus came up with two parables that illuminate certain aspects of the kingdom of God. First, the mustard seed. "It is like a grain of mustard seed which a man, having taken, cast into his own garden; and it grew and became even unto a tree and the birds of heaven nested in its branches." The point of the parable entails the smallest of beginnings expanding to the largest of sizes among its class of garden herbs. The mustard seed was not a tree; it was a garden plant of the vegetable variety. But it grew to such size that birds would use it as though it were a tree. It was vegetable in kind but became a tree in size. Such a growth furnished Jesus with a perfect analogy with which to describe the kingdom of God from its insignificant beginning to its great growth and expansion. The kingdom is "like" that!

And does that not perfectly reflect the kingdom from its unlikely, unexpected, insignificant beginning in the teaching, life, death and resurrection of one obscure itinerate preacher of righteousness to its incorporation of peoples of every climate, culture, kingdom and nation? From Jesus it has grown until it has penetrated every nation on the earth.

Furthermore, the kingdom is "like" the mustard seed in its growth in each individual in which it lodges. From the lonely mountaineer to the criminal languishing in his dark prison cell the gospel has exerted its transforming power. The seed of the good news of Christ has found lodging in the hearts of such men. It has generated new life even in such isolating confinement. From these secluded, unnoted beginnings it has grown until the blossoms from these lives bear fruit in uncounted hundreds of other people. Such is the _nature_ of the kingdom of God. This is that to which the kingdom of God is "like." It _expands_!

The second parable Jesus used stressed a different aspect of the kingdom. Not only does it _expand_ to such _large_ proportions it also has within it _power_ to progress through any and all kinds of obstacles. Nothing can keep it from diffusing itself through the _whole_. "To what shall I liken the kingdom of God? It is like leaven which a woman, having taken, mixed into three measures of meal, until the whole was leavened." This story emphasizes a different aspect of the same truth as the mustard seed. Here Jesus underscores the power of the kingdom to produce _moral_ transformation.

The sad fact is that man is corrupt in his <u>heart</u>. So knavish is he that he will conform his outward behaviour to <u>appear</u> righteous while all the time he pursues evil ends. He hides his wicked intent by his good conduct! Changing outward conformity is not sufficient to change the inner soul. When a spring is poisoned it cannot be purified by pouring clean water into the infected water. First the toxic element must be removed. <u>Then</u> the water that flows will be pure. Moral and spiritual purity springs from within out, not from without in. Righteousness is not forced onto a man; it rises from an inward compulsion. "If the heart doesn't condemn, we have bold confidence..." (I Jn.3:21) For this reason it is necessary that the kingdom rise from within the spirit. God's reign begins in the heart and from there it ferments the whole.

Leaven is the symbol of every moral principle, good or bad, that works in the inmost sensitivity of man. The point of the parable is the <u>pervasive</u> quality with which it saturates that which it inhabits. The sovereign power of God, once inserted into a soul, will impregnate and saturate every crevice. And thus it will gradually change the moral quality of him whom it penetrates. It's the nature of the kingdom to alter radically the human heart in which and over which it reigns. The bad it either changes into good or drives it to ultimate judgment! God accepts a man where he is and in the condition in which he is. But God won't leave the man there. He saves or condemns! God rules in redemption or judgment! In either case, God reigns! He is sovereign!

As a flower stretches toward the sun the Godly life of the spirit reaches upward to higher levels of spiritual experience. It seeks the upper planes of moral sensitivity. The divine life, as announced in the Gospel of Christ, seeks to invade the <u>whole</u> of human life. First God's rule invades the individual's life. From there it penetrates the family, parents, children, siblings, relatives and friends. But it cannot stop there. It must infuse itself into and throughout the social order. By nature it is redemptive. By quality it is pervasive. It must saturate all and every sphere of human existence. It will conquer or condemn. But in any case God reigns!

Powerful politicians are hardly ones whom we expect to be superior as citizens of the kingdom of the spirit. They are not most outstanding for their exercise of moral conscience. Throughout history government bureaucrats aren't renowned for lofty spiritual or ethical standards. In the 1970-80's Charles Colson, "hatchet man" of federal administrative policy, fell from his high position in government to being a prison inmate. God found this man in his dungeon of defeat, accepted him for what he was and where he was. From that point God turned him into his spearhead for advancing the sovereignty of God not only among the prison population of America but throughout the world.

He who rules by the sword shall perish by the sword. But he who yields to the spirit of God's sovereign grace shall know freedom from his bondage to corruption.

227

God reigns in blessing over the pure in heart. He reigns as well in judgment over the impure. "Whither shall I go from thy Spirit? Or whither shall I flee from thy presence?" (Ps.139:7) Even if one wished, there is no escape from God. The inner character of one single soul works its outward effects in ever widening circles and through ever lengthening years. If it be a Godly heart the social order rises a notch in its moral, spiritual sensitivity. If it be an evil heart society feels the impact in economic depression, social crime, political death. Evil may _seem_ to be on the throne and good on the scaffold. But the fact _is_ God is ever on his throne; he is in constant control of moral forces. He rules in judgment on that evil that would ignore or usurp His righteous rule.

In 1917 Karl Marx and his atheistic, materialistic philosophy invaded Russia with its brutal anti-human, anti-God spiritual agenda. But faith in no-God, and biased belief in anti-human values do not constitute reality. Assuming God to be ultimate reality then faith in no-God and subjective belief in anti-human values do not make God disappear. If God really reigns, it does not take an inspired prophet to predict the ultimate downfall of communism. The darkness of communism descended in 1917. It's disintegration came in 1989. In his own way, using his own methods God was ruling during that entire 72 year period. Inexorably he brought communism to its self destruction. Sin and falsehood in any form carries within itself the seed of its own disintegration. It took God just 24 years to bring Romania's ruthless Ceausescu to his bloody judgment for his violation of every divine-human right! God is never absent from his sovereign throne. He does not disregard man's right to choose wrong, but he ceaselessly rules in absolute moral and spiritual authority. "The reign (kingdom) of God is like leaven, which a woman having taken mixed in three measures of meal, until when the whole is leavened!" The kingdom is _like_ that! "He who has eyes to see, let him see!"

There is nothing more _universal_ than God's rule! Men, angels, and devils are subject to his sovereign power and authority over both good and evil. Said the Psalmist, "If I ascend to heaven, thou art there! If I make my bed in Sheol, thou art there!" (Ps.139:8) Surely Theophilus could sense in Luke's report of what the kingdom of God is "like" the universality of God's kingdom in its outreach to all _human_ kind.

AN OUTLINE OF LUKE 13:22-30
Are There "Many" Who Are Saved?

A right reading of the Old Testament makes clear that "all families of the earth" are included in the divine plan. Yet the thrust of the story follows God's working in and through the sons of Abraham, Isaac and Jacob. Who actually constitutes the people of God? Are "many" to be saved? Or a few?

I. THE OCCASION OF THE QUESTION. 13:22-23
1. Jesus continues his journey toward Jerusalem. 22
2. The question raised: "Are the ones saved few?" 23

II. THE PRIMARY BURDEN. 13:24-28
1. The prime task: "Strive to enter!" 24
   (a)"Many" shall seek to enter.
   (b)But they won't be able.
2. The "narrow" entrance! 25-28
   (a)The door "shut."
   (b)The protesters' plea!
   (c)The Master's response.
   (d)Negative reaction of those excluded.

III. "MANY" SHALL BE SAVED! 13:29-30
1. "Many" from four corners of the compass!
2. Those **first** shall be last and **last** shall be first!

It is better to evaluate the _nature_ and _condition_ of citizenship in God's kingdom than to speculate on "many" or "few." Strive to enter while the door is open!

* * * * * * *

ARE "MANY" TO BE SAVED?

At 9:51 Luke says: Jesus "set his face to go to Jerusalem." Here at 13:22 he reminds his reader, Theophilus, that Jesus is renewing that journey of destiny. "And he was going through city after city and village after village teaching and making (his) journey toward Jerusalem." Everything he does, teaches, or implies relates to the coming redemptive events in Jerusalem. He omits no "city" or even "village" from his itinerary.

It is safe to say that his "teaching" was the kingdom of God in its various aspects. The most recent examples were the mustard seed and leaven! The people following him and those in "cities" and "villages" probed him with questions. One man said, "Are the ones being saved few?" Such a query arose not only from a natural curiosity of personal concern but from a background belief among Jews of the time that "all Israelites have a share in the world to come."(Mishnah, Sanh.10:1) In his teaching Jesus placed such emphasis on individual salvation it inevitably raised some question about _Israel's_ part in God's redemption. Implicit in the question was: Is _all_ Israel saved? Does salvation go _beyond_ the sons of Abraham?

Jesus does not address the questioner. He "said to them" the people. Jesus won't answer the curiosity seeker. And he holds in abeyance the question of "beyond the sons of Abraham." He uses the question to "teach" the imperative of entering.

229

The Primary Task!

For anyone who wishes to share in the kingdom of God and its salvation the primary task is _finding_ and _assuring_ his or her place in that kingdom. It is _not_ determining how many or who are to be there. Why be curious about the "many" or "few" if my own standing with God is not secure? Hence it is that Jesus did not address the question but said to the crowd, "You be striving to enter through the narrow door..."

The man who asked the question, "Are there few..." surely was reflecting the human trait of fixing attention on the minutia of trivialities even though interesting. We fasten our minds on whom or what to blame when life turns sour. Or we praise the "luck" of those who enjoy successes on life's uneven journey. If we fail, it is not ours, but always someone else's fault. If fame or fortune is our lot it's fate not effort that brought the blessing! It is "chance," that determines whether the coin of life falls heads or tails! It's happenstance that decides whether I go up or down in the scale of human worth. It seems that neither God nor I make any difference! Such negative ideas have sprouted and flourished from time immemorial. We assume that man is born under and subject to the whims of the way the dice roll! Human initiative or God's presence has little if any effect on the outcome. Just such reasoning underlay such a question, "Are there many who are saved?"

Jesus repudiated such a view. He taught the contrary; accept responsibility for your own actions. Keep striving to enter! The entrance is restricted, narrow, limited! And the Master decrees when the door to his house stands open and when it is to be shut! You have the responsibility to enter while it is open!

In his parable Jesus did not stop at this point. He warns that "_many_" shall _seek_ to enter and they won't be able!" The Lord does not tell just _why_, though trying, they aren't able to enter. Prejudgment as to the nature of the kingdom was one reason. A man cannot force his way in by imposing his materialistic ideas on what God's kingdom ought to be. The subject is not to dictate to the king! Arrogance, pride, ignorance, willful disobedience, lack of integrity of character, and all such qualities of the spirit hinder human enjoyment of God's kingdom. It's a moral kingdom, not racial, national. It takes character not culture to be a citizen in the kingdom of God. Hence, "many" who do "seek" to enter "won't be able!"

Jesus insists that each human being is accountable for his own effort. _You_ be striving...! If you don't _try_ to get in you won't get in! On the other hand some things lie beyond man's possibility. In the first place it is the Master who built the palace, designed the house, owns and controls it. It is _his_ house! He chooses who will come in and on what terms he will enter. All conditions for sharing in the Master's house are in the Master's control. If he did not want servants or guests _no_ _one_ could enter no matter what the effort. Hence it is that the Master of the house shuts and opens the door! It is by his _grace_ that any enter!

When the "door was shut!"

In a palatial house of a distinguished Master we would expect the portal to be beautifully adorned. Certainly one wide enough to offer easy access! The fact that it was "narrow" and difficult to enter suggests that it was a postern, a low back entrance used mainly for suppliers or servants. Such a door had special need for care lest thieves and other unworthy might gain entrance. At any rate the Master assumed the care of the door. He opened and closed in keeping with his will and purpose. He kept it open as long as servants and suppliers needed it. But when those for whom it was designed failed to take advantage of it the Master "shut" the portal to thwart robbers and riffraff! Thus when some, who refused to "strive to enter" while the door was open, found themselves excluded from the Master's house.

Quite to be expected was the protest of those servants and suppliers when they found themselves outside with no way to fulfill their tasks. The foundation of their plea was their acquaintance based on their former engagement for service. Groceries and other necessities could not be delivered without their entrance. Servants' tasks in the mansion would go undone without their presence! They pled personal worth and former familiar association as a basis for entrance. They began "to stand outside and to knock at the door, saying, 'Lord, open to us.'" But the Master answered, "I do not know from whence you are." Then the protesters exclaimed, "We ate and drank in your presence, and you taught in our streets." In other words, they pled on the basis of their past personal relationship. They presumed on personal friendship; they ignored responsibility. Friendship without responsibility is not enough to insure access to the Master's house. Personal association of any kind involves obligations and duties. And when these liabilities are not honored the shut door will not be opened. Unfaithful servants are permanently excluded. Untrustworthy servants have forfeited their relationships.

The Master's response was, "I do not know whence you are. Depart from me you workers of iniquity!" Failure in a trust given is the worst kind of sin. It makes of one a "worker of iniquity!" To fail in a trust is equal to rebellious behaviour. It only wins exclusion from the Master's presence.

Refusal to enter the "narrow" door when open really reflected the delinquent character of those who missed their opportunity. And that rebellious nature shows up in their reaction to their exclusion. "There shall be the weeping and gnashing of teeth whenever you shall see Abraham and Isaac and Jacob and all the prophets in the kingdom of God and you being cast out.." Men "weep" when despair settles over them. They "gnash their teeth" when provoked to anger. Those who neglect their opportunity to enter the kingdom vacillate between hopeless despair and explosive anger. In either case they are blaming the Master or someone other than themselves for their unhappy plight. They still can not see any blame on themselves for _their_ failure.

The Question Answered!

Though Jesus did not directly answer the man's question he did give an answer! Though many of Israel would fail to enter a vast number not only of Israel but also "many" others would enter. "And they shall come from east and west and from north and south and they shall sit down in the kingdom of God." By noting the four points of the compass Jesus was implying that peoples beyond the confines of Israel's home land would take part in God's kingdom. And though "many" in Israel would exclude themselves others of Israel would welcome an inheritance in God's sovereign rule! But also "many" outside Israel would be citizens in that same reign of God. And the amazing thing was that so "many" beyond Israel would share the kingdom! In a word, Gentiles would be blessed equally with Jews and they in great numbers!

The shocking idea in the teaching of Jesus was the prospect that non-Jews were equally in the program of God. Racial, religious, cultural distinctions were to be entirely eliminated. "Behold! last (ones) shall be the ones who shall be first; and first (ones) shall be the ones who shall be last." Which is Christ's way of saying that Gentiles, who now are "last" in hope shall in reality enjoy the privilege of being the first. They, in great numbers, shall enter before Jews! And Abraham's sons shall find themselves latecomers. Those who were first in privilege become last in citizenship!

Thus the original question, "Are there many who are to be saved?" was answered! Yes! there are many; but in reverse order. The Jew is not to be "first" because of his historical privileges. In spite of his advantages he neglected to "strive to enter" God's kingdom. Now the time has come when those who enter shall do so, not because of religious, racial, cultural advantages, but on the basis of their humanity. Faith in God, obedience to Christ are open to all as human beings. It is better to measure the nature of the kingdom; better to submit to the conditions of citizenship than to speculate on who or how many shall enter. It is much better to "strive to enter" than to guess on possibilities!

As he reads Luke's story the fact that God has provided redemption for humans as humans is becoming increasingly clear to Theophilus. Racial barriers and cultural limits cannot prevail in the presence of God. They may have their place in national identity. They may even help the individual in strengthening himself in search of family unity. But the kingdom of God rises higher and stretches farther than such limits as men make. God's kingdom is divine in origin, outreach and destiny. He who enters becomes more than a world citizen. He becomes a child in the family of God, a citizen in the universal kingdom of the one, living, eternal God of all creation!

232

AN OUTLINE OF LUKE 13:31-35
"Herod Wants to Kill You!"

As leader-governor in Israel Herod was protector of the people, provider of law, order, justice and equity! Why would he wish to kill Jesus? Why does dark do away with light? Or evil eliminate good? It's not the office but the integrity of him who governs that determines whether justice prevails.

I. THE WARNING DELIVERED. 13:31-33a
1. "Certain Pharisees." 31
2. Destiny not intercepted by Herod or his kind! 32
3. Persistent move toward destiny. 33a
II. JERUSALEM, CITY OF VICTORY THROUGH VIOLENCE. 13:33b-35
1. Jerusalem, rejector of God's emissaries. 33b-34a
2. Christ's attempts to protect the people rejected. 34b
3. "Your house is left to you" unprotected. 35a
4. Time of acceptance will come! 35b

Herod wanted to kill the Christ. When face to face with him he held the Christ in contempt. He still seeks to kill and hold contempt! But the Christ still says: "I am casting out demons and performing healings today, and tomorrow, and on the third I am completing my mission!"

* * * * * * *

HEROD WANTS TO KILL CHRIST!

The crisis of his Jerusalem destiny with its humiliation and insults, not to mention the shame of the cross, dominated the mind of Christ as he resolutely trudged toward Jerusalem. His popularity with the people was undiminished. Opposition from civil and religious leaders was increasing. Tension was rising! Cities and villages along the borders of Galilee and Samaria welcomed him. Here "certain Pharisees" warned Jesus, "Get out and make your journey elsewhere." In spite of the plaudits of the people danger from authorities was growing. "At that very hour certain Pharisees" offered their warning admonition.

Why would Pharisees seek to protect Jesus from the threat of the governor? Were Pharisees not among those who not only resented the doctrine and influence of Jesus, but now were among those "authorities" who were seeking his death? Some say that they were secretly plotting with Herod to get Jesus out of Galilee into Judea where their plotting might more quickly materialize in his death. But there were some Pharisees, like Nicodemus, who were more willing to hold open minds as to Christ's claims. They preferred, at the least, to see fair play prevail until all evidence of his person could be considered. The use of the term "certain" identifies these Pharisees as a group other than those who sought the death of the Lord. These were friendly to Jesus. At any rate, motive aside, they alerted Jesus to immanent danger to life at the hands of Herod.

The response of Jesus to Herod's threat reveals his faith in God's destiny for his life and mission. "You tell that fox, Behold! I cast out demons and healings I complete today, and tomorrow, and on the third I fulfill my mission!"

233

Divine Destiny Inviolable!

Jesus referred to Herod as "that fox." By that term Jesus recognized in the king the sly trickery with which he maneuvered people and events for his own selfish ends. Herod worked every ploy to enhance his power, advance his prestige, and to protect his person. He was a consummate crook, a knavish rogue. By this one word, "fox," Christ characterized this evil man!

With it all such perverted power in one recreant king could not divert the Christ from his God-given destiny. Such is the core of Christ's answer to Herod's threat. "Behold! I am casting out demons..." That is to say, "I am going to continue rebuking the moral evil that controls men, ridding them of its choking tyranny." Furthermore, "I am going right on exercising cures on the physical ills that bind and buffet so many of the people." In effect Jesus was saying that the heavy hand of Herod nor any of his kind could hinder him from doing that for which he was sent into this world. Human governors may threaten, hurt, and even delay God's redeeming will but nothing Herod does can defeat it. And to underscore this idea Jesus added, "...and on the third (day) I will bring to successful fulfillment the mission for which I was sent into this world." By this enigmatic answer the Christ was affirming that God's will cannot be defeated nor can God's messenger be diverted from his calling by threats from evil conspirators.

God created man "in his own image" and "after his likeness." Whatever else that means it includes the idea that man is free to make choices. God does; so man can! And God never violates that in man. On the other hand God, being God, makes his free choices and has the capability to see that his choices prevail. God exercises his will (choices) without abusing man's choices. If a man makes evil choices God uses that evil choice to overrule its evil consequences in order to accomplish his own divine good goal. If the man makes wise, good choices, God's will in that man realizes its end in blessing. But if the man makes a wicked choice, God still uses the bad consequences for his divine ends but judges the man as worthy of chastening if not death.

God is involved personally with each human being. If flowers and grass "which today is and tomorrow is cast into the oven" are a part of God's concern surely no human being is beyond his design. No human being has been sent into this world without a divine end. Each man has a God-designed purpose for being here. In this respect also Christ is our example. He came into this world by God's design and on a mission peculiar to him. But that very fact reveals that every other person comes to fulfill his or her own peculiar place in the scheme of things. Hence that which Jesus said to Herod may be said by each of us. No threat from evil, no tragic reversal, no pain-ridden event can keep me from fulfilling my task in life. Today I rid this element of evil from my life and area of influence. Tomorrow I heal a hurt in someone's life. And in the end (on the 3rd) I accomplish that for which I was sent. God governs; not the Herods of the world! He governs in blessing my obedience or in using my mistakes!

234

Jesus pursues a companion idea. That each human has his own peculiar mission is reassuring, confidence-building, and spurs to action. "Spurs to action" is the point of emphasis. The fact that each man has his God-given destiny is no grounds for sloth. God may have his design for my life but that does not mean that I can be slack in making my effort to fulfill my mission. So Jesus added, "But it is necessary for me today, and tomorrow and the coming (day) to keep on journeying (moving) toward my destiny..." Since God has assigned for me my goal, then it's only logical that I do my part to keep on keeping on regardless of Herod or any other threat. Nothing must distract me from moving ever onward toward the accomplishment of my mission! Life's tragedies, and even more decisively, life's bounties must not keep us from making our resolute efforts in realizing the divine destiny in our lives. There must always be persistent movement toward our goal.

Jerusalem, City of Victory Through Tragedy!

Aware that he had his specific portion of God's plan to fulfill Jesus erupted in a flood of emotions. History had marked Jerusalem as the most holy spot on earth. At the same time it was the most violent against God's holy servants. "It is not acceptable that a prophet perish outside Jerusalem." Man's crimes of rape, robbery, murder, mayhem, and massacre have been most savage in association with man's most holy places and rituals. Contradictory as it may seem religion has been the occasion for humanity's most cruel madness of man's brutality against man!

Even before Abraham's time mount Zion had been a holy shrine. The greatest of Hebrew prophets had met their fate at Jerusalem. Isaiah, Jeremiah and the blood of countless others of God's servants drenched the walls of the "holy" city with their life's blood. Jerusalem was the locale where God's messengers traditionally died. Could it be that God's "only begotten" son should perish somewhere other than Jerusalem? Never! Jesus must press on his journey, he must trod the lonely path to Calvary. He must keep moving! No threat of violence or any other distraction must thwart his relentless advance to his redemptive destiny of death!

The vision of his final sacrifice was too real! It flooded his mind and consumed his soul. In unmatched pathos he cried out, "Jerusalem! Jerusalem! the one killing the prophets and stoning the ones sent to her, how often I wished to gather together your children in which manner a bird (gathers) her brood under her wings, but you did not wish it." The strong contrast between "I wished" but "you did not wish" is to be marked. Jesus deliberately called attention to his divine will and their rebellious human will. God wanted but you didn't want that protection and salvation which he sought for you. As in past history the present generation of Jews was in the process of plotting the murder of God's representative prophet, this time God's Son! The redemptive will of God and the rebellious will of man meets its climax at Jerusalem's Calvary!

235

The figure of the bird protecting her brood was that of the Christ trying to protect God's people. They were symbolized by and centered in Jerusalem, murderer of the prophets. To protect God's people and bring God's redemption was the purpose of Christ's public service. This the goal of "that which I would!" But "you would not!" It was his will opposed by their will. It was the clash between the divine will and the human! God allows the human will to exercise its right as human. But by so abusing free will in refusing God the result is, "Behold, your house is left to you!" Since you've chosen to stand on your own without God's protecting Christ, you must endure the consequences, loss of freedom, abandonment to military defeat, national disintegration, and scattering among the nations of the earth. "Your house is left to you."

Sin takes many forms but at bottom it is one and the same. Its varieties are merely manifestations of an underlying unity, the human will demanding its own way in opposition to the divine will. This being true, any sin embodies every sin; each sin is, in principle, the killing of the Christ. Herod was jealous of his own place on the throne of Israel. He saw in Jesus a threat to his throne and its power. He would kill Jesus! Thus it is that every sinner sees in Jesus a threat to himself, his own independence. He must submit to the will of the Christ for his own redemption. But he is fearful of giving up himself to the will of another, even the Christ. Nevertheless, Christ came to protect man from himself. By capturing my will Christ sets me free to choose the divine will and thereby be free from the ill effects of my own willful sin. Christ is daily saying to me, "I cast out demons and effect cures, and the third I fulfill my mission (of setting you free.)" The choice is mine! Shall I submit my will to him and thus be really free? Or shall I reject his protection, murder him, as it were, and hear the judgment, "You are left to your own!" The issue is crucial; my will opposed to God's!

The issue does not have to end in judgment. "You shall not see me until when you shall say, 'Blessed the one coming in the name of the Lord.'" Whether Jesus, in these words, referred to his "second" coming or the ongoing possibility of acceptance of the will of God after their national destruction is a matter of debate among students. But in either case salvation in Christ is still open to the people of Israel. The time shall come when they in great numbers shall respond to the Christ whom their fathers rejected at Jerusalem's calvary. Redemption has always been universal in the plan of God. It is actual in individual lives from "all the families of the earth."

236

OUTLINES OF LUKE 14:1-24
Luke reports distinct points in these three episodes. Yet
they are united by place and an underlying thesis. The place:
The "house of a certain one of the rulers of the Pharisees."
The thesis: The kingdom and its personal relationships!

AN OUTLINE OF LUKE 14:1-6
Use and Misuse of God's Laws!
Shall the laws of God be used to guide me in improving the
quality of life? Or may I manipulate them for selfish gain? One
is the proper use; the other the abuse of laws.
I.   LAWYERS AND PHARISEES "WERE WATCHING HIM!" 14:1-2
     1. Sabbath dinner in a Pharisee's home. 1a
     2. They "were watching him critically." 1b
     3. Presence of a man afflicted with dropsy. 2.
II. THE "ANSWER" OF JESUS! 14:3-4
     1. "Is it lawful to heal on the Sabbath?" 3
     2. "They got silent." 4a
     3. Jesus "answered" with a deed! 4b
III. THE NON-ANSWER OF THE LAWYERS AND PHARISEES! 14:5-6
     1. The challenge of Jesus. 5
     2. They "were not strong to answer back!" 6
God's laws are for self-discipline, self-improvement rather
than manipulation for selfish ends. We are not to manipulate
God's law for our indulgence. We are to obey for our good!

* * * * * * *

THE USE AND MISUSE OF GOD'S LAWS!
     Laws are the glue that hold society together. Without laws,
rules and regulations, not only society, but all groups within
society would turn into chaos and confusion. We need laws! But
human nature is such that it can and does abuse good laws by
making them tools for evil ends. A selfish soul can take God's
description of right behaviour and make it his own personal
instrument to advance his own selfish ambition. Law, designed
to protect man against self-destruction, becomes the means of
that self-destruction that it is intended to prevent.
     Lawyers "were watching him!"
     The friendly gesture of the Pharisees who warned Jesus to get
out of Herod's territory was not the attitude of most Pharisees,
certainly not "the rulers" in the sect. "It came to pass that a
certain of the rulers of the Pharisees" invited Jesus to dinner
after a Sabbath morning worship in the synagogue. It possibly
was some Perean city along the route of Jesus' journey to
Jerusalem. No matter the motive of the Pharisee, good or bad,
it took courage and kindness on the part of Jesus to honor the
Pharisee's home with his presence. Hostility or not Jesus would
keep pressing the claims of his mission to them. Calvary and
its cross was just over the horizon and at their hands! Yet
Jesus kept mirroring their inconsistent behaviour and their
habitual hypocrisy right unto the end. He would reach out to
heal not only crippled bones but also crippled hearts!

237

That Jesus was a special guest in this house of a "certain" one of the "rulers" marks him as special if not honored! He was not the host; but an invited guest. We wouldn't expect Jesus to be dishonored by any sort of embarrassment, at least not purposely. But some features Luke includes in this story raise questions. First, how did it happen that a "certain man with dropsy was before him?" Why was that man at this feast? Was he uninvited? Was he a relative of one of the "rulers." But even so, how did he happen to be there? Some have suggested that, in keeping with local customs of the time, he just walked in self invited. Friends or even strangers might drop in to witness prominent people at such festive occasions.(cf.7:37) There is no certain answer. And for that very reason it isn't important to Luke's point in reporting the story.

But there is another feature that suggests a possible reason why such a sick man might have been present at such a feast. It is said, "they were watching him!" The verb "watching" is compounded of "watch" and prefix "carefully" or "critically." These "lawyers" were interested in how Jesus would deal with the law, the law of the Sabbath! The appearance of honoring Jesus hid hostile hearts.

Jesus "answered!"

It should be noted that Jesus "having answered spoke to the lawyers and Pharisees." To whom did Jesus "answer"? The record does not state that anyone had "asked" Jesus anything. So why does Luke take pains to point out that he "answered?"

When he did "answer" the content of his "answer" cues us in on a possible reason why the dropsical man was present. Was it that he was purposely planted there that they might "watch" how Jesus would handle the Sabbath law? In view of their past hostility that certainly is a possibility. But even if the man just walked in these legalists took advantage of his presence to "critically watch."

If Jesus was annoyed at their entrapment he didn't show it. He took up the situation and directly challenged these "lawyers" by asking, "Is it lawful on the Sabbath to heal or not?" They as lawyers ought to be able to handle that question of law! He put them on the defensive. Now they had a question as to how they would observe the Sabbath law.

The answer to the question of Jesus was met with a non-answer. To the question Jesus proposed the text reports, "They got silent." In a word, they refused to incriminate themselves. They knew the law! They knew the traditions which had been added as a hedge about the law. They knew their own practices that sought to obey the letter while violating the spirit and intent of the law. So, rather than expose themselves to such hypocrisy "they got silent!" What a dramatic scene! A Sabbath festive occasion! Food, fun, fellowship of a gala occasion! A "situation" in which a dropsical man poses a problem of law. Jesus proposes a simple point of law, "Is it lawful to heal on the Sabbath or not?" The silence was loud! The joy and laughter was choked by sullen silence.

Since they would not answer Jesus did! But he answered, not by word but by deed. "Having taken hold (of the man) he healed him and sent him off." Jesus touched the man! He offered him the encouragement and warmth of human touch. Then immediately he got the man out of the tension-filled, hostile environment. The man should not have to become embroiled in anxieties hatched by Pharisaical nit-picking over Sabbath traditions.

The Non-answer of the Pharisees!

The "silence" of the lawyers spoke more than words. Their non-answer was their answer. Their practice on the Sabbath was at variance with their doctrine. They "worked" to protect property but censured the curing of a crippled human.

Jesus took the offensive. He drew an incriminating picture of their answer to his question. "Which of you whose child or ox shall fall into a pit and he will not immediately pull it out on the Sabbath day?" The force of the question is apparent when we recall that some Jewish parties explicitly forbade such labor on the Sabbath. "Let no one assist a beast in giving birth on the Sabbath day. Even if it drops (its newborn) into a cistern...one is not to raise it up on the Sabbath."(Anchor Bible, Luke, pg.1040) Jesus is conceding his present adversaries as having a more merciful practice than such extremists. If even _they_ would salvage a child of their own, or even an animal, surely they would not fault his healing a fellow man! Thus Jesus appealed to their deepest humanity. He sought to lift their vision beyond the letter of the law to its spirit and purpose. People and laws are not "things" which we manipulate for selfish advantage. They are for guarding against our own self destruction and to alleviate the pain of others entrapped in their own folly.

But once again "the lawyers and Pharisees" failed to voice an answer to his challenge. The text declares, "And they were not able to be strong to answer back." The wording, "they weren't strong to answer," is significant! They lacked the moral courage to speak their opinions out loud! They were ethical pigmies, moral mutes. They had no strength of character to accept, much less confess defeat on points of their own law. To them the law was an instrument for manipulation, not a pattern for practice. It was to be used, as opportunity afforded, for getting rid of opponents in court of law, for advancing one's own self-serving ends in the market places of life. Law was to be upheld at all costs; people were to be controlled, managed, and used! God's laws were given to help, not hinder, human lives. "You shall not see your brother's ass or his ox fallen down by the way and withhold your help." (Deut.22:4)

Christ's ability to cut through entanglements of man's manipulation of law would appeal to the noble Theophilus. The wisdom of Jesus getting to the core of truth as it winds its way through the maze of partisan scruples could only inspire the heart of any noble person, whatever his race or nation. The themes of _humanity_ and _universality_ are the threads that make Luke's Gospel the "most beautiful" of all literature!

AN OUTLINE OF LUKE 14:7-14
Status and Recompense!
Status and recompense are two matters with which people are concerned. What is my position in society, employment, scale of values? What rewards do I get for service rendered or status obtained?

I. METHODS OF SEEKING STATUS! 14:7-11
   1. Banquet guests grasping for places of status. 7
   2. Christ's counsel to the guests. 8-10
     (a)Not self-serving seizing. 8-9
     (b)Respectful, self-effacing choices. 10
   3. The God-implanted principle! 11
II. OBJECTS OF RECOMPENSE! 14:12-14
   1. Those who have no need. 12
   2. Those who have no opportunity. 13
   3. Real recompense. 14

Both status and recompense are imbedded in the universe of which we are a part. They are built into the nature of things. They are not capriciously or arbitrarily given. They're inherent in the quality of life of kingdom citizens! Both recompense and status shall be bestowed "in the resurrection of the righteous."

* * * * * * *

STATUS AND RECOMPENSE!
Where do I stand in the scale of success? What is my status? What is my reward for the service I render, the status I occupy, the values to which I hold? My position and my pay, right or wrong, loom large in my view of my worth!

These two factors are the subjects of Jesus' counsel at that Sabbath feast at which "lawyers and Pharisees" were "watching" him! Their position in society as leaders made their behaviour doubly important as examples.

Methods of securing status!
The man with the dropsy had been healed and dismissed. It was time for festivities to begin. Though the positions of prestige were the host's to bestow, many guests were maneuvering into positions in the banquet hall from which it would be natural for the host to point them to the nearest seat of prominence. In fact, some were bold enough to drop down into the "chief seats." Jesus, "observing how they were selecting for themselves" spoke a parable. It was a scene of avaricious grasping for social level so openly greedy as to make noble men blush with shame. At least it gave Jesus an opportunity to give counsel on such abuse of seemly behaviour. Egoistic grabbing ill reflects the "image of God." "Whenever you're invited to wedding festivities, don't rush to grab the prime place of honor, elbowing others out of your way...!" Such self-asserting greed for primacy leaves you helpless when the host has already designed that high place for someone else. If the host publicly says, "You give the seat which you have grabbed to this fellow of my choice," then you shall endure the public shame of your arrogant presumption.

240

In every period in history, in every culture throughout the centuries there have been "chief seats." Pestigous places of honor, positions of power, social, economic, political have at all times been available. There have been no lack of ambitious, self-centered, self-seizing people, gluttonous for honor. They covet the number one spot however insignificant their team! And often such men stoop to any level to gain the "chief" seats.

In that ancient first century the Jewish Pharisaical host held the privilege of assigning the gradation of "seats" to his guests. Just to get an invitation to a festive occasion was itself a coveted honor. But to occupy the "chief" seat was glory beyond measure.

Two methods were available with which to attain the desired distinction; maneuver, manipulate, push others aside, grab it for yourself! Or lie back, relax, wait for the host to appoint you to the "chief" seat! Aggressively seek the seat or await the will of the host! Disregard the value of others and push them aside! Or allow them their opportunity!

It was just such a case that drew forth Jesus' counsel to the guests of that Sabbath feast. The basic problem was the conduct of human beings toward each other. Jesus rebuked fellow-guests for maneuvering the other guests as they sought for <u>themselves</u> the best places. True lasting honor does not come from self-seeking! It rather derives from someone other than one-self. Honor gained by self-seeking is temporary, fading and fleeting. It's like a fist full of air perishing in the hand. Real honor springs from that which someone else bestows. It rises from recognition of service rather than how one outdistances others.

In the present instance Jesus points out the advantage of the self-effacing choice of taking the lower seat, even the lowest, and trusting the host to recognize true worth by inviting to the "chief seat" of honor. Such glory will be acknowledged universally, will have permanent value, and enhance genuine personal relationships. By thus recognizing the value of others at the feast one really secures a warmer, more wholesome, more humane place in the hearts of men.

Thus Jesus teaches the universal principle of true personal relationships. "Everyone exalting himself shall be humbled, and the one who humbles himself shall be exalted." This is as true as the force that guides the stars in their course. This principle governs all of life in all its forms. The seed gives itself to the soil, sun and rain. And in thus losing its life it gives life to plant, animal and human lives. The fish of the sea, the foul of the air, the beast of the forest have their vital place in the ongoing of all other life on this planet. But it is in the giving of their life that they live on in the lives of others. There is one vital difference between plant-animal and man. Man can <u>choose</u> to give or grab. He is not impelled by an unyielding nature to give. He enjoys the moral freedom of <u>giving</u> or not giving! The mother gives her life in devotion to her children. She finds herself living in the lives of those selfsame children. When she sits in the stands and sees her son score the winning points her heart bursts with pride! Or when she is present at the induction of her son into elected public office, her life finds fulfillment. Life overflows in a parent with a sense of satisfaction when a son gets glory.

"Pride goes before a fall" is proverbial truth. It reflects a universal law of life. And that "the meek shall inherit the earth" is as inevitably valid as are all just and moral laws that guarantee ultimate justice in this universe. That the humble and the meek shall be exalted to honor is as certain as the sun shall rise each day. It's the way God has constructed the moral world. It's not the manipulation of a man that gains the "chief seat." It's rather our divine host who assigns the positions of power, glory and honor!

Self-effacing service is the source of moral strength, the basis of personal power, the foundation of lasting glory. After the sun is a burnt out cinder and the stars have faded into eternal gloom, after man's final parliament has assembled and human governments are no more, it shall still be true that he who exalted himself shall have paid the price of being brought low. Eternal reality confirms the fact that "the one humbling himself shall be exalted." Such moral facts make of this a universe, not a chaos! Languishing on Elba could have been avoided had Napoleon heard and heeded the maxim, "Everyone exalting himself shall be humbled." Jesus Christ was crucified by the courts of man but two milleniums later he lives in the hearts of millions. Why? Because "the one humbling himself shall be exalted!"

Who shall be recompensed?

He who was the invited special guest so that his behaviour might be "watched" himself became the "watcher" of offensive human behaviour; conduct that was unbefitting nobility of character, distasteful to God.

Having rebuked the guests Jesus turned his attention to the host. He too might lift the level of his conduct as a host. In his economic status and his religious position he should consider critically whom he appointed to "chief seats" at his banquets! In fact he could well revise his list of invited guests. "He (Jesus) was saying to the one having invited him, 'Whenever you make a dinner or banquet quit calling your friends, neither your brothers, nor your relatives, nor rich neighbors; lest they return the invitation to you. Thus repayment comes to you!'" Those listed here by Jesus have personal posessions or human relationships which leave them no need for the physical demands of life. Without doubt they had other human needs for emotional and social support, though even in these they were surfeited. But in the bare necessities such as food, clothing and shelter these people felt no want. What Jesus was saying is that he who has much is obligated to serve, not the haves, but the have nots! To whom much is given much shall be required!

Jesus then made a second list of possible guests, those who lacked the most basic needs for human existence. "But whenever

242

you give a reception call the poor, maimed, crippled, blind, and you shall be blessed, because they do not have anything with which to repay you." Here again the "blessedness" which comes from giving to those who cannot give back is built into the act itself. A man can only eat so much before food becomes a hazard to health. He can wear only one suit at a time. To have two cars in the garage while he is driving a third is a misuse of capital which could be earning if invested. The sensible way to share is to give the oversupply to him who lacks. He who lacks is to be filled with my surplus. This not only fills his stomach but it fills full _my_ soul! _I_ become more like the God in whose image I have been made when _I_ give like God gives, that is, to him who can't provide for himself. That's what grace means! The purpose for which man was created in the beginning finds fulfillment when a man reaches that lofty level of life. We were given life to give life, created in order to create, we work that others may work, eat that others may eat. In other words everything man does is to be done that others may partake. People are channels through which the water of life flows so that others may freely drink. It's those who don't have who are to be compensated with that which we have.

In giving we get our own reward. The reward which _we_ get comes both here and hereafter. Here my giving is rewarded with an ever expanding vision of purpose, an ever increasing depth of character, an all encompassing sense of meaning and purpose, a deep sense of satisfaction in a life well spent.

But this is not all! Jesus indicated that a larger reward was lying just over the horizon of life. "For it shall be returned to you in the resurrection of the just." Take the long view! Remember that death is an intrusion, a flaw man has made in God's masterpiece. Death was never intended to be; it was interposed by man's meddling in God's project of creation. Death is an impertinence! It has been corrected by Christ's resurrection and shall be eliminated completely by "the resurrection of the just." At that point recompense begun here shall be completed there. Eternity reveals and completes that which God gives to those who have learned to give. It is at the "resurrection of the just" that both status and recompense find ultimate fulfillment. It is only when we take the long view that we learn what position and pay really are!

Once again Luke is able to uncover to Theophilus that God's gifts to men are both _universal_ and open to all _human_ beings! Nothing is sectarian, cultural, national or racial about sharing what I have to those who need what I possess. And certainly nothing is limited or restrictive about giving another his opportunity for preeminence! Self-effacing giving has within it the possibility of infinite worth. He who gives gets!

Eating Bread in the Kingdom of God!
"God is love" and God is gracious to all! Why then are not all saved? Cannot his redeeming love assure redemption to every person! That does not appear to be! Why not?

I.   BLESSEDNESS OF HIM WHO EATS BREAD IN THE KINGDOM. 14:15
    1. The eschatological Kingdom of God!
    2. "Blessed " is he who enjoys that festive food!
II. THE INVITED GUESTS! 14:16-20
    1. The feast prepared and ready. 16-17
    2. Excuses of the invited guests. 18-21
    3. The actual guests. 21-23
      (a)Those from the "streets and lanes."
      (b)Those from the "highways and hedges."
III. DESTINY OF "THOSE HAVING BEEN INVITED."
    1. "They shall not taste of my dinner."
    2. Why excluded?

God is capable of saving all. He is willing to save all. He will yet save "all who will" to be saved! But men must choose to enter the banquet hall prepared for all!

* * * * * * *

EATING BREAD IN THE KINGDOM OF GOD!
It is still the Sabbath day. Jesus is still at the festival of the Pharisee who invited him home for dinner. His healing of the dropsical man demonstrated how properly to observe the Sabbath. The advice of Jesus how to be a good host and good guests prompted one of those assembled to envision, "Blessed is he who eats bread in the kingdom of God."

Blessedness of the Kingdom festivities!
This guest at that Sabbath dinner was impressed with the insight of Jesus about how to behave as guests and with whom to share one's bounties. Self-serving maneuvering for places of honor was ill becoming for a man. And hosting those in need rather than those who lacked nothing was soul expanding and character building. Some at this Sabbath meal saw sense in what Jesus was teaching. "A certain one of those" spoke up to observe the blessedness of anyone who might share the festive table in "the kingdom of God." Jesus had just mentioned compensation coming in "the resurrection of the just." It was this eschatological feast at the end time, the heavenly life of festivity with God and the saints to which the man's mind turned. "To be congratulated (blessed) is he who eats bread in the kingdom of God." There is to be a festive life after this sordid human experience. There is to be a place and time when every need of the most destitute shall find full satisfaction at the table of God. Whatever the fallacies about God's kingdom might obtain it was an unquenchable dream that on occasion broke into the open. The man burst out with a sudden inspiration of hope in a future blessedness. He voiced the deepest longings of humanity. The reality of the kingdom of God does not die!

Nevertheless, this same man was a Pharisee, one who by virtue of being of that party expected preferential treatment because he kept the traditions! He was of the "elect" without which there would be no feast! So when he voiced assurance of being at God's kingdom festival Jesus responded with adversative, "But that one (Jesus) said to him..." The parable following was fair warning not to take for granted standing in the kingdom! A man cannot share in the kingdom feast apart from God's grace. But he can damn himself if he chooses not to accept the invitation.

The guests invited!

In oriental custom a man of wealth and social standing would issue invitations to a number of his peers to celebrate a banquet at his home. At the proper hour he would send a servant to remind the invited guests that the supper was ready; come without delay. Jesus depicts just such a situation.

In view of the remark that drew forth this parable the characters in the story reflect realities of the kingdom of God. The parable is peopled with: host, invited friends, a servant, city dwellers in "streets and lanes," and rural residents of "highways and hedges." Obviously God is the host. His kingdom is the feast. It is first announced through Old Testament prophets. The servant offering the final announcement "all things are ready" is Jesus. Those of "streets and lanes" are street people, the "poor, maimed, blind, lame" of Judaism. Those of "highways and hedges" depict humanity aside from God's historic people, in other words, Gentiles!

This parable was drawn from Jesus as he journeyed toward Jerusalem and its redemptive cross. He had been declaring the kingdom feast for three years. In effect he was saying, "all things are now ready."

The great tragedy was that he and his message of invitation were being rejected by the leaders of the Hebrews. Their rejection is depicted in three excuse-makers. "They all with one (similar evasive pretext) began to make excuse."

A fellow does not purchase a plot of land before he has investigated its location, its ability to grow crops or otherwise produce income. Yet this first man cloaked his refusal with obvious hypocrisy, "I bought a field, I need to go see it!" What he actually was saying is: "I decided long ago that I was not going to accept my friend's invitation to dinner. This 'excuse' is a cloak to hide my determined rejection."

All three were "of one" attitude, united in their determination to reject the invitation; they were of one in the pattern of refusal. The second said, "Five yoke of oxen I bought and I go to test them; hold me as one having begged off." To buy oxen unseen and untested is a model of stupidity. Had he not examined his purchase before laying out the purchase price? Had he not investigated the strength, health, and market value? Did he wait until after the purchase to "test" the five yoke? His "excuse" was as invalid as the first. His "excuse" was no excuse; it was a blind behind which he could cover his refusal to attend the friend's feast.

The third was the most blunt! He responded, "I married a wife and I'm unable to come." When a man marries he does add unknown and unexpected duties. But they do not nullify social debts. In fact they increase the need for social contacts. So this man confirms what the other two said. I don't intend to go! My wife is as good an excuse as I need. I just will not go!

Human beings seem to think their beliefs or disbeliefs fix and determine truth. There is no greater illusion! Truth is that which is real, genuine, factual, authentic. It is not subjective, opinionative, theoretical. What I believe may or may not be true. Truth is true regardless of my opinion or belief about it! My belief affects my actions but it doesn't determine reality. Truth is truth in spite of what I believe.

All this is to say that the reality of God and his kingdom isn't determined by majority vote of men. If God be real he exists whether men believe or disbelieve. His sovereign rule exists independent of what men think. Furthermore, his kingdom will be realized in history in keeping with his will, not man's beliefs. The text says, "the master of the house, having got angry said to his servant, 'Go out quickly into the streets and lanes of the city and bring the poor, maimed, blind and lame in here.'" The festival of God's kingdom is a reality of history even if men treat it with contempt. Regardless of man's rejection God will and does have a kingdom. If wiseacres refuse it, then street people will enjoy it. If privileged reject it, underprivileged will have it. In fact the rule of God is not for "classes." God's kingdom is for men as men aside from class distinctions. "Street people" are not urged into the kingdom because they are of the street but because they are people.

To enforce the universality of the kingdom the parable goes on to report, "The servant said to the master, 'Lord, that which you commanded has been done, and there is still room!'" To that the master responded, "Go out into the highways and hedges" in the countryside and constrain them to enter. And this that my house may be filled." The kingdom of God is not only a reality of history, it's festive purpose shall be enjoyed by a full complement of humanity for which it was designed. City people (Jews) and rural people (Gentiles) alike embody the citizen guests of God's eternal banquet hall.

Those excluded!

Jesus makes clear: God is capable of saving all, willing to save all, has provided redemption for all with no exceptions. He makes no prejudgment by race, nation, economics, culture, color, or any other human limitation.

The point of unity in Christ's story is that the three men excluded themselves. It was not the host but the choice by invited guests that kept them from the festival. "I say to you that no one of those men, the ones invited, shall taste of my dinner!" "Those men" are all for whom the kingdom has been made ready from eternity yet have dishonored the king, violently rejected his servant, the Christ, and refused his continuing appeals. Even "street people" must choose. No man is to be forced! He is to be constrained by persuasion, argument, appeal.

246

AN OUTLINE OF LUKE 14:25-35
The Cost of Discipleship!

As everything worthwhile discipleship to Jesus has its price!
It means more than to regard with favor or admire with esteem.
Discipleship involves commitment to the person of Christ. And
that is costly!
- I. THE WILL TO CUT THE BONDS OF BLOOD. 14:25-26
  1. Discipleship distinguished from following Jesus! 25
  2. The cost of family ties. 26a
- II. THE WILL TO COMMIT ONE'S OWN SELF! 26b-27
  1. Radical self-denial. 26b
  2. The ultimate cost: "bearing one's own cross." 27
     (a)Crucifixion of self.
     (b)And "coming after me!"
- III. THE WILL TO REJECT MATERIAL POSSESSIONS. 14:28-33
  1. Examples of counting costs. 28-32
     (a)Building a private tower. 28-30
     (b)Waging public warfare. 31-32
  2. The teaching applied. 33-35
     (a)Covenant to commit possessions. 33
     (b)Commitment to retain purity as good salt! 34-35

Then as now "many crowds were following along with him." But
discipleship to Jesus calls for more than "following along." It
requires stern conditions of personal sacrifice.

* * * * * * *

THE COST OF DISCIPLESHIP!

As a Christian believer am I to do what the Bible says? Or
is it better that I do what the Bible means by what it says? In
his effort to discourage shallow, superficial followers Jesus
uses a startling figure to highlight the total cost discipleship
entails. "If anyone comes to me and does not hate his father..."
Hate is a strong word! It involves "extreme feelings." It
implies radical aversion to some thing or some person. So when
Jesus tells those "many multitudes" who were "following" him
that discipleship embraced "hate" to parents, siblings, and
spouses, without question it had a shocking effect. In order to
be a disciple of Jesus must one carry hostile feelings toward
those whose bonds of blood bind soul to soul? Yet to water this
down so as to remove all feeling is to empty it of substance.
Just what does Jesus mean by that which he says?
The Will to cut the bonds of blood!

Hate(μισέω)is the reverse of love(ἀγαπάω). "No house-servant
is able to serve two masters; for either he will hate the one
and despise the other, or he will cling to one and the other he
will despise."(Lk.16:13) The Greeks made subtle distinctions in
"love." They enjoyed different words for differing shades of
emphasis. Love of affection found expression in φιλέω. ἀγαπάω
marked love in which the will came to the fore. This is not to
say that either affection or will was entirely absent from
either one of these words. The human soul cannot be totally
departmentalized. But if one wanted to stress the will ἀγαπάω

247

was the word to use. When Jesus said "Love your enemies" he was not advising us to _feel_ good but to _do_ good toward our enemies. "God so loved (_willed_ redemption for) the world that he gave (did something)..."

Hate is the opposite of _love_! To "hate" one's father when confronted with loyalty to commitment to Christ is to exercise the _will_; that is, if faced with a choice between my "father" or my "Christ" I choose Christ. That is what Christ _means_ when he asks me to "hate" my father!

A father threatens to disinherit his son if he acknowledges faith in Christ. But the young son trusts his life and future to God in Christ in the face of such menacing opposition. He _chooses_ Christ rather than acceptance of an inheritance from his father. That is what Christ _means_ when he speaks of _hating_ one's father. In this sense "hate" is not so much _feeling_ malice as it is _choosing_ Christ when the father has demanded rejection of the Christ.

Thus it is clear that discipleship involves much more than just "following" Jesus. "Many crowds" were "going along with" Jesus. They were attracted by his miracles, his skill in debate with obnoxious leaders, the warmth of his person, the insight and depth of his teaching. But they ill-understood the implications of those teachings for their own _personal_ choices. They were ignorant of his destiny at Calvary, particularly as that cross related to _their_ lives. They were "followers" but not yet "disciples."

It was in such a context that Jesus thrust before these shallow, thoughtless "crowds" the cost of being a disciple. In effect Jesus was saying, "If confronted with a choice between the closest ties of family and being a learner (disciple) of mine you must be able to choose me over your family." This is the cost of being a disciple! And though not everyone throughout history has actually been called upon to make this radical choice everyone _has_ been asked to commit himself to such a possibility. For discipleship Christ can not be a second choice. He is all or nothing; first without exception! To love Christ is to "hate" the closest family bonds!

The ultimate cost!

One bond closer than any family tie is that to self! In pressing home the drastic cost of being his disciple Jesus went beyond hate of father or mother: "yea, and even (if he hate not) his own soul, he cannot be my disciple." To be a disciple of Jesus one must be able to make the radical and painful decision to choose martyrdom. A man may not want martyrdom, he may shrink from its pain, he may in fact escape such an ultimate issue of faith. But from the beginning of his Christian commitment he must accept the possibility of martyrdom. If Stephan was stoned to death for faith in Christ the potential lies before _any_ disciple! The choice of martyrdom must be made _before_ one faces the fact. He who rejects the possibility will fail the fact should he face it

Lest the "follower" miss the radical cost of discipleship

248

Jesus added in specific words exactly what discipleship implies. "Whoever shall not bear his own cross and come after me, is not able to be my disciple." In that time and place and culture the "cross" meant only one thing, _death_! A shameful, painful criminal's death! Discipleship to Jesus means total, complete rejection of self and one's own advantage, even life itself, when the situation demands it. No middle ground is possible, no compromise is permitted. Cutting family ties may seem harsh but that is trivial compared to giving of one's self!

"If anyone wishes to come after me, he is to deny himself and take up his cross _daily_ and (thus) follow me."(Lk.9:23) In that statement Jesus points to two elements in self-giving. (1)The negative is "to deny self." That means a repudiation of self as the center to which all else and all others must subserve. (2)"Take up his cross" is the positive side of self-crucifixion. The disciple is to give **agressive**ly to the need of Christ, his cause and kingdom as it appears in the needs of others. Denial of self without cross-bearing would create a hermit, at best a monastic, secluded, segregated community. Choosing the cross without denial of the self would create a display of egotistic pride. Sometime martrydom has been accepted, not for the sake of Christ, but to demonstrate one's _own_ pride of commitment. Discipleship _loses_ the self in the cross.

Choosing the self-denying cross is done once-for-all. But that chosen with such finality becomes in practice a _daily_ experience. The choice is decisive; the performance is repeated!

Rejection of material possessions!

Self-denial and cross-bearing _can_ be so abstract. It can be romanticized. We can revel in the idea without getting down into the dirt and incarnating it in a deed. We warm to the idea but shrink from performance. I can "love my neighbor" in thought and word but turn away from him in his desperate need. I can tell him to "be filled!" But I ignore sharing my food when he is hungry or my affection when he is hurting. Hence Jesus painted two pictures of the need to count the hard cash before attempting to build a house.

"For which of you wanting to build a tower does not first, having sat down, count the cost, if he have enough for completing?" In all such affairs of life demanding financing it's only a fool who won't evaluate his capital and credit. If he doesn't he throws himself open to ridicule from the public as one who has big ideas but few "cents"(sense). His scoffing neighbors will contemptuously taunt, "_This_ fellow began to build but wasn't able to complete!"

That which is true in building a castle is also true in public affairs. "What king, going against another king to wage war shall not, having sat down, counsel whether with 10,000 he can meet the one coming against him with 20,000?" A government runs on taxes, not fleeting wishes! It's a matter of prudence. The whole government process costs sheckles! Thus one must come to terms with cash costs if he launches any kind of venture in this world.

249

At this point Jesus presses home the utmost cost in terms of self-crucifixion! "Family" represents the warmest ties of personal affection. One's "self" represents the single most exclusive, inherent, private, inner attachment. To "hate" one's self is the most radical of hatreds! But the supreme test of self-hating crucifying is to part with one's possessions. Climax of this lesson on the cost of discipleship is: "Thus therefore anyone of you who does not renounce (say good-bye to) all his possessions is not able to be my disciple." What is more radical in a material world than to "say good-bye" to all material things? The test of self-denying crucifixion in this kind of world is how one uses possessions, money, "things."

To the "many crowds" who "were following" no illusions were offered to manipulate them to be disciples of Jesus. He insisted in the plainest, most severe language the cost of discipleship.

Whether Jesus added verses 34-35 to his examination of discipleship or not may be questioned. But at least Luke felt these words a fitting close to the subject under discussion. "Salt is good! But if the salt has lost its taste, in what can it be made salty? It is fit neither for land or dunghill! They cast it out!" Some students of the text have thought this is "loosely" connected with the text. Yet it is a pointed comment on conditions of discipleship.

In spite of the severity of the cost, disciples of Jesus make the world more palatable. The "taste" of life in this world often becomes sour, bitter, unsavory. On the other hand, when Christ and his disciples intrude faith in God and his lifestyle into the social disorder life becomes more appetizing, even delicious. When the moral quality of life becomes tasteless, human existence is coarse, barren, insipid, unsavory. But let the leaven of Christ in his disciples infiltrate a society then life becomes fruitful, luscious, tasteful. Such is the harvest when the seed of Christ comes to maturity.

What imprint would this discussion of the cost of discipleship make on a Greek of the status of the "noble" Theophilus? On examination of the principles of discipleship herein portrayed nothing national, cultural, sectarian or limited can be noted. The moral and spiritual realities that invade and saturate human existence on this globe are common to men everywhere. They are omnipresent, catholic, uncircumscribed. That which is universal is true and that which is true is universal. And that which is true is human and that which fits every human is universal! These facts may not be explicitly stated in the text but they lie implicit within it. "The one having ears to hear is to hear!" He who has eyes with which to see can see!

250

AN OUTLINE OF LUKE 15:1-32
The Joy of Finding That Which Is Lost!

The three parables that, for the most part, form chapter 15 all address the grumbling remarks of verse two. "Both the Pharisees and the scribes were murmuring, 'This man receives sinners and eats together with them!'" The three parables join in an answer to such biased ignorance.

  I. THE CARPING CRITICISM. 15:1-2
     1. "Publicans and sinners were drawing near!" 1
     2. The grumbling of "the Pharisees and scribes." 2
 II. CHRIST'S THREE PARABLES IN ANSWER. 15:3-32
     1. The lost sheep! 3-7
     2. The lost coin! 8-10
     3. The father who had two lost sons. 11-32
        (a)The younger son and his inheritance. 11-19
        (b)The father and the repentant son. 21-24
        (c)The elder son and the father. 25-32

All three stories stress the joy of finding that which has been lost! Christ came to reveal the mercy, grace and love of God in redeeming lost man. This chapter relates the logic of accepting, receiving, and "eating" with social outcasts.

* * * * * * *

THE JOY OF FINDING THAT WHICH IS LOST!

Luke's artistic skill as a writer reaches superb heights in chapter 15. Here Luke displays his theme, the love of God in saving the lost! The theology of how God saves sinners is left to other scripture. But the fact that in Christ God came "to seek and to save" the lost is nowhere more beautifully portrayed than in this perfect picture.

The carping criticism!

Jesus continues his steady pace toward Jerusalem and its Calvary. His message of mercy was being welcomed by increasing numbers of "tax-collectors and sinners." Such people were by no means the poor "street people" of the times. Just the opposite! By the nature of their job tax-collectors had many opportunities to line their own personal pockets. And human nature being what it is many took full opportunity to do just that. The others rewarded themselves quite well from the government revenues they collected. As for the social pariahs called "sinners" their very sin was the means of wealth! Prostitutes and pimps are not numbered among the poor! These rejects Jesus welcomed to his company and went so far as to socialize with them. He "was eating" with them. In the Orient, then and now, to join at table was to recognize social equality, even personal acceptance and friendship.

Unable to disparage his teaching the Pharisees and scribes increasingly "grumbled" at his social conduct. And they "kept on grumbling." Their sarcasm heightened with their repeated murmurs, "This fellow welcomes sinners and eats with them!" Whatever "this" fellow's teaching may be his social deportment marks him a fraud! The facts betray him.

251

Christ answers in three parables!

Christ's answer to the censure of his critics is couched in three parables. The parables vary in details and each has its own emphasis. Yet together they form a complete answer to the charge of the grumblers. They may, and many expositors do, treat them as separate messages. Yet they remain one, each providing its own emphasis to the common theme. All unite in revealing the joy that God has in searching for and finding that which is lost. Heaven is not indifferent to the feelings of earth, its lostness in guilt, frustration, despair, defeat, yet coupled to hope of a rise to better fulfillment of life's possibilities. In fact the third parable probes the depths of the human psyche in its downward fall and its penitent renewal.

They all reveal the logic of Christ's efforts to reach out to save those who are lost. It's the very lostness of the lost that makes fraternizing with them logical. It's because they have "squandered their substance in riotous living" that presents the reason for associating with them. Furthermore, to find fault with such social conduct is itself ample testimony to the very lostness of those who grumble at such behaviour.

The Lost Sheep!

"Which man of you, having a hundred sheep and having lost one of them, does not leave the ninety nine in the desert and go after the lost until he find it?" Any shepherd worthy of the name would do this. A good shepherd is willing to take the initiative in going out into the desert to hunt for lost sheep. Certainly no shepherd would expect a sheep to be able to search for its shepherd. So, it's in keeping with Christ as the shepherd of God's flock to search out the lost. This cannot be done by isolation from the lost sheep. On the contrary, not only must the shepherd search but he must be resolute and persistent in the search "until he find it." The shepherd is not unmindful of the ninety nine. They are secure in the fold. But his chief immediate concern is to find the one that is lost. "Until he find it" that task occupies all his energy.

Besides, once having found it he "puts it on his shoulders." That is, he approaches the lost with the tenderest of care. Any wounds, scars, broken bones, or damage to the wool must be considered in the rescue from mountain crag.

Besides that, when the shepherd with his prize gets back to the fold he wants his family, neighbors and friends to share in his jubilation. He invites them, "Rejoice with me, because I found my sheep, the one which was lost." The thrill of finding the lost must be shared. Heart rejoices with heart as friends enter into the feelings of the shepherd. There's no lack of love for the ninety nine. But the point of concern is the lost, not the secure! Because the sheep was lost is reason enough to search it out and rejoice in its finding! God himself feels that way! So why do you grumble?

The Lost Coin!

"Or what woman having ten drachma, if she lose one, will she not light a lamp and sweep the house and seek carefully until she find it?" The dress is different but the stress is the same.

The shepherd with one lost sheep and the woman with one lost drachma lived on different economic levels. He was relatively well off compared to her. Unless she were a coin collector one coin could represent a tenth of her economic resources. A sheep worth one drachma represented one hundreth of the shepherd's economic worth. In modern terms he was middle class moderately wealthy. She bordered on povery. But that in which they were equal was the initiative which each exerted to search for the lost, the persistent effort each put forth and the joy each felt over finding that which was lost. "Does she not light a lamp and sweep the house and keep on searching carefully until she shall find it?"

She also shared the human desire to invite relatives, neighbors and friends to enter into her joyful elation over her recovery of the lost. In normal human relationships to feel pleasure over the good fortune of a fellow human being with whom there are close emotional bonds is the usual. It's this very universal human trait that sets the grumblers apart as inhuman. It was a back-handed yet potent way for Jesus to show up his critics as illogical, inhuman eggheads. It's one thing to be a scholar who fills his head with knowledge. It's quite another to fill the heart with love for the unfortunate outcast.

And the point of the parables thus far given is that God is just like the good shepherd. And the woman's abandoned interest in her lost coin precisely reflects the feeling of God for the outcast abandoned by the synagogue pundits. If the "Pharisees and scribes" be righteous then why be critical of him who searched out the unrighteous that they might become righteous? The righteous are the very ones who ought to be taking the lead in seeking out such people. God does! Why not they?

The Father with two lost sons!

This third parable raises the level of intensity of feeling as well as revelation. The story does not deal with the loss of "things." Now we are dealing with human beings and the interplay of emotional bonds. The story is not about a "prodigal son" nor an "older brother." The theme is embedded in the opening remark, "A certain man was having two sons." The father is the main focus! Both sons are important but they are not the reason for the story. It's the father and his relation to each son that is the core of Jesus' teaching. The prodigal demanded and got his portion of the inheritance and went off into a "far country." There he "wasted his substance in riotous living." The older son stayed at home, labored faithfully in the father's fields. But both sons were lost to any real relationship to the father. The "prodigal" finally "came to himself," saw the value of life back on the farm and came home. He was "found." The older son refused to welcome the wayward brother nor would he enter the father's joy. He was lost to any family relationship and was thus denied fellowship with his father. The story does not reveal whether the older ever "came to himself." If he ever entered into the joyful festivities is left open. But as long as he refused to enter it left him outside the family fellowship. He was as much lost as the younger son ever had been! The point of the parable is that the <u>father</u> reached out to welcome <u>each</u> <u>son</u>. The story reveals <u>God's</u> actual attitude toward the wayward and the <u>divine</u> <u>pattern</u> for man's obligation toward the outcast!

We leave more detailed exposition of these parables to the standard commentaries. Here we note essentials of all three as they relate to the opening verses which relate the occasion that drew them forth. In answer to his critics Christ is saying: When I consort with "sinners" I reveal heaven's will! This is the reason for God invading this world, that is, to reach the outcast by identifying with him in his miserable existence and thus bring him back to the Father's home. Indeed, God is <u>so</u> human!

As to the impact of this chapter on Theophilus how could he miss the upsurge of human feeling for the unfortunate? To lose precious possessions is an experience common to all men. And the pain of loss of a beloved child is anguish that in some form or other is an experience embracing all humanity. Sooner or later it touches every family! And when the lost returns joy is also a common human feeling. Furthermore, it isn't difficult to feel the force of the lostness of the self-righteous who fails to accept the joy of the returning brother who "was dead and lived, and was lost yet was found." God is the Father who would welcome <u>every</u> son who has been lost at <u>any</u> level!

AN OUTLINE OF LUKE 16:1-13
God or Mammon?

Which is of supreme worth, God or mammon? In a material world there is no escaping the need for material possessions. But the question is: shall possessions be the object of supreme value or is God, who lives above and beyond and who created the material, have my ultimate loyalty. Is it God or mammon; the divine or the material?

I. PARABLE OF THE DISCERNING STEWARD. 16:1-8a
   1. Accused of mismanagement. 1
   2. Called to give an account. 2
   3. Facing the future! 3.
   4. Plan for security executed. 4-7
   5. Recognition of his shrewd use of his opportunity. 8a
II. APPLICATION OF THE PARABLE. 16:8b-12
   1. "Sons of this age" use material opportunities. 8b
   2. Follow their wisdom, not their morals. 9
   3. Three contrasts. 10-12
      (a)Faithful in small versus much.
      (b)Faithful in ordinary versus exceptional.
      (c)Faithful in another's versus one's own.
III. LIMITATIONS OF STEWARDSHIP OF POSSESSIONS. 16:13
   1. "No one is able to serve two masters." 13a
   2. "You are unable to serve God and mammon." 13b
   3. Serve God with mammon!

Material possessions are so much a part of life in this world, even a necessity, that they have a built in tendency to take the place of God. Their very necessity and what they supply create an inevitable illusion of their importance. They very easily become a substitute for God. Hence the issue of life is: Shall we serve God or mammon? Or shall we serve God with mammon?

* * * * * * *

GOD OR MAMMON?

The term "mammon" in English has become synonomous with "riches" or "possessions." This text presents the relationship of a man to possessions and the effect which his possessions have on his relationship to God. The final sentence of the paragraph states unequivocally, "You are not able to be serving God and mammon." On the other hand the whole point of the parable and its application is that we are not only able but obligated to serve God with mammon.

The Discerning Steward!

In verse 8a the text reports, "The master became pleased with the dishonest steward." Certainly he was not pleased with his standard of morality, questionable to say the least, but he was fascinated with the shrewdness with which the steward used possessions, even someone else's, to assure his future security. The point of the parable is not how he used the possessions but rather the fact that he saw in possessions the means by which he could guarantee his future welfare.

255

To name this story "The Parable of the Unjust Steward" is to misjudge the point. It is not the dishonesty of the steward on which Jesus focused. That is clear from Christ's own exposition in verse nine, "<u>I</u> say to you, Make for yourselves friends of the unrighteous mammon." In other words, "Take advantage of wealth to prepare for your future, particularly the future "in the eternal tabernacles" that lie beyond the grave. The parable graphically reveals that material things are a tool in the hands of a wise and skillful craftsman for building a heavenly home. Possessions in themselves are never evil. It's the disposition of the heart of a man who possesses them that determines their moral value.

The flow of the story makes this plain, "A certain man who was rich was having a steward, and this one was slandered of scattering his goods." The steward was mismanaging the estate that had been entrusted to him. That he was dishonest is not stated. But for one reason or another he was bungling the assets entrusted to him. And, being accused, the master demanded an accounting. Threatened with loss of a job the steward faced his future with forboding. He contemplated "in himself, I am unable to dig, to beg I am ashamed." Construction work was too heavy. Emotionally, "I am ashamed to beg." Pride stood in the way of street begging. Then a bright idea struck him. His managing the esate wasn't a total loss. It acquainted him with the usefulness of money. He would take advantage of his knowledge of the power of money and human nature to provide for his future welfare. So, he called each of the master's debtors. To the first he asked, "How much are you owing my master?" To which the answer was, "868 gallons of oil." The steward, still in control of the master's affairs, offered the savings of half the debt. "Take pen and paper and pay half your debt and we'll call it square!" And thus to each debtor he submitted an appropriate trade-off. The upshot of his shrewd bargaining was to get viable cash in the master's coffers not to mention gaining the good will <u>for himself</u> of burdened debtors.

Even the master was impressed with the astute expediency of his steward. "The master became pleased at the scheming steward because he did wisely." It is worth repeating that it was not the questionable method the steward used but rather the fact of his insight into the <u>use</u> of possessions to prepare for one's future. The proper use of money always finds admiration in the view of those who know business principles. God is the creator of all laws including those of the economic world. In dealing with the master's money the steward had failed. But he had learned his lesson for in providing for himself he proved to be quite shrewd in the use of principles which he had misused in the affairs of the master.

Application of the Parable!

No parable is an end in itself. It has a practical purpose, a point to be applied. Jesus guides his hearers to the point. "<u>I</u> say to you, Make for yourselves friends of the unrighteous mammon, <u>in order that</u> when it fails <u>they</u> (God) shall receive you into the eternal tents." Possessions are not the goal of life,

256

they are its servant. Mammon is morally neutral. It is neither "right" or "wrong," "good" or "evil." It is called "unrighteous mammon" only because of its abuse, not its proper use. In fact at this point (vs.9) Jesus urges that the "unrighteous mammon" be used toward righteous ends. He exhorts kingdom people to "make for yourselves friends" by the right use of "unrighteous mammon in order that (purpose) God may receive you into his eternal tabernacles."

How could Jesus be more clear than that? Material things of necessity must have their rightful place in what is in essence a moral, ethical, spiritual universe! Having severed his moral and spiritual relationship to God, man has substituted the objective visible material riches for God. He has blinded himself to the spiritual realities of which the material is but an outward form. He has made money an end in itself instead of an instrument to a higher end. In this parable Jesus restores material "things" to their rightful place, "Make for yourselves friends with the unrighteous mammon..." We are to follow the wisdom of "the sons of this age" but not their morals.

In order to enforce this principle Jesus introduces three striking contrasts. First, "the one faithful in the least is also faithful in much." The amount of things with which a person is entrusted has little if anything to do with his ability to be faithful. Character is not determined by "much" or "little" but by moral and spiritual qualities. To be "faithful" is a trait of character. It's opportunities are limited only by whether "much" or "little" is in the hands of him who is "faithful." This initial contrast plainly declares that "he who is faithful in little" by his faithfulness in the "little" demonstrates that he can be and will be trusted with "much."

The second contrast states, "he who is unjust in least is also unjust in much (greatest)." In this Jesus raises the level of opportunity. It's the "usual" versus the "unusual," the "ordinary" versus the "exceptional," the "material" versus the "spiritual," the "human" versus the "divine." Once again faithfulness is the basic issue, not the level or sphere in which the trust is exercised. And the test of faithfulness is from the lesser to the greater. If one be trustworthy in the material he can be trusted in that which is higher, the matters of the spirit. When I am reliable handling ordinary possessions then I can be entrusted with sublime responsibilities. If I use God's goods for God's glory then God will entrust me with His kingdom's assets, His peoples' needs!

The most basic contrast is: "If in another's (possessions) you do not become faithful, who will give to you your own?" The startling thing is that faithfulness in another's is the measure by which one comes into possession of one's own. In other words, the "possessions" which pass through my hands in this life are really not mine, they are God's. When I have displayed that I can be trusted to handle God's goods, then can I be trusted with that which God has planned for me. The supreme test of faithfulness is handling that which is another's.

Limitations of Stewardship!

Human responsibility in a steward's relation to his master has built in limitations. Expressed in a logical syllogism the major premise is: "No steward is able to serve two masters." If a man makes mammon "master" then he can not serve God as "master," for "he would hate the one and love the other." The conclusion is: "You are not able to be serving God and mammon."

The inference involved in the minor premise is that mammon is given the value of God in a man's life. If so, then God cannot be God in his life. God is effectually eliminated from his rightful place as Creator-Lord. In order for God to reign as God mammon cannot be treated as supreme Lord. It must be one or the other since "no steward can serve two masters."

But there is a secondary minor premise in this logic. Mammon has its rightful place in this material created order. It is necessary for the ongoing of our physical well-being. The place of "mammon" is essential and to be respected. But to raise mammon to the position of God in the scale of values is to dethrone God. It becomes idolatry of the most subtle and vicious kind. "No one can serve two masters." God is the sole rightful master. Yet mammon has its acknowledged rightful place in human needs. The conclusion we draw is that a steward is to serve God with mammon. And that is the point of the parable. We glorify God when we wisely use mammon in his service. Mammon is a practical instrument of service in the life of a faithful and wise steward.

This is a material world. The flora and fauna cover the earth with living organisms of delightful beauty. The fish of the sea, the fowl of the air, the animals of the forests, the minerals in the ground make a paradise of wealth for man to explore, mine, and possess. These resources of God's "mammon" are given to bless man. They are to enable all men to live healthy, full lives while on the earth. They provide food and energy. They are everywhere present and have the power to renew themselves indefinitely. They are given for service to man's universal needs, but certainly not as his object of worship.

"God is spirit" and man has been made to be "in the image and likeness of God." "It is necessary for the ones worshipping him (God) to worship in spirit and truth."(Jn.4:24) When a man places mammon on God's altar with his whole mind, heart, soul and spirit then it is that a man worships God with mammon.

This is Luke's word to Theophilus! Worship of the living God is open to men of every nation, culture, and race. It is vitally human that worship is to be offered with mammon not to mammon!

258

AN OUTLINE OF LUKE 16:14-18
How to Sanctify an Abomination!
"That which is exalted among men is an abomination before
God!" So said Jesus. But as unlikely as it is there is a way to
get the abominable thing sanctified "before God."
I. WHAT OCCASIONED JESUS' STATEMENT? 16:14-15
    1. Pharisaical "lovers of money." 14a
    2. "Mocking" Jesus for his teaching about mammon.14b
    3. Two views about justifying human beings. 15
       (a)"Ones justifying themselves." 15a
       (b)"God knows your hearts!" 15b
       (c)That "exalted" by men is foul "before God." 15c
II. INTRINSIC PERMANENT VALUE OF THE LAW. 16:16-18
    1. "The law and prophets (were) until John." 16a
    2. "From then the kingdom of God is evangelized." 16b
    3. The law transcends creation in inherent value. 17
    4. The marriage bond an example. 18
That on which humanity places high regard is an abomination
before God! And yet in the face of that as fact God can purify
the human heart so that which is an abomination can become
sanctified purity! As he works in the hearts of men all things
corrupted by man can be cleansed by God.

* * * * * * *

HOW TO SANCTIFY AN ABOMINATION!
Some students are troubled because the "sayings" of Jesus in
Luke 16:14-18 seem unrelated to the context. Stories of 15:1-32
(joy over the found), 16:1-13 (the discerning steward) and
16:19-31 (rich man and Lazarus). What's the connection between
those and the law and prophets, marriage and divorce and such
teachings?
There seems little doubt that Jesus said these things but did
he declare them at this time in this context as he moved
relentlessly toward Jerusalem with its climax of the cross?
Suffice it to say that Luke saw fit to record these sayings at
this point. To him there was a meeting of ideas. And he is the
author who in his narrative is telling the story of Jesus as he
understands its meaning.
The Occasion of Jesus' Statement!
However obscure, there is a conjunction of thought. After
the practical logic of rejoicing over finding that which is lost
Jesus pressed on the Pharisees the folly of making mammon an
idol replacing the living God. He struck an exposed nerve when
he taught, "You cannot serve God and mammon." At this the
Pharisees abandoned their contained hostility to "mock" both him
and his views. "The Pharisees, being lovers of money, were
listening to all these things..." "These things" to which they
were listening cut the foundation out from under the practice of
their lives. To them money was a sure sign of the blessing of
God on their lifestyle. Poverty merely marked one's failure to
follow the righteousness of God in one's life. Thus they began

259

to sneer at him openly. Their contempt for him and his notions was written in their looks, voice, gesture and general conduct. Their entire philosophy of the place of mammon was at variance with his. But beyond that they showed contempt of his person as a teacher "come from God." They literally "turned up their nose" at him as God's representative. It was an ugly confrontaton.

But Jesus accepted the challenge. "You are those justifying yourselves before men." Mammon, possessions, riches, money, may be neutral so far as morals are concerned. But the motive for which it is sought, the methods by which it is gained, and the use to which it is put, once secured, determines the moral value of the man who has it.

Men become "lovers of money" for a variety of reasons. More than to keep body and soul together, more than for clothes on the back, more than a house to shelter from sun, rain, and storm, the amount, quality, variety, and social standing these possessions give breeds a sense of self worth. By amassing fortunes that separate them from the degrading levels of the masses men "justify" themselves as being "superior." Money separates; it ceases to serve. It becomes a tyrant instead of trusted steward. The kind and size of house, its location in the community, the brand of its appointments become the measure of a man's position amongst his fellowmen. These are the "things" that give security, power, prominence; they give the appearance of quality, the marks of "class." By these methods and in these ways men universally have buttressed themselves, hidden their weaknesses, covered their blemishes and, relieved their sick souls and deadened their moral conscience. Thus do men "justify themselves among men."

But there is another way. Said Jesus, "God knows your hearts!" God looks beneath the material wealth, the outward display, the public show. He looks to the secret motives of the inner man. <u>How</u> did you get the money? <u>Why</u> did you seek the fortune? <u>What</u> are you doing with it and why? Such secrets shrouded in the heart can be concealed by pompous show. But God knows the heart. As he looks into each soul no smoke screen of appearance can cast a shadow on reality. Motives are naked; purposes are clear; laundered money is detected by the searching eye of God. "Whither shall I go from thy Spirit, Or whither shall I flee from thy presence?"(Ps.139:7)

That God "knows" the heart is itself enough to undercut the superficial "justification" that men claim for themselves. But total devestation of man's self-justification derives from the fact that "the thing exalted among men is an abomination before God." For the Pharisees coveting and obtaining mammon was sufficient to justify them among men as being blessed of God. Yet Jesus was asserting that coveting mammon was itself an "abomination before God." The sign of salvation was in reality the sign of their damnation. Furthermore, acquittal of wrong in the sight of men means absolutely nothing before God! Why? Because "God knows the heart!" Mammon gains esteem in the sight of men. But approval of man weighs nothing on God's scales. The

260

deepest recesses of human hearts are open to the sight of God. The Creator knows man's desires, hates, loves and these constitute a man's real worth. Pride leads to false estimate of worth. Even when a man seeks mammon with the best of motives it can become a cause for pride and self worship. And here too God "knows the heart" and judges rightly a human's worth! The heart is the subconscious level of human feelings, emotions, and reactions. That which is "high" in man's feelings is "low" on God's chart of values! Hence self deception as to one's own worth is a part of every man's experience in this kind of world. That which seems good is really an "abomination."

The Intrinsic Value of the Law!

The law says, "Thou shall not covet!" To that Exodus adds specific things that men should not covet: "....your neighbor's house,..wife,..servant,..ox, ass, or anything that is your neighbor's." (20:17) The "things" that your neighbor possesses are _his_ mammon for which _he_ shoulders responsibility. Don't invade his mammon to increase your own!

Of all the commandments the tenth deals most directly with the _heart_. It is possible to conform to the others in outward display while violating the purpose and spirit of every one of them. But the tenth penetrates the heart. And God "knows the heart!" There's no way to masquerade covetousness under the guise of obedience! "As a man _thinks_ in his heart so is he."(Prov.23:7) What a man _thinks_ is the measure of what he _is_!

The scripture is quite pointed in saying, "The law was _given_ through Moses, the grace and the truth _became_ through Jesus Christ."(Jn.1:17) Note that "law was _given_" but "truth _became_." In other words, law was imposed from without. _Truth_ (reality) springs from within! A master artist can paint an orange tree with such skill and beauty that his picture imitates the real thing with exact detail. It draws the critic's admiration. But if we want to drink orange juice _no_ painting however well done can quench the thirst or nourish the body. Life springs from within beginning with roots absorbing nutrients from the soil. The branch gets its sap from the vine. Blossom and fruit follow as light and heat flow from the sun. Law is righteousness _painted_ on; life is grace and truth springing from within. "Grace and truth" rise from the depths of the heart as sap rises from root through vine to branch to fruit. Law is "painted" on to imitate the real thing; "truth" (reality) emerges from within the heart and produces obedience as sap generates fruit.

From another point of view law is but the description in literary form of right behaviour. As such it can never be outmoded. "Thou shalt not steal" or "thou shalt not murder" are not true because of democratic vote. On the contrary, these laws of moral conduct rise from the moral nature of God as Creator. Hence they are intrinsic within the nature of human beings as creatures made to be "like" God "in his image." They can never be outdated. But they must spring from "grace" within not forced from without. They rise out of moral necessity, not imposed by coercion. Thus it is that "the law and the prophets

261

(were) until John." The law "given" by Moses and impelled by the prophets represented God's sovereignty until the appearance of John the Baptist. But "from then the kingdom of God is evangelized and all are pressing into it..." With the coming of the Christ no longer is the law "given." Now God's sovereign grace and his eternal truth transform men into his image by recasting them from the heart out. Instead of conforming to law men are now realizing fulfillment to law by grace working truth within them. Law still describes the pattern of what human life should be. And any deviation from the law carries its own destruction. It decays the person from within. For that reason "grace and truth" rise from within that men may fulfill the ideal social behaviour as described by the law.

The law is so eternally present that it transcends creation itself. "It is easier for heaven and earth to pass away than for one horn of the law to fall." The very least "jot or tittle" of the written law so identifies with the moral nature of God that even the created order, symbol of solid permanancy with men, shall "pass away" before God's moral nature should altar, decline or erode! Nothing is more abiding, eternal or permanent than God, his moral essence.

Because of the intrinsic value of God's moral law society holds together so far as God's law prevails in human practice. The family is the basic unit that glues society in some degree of harmony. That fact links the thought of Luke 16:18 to the ideas of verses 15-17. "Everyone divorcing his wife and marrying another adulterizes; and the one having been divorced from a husband, marrying, adulterizes."

The law states, "Thou shalt not commit adultery." To covet and take another person's spouse is adultery. It breaks one of the most basic units of society, the family. Faithfulness in the marriage bond still reflects the "will of God" as it relates to the law of adultery. Man is free to ignore, violate or otherwise change the law. But he is not free to escape the consequences of his choice. As representing God the law of adultery is inviolable. And though divorce may be inevitable, even necessary, for human peace and safety, but the consequences leave a radical scar. It is not a matter of being denied forgiveness in God's grace; nor does divorce necessarily bar one from heaven. It underscores the fact that its consequences, both individually and socially, remain a scar. Under God's grace even a violation of the marriage bond may be transformed into a channel of blessing. God is ever "working all things for good!" He can turn even an "abomination" into thing of beauty!

16:15-18 communicates the author's dual emphases on the universality and humanity of God's revelation. Nothing in human experience is more permanent, universal or human than the moral law of God. But it's God's grace that brings the law to completion in a man's experience.

AN OUTLINE OF LUKE 16:19-31
A Dialogue Between Heaven and Hell!

Luke continues the theme of possessions and man's relation to them. Moving toward Jerusalem Jesus tells of "a certain rich man" and "a certain poor (man) whose name was Lazarus." They had contrasting lifestyles here and in life beyond life.

I. CONTRASTING LIVES IN THIS WORLD. 16:19-22
    1. The life of "a certain rich man."
       (a)His mansion: The "gate" of entrance!
       (b)His clothing: Royal "purple and fine linen."
       (c)Social life: "Daily merry-making."
       (d)Nameless in the parable. No identity!
       (e)He "died and was buried."
    2. "A certain poor whose name was Lazarus!"
       (a)His name identifies; he was a person!
       (b)His home: The rich man's "gate."
       (c)Food: "Crumbs from rich man's table!"
       (d)His health: "Full of ulcers."
       (e)Social life: "Dogs licked his sores."
       (e)He died, "taken by angels to Abraham's bosom."
II. THE CONTRAST IN LIFE BEYOND LIFE. 16:23-31
    1. The rich man:
       (a)"Being in torments!"
       (b)"Sees Abraham...and Lazarus in his bosom!"
    2. The Dialogue:
       (a)Admonition: "Have mercy...send Lazarus!"
       Answer:"Son remember: Moral justice! Moral chasm!
       (b)Request: "Send him to my ...five brothers!"
       Answer: "They have Moses & prophets!"
       (c)Objection:"They'll believe one from the dead!"
       Answer:"If they hear not Moses...they won't be
              persuaded if one rise from the dead!"

Neither poverty redeemed Lazarus nor did wealth condemn the "rich man." It was each man's relationship to and use or abuse of his moral opportunities that determined his eternal destiny. Character formed here will not be transformed hereafter. Mammon offers opportunity to shape and reveal character!

* * * * * *

A DIALOGUE BETWEEN HEAVEN AND HELL!

Character formed here cannot be transformed hereafter! Man's eternity is forged in time. The ripening of the human spirit comes by the management of mammon during years of toiling with material things. Evaluating possessions, managing money, the use or abuse of riches, responsible choices in acquiring wealth forms and transforms character. Eternal destiny is the fruit of such choices. These fashion the undercurrent embedded in the parable of the rich man and Lazarus.

Lives in Contrast!

"There was a certain rich man" and "there was a certain poor (man)!" But it was not the wealth or poverty that proved their greatest contrast. The "great chasm" that separated them was moral character. In that regard the poor displayed the "image" and "likeness" of God more than the rich man. He did not find himself in hell because he was rich. Nor did Lazarus enjoy the bliss of Abraham's bosom because he was poor. Nothing in the immediate story nor in all scripture assumes or teaches that wealth is immoral or that poverty is virtuous! Abraham, Isaac and Jacob, were men of wealth, yet they are the forefathers of faith. In spite of faults they became progenitors of the rich religious heritage of the Hebrews, indeed of all mankind! Lazarus was caught in a world system that often deprives the righteous of material reward yet scatteres its riches without regard to moral merit. We look beyond the wealth or poverty for the point of the parable.

The lifestyle of the "certain rich man" is suggestive. His palatial home was entered by a gate broad and ornate enough for Lazarus to find a make-do "home." The "gate" matched the mansion in elegance of style. Futhermore, his clothing was of royal "purple" and silken "linen" setting him apart from the tattered apparel of the common man. Both his house and dress walled him off from the crowd! They tended to remove him from the struggle which burden most men. He wasn't a man among men, but a man above men. The bond of human kinship waned under the weight of his wealth.

To compensate for the loss of such human identity the rich man created an aura of social activity. He became a party man! Day after day he created brilliant parties for his cronies. He replaced his loss of identity with a circle of private chums of his own choosing. He thus drowned out the cry of suffering man with the bawdy songs of daily fancy balls at the mansion. "He made merry daily in sumptuous living.!"

The "rich man" remains nameless! That is a subtle yet suggestive touch by Jesus (or the author). Such a striking contrast to the poor man, Lazarus, the rich is left in the story with no distinctive, personal identity. He's just one of a class, human, yes, but no name, no personality. Wealth and its power has built a shell around him. His self protection from society has left him a non-person; nameless!

But his indivisible, undeniable humanity finally came and placed its inevitable mark upon him as mortal man, "he died!" That without question identified him as human. Man is born to die! At the moment of birth he begins his long trek to the grave. Wealth or poverty may hasten or slow the process but the process moves on irretrievably. So the rich man "died." The abscence of any report of the funeral serves to stress the fact of death. The point is that his mansioh, clothing, merry-making came to its predictable end, "he died!" Life is over! If there is any meaning or purpose to his having lived it must now be evaluated and its fruit harvested. If life has no fruit nor sets forth any meaning then nothing remains but a total blank, an absolute obliteration of personality.

But a "cerain poor (man), by name, Lazarus,.." The very name indicates the character and bias of the poor man. "Lazarus" means "God has helped!" That which man denied God gave; bond of friendship, fellowship of love, security of soul amid poverty of possessions. Moreover, the fact of designating him by name certified that he was not forgotten as a distinct person. He was a "somebody" to be remembered in the counsels that counted. He was not a "certain poor," lost among multitudes of a class. He was one who included God among his acquaintances and from whom he got succor where men refused to help! So far as the "certain rich man" was concerned that which alone identified him was his self-centered use of his wealth. But the poor man was close enough to God as to be identified as recipient of divine aid! Forgotten by his followmen, God knew him by name.

The story lists the limitations of the "certain poor man." He was one of the "homeless" who are a part of every civilization since history began. His house, home, and bed was the rich man's "gate." There he was "dumped" by nameless friends that he might possibly gain sustenance from the rich man's bounty. He grasped for "crumbs that fell from the rich man's table." His food was the rich man's garbage.

Such existence hardly provided a healthy life. A rash of festering ulcers laced his meager frame. Lice gnawed his putrid flesh. Poisonous pus oozed from the irritating sores. They clothed his flesh like tattered rags. His social companions were dogs, scavengers of the alleys. They "licked his ulcers" like soothing medicine and comforted his sagging spirit more than human friends. When Eden's first parents challenged God's will by eating the forbidden fruit they did not anticipate the meaning of the threatened "death." Focused in this poor man was the curse of the pre-announced "death."

In due time, Lazarus "died and was taken off by angels into Abraham's bosom." Though nothing is recorded about it, no doubt, the rich man was honored among men by an opulent funeral. We are only told that "he died and was buried." Yet when Lazarus died heaven sent a bevy of angels to carry his soul to the halls of heaven. The difference in quality of spirit, not possessions, forged the disparate destination of the men.

Contrast in the life beyond life!

The contrast continues in life beyond life. In this world life finds time for growth and development of the "image of God" in man. The ups and downs, victories and defeats, good and bad contribute to the end result. Character is shaped on the wheels of the divine Potter. The heat of life's oven bakes character into each living soul. That's why life formed here is not transformed hereafter.

The state of the rich and the poor is reversed! "In hades," in his poverty of spirit, "the rich man, being in torments, having lifted up his eyes sees Abraham from afar and Lazarus in his bosom!" The unnamed "rich man" is conscious! Life beyond life retains intelligent recognition. He is aware of moral differences. He experiences flaming "torments" and is aware of Lazarus at rest in "Abraham's bosom."

The Dialogue!

A conversational exchange takes place between the rich man in Hell and Heaven's spokesman, Abraham. Writhing in his torment the rich man hardly avoided surprise if not resentment at seeing the beggerly Lazarus reclining at ease in Abraham's bosom. He contemptuously ignored Lazarus and addressed Abraham. "Father Abraham, have mercy on me and send Lazarus that he may dip the tip of his finger in water and cool my tongue." True to character he demanded that the poor be his slave. As in life so in afterlife he expected to be served rather than to serve.

That he recognized Lazarus and called him by name is notable. When he had passed his palace gates he was conscious of the beggar and his distressed condition. He even knew his name. Could he himself have been a cause of the destitution of Lazarus? At least his wealth had blinded his eyes and calloused his soul. He ignored his duty to others' needs! In torment his selfish soul acts out his selfish concern by demanding, "Send Lazarus to serve my needs!" He was still blind to moral distinctions between himself and Lazarus.

Heaven responds to Hell's request. "Son remember that you got your good things in your life and Lazarus similarly got the bad!" Then Heaven pointed out that the real difference between the "good" and the "bad" was more than material. Abraham said, "Amid all these things between us and you a great chasm has been established..." The gulf between Hell and Heaven has been fixed once for all, permanent, irrevocable, not to be annulled. So fixed is it that "the ones wishing to go from here to you are not able, neither shall they come over from you to us." The distance between us is not measured by miles or money, it's a moral chasm and that is fixed by the use or abuse of moral opportunities during life. "Son remember the number of times you failed to use your money when you ignored the muted appeals of Lazarus' need as you passed in and out of your gate?" Moral worth fixed in life won't be transfixed in life beyond life! In view of the moral character you developed during life, rigid and fixed, "now here he is comforted, but you are in torments!"

Hell resolutely persists in his selfish demands. "I ask you father, send him unto my father's house..." From Hell the "rich man" still claims Abraham as "father." He still insists on spiritual kinship. He assumes that Heaven should take special interest in my father's family. "I have five brothers! They should be warned (witnessed to) lest they shall come to this place of pain." Not only does the rich man complain of his pain but he implies that he was not sufficiently warned about the moral consequences of his earthly behaviour. "Give my brother more and better warning than you gave me!" His self-centered soul continues to express itself in his "fixed" moral condition. In effect the rich man was claiming, "It was Heaven's fault, not mine, that I am in this place of pain!" The moral destiny of human beings is determined by Heaven, not man! You made me thus; you failed to warn me adequately; how could I help being here?

Heaven refuses the complaint. Abraham responded, "They are having Moses and the prophets. Let them hear them." The writings of Moses record the events surrounding the giving of the law as well as tokens of God's presence in leading Israel out of Egypt. The moral holiness of God is stated in three commandments, "no other gods," "no graven images," don't take "the name of the Lord God emptily." Two commands guard the moral sanctity of time: (1)regularly, "Remember the sabbath day to keep it holy," (2)in your heritage, "Honor your father and mother." Four commands reveal moral responsibilities in social relationships: toward life, "You shall not murder." In the family, "You shall not commit adultery." In respecting property, "You shall not steal." By the sanctity of the pledged word, "You shall not bear false witness." Above all in purity of the heart's desires, "You shall not covet."

The prophets have recorded how God dealt judgments through centuries against individuals and nation when his moral values were ignored. Yet he rained blessings, material and spiritual, on both nations or individuals who honored in life his moral standards. The scrolls of Old Testament have stood as bulwark against the tide of rebellion and sin. To every generation they have been the word of warning. But, if one is to avoid the inevitable torture of disobedience, he must read, hear, and heed! Don't blame Heaven for failure to read and heed the warnings of "Moses and the prophets!"

The word of God is designed as light for those who walk in darkness, as guide for those lost in arrogant self-serving. It is antidote to sin. It is the necessary warning. Man cannot escape moral blame while "Moses and the prophets" stand.

The rich man persists in refusing Heaven's argument. "No! No! father Abraham. That's not enough! But if anyone go to them from the dead, they will repent!" The supreme warning, according to Hell, is one who repudiates death by denying its permanent power. "Send one risen from the dead and that will do." Little did the rich man recognize how he was an example of the chains of unbelief. He was even now rejecting the idea that he had been adequately warned. He now knew by experience the judgment of Hell. Yet he didn't yet "believe" that the word of God was fair warning. He demanded the miracle of a resurrection. He didn't accept that "character formed here would not be transformed hereafter." He was insensitive to the moral chasm.

Heaven speaks its final word. It dismisses the persistent unbelief of Hell. "If they do not hear Moses and the prophets, they will not be persuaded even if one shall rise from the dead!" Unbelief, once hardened, will not be changed! The "rich man" in Hell demonstrated that unbelief persisted beyond life on this earth. When anyone wills not to believe no evidence will alter the fixation of soul. Later experience confirmed this by the resurrection of Jesus. Even though presented by many intelligent, eye witnesses who sealed their honesty with their blood yet men continue in unbelief and moral disarray.

Moral responsibility is the common denominator to which every human being is subject and for which he shall answer here and hereafter. Moral responsibility is universally human. Moreover, as indeed all _truth_ is, it is timeless and eternal!

* * * * * * *

AN OUTLINE OF LUKE 17:1-10
Problems of Christian Relationships!
Real Christianity consists of relationships! Relationships between God and a man, between believer and believer, between Saviour and saved! Even among evil men their lostness is created by relationships between the lost and Lucifer. Many are the problems created by relationships.
I. STUMBLING BLOCKS. 17:1-3a
    1. Stumbling blocks are inevitable. 1
    2. Consequences on those causing them. 2
    3. Be ever on guard! 3a
II. FORGIVENESS. 17:3b-4
    1. He who creates stumbling blocks needs forgiveness.
    2. Be ever ready to forgive. 3b
    3. Boundless forgiveness! 4
III. FAITH. 17:5-6
    1. "Add to us faith!" 5
    2. Living, growing, expanding faith. 6
    (a)Faith is a _seed_.
    (b)The power of living faith.
IV. DEFICIENT SERVANTS! 17:7-10
    1. The Master-Servant relationship. 7-9
    2. A Dutiful servant does that which he ought. 10
Christ relieves tensions and resolves problems in the lives of Christian believers. One must be "in Christ" to experience him as the problem solver!

* * * * * *

PROBLEMS OF CHRISTIAN RELATIONSHIPS!
In its very nature moral responsibility implies someone other than me. Moral duty implies "ought" on my part. But that which I "ought" to do presupposes _someone_ to whom I "ought" to do it! It's in these areas of the "ought" where tensions arise between people, including believers. Thus it is in such relationships that Christ can resolve problems. It is here that salvation "in Christ" comes to full fruition.
The story of the rich man and Lazarus sharply focused in on the moral responsibility of men not only toward possessions but also toward other human beings. In this text Jesus extends his teaching over a series of matters in which people, especially believers, are _obligated_ (ought) to relate to one another in a spiritually healthy, wholesome, redemptive way.

268

Stumbling Blocks!

"And he said to his disciples!" The four topics of this text were addressed to "the disciples." In the state into which we as human beings are born in this world no escape from moral entanglement with others is possible. And though it is true that each man must bear his own liability for his own decisions part of that liability is the effect which his decisions have on others as they make their decisions.

We do not live in isolation. Each human is a single thread, but one that is woven with other threads into a whole cloth! The strength or weakness of the fabric is affected by how I do or do not contribute to the whole. As an individual I am entwined with other human beings, especially to those in the household of faith. That which I think, believe, do, and practice influences that which "these little ones," think, believe, do and practice. Those who are babes in belief are dependent for guidance and support, from those who are more mature in the family of faith. I cannot "do as I please." On the contrary, as a mother is responsible for the babe to which she gave birth so each Christian bears some responsibility to the new babe in the family of Christ. He must be fed the milk of the word, cleansed from his own self-inflicted sins, loved, nourished, forgiven, and restored until he can walk firmly on his own feet.

Jesus is teaching the disciple's responsibility of using personal influence in the stability of fellow-believers, especially newly born ones. "It is impossible that stumbling blocks not come!" That is to be expected. But one must not forget the awesome responsibility entailed! "Woe through whom the snare comes." Not to assume my responsibility in the life and moral welfare of the spiritual development of one "of these little ones" exposes me to horrible judgment. "It is advantageous if a millstone be hung around his neck and he be hurled into the sea!" Death is more inviting than life if I desregard my involvement with the needs of other believers, particularly those recently born into faith!

Severity of punishment implies severity of crime. This teaching of Jesus points to seduction to sin in general. But the immediate context involves ensnarement to apostasy. Having confessed Christ as Saviour so to lead the new confessor into repudiation of that faith is worthy of the most humiliating, shameful, public punishment. Better for that one "to be hurled into the sea with a millstone laid around his neck!"

Such an obligation demands constant care. Jesus urges, "Take heed to yourselves!" Be ever alert to opportunities to meet the needs of others less grounded in faith. An island in mid-sea is linked to the mainland by the land mass below the surface. The waters of the seas fill in the depressed areas. Thus each believing Christian is linked to every believer in the community of faith. "Be always alert" to be keeping the unity and stability of the faith strong in the hearts of all believers!

Unlimited Forgiveness!

"Take heed to yourselves" (3a) hinges the preceding to the following teaching. "Be ever alert" not to be a snare to the weak and unwary but "be watching" lest your very maturity in Christ ensnare you into failure to forgive "one of these little ones."

One of the most demanding, most difficult duties for any Christian, new or old, is to forgive! That is a source of innumerable stumblings. That is the bait that dupes the frail and faint. When he nibbles the bait the trigger snaps the trap and he's caught in its steel jaws. No sin surpasses in its deceit more than the unwillingness or inability to forgive.

For forgiveness to transpire three ingredients must always prevail. "If your brother sin, rebuke him; and if he repent, forgive him!" Forgiveness embraces much more than appears on the surface. The process includes: (1)rebuke, a pointing out of the offense; (2)repentance, a change of mind by the offender; (3)forgiveness, releasing of the feelings spawned by the wrong. In other words, for forgiveness to remove any barrier between brethren it takes more than just withholding ill will! Both offended and offender have equal but different roles to play in renewing brotherly relationships. And for each to discharge his duty it takes more than ordinary spiritual assets. In fact, at any level, in any place, era, or culture forgivenss is the crux of Christianity. Since "all have sinned" forgiveness by God toward man is the essence of salvation. And if man's offense against man is to be rectified the same process must take place between offender and offended, between wrong-doer and him who is wronged.

As in all things God gives the pattern for forgiveness. He demonstrates how! First he "rebukes." He must bring a man to face his own responsibility in his sin. "If we say, 'we do not have sin (guilt) we deceive ourselves...'" "If we acknowledge our sins, he is faithful and just that he forgive our sins..." (I Jn.1:8f)

God is ever so willing to forgive. Indeed he has provided for my redemption at the cost of the life of his only begotten Son. Yet he cannot forgive unless and until I accept the fact of my need of forgiveness. To that end God must "rebuke" "admonish" "convict" of my responsible guilt in wrong-doing. God is absolutely intolerant of evil. But he is equally anxious, able, and willing to forgive him who sins. But his hands are tied until I accept my need.

Thus it is when I have wronged a brother in Christ. Some way must be found to get me to face the wrong I have committed. In the words of Jesus, He who is wronged is obligated to "rebuke" me. Now that takes a quality of humility, sensitivity, and spiritual maturity beyond the usual. To "rebuke" without compounding the already irritating sore takes spiritual skill that only God can supply. The words of Paul are so appropriate here: "Work out your own salvation with fear and trembling; for it is God who works in you both to will and to work his good pleasure."(Phil.2:12f)

270

Once I have looked into the mirror of my soul and faced my wrong the next step is mine. I am to change my mind about my responsibility in guilt and my approach to him whom I have wronged. In a word I am to repent!

We must not forget that two are involved in forgiveness, the offender and the offended. There can be no forgiveness without both moving together toward each other with sympathy and understanding. For the one who is hurt to withhold resentment is not forgiveness. First must come rebuke! Then repentance of wrong-doing! Finally comes reconciliation, a healing of the breach by forgiveness. When such a process is consummated the restored fellowship becomes more firm, more binding than before the breach. Forgiveness that does not cost is not real. It is shallow sentimentality!

How often and how much must I forgive? Jesus said, "If he sin against you seven times in the day and shall return to you saying, I repent, you shall forgive him." The Lord is not urging that we limit forgiveness to an exact mathematical formula. It is his way of teaching that forgiveness has no limits! As God is boundless in his forgiveness of a man who repeatedly asks, so in human relations forgiveness is to be measured by the divine standard. It is to be boundless! He who will not forgive need not expect God's forgiveness.

"Add to us faith!"

The call to forgive demands the highest quality of faith! Forgiveness is too lofty a mountain for a disciple to climb alone. The obligation to forgive prompted an immediate prayer from the apostles. "Increase our faith." It was at once a cry of despair, yet a recognition of their obligation to forgive. "Lord, if we are to forgive like that we need more faith! Give us the amount of faith that will enable us to forgive." "Faith is assurance of things hoped for!"(Heb:11:1) How can we ever forgive as we ought without a quality of faith that propels to reconciliation? The plea of the disciples is, "Add faith to that which you already have given us!"

The immediate response of Jesus to their plea made clear that genuine faith has inherent within the power to increase itself. Faith never stands still; it is never static; it must grow or wither. Said Jesus, "If you were having faith as a grain of mustard seed, you would say to this sycamine tree, 'Be rooted up and planted in the sea!' And it would obey you!" The amount of faith, be it ever so small, is not so important as the quality. Genuine faith, honest faith, pure trust, by its very nature, must grow until it demonstrates power beyond limit. With God in Christ as the object of the Christian's faith, even though small, it will increase until its power propels the unexpected, even the impossible. The Gospel of Thomas relates forgiveness to similar mountain moving power: "If two make peace, one with the other...they will say to the mountain 'Move away,' and it will move away."(§ 48) Thus it is Jesus points out to the twelve that it's the quality as much as the quantity of faith that provides power to forgive.

271

The Servant Master Roles!

This bundle of texts continues with a story of a servant in relation to his master. A servant's role is to <u>serve</u> not rule. And while a servant may be commended for rendering his service <u>well</u>, he need expect no praise for performing his role as servant. <u>That</u> he <u>ought</u> to do with or without praise for <u>how</u> he does it. A carpenter, brick mason, lawyer or doctor may get plaudits for performing their services <u>well</u>. But they need not look for accolades merely because they discharge the vocational task for which their talent and training have equipped them. So Jesus pictures a plowman or sheep herder after a hard day's labor in the field coming to the Master's table. He does not get out of his servant role by elbowing the Master away from his own dinner table. The Master of the house has <u>his</u> role to play as much as any servant. The point of the story is that each person in a society need expect no extra distinction merely because he has done that which he is assigned and equipped to do! The plowman is not thanked for plowing nor need the shepherd expect surplus praise for caring for the sheep. What else should a plowman or shepherd do than plow or care for sheep? And for that matter, what should a Master of a household be expected to do other than give direction and set goals for the entire household with all its various servants. What is a society but just that, a society, with each person faithfully performing his own special function in the whole.

Jesus declares the underlying principle by which his society, his kingdom, shall operate. "Whenever you have done all that has been commanded you, you are to say, 'we are profitless slaves. What we were obligated to do we did.'" That which the slaves were voicing was that they merely performed their assigned task in the family community of which they were a part. But having performed that role they had no other claims to profit.

Such is the role that the Christian believer plays in his relationship to God as creator-king. When we function as God's servant in God's kingdom we have done that which we "ought," nothing more! The destiny which the faithful servant gets is not due to his performance as a servant but rather on the grace of the Master. A servant can make no just claim for having more than he ought! No matter how adequately a person serves in God's kingdom, he still does not accrue any personal <u>profit</u>. He has done only what he <u>ought</u>! No man is awarded redemption just because he is a <u>human</u>. His humanity is a "gift" of God's grace!

Without doubt Jesus spoke these "teachings" which make up this cluster of four. No logical reason can be found for his not having taught them on this last journey to Jerusalem. But even so, Luke, who framed this story, felt a connection between these ideas and his unfolding account of the redemptive ministry of Jesus. Each text sounds a universal chord that runs through men of all nations and cultures. Luke keeps stressing his major themes for his reader, Theophilus.

AN OUTLINE OF LUKE 17:11-19
A "Stranger" Made Whole!
Gratitude is neither national nor racial; it is human and
therefore universal! It may be crusted by pride of party,
smothered by arrogance of race but it will surface in most
unlikely hearts at most unusual places. The healing of ten
lepers exhibits gratitude at its best contrasted to ingratitude
at its worst.
    I. A COMMUNITY OF SUFFERING. 17:11-13
        1. The continuing journey to Jerusalem. 11
        2. A community of suffering. 12-13
    II. CURING THE COMMON SUFFERING. 17:14-16
        1. The command. 14a
        2. The cleansing. 14b
        3. The gratitude of "one of them." 15-16
           (a)He "saw" he was healed."
           (b)He "turned back."
           (c)He "praised God."
           (d)He "thanked" Jesus.
           (e)He "was a Samaritan," a "stranger."
    III. THREE QUESTIONS OF JESUS! 17:17-18
        1. "Were not the ten cleansed?"
        2. "Where are the nine?"
        3. Did "none...give glory to God save this stranger?"
Suffering demolishes differences but fundamental attitudes
surface when the pain is abolished. The soul must be "saved"
from its basic disposition to the evil of ingratitude. "Be on
your way, your faith has saved you!"

                    * * * * * * *

A "STRANGER" MADE WHOLE!
    Men display their basic self-centeredness in various ways.
Wealth, houses, clothes, jewelry, vocation, social position,
race, formalism, religion all have at times served a selfish
covering of man's true position before God and man. But let
men of essential differences fall into common pain that has
social stigma then misery breaks all barriers. Agony generates
unity. Felt unity leaps all walls and makes fundamental
differences disappear. But the test of the unity comes when
cure eliminates the common pain. Community that cannot endure
cure dwarfs into its selfish cells.
    As Jesus was going to Jerusalem he was journeying "between
Samaria and Galilee" toward Perea. He was moving persistently
toward his God-given destiny. The cross with its redemptive
power dominated the situations which confronted him day by day.
And "as he was entering into a certain village ten leprous men
met him." Leprosy was the AIDS of Biblical times. It was slow
but sure death. It meant segregation from family, friends and
ostracism from and by society. It assured a slow permanent
total abandonment of hope. It carried a stigma permanent and
terminal. It created physical and psychological communities
dwelling apart.

273

"And as he was entering into a certain village ten leprous men met him." Just before crossing into Perea while yet along the border between Samaria and Galilee this collection of suffering abandoned men confronted Jesus as a cloister needing his mercy! Their tattered attire, putrid flesh, protruding bones, stumped feet, shrill creaking cries marked them as a clan of pain. They formed a society apart. Their mutual agony made them one! They lived, cried, despaired, hoped, moved, slept and ate together! They were a community unto itself. Yet never without longing for their lost place in the society of men. But as a society unto itself, segregated and solitary, in keeping with Levitical law, they "stood afar off." Though ten in number their forced exile left them lonely men. That they "stood afar off" marked not only their physical disease but their spiritual isolation. Unless one personally experiences such a diseased association this is an unthinkable, incredible, inconceivable unit of society! The physical, bad as it was, was outstripped by the mental, psychological anguish.

When the ten came face to face with Jesus they lifted their voices as one, "Jesus, Master, have mercy on us!" The text presents the subject "they" with unusual emphasis. And it uses the singular "voice" though the "they" is plural. In other words, the ten felt, thought, responded, and spoke as one! Their miserable condition bonded them into a singular oneness of action, "Master, mercy us!"

Curing the Common Suffering!

The response of Jesus to this plea is as astonishing for what it does not say as what it does report. Jesus never said that he would cure them. He never demanded faith, at least not in so many words. He inquires nothing as to their national, cultural, economic, social, or family conditions. The text merely states, "Having seen he said to them, 'When you have gone, show yourselves to the priests!'" If he explained why they should go to the priest the text doesn't say. He assumes they must know the why! That assumption is the nearest thing to any demand for faith. Why must they go to a priest except to be examined as to their cure?

Without question this is a remarkable and an unusual healing. By a word of command, though not of healing, without a touch, Jesus cured all ten men. But the men did not know they were healed until "while they were going they were cleansed." And though the record only tells us that "one of them, having seen that he was healed" we may assume they all saw "as they were going" that they were healed! The healing took place enroute to the priests. In other words, it took place while they were obeying the command to "go, show yourselves to the priests." The fact that so little is told about what surrounded this miracle story leads to the conclusion that the healing is not the main point of the narrative. The thrust of the story is the gratitude of one and the ingratitude of nine. And that "he was a Samaritan" and the nine were sons of Abraham!

274

No doubt is left but that "they" (all ten) "were cleansed."
"But (only) one of them, when he saw that he was healed,
returned..." That he saw means he personally experienced. It
was a sensual observance of returning health that transpired
before his own eyes. This was not someone describing healing
but a transition going on within his own senses. No one need
tell him, he knew, felt, sampled, endured the marvel of
returning wholeness. He who has suffered the stygma of social
disease is capable of appreciating health better than he who
has never been sick. He who has known the shame of prison can
know better the opportunities of freedom. He who has lived
three score and ten years can be more perceptive of the real
meaning of life than the infant who has not yet begun the
entangling trail. This "one" man's heart brimmed over with
joy, appreciation, and thanksgiving. He "turned back!"
     That he "turned back" speaks volumes, especially since the
nine did not. The lesson lies in what he felt and did when he
"turned back." He returned with "great joy!" That's how he
felt. He began "glorifying God" and he "fell before the feet"
of Jesus "thanking him." That's what he did!
     The experiencing of health after sickness clamors for a
reevaluation of life and its meaning. Returning health brings
the opportunity to change health habits. Health-giving foods
supplant snacks, exercise replaces endless sitting at a desk.
After lapse into sin and its dehumanizing effects vision and
purpose rise on the moral and spiritual horizon! When one
"sees" healing, he changes his course in life; he "turns back!"
     But to turn back leaves a spiritual void unless something is
done! The healed leper "glorified God" and began "thanking"
Jesus. A healing from physical sickness or moral sin opens up
the potential of recognition of our dependency as creatures on
God as Creator. To see life and to see it whole is to see us
as human in our creaturely dependence on the divine ordering of
life. In him "we live, move and have our being." We must not,
yea, we cannot live apart from God. And though we may deny
him, ignore him, reject him, he remains as Creator and we are
his creatures! Health after sickness brings back that
wholesome sense of our place in God's scheme. Thus we can
"glorify God" as God
     Furthermore, we may be "thanking" Jesus, God's agent in the
whole redemptive process. "Christ died for us!" "I came that
they might have life and have it more abundantly!" It is
because of his redeeming labor that we are healed from the
sickness of sin. Gratitude is the instinct of the saved,
physical and/or spiritual! As life in the growing grain rises
toward the sun, so renewed life in a man rises to its rightful
relationship to the life-giver!
     "And he was a Samaritan!" That he was a "stranger" from the
commonwealth of Israel gives all the more emphasis to the fact
that thanksgiving springs from a human heart, not a cultural
heart crusted over with selfish racial pride or religious
superiority.

275

Three Questions of Jesus!

Whenever Jesus asked questions it was to stimulate thought and draw forth truth; it was not to gain information. He asked three questions, the first proposing, "Ten were cleansed were they not?" The framing of the question was such as to show that he was expecting "Yes" as the answer. Certainly there were ten lepers and all were cured were they not? God doesn't do things half way! Christ's healing of all ten reveals a pattern of divine behaviour. Healing is not to be denied to anyone who has legitimate needs. As with the lepers so with the leprousy of sin. Though "all have sinned" yet God's redemption in Christ is open to all without distinction. No cry for mercy is forgotten, overlooked, or ignored. Salvation is universally available! Sunshine and rain fall alike on the "just and the unjust." Life, healing, and health are gracious gifts to the whole human creation.

But Christ's second question discloses that "all" do not respond to God's grace in equal measure or with the same spirit. He asks: "Where are the nine?" The flesh of the nine was made as fresh, firm, and full as that of the "one." Restoration to social acceptance was as much a reality to them as to the "stranger." But they took the healing with no recognition of the Healer. They accepted it as a "right" not a gracious gift of God's glory! At least their behaviour would indicate such. Cleansing from leprosy or sin involves two persons, the redeemer and the redeemed! It is a relationship between Saviour and sinner, the living God and a decaying dying man. The nine obeyed in the sense that they went to show themselves to the priests. But that was the formal, legal, ritualistic social requirement. They forgot the Person through whom their restored health came. And that is ingratitude which itself denies the full value of the cure. Ingratitude endangers, if it does not destroy, gracious relationships between living persons. And wholesome relationship is the essence of salvation between man and God.

It was only the "one" who returned "glorifying God" and who "fell on his face at his feet thanking him." And Luke pointedly observes, "He was a Samaritan!" This fact prompted the third question, "Were they not found, those who returned, to give glory to God except this stranger?" We should expect that of ten who were healed ten would express praise and thanksgiving. Jesus appears amazed and puzzled that the nine failed to show in spiritual terms that cleansing which they experienced in their physical bodies. They missed the most important part of the healing, that of the inner man. Joyous gratitude is the mark of the saved man. Selfish ingratitude is the mark of the lost.

Furthermore, he was a "stanger" not one of the "chosen" race who expressed his spiritual healing. Salvation is not for the Jew as a Jew or a Samaritan as a Samaritan. It is for a human being as a human! Hence Jesus recognized the saved condition of the "stranger." He said, "Get up, be on your way, your faith has saved you!"

276

AN OUTLINE OF LUKE 17:20-37
When, How, and Why the Kingdom of God?

The answer to a question is often influenced by who asks? The Pharisees asked, "When is the kingdom of God coming?" Jesus gave a somewhat different answer to them as that spoken to the disciples as he journeyed toward Jerusalem.

I. THE KINGDOM WITHIN. 17:20-21
1. The question asked. 20
2. The answer: The inward nature of the kingdom. 21
   (a)Not by observation.
   (b)It is "in your reach."
II. THE KINGDOM WITHOUT. 17:22-37
1. The answer determined by whom addressed. 22-23
2. The kingdom has its outward effects. 24-33
   (a)Analogy of lightning: sudden and universal. 24
   (b)A necessary condition, rejection of the king. 25
   (c)Two illustrations of when! 26-30
   (d)Urgency of "that day." 31-33
   (e)Selectivity on "that day."
3. "Where the body is there shall the eagles gather."

If there be in fact a "kingdom of God" and we assume there is. And if this be a world universally corrupted by sin, and we accept that as fact, then it follows as night the day there must be judgment, a sifting, a separating. This is why the kingdom of God must come! The kingdom is an inevitable reality, the hope and destiny of man!

* * * * * * *

WHEN, HOW, AND WHY THE KINGDOM OF GOD!

The kingdom of God occupied the thought and teaching of Jesus during his public ministry. In fact the kingdom was the reason why he came, to reestablish the rule of God over men.

The Kingdom Within!

On a number of occasions Jesus had spoken about the kingdom of God, its reality, its near approach, even the fact that it has "already reached you!" It is not likely that such teaching had failed to reach the ears of his Pharisaical enemies. Why should they now inquire, "When is the kingdom coming?"

The way in which Jesus answered indicates that their real problem was not when but what! Their understanding was a misundertanding of the nature of the kingdom. It wasn't time but kind of kingdom they really needed to know. It is that which Jesus addressed in his reply to their query. "The kingdom of God does not come with observation. Neither shall they say, 'Behold! Here or there!'" Omens, signs, visible tokens or portents do not attend the coming of the kingdom. Such things will not enable you to point your finger, "Here!" or "There!" You're not to look for time or place nor speculate about when or where. Such matters are inobservable! Eye, ear, or touch cannot identify God's kingdom. Its nature and quality are not subject to such criteria.

277

The obverse side of that coin is, "The kingdom of God is within you!" Just exactly what Jesus meant by "within you" is a subject of debate among honest, serious students of scripture. But whatever he meant one thing is certain, the kingdom of God is _internal_! It has external aspects but in its essence God's kingdom is spiritual. Material or physical standards do not determine where, when or what the kingdom of God is. The spirituality of that kingdom evades such measuring rods.

In a world such as this externals have their place, so much so that what cannot be seen, tasted, touched, heard is often assumed to be unreal, non-existant. As a matter of fact the externally physical is the manifestation of the more basic reality of spirit. A corpse is visible to eye and sensible to touch but without spirit we designate it as _dead_. Money, food, clothing, and houses are visible externals yet have no real significance except as they minister to the _essence_ of what human beings _are_! "God is _spirit_." It is not only true that "it is necessary for the ones worshipping him worship in spirit and truth" but also that they be related to God's physical creation as God himself is related. The physical not only is servant of the spirit it displays the spirit, its ideas, goals, and intents. In a real sense "the kingdom is _within_ you."

There is a sense that the kingdom of God is "within your reach." The context suggests that that idea not be overlooked. In koine Greek, current among the people of the first century world, "within you" was a phrase used by the people to mean, "within reach." It did not mean "inside you" in a physical sense, but rather "available" to you.

The kingdom of God, as Jesus had indicated, "has arrived." It was already present in his person as a redeeming power and judgmental force. And though the kingdom was yet to come finally on "that day"(vs.31) still, it was _now_ available to anyone who was sensitive to his message and person. It was "in their midst" and quite accessible. That which was needed was a spiritual sensitivity.

The Kingdom Without!

Surely the kingdom of God in its essence is an inward spiritual sovereignty. Yet of necessity it must thrust itself into outward, visible, forms perceptible to man's experience in this mundane world. In verse 20 it was Pharisees who proposed the question about the kingdom. In verse 22 we are told that Jesus, "said to his disciples..." He proceeds to develop the kingdom theme in its outward visible expression. Such a variance is there between the ideas of 20-21 and 22-37 that some students detect a contradiction. It was rather the different _audience_ that determined his emphasis. He first corrected the Pharisees' fallacies. Then to his trusting disciples he exposed the need for preparation for the sudden universal consummation of the kingdom. It's one thing to have the kingdom available; it's another to be _ready_ at the crisis of history when God's kingdom comes to its _final_ fulfillment.

As history advances circumstances will arise when "you will desire to see one of the days of the son of man and you shall not see it." In such wearisome times when faith wears thin "they shall say to you, 'Behold! there, Behold! here." Many dark days shall cloud your vision so that you may be tempted to find the kingdom of God in political, economic, and social reforms. "Don't go off neither pursue" such illusions! The kingdom won't come that way! The visible appearance of the kingdom is too much like lightning for such to delude you. "As the lightning flashes and lights up the heaven from one horizon to the other thus shall be the son of man in his day." In three particulars lightning is analogous to the kingdom: it can be seen, it is sudden, it is universal from east to west. When the "day" of Christ comes it will be <u>sudden</u>, <u>visible</u>, and <u>universal</u>. Whatever signs may herald his coming they will be too general for preparation to be made at the moment. Hence it is imperative that men be ever on the alert, be always ready, be continuously prepared for that consummation of the kingdom.

Some general tokens will appear before "that day" of the king's final coming. First an immediate precondition is "that he suffer many things and that he be tested and rejected by <u>this</u> generation." There will be no sovereign rule of God unless and until he, <u>the</u> <u>king</u>, prepares the essentials of moral, spiritual triumph over the reign of evil. To rule <u>in</u> this world he must rule <u>over</u> this world. He must conquer its most visible power, <u>death</u>! To that end he must confront evil at its worst in the nation's leaders. He must be subjected to the most Satan can produce, criminal rejection and execution. This that he might rise to demonstrate his power over death.

Beyond his trial, rejection, death and resurrection there lies before believers an indefinite period of carrying on the necessary functions of life. But even so preparation for his <u>sudden</u>, <u>visible</u>, <u>universal</u> coming is imperative. Don't allow the daily necessities of living drug you to sleep. Be always alert to the very dangers inherent in normal living.

Jesus reminds of two historical events that enforce this. "Just as it happened in the days of Noah, so shall it be in the days of the son of man. They were eating,..were drinking,..were marrying,..were giving in marriage until the day in which Noah entered the ark and the flood came and destroyed all." A similar sudden destruction came in the time of Lot. "They were eating,..were drinking,..were buying,..were selling,..were planting,..were building...But in the day in which Lot went out from Sodom fire and brimstone rained from heaven and destroyed all." Two details we note. First, the activities of Noah's and Lot's generations were innocent, even essential activities. Nothing was sinful about any of them. Any wrong grew out of being so involved in the necessities so as to dull one's sense of spiritual imperative. A disciple must keep himself ready for the <u>sudden</u>, <u>visible</u>, <u>universal</u> appearance of the Son of man and his kingdom. The danger is not the worst versus the best but the innocent against the highest!

279

In view of the sudden, visible, universal appearance of the "son of man" on "that day" the necessities of earthly life will be as trifles. Nothing shall be more urgent than the king and his kingdom. For the subjects of the king what could be more crucial than their personal relationship to Him, their king? Eating, drinking, marrying, giving in marriage, planting and building, all so life-consuming now, will be so irrelevant then. When the flood waters inundated their houses and swept away all food, family, and belongings of Noah's generation was there any greater "necessity" than life itself? And for Lot and his family what possibly could have been more important than moral maturity when fire and brimstone hailed down from the heavens? On "that day" life and its moral, spiritual relationship to God will supersede all sensual, economic, physical "necessities" so important to life as we now know it. Our urgency for vigilance on "that day" is beyond imagination!

So grave will it be that no time will be allowed to "save" the "necessities" of this world. "On that day he who is on the roof top and his goods in the house, is not to go down to get them." Of what believable value can equipment, utensils, keepsakes, stocks or bonds be at the crisis when time and eternity meet "that day"?

"That day" itself will be a time when moral selections become final. A permanent separation shall divide the most familiar friends and relatives. "On that night two shall be upon one bed, one shall be taken and the other left. Two shall be grinding together, the one shall be taken and the other left." It is noteworthy that the word translated "other" indicates "other" of a different kind, not of the same kind. In other words, though in outward appearance the "two" seem the same, the inward moral characters are as different as night and day. In spite of similar form and appearance the spiritual differences between people are the abiding, basic matters that make eternal separations.

So radical did these character differences seem to the disciples that they entreated Jesus, "Where, Lord?" Their startled query indicates their failure to understand clearly. Thus Jesus gives answer in a proverbial statement, "Where the body is, there the eagles gather." In other words, as carrion is consumed by eagles so it will be for those who have abandoned themselves to the dead-end "necessities" of this world's concerns. Corruption attracts birds that feed on putrefying flesh. Judgment shall devour those who have become carrion in character.

The more humanity changes the more it is the same. Science, technology, culture is ever altering, growing, changing yet beneath it all human nature remains ever the same, addicted to evil and reaping in moral judgment that which it sows. Outward advances hide the unvarying corruption within. Only he who has a living relationship with God abides to survive the dissolution of death.

280

AN OUTLINE OF LUKE 18:1-8
Justice and Prayer in God's Kingdom!

In verse one Luke designates the point in the parable of a "widow" and a "certain judge." The lesson is: It's logical "to be praying always and not to faint." The oppressive, increasingly brutal world will induce believers to grow weary in faith and forsake prayers to God. This parable addresses this temptation.

I. A WIDOW BEFORE A JUDGE. 18:1-5
   1. A "certain judge."
      (a)His responsibility as judge.
      (b)His faith toward God and attitude toward men.
   2. A "widow in that city."
      (a)Her plea.
      (b)Her persistence.
      (c)The results.
II. APPLICATION: BELIEVERS AND THEIR JUDGE. 18:6-8
   1. God's justice.
      (a)Towards his "elect." 7a
      (b)His longsuffering towards the oppressors.7b
      (c)His decision comes with dispatch. 8a
   2. Drain of faith due to delay of "that day." 8b

The judge was a person with bias toward God and man. God is personal, living, just. He deals with us as individuals and as a community of faith. He welcomes communion with his own!

* * * * * * *

JUSTICE AND PRAYER IN GOD'S KINGDOM!

Luke inserts this story of "a certain judge" and a "widow" as a climax to his report of "When is the kingdom of God coming?" Christ's rejection by "this generation" followed by the long delay before his second coming would place his believers' faith under severe strain. They need reminding that, while waiting disposal of divine justice, persistent prayer sustains faith.

Luke leaves no doubt as to the primary point of the parable. In 18:1 he clearly stresses: "But he was speaking this parable to them that they always be praying and not be fainting!"

The Widow Before the Judge!

"A certain judge was in a certain city..." The twice-used "certain" indicates that _this_ judge in _this_ city held a reputation of some distinction. The position of _judge_ was one of grave responsibility. On him rested dispensing of fair play between citizens contending their "rights" in courts of law. Such trust demanded a keen sense of judicial honesty. It was normally a function of great prestige. And judges who discharged their task with prudence were held in high esteem.

But being human, judges lived under similar frailties as all men. On occasion personal bias distorted good judgment. So this judge was "not fearing God or reverencing man." His faith in God was faulty; his respect for men was cynical!

This judge, scornful of human nature and with flawed faith in God, was confronted by a determined widow who refused to take "No" in a suit against an adversary. "There was a widow in that city, and she was coming to him saying, 'Render justice to me from my adversary!'"

When James spoke of (1:27) "orphans and widows in their affliction..." he was reflecting the exposed vulnerable status of the most helpless in human society. But this widow's asset "in her affliction" was a stiff backbone and an unbroken will. If her "adversary" were male she well knew the odds against her in this judge's court. In a man's world before a judge who "reverenced not man" the cards stacked against her were mountainous. Her one weapon was perseverance in the face of all obstacles. Her will was as granite; her firmness as iron. She came before the court day after day, week after week, until the carping judge became conscious of her persistent presence. As a professional he was losing face. He was coming under adverse criticism from his peers. She was an embarrassment!

Her plea was simple, explicit, unmasked! She requested justice, obvious to all! Appearing daily to demand her right she refused to be silenced. On his part the judge sought to ignore her. Failing this, he put her off by suggesting later action. Her persistent pleas consumed his time and became a blemish on court records. At any rate, when his delaying tactics failed, the judge grudgingly conceded and said in himself, "Though I do not fear God or reverence man, yet because this widow supplies trouble to me I will grant to her justice lest coming unto the ultimate end her persistence shall cause me to lose prestige before men!" Her perseverance paid dividends. In a man's world this woman gained the kind of justice due each person as a human being. Though this judge was unjust he rendered justice because of social restraints largely fomented by this widow's persevering tenacity. At times God's justice manifests itself in man's injustice!

Believers and their Judge!

Jesus himself pointed out the obvious application of his parable. He said, "Hear what the unjust judge says! Shall not God even do justice for his elect, the ones calling to him day and night? And shall he not be longsuffering over those, (the ones oppressing them)? I say to you that he shall do justice for them, and with dispatch!"

By nature a parable presents one core point. Details give background and color, the sense of reality in a given setting. But only one point is major. In this parable both the judge and the widow are the true to life details. This situation commonly occurred in the courts of men. Specifics varied but persistent patience is the central theme. In his response to prayer God is neither unjust nor does he need social pressures to arouse him to action. By nature God is just! He gives justice with an even hand apart from multiplied human pressure. God does respond to persistence on the part of his "elect," those who have accepted his grace in redemption.

"Will not God do justice for his elect, the ones crying to him day and night?" The question is framed to imply the answer: "Yes, he will certainly render justice to his elect." If a bogus judge can be coaxed to do justice, how much more will the righteous God respond to persistent prayer of his elect? Certainly he will hear and heed!

A textual variation in verse 7b forces a decision on those who would exegete this parable. Is verb rendered(AV)"bear long," (RSV)"delay long," (NEB)"listen patiently," indicative or participle? Does the pronoun, "them" of vs.7b refer to the "elect" or the oppressors?

Taking the participle as the preferable reading we translate, "...even while being longsuffering over them, the oppressors." Even if God restrain his wrath on account of his oppressed, he holds back giving justice immediately, "being longsuffering toward them, the oppressors." In God's concern over rendering justice to his "elect" we must remember that the oppressors are also his concern. They too are objects of his redemptive love. He would allow them time for repentance!

The position of believers after the Lord's departure and during the long period before his second coming is such that they are like a "widow" deprived of her rights. And they must claim without ceasing their just rights to the judge of the universe. In the application of the parable Jesus promises that he will answer their pleas. But he will restrain his answer for a time. He will not insert his justice immediately, not from indifference to their pleas, but rather because of his longsuffering in behalf of their persecutors. "The Lord is not slack concerning his promises; but is longsuffering...not wishing that any should perish, but that all should come to repentance."(II Pet.3:9) No hint appears in the parable that the object of the elects' praying was that the oppressors be punished. It is rather for their own justice to which, not only as his elect, but as humans they are entitled. God will be just! To that end pray repeatedly!

But the point must come when God's wrath on unjust persecutors will be exercised. The promise is, "He will perform justice upon them in quickness!" The "in quickness" says that once the wrath of God is executed upon which deliverance for the oppressed comes it will be effected with no delay. It will be done in a bat of the eye! It will be "with dispatch."

The long period of time "until he come" on "that day" will try men's faith. "But the son of man, when he comes, will he find faith on the earth?" Under the pressures believers must endure until "that day," they must learn the "need to pray always." Their constancy in prayer is related to the health of their faith. Luke suggests, "I am not concerned lest the judge (God) fail in his role. That with which I am concerned is whether the widow (the believer) fail in hers!" When he comes will there be the kind of faith that sustains prayer; and will there be prayer that sustains faith? There is no victory without faith that withstands the onslaught of unbelief!

283

AN OUTLINE OF LUKE 18:9-14
Two Prayers: The Pharisee and The Publican!
On what basis may a man be justified before God? By deeds or
disposition? Conformity or humility? Of the "two men who went
up into the temple to pray" the position of the men and content
of the prayers revealed their real relationship to God.
  I.   THE PHARISEE. 18:10-12
       1. He was "a Pharisee!"
       2. He "went up to the temple."
       3. He "having taken a stand."
       4. He "was praying." Descriptive, iterative or both!
       5. He "was praying to himself."
       6. His was a prayer of thanksgiving.
       7. Content of his prayer:(a)Negative (b)Positive.
  II. THE PUBLICAN. 18:13
       1. "Having stood afar off!"
       2. "Not even willing to lift his eyes to heaven."
       3. He "was beating his breast..."
       4. Content of his prayer:(a)what it was not! (b)A plea
          for mercy for "the sinner."
  III. THE CONCLUSION OF THE MATTER. 18:14
       1. Each man "went to his house."
       2. Each man got different results.
The rational was "because everyone exalting himself shall be
humbled, but the one humbling himself shall be exalted.

* * * * * * *

TWO PRAYERS: THE PHARISEE AND THE PUBLICAN!
     Prayer is one of the most delicate, sensitive, spiritual
exercises of the soul. In prayer one can cover from others any
lingering hypocrisy. It's more difficult to hide hypocrisy
from oneself. To the inner man prayer tends to tear away any
sham pietism encasing the spirit. Prayer bathes the soul as
water bathes the body. If conditions are right prayer
cleanses. There's a bit of self-righteous Phariseeism in most
men. Prayer, when allowed, may be an antidote to such self
righteousness! This parable of the "two men who went up to the
temple to pray" mirrors just such a possible cleansing.
                        The Pharisee!
     That he was a Pharisee presents a man encased in a hard
shell of pretentious self righteous vainglory. Pharisaic
dedication to Mosaic law blossomed from the great Babylonian
captivity. Convinced that disregard for Mosaic legal system
had brought on the tragedy of national captivity these pietists
resolved that it would never happen again. Out of their
commitment to precise conformity to the minutest letter of the
law the party of the Pharisees became the most rigorous
practioners of the mass of traditions hedging the law in the
first century of the Christian era. To be a Pharisee was to be
environed, shaped and committed to outward conformity to every
detail of the tradition of the elders. This Pharisee's prayer
reflected his upbringing and his personal commitment.

284

Such a philosophy of piety impelled him to go "up into the temple to pray." He sought the place where his piety should be practiced. Though "God is spirit" he felt the place ought be holy if his prayer was to be holy.

Furthermore, in that sacred place, "having taken a stand..." The phrase indicates that he positioned himself with all possible detailed flourishes to call attention to the fact he was about to pray. He stationed himself in the temple nearest the most prominent priest where he could get the most attention from the public. Here "he was praying!" This expression "was praying" describes the detailed movements involved in the exercise of praying. It also indicates that he repeatedly "was praying." Over and over he went through the formal exercise of prayer. He wished men, not to say God, to be aware that he was giving time to prayer.

The most significant detail in the report is "he was praying to himself." In appearance his prayer was to God; in fact it was "to himself." The content of his prayer became a recitation of his own virtues, the wrongs he avoided and the good he did! It really was a prayer about himself. His prayer glorified himself, not God. If it reached the ear of God it informed God what a great and good worshipper he had in such a pious Pharisee! Even the "thanks" he offered turned to self emulation. "O God I thank you that I'm not like the rest of men..."

Lest God overlook his virtues the Pharisee spelled out in detail exactly how he "was not like the rest of men." Other men he lumped together under three categories, "robbers, unjust, adulterers!" These are what he was not! And we have no reason to assume otherwise. These are legitimate negative values. A son of God ought not be a thief, unjust, or adulterer! This is laudable! Even essential qualities of a righteous person.

The Pharisee even gave a contemptuous back-handed compliment to the publican when he added, "or even this publican." It was a veiled way of saying that "this publican" was a notch above being a "thief, unjust, or adulterer" and yet still much below the high plane of righteousness that he, the proud Pharisee, had attained!

For proof of his lofty level of righteousness the Pharisee listed his positive credits. "I fast twice a week; I tithe all things which I get!" Not a Monday or Thursday but that he disciplined himself in devotion to God in the proscribed fasts. And the treasury knew the weight of his gifts down to the least "mint, rue, and herb." The practices of this Pharisee equals if it doesn't surpass many people in the modern church. In form he was an exemplary devotee to God!

The Publican!

Of the "two men" of the parable "the other was a publican." The term "other" exemplifies "another of a different kind" than the Pharisee. The very choice of this "other" tips us off to the contrast between the "two men." The publican was radically different!

Just how different he was the publican shows when he too, "having stood," placed himself "far off" from the Pharisee and other worshippers. He too "went up into the temple" to seek the place of prayer. But the weight of guilt and shame fenced him off from other worshippers. They _seemed_ far above him in decency of soul. He was one with them in worship but "far off" in belief in his personal worth. The Pharisee thanked God that "he was not as (guilty) as other men." This publican confessed his _own_ guilt. As he searched his soul "other men" were not in the range of his thought. So isolated in spirit was he that he was "not even willing to lift his eyes to heaven." He couldn't bring himself to look God in the face! He avoided the searching insight of God's penetrating eye. His guilt was overwhelming. The Pharisee sought release from sin by finding "other men" less righteous than he. This publican "was beating his breast" as sign and symbol that he alone was the sinner deserving of punishment for his own guilt. His was _not_ a display of his superiority but a demonstration of his own sense of guilt. Such is the mark of true contrition.

We note his use of the definite article "_the_" in his prayer. "O God, be propitiate toward me, _the_ sinner." The Greeks did not enjoy the luxury of an indefinite article "a" though εἶς (vs.10)may be substituted. He did not refer to himself as "a" sinner." In the confession of prayer in the absolute light of God's infinite moral purity the honest man does not see himself as "a" sinner, one among many. He alone is "_the_" sinner who occupies the entire horizon of his vision. He who is under deep conviction of his own guilt has but _one_ sinner in mind. He and he alone is "_the_ sinner above all sinners! "O God _I_ am the sinner for whom I am asking." This is the very point of the contrast between the prayers of the "two men who went up to pray."

The Conclusion of the Matter!

Each of the "two men" had put himself in the place of prayer, had delivered his burden to God and thereby laid _himself_ open before God. Having prayed each "went to his house" filled with some sense of relief. But justification does not take place subjectively in the heart of the one who is justified. On the contrary, it is God, the justifier, who pronounces the word of justification, "Not guilty!" According to Jesus, "This man, the publican, went down to his house having been justified rather than that one, the Pharisee!" The import of the whole story is that he who accepts, acknowledges, confesses his own responsibility in his own wrong-doing is the one God justifies. Whereas he who finds his release from guilt only in uncovering the guilt of others goes down to his house still under the self-delusion of his own righteousness. The obvious conclusion is: "Everyone exalting himself shall be humbled, but the one humbling himself shall be exalted." God's estimate of moral character prevails in spite of a man's estimate of himself! It is the presence of humilty more than the absence of evil deeds that gets justification!

AN OUTLINE OF LUKE 18:15-17
Children and the Kingdom!
"But even babes they were bringing!" The "even" points to humility as the apex of spiritual qualities in a believer in Christ! It is foremost for mature Christians because it is primary in the child.

I. THE OCCASION. 18:15
1. "They were bringing babies!"
2. "That he might hold them!"
3. The "disciples were rebuking them."

II. THE REACTION AND TEACHING OF JESUS. 18:16-17
1. Jesus "called to them!"
2. Teaching relative to little children.
(a)Why this is true!
(b)Importance of this truth.

Love is the heart of the gospel, the overflow of God's nature. Yet love in human relationships displays its highest expression in humility. In building and strengthening the community of Christ nothing surpasses the tender, receptive, self-yielding power of humility.

* * * * * * *

CHILDREN AND THE KINGDOM!
In the preceding story of the prayers of the Pharisee and Publican nothing good done by the Pharisee was able to justify him before God. And nothing bad done by the Publican kept him from being justified! The flood gates of God's grace opened to the Publican when he turned in humility toward God. That, in this seemingly unrelated experience with children, is the very point of Jesus' teaching about children and the kingdom. Luke, master story-teller, selected this episode of "babies" blessed by Jesus as strong confirmation of the necessity of humilty for him who would "enter" the kingdom of God.
The Occasion!
That which occasioned this was the persistent coming of many mothers with their "babies" that Jesus might give his blessing. "They were carrying even their babies..." The grammars call this use of conj. καὶ the ascensive. It presents the idea as the very pinnacle of whatever is under consideration. "But even babies" implies that various other kinds of human beings sought the blessing of Jesus. But "babies" too! What could a suckling baby get from Jesus? When talking about the kingdom of God some intellectual capacity is expected if one is to "receive" anything of value from teaching about the kingdom. Is it really appropriate to have nursing "babies" take the time and energy of Jesus when they aren't yet old enough to appreciate "adult" ideas? But Luke apparently with deliberate choice used this experience to stress the point that the receptivity of humility is the most important element in kingdom citizenship.
"But even nursing babies they were bringing...!"
The purpose of these mothers bringing their babies was "that

287

he might touch them." We note two details. First, Luke alone
inserts the term "babes." In the reports of Mark and Matthew a
word referring to a child older than a nursing babe appears.
Though παιδία also appears here in verse 16, it's vital to
Luke's emphasis that he first insert "babies."

A second detail is the term "touch." It carries more than
simply to feel as with the touch of a hand. It means to
"handle," "take hold of," "critically grasp." In Matthew's
account Jesus was asked to "place his hands on them and to
pray." As Luke tells the story the context suggests that Jesus
actually took the babies into his arms. This took valuable
time and energy from teaching more mature people. To the
twelve this appeared a misuse if not abuse of precious hours.

As for Luke's word "babies" it was vital to his emphasis.
The point of the incident is more dramatically pictured by
"babies." The very fact that these were infants not yet wholly
weaned from their mothers' breast is important to Luke's idea.
The very fact that this age group of children was not yet able
to grasp with the intellect yet was so trustingly responsive to
the mothers' supplying their needs is the very point that makes
them role models for "mature" people seeking entrance into
God's kingdom of spirits. Their fresh warmth, their want of
distrust, their failure to be suspicious, their inability to
claim some achievement in life made them perfect patterns for
kingdom citizens.

Luke is not at all denying the value of intellectual thought
nor is he downgrading the value of the profound doctrines of
Christian theology. But even disciples with such advance
learning must never get beyond the kind of loving receptivity
or humble trust of God as Creator-Father! That's the point of
similarity between the adult believer and the babe! If
advanced understanding erodes faith it becomes a snare; not an
enlightening of the heart! Who really is righteous, he who
knows only to trust as he receives the blessings of the
kingdom, or he who has learned the profound things of God but
doesn't know enough to trust with uncritical humility! A
suckling baby is nearer the kingdom than that!

Little did the "adult" disciples understand the nature of
the kingdom. "They began and kept on rebuking" the mothers who
burdened the Master with their infant babes. Men are too taken
with their own importance to perceive the simplicity of trust.
Adults have a hard time seeing the unblemished soul apart from
its corruption by years immersed in materialism. It's
sophisticated grown ups who call the sensual "adult" and the
innocent "childish."

The Reaction of Jesus!

When Jesus saw the disciples "rebuking" the mothers he
"called them," both mothers and disciples. With strong feeling
he said, "Permit that the children come to me and quit
hindering them." Such conduct betrayed a lack of "mature"
understanding of the kingdom. It also was destroying the
foundation on which it was built.

288

When Jesus gave the logical reason as to why the disciples should "quit hindering" children from coming he said, "for of such (quality) of human beings is the kingdom of God." His use of the qualitative demonstrative τοιούτων is significant. It gives clear emphasis to the quality of those who make up the citizenry of the kingdom of God. The fact that people are old, crusted over with scabbed husks plastered on the human soul by many years in this sin encased world is reason enough why adult people must "be born anew" if they are to enter the kingdom! The adult, hardened by long exposure to a sinful environment, has to become as a child in order to start life all over again as it were. If he has lost this quality, he must turn again and reestablish it.

Living as a citizen in the kingdom of God implies growth! To grow one must first and foremost be born. To be born implies the beginning of life. The logic is that a citizen of this world must become (in quality) a citizen of God's world of the Spirit. It's not the immaturity of the child that makes him a role model for the kingdom man. It's his receptivity, his utter sense of dependency, his emptiness of self-attainment. A child has as yet had no "success" to blur his view of his dependency. All his "growth" is ahead of him. And that "growth" must be in spiritual experience, not the physical-material. He must grow "in Christ" rather than under "the ruler of the power of the air." Such is the quality of those who inhabit the kingdom of God.

So important to the kingdom is this "quality" that Jesus added, "Whoever shall not receive the kingdom of God as a child (receives it), he shall not enter into it." The unspoiled child cannot enter the kingdom any other way than unspoiled. The adult must enter "as" the child enters. In effect he becomes a child again!

Furthermore, Jesus accentuated the negative by the intensive double negative οὐ μὴ "he shall not at all enter..." There's no way on earth or in heaven to permit anyone entrance who refuses to come "as" a humble little child!

In building and strengthening the community of Christ in this world nothing surpasses the self-yielding, tender, receptive power of humility. And the most obvious example of humility in human beings is a little child.

Underlying this teaching are Luke's major themes of universality and humanity. All human beings have had to be "little children" before they became weighted, even retarded, with the encumbrances of materialism. Nicodemus, sophisticated Pharisee, needed "to be born again" not to mention the salty seaman, the apostle Peter. It takes every human a long time to grow in grace. But before growth it's necesary to be born!

AN OUTLINE OF LUKE 18:18-30
Possessions and Dependence!
For dramatic reasons, if not chronological, Luke relates the
incident of the rich young ruler to Christ's blessing of the
babies. There is a bond between the two. In different ways
each event exhibits the imperative of dependence.
I.   A "CERTAIN RULER" ASKS A PERSONAL QUESTION. 18:18-23
     1. "What, having done, shall I inherit life eternal?"
     2. Jesus challenges the ruler's term of address! 19
     3. The primary command: Obey the Decalogue. 21f
     4. The "one thing lacking." 22
     5. The young man's failure! 23
II. A LESSON FOR THE DISCIPLES. 18:25-27
     1. Observation about possessions & dependency. 24
     2. An illustrative metaphor. 25
     3. "Who, then, is able to be saved?" 29-30
III. THE COMMITMENT AND BLESSING OF THE TWELVE. 18:28-30
     1. Peter: "We, having left our own, followed!" 28
     2. Jesus' observation and promise! 29-30
In point of fact a man is dependent for everything. Yet he
is the only creature in the whole of creation that may
recognize and choose his dependency!

* * * * * * *

POSSESSIONS AND DEPENDENCE!
Babies being blessed and a prominent magistrate's problem of
personal salvation would not appear to have much in common. And
they are not related in any personal way. But as a skillful
story teller Luke places them side by side for dramatic and
stylistic effects. Dependency is the point of connection!
Children, most especially babies, are perfect examples of
dependency. They have no choice for of necessity they must
look to mothers for life itself as well as the ongoing
necessities of life. The rich young magistrate, because of his
wealth, had lost his feel for dependency on parent, God or
anyone other than himself. He too was dependent, but had lost
his sense of being dependent! This proved to be his downfall,
the "one thing lacking" in his quest for "life eternal."
His Personal Question!
"And a certain magistrate asked him saying, 'Good Teacher,
What shall I do to inherit life eternal?'" The young man had
lived an exemplary life. Moreover, he was a man of commanding
wealth. That itself, from the viewpoint of current belief,
implied divine blessing. Yet his restless heart knew no real
peace. He felt something was "lacking" but he knew not what.
His soul knew no abiding comfort. So he was drawn to this
itinerate teacher whose wisdom and kindness had become famous.
He approached Jesus with his personal question, "What must I
do, (that I haven't yet done) to inherit life eternal?" He
wanted something more than routine rules. Possessions and
exemplary behaviour simply did not satisfy!

290

In his initial response to the inquiry Jesus challenged the young magistrate's use of the term "<u>Good</u> Teacher." It is not in keeping with the known spirit of Jesus to think he "bristled" at this address. And the notion that Jesus here conceded his own sinfulness misses the point of the story. In fact, if he in any way is directing attention to himself, it's his unity with God, his sinlessness, to which he is calling attention. Jesus was aware of his divine nature and he very well could have been calling on the young man to recognize such an implication of his term "<u>Good</u> teacher!"

But in fact there seems to be a yet deeper meaning to the answer of Jesus. From the human point of view this young ruler was genuinely good. Jesus didn't question the young man's claim of obedience to the decalogue from his "youth up."(vs.21) And Mark in 10:21 reports that Jesus "loved him." Jesus recognized in the young ruler a genuinely sincere searcher of truth and He, Jesus, felt favorably toward him. But the man's fundamental view of human nature was at fault. Jesus was determined first to rectify the man's radical mistake.

The man thought that humanity was essentially "good." That's why he thought he, on his own, could "<u>do</u>" some one great deed and thereby attain life eternal. When he addressed Jesus as "Good master" he was addressing the <u>human</u>, the <u>man</u> Jesus. Jesus is here challenging the young ruler to grasp the fact, to perceive that all good in man, any man, flows from the presence of God. He thus strikes at the man's basic error. At the same time he points out that the "good" in Himself as the "Good teacher" is from God. Even Jesus himself is dependent for his goodness on God's presence and work within him. There's no question about the divine nature of Jesus as everywhere established throughout Luke's gospel. But in this present episode his deity is not the main stress. It's the idea of "good" not only in Jesus but in any man, including this young man's view of himself as essentially good. No man is good except as the <u>good</u> God is at work in him. Man, every man, is <u>dependent</u> on God for any goodness that rises within him.

After clarifying the inquirer's thinking about "good" Jesus turned to the question asked. "You know the commandments, Don't adulterize, don't murder, don't steal, don't lie, be honoring your father and your mother." This part of the decalogue deals with personal, social relationships. If you're looking to <u>do</u> things, attend to those matters that relate to other people. To serve the rights and needs of other human beings is the thing to <u>do</u>! Even one's relation to God, as stressed in the earlier part of the decalogue, in part finds fulfillment in serving God's children.

But the young man was disappointed at this reply. The fact he had kept the commands from his "youth up" yet still felt a lack in his life was the reason he had come to Jesus. "This I have done! But I feel the need of something greater. What must I <u>do more</u> than this?"

Having led the young man to profess openly that obedience to the ten commandments left him unfulfilled Jesus could expose the lack in his life. Jesus said, "One thing is yet lacking to you! All howevermuch you are getting, sell and distribute to poor people and you will get treasure in heaven, and come be following me." In Luke 18:22 the standard versions read "all that you have (ἔχεις)...and you will have (ἕξεις)..." But the root idea in ἔχω is punctiliar "get" not "have." In other words, "All that you get is not for self indulgence but is God's gift of trust." The young magistrate must recognize that he is God's agent to use material things for the service for the people of God.

But Jesus does not leave the matter merely as an exercise in management of money. With significance he adds, "and come, be following me!" The young ruler had been adhering to a list of rules from his "youth up." Jesus would not call him to a different but still a set of rules regulating material possessions. One best obeys "rules" when they are embodied in a living person. That's the force of Jesus' word, "Follow me!" The warmth of a living person in whom the "rules" are demonstrated gives form and power to the rules. By following the person one obeys the rules. But rules without the person become a dry burden, a hollow exercise in self-will, a lifeless conformity that leaves one still empty in heart and soul. The crux of Jesus' answer was, "Follow me." Moreover, to "follow" was more than the initial commitment. It meant a continuous, repeated, regular, "following" as each day brought situations that involved self-denying choices. That was the "one thing yet lacking." That was what he must yet do to inherit life eternal.

To put Christ's answer to the magistrate in another way we paraphrase, Separate yourself from the false worship of self, the idol of material possessions, or any illusory substitute for the living God. Sever yourself from whatever holds the supreme loyalty of your heart. Do that, then "Be following me!"

The tragedy of the story is the failure of the rich ruler to yield to the challenge of Jesus. He was too dependent on the gods of his own making, specifically his wealth. To turn loose of things for the fellowship with God as revealed in Jesus was more than he was willing to do! When he discovered what the "one thing yet lacking" was he found that he was not willing to do it! The need he felt; but the doing he denied! "That one, when he heard, became exceedingly sad, for he was very rich." Literally, "he was sorrounded with sorrow!" The goodness and sincerity of the youth is seen in the depth of his disappointment. He was overwhelmed with sadness. He really wished to do that which was offered. He lacked the will to accept dependency on God rather than his self-established reliance on the false god of wealth. How many times this has been repeated through the centuries?? Shall I depend on the gods created in my image? Or shall I rely on him who created me to be in his image?? This is the issue.

A Lesson for the Disciples!

"Having looked on him, Jesus said, 'With what difficulty do the ones getting possessions enter into the kingdom of God!'" The obvious lesson from the failure of the young man to thrust himself in dependence on the goodness of God was not to be lost. The magistrate's loss could dramatize their gain. His failure was typical of this world's choices. The world gets; God gives! To "follow" Jesus means to possess property in order to distribute it. There's no point in "getting" unless there are human beings to whom to give! Such is God's program of possessions. Men "with difficulty" rise to this view. So visible, so presently real are possessions that few men see beyond to the God who gives them.

So much do possessions blind man to his condition Jesus had to use a metaphor to make clear the truth. "For a camel to go through a needle's eye is easier than for one who is rich to enter the kingdom of God." It's possible for this to picture a camel weighted with a commercial load approaching a low, narrow city gate through which it cannot enter. But we should not forget that Jesus deliberately chose to describe an impossible condition. He intended a predicament so drastic that it was beyond human achievement. The main idea was neither camel or needle's eye but the <u>impossibility</u>! A man who <u>depends</u> on his possessions <u>cannot</u>, in his own will, inherit life eternal!

Jewish thought of the time felt that wealth signified God's favor. The shock of Jesus' image is seen in his hearers' agitated response. "And who is <u>able</u> to be saved?" If the rich, favored of God, can enter the kingdom no better than a camel can go through a needle's eye, the inevitable conclusion is that <u>no one</u> can be saved! And <u>that</u> is the very point! <u>No one</u> by his own efforts, without the grace of God, <u>can</u> be saved! Rich and poor, wise and fool, homeless and healthy, <u>all</u> alike depend on God to do that which man cannot do. Jesus said as much, "That which is impossible with men is possible with God." The impossible becomes possible!

From blessing babies to the challenge to the ruler one idea unifies. <u>Depend</u> on God's grace for every need from mother's milk to spiritual wholeness. Essentially religion is self-denying, self-fulfilling reliance of creature on Creator! In a child it's instinctive. In the man it's by choice.

The Commitment of the Twelve!

Peter, seeing the emotional struggle of the rich ruler, observing Jesus' affection, spoke for the twelve; "Behold, having left our own, <u>we</u> followed you!" Fishermen's nets, accountants' desk, family wealth had been left behind when they responded to Jesus' call to "Follow me." Such surrender of possessions may not have occurred to him as sacrifice. But the young magistrate's return to dependency on his bank account focused attention on the choice <u>they</u> had made. He wasn't seeking praise. He merely observed that they <u>had chosen</u> that which the young magistrate had refused.

293

The rich ruler had gotten for himself and refused to give up that which he had gotten. On the other hand, Peter and his companions had given up wealth-rewarding careers to "follow" Jesus. But they got ample compensation for what they gave. Jesus said, "Truly, I say to you there's no one who left home or wife or brothers or parents or children on account of the kingdom of God who shall not receive many times more in this season and in the coming age life eternal." God calls men to give up idolatrous loyalties. In return they get multiplied bonds far surpassing that which they have forfeited. The security of possessions is replaced by the protection of God's family of faith. Any human relationship men sacrifice for the sake of "the kingdom of God" the citizens of that kingdom return many times in many ways. Jesus already had advanced the idea of a community of faith superseding the bond of blood. When his mother and brothers sought to limit his activity he said, "My mother and brother are these, the ones who hear and do the word of God."(Lk.8:21) The bond of Christian fellowship binds closer than the bonds of blood! The history of the church is replete with testimonies to this fact in "this season." Besides, in "the coming age" the compensation is "life eternal." Who can compare <u>that</u> to present suffering?

Luke avoids Mark's (10:30) mention that the compensations must make room for "persecutions." That too shall accompany the sacrifices which those who "follow" Jesus shall give. Luke is aware that "persecutions" accompany the compensations for kingdom commitment. But in his story he ignores them because they do not nullify the fact of the vast compensations that outweigh the costs. For every home, wife, parent, sibling, or child lost "on account of the kingdom of God" there are untold others who more than fill the void. Nothing in time or eternity is stronger and more permanent than the family of God in Christ!

He to whom Luke penned this story was a high born Greek, Theophilus. And though the cultural differences between Greek, Roman and Jew were decidedly different, the differences did not nullify their unity as human beings. They were equally children of God's creative genius. They were equally <u>human</u>. Though in different forms they faced the same human problems, one of which was the materialism of possessions. The arts and sciences of the Greek, the organizational and legal skills of the Roman and the religious faith of the Jew did not release any of them from facing the fact of materialism. All were tempted to depend on their own skills in opposition to dependency on God. This was the <u>universal human</u> problem facing Theophilus. The story of Christ's blessing the babes and challenging the rich young ruler addressed this problem of dependency!

AN OUTLINE OF LUKE 18:31-34
"Going Up To Jerusalem!"

Three times during his public appearances Jesus plainly told
what the issue of his ministry among men would be. Three times
his closest companions could not grasp the truth. Nonetheless,
he insisted they hear the unwelcome facts.

I.   THE CHRIST'S DESTINY IS AT HAND! 18:31
     1. He "took aside the twelve..." 31a
     2. He declared: "We are going up to Jerusalem!" 31b
     3. Fulfillment of "all things written through the
        the prophets." 31c
II. PRONOUNCEMENT OF WHAT WILL HAPPEN AT JERUSALEM. 18:32
     1. Shall be "delivered to the gentiles." 32a
     2. Personal abuse. 32b
     3. Scourged and judicially killed! 33a
     4. He "shall rise on the third day." 33b
III. DULLNESS OF THE TWELVE. 18:34
     1. "They understood none of these things." 34a
     2. "This matter was hidden from them." 34b
     3. "They were not knowing what was being said." 34c

That he must die Jesus stated at least three times. Three
times it was hidden from the twelve. Jesus did not explain why
he "must" die. He expressed its necessity! It was after the
fact that the why would become clear. But he did teach that
these things were in harmony with "all that had been spoken
through the prophets." This was God's plan; Christ's destiny!

* * * * * * *

"GOING UP TO JERUSALEM"

That which men learn about life they must learn in life. And
that's an ongoing process. We aren't born fullgrown physically,
mentally or spiritually. Even when the "Word became flesh" he
"learned"(Heb.5:8) The early disciples had to unlearn much
before learning basic truth. When Jesus first called them they
followed him, not the truth which he came to reveal.
     It wasn't until Peter voiced faith in him as "the Christ of
God"(Lk.9:20) that Jesus ventured to disclose that it was
"necessary that the son of man suffer many things and be
rejected..."(9:22) Later he withdrew the veil a bit further
with the urgent, "You put in your ears these words, The son of
man is about to be delivered up into the hands of men."(9:44)
But again they didn't understand for "it was hidden from them."
Shortly after Jesus resolutely "set his face to go to
Jerusalem."(9:51) The cross cast its ominous shadow over the
remaining months of his ministry. The twelve sensed a new
seriousness in the Master's manner. But they did not understand
for the cross "was hidden" from them. Too long had they
anticipated a kingdom based on force of arms and the power of
politics to entertain any idea of a spiritual kingdom of truth.
The strength and authority of moral and spiritual power could
not penetrate the hard crust of material might of political
governments.

295

Christ's Destiny at Hand!

The time had arrived when Jesus must make clear his tragic destiny. However difficult, the twelve must face facts. The text testifies, "Having taken them aside..." There was need for a private lesson without the distractions, noise, and turmoil of crowds. At times it is better strategy to teach the few that the many may be reached. Jesus must be sure the disciples have adequate exposure to the lesson on the cross (and resurrection) if later the multitudes are to hear. Thus he "took them aside!"

Jesus and the twelve, after some six months with face "set toward Jerusalem," had arrived at the outskirts of Jericho the final city before the ascent to Jerusalem. The moment had come when he must announce, "We are going up to Jerusalem!" By no means was this their first sojourn to the capitol but there was a difference. This time all the other visits gathered meaning as tributary streams emerge in a mighty river. His separate sessions of teaching, his mighty miracles, the variety of experiences with people and disciples are now to unite in the saving events of one week. This is not only Christ's week of destiny but through him that of the world! Eternal issues are to be concluded and accomplished. There were portentous overtones to the words of Jesus, "We are going up to Jerusalem!"

Formerly when he taught them about these matters he had mentioned suffering "many things" and being "rejected of men." Now at the outset he revealed that "all the things having been written through the prophets shall be perfected (brought to their intended goal)."

The Old Testament prophets kept the notion of the kingdom of God from sinking to the level of a crass materialism whose sole end was political power. They were those who called Israel to judgment before the court of moral, ethical, and spiritual standards. And it was the prophets who insisted on the individual's moral liability before God. According to prophetic teaching a man cannot escape his own moral responsibility by blaming ancestral genes or environment. "The soul that sins it shall die!"(Ezk.18:4) According to the prophet's word it was not the national cult that made God available to the citizen of Israel. In the great captivity, after temple and cult lay naked and destroyed, God spoke through the prophet Jeremiah, "You shall pray to me...you shall seek me and find me, when you search for me with all your heart!" (29:12f) And it was the peer of all prophets, Isaiah, who painted with glowing colors the Servant poems that sketched in spiritual outlines the Messiah as "light to the Gentiles." (Is.49:6) His prophetic picture of 53 sounds the notes of a New Testament prophet: "He was despised and rejected of men; a man of sorrows, acquainted with grief...He shall see the travail of his soul, and shall be satisfied; by the knowledge of himself shall my righteous servant justify many; and he shall bear their iniquities."

296

What Will Happen at Jerusalem!

Jesus did not recite specific texts from the prophets. He did speak of "all" judgments written "through the prophets" that would fall on the Christ. He would "be delivered to the Gentiles!" Submerged in "all" Old Testament scripture was the purpose of God to reach Gentiles. In Ur God said to Abraham, "in thee shall all the families of the earth be blessed." And no prophet ignored the universality of the goal of God as he dealt with Israel. He chose one people through whom he sought to reach all peoples. When Isaiah spoke of the coming Servant as "light to the Gentiles" he was voicing more clearly the note underlying every prophet. Thus in the redemptive events of this "going to Jerusalem" the Gentile became as faulty as the Jew in the final fatal tragedy. Guilt falls on both Gentile and Jew as indeed redemption is for both Jew and Gentile! There are "none righteous!"

From both segments of humanity "he shall be mocked, he shall be insulted, and he shall be spit upon." No perversion of man's abuse against man shall escape the arrogant mauling. Nothing faded from the vile imagination of those who outraged "the Christ of God." Every generation has seen men in authority who, finding themselves in power over the poor, weak and/or innocent have toyed with them before executing them. The conduct of these authorities, Jew and Gentile, would more than imitate the typical behaviour of humans against humans! Having trifled with the Christ they would then "scourge and kill him."

Was such the "intended end" proscribed by God for his Christ from the beginning? Was this God's goal for history? Is this that which "all that had been written through the prophets" about God's sovereignty in history? What justice, what victory, what power does God display by allowing such abuse to his chosen One? Can salvation come from such deplorable defeat?

As little as the twelve could grasp the answers to these questions so did the final promise of what awaited him at Jerusalem slip unnoticed by them! He "shall rise on the third day!" The abuse and death of their Teacher disturbed their emotions and blinded their minds. Without the resurrection there would be no justice. With it tragedy turns to triumph, humiliation changes to jubilation, defeat becomes victory! The weakness of death erupts in the power of life. The bad news becomes good news, "the power and wisdom of God."

The Dullness of the Twelve!

The total inability of the twelve to admit entrance to any of this humiliation of the Christ Luke emphasizes in three different ways in verse 34. "And they understood none of these things." Intellectually such prospective abuse made no sense. It was incomprehensible. Nothing in the background of any of the twelve could lead them to think in terms that would put God or "the Christ of God" in such a weak, humiliating, helpless situation. Given Christ's divine origin and powers they would not allow such injustices to take place. They simply "did not understand!"

297

Luke repeats his description of the dullness of the twelve though he alters both verb and tense. Literally he says, "and this matter was having been hidden from them." The periphrastic past perfect tense looks to a point in the past at which it became hidden and then suggests that it remained hidden even to the present moment. They were in the dark about this thing and they'd been in the dark for quite some time. So far as seeing an abused, insulted, clobbered, Christ is concerned their past blindfolded them. It had been and still was "hidden" from them! Their mental eyes had been scaled over. The light of prophetic truth could not penetrate their spiritual blindness.

Futhermore, Luke is relentless in his pressing on his reader the dullness of the disciples. He adds: "and they were not knowing the things being spoken." Imperfect tense with negative "were not knowing" indicates continuous ignorance. The context even suggests that this ignorance was self-imposed. They didn't know because they would not know. They could have perceived had they willed to see. But they were remaining ignorant for the simple reason they didn't make the effort to see.

It seems apparent that Luke makes this three-fold insistence on the dullness of the disciples because it is so typical of the human race. Moral and spiritual ignorance is the product of human bias. Men are so prepossessed of themselves, their knowledge, their own ideas about self, sin, God, and life, that no place is left for revelation from other sources. Human bias is based in rebellion against any moral dependence on God.

The fact is, "they didn't understand." The reason was because, "it had been hidden from them." And that lay in their continuous refusal to "recognize (know) the truth of those things being spoken" to them. And this entire process is universally typical of men of all places, times, and cultures. Men are blind about the Christ and the nature of his kingdom because they will not see.

The fact of the matter is that it was inevitable and logical that "he shall be delivered over to the Gentiles and that he be mocked, and insulted, and spit upon, and scourged and killed." What else should one expect of light in a dark world? This is that which Jesus had said, "We are going up unto Jerusalem, and all the things having been written through the prophets will be brought to their intended redemptive end." Yet men still "don't understand, and this thing has been (and still is) hidden from them, and they're not knowing the things which have been spoken!"

It remains for those who know to keep on telling those who don't know!

AN OUTLINE OF LUKE 18:35-43
When Blind Men See!
Differences in the reports of the blind man of Jericho are a
challenge to intellect, faith, and honesty. He who wills to
find discrepancies will. He who seeks truth can find it!
I.   WHAT IT MEANS TO BE BLIND. 18:35-39
     1. Must beg for necessities. 35
     2. Is denied firsthand knowledge of activities. 36
     3. Is limited in participation. 37
     4. Seeks participation, having learned. 38-39
II. JESUS AND THE BLIND MAN. 18:40-42
     1. Jesus commanded that "he be brought to him." 40
     2. "What do you wish that I shall do?" 41
     3. Sight restored. 42
        (a)The sight given. (b)Your "faith has saved you."
III. WHEN BLIND MEN SEE! 18:43
     1. The blind "glorify" God. 43a
     2. The multitudes "praise" God.
Christ came that men might see! Though the twelve(Lk.18:34)
"understood none of these things" and it "was hidden" and they
"were not knowing the things being spoken" yet after the cross
and resurrection became facts of history "faith" would restore
their dulled perception. Thus Christ gives sight to the blind!

* * * * * * *

WHEN BLIND MEN SEE!
     The final journey to Jerusalem, city of destiny, is almost
over. Jesus and the twelve arrive at Jericho just a few brief
miles and days before the cross. Matthew and Mark are joined
by Luke to record this story of Bartimaeus the blind beggar.
They tell the same story but with different details. Some see
contradictions; all readers must decide why the differences.
     The simple solution is found in the particular viewpoint,
purpose, and stylistic stress of the three authors. Each must
be allowed to present his own emphasis in terms he chooses.
     Matthew speaks of two blind beggars; Mark and Luke mention
only one. This is a difference but not a contradiction. If two
beggars were there that assures that one was there. It suits
Luke's purpose to emphasize what Jesus did for one. That he did
the same for a second Luke doesn't deny; it just doesn't add
anything to the fact that Jesus made the blind to see!
     Matthew reports that "two blind men were sitting by the road
side" as they "went out of Jericho." Mark agrees that Jesus
"was leaving Jericho..." Luke states that "as he was drawing
near to Jericho a certain blind man was sitting along side the
road..." Luke does not tell when or where Jesus gave sight to
the blind man. He may have done it when entering or when
exiting the city so far as Luke reports the incident. The
differences reflect dissimilar but not contradictory views. He
who wants to discover contradictions can. He who wants to see
truth may enjoy that privilege!

299

What Blindness Means to the Blind!

At the very least blindness is an obvious handicap. It does not make a man any less a human but it does remove him from the mainstream of life. It well nigh destroys his freedom of movement, it makes him abnormally dependent on the good will of his fellowman. In the case of the blind man of Jericho it forced him to become a beggar for the very necessities of life. Food and clothing came to him only through the generosity of the passerby. What shelter he had we are not told but we safely assume that a beggar's income would hardly offer more than a hovel. True, being a beggar didn't necessarily lessen his humanity but it certainly tended to dehumanize him. It could only hurt his pride, self-esteem, and sense of acceptance by "normal" human associates if he had any.

Another limitation inherent on the blind is that it denied him firsthand knowledge of the life swirling all about him. Of this blind man at Jericho the text states, "When he heard the crowd going by he inquired what this might be?" Unless someone took time to tell him he could only guess at the meaning of sounds, voices, scuffling feet, shouts, and all such normal activities. Social processes at best could only be a noisome blur.

In the present instance when the blind man of Jericho sought the meaning of the shouts and noises some from the crowd, "declared to him that Jesus the Nazarene is passing by." So widespread was knowledge of Jesus that his reputation had reached the ears of the disenfranchised of Jericho. Without hesitation Bartimeus began to cry aloud, "Jesus, son of David, have mercy on me!" Both the title, "son of David," and his urgent cry, "Have mercy" testify to the blind man's knowledge of and faith in Jesus as the long looked for Messiah. That he believed Jesus to be Messiah and that he was a merciful Messiah is confirmed by Jesus' response in giving him sight and the direct statement, "Your faith has saved you!" Formerly Jesus had carefully avoided allowing disciple or friend to use openly any Messianic title lest he be indentified with the current popular belief that Messiah was a political power to lead a material kingdom. But now the spiritual nature of his kingdom was about to be made clear by his imminent death. He willingly accepted this open declaration of him as King-Messiah, David's promised son.

That it was a blind man who could see this truth was itself a welcome sign of the spiritual nature of Christ's mission. The kingdom of God is for the deprived, the handicapped, those whom evil has scarred. For a blind man to "see" both physically and spiritually was fitting revelation of the spiritual reality of the kingdom of God. In other words, when the blind man learned the meaning of the noises of life going on around him he participated in them to the limit of his potential. He even persisted in spite of many in the crowd who "rebuked him that he should get silent." Having learned, he was determined to share in the Christ as best he could.

300

Jesus Responds to the Blind Man!

We do not question the historical reality of this story of the blind beggar of Jericho. But the time, place, particulars and especially Luke's placing of this episode in relation to the preceding account of Christ's teaching about his impending death make it suggestive of deeper truth. Examine verse 34 which tells that the twelve "understood none of these things." And that "this matter was hidden from them and they were not knowing the things being spoken." In a word the twelve were blind to the nature of the kingdom and its methods. Yet in this story we meet a severely handicapped man who, with all his limitations, grasped the essence of the Christ's person, message and kingdom. He could "see" the truth where others more privileged were blind. Moreover, when he saw he vigorously pursued the opportunity to lay hold on what he saw.

Jesus heard the cry of the blind man above the confusion of the crowd. The appeal, "Son of David, have mercy on me" was the cry of humanity's desperate need. To such Jesus never was deaf. For just such a plea he had come. Other noises were a distraction, an intrusion. The real need of mankind was voiced by this blind beggar, "Son of David, have mercy!"

So "Jesus, having stopped, commanded that he be brought to him." From the moment he began his public campaign Jesus kept calling men to be brought to him. Even the call of the twelve involved an invitation to become personally attached to Him who could fill every human need. Everywhere he went Jesus kept calling for men to be brought to him.

Having come, next came the question, "What do you wish that I shall do for you?" We hardly suppose that Jesus was asking for information. Surely he knew that the blind man wanted sight! Yet Jesus insisted that the man formulate a statement as to his need. For the needy it's important that he be able to formulate his need and voice it. Men need to ask for more than "blessings" in general. They need to specify which blessing. Thus the man said, "Lord, that I see again!" The man quite obviously wanted his physical vision. And that Jesus freely gave: "See again!" But it is noteworthy that Jesus added, "Your faith has saved you!" There's more in that remark than "saved your sight." True, the man got his sight back. But he had already obtained more than he had sought. His faith that drove him to Jesus and overcame all obstacles had already given him insight into the nature of the person of Jesus and the spiritual quality of Jesus' reign as "son of David." The man got more than physical sight. He got both physical and spiritual sight. And that was something that even after three years of companionship with Jesus the twelve had failed as yet to attain. Quite often handicaps prove to be blessings in disguise whereas normal blessings can become hidden hindrances to fellowship with God. That this blind man "see" so clearly the true nature of the King and Kingdom is remarkable testimony to the purpose of Christ's coming. And that Luke place it here in his story makes it even more clear!

301

When Blind Men See!

Besides the immediate return of sight verse 43 reports some facts that followed the healing. First, "and he was following him..." On the spot the blind beggar became a disciple: "he began to be following..." His was an immediate but a commitment that was to be continuous. Jesus got a new dedicated disciple whose life was from henceforth totally altered. We may wonder how the freshly won sight and insight would weather the coming tragedy of the Christ's death! If we have construed aright the newly gained insight of the blind man into the nature of Jesus and his kingdom we may assume his faith could carry him through the ordeal of death. Without question the trial and death of Jesus would severely strain his faith but it wouldn't break it. If the twelve with their lack of understanding could survive the events of the week, certainly he who "saw" so clearly at Jericho could endure the reverses of the week.

It is also said that the blind man "was glorifying God." It is Godet (Com.on Lk.,pg.416) who observes, "δοξάζειν relates to power, αἰνεῖν to the goodness of God." The man "was glorifying God." "All the people, having seen, gave praise to God." The blind man was overwhelmed with the power of God revealed not only in giving him sight but in God's wisdom and power in using Messiah's death to confound the powers of this world. On the other hand the "people were giving praise to God" because of his manifest goodness toward the handicapped outcasts.

According to Luke the significance of this narrative is seen in its relationship to the dullness of the disciples to see the necessity and meaning of the approaching death of Christ. That the disciples, not to mention the world, should ever grasp the meaning of his death Jesus must endure alone the suffering of Gethsemane, Calvary and the prison of the tomb. Nevertheless he came that men might see that which they didn't "understand" and what was "hidden" and all they "were not knowing." The events themselves with the coming of the Holy Spirit would rightly reveal the meaning of these redemptive events. Their faith would then restore their dulled perception, their blind eyes of the heart.

AN OUTLINE OF LUKE 19:1-10
When Lost Men Are Saved!
Luke sums up the experience of Jesus with Zaccheus with "The son of man came to seek and to save the one having become lost. What happens when the lost are saved?

I. THE "LOST" SEEKS TO SEE THE SAVIOUR! 19:1-4
 1. The occasion: Jesus going through Jericho. 1
 2. Zaccheus, the "pure." 2
 (a)A chief publican.
 (b)He was "rich."
 3. He kept on seeking. 3
 (a)The crowd thwarted his efforts.
 (b)His dwarfed stature was a hindrance!
 4. His successful strategy. 4
II. JESUS, AS GUEST, CONFRONTS ZACCHEUS. 19:5-8
 1. Jesus, self-invited guest. 5
 2. "Rejoicing" Zaccheus "received" Jesus. 6
 3. The crowd "was murmuring." 7
 4. The commitment of Zaccheus. 8
III. SALVATION REALIZED. 19:9-10
 1. Salvation as fact. 9
 2. Salvation as purpose. 10
The idea "saved" appears in both Jericho episodes, the blind beggar and the chief publican. Of the blind, "Your faith has saved you." Of Zaccheus, "Today salvation came to this house." Jesus brings salvation, body, mind, soul and spirit, to the outcast poor and the outcast rich. Both needed it; both got it!

* * * * * * *

WHEN LOST MEN ARE SAVED!
To give a perfect picture of God as human and universal saviour, Luke sketched in bold strokes of his pen the colorful story of Zaccheus, chief publican of the Jericho district. He was a fellow-citizen of the same city as Bartimaeus, the blind beggar. He had the same need. One was clothed in beggar's rags; the other dressed in the wardrobe of wealth. Both were castoffs of society; one by physical handicap; the other by social blemishes. Underneath outward appearances they both were blinded by the moral distortions of life in this kind of corrupt world. They needed to be "saved." And that's why Jesus came, "To seek and to save the lost!"
The Lost Seeks to See the Saviour!
When Zaccheus heard that the celebrated Teacher was passing through the city of Jericho he sought to see him. This was his opportunity! He wouldn't allow anything to stand in the way. In fact, he "was seeking to see Jesus, who he was!" He made repeated efforts. Each rebuff or hindrance was but another tantalizing temptation to lure him on in his quest to "see Jesus." He wanted to see "who he was." Zaccheus wished to size up this Jesus for himself. So much hearsay concerning the man must be evaluated by his own judgment. He who wants to be saved must seek to be saved!

303

It may have been by coincidence or design but the man in whose home Jesus brought salvation bore the name Zaccheus which means, "clean," "pure," "innocent." Jewish society considered a "publican" anything but "pure." He who betrayed his people by serving Rome as toll-collector was deemed worse than morally depraved. He certainly was not "clean." Yet it's the point of the story that Jesus purposely invited himself into this home that he might declare the man clean in God's sight.

Zaccheus was not only a publican, he was "chief publican" of the entire district of which Jericho was headquarters. The balm which grew profusely in the Jericho oasis plus the sizable traffic which moved along this highway from Perea through Judea to Egypt made for a large community of tax-collectors. Zaccheus obtained much of his wealth from his being the "chief" of all these tax men. He not only made money on his own but made an over-ride on those who worked under his oversight. At any rate the text, not without purpose, states that "he was rich." But his riches did not deter Jesus from inviting himself into the toll-collector's house for an evening of fellowship and over night lodging. Nor did the fact that Zaccheus was "a sinner" keep Jesus from forming a friendship. On the contrary, Jesus was as determined to _seek_ Zaccheus as the tax collector was to seek a sight of Jesus.

Little did Zaccheus foresee what his catching sight of Jesus would bring into his life. Compared to most men Zaccheus was a dwarf in stature. His lack of height made it easy for the crowd to thwart his every effort to catch sight of the great Teacher. But he circumvented their rebuffs by circling the city, climbing up to the broad branches of a sycamore tree, and there waiting until Jesus should pass just below his perch. He who "seeks" will find a way! But he hardly could have expected to be the center of such attention. Of all residents of Jericho, prominent or obscure, leader or layman, poor or rich how could it be he who might expect such attention from the renowned rabbi! But his very hindrances became the steps by which he rose to the fellowship of the saved.

We have noted how Zaccheus took the initiative in overcoming every roadblock set in his way to catch a sight of Jesus. Equally important is it that Jesus responded with his own initiative. Jesus would not ignore such efforts to "see" him. Jesus did not resent nor condemn the man's wealth. Zaccheus' view of himself and his wealth was vastly different from that of the rich young ruler of 18:18-30. And even when this chief publican offered to "restore four-fold" any ill-gotten gain the Lord did not ask him to "bestow _all_" his possessions on the poor. Though it might contribute to his spiritual lack, the man's wealth wasn't what made him an outcast. Nor did his riches create his poverty of spirit. His great need was salvation from sin, basic to every man. Not in his memory had Zaccheus enjoyed such honor as offered by Jesus. "When he came to the place, Jesus looking up said to him, 'Zaccheus, hasten, come down; for today in _your_ house it's necessary that I stay!'"

Jesus Confronts Zaccheus!

The physician who heals the deadliest disease thereby shows that he may heal the less serious sickness. If Zaccheus was the most infamous of Jericho's citizens it was most logical that the saviour choose his home into which to bring salvation. If the Christ can save the worst he can save any! By so honoring this man he was saying to every soul, "You are worth saving!"

Though the chief publican with repeated efforts sought to see Jesus, it was Jesus who engineered the night's fellowship. It was Jesus who proposed, "Today it's necessary that I lodge in your house!" Though men must "seek God in the hope that they might feel after him and find him," in the final analysis it is God who seeks men. As men open themselves to him God finds men and invites himself into their lives. He won't force himself but he will invite himself into every seeking heart.

It didn't take Zaccheus long to overcome the initial shock of being chosen as Christ's host. "Having made haste he came down and received him while rejoicing." Men may be astonished at God's initiative in "so loving" sinners as to want to come into their hearts and homes. But it needn't take long for those who sincerely seek to "receive while rejoicing." As men we may feel lonely, rebuffed, rejected by our fellow-men but to be the host for God's Christ restores self-confidence and self-esteem. In a word, we are "saved." When men "receive" Jesus they "rejoice" with the joy of salvation.

That Zaccheus be "rejoicing" is an expected reaction to his hosting the Saviour. When the Christ became his guest he became God's guest. But the people viewed Christ differently. "And all having seen were murmuring saying, 'He went in to lodge with a sinful man.'" The ways of God are not the ways of man. For man, to associate with a "sinner" implies one partakes of the sinner's sin. For God, there's no way to win a sinner from his sin apart from associating with him where he is. God goes to the sinner while he is sinning in order to rescue him from his sin. Such is the logic of Jesus, "Today I must remain in your house." Let the crowd keep on murmuring, you and I have an experience of salvation to inaugurate!

There is something defiant, resolute, definitive about the way in which Zaccheus responded to the crowd's murmuring." Furthermore, Jesus' self-invitation to honor an outcast broke down all barriers to his soul. "Zaccheus, having taken a stand..." He gained more than "seeing" Jesus. He found a new vision, new goals, new life, the power of a redeeming person! In defiance of all past and present criticism, "having stood," became a decisive moment of rebirth!

A new birth demands fresh commitment. And at this point Zaccheus was not lacking. "Behold, the half of my possessions I give to the poor." Zaccheus, in contrast to the rich ruler, readily grasped the implications of salvation in Christ. The need for radical change in life habits was too obvious for temporizing or delay. Commitment is inevitably involved in conversion to Christ!

305

But the commitment of Zaccheus went much further than half his possessions and income. It included a resolve to make moral amends at any point in which he had unjustly taken from others that which was rightfully theirs. Insofar as possible to host Christ in the heart is to reshape moral behaviour, both in relationship to God and men. "Everyone having been begotten of God does not keep on doing sin, because his seed is abiding in him; and he is not able to go on sinning."(I Jn.3:9) For the moral life to be changed is as normal as the full grain in the ear to spring from life in the seed. Whether Zaccheus had actually defrauded or blackmailed anyone is not necessarily implied in the text. But the structure of his sentence (1st class condition) assumed the condition to be true for the sake of the argument proposed. In a word Zaccheus said, "If I have wrongfully defrauded, and let's assume that I have, then I pledge myself to return four-fold." Restitution is the best proof of conversion to Christ! Could there be any doubt that "salvation has come to this house?" Works may not be the justifying basis for salvation but they give good evidence of its reality!

The word "faith" is not mentioned in this story. Luke did not need to mention it. "Faith is completed (made perfect) by works."(Jas.2:22) When Jesus said, "Salvation has come to this house because he also is a son of Abraham" he was not calling attention to Zaccheus as a Jew. It was that faith of Abraham that was imitated in Zaccheus that made him a "son of Abraham." It's the "lost" Jesus came to save, not Jews (or Gentiles) as such.

Moreover this story of Zaccheus is companion to that of the blind beggar in which Jesus made clear the role of faith by declaring "your faith has saved you." Both men gave kindred evidence that they detected the moral and spiritual qualities of Jesus and his kingdom. Salvation as fact was demonstrably present in both men. Furthermore, each man perceived that salvation was in some way related to the coming redemptive events in Jerusalem. These two men, outcasts on the garbage heap of humanity, were able to read aright the significance of this Christ even when more privileged disciples were faltering under the weight of the abuse heaped on him and the death which followed.

That these men were "saved" at Jericho near the ascent to Jerusalem at this time is part of the significance of Luke's placing these stories here. The story of Zaccheus climaxes the entire public ministry of Jesus. Before the week of Calvary it demonstrates that "the son of man came to seek and to save the one who has become lost!" And without the coming week's events no saving the lost would be possible.

306

AN OUTLINE OF LUKE 19:11-27
A Time For Testing!
Why tell this tale here? Luke states two reasons. "And they hearing these things (in reference to Zaccheus), he added and spoke a parable because he was near Jerusalem and because they were supposing that the kingdom of God was immediately about to appear." These are the reasons why Jesus presented the parable just at this point in time. They are equally the reasons why Luke placed this episode here in his unfolding narrative about the son of Mary, Son of God!

   I. THE OCCASION FOR THE PARABLE. 19:11
     1. The historical framework.
     2. The moral need.
  II. THE PARABLE: TESTING RESPONSIBILITY. 19:12-24
     1. Responsibility given and exercised. 12-15
     2. Responsibility examined. 16-21
     3. An accounting demanded. 17, 19, 22-24
 III. THE PRINCIPLE GOVERNING MORAL RESPONSIBILITY.19:25b-27
     1. "To everyone getting it shall be given." 25b-26a
     2. "From everyone not getting even that which he has shall be taken away." 26b
     3. The king's "enemies" self-destroyed! 27

"To every action there is an opposite and equal reaction." This principle in the physical universe holds true throughout the entire moral-spiritual universe. Jesus recognized a spiritual force in the world with moral implications. There's no neutrality. Each action meets with an equal and opposite moral-spiritual reaction. It's a law of the kingdom of God!

        * * * * * *

A TIME OF TESTING!

After Jesus' refusal of a kings' crown at the feeding of the 5000 enthusiasm for him subsided. But since starting a steady movement toward Jerusalem, his final to that city of destiny, excitement gradually rose. "Many multitudes were going with him..."(14:25) In Jericho the crowds" "were going before him..."(18:38) The press of people was so great that many could not get a glimpse of Jesus. Signs of growing enthusiasm for the Teacher and anticipation of critical confrontation excited the thronging people. The self-possession of the Lord gave striking contrast to the excitement rippling through the press of crowds. As the people were "hearing these things" to, from, and about Zaccheus he "added and spoke a parable." Their nearness to Jerusalem prompted the story. He was approaching a confrontation with the Jewish authorities. The air was electric with activity. Something must channel and control the growing agitation. Jesus used a parable to do just that.
The Occasion for the Parable!
The story which Jesus chose to tell, while being independent enough to stand alone, nevertheless was set in an historical situation familiar to his audience. At the death of Herod the

the Great his oldest son, Archelaus, according to his father's
will, inherited the kingdom. But Archelaus could in fact only
be sure of his kingship at the will of Rome. To make his title
firm he journeyed to distant Rome in an attempt to get his
kingship authorized by Rome's consent. So harsh had the rule
of Herod been that the Jewish subjects "hated" the Herods. Thus
an embassage of 50 Palestinians, Jews and Samaritans, were
commissioned by the people to appear at Rome to protest the
appointment of Archelaus. They were to plead for autonomy in
government. Though Rome denied Archelaus the title "king" he
was given the role of ethnarch. Within the "fourth" thus
granted Archelaus in effect became "king."

Jesus did not hesitate to frame his parable on this
historical incident. He was now at Jericho ready to ascend to
Jerusalem, symbolic of a much loftier "ascent" to a higher
Jerusalem. This last lap of his journey and the coming week's
events would make possible that ultimate ascent! Yet between
his steep climb to Jerusalem with its throne a cross, its crown
of thorns and his coming again as empowered sovereign of God's
eternal kingdom he would be a "long time in a far country," as
it were. The historical setting for the parable lent it
authenticity and realism. The place and time of delivering the
parable are significant for its meaning. But the introduction
given in verse 11 indicates the moral import of the parable.
"He spoke a parable because he was near Jerusalem and because
they were supposing that the kingdom of God was about to appear
immediately." Though there is a real sense in which already
"the kingdom of God is among (in) you" there is another very
real sense in which it will not come in its fullness until the
king shall return from the "far country" as duly appointed
monarch! At that consummation of history an accounting shall
be demanded of all the king's subjects.

The Testing of Responsibility!

Immediately preceding the parable of the pounds is the story
of Zaccheus with its continuing emphasis on responsiblity for
material possessions. Immediately following is Luke's account
of the Christ's "royal" entry into the capital city! Thus the
proper use of possessions and Christ's kingship are united in
the giving of this parable. It also serves to clarify the
current mistaken notion of the kingdom's immediate appearance
as a political power in world affairs. It is a spiritual
kingdom! And though it is already "among you" it is not to
appear in all its full glory until he, the Christ, goes into a
"far country" and after a long period of time "comes again"
with full eternal sovereignty. All illusions of temporal,
material, political power must be discarded.

The parable tells of a "certain nobleman" who entrusts to
his servants ten pounds. Then he exhorts each to "do business
while I am coming." The amount of money is not really a large
sum. But the point of the parable is, not the size, but the
ability to show an increase with such a meagre start. This is
a time of testing the integrity of each servant.

Thus it is that while the nobleman went to the "far country" his servants "did business" with the money entrusted to them. The embassage, failing in its mission, the nobleman returned as king and sought an accounting from his servants. Typical of the ten, three reported on their business ventures. One said, "Your pound produced ten pounds." To whom the king responded with grace, "Indeed, well done, good servant! Because you became trustworthy, you are to get power over ten cities." A second servant, though less bountiful, nonetheless, reported a good gain of "five pounds." To him the king pledged, "You will get authority over five cities."

When a third came to make his report he is described as "another" servant." The term "another" means "another of a different kind." His character and disposition was radically different from the first two. He saw the Master in a different light, austere and harsh; he viewed himself as well as his responsibility differently. His trading methods were different.

A king, in order to rule well, needs good administrators over populous territories, especially cities. This third servant had proved himself honest but quite useless as an administrator. He was strictly honest in the care with which he "did business." He guarded against loss by not speculating with the Master's money. He guarded his trust with conservative care. He wrapped the money in a "sweat rag" and hid it safely away. That he steal never occurred to him. He would protect his trust against any possible loss. But in so doing he failed to demonstrate any administrative ability over other people. The earlier two were rewarded with administrative power over cities, not money. The entrustment of the "pounds" was really a test of their capacity as managers.

Though the "other" servant was strictly honest he was judged "wicked" because he failed to make good decisions in managing money. He failed the test of reliability. Hence his harsh punishment! Failure to use opportunity led him to self destruction! He was condemned by his own words. "Evil servant, out of your own mouth I will judge you. You were knowing that I was an austere man, taking that which I didn't plant and harvesting that which I didn't sow? Then why didn't you give my money to the table bankers? And I, when I came, would have collected it with interest?" The man, though honest, was "wicked" because he did not use the opportunity with which he was entrusted. Virtue is a positive quality, not negative. Virtue is not avoiding the bad; it's submission to positive qualities of character! To be wicked is to do nothing when doing something is possible. Virtue is not preserving security behind barred doors. It's to enter an open door when it's open.

The Principle Governing Moral Responsibility!

The parable has more to say about reliability in the king's kingdom! At the accounting the king said to his attendants: "Take from him the pound and give it to the one having ten." In shocked surprize they urged: "He got ten!" Ignoring them, the king proposed a principle of responsible action. "To everyone having it shall be given, but from the one not having even

309

what he has shall be taken from him." English versions usually render ἔχοντι, ἔχοντος, ἔχει, "having," "having," and "has." But the Aktionsart (action native to the verb root) is not have but get. "Have" is a linear idea; "get" is point action. To render this verb by our "get" is more accurate. Besides, how can we "take from" someone that which he "does not have?"

The servant who wrapped his master's money in a "sweat rag" possessed (had) nothing! Though he imagined he had protected the trust, on his own he had gotten nothing! That which this royal Master was teaching was: "To everyone who gets" and keeps on getting through his very getting reveals that he is a "go getter" and can thus be called upon to manage property, people, money or any other thing with which he is entrusted. On the other hand the "non go-getter" by his very nature shall lose anything he thought he had. If he ever "got" anything his attitude and disposition insures that he won't keep it long. Even what he "got" he will lose! This is a law of life, a kingdom law! It can be found throughout the entire universe, physical, moral, psychological, spiritual. Inherent within the "getting" is the promise of more. Imbedded in the "non getting" is the loss of anything already gotten.

Lying within this principle is the explanation as to why the servant who gained ten pounds was entrusted with the one forfeited by the non-getting "evil" servant. When one demonstrated that he could "get" so much increase from so small a beginning he was given more. Because he had gotten ten pounds from ten invested the royal Master felt it a better business venture to give another pound to him who had ability to gain the most. He who had gotten ten was a better producer than even he who had gained but five.

It is worth repeating! It's a law of life, "to him who gets, more shall be given; but from the one not getting even that which he (thinks) he got shall be taken from him." He who succeeds shall be rewarded with more success. He who fails shall be weighted down with more failure. This is not to say that "getting" and "non-getting" can not be reversed. But in general success breeds success and failure begets failure. That's the point in the parable.

Having made the "evil servant" an example of his justice, the king turns to all his "enemies" who "hated him" and had sought to dethrone him from his royal right as king. "But to these my enemies, the ones not wishing me to reign over them, bring them here and slaughter them before me." This is more than mere failure to "do business" for the king of God's kingdom. Determined and open rebellion gains a more dreadful destiny than failure. It harvests personal elimination, a violent and permanent banishment. He who wills not to have God as king forfeits his moral and spiritual self "before me." Banishment from God is the ultimate death sentence.

Nothing is more universal or more human than the law governing human responsibility. It crosses national, racial, cultural, moral and spiritual boundaries. How could Theophilus miss the point?

310

AN OUTLINE OF LUKE 19:28-48
The Christ's Royal Entry into Jerusalem!

If "Triumphal Entry" means that Jesus entered Jerusalem as a victorious Roman General given a "Triumph" then it's a misnomer The battle had not yet been fought or won. That would come at Gethsemane, the courts of men, Calvary, the open tomb, his ascension and coronation above. This entrance was the Christ's first and only public claim for himself as King! This was his royal entry!

I. THE ROYAL APPROACH TO JERUSALEM! 19:28-40
1. "Going before, he was journeying to Jerusalem." 28
2. Preparation for the royal entrance. 29-34
3. Jesus honored as king by disciples and people. 35-38
4. Rejected by "certain of the Pharisees!" 39-40

II. THE CHRIST'S LAMENTATION OVER THE CITY. 19:41-44
1. Christ's emotional outburst. 41
2. The words of his lament! 42
3. Prophetic destiny of the city! 43-44

III. ASSERTING HIS AUTHORITY AS KING! 19:45-48
1. Cleansing "my house," the Temple of God. 45-46
2. He "was teaching daily in the Temple!" 47a
3. Opposition aroused to destroy him. 47b-48

With the Christ's public presentation of himself as King of God's Messianic kingdom the hour of the world's destiny is at hand. The critical events of human redemption occur during this final week. They display once and for all the nature of the king, the kingdom, the subjects of that kingdom and their utter contrast to human expectations! Herein are revealed the real issues of human life and destiny!

* * * * * * *

THE CHRIST'S ROYAL ENTRY INTO JERUSALEM!

That Jesus was conscious early in life of his divine nature is clear from Luke's gradual unveiling of the life of Jesus. No doubt Mary had occasion to tell her son some of those events environing his birth, things she kept "pondering in her heart." Even at twelve years he was conscious of his ability to cross verbal swords with the intellectual leaders of Israel. When in his native town of Nazareth he quoted Is.61:1 Jesus was quite conscious of his nature and mission, "Today this scripture has been fulfilled in your hearing."

Yet in spite of his ever increasing awareness of his holy nature and mission he was ever so cautious in making claim of his Messianic calling or divine nature. In fact, until Peter confessed "Thou art the Christ" Jesus did not admit the title. Certainly not openly. And even then he commanded Peter and the others: "Tell this to no one." It was only then that he began teaching in private, "The son of man must suffer many things, and be rejected...be killed...and be raised..!" Though they couldn't comprehend, he knew his nature, his mission and the cost to accomplish it!

311

The Royal Approach to Jerusalem!

When Jesus heeded the cry of the blind beggar of Jericho, "Jesus, son of David!" he signaled that the time had come when he would openly seek his reception as King-Messiah. Secrecy, caution as to his divine person and his God-given mission of redemption was a thing of the past. Henceforth he would publicly proclaim his deity and Lordship. From now on men must choose or reject him as king! "Having said these things..." about the "certain nobleman" journeying to a "far country" to "seek for himself a kingdom" Jesus now deliberately presented himself as king with full regal powers. He "was journeying, going before unto Jerusalem!" He with purpose led the glad procession to Jerusalem "going before!"

"And when he drew near to Bethphage and Bethany at the mount of Olives" he executed a prearranged plan for a formal entrance that would signify the stamp of his kingship. He dispatched two of his faithful followers to the village of Bethany in which was a tethered colt "on which no man had ever sat." That he had arranged for the use of the colt is clear from the unquestioned yielding by the owner to the statement of the two disciples, "His master has need" (of it)! That it was a colt, symbol of peace, and not a beast of war, testified to the kind of king and kingdom he was heralding.

Immediately on the disciples' bringing the colt to their Master they shed their cloaks, cast them on the colt and lifted Jesus astride the animal. They thus showed the high honor and royal esteem they had for their Teacher. In addition "as they were going they were spreading their garments on the roadway." The dullness of the disciples as to the necessity of his being abused, rejected, and killed (Lk.18:34) left them with their notion of his kingdom as grossly materialistic. And now it was quite clear that he was openly announcing himself as king! Their loyalty and enthusiasm knew no bounds. Their trust in him had no limits! Their own garments, spread before his royal mount, was testimony to their excitement at his open declaration as king! Their enthusiasm was contagious! For "as he was drawing near to the descent of the mount of Olives, the multitude of his disciples, rejoicing, began to praise God in a great voice..."

The enthusiasm of the crowd, generated by his open declaration of his kingship, found support in "all the signs which they had seen" throughout his ministry in Galilee including the sight given to blind Bartimaeus. Though Luke omits the raising of Lazarus John's Gospel notes how that sign in Bethany stirred the people. The crowd praised Jesus in the words of Psalm 118:26, "Blessed be the one coming in the name of the Lord." Luke includes the title "the king!" Thus he leaves no doubt as to the meaning of "the one coming!" And as to the kind of kingdom the voice of the people defined it as "in heaven peace, and glory in the highest!" Genuine peace arises in "heaven," the peace of reconciliation between God and man. And the "glory" due God resounds in the "highest" places!

312

Rejected by "Certain of the Pharisees!"

The enthusiastic praise of the multitudes pricked the hearts of "certain of the Pharisees." Opposition from the Pharisees was not new to Jesus. They had scrutinized every "sign" and had harrassed him at every step of the way toward Jerusalem. It was beyond their mental or emotional capacity to keep quiet in the face of such universal acclaim for Jesus. His plain claim of Lordship over God's kingdom they could not let pass without a challenge. They themselves were helpless before the rolling tide of the peoples' popular acclaim. The one possibility open to them was an appeal to his sense of concern for the peace and unity of the nation. If he could control the tidal wave of emotions, then they could proceed with their orderly political power in the presence of Rome's constant threat. To them it was the political hopes they sought to protect. To him it was the redemption of humanity that was at stake. These Pharisees were "from the crowd." Without acknowledging him as King-Messiah they presented their appeal, "Teacher, rebuke your disciples." Muffle the mouths of these your misguided followers!

This was a confrontation between two fundamentally opposed views of the nature of the kingdom. Was the Christ destined to redeem and rule the hearts of men as sovereign? Or would those who clung to political power, financial freedom and military might dominate? The issue was as old as creation! It's Eden all over again. "Enjoy the paradise of God's will and live or eat of the tree of self-serving indulgence and die!"

The reply of Jesus to the attack of the "certain Pharisees" appealed to the inevitability of truth! On the scaffold truth may "forever be" but the scaffold itself will collapse under the force of the reality of truth. Thus said Jesus, "If these (people) shall keep silent, the stones shall cry out!" The hour is at hand when the truth can no longer be repressed. The unconscious forces of creation will burst forth! There's no way to suppress the true nature of God's kingdom or king! Even if someone keeps silent, something will speak! How can truth be thwarted forever in a world ruled by the good God? This is the final gasp of Pharisees in Luke's Gospel. For the moment they were "silenced" by the testimony of truth!

The Christ's Lamentation!

The union of the divine and human in Jesus breaks forth in his sudden burst of emotion. "And as they drew near, when he saw the city he wept over it!" No doubt entered his mind as to his weathering the coming storm. Knowledge of his Father's will, his coronation beyond the cross, empty tomb and ascension sustained his battered spirit. But the sight of the city, its years of historical connection with God's people, its identity with divine redemptive promises set aflame his imagination. Contrast between what might have been and tragic reality of present bitter, stubborn, rebellious rejection was more than his wounded heart could shoulder without mountains of emotion. Great sobs shook his frame as he empathized with lost humanity!

313

"If this day you knew, even you, the things facing peace!" The great tragedy, not just of the Jew but of man, is not the manipulation of political powers, but the corruption of the moral and spiritual forces that lie unseen below the outward levels of life! This failure to resolve the moral disruption between God and man is the underlying root of human pain and discord. "If only you knew, even you, these things producing peace!!" But the sad reality is, "they are hidden from your eyes." Your prepossession of grasping of outward powers has brought on your moral blindness aborting your spiritual vision. When personal profit transcends moral character then moral decay follows as sure as fruit rots when severed from life giving sap of the tree. And when the spirit of a man is blinded to the spiritual realities lying unseen but potently dominating and controlling the physical universe darkness follows as surely as night follows the setting sun. "But even now they (the things of peace) are hidden from your eyes!" Their eyes were scaled over because of self-inflicted moral perversions. They could not recognize God as he is because they had shaped Him into God as they wished him to be. Their self-made God blinded them to the God who walked among them.

In view of such blindness prophetic insight as to the tragic destiny of the Hebrews as God's people was clear. "For the days shall come upon you that your enemies shall cast ramparts against you and they shall encircle you and press you in, and they shall hurl you and your children to the ground, and they shall not leave among you stone upon stone, because you did not recognize the time of your visitation." In these words Jerusalem's king becomes its prophet. He considers its sad condition in contrast to its history of hope. Furthermore, as prophet he is not now concerned with <u>his</u> fate but the city's inevitable destruction. "Daughters of Jerusalem, quit weeping over me; but weep over yourselves and over your children!...if they do these things to the green tree, what shall happen to the dry?"(23:28,31) What shall become of all the hopes treasured through the centuries centered in Jerusalem? Here again the moral circumstances forces on the mind the nature of the kingdom and its king. These historical hopes can only be realized in a <u>different</u> <u>kind</u> of kingdom than the world's idea of political, military, economic sovereignty!

<u>Asserting the Authority of the King</u>!
Having presented himself as king of God's kingdom he proceeded to assert his royal authority. Not a throne room but God's temple was the appropriate place for such a display of regal power. "Having entered into the temple he began to cast out the ones selling, saying to them, 'It stands written, Indeed, my house shall be a house of prayer, but <u>you</u> have made it a den of thieves!'" By taking advantage of the pilgrims' need for sacrificial animals the priestly custodians of the temple prostituted their trust for financial gain. God's house was turned into a trading market with all abuses typical of human greed. As king he "threw them out!"

314

When a contractor builds on a site preoccupied by another structure he must first destroy before he can build. Having "cast them out" Jesus begins building by laying solid footings. He "was teaching daily in the temple." The decaying formalism must be replaced by vital personal relationship with the living God. Stifling effects of corrupt institutional religion needed replacing with dynamic of God's Holy Spirit empowering the human spirit. Authority must be centered in the person of God's Christ rather than impersonal rules of "law." This could only be effected by enlightening the mind, purifying the emotions, and motivating the will of those who, submitting to Messiah, would enter the kingdom. Hence Jesus instigated his royal rule by launching a Jerusalem ministry of education. "He was teaching daily in the temple!" That which he taught is detailed in chapters 20-21. But reaction from the leaders was immediate. "The highpriests and the scribes were seeking to destroy him, and the chief men of the people." Long centuries of human misreading the role of Israel in God's goal for universal redemption rendered these leaders blind to the reality of the spiritual nature of their national mission in the world. To them destroying the forms of religion destroyed the reality of religion. Structure hid the spirit. Pulverizing the temple of stone despoiled the Spirit of God! Robbing the ritual was to discard the righteousness symbolized in the ritual! Thus they "kept on seeking to destroy him."

Nevertheless, "all the people, hearing him, were hanging on" his every word. The people may not have appreciated the full impact of what he taught. But they liked him and that which he taught. The power of the people thwarted every murderous attempt of the "chief men of the people." His popularity gave time to lay solid footings for the new spiritual temple.

The nature of the kingdom of God had been determined from creation. The words, "Let us make man in our image" provided the spiritual constitution of any kingdom God might inaugurate. "God is spirit" and any kingdom he would establish would of necessity be spiritual. But in addition, man's sin with its consequent death imposed on human kind made the elimination of death an inevitable necessity. There can be no eternal life until death is removed. This is the logic of the Christ's death. To eliminate death he must conquer by enduring and surviving it. The reality of the spirit world must break through the illusions of this material world. Christ's royal entry with his public claim of kingship, the asserting of his royal authority and the ensuing clash was the tragic, but victorious conflict of this climactic week of his ministry on earth. It was his most divinely human display of God's redemptive plan of love. It unveiled the most universal aspects of the entire ministry of Jesus as the "Christ of God."

AN OUTLINE OF LUKE 20:1-8
The Question of Authority!
Life's paramount problem is authority! Who or what has the
right to invade the human personality with power to command?
Who or what determines moral, spiritual, or personal power to
demand and expect obedience?

I. THE QUESTION RAISED. 20:1-2
    1. When raised? "One of the days while teaching!" 1a
    2. Who raised the question? 1b
    3. The question as proposed. 2
       (a)"In what kind of authority?"
       (b)"Who is he who gave this authority?"
II. CHRIST'S COUNTER-QUESTION. 20:3-6
    1. The question answered with a question. 3-4
    2. The horns of the dilemma. 5-6
       (a)Of divine origin?
       (b)Of human origin?
III. RESULTS OF THE CONFRONTATION. 20:7-8
    1. Dodging the issue: "We don't know!"
    2. Christ's answer: John's witness sufficient!

John drew to himself all that had been spoken "through the
prophets." He testified of Jesus that "he is mightier than I."
This was sufficient testimony to the Christ's authority as
Messiah, Son of God. He who accepts John's witness as of God
accepts me as of God. He who denies John's witness will not
accept any other. Hence there's no point that "I tell you in
what authority I do these things."

* * * * * * *

THE QUESTION OF AUTHORITY!
The question of authority is primary for human beings. No
question of human values can be of more importance. To whom or
what power shall I submit for guidance? Is there some person,
body, or thing that can be for man a rule of conduct? Shall it
be king, conqueror, council, parliament, or tyrant? Or shall
it be the voice of inner conscience to which each man shall
give final loyalty?
   And then there is God! By virtue of being Creator does he
not hold absolute and ultimate authority? In view of who He is
does not all authority of any kind flow from his creative hand?
Such would seem to be the case if he be the living God as seen
in the biblical records. But one feature must be observed
about God's authority over man. Though absolute he exercises
it in keeping with the "image of God" in man, that is the "free
will" given to each human being.
The Question Raised!
   When Jesus entered the capitol city as King he at once took
charge of cleansing the Temple and inaugurating a teaching
ministry. He apparently joined some "signs" to his activity as
royal temple keeper and teacher. This unusual assertion of
royal authority was disconcerting, to say the least, to the

316

appointed authorities. For a time they felt paralyzed, their authority challenged. They were in disarray, confused over the sudden turn of events. Entering Jerusalem as king, and more important, his taking charge of kingly functions unnerved them. They were unable to negate the power of the people who were now acknowledging the royal leadership of Jesus as their Christ. "The highpriests, the scribes with the elders" felt control of Judaism slipping rapidly from their hands. From their point of view something must be done and done quickly to protect their domination and Israel's survival. And whatever they did must discredit Jesus and restore their supremacy.

"The highpriests and the scribes and the elders" constituted the Jerusalem Sanhedrin. For all practical purposes this institution held sovereignty over Hebrews as the people of God. They weren't about to allow Jesus to wrest control from them. Hence it was that during "one of the days while he was teaching the people in the temple, and evangelizing," they plotted to discredit Jesus. They agreed to propose a dilemma that would embarrass and tarnish the image of Jesus in the eyes of the people. Moreover, as members of the Sanhedrin it was their responsibility to safeguard the temple, its customs, rituals, and religious heritage. At a time and place of greatest publicity they inquired of him, "Tell us, in what __kind__ of authority are you doing these things, or who is he who gave you this authority?"

This double-barrelled question was carefully constructed. "These things" allude to the "things" Jesus had done within the last day or two. His open claim to be king by riding on a colt as did ancient king David; accepting the plaudits of the crowd as king does his subjects; cleansing the temple as though __he__ were God's temple keeper; his signs and his teaching as though __he__ were authorized to dogmatize the truth of God; His priestly control of who or what might pass through the temple; all "these things" were an offense coming from a rural, itinerant, unauthorized man from the masses. If the people could see the arrogant blasphemous conduct, his uncredited assumption of powers that didn't belong to him, they might loosen his grip on the people. If Jesus claimed his authority came from God they could demand immediate, visible, incontrovertable proof. If he failed to claim divine approval then the falseness of his behaviour would be manifest. If they could shake the affectionate, emotional tie of the people these "priests, scribes, and elders" could reestablish their authority and cast Jesus out.

Important is the fact that they challenged him as to the "__kind__" of authority! In other words, none of those recognized, accredited rulers in Israel had authorized him as King-Messiah. Did his actions rest solely on the popular will of the people? The only other kind of authority would be divine. The power he was exercising demanded that kind of accreditation. It was on this issue the Sanhedrin hoped to impale Jesus before the people.

317

The fact was that the <u>kind</u> of authority that Jesus exercised was inherent in <u>who</u> he was. This word ἐξουσία is made from the preposition ἐκ "out of," "from" and present participle of εἰμί "I am." The power that springs out of the essence of his nature is the authority which he was in fact exercising. The Son of God partakes of the nature of the Father. That which he does is as inevitable as life in the fruit springs from life in the seed. It is inherent within! Enwrought in the Son is the power to exercise the rights of the Father.

At this point of power the "priests, scribes, with the elders" challenged him! And that was what lay behind their companion question, "<u>Who</u> is he who gave you this (kind of) power?" The temple authorities certainly have not given it. The power of the people is fickle and passing. Besides, they have no innate right to bestow such powers. <u>Who</u> then could bestow this right? If God, then give evidence beyond question!

Christ Answers with a Counter-Question!

To answer by direct appeal to his miracles, daily teachings, or ministry among the multitudes would be fruitless. It was just such things that prompted their opposition in the first place. This evidence they already had discounted. Their presuppositions regarding the political concept of God's kingdom was too ingrained for them to acknowledge his notion of a spiritual kingdom. His emphasis on truth, honesty, integrity of mind, heart and soul was in itself proof that he needed to prove he could be king of <u>their kind of a kingdom of God</u>! With them the issue was not spiritual versus a material kingdom. It was rather <u>who</u> was to exercise the power. Was it to be the priestly leaders authorized by the duly appointed Sanhedrin? Or should it be Jesus, an unaccredited outsider?

For this reason Jesus refused to appeal to his signs, teachings, or other such proofs. He countered with a question. "<u>I</u> indeed will ask <u>you</u> a word. The baptism of John, was it of heaven or of men?" Jesus reversed the roles. He took the offense. He placed them on the defense. In the last analysis even their present tyranny depended on the good will of the people. In private counsel they reviewed their dilemma: "If we say, 'Out of heaven,' He will say, 'Why did you not believe him?' But if we say, 'Of men!' All the people will stone us, for they have been persuaded John to be a prophet.'"

This was an incisive answer. First, it turned the attack from himself. He made no direct defense. He avoided making himself the issue. Second, it unveiled their hypocrisy. They were not interested in "<u>who gave</u>" this authority. They were protecting their own role as keepers of the Temple and rulers over Israel. Third, by this answer they were forced to face the witness of John as to who and what Jesus was in the life and hope of Israel. John testified and the people believed that Jesus was "the coming one," Messiah and king of Israel's promise! From the testimony of John the "people" gathered that Jesus was "of God!" Christ's response was not an evasion but a forthright answer to their attempt to entrap him.

318

Results of the Confrontation!

By his counter-question Jesus had completely boxed them into a corner. There was no escape from their making a statement before the populace. As far as the people were concerned John was a bonified prophet sent by God. And John's witness included "One mightier than I comes, the thong of whose sandals I am not worthy to unloose: he shall baptize you in the Holy Spirit..." And John heard God's voice declare of Jesus, "You are my beloved son..."

John's was a clarion call to follow Jesus as God's Son, the long awaited and clearly promised "son of David," king of God's Israel! But for these "Pharisees, scribes, and elders" to accept Jesus as such a Christ was to dethrone themselves and thwart their determined political aspirations of sovereignty. Such ambitions they were unwilling to sacrifice.

On the other hand any effective rule must find support from the people. Even a despotic government must enjoy the support of public opinion. For them to renounce John's testimony would throw them open to loss of this very necessary public support. This too they were unwilling to abandon. They could not afford the loss of people power. Nevertheless, an answer was expected. The situation demanded it! So by declaring, "We don't know!" they dodged the issue. It was an attempt not to compromise themselves. It was their attempt to hide their self interest not to mention their lack of basic honesty.

And how did Christ deal with their answer to his challenge? Jesus said to them, "Neither do I on my part tell you in what kind of authority I am doing these things." At first sight Jesus might seem to be piqued at such an obvious dodge of the issue. But such is a shallow view of both Jesus and his answer. He had no reason to be irritated. He was in control! They were to be pitied; they had dishonored themselves and their trust. What he realy was saying was, Since you are unable to recognize or accept John's clear witness about who I am and whence my authority, you are in no position to be able to judge even should I give direct answer to your question. You are incapable of judging authority! For me to attempt an answer would be as futile as offering a child that which is suitable only for the adult mind! It would confuse more than help you. If you can't understand John's witness it would only confound darkness to listen to mine!

The kind of authority resident in the Christ springs out of his nature as divine. No man spake as he spake, lived as he lived, taught as he taught or died as he died. And no man, other than he, rose as he rose in triumph over death! He is unique in all history. Yet he identifies with all humanity as a human. No one is more universal than he. All this is inherent in who and what he is. He is wholly divine, completely human, entirely universal. God, "This is my beloved son!"

319

AN OUTLINE OF LUKE 20:9-19
A Landowner and His Renters!

Having addressed "authorities" of Israel on his authority,
Jesus turned to tell a parable to the people! It clarified to
them the kind and source of his authority. It also identified
the deadly unbelief of the Jewish leaders who were in the
process of murdering the owner's "son."

I.   TO AND ABOUT WHOM THE PARABLE ADDRESSED! 20:9a, 19
      1. To whom: "the people." 9a
      2. About whom: "the scribes and chief priests." 19
II.   THE PARABLE: 20:9b-15a
      1. An owner leased his vineyard to farmers. 9b
      2. Three attempts to collect the rent. 10-12
      3. The owner appeals to sense of respect! 13-15a
      (a)Owner sends his son.
      (b)The renters' plot!
      (c)Renters murder the son!
III. DIALOGUE WITH THE "PEOPLE." 20:15b-19
      1. Question proposed to the "people." 15b-16a
      (a)The question.
      (b)The answer.
      (c)The peoples' response!
      2. Jesus judgment in view of scripture. 17-18
      (a)"The stone the builders rejected." Ps.118:22
      (b)Judgment pronounced.
IV.   RESULTS OF THE PARABLE. 20:19
      1. On "the scribes and chief priests."
      2. On "the people."

No longer was there doubt as to his authority, its source
and kind. The leaders clearly saw themselves in the parable
and "sought to lay hands on him." The "people" with equal
clarity saw the point of the parable. For the moment they
were able to protect Jesus from judicial murder.

* * * * * * *

A LANDOWNER AND HIS RENTERS!

There's a close relation between the story of some abusive
renters of a vineyard and the question of Jesus' authority.
Some students treat the two paragraphs as part of the same
story. To a close reader the connection is obvious, even
vital to the question of authority. Certainly in Luke's mind
the account of the murderous tenants sheds light on the source
and kind of the Christ's authority. The parable skillfully
enables Jesus to answer the question without direct personal
attack. But none the less Jesus made perfectly clear that he
was the "son" and they, the leaders of Israel, were the
unfaithful abusive vinedressers; their murderous behaviour was
leading the "owner" to "give his vineyard to others."
To and About Whom the Parable Was Addressed!

When Jesus addressed the issue of his authority by asking a
question he did not let the matter drop. He wanted his answer

320

to be unequivocal, especially to the "people." While the motive of "the chief priests, scribes and elders" was vicious, their question was important. It needed a clear, conclusive, unhesitating answer. The "people" should know exactly who he was and why he claimed authority as king. Hence Luke states that Jesus "Began to tell this parable to the people."

They who challenged "in what sort of authority do you do these things?" had been effectively silenced. But though these professionals were not excluded from Christ's redemptive mission it was "the people" who must know beyond question his redeeming person. His world mission would be completed through "the people." Theophilus must realize the power and place of the people in God's plan for humanity. The gospel is not a power ploy for a chosen few. It's for "all the families of the earth." It can only be entrusted to the people!

On the other hand the parable was told in the presence of "the chief priests, scribes, with elders." And it was told about them! In dramatic form it answered their original question about his authority. But more, it dramatized the place they, the leaders, would play in the murder of their king. They clearly caught the force of the parable "for they knew that against them he spoke!"

The Parable!

With a few bold strokes Luke displayed the plot. "A man planted a vineyard, and he leased it out to farmers, and he went off for a long time." Numbers of Palestinian landowners did just that. For various reasons they would rent property to local workers while they went to Athens, Rome or other distant centers for governmental, social, or personal service. They used their income from their rented lands to undergird the income from their service. Such was the case of this "certain man." At the appointed season when the fruits (rents) were due he "sent a servant to the renters in order that they might give him the fruit (rent) from the vineyard."

At this point an unexpected twist in the story occurs. When a servant of the absent landowner arrives to collect the rent the workers of the land "flayed" him unmercifully and "sent him away empty." The quality of the labor of the renters is not at issue. Clearly the land produced well and the toil of the laborers was rewarding. So the issue is the shocking behavior of the rental farmers. To put it mildly, this conduct toward a landowner's rights was unacceptable. We would expect strong reprisal from a landowner. He would make legal moves against their breech of contract. And we would expect him to proceed with personal revenge. Yet, contrary to all expectation, as though nothing deviant had happened, the landowner sent another servant to collect the rent. He made no effort to bring these abusive farmers to justice! Nor did he oust the renters! If this reaction seems unreal let it be noted that it is unreal. That's the point of the story. It is such unexampled behaviour that is the power of the parable.

321

The patient grace of the landowner equalled and surpassed the unconscionable actions of the leasees of the farms. He sent even a third servant to collect the agreed-on rent. But of this one too the renters, "having brutally bruised him, cast him out." With the coming of each servant these savage hirelings stepped up the level of their barbaric behaviour. The first servant they "flayed." On the second they heaped shameful treatment on top the flaying. On the third, having mutilated him with disfiguring bruises, they "threw him off" the land as an unlawful intruder. There seemed no limit to the inhuman disregard for their legal contract not to mention the cruel treatment of fellow human servants.

But even more amazing is the incredible, incalculable grace of the landowner. The "people" to whom Jesus first addressed this parable thought, if they didn't say, "Impossible! We have never heard of such a thing! No landowner, in his right mind, could conceivably let renters get away with such atrocious contempt of contract." It was unheard of!

But it was the purpose of the parable to get the people to see that, though unheard of, it was transpiring in their very presence, before their own eyes. To catch their attention and to implant it permanently in their conscious minds Jesus sketched with bold black strokes the caricature of this landowner. Indeed he was _different_! Jesus overlaid this parable with some bolder lines of allegory. As he develops the parable it becomes increasingly obvious that by these "servants" Jesus alludes to some Old Testament characters, particularly the prophets. After all, Israel, as the people of God, was his "well-beloved vineyard in a very fruitful hill."(Is.5:1) Their own scriptures stated, "Since the days that your fathers came forth out of the land of Egypt...I have sent to you all my servants the prophets..."(Jer.7:25) And Luke would report, "Which of the prophets did not your fathers persecute? and they killed them that showed before of the coming of the Righteous One..."(Acts.7:52) In his story Jesus was clearly depicting the fact that God, the landowner had entered into a covenant-contract with Israel and its leaders to farm his vineyard. Furthermore, he had sent repeated "servants, the propehts" to enforce the terms of the contract. These prophet servants were unmercifully abused and rejected by the keepers of the vineyard.

But the climax of such violent rejection Jesus had yet to sketch. Thus in a soliloquy Jesus has the landowner say, "What shall I do?" To which he immediately lights on the grotesque idea, "I will send my son, the beloved son. Perhaps they will surely respect this one!" If sending three _servants_ was unseemly, the dispatching of the _son_ was beyond comprehension. Not only was it illogical, it was contrary to all oriental family tradition, it was inhuman on a father's part. It was totally irrational! But it's this irrationality that makes the story so vivid to the listeners. Jesus is describing a fact in process; not an imagined impossibility!

322

"But the farmers, when they saw him, began to reason with themselves saying, 'This is the heir; let's kill him that the inheritance become ours.' And when they had thrown him out of the vineyard, they killed him." This sad story worked itself out in real life. The murderous renters, "priests and scribes" threw "the Son" "out of the vineyard" and "killed him." "Jesus suffered outside the gate..."(Heb.13:12), the final fulfillment of the details of the allegory. The "priests and scribes" crucified Jesus "outside the gate." So Jesus "began to tell this parable to the people" that they might know the villainous nature of the keepers of Israel.

The parable's point was too plain to be missed by either people or leaders. But Jesus pushed the analogy to its fatal end. He asked the people, "What then shall the Lord of the vineyard do to them?" To this rhetorical question Jesus himself gave answer. "He will come and he will destroy these farmers, and he will give the vineyard to others." Such is the inevitable end of faithless farmers! He who cannot or will not be loyal to trust given must forfeit the trust.

When this principle arises in human experience it comes as a shock. The tragedy overwhelms the emotions. To the people of Israel it appeared impossible. To Christ's picture of dispossessed leaders of God's garden they burst, "May it not become!" That Israel be evicted as God's people was beyond belief. That the keepers of God's vineyard be denied their place was to repudiate history and God's place in it. In disbelief they cried, "May this never be!"

Jesus confronted their doubt with the mirror of the scripture. "What then is this which stands written? (The) stone which the builders rejected, this became head of the corner?" (Ps.118:22) The Psalmist points to when your own workmen reject the cornerstone that gives proportion and strength to your nation, a foreshadow of my spurning by these your leaders!

But this particular cornerstone does more than determine the angle in the foundation wall. In two ways it harbors judgment! The citizen or builder who "trips" over it shall break himself. If you don't recognize it for what it is you will destroy yourself. Moreover, "That stone will pulverize the one upon whom it shall fall." It shatters into tiny bits the careless, ignorant, rebellious builder. The cornerstone guarantees a strong, straight, secure building or it becomes the instrument of judgment on him who ignores its place. Jesus points for the people the drama being produced by these faithless "chief priests and scribes." They writhed in the heat of the truth he taught. "In that same hour they sought to lay their hands on him but they feared the people. They knew that against them he spoke this parable."

By the parable Jesus taught the people, warned the leaders, affirmed his own place as son in God's plan and revealed that God was giving his vineyard to "others." Theophilus would react well to the idea of "others."

AN OUTLINE OF LUKE 20:20-26
Giving to Government and God!
Though Israel's leaders "feared the people" and thus failed
to "lay their hands upon him in __that__ hour" they proceeded to
elevate their efforts to entrap Jesus. At the same time they
sought to foil the power of the people.
I.   THE QUESTION OF ATTACK! 20:20-22
      1. Their motive: entrapment! 20
      2. Their manner of attack: flattery! 21
      3. The question: "Lawful to give taxes to Caesar?"
II.   THE CHRIST'S ANSWER. 20:23-25
      1. His evaluation of their motive. 23
      2. His method of measuring the answer. 24
      3. His answer to __their__ question. 25a
      4. His answer to __his__ concern. 25b
III. RESULTS OF THE CONFRONTATION. 20:26
      1. The leaders defeated "before the people." 26a
      2. They (a)"marvelled" (2)"Got silent!!"
To the question Jesus gave full answer. Besides, he taught
the "people" to return to God "the image of God" in them.

* * * * * * *

GIVING TO GOVERNMENT AND GOD!
The "scribes and chief priests" became infuriated at Jesus
because he so plainly identified them as murderers of the
"son" and who cast him out of God's vineyard. And though they
"sought to lay their hands on him in that very hour" they
restrained themselves because they "feared the people." But
this only fueled the fires of their hate. They immediately
plotted a series of attacks. Both political and religious
doctrines furnished points of attack. Pharisees, Herodians,
Sadducees joined forces in several waves of assault, the first
of which is the question of tribute to Caesar.
The Question About Tribute!
Luke ignores the fact that the Herodians and Pharisees
joined forces in this attempt to discredit Jesus. Their aim
was to drive a wedge between Jesus and people. They also
hoped to snare Jesus in words disloyal to Rome.
Clearly their motive was entrapment. They "watched him
maliciously." With unremitting persistence they scanned every
move, listened to his every word. They wanted to "catch" some
inadvertent self-betrayal in deed or speech. They employed
spies to counterfeit loyalty to him. They hired "liers in
wait" who pretended dispassionate fairness and justice. They
"played the hypocrite" feigning fair play but with the secret
purpose of "laying hold of his __word__. The ultimate aim was "to
deliver him to the jurisdiction and power of the governor."
Evil always conceals its real goals under the cover of the
pretense of justice. Ill-will displays its evil as though it
were good! Sin likes to be seen as righteousness!

With honeyed words these hypocritical politicos tried to play on the ego of Jesus by saying, "Teacher, we know that accurately you are speaking and teaching and do not receive the person. But upon truth you are teaching the way of God." Such fawning flattery hopefully would leave Jesus vulnerable to the trap set. Every man's insecurity is open to such stroking. With their view of Jesus why should he be any different from other men? So this slathering adulation was intended to disarm him from any defence against their attack.

Having executed their strategy of cajolery they proceeded with their baited question. "Is it lawful to give tribute to Caesar?" Among the people of Israel this was a burning issue. To pay or not to pay the detested Roman conquerer the hated poll tax provided constant controversy and induced sharp divisions. The party of Zealots violently opposed any tax to the overlord Gentile. The Herodians, ever loyal to the family of Herod, advocated payment. The Pharisees, while tolerant of the tax, would just as soon it be withheld. To them it contradicted Mosaic law and the traditions of history. By publicly proposing this live divisive issue the scribes hoped to force Jesus to identify himself with one side or the other. They could then charge him either with denial of the laws and traditions of Israel or with fomenting rebellion against Rome. In either case they could hand him over to the "jurisdiction and power of the governor." Was he a rabble rouser or a rebel against Rome?

The Christ's Answer!

Jesus met the question head on. He not only honestly answered _their_ question, but added a more basic factor. He used the opportunity to teach a more positive, more constructive foundation to human life. There is more to life than immediate current political issues. Life's foundation lies deeper than religious differences of the day. One's relationship to God is greater than that to government. In fact, a man's relation to God determines the validity and stength of his involvement with government.

Jesus turned the question back on the questioners. First, he challenged their intentions. With perceptive eye and penetrating thought he perceived their hypocrisy. He thought through the implications of their question. Luke avoids detailing that Herodians and other parties were among the questioners. He seems more interested in the question than the parties. Luke reports that Jesus, "Having perceived their craftiness..." In the face of such trickery Jesus disarms them by giving an honest forthright answer. "Show me a denarius." By asking for a denarius Jesus demonstrated that he did not have one. For them to delve into a money bag indicated that _they_ did have and use Rome's coin. In that society, as presently constructed, they could not do daily business without _using_ Rome's coin. If you oppose the _use_ why are you carrying and _using_ it? By so doing you acknowledge your dependence on Rome.

From the inconsistency of their usage Jesus turns to the basic principle involved. "Whose image and inscription does it have?" More than the abstract idea of government, or even Rome, is at stake. The Emperor as a person symbolizes the ideas and ideals of Roman society. The coin of the realm is more than a medium of exchange. It symbolizes by the image with which it is imprinted Roman law, order, and social values. Hence Jesus asked, "Whose image is inscribed on the coin?" The ideals of Roman society and authority were embodied, at least symbolically, in the living Emperor. So, the obvious answer of the interrogaters of Christ had to be "Caesar's!"

To this Jesus declared, "The answer to your question is clear. If this is Ceasar's, give it to Caesar. He furnishes a variety of services. You ought then pay back for those services. Return to Caesar what Caesar has given to you." (ἀπό compounded with δίδωμι "give" means "give back")

Had Jesus stopped at this point the questioners would have had their answer, complete, definitive and final. But Jesus had a greater concern. Government has its place, a divine place. "Be subject to the governing authorities. There is no authority except from God, and those that exist have been instituted by God."(Rom.13:1) Nations and their governments play an important and ongoing role in history as his eternal plan unfolds. Nevertheless, there is something more basic to God than governments. It is the recreating of that "image" lost in Eden. When Jesus asked, "Whose image is inscribed on the coin?" it not only brought to mind Caesar's image but prepared for Christ to introduce the greater "image" of one who governed where human governments fail. In the beginning, at the threshold of creation God stated, "Let us make man in our image..." And man was made with that lofty stamp. In fact, man began his career actually in the divine image. Had he not faltered by self-willed rebellion history would have been so different. Man would have ruled sublime at the head of a benign kingdom of gentility and righteousness. But alas! Eden became a disater. Man not only fell from his lofty "image" but he bequeathed sin as heritage to his descendents. And with sin came its accumulated suffering ending in universal death.

So it was not without design that Jesus added "...and (give back) the things of God to God!" Without question this addition was of special significance to Jesus. The bounty of God's giving to man is immeasurable. The creation with its myriad forms of living things are among God's gifts to man. But these fade into insignificance when we recall the divine image with which we were bequeathed. That is the "tribute" most pleasing to God and most helpful to man. With all your giving to governments don't fail to give back to God that which reaches his goal, not to say your highest privilege.

With what skill Jesus turns the shafts of evil into instruments of blessing. A venomous attack he transformed into

326

a reminder of man's creation "in the image and likeness" of his Creator. And by so doing he thwarted the attack of the leaders against him. Instead of his losing face it was they who felt the sting of defeat in public forum.

But it was more than defeat of enemies that Jesus achieved. If he didn't actually win some of his opponents as disciples he at least gained their admiration. Luke testifies that they "weren't able to ensnare his word...and they marvelled at his answer..." They recognized in him a skillful thinker, debater, intellectual whose grasp of God and human nature lay beyond the ordinary and usual. They "marvelled" not only at the content of his answer but the manner of his handling their advance against him.

We can only wonder whether any of these leaders of Israel became committed to him and his cause, if not before, at least after the Pentecost of Acts 2! At any rate Luke reports that for the present they "got silent." There was nothing more to be said. They were completely foiled in their effort to embarrass him or to distract the people from him! They retreated with chagrin.

In this episode the term "image" is the key to unlocking its secret. Nothing is more universal than the "image" of God in human nature. Even though it may seem marred beyond recognition nevertheless in each human being the image of God lies latent. Under proper conditions it may be roused to return to the image for which and in which it has been created. No one lies beyond the prospect of redemption. God has placed within each human the capability of recapturing the image of God for which he was made! In that lies the story of Jesus, his purpose in coming, his goal in suffering, his triumph over the tomb. In this figure of the "image" lies the summation of Luke's gospel for Theophilus. God became so thoroughly human that he might remake man to be thoroughly "like" him in his "image."

327

AN OUTLINE OF LUKE 20:27-40
Life in This Age and the Next!
"If a man die shall he live again?" And if so, under what
conditions? And what the relation, if any, between "this age
and the next?" Such issues are displayed in the question of
the Sadducees to Jesus relative to leverate marriage and life
that follows life!
- I.   A PROBLEM PROPOSED! 20:27-33
  1. The Sadducees' view of resurrection. 27
  2. Leverate marriage and life beyond life. 28-33
  (a)Moses' teaching.
  (b)The practical problem. Seven men having the
     same wife.
- II. THE ANSWER OF JESUS. 20:34-38
  1. "This age" and the "next age" contrasted. 34-36
  (a)Marriage in "this age" versus the "next."
  (b)Death in "this age" versus the "next."
  2. Moses said God is "Lord" of Abraham, Isaac, Jacob.
  3. God the "God of the living, not the dead."
- III. CONSEQUENCE OF THIS CONFRONTATION. 20:39-40
  1. Commended by "the scribes."
  2. "They were no longer daring to question him."

Ignorance of life beyond life furnishes no basis on which
to determine truth about "that age." Besides reading what
Moses says we must pierce the meaning of that which he says.

* * * * * * *

LIFE IN THIS AGE AND THE NEXT!
"If a man die shall he live?" That question furrowed the
brow of Cain when first he looked on the cold corpse of his
murdered brother. It knotted the soul of Adam and broke the
heart of Eve when they gently laid their dead son to rest in
the first grave known to man. No one has passed through this
vale of tears without facing for himself that question.

Man has come up with a variety of answers no one of which
sprouts from any first hand knowledge. The nature of the
problem, the almost total absence of hard evidence opens up
all manner of speculation. Prejudice, ignorance, desire,
personal experience in this age are the ingredients from which
we pool our ignorance to get uncertain answers about "that
age." Who has penetrated the life beyond life and come back
to give assured answers? Only in Jesus the Christ do we have
positive conclusive answers. And even his testimony is
questioned by much of the human race. Yet he alone claims to
have journeyed beyond the grave and returned with a sure word,
"Because I live you shall live!" On what grounds does he
build belief that life lies in "that age" beyond "this age"
here and now?

A Problem Posed!
In the present text for the first time in Luke's gospel the
Sadduccees are mentioned by name as among the opponents of

328

Jesus. The Pharisees were the more numerous party, occupying the synagogues and being the teachers of the people throughout the land. In contrast the Sadducees composed a nucleus for the Jerusalem temple priesthood. Tracing their lineage back to Eleazar, son of Aaron, they became a priest-lay aristocracy, a rigidly restricted circle of Hellenized Hebrews. They held the esteem of the well-to-do yet lacked any following with the people. They received as authority the five books of Moses but regarded the rest of the Old Testament with less force. Since they could discover no specific allusions to a resurrection in Moses they felt no compulsion to adopt a doctrine about a resurrection. That they had a continuing debate with the Pharisees as to a resurrection is not hard to imagine. And the argument with which they attacked Jesus appeared unanswerable. With such seemingly irrefutable logic they often discomfited the Pharisees. In it they had perfect proof, placing their viewpoint beyond denial.

Against this background Luke reported, "Certain of the Sadducees who were claiming there was no resurrection, asked him, saying, 'Teacher, If someone's brother should die, having a wife, and this one be childless, Moses wrote us that his brother should take his wife and raise up seed for his brother.'" Such a practice of leverate marriage (Deut.25:5) was still practiced by some in the first century A.D.

This reference to Deuteronomy 25:5 furnished the Mosaic authority for leverate marriage. To these Sadducees it also furnished the logical premise on which their denial of resurrection rested. To them the following dilemma admitted no possibility of resurrection. "There were seven brothers. And the first, having taken a wife, died childless. And the second and the third took her, but likewise also they did not leave children; and they died. Later the wife also died. So then, the woman, in the resurrection, became the wife of which one? For the seven got her as wife!"

We have observed that this was a stock argument in the Sadducean arsenal for warfare. It was their most lethal weapon in the battle of the resurrection. But their motive for using it against Jesus was to discredit him, not with the Roman governor, but with the Jewish people. They wished to vanquish Jesus with ridicule as a teacher of Mosaic law. If they could humiliate him as a teacher of the Deuteronomic code they might hope to undercut his influence with the public. Now Jesus must escape from the theological corner into which they had driven him.

The Answer of Jesus!

Matthew and Mark tell of the sharp rebuke with which Jesus turned on his adversaries. Luke emphasizes the substance of Christ's answer. Jesus' patient dignity comes through as he, without insult, reminds them of their ignorance. "The sons of this age marry and give in marriage, but those having been deemed worthy to obtain that age and the resurrection, that from the dead, neither marry or give in marriage."

329

We first note in Jesus' answer his dealing with "this age" and "that age" as axiomatic. That there be two such "ages" was self-evident to him. A "this age" without "that age" would leave God's creation corrupted and demonstrative of divine impotence and folly. What kind of Creator would allow such a world as "this age" and prepare no "coming age" to reclaim and redeem such an age as "this" has proved to be? To assume the two "ages" contributed to his answer to the dogmatic assertions of the Sadducees. Jesus did this by the authority expressed in voice and gesture.

But then Jesus called attention to the fact that they were uninitiated and hence unacquainted with "that age." Something as commonplace as artificially made ice and refrigeration in 20th-century America has been judged "impossible" by primitive peoples of undeveloped lands in this same century. Until I experience something it is "unusual" to say the least if not impossible. It is "unrealistic" until I personally experience its reality!

The Sadducees, with all their intellectual sophistication, were in precisely this condition. With only experience in "this age" they attacked One who had knowledge of "that age." And, according to Jesus, fundamental differences obtain between "this age" and "that age" that make it impossible for anyone who knows only "this age" to pass judgment on either the existence of or the differing conditions in "that age." Thus Jesus pointed to the practical value of marriage in "this age." In contrast marriage would be entirely extraneous to the conditions of life beyond this life. In picturing "that age" Jesus characterized it as "the resurrection from dead (bodies)." From a moral, spiritual point of view the "age to come" is already here having begun with the incarnation of the Christ. Yet from a physical point of view the "present age" extends until "the resurrection of dead (bodies)" of those "having been deemed worthy" by God "to attain that age." And after the resurrection of those dead ones, "they neither marry nor are they giving in marriage." Marriage has no place in the world to come. Jesus sustains that fact by declaring, "for they are not able to die any more." Death, being a thing of the past, marriage has lost its practical value. Furthermore, Jesus also states why these risen ones don't die any more: By the absence of death and the absence of marriage, "they are equal to angels."

Marriage in "this age" is for the stated purpose of preserving the human species. In the very beginning God said to "them," the male and female whom he had created, "Be fruitful and multiply and replendish the earth." (Gen.1:28) The male and female became "one flesh" in the marriage bond. Without marriage death would soon put an end to human kind. The family sustains the ongoing race. Apart from marriage, male and female have no distinctive function in the kingdom of God. Hence it is that "marrying and giving in marriage" has no place in the world to come.

Jesus points to another difference between the two ages. He gives the reason why marriage and death are no longer part of the life pattern of those who attain to the resurrection. He says, "and (they are) sons of God, being sons of the resurrection." He so indicates that men born into "this age" are sons by birth from marriage of a male to female. But in "that age" men are "sons of God" in that God gave them life and body by means of raising their dead bodies. In other words, the resurrection is effected by the command of God, not the marriage of a man and woman. Being "sons of the resurrection" they are "sons of God" and therefore not sons of a marriage relationship. This confirms that the "sons of resurrection" are "equal to angels." What bodies angels have come directly from the immediate omnipotence of God. So too do the bodies of men raised from the dead. God's creative power, not marriage, gives his "sons" bodies.

Having now established that the conditions of "this age" are not the critera on which the circumstances of "that age" can be determined, Jesus next turned to what Moses said about life beyond life. Since the Sadducees looked to Moses as their authority they should give strict attention to that which Moses actually said about living beyond "this age." "But that the dead are being raised Moses also revealed at the (burning) bush when he called the God of Abraham and God of Isaac and God of Jacob, Lord." It was an observable fact of history that Moses lived several centuries after the great patriarchs who formed the fountainhead from which flowed Israel, the people of God. Was God ruling over dead corpses all these years? To ask such a question is to answer it. "He is not God of dead (bodies) but of living (people!)." It's "living" spirits of living people with whom God has to do in the life beyond this life. The concept of God administering to dead bodies is implausible and unacceptable. To think of God as reigning over a cemetary is to make him a no-God! Bodies, not spirits, are buried in cemetaries. The spirit (breath) leaves the body at death. The spirit goes to live in the presence of God for, says Moses, "All are living to him!"

The dative idea of personal interest is prominent in "all are living to him." They live "for the praise of God," "the sake of God," "the service to God!" It could convey the idea of association "with God." In any case these people are not corpses. God is "living" and those of his creation, being in his image, are therefore "living to him."

Consequences of the Confrontation!

The threat of entrapment Jesus again turned into victory. Those who baited him were caught in the trap which they themselves set. His teaching ministry this final week thus became an offensive strike for truth. And some Pharisees, though opposing him during his ministry, praised the skill with which he routed the Sadducean hecklers. "Teacher, you spoke well." He won their respect if not their discipleship.

331

But even more important Jesus silenced all attempts to discredit him with the people. "For no longer were they daring to ask him anything." Their scheming plots to entrap Jesus left them as an army without arms or ammunition. They must either make peace or use more violent methods. From now they must mount a direct offensive through the religious and civil governments available.

So it has remained through the centuries. Each generation faces the reality of the Person of Jesus as God's Christ, man's saviour. The plans and plots of men to discredit him as God's message of redemption are foiled by the facts of history. When we listen to his answers to attempts to downplay the evidence we are left in the same situation as his questioners of old. We "no longer are daring to ask him anything!" We must accept what in fact we are, rebels against God, or yield to Him as Son of God, our Saviour!

* * * * * * *

AN OUTLINE OF LUKE 20:41-44
Why David Called His "Son" LORD?

God's ways are not man's ways. He made David's son and heir David's divine Lord. That reverses man's way. Men look on the son as heir apparent, not Lord Master. The father is the Lord Master!

I.   JESUS ASKS A QUESTION. 20:41
    1. "He said to them." 41a
    2. "How are they calling the Christ David's son?" 41b
II. THE WITNESS OF PSALM 110. 20:42-43
    1. The message of Psalm 110.
    2. David's witness in Psalm 110. 42b-43
III. A SECOND QUESTION OF JESUS. 20:44
    1. David Calls him "Lord."
    2. Why?

The Old Testament testifies to the divine nature of the promised Christ. If the scribes accept the witness of the Old Testament they must expect David's "son" to be divine in nature. That is the crucial issue.

* * * * * * *

WHY DAVID CALLED HIS "SON" LORD!

Jesus dealt with his Jewish enemies firmly but not with revenge in heart. His purpose at all times, even when reproving, was to bring them to repentance, a change of heart toward him and his word of redemption. He does not weep over their coming judgment. On the contrary he weeps over their blind resistance to God's offer of redemption. (Lk.19:41-44) In the present text he asks "them" a question, not trying to entrap or embarress them, but to enlighten them as to his nature as God's Messiah, their Saviour.

332

Jesus Asks "them" a Question!

At the baptism God identified Jesus as "my beloved son." John testified Jesus to be "he that cometh." One who "shall baptize you with the Holy Spirit." With growing clarity the Person of Jesus became the focus of conflict. Who is this Man? What is his relationship to God, Israel, Messiah?

Christ's was a bold thrust. During these days of teaching ministry in temple and Jerusalem he had openly demonstrated his right as keeper of the temple. He claimed divine sonship to God! In the parable of the wicked servants he had pointedly pictured himself as "beloved son."(20:14) And "they perceived that he spake this parable against them."(20:19) He survived wave after wave of attacks from every side turning each question into a teaching session. It was this bold assertion of sonship to God that formed the crux of the issue between Jesus and the scribal leaders of Israel. Their view of Messiah was faulty. Their reading of the Old Testament was colored with the current political, economic overtones.

That Messiah be king they saw aright. In his message of consolation to exiled Israel Jeremiah promised, "They shall serve the Lord their God and David their king, whom I will raise up for them."(30:9) Hosea speaks of the time when "after" being without "sacrifices" and such devices of worship Israel "shall return" and "seek the Lord their God and David their king."(3:5) From such texts how could Israel's leaders not expect Messiah to be king, "son" of David? Furthermore, Isaiah had said "a child is born, to us a son is given" who should be more than a mere mortal king. He would be "Wonderful counselor, Mighty God, everlasting Father..." (Is.9:10) It would indeed be difficult not to perceive prophetic intimations of a Messiah more than a frail human being in such words. The rigid monotheism of Israel made it difficult if not impossible for them to think of David's son, their Messianic king, to be more than a man, certainly not deity! Moreover, their materialistic, political environment dictated to them the kind of Messiah king they might expect. And that his kingdom was to be established as sovereignty over men's hearts was too spiritual for their sensual souls to grasp. They did not read the Old Testament prophecies clearly enough so as to see him as anything other than an earthly king of an earthly kingdom. Messiah as deity? the God of Abraham, Isaac, and Jacob? No way would they think a mere man to be the God of Israel! Could such instruments as kindness, gentleness, purity and love clash victoriously with Rome's mighty army and overcome? Preposterous! Perish the thought! And these leaders determined that any man who suggested such a thought himself should perish.

This situation lay at the heart of Jesus' question when he asked them, "How say they that the Christ is David's son?" By his question Jesus would divorce his enemies from the idea of a political Messiah. They must rid themselves of the error that the "son of David" would be only a human ruler.

The Witness of Psalm 110!

Luke reports, "But he said to them!" But he does not identify who this "them" is. He wants Theophilus to know that anyone who fails to perceive Jesus to be the Divine-Man misses the point of the incarnation. Man as man could never save man. It was God as man that opened the way to restore in man the divine image which he scarred and marred in Eden.

Together in individual lives, in sacrifice and institutional ceremony, in prophecy, psalm and symbol the person and work of Israel's Messiah-King was foreshadowed. The Hebrew world was amply provided with signs pointing toward the promised King. Embedded in the Old Testament lay Psalm 110, unmined. From it Jesus brought forth a sparkling jewel of truth that identified David's son as divine Lord!

Psalm 110 divides into two sections: (1)The Priest-King and his army(vss.1-4), (2)the king's triumphant warfare.(5-7) In the tradition of first century Israel David was the author. If not, the argument Jesus made was void of force since then David did not call his "son" "Lord." From Jesus' point of view David said, "The Lord (God) said unto my Lord (Master)." The term "Lord" was used when speaking to a superior. It certainly was not normal that a father speaking to a "son" would address him as "Lord" (Master). In the light of this the question Jesus raised is, Why "did the Lord (God) call my (David's) Lord (Master)...?" Since this was a Messianic Psalm on what grounds would David be speaking of his royal descendent (son) as "my Lord?" Not only was he, according to the Psalm, David's "Lord" but he was invited by God to share his divine throne as co-ruler. The authority and power of David's "Lord" was equal to and shared with that of the "Lord God." Such quality of rule would not be imposed on him as a mere human. He was something more than that!

In the ancient Near East a conquering king would often make a foot rest out of precious stone. Figurines carved in the pattern of enemies conquered on the field of battle served as shameful reminders to the king's enemies. With these sharply pointed words Jesus faced his enemies, "...sit thou on my right hand until I put your enemies as the footstool of thy feet." The chief point at issue was David's relationship to his "son." But Jesus kept before these "enemies" the part they were playing in rejecting David's "son." It was all a part of identifying David's "son" as someone more than a mere man.

A Second Question of Jesus!

Having thus prepared the groundwork for a final thrust, Jesus proposes a second and clinching question. "So then David calls him Lord; and how is he his son?" In the light of the Old Testament texts only one way can David call his son, a descendent, his superior "Lord" and Master. And that is if that "son" the divine co-ruler with the Lord God of Israel were in fact equal in nature, authority and power with God!

334

This analysis of the Psalm left Christ's enemies with no foundation. Either acknowledge him divine in nature, son of God, Messiah of promise, David's son and their king or become aware that they are confirmed rebels against Yahweh, the God of Israel's history. Jesus was God's son, their Christ or they had no Christ. Their whole history was a lie! Their scripture and his logic devastated them.

The Old Testament testifies to the divine nature of the promised Christ. Psalm 110 explicitly called David's son "Lord" thus identifying that son as God's divine Christ.

Not only is he Messiah, David's son, but he also shares sovereign rule over the universe, including the moral and spiritual universe. And as such he functions for fallen humanity as its only true priestly sacrifice. He offers himself as both sacrifice and priest in removing the stain, guilt and power of sin which has corrupted the whole human race. For that reason David recognized in his "son" the merging of the kingly and priestly functions. "The Lord has sworn and will not repent; You are a priest forever after the order of Melchizedek." (Ps.110:4)

The Person of Jesus was the crucial issue of the conflict between Jesus and the leaders of Israel be they Pharisees, Sadducees, scribes, or lawyers. This brief paragraph with the prominence it gives to Psalm 110, sums up in brief the entire ministry of Jesus not only to the Jew but also the Gentile. It appears obvious that Luke, being a Greek, writing to Theophilus, a noble Greek, wished to convey the universality of this Saviour for all mankind.

* * * * * * *

AN OUTLINE OF LUKE 20:45-47
Pretense and Practice of Piety!

The most effective tool for leaders is the practice of the ideal. Rhetoric is helpful, but example is the better teacher. Demonstration is the best description!

I. THE AUDIENCE ADDRESSED. 20:45
   1. While "the people were hearing!"
   2. He "said to the disciples."
II. THE DISPLAY! 20:46
   1. "Walking in robes."
   2. "Salutations in the marketplaces."
   3. "Chief seats in the synagogues."
   4. "First places at the banquets."
III. THE PRACTICE. 20:47a
   1. "Devouring widows houses."
   2. "Making long prayers."

To teach the truth is part of the function of a good leader. To demonstrate it in practice is even better. But God's greater verdict of judgment is on him who fails to practice the truth which he preaches!

PRETENCE AND PRACTICE OF PIETY!

The scribes, lawyers, Pharisees, and Sadducees have all been silenced. Jesus now turns to the task of warning against the life pattern of these professional religionists. "Take heed from the scribes" is his exhortation. Separate yourself from the pretense of piety! Nothing wrong in that which they say. Just don't be doing that which they do! Piety they describe but they don't demonstrate it!

The Audience Addressed!

"As all the people were hearing..." That to which the "people" had been listening was the war of words between Jesus and "them," the scribes, lawyers, and all who presumed authority over the "people." Most recent was his rout of the scribes by his question, "So David calls him Lord; how then is he his son?" As Luke develops his story this is that which "the people were hearing." Jesus was aware of "the people" and their need for warning. After all, it was people for whom he came into the world; it was people for whom he gave himself a sacrifice, it was people who were the goal of redemption. Jesus was not unaware of the people.

But in view of what "the people were hearing, he said to the disciples." It was "the disciples" who would fill the leadership roles in the kingdom of God under the New Covenant. The disciples must rise above the low level of purity seen in Israel's leaders of the Old Covenant. Leaders by the nature leadership are always subject to the temptation of show without substance. Thus the immediate audience of special need was his "disciples." To them he gave this warning!

The Display!

"Take heed!" Place your mind on the behaviour of Israel's leaders. Separate yourselves from their practice of piety for they display but don't do! They substitute appearance for reality. So separate yourselves "from" them in your conduct.

In four features they fake purity. They are "the ones wishing to walk in robes." These are those who believe that "dress makes the man." The "long robes" of which Jesus warned initially referred to clothes in general. But over time the word came to indicate priestly robes until it took on the meaning of the "outer cloak" which priests, lawyers, and public officials adopted as a fashionable mark a distinction. In modern circles the gaudy colors of academic doctoral robes may be cited as comparable. Any "wrong" in such a display was not in the robe, its brilliant colors, or its symbol of academic excellence. These things were and are morally neutral. The warning of Jesus was addressed to the personal love for such garish ostentation. Clothes are essential for refined graceful living. But they are to reflect the good taste and moral integrity of the wearer. Ornate display reveals a sickness of soul unbecoming to a follower of him who "had no place to lay his head." He whose purity of heart lies no deeper than the robe he wears lacks the "image" of God in which he was created!

336

They are also "ones loving salutations in the agora," the
marketplace. To be recognized by name at the super-market, to
have your name flashed on the marquee above the noisy hub-bub
of the stock exchange, the filling station, Wall-Mart or
Sears; to be so heralded as prominent in the commerce of the
day gives these self-seekers much social satisfaction. Their
ego loves it, devours it, can't live without it! One of their
chief aims is to have their names respected in bond-markets,
banks, and business houses. And to have their pictures appear
in the daily newspaper is the acme of social delight.

Besides that, they are the "ones loving the chief seats in
the synagogues." Their ego craves fulfillment in the local
places of worship. It's not so much God they seek to serve as
the prominent places in the front pews that men, not God, may
see them there. They like to _get_ worship, not _give_ it! Their
position _at_ the service determines the value of the Sabbath
rather than their relationship to God _during_ the worship.
They love the "chief-seats" not the truth! This is idol
worship at its worst. They have become their own god!

Finally they are the "ones loving the first places of honor
in their banquets." The constant round of evening dinners
were a regular part of these leaders' social activities. The
highest place of honor was that immediately across from the
host. Socially, it was worth a month's maneuvering to be
ennobled as the one chosen for the "first seat." To outrank
all other guests was an honor beyond which, socially, there
was no higher! What more could life offer than these four
prizes? Dress, public salutations, prominence in public
worship, lionized at country-club banquets! To attain first
rank in these areas of life identified them with "success,"
"righteousness," "piety."

The Practice!

As in all cultures through the ages these marks of human
values have been reserved for the few, not the masses. The
"people" may be more often identified with the poor, the
outcast, the handicapped. In ancient Hebrew society such
classes of "people" would be represented by the widow and
orphan. They had no one to champion their rights before king,
court, or society. They were the most helpless!

Jesus painted a picture of the scribes' conduct as they
related to widows. He pointed to two patterns of behaviour.
They, "devoured widows houses" and they "made long prayers."
Such practices hardly matched the "righteousness" of their
four dimentional display of personal "success."

"Devour" is a strong word. It literally means to "eat
down," "consume." The way these "pious" persons practiced
their widow-devouring" pillage took a variety of forms. They
might extract exhorbitant pay for legal aid. As lawyers the
scribes could and sometimes did, as legal guardians, cheat
widows of their rightful possessions. Or like gluttons, they
would scrounge like a parasite off of the limited means of a
widow. Some scribes would take as pledge the house and goods

337

of widows knowing full well that such women could never pay off the obligation.

As for the practice of "making long prayers for a pretext" the scribes found this as a perfect cover for their "devouring widows' houses." In public they made elaborate pretentious prayers pleading the cause of widows. At the same time, by their own duplicity, _they_ were "devouring widows' houses."

Such practices showed these pious frauds as samples of hypocricy nauseating to the "people." To these scribes the pompous display of dress, homage, prominence in church and club while consuming the resouces of widows seemed quite compatable. Any contradiction between flamboyant display and egoistic practice escaped them! To them, show and substance were one and the same. It is against just such muddled thinking and irrational practice that Jesus would warn his disciples. "Take heed from the scribes" was and is a constant concern for any who would accept leadership authority in the kingdom of God.

Where men are blind to the inconsistencies of their moral behaviour God's view is crystal clear. His verdict is fair but firm. Men judge "success" by outward appearance. God determines "success" by the moral and spiritual purity of motive and act. The thought of the heart, the purity of the intent, the chastity of the feelings, determine the virtue of the deed.

The warning of Jesus was justified because "These shall receive greater sentence of judgment." Between the scribes' display of righteousness and their practice there was an impassable chasm. Yet we note that both the display _and_ the practice were at fault. Such "success" in appearance was failure in fact!

"These shall receive greater judgment" raises the question, "Greater than _whom_?" It would have been better for these scribes had they not _pretended_ to be pious. Their pretence made judgment heavier. As scribes they had so many more opportunities for practicing purity than their fellow Israelites. Light or heavy judgment follows opportunity, little or much! Because they claimed greater "success" in righteousness they received greater verdict of guilt.

God's judgment on moral and spiritual deeds falls on every human being without favor. But part of each "deed" is the sincerety of the _motive_ that prompts the particular deed. "These (who pretend with no substance) shall receive greater sentence in judgment.

AN OUTLINE OF LUKE 21:1-4
Successful Giving!
How shall I dispose of the money that passes through my hands? Shall I save it? spend it? invest it? give it? What determines the successful management of money?

I. WHAT JESUS SAW IN THE TEMPLE! 21:1-2
   1. He saw the rich casting gifts into the treasury.
   2. He saw a poor widow casting in her living!
II. WHAT JESUS SAID IN THE TEMPLE. 21:3-4
   1. "This widow gave more than all!"
   2. Quality, not quantity measures the gift.

With God, more or less, is not measured in the number of dollars. It's indicated by the nobility of the giver!

* * * * * * *

SUCCESSFUL GIVING!
Money! How we acquire it? how we spend it? how we keep it? how we give it? how we dispose of it? These things not only make the man, they reveal the man. What money does to him who handles it is more important than what one does with the money he has! Life teaches that the money we keep we lose; that which we spend we have; that which we give we keep. In every respect money measures the man! When I spend money to purchase food, clothing, a house, a car or a book, I possess usable things vital to living in this world. I thus have what I've spent. But when I keep my money it is of no value in and of itself. It lies useless in the safety vault, bank, or pocket until I spend it or give it away. It is lost to me! And even when it is spent it begins immediately to decay and disintegrate and disappear. But the only permanent money I possess is that which I give away. The money I give supports life in all its needs to someone else. As long as the life to whom I give goes on living it is mine to enjoy. In the knowledge that I have contributed to that life I live in someone else. No one can rob me of that joy. It is part of me forever!

What Jesus Saw in the Temple!
"And when he looked up he saw the rich casting into the treasury trumpets their gifts. But he (also) saw a certain needy widow casting there two thin coins!" Jesus saw the rich and the poor giving gifts.

In the preceding paragraph Luke mentioned both the wealthy and the widows. Jesus thoroughly castagated the life style of the well-to-do "scribes." He particularly noted their "devouring of widows' houses" while hiding behind the veil of "making long prayers." After his long teaching sessions ended he "sat" exhausted and in pensive meditation. He watched the people, rich and poor, cast their gifts into the thirteen trumpet-shaped "treasuries." He measured both the motives and the gifts of the givers. The sum which the many "rich" gave differed from the sum which a "certain widow" gave!

339

What Jesus Said in the Temple!

Jesus saw the liberality of the rich (plural) casting their gifts. He heard the clinking of their many coins clattering down the metal treasury trumpets. He casually summed up the total of their many sizeable gifts. It was an unusually large sum of money! The functions of the temple could not be fulfilled without this generous support.

Then he fastened attention on a "certain poor widow" as she cast in her "two thin coins," (a "mite"). He calculated the sum total of her gift as measured against theirs. And ever since, what he said has startled the world. His observation seems unreal to the "real" world. It appears out of keeping with the standards of the business community in any age. It is irrational, illogical, unsound, not to say insanely stupid.

If we speculate on the differences between the gifts of "the rich" and that of this penurious widow the incredible absurdity of what Jesus said appears clear. To one whose income is measured in thousands and whose possessions total in millions a gift of one thousand dollars is hardly a ripple on the surface. By such a gift no one could conceivably experience a shortage of money. By material standards "sacrifice" is foreign to vocabulary or thought. It was of such people as these whom Jesus watched with increasing gravity. Yet that which amazed him most was not the amount of the gifts of the wealthy. It was that of the lone widow. That which he said was: "This poor widow gave more than they all."

No standard by which "success" is measured in "this age" can justify Jesus' judgment. The gift of even one "rich" person would be a greater amount than the gift of one such destitute widow. How could Jesus possibly say that she gave "more" than they all?

Jesus does not ignore this problem which his words would provoke. His full statement is, "Truly, I say to you that this poor widow cast more than they all, for these out of their abundance cast unto the gifts, but this one, of her lack, cast all her livelihood which she was having." We need not think that this frail woman gave her grocery money or that she failed to pay her rent. Not at all! She hardly had enough to pay these necessities for eaking out a bare living. But out of this meagre allowance, she kept nothing beyond for herself. She gave her entire remaining livelihood. In contrast "the rich" did not have to calculate carefully whether they would have enough for groceries, rent, clothing, health, insurance, or retirement. They had a superfluity of invested money to care for such things and more! They gave out of their "abundance." Out of her lack she gave beyond her means!

Considering all these factors the question still remains: How can Jesus say that this widow gave "more than they all?" The sum of all their gifts would be in the thousands of dollars. That which she gave remains "two small coins" about one cent in value!

340

Jesus' standard of measurement is radically different than that of "this age." The total which "the rich" gave was not the sum that went into the temple treasury. It is rather to be gauged by the amount which is left after they cast their money into the receptacles.

He who gets $500 each week for labor done, if he tithes to the Lord, gives $50.00. He retains $450. When he who earns $100 each week tithes he gives $10.00. He retains $90.00. In terms of dollars given the $500 man gives $40 more than the $100 man. But in terms of that which each had left after giving, the $100 man had $90 while the $500 man had $450. Percentage wise each gave the same. But in terms of what is held back the $100 man gave about four and a half times _more_ than the $500 man. Besides, "the rich" retained abundant capital for safety and investment. So he who has nothing after giving gives _more_!

Thus with the poor widow. She had nothing left after she cast in her "two thin coins." The rich felt no depreciation in their ability to carry on investments, business, social obligations or any other such normal human activity. The rich gave little out of their enormous surplus. Out of her poverty the widow gave "all her living" and had nothing left over. By kingdom standards she gave the "most."

The story of this unnamed widow leaves another imprint on Theophilus, the reader. The glory of man as a creature of God is his recognition and sensitivity to his dependence on God as Creator. Poverty may be a curse if a man allows it to give birth to anxious care. The presence of much money tends to generate dependence on the money rather than the God who gives us the means to accumulate money. We tend to look to money as our security. Poverty becomes a blessing in disguise if and when it compels us to cast ourselves on God who governs all providences in human life. "Cast thy burden on the Lord, and he will sustain thee: he will never suffer the righteous to be moved."(Ps.55:22) That promise of God takes root more readily in the heart of the helpless "poor widows" of the earth than in "the rich." The very presence of poverty leaves one consciously dependent on the promises of God.

Money may be the "root of all evil" but the lack of it is the soil out of which grows much good!

AN OUTLINE OF LUKE 21:5-37
Signs of Judgment and the Kingdom!
When Jesus said "The kingdom of God is within you" he spoke
of God's sovereign rule <u>within</u> the hearts of believers. But
the kingdom also has outward visible aspects. "Signs" signal
it, particularly its visible coming at the consummation of
history when Messiah comes in his "second" advent. Ever since
the Christ's first advent ending in his violent rejection by
Israel such signs have appeared repeatedly.
- I.   JESUS ANNOUNCES COMING JUDGMENT. 21:5-7
    1. "Certain ones" admire the magnificent temple. 5
    2. Jesus says, "stone on stone shall not be left!" 6
    3. A two-fold question: 7
       (a)"When shall these things be?"
       (b)"What the <u>signs</u> when these things shall come?"
- II. JESUS ANSWERS THE TWO-FOLD QUESTION. 21:7-24
    1. Don't read signs superficially! 8-9
    2. Persecution amid tumult of nations. 10-19
       (a)Conditions of the persecutions.
       (b)Promises during persecutions.
    3. Signs of judgmental destruction of Jerusalem.20-24
       (a)Armies encircling Jerusalem. 20
       (b)Behaviour & condition of citizens. 21-24
- III. THE COMING OF THE SON OF MAN. 21:25-30
    1. Signs of "the son of man coming!" 25-28
    2. Lesson from the fig tree. 29-30

Be watching! Be alert! Don't allow personal pleasures,
social indulgences or business interests to trap you unawares!
Don't allow international "tumults" and warring rivalries
terrify you, "for it is necessary that these things be first,
but the end (goal) is not immediate." God's eternal goal must
be attained before the termination of history.

* * * * * * * *

SIGNS OF JUDGMENT AND THE KINGDOM!
When God said, "Let us make man in our own image" he had a
well defined goal in mind. In the words of Paul, "he selected
us in him before the foundation of the world <u>that</u> we should be
holy and blameless..."(Eph.1:3-4) His goal was and is to have
a family of children fashioned "in his image." History shall
not terminate until that goal is achieved. God is present
providentially maneuvering "all things together" to fulfill
his goal. He is weaving a pattern and, in spite of broken
threads, will not stop until the fabric is complete.
Jesus Announces Coming Judgment!
In Christ's last week of public ministry while teaching in
the temple "certain ones" were admiring the architectural
beauty of the temple. Its adornments and votive offerings
enriched greatly this holiest house of Israel. Its immense
stones and measurements made it one of the wonders of the
world. Jewish pride over this temple atop Zion knew no
bounds. It was the heart and core of Israel's sense of unity

as the people of God. From their point of view if that temple should fall it would be the end of the age, the consummation of history.

As Jesus heard the spoken words about "beautiful stones" and how the temple was adorned with "votive offerings" he saw behind the beauty to the sad moral conditions that told of impending doom. He declared, "These things which you are beholding, days shall come in which a stone on a stone shall not be left which shall not be cast down!" What a shocking impossibility! Not only was the temple the symbol of God's presence but thereby the sign of the stability of Israel and it's place in history.

For the temple to fall was for the world to fall! Yet in this very discourse Jesus claimed his authority as that of God: "My words shall not pass away!" His demeanor, voice, gesture and person gave conviction to his word, "stone on a stone shall not be left which shall not be cast down."

To this appalling announcement the disciples responded with a wondering question. "Teacher, when then shall these things be? And what the sign whenever these things are about to become?" To them the threatening announcement of Jesus could only refer to two simultaneous events, namely, the destruction of Jerusalem and the end of the world. Therefore, they posed a double-barrelled question. "When shall these things be? And what the sign when these things shall happen?"

We who live in the 20th century know that the pulverizing of Jerusalem by Rome occurred in 70 A.D. We also recognize that, though throughout history the world has seen many such cities and civilizations crumble and fall, the world still stands, howbeit on tottering foundations. Without question Jesus knew that it would be a long time, as men count time, before God reached his predetermined goal. God is patiently long-suffering as he works out his eternal purpose. It would be a long time before he, as the Christ, would return to inaugurate the final phase of the kingdom of God.

Jesus Answers The Two-fold Question!

In his answer to their inquiry Jesus first warns against a hasty attachment to anyone who presents himself as a national leader or world saviour. The desperate need of humanity and the prophetic hope for a Messiah leaves the door open to charlatans to deceive the hurting hearts of human beings. "Beware lest you be led astray!" Don't let your need blind you to the selfish exploitation of false Messiahs. Jesus has always had imitators who rob the souls of men. Self-centered egos are quite capable of fakery, deceit and false imitations. The reality and fact of the perfect Christ makes possible counterfeit Christs! "Many shall come in my name!" Late in the first century A.D. the venerable apostle John gave testimony to the need for this warning of Jesus. "Just as you heard that antichrist comes, even now many antichrist have come."(I Jn.2:18) Such false Christs have appeared in every generation since. The warning is still pertinent!

343

The tumultuous times surrounding the doom of Jerusalem pointed immediately to the destruction of the temple and all semblance of Jewish nationalism. That took place in 70 A.D. But beyond this primary reference such savage ragings were a pattern to be repeated in the judgment and fall of many succeeding cultures. Moreover, they embodied similar signs and pains that would appear at "the end" when the Christ would return for judgment and salvation. What Jesus says here about the coming destruction and desolation of Jerusalem has within it the wider revelation of "the coming of the son of man."

"Whenever you hear of wars and tumults, don't be terrified; for it is a logical necessity that these things happen first, but not immediately is the end," the destiny for Jerusalem or the world! The final destination of temple and its city must be judgment or redemption! Jesus declares that because of Israel's failure to obey the moral forces of God's law, judgment was inescapable. God must develop another "people" to reach his eternal goal (end).

Jesus continued his warning! "Nation against nation and kingdom against kingdom shall rise up, and both great earthquakes and plagues and famines in place after place shall come. And both terrors and great signs from heaven shall be!" Such turmoil must preceed the "end" of Jerusalem, not to say the "end-goal" of history. To his immediate audience Jesus was alluding to the ominous signs of Jerusalem's demise just over history's existing horizon. But these self-same signs would reappear as the end-goal of history approached.

For the coming judgment on Jerusalem a warning about persecutions was timely. "Before all these things they shall cast their hands on you and they shall persecute, delivering into synagogues and prisons, leading you off before kings and governors on account of my name. It shall turn out to you for a testimony, an opportunity for you to witness to your faithfulness to me. So don't put in your hearts to prepare a defense. I will give to you word and wisdom by which all opposing you shall not be able to withstand or answer."

Once again, the immediate application of this warning was the fierce persecutions that the enemies of the Christ would heap upon believers as the "end" of Jerusalem drew nearer. Official persecutions were to be expected. That darkness resent light is no surprise. And that evil use violence against the good is to be expected. But the source of some of the deadly torture is surprising. It would add emotional hurt to physical violence. "You shall be delivered up by parents and brothers and kinsmen and friends." For Satan and his minions to attack God's people is not surprising. But for family and friends to betray, persecute and kill would be more than surprising; it would be shocking to the heart! Luke's Acts of the Apostles witnessses to the beginning of these persecutions before 70 A.D. That "you shall be hated by all on account of my name..." has distressed every generation since!

Signs of Destruction of Jerusalem!

But there were certain signs that clearly would indicate that the "end" of Jerusalem was imminent: "Whenever you shall see Jerusalem surrounded by armies of footsoldiers, then you may recognize that her desolation has drawn near." When Rome's armies appeared encamped around Israel's ancient holy city the divine goal for that center of Israel's history shall have been reached. From then it, at most, shall serve as symbol of the real center of God's goal for all His Israel, people of all ages, nations, and cultures.

But that generation must take heed and recognize the "signs" and act appropriately. "Then those in Judea are to flee unto the mountains, and those in the midst of her must get out, and those in the fields are not to enter into her, for these are the days of vengeance to fulfill all things having been written. Woe to those pregnant and those nursing in those days for there shall be great distress upon the earth and wrath against this people. And they shall fall by the mouth of the sword and they shall be captured by all nations, and Jerusalem shall be tramped down by nations until the times of the nations shall be fulfilled."

Whatever "the times of the nations" may mean there is no question but that this passage clearly alludes to the fall of Jerusalem at 70 A.D. This primarily describes the suffering of Jerusalem and its population as the moral result of having such open opportunity of knowing the promised Christ, yet having rejected him as the Christ.

Thus Jesus answered the basic question as to "when these things shall be?"(vs.7) Luke is writing for a Gentile reader. The moral principles that led to the downfall of Jerusalem he clearly sets forth. Ignoring those principles, either through ignorance or deliberate intent, issued in the inevitable fruit of carnage and razing to the ground. In the case of Jerusalem the fruit was utter destruction. But the moral conditions that prevailed and brought on that destruction are universal and repeat themselves each time a civilization embodies the same immoral elements. God reigns! He reigns in each city, people, nation on similar moral principles. The harvest is always the same. The rise and fall of each empire is written in the history of Israel and its holy city. But the final "end-goal" toward which history is working is "not yet!"

The Coming of the Son of Man!

Though his questioners thought the "end" of Jerusalem was to be identified with the "end" of the world these two events, as time has testified, were in fact many centuries apart. Jesus was well aware of that fact. So beginning at verse 25 Jesus began dealing with the signs relating to "the coming of the son of man." He declares, "And signs shall be in sun and moon and stars and upon the earth distress of nations in perplexity in roaring of the sea and tossing; men fainting from fear and expectation of the things coming on the inhabited earth, for the powers of the heavens shall be

345

shaken." These "signs" are different from those heralding the destructive "end-goal" of Jerusalem. These are world-wide, universal in scope. Here before the "end-goal" of history the entire inhabited earth shall fall headlong into grievous turmoil. Noticeable disturbances in the heavenly bodies shall appear. Tidal waves at sea shall leave human beings "fainting from fear and expectation of the things coming on the entire inhabited earth; for the forces of the heavens shall be shaken." All these powers of creation shall terrify all peoples! But it is "then that they shall see the son of man coming in a cloud with power and great glory." In spite of delays and seemingly disruptions in ongoing history there is in fact a predetermined goal toward which God is directing history. And the point of demarcation is the public, visible appearance for the second time on this earth of "the son of man," Jesus the Christ. Not only here but Luke states again in Acts 1:11, "This Jesus, the one having been taken up from you into heaven, will come in similar manner as you beheld him going into heaven." A second visible appearce of the Christ shall mark the "end-goal" of His-story launched at Eden and consummated at a specific point in time! And at that point time shall yield to eternity!

When these cosmic signs emerge into view and they "begin to happen," as believers you "shall stand up straight and lift up your heads, because your redemption draws near." The term "redemption" literally means "release." Quite a picture! At best, life in this world is a binding and hindrance of our God-given creative powers of life. Sin restricts our freedom to reach latent divine goals within us. Once sin has been slain, bound, and cast, with its author, into the lake of fire and brimstone, the redeemed shall be truly "released" to the freedom for which children of God(man) have been created. When these cosmic signs become visible Christian believers may take heart that the "end" is at hand.

Such "signs" will be visible, concrete, defineable. To enforce this Jesus added a simple parable that would be clear to any person sensitive to the spiritual realities. "Behold the fig tree and all the trees! Whenever they shall blossom forth, you shall recognize from yourselves that already the summer is near. Thus also you, whenever you see these things happening, you recognize that the kingdom of God is near." Though the signs indicating the tragic fall of Jerusalem fit its peculiar judgment, yet reappear in the fall of any similar civilation's demise, the "signs" of the "second coming" have a broad universalism peculiar to the ultimate "end" of history. They will be distinctly recognizable!

According to this word of Jesus these "end" signs are such that they announce "the kingdom of God is near." We note that "kingdom of God" may refer to the reign of God "within" the human heart. But it also, as here, may refer to the outward, visible, politico-religious institution of God's reign over redeemed society. It's just such a final society of the

346

redeemed to which Jesus alludes here in speaking of "the
kingdom of God is near." It is one and the same as that of
which John speaks in Rev.21:2,5, "I saw the holy city, new
Jerusalem, coming down out of heaven...Behold I make all
things new." And that this is as certain as God himself Jesus
underscored with his personal assurance: "The heaven and the
earth shall pass away, but my words shall not pass away."

Whether the reader of Luke's Gospel be the generation
living at Jerusalem's destruction in 70 A.D. or that at the
second advent, an appropriate exhortation would be similar:
"Take constant heed to yourselves lest your hearts be weighted
down in carousing and drunkenness and cares pertaining to
livelihood, and that day shall rush upon you as a snare." But
the "second coming" would have distinctive features suitable
only to a cosmic universalism. "For it shall come upon all
those dwelling on the face of all the earth."

Time and eternity are two dimensions of existence. For
those of us who have only experienced time, eternity is
difficult to envision. Our minds "stop" at a given point. We
measure time with a beginning and an end; by seconds, minutes,
hours, days, weeks, years, etc! Eternity has neither
beginning or end. That's hard to conceive! The very fact that
each day comes and goes in our experience as it always has we
expect time to keep moving along at its regular pace. It's
for that reason we can be lulled into false security. Twenty
centuries have come and gone and time moves along at its
steady pace. Yet there stands the word of Christ, "You shall
see the son of man coming in a cloud with power and great
glory."

There comes a point at which "time" and "eternity" meet and
time shall be swallowed up in eternity. Time shall cease to
be. It is at that point when Christ shall come again to
earth. For all practical purposes each generation of humans
as it lives during its "time" is the "last" generation. For
the period of "its" appearance on earth it is its own "last"
generation. Therefore Jesus exhorted, "Be always taking heed
to yourselves..." Don't be overcome with "carousing parties
and drunknness, and business cares pertaining to living."
Should the believer's heart be doped by these distractions,
"that day shall rush upon you like a snapping of a baited trap
upon all those dwelling on the face of all the earth." He
shall make a sudden universal appearance.

Two areas of Christian experience must be maintained
without break: (1)"Watch!" Be ever alert! (2)"Praying..!"
Keep your eyes open and your heart praying. And this watchful
praying shall encompass two specifics: (1)strength "to flee
all these things about to happen." (2)Strength "to stand
before the son of man." To escape the down-drag of the
world's attractions and to gain power to stand before the Lord
Christ as redeemer of conscience is the reward for always
being alertly watchful. These are the concerns of time and
eternity!

347

SPECIAL NOTE ON LUKE 21:32!

"Verily I say unto you that this generation shall not pass away until all things happen!"

To what does "this generation" refer in this passage? Various commentators have come up with a motley assortment of interpretations. They include:(1)The contemporary generation of which Jesus was a part. (2)The Jewish people as a race. (3)All humanity. (4)The generation living at the appearance of the "end" signs. (5)A kind of men, a type that reproduces and duplicates itself in many life-spans from his first coming until the second coming.

Any one of these meanings has its supporters. That very fact suggests that each explanation appears logical, given a specific context and a personal point of view from which to start. A determining factor must include the significance of the expression, "end-goal is not yet" of 21:9.

At creation God had a goal in mind. Though the sin of Eden thwarted, it did not defeat God's goal. It changed his method. No longer creation in Christ, now it must be redemption in the Christ, the λόγος!

In the synagogue at Nazareth Jesus stated: "Today this scripture has been fulfilled."(Lu.4:21) That which happened in Israel's rejection of their Christ found its fruit in the destruction of Jerusalem in 70 A.D. But in his crucifixion and resurrection lay the seed of redemption, the "end-goal" of God's eternal purpose before and at creation. The signs that marked the destruction of Jerusalem were a prefiguring of the "end" toward which God moved throughout history. The same signs are to appear with added heavenly universal portents when men "shall see the son of man coming in a cloud with power and great glory."

In view of this fact any one of the five meanings listed above has some merit. If the expression "this generation" appeared in verses 20-24 in which the fate of Jerusalem was described, the logical reference would be to the generation then living of which Jesus was a part. But it appears here in the verses that describe disturbances in heavenly bodies of creation, universal disturbances. Furthermore verse 31 just preceding the phrase "this generation," speaks of "the kingdom of heaven is near." The "this generation" of verse 32 seems to be related to and based on the thought in verse 31 about the nearness of "the kingdom of God."

Luke was writing to a Gentile audience. To such an audience he says, "This generation shall not pass away until all things come to pass (happen)." The other Synoptics state, "all these things." Luke doesn't limit which things "shall come to pass" by "these." He makes it universal when he says, "all things.

Explanation number four(4) above seems the most natural meaning in Luke's report of this saying of Jesus.

Responsibility in the Plot to Kill Jesus!
Are men pawns or puppets in fulfilling the will of an Evil
Despot? Or are they self-willed actors creating the tragedy
that is life?
I. THE PLOTTERS. 22:1-2
1. The occasion: Passover Feast. 1.
2. Man's search: "How they might destroy him!" 2
3. Restrained: "For they were fearing the people." 2b
II. SATAN AND JUDAS, THE HUMAN! 22:3
1. The Role of Satan. 3a
2. The role of Judas, "being of the twelve." 3b
III. THE "WILL" OF GOD AND THE PLOTTERS. 22:4-6
1. The pact made: "How he might deliver him!" 4
2. The price! 5
3. The search for a suitable opportunity. 6

Sin and its awesome quality of evil finds its origin in the
universe of spirit that environs the moral world of man. But
man must bear his individual responsibility for its powerful
presence in his own experience. Satan may be the author but
man is his willing tool. And even being "called" to the Lord's
most intimate company cannot, of itself, guarantee freedom
from the corruption and destruction of sin.

* * * * * * *

RESPONSIBILITY IN THE PLOT TO KILL JESUS!
Of the Synoptic writers Luke is the only one who reports
that it was Satan who "entered into" Judas and led him to the
betrayal of Jesus. That raises the important question as to
human responsibility for sin. Are we puppets whose movements
are dependent on him who pulls the strings. Or are we "free"
to make choices for which we alone are responsible. Are we
pawns on the chessboard of life or are we soldiers who fight
our own battles and determine our own destiny?
The Plotters!
"The feast of the unleavens, the one being called Passover,
was drawing near." This is the setting in which the supreme
drama of human history takes place. It was a sacred time
commemorating the deliverance of Israel from the Pharoah's
Egyptian captivity. It was during this holy feast that the
present leaders of Israel "were seeking how they might destroy
him" whom God designated as "the lamb of God."
That Jesus was to be destroyed was already determined in
the minds of these "chief priests and scribes." "Were
seeking" indicates repeated action. Theirs was a complicated
and ongoing problem. When, where and how were they to get rid
of this pretender to Messiah's claims? Their position was
aggravated by the favor in which Jesus was held by "the
people." And these leaders "were fearing the people." A
revolt by the "people" would jeopardize their position not to
say their bodily safety. What were they to do?

As the "chief priests and scribes" weighed and discarded each possibility they drifted into sharp conflict on <u>how</u> to rid themselves of Jesus. One proposal after another was dismissed as impractical or too perilous. The presence of many from Gallilee where Jesus was popular with the people made their task treacherous. They found no agreement on how to proceed. Nothing was fool proof; they were stymied in their efforts to destroy Jesus.

<u>Satan and Judas</u>!

An unexpected windfall resolved the perplexity. Judas, one "of the twelve," startled the schemers with a singular yet welcome solution to their evil conspiracy. "Satan entered into Judas, the one called Iscariot, being one of the twelve." In their conspiring it seemed unlikely that one of the intimates of Jesus could resolve their depraved intent. Yet here was a man fully aware of all movements, plans, and purposes of this Jesus. And by his very offer of betrayal, he revealed his own disenchantment with Jesus. In a word, he was actually changing sides between the pretender and their purpose. "And he, when he had gone off, spoke with the chief priests and soldiers <u>how</u> he might deliver him to them."

Luke is the sole Synoptic writer who introduces "Satan" as the motivating cause of this disciple's betrayal of his Master. To his Gentile reader Luke was suggesting that spiritual powers beyond the human personality were at work in the moral atmosphere in which humanity must live and work. The diabolical deeds, the wicked imaginations, the moral depravities of human behaviour could only be accounted for by such a dominant spirit as a <u>Satan</u>. Luke seems to say that "Satan <u>entered into</u>" Judas and took possession of him to the extent of controlling him! How can this be and yet Judas be responsible for his heinous deed?

Two factors must be considered. First, The statement by God at creation concerned making "man in our image." Though man was and is a "creature" he is "like" his creator. That is, he is capable of weighing moral values and choosing between right and wrong. However the evil Satan exercises his poisonous powers he must persuade, motivate, influence a man to do his knavish bidding. God's exhortation to our fallen ancestor was "sin couches at the door:and unto you shall be its desire, but <u>do thou rule over it</u>." Even though fallen under the power of evil, man has the moral power and responsibility to "rule over it." Though weakened, wounded, and bruised man retains the obligation to choose.

An analogy of Satan "entering into" a man may be seen in relationships between two men. A friend comes and "enters into" a fraudulent scheme with a friend. The stronger person makes decisions that effect the integrity of the less dominant. But before a court of law, not to say human conscience, each is responsible. Every man is answerable for allowing another to make <u>his</u> choice in any matter. When "Satan enters" <u>we allow</u> it!

350

A second factor underscores and thus emphasizes that drawn from the first, "We allow it!" True, "Satan entered" but only by permission of the one into whom he sought entrance. When Satan knocks at the door of my soul I am not forced to open; I can ignore him; I can refuse to listen to his urgent thumping. It is he not I who asks for entrance. No one compels me to respond! Man still controls his own destiny.

But forces of righteousness are available to encourage and strengthen a man in his resistance to Satan's advances. The fact that a man fails to call on these positive powers of God reflects the degree to which Satan can "enter" a human. That Judas was "of the twelve" shows how deeply he had welcomed Satan's approach. Judas abused the brotherhood which "the twelve" offered. He had become calloused, resistant to the call of fellowship, blinded to the power of the Person of the Christ. The soil of his soul became pliable toward evil suggestions of a Satan! To betray a friend is a lower moral level than to attack an enemy! Judas fell deeper into depravity than those to whom he betrayed the Christ.

The Will of God and That of the Plotters!

Judas came with a definite plan as to "how he might deliver him." The plotters "rejoiced and arranged to give him money." That Judas would perform his perfidy "apart from the crowd" relieved the priests of personal danger and assured the success of the plot. Judas' plan lifted them from prime moral liability. The price in money was minimal; in moral value, though it left its' dark scar, it shifted the major role to the betrayer. Who was betrayed spread moral responsibility to "man" in equal measure.

But the chief point of this whole perverted event lies in the fact that man's plot became God's method of fulfilling his goal. That God "works all things for good"(Rom.8:28) is a dictum of Paul. And he wrote it before Luke penned his Gospel. The plotting of the Jewish leaders, the betrayal of Judas, and God's meshing together of these human forces reveal God's providential rule. "The priests and scribes were seeking (repeatedly) how they might destroy him." "Satan entered..." and Judas "spoke with the highpriests...how he might deliver him." And God, the master weaver, "worked all (these) things together for good," God's goal, which is man's redemption!

Though startling such is God's normal way of working "all things for good." Among the ills to which man is heir death is the ultimate. At creation it was not God's intent that human beings die. That was man's choice! Our first parents were fully warned: "You shall not eat...lest you die." But they "did eat." At that moment they "hid themselves" from God and death began its lethal assault. Yet from the beginning God turned humanity's ill choices unto his own divine ends. The pains of sin God recast into lessons of life. Men of God have profited in character from their own loss of rectitude. By living through this mortal experience they have learned to live for immortal hope.

Babylon, its political power and military might, proved to be one of the greatest empires in the ancient world. It stood in fact and symbol as the giant enemy of Israel, God's people. It became the power that defeated Judah on the field of battle and carried captive the strength of its citizenry in 586 B.C. It was Babylon's purpose to destroy Israel's culture from the roots up. Yet Babylon impressed itself on Hebrew destiny as much or more than any other in antiquity. Besides earlier ideas, influences and persons the great Captivity of 586 helped shape the religion, economy, and forms of thought on all succeeding generations of Jewry.

A specific example is the Hebrew concept and practice of God. The sin of Israel from the days of the wilderness was idolatry. They adopted the gods of the Canaanites. But since the Captivity no Jew can be found who is an idolater. He may be atheistic but never an idolater. For the Hebrew mind and heart the Captivity settled that issue once and for all. God is active in human history. That which men devise against him or his people God uses for his own ends. Babylon purposed to destroy a weak neighbor but God used that destruction for his own purpose, to purge his people of idolatry.

At a more personal level we note the history of David. As a youth, fresh from the fields of Bethlehem, he was thrust into the powerful cross currents of political power as king of a united Israel. But there came with the territory the strong winds blowing him into the curruption of social enticements. His personal life fell under the sway of the demands of the flesh. He yielded to the seduction of adultery followed by murder to cover his guilt. Yet these very failures were the tools in God's hands to turn him into the "sweet singer of Israel." He became the poet who voiced the hopes and feelings of every sinner who seeks in God forgiveness. Who but a David could sing: "Create in me a clean heart O God; and renew a right spirit within me. Cast me not away from thy presence; and take not thy Holy Spirit from me."(Ps.51:10f)

It is a constant principle of God's involvement in human affairs that he uses the plans and people who would oppose him to accomplish his purposes of love in redemption or judgment. Thus in this plotting against the life of the son of God the leaders of Israel "were seeking how they might destroy him." And Judas came and proposed "how he might deliver him to them." Such were the plottings and plans of those who opposed themselves against God's anointed. On the other hand God could not conquer death in behalf of humanity except His anointed one die. Hence he used the evil machinations of men to push forward his own plan to conquer death.

The entire episode, as disheartening as it might appear, gives assurance of God's ever-present activity in behalf of man. Give us eyes to see and hearts to respond to God's involvement in the affairs of men!

AN OUTLINE OF LUKE 22:7-23
God's Passover!
In Jesus God clothed himself with flesh, identifying with
human nature. God became so human he sampled how a man
thinks and feels!
I.   PREPARING THE PASSOVER. 22:7-13
     1. Two designated to "Prepare the Passover." 8
     2. Prearranged for privacy & secrecy. 10-13
II. EATING THE PASSOVER! 22:14-20
     1. "When the hour came, he & apostles reclined." 14
     2. "With desire I desired to eat this Passover."15f
     3. Institution of a "new covenent." 17-20
        (a)Distributing the 1st cup. 17
        (b)The bread: "This is my body." 19
        (c)A 2nd cup fulfills the Passover. 20
III. THE BETRAYER, THE CHRIST & RESPONSIBILITY! 22:21-23
     1. The presence of the betrayer. 21
     2. The designed destiny of the Son of Man. 22
     3. The concern of the disciples. 23
Gethsemane and the cross, alone in the Synoptics, surpass
this scene to disclose the total humanity of the Deity in his
fleshly sojourn. "With desire I have desired to eat this
Passover" reveals the intense feeling of Jesus, God's son.
That God feels as we feel is assured in this episode.

* * * * * * *

GOD'S PASSOVER!
Woven into a people's national festivals are the values
peculiar to that culture, nation, and civilization. It is so
among the Hebrew people. At the threshold of Hebrew history
lies the feast of the Passover. The meaning of the existence
of that peculiar people lies embedded in the Passover, its
origins, rituals, traditions and customs. God, freedom, life,
national destiny, worship, and other similar values are
entwined in the Passover festive week. It was the festival
more than any other that incorporated the entire meaning of
Hebrew national existence. To destroy the Passover would
eliminate that which was distinctively Hebrew.
Preparing the Passover!
Jesus came to fulfill Old Testament aspirations, not to
destroy them. We are not surprised then that he should
arrange to celebrate this symbolic ceremony of Hebrew
heritage. He sent Peter and John, "Go, prepare for us the
passover that we may eat." Because of the thousands
thronging Jerusalem from throughout the world the slaying of
the paschal lamb was no longer confined to the temple
priesthood. Private rooms and family heads often became the
scene and persons preparing the feast. Thus Jesus, desiring
to protect his privacy, especially from the traitorous Judas,
made secret arrangements for a special "large upper room"
where he might celebrate the Passover with his disciples.

353

As the paschal supper was celebrated in the time of Christ four elements were present. After prayer the father of the family presented to the table guests a cup of wine followed by bitter herbs. Next the father circulated a second cup accompanied by an explanation of the _meaning_ of the feast. Third, the leader took two unleavened loaves, broke them and placed the pieces one on the other. Taking one of the pieces, with thanks, he dipped it in sauce and consumed it along with a piece of the paschal lamb with bitter herbs. Each person followed that pattern. Finally, the father led in the singing of the Hallel(Psalms 113-118).

It was the responsibility of Peter and John along with the owner of that "upper room" to see that all arrangements for the proper celebration of this feast were complete. It was Jesus' desire that knowledge of these plans should be kept from his enemies, among whom now Judas must be numbered.

Jesus arranged with the owner of the "upper room" to reserve that space for his final feast before his struggle on Calvary. That he arranged beforehand finds support in that when Peter and John should enter the city, "a man shall meet you bearing a jug of water. Follow him into the house into which he shall enter." Women, not men, were the bearers of water in that society. That a _man_ would be carrying it was a prearranged sign. The owner of the house shared in the plan to preserve privacy.

Eating the Passover!

"And when the hour came he reclined, and his apostles with him." The carefully arranged feast was at hand. Jesus and his twelve were together for _this_ solemn historic occasion. Christ's crucifixion, within 15 hours of this meal, would change the entire significance of the Passover. And such a change would alter the whole course of the kingdom of God in the world. _That_ is the reason why Jesus said with such depth of feeling, "With desire I desired to eat _this_ passover with you before I suffered."

The doubled term "desire" indicates "heated" passionate longing. Mingled with Jesus' knowledge of his place in God's redemptive program for human redemption was the quite human _feeling_ about his personal suffering, particularly his death by crucifixion. Not only the physical _pain_ but the mental, moral, emotional anguish took possession of his soul. All the strands of humanity's hurting gathered into one supreme throb at Calvary! And the meaning of the Jewish _Passover_ was to get its finest illumination in _his death_ as a sacrifice offering for all men. In fact the Hebrew Passover would find its highest, truest, real explanation in his death. It was to be God's Passover! "This" Passover filled the mind, heart and soul of Jesus in anticipation, not to say in fact! No other passover could in any way equal in import _this_ passover. From God's perspective this was the only genuine passing over of man's guilt! Israel's Passover of Old Testament times was symbolic; Christ's was the real thing!

354

But Jesus inserted more in this eating of this passover than was seen in other celebrations of the festal event. Old symbols took on added, altered substance. In fact the importance of this passover came in its reinterpretation. Jesus explained the meaning of the elements of the ancient feast in terms of himself, especially his death as God's means of passing over the sin of man.

For Luke's intended meaning of this gathering of Jesus with his disciples it cannot be overstated that Jesus deliberately gave an interpretation of the Passover radically different from the customary. It was indeed a celebration of the historic passover. But the Christ infused into its liturgy his own new elements. He reinterpreted the older items but with new connotations. He injected new particulars with fresh truth about himself, his body, his blood, the redemptive meaning of his death. While the passover served as background, specific ingredients are highlighted by Jesus and put forward as new truth, at least deeper meanings of the truth embedded in the old.

Important to understanding of this paragraph is the fact that a severe textual problem obtains as to 22:19c-20. These verses do not appear in some of the underlying Greek manuscripts. Consequently versions vary depending on the translator's judgment. The Authorized Version retains them, "...that being given for you. Be doing this in memory of me. Likewise also the cup after supper, saying, This cup is the new testament in my blood, which is shed for you." But these verses do not appear in the RSV and other modern versions.

It is not possible or appropriate that we here evaluate the external or internal evidence as to these verses. For the present purpose we observe that Nestle's text carries them. And as the text stands verse 17 states that Jesus, "having received a cup, having blessed he said, 'Take this and distribute among yourselves...'" Then, having "taken bread" he offered instruction to "do this in my memory..." Then he took a second cup(vs.20)saying, "This cup (is) the new covenant in my blood, that being poured out over you." Students have been concerned about "instituting" the "Lord's Supper" with two "cups" rather than one!

The reader should remind himself that Jesus is not instigating a new institution in place of the passover. He is reinterpreting the old. He is not instituting the Lord's Supper. He is eating the passover and explaining the deeper significance of that centuries old memorial feast. He used the "cup" of the old passover and interpreted it in the light of his approaching death. He was actually casting the light of fulfillment on the shadows lying buried in the forms of the old. That which was "new" was the fact of his death as Messiah, the only real escape from the bondage of sin that held man vice-like in its deadly hold. That is the ultimate significance of the passover. The "Lord's Supper" is the new interpretation of the old passover!

If Nestle's text reflects the original we still face two "cups." Between the two was the breaking of the "bread" which Jesus described as "my body." Again we recall that the entire repast was the passover, but as illuminated by the new features of the Christ's "body" and "blood" offered in sacrificial death. As noted above the passover, as practiced in the first century, included a "cup" with bitter herbs. A second "cup" followed. At this particular "upper room" gathering the second cup is described as taking place "after the supper." During this second cup the leader dramatized the meaning of the historical feast. It seems that "after the supper" the group enjoyed a time of informal visiting. Then the _meaning_ was explained. Thus when the festivities arrived at the point of the _explanation_ of the _meaning_ Jesus with deliberate intent introduced the "new" covenant in "my blood."

"My body" and "my blood" are fresh, new factors that the old passover could not have included. The "body" and "blood" of Messiah could have meant nothing to the celebrants who left Egypt or any other generation before Messiah came. But at "_this_" passover Messiah was present. He was on the threshold of being the literal passover lamb. Thus he inserted into the memorial feast _himself_ as the object of memory. _HE_, not a lamb slain in Egypt, was the "blood" that assured God's passing over. Moreover, it was a passing over for human redemption from sin, not escape from death of the first born of a generation of Egyptian slaves.

This transformed meaning of passover is enhanced when "body" and "blood" are clearly defined. In classical and koine Greek σῶμα refers to the "self" more than the physical frame of bone and flesh. In Romans 12:1 Paul exhorts to "present your bodies a living sacrifice." He is pleading for them to give them "selves" to Christ without reserve. Here when Jesus declares "this is my _body_" he refers to _himself_ as the bread of the covenant.

Also the term _blood_ refers to more than physical elements. Lev.17:11 says, "the life...is in the blood...it is the blood that makes atonement by reason of the life." Thus when Jesus explained the meaning of the passover, the elements of _bread_ and _blood_ picture the _self_ and _life_ of the Saviour with power to redeem from sin and death. Had he withheld the sacrifice of self or life there would be no redemption. In the passover fulfilled, the Lord's Supper, that which believers are to remember is the humiliation, suffering, death plus the resurrection of the Christ."

Twice Jesus states, "I shall no longer eat of it until the kingdom of God shall be fulfilled."(16) And "I shall not drink from the fruit of the vine until the kingdom of God shall come."(18) Once the kingdom "is fulfilled" Jesus will share with believers in the memorial as newly interpreted. He is present whenever the memorial feast is eaten be it at appointed worship or when "he comes again!"

The Betrayer, the Christ and Responsibility!

In view of God's sovereign rule over history, particularly redemption as it threads its way through history, the choice Judas made to betray his Master poses the basic question of God's rule and man's freedom. The ignoble betrayal by Judas, one of the twelve, contrasts vividly with the warm trust, strong bond of friendship cementing the group. Jesus is sadly aware of Judas' basic choice to break the trust of a disciple. But he was equally aware of God's sovereign plan for redemption. "<u>Yet</u> (in contrast) behold (surprising as it seems) the hand <u>of</u> the one betraying me is with me on the table." How remarkable God's predetermined unyielding plan uses the free choices, good or evil, of men in working out His purpose! This is true in the present instance "<u>because</u> the son of man goes according to that having been determined, <u>but</u> woe to that man through whom he is betrayed." God has predetermined the purpose and plan! But each man bears his own personal responsibility in the choices he makes for good or ill. And "that man" whose false hand is on this table is wholly liable for his own shameless betrayal.

The depth of man's depravity is thus pictured in lurid colors during the holy feast. The closest friend becomes the prime example of man's lowest, farthest fall! Sharing even in the Lord's passover can't of itself guarantee freedom from evil, soul-destroying choices.

The twelve immediately reacted! "They began to question among themselves whoever of them this might be about to do this thing!" The fact that each disciple reflected on his own loyalty shows how well Judas covered his villainous purpose. It seemed, as indeed it was, so out of keeping with the love, warmth and affection of friendship, not to say discipleship. Yet it was the keenest kind of revelation of the human heart's capacity for base behaviour. It became a warning to any redeemed person who would presume on God's grace.

So much of the <u>humanity</u> of the son of <u>God</u> is revealed in this episode. Nothing in the Gospel records discloses the human quality of God in the flesh better. The deity's capacity for being human is unsurpassed, unless it be Gethsemane's suffering or death on the cross. God became thoroughly human that man might obtain his divine destiny, the "image and likeness" of God!

AN OUTLINE OF LUKE 22:24-30
The Rewards of Discipleship!
If a disciple within the inner fellowship could stoop to
the depth of betrayal as did Judas, may not a disciple rise
to heights of loyalty? Who, then, has risen the highest?
That begets a natural inevitable conflict among the twelve!
I.   THE DISPUTE: "WHO IS THE GREATEST?"
     1. The occasion of the dispute. 24
     2. Standard of greatness among the "nations." 25
     3. A different society. 26a
II. THE KINGDOM MEASURE OF GREATNESS. 22:26b-27
     1. "The greatest among you!" 26b
     2. The servant-master relationship. 27a
     3. "I am among you as one who serves." 27b
III. RULERS IN THE ISRAEL. 22:28-30
     1. Discipline: Learning to rule. 28
     2. Entrusted with sovereignty. 29-30a
     3. Judges on the thrones of the Israel! 30b
As was their Master the apostles were beaten, buffeted,
and broken through years of service. All save John died a
violent death. Yet who rules in the lives of more people
than the twelve? The moral, ethical, and religious truth that
reigns in the lives of millions flows from the lives and pens
of the apostles. Rulers of the world's kingdoms fade and
die. But the "apostles' teaching" still rules over the
hearts of myriads of believers.

* * * * * * *

THE REWARDS OF DISCIPLESHIP!
Three factors motivate men to rise in the human scale of
greatness: money, power, and fame! And these are quite close
in relationship to each other. Money brings power; power
leads to money; and each or both can lead to fame! On
occasion such motivaters will lead a person to tramp on the
rights of others in order to advance his own interests at the
expense of the other. Judas decided that he would get
neither fame, fortune, or force from association with Jesus.
So he betrayed him for thirty pieces of silver. He thus
became infamous, the classic example of a conniving traitor.
When Jesus, at the passover supper, indicated that "the
hand of the betrayer is with me on this table" the apostles
were shocked. It was a time of soul searching! They began to
question, "who of them this might be!" It doesn't take much
imagination to hear Peter (and the others) protesting the
possibility of doing such a dastardly deed. In fact later at
this very supper Peter would affirm that he would die before
denying the Master. So, human nature being what it is, the
point at issue became, "who is the greatest." None would
concede that he was the lowest. But, in denying that, each
grabbed the opportunity to declare his own supreme loyalty.

358

The dispute:"Who is the greatest?"

"But also a contention of envy arose among them as to who of them **seems** to be greatest!" At this point the eleven were not aware that Judas was the "hand" that would betray. So no one was willing to acknowledge that **he** was traitor. In an effort to claim loyalty each raised his voice to declare that he had the loftiest fealty. Without realizing the level to which they were stooping each man became juvenile. It became a contest in bragging. Ill-feeling, resentments, anger grew as self-love splashed over unashamedly. In view of the intense stress of Jesus' coming suffering the contention was rude, discourteous, infantile. Besides, that over which they were contending was a subjective sentiment by each man. The text reads, "who of them **seemed** (δοκεῖ) to be greatest." Of verbs relating to **thought** "seem" is the most subjective. It was a personal argument of twelve men each of whom was claiming what "seemed" to **him** to be greatness!

Each man was entrapped by the normal standard of greatness as reflected in world society. Jesus dampened their ardor by reminding them of the world's model of greatness: "The kings of the nations are lording it over them, and the ones exercising authority over them are called Benefactors." Brute force and bold authority is the rule among "the nations." That is the accepted pattern, the sanctioned way to control the masses. Without a name(fame); without mastery of the economy(money); without military force(power) what government, national or local, could survive? To ask is to answer the question.

The kingdom measure of greatness!

Jesus paints strong contrasts between kingdom standards and that of "the nations." He inserts the graphic 2nd personal pronoun, "But among **you** (it is) not thus!"(vs.26) He continues the contrast,(28) "But **I** on my part..." Jesus, with sober intent, marked the difference between God's kingdom and that of "the nations."

And what are those standards so at variance with the world? "But the greatest among **you** is to be as the younger and the one governing as the one serving." **Service** is the measure of greatness in the sight of God. In fact, God's path to greatness subordinates fortune, fame, and force to serving **others**! We cannot eliminate money, fame or power. But they don't determine greatness. They're tools that **serve** him who is great by God's rule.

The Lord enforces his idea of greatness by the example before them. "Who is greater, the one reclining (at table) or the one serving? It's the one reclining is it not?" The Master who owns house and land doesn't first serve his house slaves before he himself eats does he? No! He is served first by the house boy! So, take note, "**I** am among you as the one **serving**." I may have power to work miracles, a name known country wide, and ample money to feed, house, and clothe me. But it's my **service** to the needs of human beings that is the base of my power, the worth of my name, and the sustenance of my spirit. Fame, fortune, and force without service breed death. They are to be instruments in the hands of "one who serves." They are channels of life!

Though Luke does not report it, at a point during this upper room scene, by washing the disciples' feet(John 13:3f) Jesus displayed the labor of a menial servant. Such was their pattern for greatness. The greater the service the greater the man!

As to these disciples Jesus acknowledges, and thereby encourages, his followers as faithful servants. They have had three years of schooling under the master teacher. It was a period of discipline. The time of graduation was anticipated. The rewards of learning are to be experienced. "But you are the ones having persevered with me in my trials." Through the peaks and valleys of his ordeals all, save Judas, had proved steadfast. And that devotion would be rewarded in kingdom terms and on kingdom standards. Jesus promises: "And I deposit with you just as to me my father deposited with me a kingdom. You shall eat and drink at my table in my kingdom, and you shall sit on thrones judging the twelves tribes of the Israel."

Whatever else he meant, this certainly says that God's kingdom is the heritage of the earliest disciples. By implication it would include all believers as heirs of the kingdom of Christ.

Two facts he affirms. First, the joys and rewards of God's sovereignty in their lives would be their personal possession. The reign of God deals primarily with moral, ethical and spiritual values. Faithfulness through trials brings the highest personal rewards: forgiveness, strength, moral character, clear vision of eternal values, and other qualities of the spirit. Basic to all external, material expressions of life is the health and strength of the spirit, the image of God in man. "God is spirit" and he rules in spirits! In this first promise Jesus declares: I give you sovereignty in spiritual values! This is "to eat and drink at my table in my kingdom."

A second promise is: "And you shall sit on thrones judging the twelve tribes of the Israel." A ruler rules from a throne. It's the source of principles and laws of authority. Have the apostles of Christ ever exercised this royal responsibility? And has their dominion extended over "the" Israel? If so, how, when and where?

The promise finds fulfillment in ways not always visible in material, outward forms. Later in Acts this same Luke describes the earliest band of believers as, "continuing stedfastly in the teaching of the apostles..."(2:42a) In that early group there was no creed, no organization loaded with tradition, no institution, no property - only the presence of the apostles and their "teaching." For an entire generation no written word guided the early church. Only the "apostles' teaching." As needs arose the apostles wrote to answer those needs. As first generation of believers began to die Gospel records appeared. The need for eye-witness accounts of the life and deeds of Jesus became apparent. These were written either by apostles or their close companions. Luke reflects the teaching and viewpoint of his associate Paul. Mark presents Peter's view of the Christ. The "apostles' teaching" formed the standard for both life style and doctrine in the early church. Since then the New Testament, the "apostles' teaching," has been the rule of "faith and practice" for the entire Christian community. No king or governor has exercised his thronely authority with greater firmness or more widespread acceptance than have the apostles! Not by physical force have they ruled. Rather through moral persuasion and spiritual power have they exercised their royal authority in the lives of believers. They rule in the realm of truth, not politics. They rule in the kingdom of God, not the world of fallen humanity.

The apostles were given the privilege of walking, talking, hearing, seeing, touching ("handling") the Lord Jesus, the "Word made flesh." This went on for three years or more. They were vouchsafed a degree of intimacy with Jesus beyond others. After his resurrection they were given a forty day seminar reminding and explaining the facts, meaning and significance of His earthly appearance. They were promised God's Holy Spirit to "guide them into all the truth." The records they left constitute our New Testament. They are the instruments of God's revelation to man. Their word is the reigning authority because reality of truth is authoritative. Whatever else Jesus may have meant by, "you shall sit on twelve thrones" he at least meant this much, that the "apostles teaching" is decisive in matters of Christian faith. Their teaching still rules over the minds and hearts of millions of believers.

They are the greatest because they serve the most! If ever any should be greater it will only be because they serve more. Jesus said, "_I_ am in the midst of you as one who serves!

Dangers Of Discipleship!
In 22:7-38 Luke describes the "upper room" gathering from
its preparation by Peter and John (7) until they dismiss to
the Mount of Olives and Gethsemane.(39) Thus the warnings of
31-38 form the closing instructions before the sufferings of
his "passion," Gethsemane, the trials, and the cross.
- I. DANGERS TO THE SPIRIT. 22:31-34
  1. "Satan asked to sift you." 31
  2. "I prayed concerning you." 32a
  3. "Having returned, establish your brothers." 32b
  4. Peter's protest of loyalty! 33
  5. A prophetic warning. 34
- II. DANGERS OF PHYSICAL VIOLENCE. 22:35-38
  1. Their security during his present ministry. 35
  2. "But now" a change of tactics is needed. 36-37
     (a)Need for a "sword."
     (b)That "having been written about me has
        reached its goal."
- III. THE TWO "SWORDS." 22:38
  1. The disciples' misunderstanding! 38a
  2. The response of Jesus. 38b

Satan attacks any who align themselves with God. He tries
to "enter" all disciples of Jesus. Being a close disciple
does not eliminate the attacks. In fact, it assures that he
will make every attempt to destroy the faith of the believer.
Two dangers to discipleship are: that Satan enter within and
that he assault from without; that he corrupt the spirit, and
that he pain the body to the point of apostasy.

* * * * * * *

DANGERS OF DISCIPLESHIP!
Evil as a fact of life is beyond dispute. It shows up in
physical pain, moral depravity and spiritual vice. From the
biblical viewpoint these forms of corruption stem from a
personal source outside the human. This evil One appears
under various names such as "the devil," "the old serpent,"
"Satan." That he enters into man does not relieve the human
of his responsibility for evil. God warned man of his
liability: "...of the tree...you shall not eat...lest you
die."(Gen.3:3) "Sin couches at the door...you rule over
it!"(Gen.4:7) Still, it was this "serpent" who enticed man to
choose death over life. And though the consequences have
followed to this day "the old serpent" still seeks "to enter"
each human, especially believers.
"The devil, having completed every temptation, departed
from him for a season."(Lk.4:13) Without doubt Jesus felt
the force of the "accuser" throughout his ministry. But in a
special way this evil One attacked the twelve with satanic
power this eve before the crucifixion. He succeeded in
entering Judas. Only the prayer of Jesus thwarted his

permanent capture of Peter. Of the disciples He focused his
attack on Peter. Though cut of the same cloth his onslaught
against Peter was second only to his assault on Jesus, the
leader and spearhead of the entire redemptive program.
Satan's strategy entailed blitzing the moral integrity of the
Christ. Companion to that was his vigorous invasion of each
in the disciple band. He launched a two-fold attack. He crept
within to cloud the heart's vision. From without he battered
the body so as to induce apostasy.

Dangers to the spirit!

Being aware of the issues Jesus forewarned the twelve.
"Simon Simon, Watch out, Satan has sought out you to sift you
as one sifts grain." In reporting Satan's advance on Peter
Jesus uses the plural you. Satan not only wants you Peter, he
seeks each of you, all of you. He seeks control of anyone
into whom he can get entrance. His strategy is to enter the
leader.

Because the evil One wants Peter, Jesus throws up a
protecting prayer in behalf of this prime apostle. "But I
prayed concerning you(sg.) that your faith fail not." In the
case of Job when Satan appeared before God with "the sons of
God" he sought to destroy Job's faith and integrity. As with
Peter Satan's attack against Job aimed at his inner heart and
his outward health and wealth. The undermining of man's
faith in God's care is the goal of the tempter. He who is
under Satan's fire needs all available support, human and
divine. Job's wife advised her husband to "curse God and
die." In accusing Job of secret sin his friend, Eliphaz,
offered little better, "Your iniquity teaches your mouth."
Not so with Peter. In Jesus he had a friend who looked
beyond the fault to the potential Peter could become.

But Satan's assault on Peter was real! This is not
fiction, a story about imagined people. Judas had already
fallen prey to the intrusion of Satan. Without divine
support the salty impetuous Peter would be no match for the
devil's wiles. So Jesus disclosed "I prayed concerning you!"
The word for "prayed" gives emphasis to the desperate need of
Peter. After all, Satan had "asked" God for the opportunity
to "sift" Peter as a farmer "sifts grain." Satan's
assumption is that at bottom even the finest of disciples is
a Judas. God is always in control. He allows Satan's
invasion of human personality for purposes of trial and
temptation. But he sets limits beyond which Satan cannot go.
From the divine point of view Satan's invitation to evil is
also man's opportunity for good. An invitation to become
embroiled in sin is equally a call not to commit sin.
Temptation has its up side. "Count it all joy when you fall
into manifold trials; knowing that the proving of your faith
works stedfastness.(Jas.1:2f)

For such reasons prayer is effective in the moral
struggles in human life. God is personal! He isn't aloof,
inaccessible to human appeal. He responds to thoughtful

appeal from his children. This for certain would include his "only begotten" son. God does not have to be persuaded to be concerned about the moral welfare of his sons. But, being the model on which men in his "image" are to pattern themselves, he desires that they talk to him, counsel with him, express their longing for victory for their brethren. Prayer contributes moral fiber to him who prays as well as him for whom he prays. True, God may not need to be persuaded but he does wish to be recognized as partner who plays an important role in the human struggle for triumph over the tempter. Hence Jesus, with sympathy for God's part in Peter's moral struggle, prayed for him in his urgent need.

There's no doubt as to the power of Jesus' prayer. Upon informing Peter of his prayer support Jesus immediately exhorted, "And you, having turned, strengthen your brothers." Judas was already bound, completely captured in the clutches of Satan. But Peter, though tried as by fire, would rebound from his ordeal unscathed with any permanent harm. In fact that shameful experience would strengthen the sinews of his soul. "When you have returned," said Jesus, "make strong your brothers!" Peter's trial would be the "proving" of his faith and thus equip him to help others in their battles for faith. And this Peter did as seen in Luke's sequal, Acts.

Little do we grasp the depth, intensity of moral reality with which we contend. Peter is a perfect example of this lack. With bravado he boasted of his strength. "With you I am willing to go even unto prison and death." We have no reason to doubt the intent of Peter. He meant every word of his boast. Though limited in knowledge of Jesus or his kingdom, thus far Peter's entire discipleship testifies to his undivided devotion to Jesus. Without question his purpose was to submit even a criminal's cross if discipleship demanded. In this too he would be leader.

The point of Jesus' reply to Peter's claim was, not to deny Peter's intent, but to reveal the immensity, intensity, and nature of the warfare. Hence Jesus warned, "No cock crowing today (shall be) until three times you shall deny having known me." How well Jesus knew human nature's tendency to underestimate the frailty of its own ego. Such weakness is confirmed by Peter's three-fold denial that night. It is verified by numerous such denials through succeeding centuries. Many, having begun discipleship, have denied. Some have "returned" because someone prayed!

Dangers of physical violence!

Satan's attacks on the soul are subtle, sagacious, crafty. His assaults on the physical frame are open, overt, unbounded exhibitions of violence. To prepare the twelve for these onslaughts Jesus points out that his coming death and consequent physical absence from them would bring a different situation. This would involve need for better insight of the nature of spiritual armament than hitherto. He reminded them, "When I sent you off without purse and alms-bag and sandals, you didn't lack anything did you?" They testified, "Nothing!" He noted a decided change from the earlier incidents as they moved among people. "But now, the one having, is to take purse, likewise also an alms-bag, and the one not having is to sell his cloak and purchase a sword."

During his ministry Jesus was a popular figure. His favor with the people threw a sheltering wall around his disciple band. His miracles, healings, purity of life and lofty teaching warded off negative influences even from those among the Jewish leaders who threatened him. As the power of public opinion sheltered Jesus so it veiled the disciples from physical harm. "But now" he was entering a new phase looking toward the end-goal for which he came into this world. He was on the threshold of public trials before both Jewish and Roman authorities. He was about to be maligned, abused, rejected and crucified as a common criminal. Association with him as disciple, rather than protecting, would be a badge of criminal guilt. Henceforth they must rely on their own ingenuity for protection. They must equip themselves with armament fitting the kind of violence they were about to face. The enemies of God's rule would spare nothing, not even murder, to embarass, harass, and destroy their testimony to the kingdom of God. Accordingly Jesus warned, "But now, the one having a purse is to take it, likewise also a money-bag, and the one not having is to sell his cloak and buy a sword."

To support that a radical change was at hand Jesus quoted Is.53:12 as finding fulfillment in that which was to happen to him. "For I say to you that it is necessary that this having been written shall be brought to its goal in me: 'and he shall be counted with outlaws.'" In contrast to his popular acceptance with the people the Jewish leaders would invoke upon him the utmost dishonor, a criminal's execution by crucifixion. And that which is imposed upon him shall extend to his followers. Jesus would forewarn the disciples that they must prepare for active warfare. As the leader so they would fare! In so warning Jesus exhorted: "Get purse, money-bag, and sword." So important was the sword as part of essential equipment he added, "If you don't have a sword, sell your cloak and buy one!"

In spite of years of teaching and association with the person of Messiah the twelve were too much saturated with this world to recognize what he was saying. By his non-violent resistence to arrest and execution he would show that he did not mean the sword of worldly warfare. He meant the "sword" of the word as revealed in him and his testimony to truth. He would exhibit it yet this evening in Gethsemane by restoring the ear to the servant of the high priest. But the disciples, yet under the illusion of this world, said, "Lord, Behold! two swords!" To which in sad irony Jesus answered, "That's enough!" Thus the conversation ended. It was time to enter Gethsemane and begin the final phase of his ministry. How much more human can the divine Christ reveal himself to be?

365

AN OUTLINE OF LUKE 22:39-46
Jesus In Gethsemane!

Nothing in the gospel records reveals the true humanity of the Lord more than when in Gethsemane. Even his death does not surpass Gethsemane in sounding the depths of the mystery of God in relationship to the human soul.

I.   WHY PRAY? 22:39-40
     1. He went "according to custom" to Mt. Olives. 39
     2. He suggested content for the disciples' prayer.40
II. THE PRAYING OF JESUS IN GETHSEMANE. 22:41-44
     1. He was "drawn apart" from them. 41
     2. His struggle! 42
     3. Angelic support. 43
     4. Increased intensity of his praying. 44
III. THE DISCIPLES AND PRAYER. 22:45-46
     1. He "found them sleeping from grief." 45
     2. Renewed exhortation to prayer. 46

Jesus, "who in the days of his flesh, having offered up prayers...with strong crying and...heard for his godly fear...though he was Son, yet learned obedience from which things he suffered..." Being human, Jesus instinctively shrank from death. But "having been heard" he was delivered from fear of failure in his mission. Though death was still his mission, he walked in perfect possession of his soul through trial, cross and tomb.

* * * * * * *

JESUS IN GETHSEMANE!

True to his medical perspective Luke points up the physical pain in the Gethsemane ordeal of Jesus. The consequence of Adam's choice to sin was death. The bleating rebellious sacrificial lamb was symbolic but hardly an acceptable real sacrifice sufficient to rebut sin's deadly sequal. Redemption demanded a free acceptance of the fatal consequence of sin. Jesus, as embodiment of Life, must give his consent to death. Life must freely choose death if death's chains were ever to be shattered. He must accept death! In his own unique way, Luke, the good physician, spotlights the intense human struggle of Jesus in Gethsemane.

Jesus, as man, is surrounded by all that limits every human being. On the other hand, he has open access to God and all that God can be to every human being. The problem of man is to keep his human spirit free and open to God within those limits of being human. This is the struggle with which Jesus wrestled in the garden. Satan had already ensnared Judas. He was presumptious to invade the person of Jesus. The humanity of the Christ left open to Satan the possibility of his capturing Christ. Luke does not give a literary sketch; he describes the real historical battle of God's man crossing swords with Satan. Christ's prayer in Gethsemane was the honing of the sword with which he would defeat the strategy of Satan.

366

Why Pray?

That Jesus sought the privacy and peace of the secluded garden for prayer testifies to the importance he places on prayer. Not only did he agonize in prayer but twice in this text he urged his companions in this crisis to pray. The text says, "Having gone out he went according to custom to the mount of Olives." To seek in prayer God's counsel in a crisis was "according to custom" with Jesus. By no means was this his first time to seek the strength of prayer. When he chose the twelve he "went out to a mountain" for a night of prayer to God.(6:12). Again, at the transfiguration shortly after he began to teach the necessity of his death, he sought out a mountain for a night of prayer.(9:28) Both by precept and example he laid on the disciples the important fuction of vital prayer.

In the present instance Jesus gave specific guidance as to the content of such prayer. "Be praying that you don't enter into temptation." When he discovered them sleeping, he roused them with the repeated exhortation, "Why do you sleep? Get up! Pray that you don't enter into temptation!" Without doubt there are many matters about which prayer is proper but in the final analysis "temptation" to evil in one form or other is implicated. At each turn (crisis) in life's road men make moral choices. Men need God's presence and involvement. "Trials" make God's patronage essential.

Prayer to God implies that choices, decisions, resolutions are not predetermined, fixed in concrete. They are subject to the "will" of free moving agents, divine and human. Moral law is predetermined by God. Right and wrong aren't negotiable. They are fixed by Him who is unchangeably pure and holy. On the other hand, as created in the "image" of God, under attack to do evil, man needs the supporting strength of divine help. But he must will to seek it; he must petition for it. If a free thinking, free choosing man won't ask for available help it won't be arbitrarily thrust upon him. The moral value of "right" versus "wrong" is to seek, choose, ask for the "right." Prayer is one free spirit asking another free Spirit to give strength in life's moral conflicts.

Jesus Praying in Gethsemane!

The full moon could not dispel the dark shadows of the soul. "Having come to the place" and having urged the disciples to pray "not to enter into temptation" he "dragged himself forward about a stone's throw." There he dropped "to his knees" and in that pose of supplication, began his prayer not "to enter into temptation." The fact that he could yield to the tempter is essential to the idea of prayer. If Jesus, by God's decree could not yield then there was no "temptation" at all; the whole story is a farce, a caricature of reality. The tension between Satan and Jesus was not theatrical play-acting. It was the epitome of every man's struggle between the higher and lower moral destiny.

In one summation Luke capsules three prayers of Jesus as reported in the other synoptics. "If you will (and I assume that you will) take this cup from me. Yet, not my will but yours is to be!" Underlying this prayer is the trustful assumption that God can will a different plan than the humiliation and death now facing him. On the other hand, the prayer reveals the trust of Jesus by declaring "not that which I will..." The human awe and dread of death impairs clear vision of "right." Since he was human, Jesus prayed that God's clearer perception be decisive. To trust God instead of any human decision typifies faith at its best. As a human Jesus recoiled from death. Being "son" he trusted God's decision more than his human wish. This was exemplary both as son of Mary, the human, and Messiah, son of God! As a man he wrestled with Evil as must every man. As a child of God he yielded in prayer, "not that which I wish but what you will." The very fact of prayer recognizes the moral limits of being a human. At the same time it discerns the place of God clarifying man's vision and securing God's helping strength in attaining moral maturity.

How severe was this clash with Satan? As with all Jesus did, it is the pattern on which every man must grapple with Satan. It was temptation par excellance! This is confirmed by the exhortation of Christ to the disciples, "Be praying that you enter not into temptation." He was feeling the force of the persuasive powers of Satan. So too were they! As was their danger of yielding to an invitation to escape the agony of a cross, so was his. If they were to pray to find strength to endure, so must he uncover that strength. Prayer is the harmonizing of the human heart to God's. Such prayer opens the door for a free flow of divine strength. The need for humiliation and death would not only be sharpened but capacity for enduring it could arise through prayer.

Christ's use of the image of "this cup" deepens the sense of the moral warfare. The idea of "cup" carries the Old Testament notion of "cup of judgment" or "cup of destiny." By the prophet God said, "I have taken out of your hand the cup of staggering, even the cup of my wrath..."(Is.51:22) "Take this cup of the wine of wrath at my hand, and cause all the nations to whom I send you, to drink it."(Jer.25:15)

Since Jesus identified himself with the sin of humanity and was set for man's salvation from such sin it became imperative that he subject himself to the "cup" of God's "wrath." This was God's plan, God's "will." Christ's struggle in Gethsemane was to attain victory over the temptation to "enter" (yield) to Satan's appeals to reject the "will" of God in the matter. His was the ultimate in humanity's struggle against the sin of Satan. That Jesus was "Son of God" in no way lessened Satan's challenge to his moral integrity. In fact, that he was God's son, born of woman, increased the intensity of the combat. Jesus was tempted "in all points." And to the limit of human endurance!

368

Nestle's text double-brackets verses 43f. Manuscripts are evenly divided as to whether they were in Luke's original. We include them because internal evidence added to the external, supports them. They suit the situation. God did not ignore the pleas of his Son! "An angel from heaven appeared strengthening him." How or in what form this "strenthening" came is not stated. It's the fact that God heard and gave answer that is Luke's concern. In crises God is always accessible to him who calls. In whatever form an angel comes, he who has eyes to see and heart to feel can comprehend. The point is, God hears and answers his children's prayers.

But the coming of the angel did not diminish Satan's assault. "And having gotten in agony, he was praying more earnestly." The "more earnestly" finds dramatic description in "his sweat like drops of blood falling upon the ground." The more God hears prayer the more Satan beseiges his prey. And greater becomes the victory! So Jesus, "having gotten up from his prayer..." From this point forward Jesus walked without fear or uncertainty through the coming ordeal of trials and crucifixion.

Prayer and the disciples!

The one remaining need was transposing his triumph to his weary grief-stricken disciples. "Having come to the disciples he found them sleeping from the grief." Luke alone of the synoptists explains the cause of their sleep as due to "grief." Their humanity overtook them; by his prayer "not to enter into temptation" he survived his humanity.

The events of the night, the threat of the hour had drained them in mind, body, emotions and soul. Not a one of them had heeded his plea to "pray that you enter not into temptation." All looked for refuge in sleep, not prayer. Startled at their failure to lay hold on divine help he adjured them, "What! are you sleeping? Get up! pray that you not enter (yield) to temptation!" In a very real sense, his trial was theirs. As he sought God's aid so must they! Human strength alone would not suffice. If they were to share his victory God must be involved. And by prayer they must get God's help just as he did! If we ask for help God gives it! But he expects us to want it!

The Gethsemane experience profoundly affected the author of the epistle to the Hebrews. Citing that Jesus, our high priest "has been tempted in all points like as we, yet without sin" he urges on his readers the place of prayer in giving hope of divine help. "Let us draw near with boldness unto the throne of grace, that we may receive mercy, and may find grace to help in time of need."(4:16) Thus he finds in Christ's Gethsemane agony a pattern for believers. As Christ gained help from on high so are we to seek divine help from the same source in the same way. "Pray without ceasing!"

369

AN OUTLINE OF LUKE 22:47-53
A Kiss, A Sword, and God!

God reveals himself, his redemptive purpose, through the actions of human behaviour. He says something in the kiss of a betrayer and the sword of "one of the twelve." Godet states, "God acts by means of history, and history is the realization of the divine thought." (Com. on Luke, pg.477)

I. THE KISS! 22:47-48
 1. The mark of love the sign of betrayal. 47
 2. The response of Jesus. 48
II. THE SWORD! 22:49-51
 1. The question of defense. 49
  (a)They observed what "was about to happen."
  (b)"Shall we strike with sword?"
 2. Violence by force! 50
 3. The rebuke by Jesus. 51
  (a)"Enough of this" violence!
  (b)Jesus, by healing, reverses the violence.
III. GOD'S WORD! 22:52-53
 1. Those "who came against him." 52a
 2. "Do you treat me as a thief?" 52b
 3. "Why not in the light of the open temple?" 53a
 4. This is "your hour, the power of darkness." 53b

This episode sketches how God achieves his predetermined plan by means of human descisions. "The son of man indeed goes as has been determined: but woe...through whom he is betrayed."(22:22) God predecided to redeem. He fulfilled it by man's choices. Judas chose to betray; Peter chose the sword. God used both wrong choices.

* * * * * * *

A KISS, A SWORD AND GOD!

What artist, be it the maestro's baton or the painter's brush, has ever surpassed God's exploiting and harmonizing human decisions for his own ends? The base betrayal of Judas and the presumptious violence of Peter, God turned into the bright light of man's salvation. He takes the broken threads of human evil and weaves from them the fabric of divine redemption. Gethsemane is a prime example!
The kiss of betrayal!
Among the Semites the kiss was symbol of affection. More than embrace or handshake it signified the bonds of strong relationship between man and man. When Judas planned with "chief priests and officers of the temple" to seize Jesus it was this mark of love they selected by which to identify Jesus. In the darkness of the garden the "kiss" to only one man would safeguard against seizing the wrong one. The moral level to which Judas sank is measured by the sign he chose. He pantomined love while harboring hate; he pictured affection while covering betrayal. His good act did not match his evil motive. Can hell invent greater depravity?

370

The long-awaited goal toward which history had moved, the God-guided end of the ministry of Jesus was at hand, the terminus of this week's emotional turmoil was overtaking them. All came to a climax before the disciples could grasp what was happening. "While he was still speaking, behold, a crowd (came)..."

In the moment of deep personal devotion, at the hour of private talk with his God, "the one being called Judas, one of the twelve, was at the head leading them..." Not only the "kiss" but the place and moment of the kiss placards the craven hypocrisy of Judas. Enemies of God never respect worship, reverance, or piety. In fact that's the very time in which the forces of darkness prefer to fire their heaviest weapons of war. And yet, as the drama unfolds, Jesus, not Judas, takes charge. He questions, "Judas, with a <u>kiss</u> are you betraying the son of man?" In thus speaking to the situation Jesus achieved two important things. First, it was at once a rebuke and an appeal. With emphasis on the form the betrayal took Jesus was making a final appeal to Judas to repent. Second, he was declaring that he, not the crowd or its priestly or goverment leaders, was in control. He intimidated them, not they him. His plan, not their plot, would rise above the surrounding darkness. The "kiss" of the betrayer was an incident in God's overruling purpose. Jesus was the one person who was calm, self-possessed, and directing events to a designed end.

<u>The Sword!</u>

Facing the crowd, the soldiers, the authorities, both religious and Roman, what kind of defense should be mounted? That was the problem when "the ones around him saw that which was about to happen!" In fact they asked, "Lord, if <u>we</u> shall strike with sword?" This question pressed on each of the eleven. They were willing, even anxious, to do that which they must. If every other means fails should we not use force? Shall not violence be confronted with violence?

So obvious, to them, was the answer that they didn't wait for Jesus to reply. "A certain one of them struck the servant of the high priest and lifted (cut) off his right ear." We learn from John's gospel the name of that "certain one" as well as the servant, Peter and Malchus. But Luke leaves them nameless. To him the principle of defense is the important point, not the particular people.

Peter was a fisherman, not a skilled swordsman. He hardly waited for Jesus to command defense; he struck with lightning speed. Had he struck with accuracy he would have split the head of Malchus. But instinctively the servant ducked and only his ear was severed. The disciples might go down fighting but fight they would for him whom they loved and in whom they believed. The world knows no other way than brute force to advance the cause of truth.

The text reads, "Jesus, having answered, said..." What he said makes clear that his defense lay in the power of truth, rather than in violence of the sword. Christ's defense was the "sword of the spirit, the word of God." Truth is its own defense. It needs not the buttress of the sword of steel! So "having answered, he said literally, "Permit unto this!" His answer might be paraphrased, "Enough of this violence!" Upon which Jesus "took hold of his ear and healed him."

Violence is not part of the kingdom method. It has no place in the divine plan. Jesus would not resort to force to propel forward the truth of God. Violence is self-defeating and so is to be avoided. When Jesus stooped to pick up the severed ear he sought to reverse the tyranny of coercion. As a matter of fact Jesus, as God's emissary, must undo Peter's explosive outburst so as not to compromise the cause of the kingdom. Before the governor Jesus would claim, "My kingdom is not of this world: if it were, my servants would fight..."(Jn.18:36) Had he not healed the servant's ear he could never have said that to the governor. Peter's act of force actually compromised the truth.

Someone asks, What would Jesus have done had Peter split open the head of Malchus? or decapitated him? Would he have healed that? There can be no doubt as to the answer. Surely he would have healed him. Not to have done so would have compromised the whole reason for his entrance into the world. Truth not only doesn't need force for its support, it defeats it. It trades the power inherent in truth as truth for the crutch of a sword. Truth is its own force! It defeats itself when it calls upon violence. If I tell a lie and resort to beheading him who accuses me, has that altered the fact? Whether I have lied or not stands whether my accuser is beheaded or not. Violence clouds the issue! The moral wrong of Peter's sword obligated Jesus to reverse the wrong. The whole reason for becoming human was at stake! No cross, no crown! "Enough of this violence!"

God's Word!

Of "those coming against him (Jesus)," Luke identifies three groups in the crowd, "chief priests, temple officers, and elders." These were the "leaders" who came to arrest Jesus. But it was Jesus who took the "lead" by accusing them. He tolerates their present purpose. He permits them to seize him. In the meantime he cuts their conscience and attacks their motives. "Did you come out as though against a thief with swords and clubs?" Do you think I am an insurrectionist? Are you fearful for your political power? "Daily I was with you in the temple (teaching) and you didn't stretch forth your hands against me!" In open daylight in face to face debate you never arrested me. Why now in the dark seclusion of this garden? What, then, are your real motives? What are you doing?

Jesus answers his own question. "This is your hour and the power of the darkness." The shadows of the night symbolize the darkness of your heart. Evil perpetrates its moral darkness under cover of night. It cannot stand the light of open day. It will not face its own dark depravity.

372

That God created man free to make his own choices meant that God would not interfere if man chose to make wrong moral choices. To be free to choose "right" man must be free to choose "wrong." Embraced in the freedom lay inexorable results. If man insisted on freely choosing moral wrong he must live with the consequences of his choice. The fruit of wrong doing is respected by Him who in creation gave the freedom. In other words, though limited, sin has its "hour" of triumph. For this reason, though Jesus controlled events and guided the action, he yielded to the momentary victory of evil. Darkness must have its fleeting "hour" and sin must exercise its temporary power. Jesus must succumb to Satan's "hour" that he may be victor over sin through an endless eternity. Darkness rules through the night until it gives way to the light of day. The authority of darkness pales at the luster of the Lord's light! Sin is colorless, toneless, anemic when faced with the blood-red health of God's grace. "This is your hour and power of the darkness." My hour and the power of "right" will overcome and reign forever!

* * * * * * *

AN OUTLINE OF LUKE 22:54-71
Man's Dealing with Deity!
Sould we not assume that man respect the God who created him? Yet if Christ's claim to be son of God is true man is anything but respectful. In fact in his dealing with God man mortifies, humiliates and otherwise demeans the Deity! Luke lists three levels of humiliation of God's son by man.
  I. DENIAL BY A BELIEVER. 22:54-62
      1. The first denial: "I don't know him." 54-57
      2. The second denial: "I am not one of them." 58
      3. Third denial:"I don't know what you're saying!"59
 II. MOCKING & FLAYING BY "THOSE HOLDING HIM." 22:63-65
      1. The "mocking" and "flaying." 63
      2. Parody of his prophecy. 64
      3. "Blasphemy against him." 65
III. JEWISH SANHEDRIN FORMULATES THE CHARGE. 22:66-71
      1. The "legal" interrogation. 66
      2. The substance of the interrogation. 67-71
         (a)A first question and answer.
         (b)A second question and answer.
         (c)Predetermined charge formulated on his claim.
    Three levels of humiliation of deity are:(1)Frailty of human nature as seen in a committed believer. (2)Callousness of human nature as viewed in "the ones holding (advantage) him." (3)Rejection by human nature as portrayed in religious bureaucrats who control "authorized" religion.

373

MAN'S DEALING WITH DEITY!

Two trusted disciples, Judas and Peter, play prominent roles in the sad scenes of the final days before Christ's cricifixion. Is the betrayal of Judas a "greater" moral debacle than Peter's denial? A cancer is a cancer is a cancer! And a sin is a sin is a sin! "Greater" is not the word when measuring moral disaster. In degree one may be "greater" but without repentance the end result is the same, death of the soul!

Judas has already abandoned himself to perdition. In the present text, in relationship to Christ, three other types of human beings are identified. They are,(1)the believer, Peter, (2)underlings, "the ones holding him," and finally (3)the assembled Sanhedrin, the "high priests and scribes," the ruling authorities. If we see Judas as a "type" four classes of men may be distinguished. Two are believers and two are non-believers. None are admirable examples of behaviour toward the Lord! One betrayed, one denied, a third mocked and unmercifully beat the accused captive, and the Sanhedrin "tried" him on the victim's own testimony of truth. This is how humanity dealt with deity!

A Believer's Denial!

Peter had the qualities of a born leader of men. Fervent in faith, strong in feelings, devoted to a cause or person, in this instance his Lord. The evening before he sincerely said, "With you I am ready to go both to prison and to death!" There is no reason to question the purity of his motives. If called upon he intended to die for the Lord!

But Peter's purpose and Peter's performance proved to be at crossed swords. His deed didn't match his devotion. When they snatched the Lord from the darkness of Gethsemane, Peter "followed from afar." He stayed as near as he dared. He intended to die if necessary. He would watch for an opportunity to serve his master! Little did he realize the frailty of the human heart, particularly his own! The darkness of the night was scarcely erased by the flickering flames of the fire with which he sought to warm himself. Suddenly with no warning "a certain maiden, having seen him sitting near the fire, having fastened her eyes on him" burst out, "This one was with him!" It was an accusation of "guilt by association." If he walked in fellowship "with him" who was accused then he too must bear the same mark of shame. Peter's denial was quick and complete, "I do not know him, Woman!" In effect Peter was saying, "There's no way I could be one with him. I don't even know him!" Such is the shameful price paid by numerous believers through the ages. Dedicated faith forgets the bondage of sin into which we all have fallen. Faith is contantly compromising itself by denial of "knowing" him.

But Peter's ordeal was not over. "And after a short while another, a different one, having observed him, said, 'You are one of them!'" After his first denial no way could

Peter accept the second accusation. To be consistent and claim some measure of integrity he had to deny (and thereby forfeit real integrity). So he made an absolute denial: "I am not!" This was more than disavowal of association "with" Jesus. It was a claim not to be "of them." The source of his world view was not to be sought in "them," the band about Jesus. Peter categorically claimed disassociation. If Peter's ideas resembled those "of them" it was coincidental. "They" were not the origin of his practices. In effect, "I am not of them!" This too has its imitators. Men may borrow their teachings or ideals from Christ and his apostles but they don't want to be identified as learning from them. Such seek moral standards of the Christ without acknowledging Him as the source. This is not guilt by association but by disassociation. I don't deny Christ's ideas but I do deny Christ!

Peter had yet further to plunge into his self-made pit of perjury. "After about the space of an hour a certain other strongly asserted saying, 'Upon truth, this one was indeed with him, for he also is a Galilean.'" Step by step Peter descended to the depth of denial. "Man! I don't know what you're saying!" Peter was a man in a storm at sea denying he was even on the water. Amid the swirling strife Peter denied knowing what was troubling people. The unhappy apostle was voiding three years of discipleship as though he were from a different world. "I know not what you're speaking!"

How quickly the human heart latches onto compromise! He who would "go to prison and die" with Christ, the same night denied knowing the Christ. He obliterated three years of lofty teaching plus an exemplary life pattern. But Christ will not leave Peter to drown in the storm-tossed waves. "Immediately, while he was yet speaking, a cock crowed. And having turned the Lord looked at (into) Peter." True, it was a look of rebuke but more, it was a look of redemption. It stirred Peter's memory of "the word of the Lord, how he said that before the cock crows you will deny me thrice." No matter how much a disciple denies or faith falters Jesus will do his utmost to invite repentance. He had given Judas a final appeal. He would do no less for Peter. Jesus had prayed for Peter(22:32). He would do everything possible to reclaim Peter from failing faith. Callous denials can be covered!

Treatment by "those holding him."

"Those holding him" were underlings, subordinate temple officers hired to do the bidding of their ecclesiastical overlords. They were the kind of "people" who sought to ingratiate themselves with the "authorities" over them. They determine their actions by the pattern of the "powers that be." They do not think; they imitate! Their minds are slaves to self-interest feelings. They practice what pleases employers, right or wrong. They do not work by moral standards but by political party.

375

"And the men holding him, began mocking and beating him."
Jesus had not been sentenced formally. Yet "those holding
him" began to humiliate him by pantomiming his own claims as
God's prophet. "Having blind-folded him they were asking:
"Prophesy! Who hit you?" With brutal beatings they showed
the point to which human nature can fall.

According to Luke's record Jesus answered not a word to
these taunting insults. From Luke's perspective they, not
he, needed pity. He, as redeemer of men, must suffer such
buffeting of body but they must face the eternal fallout from
such abuse of God's son! In a word, Jesus was in control!
They were piling up guilt upon guilt. They were being
judged, not he!

Furthermore, he was quite aware that their barbaric
brutality was part of his task of shouldering God's
redemptive love for humanity. When he volunteered to give
his life for man this kind of savage animalism was an
integral part of "giving his life." In the course of human
redemption it was simply part of "the Father's will." The
"powers of darkness" were to have their hour and this was
their hour.

These men who were "holding him" multiplied their
contemptuous barbs. "And many different blasphemies they
were repeatedly speaking against him." To "blaspheme" is "to
hurl against." These men lashed out against Christ every
conceivable kind of slander. If we can distance ourselves
from emotional judgment of such behaviour we can see that
this kind of human behaviour is the instinctive reaction of
evil against virtue. It is sinful man's only defense against
the power of purity! When darkness paints white black it is
acknowledging its own guilt!

The Sanhedrin formulates a charge!

Betrayal, denial, brutality have each exemplified their
dealing with deity. It remains only to formalize man's
disrespect for the Deity! That the Jewish official Sanhedrin
proceeds to do. "And when day arrived, the elders of the
people, both chief priests and scribes, were assembled, and
they led him unto their Sanhedrin." For months these pious
people had predetermined the death of Jesus. But all must be
done along strict legal lines. They must have a formal
"trial." Accordingly Jesus is set before the highest Council
of Judaism. As Luke relates the story no witnesses are
heard. The entire examination is directed to the culprit.
Reduced to the bare questions they asked:(1)"Are you the
Christ(Messiah)?"(67) (2)"Are you then the son of God?"(70)

Jesus' answer meets the questions but indirectly. To the
first he says, "If I tell you, you won't believe. But should
I ask, you won't answer." Which is to say, "It's useless to
answer since you have prejudged me." But Jesus added more
substantively, "From now you shall see the son of man sitting
at the right hand of the power of God." By "son of man"
Jesus denoted Daniel as pointing to him as Messiah. From this

"admission" the accusers promptly asked: "Are you, then, the son of God?" To this Luke does not report Jesus as affirming, "I am!" That would be falling into their trap. But he puts on them the burden of making that claim. "You are saying that I am." While Jesus accepts their statement he places on them any onus on such a claim. He thus escapes any legal statement in court of law as to wrong doing. His accusers rush headlong into their own trap. They multiply their guilt by stating: "Why yet do we have need of witnesses? For we ourselves heard (blasphemy) from his own mouth."

It is important to Luke's story that the maneuvering in this "trial" led to the sentence of death, not from evidence presented from witnesses, but by his mouth, the word of Jesus. He was put to death for no felony; only his holding to the truth of his being the son of God. This is the sole issue of redemption. Is he or is he not "son of God?" Christianity stands or falls on that as fact or fiction. In this interrogation Jesus maneuvered them into sentencing him on the one issue, "Are you the son of God?" If that be true, all else follows. If that be false, nothing else matters.

It must be observed that no class of men, no type of humanity dealt with deity with respect or honesty. Judas betrayed! Peter, the beloved leader of the twelve, denied. Servants of the "people of God" mocked and beat. The governing body of God's chosen condemned the Christ on his own confession of the truth about himself.

What, then, can man claim before God? On what basis can he expect mercy? What "good" can man advance before the Deity? Any hope man may have cannot come from his gracious dealing with deity! Redemption, if any, has to come from God, not man. Man's universal treatment of God offers no basis for hope of salvation at any level. "Where then is the glorying? It is excluded."(Rom. 3:27) "A righteousness of God has been manifested...even the righteousness of God through faith in Jesus Christ unto all them that believe; for there is no distinction, for all have sinned..." (Rom. 3:21ff)

We've raised the question of Man's Dealing with deity. But man's hope rests rather in the Deity's dealing with man! Man has shown nothing admirable in his dealing with God. Yet in the face of man's ingratitude and rebellion God extends his grace of redemption to man. It is now man's opportunity to respond in trusting God's grace.

377

AN OUTLINE OF LUKE 23:1-25

The Trial and Sentencing of Christ!

Trial or travesty! Was the "trial" of Christ caricature or confirmation of justice? In the answer to that question lies the truth or falsehood of the Christian movement.

I. CHRIST BEFORE PILATE. 23:1-5
   1. "All of them brought him before Pilate." 1
   2. Three accusations: 2
      (a)Perverting our nation.
      (b)Hindering payment of tribute to Caesar.
      (c)Claiming to be king.
   3. Pilate's verdict. 3f
   4. Renewed agitation of the charges. 5

I. CHRIST BEFORE HEROD. 23:6-12
   1. Pilate sends Jesus to Herod. 6-7
   2. Herod's examination of Jesus. 8-12
      (a)His joy at the opportunity.
      (b)The silence of Jesus.
      (c)Behaviour of the highpriests and scribes!
      (d)Mockery of the court.
      (e)Results of Herod's examination.

III. THE FINAL SENTENCING. 23:13-25
   1. Review of the legal procedures. 13-15
   2. Temporizing with justice. 16-19
   3. The demand to "crucify him." 20-23
      (a)Pilate "again" sought to release Jesus.
      (b)Renewed demand: "Crucify him!"
   4. Sentence pronouced as of "their" request. 24f
      (a)Pilate's official verdict.
      (b)Jesus "delivered to their will."

Luke's record, being true, the trial and sentencing of Jesus is a travesty on justice. The examining Roman tribune gave his verdict, "Not guilty!" Yet he temporized with duty and yielded to political pressure. "Their voices prevailed." God in Christ experienced human justice.

* * * * * * *

THE TRIAL AND SENTENCING OF CHRIST!

In Luke's effort to display the humanity of God in Christ he could choose no better stage than man's courts of justice. Justice in the Roman court matches the travesty in Jewish ecclesiastical courts. The human systems render miscarriage of justice more often than not.

Christ before Pilate!

"And all the multitude of them having risen up brought him before Pilate." The quickly, illegally assembled Sanhedrin had imposed their miscarriage of justice before dawn. But they were powerless to execute the verdict without sanction of Rome's judicial system. Prejudice must always seek formal legal approval. To that end the Jewish authorities rushed Jesus to Pilate before the day's traffic.

378

Luke's Gospel is one of four! Much that Luke reports may be read in the others. "Inasmuch as many have taken in hand to arrange a narrative" implies that Luke used "sources." But the prime factor is, not what he does not report, but that which he does! What each author tells is crucial to his peculiar theme. Luke has a message distinctive to him, even when he records similar material. His prime point is the humanity of the deity as he "became flesh" and walked as a man among men. Often this theme is prominent, sometimes subtle, but always present.

The chief emphasis in 23:1-5 is the verdict of Pilate: "I find no fault in this man (worthy of death)!" The reader must remember that the judge's first (and final vs.22) verdict favored Christ as innocent.

When the Jews brought Jesus before Pilate they must have at least the semblance of a viable accusation. They wished for a quick verdict of death. The immediate and general "offense" was, "We found this man perverting our nation." Rome was concerned about any unrest in the provinces. An uprising for any reason led to police action. So the accusers cloaked their murderous intent under "this man keeps stirring our people to constant rebellion."

Explicitly they defined this constant unrest as inviting failure to pay the tribute due to Rome: "...hindering to give tribute to Caesar!" This was an outright contradiction to that which Jesus had encouraged, "Give to Caesar what is Caesar's!"(20:25) But the accusers twisted Christ's teaching as though it encouraged rebellion against Rome. The animus of these Jewish leaders is seen in their resentment to this very tax. They suddenly became champions of Roman taxes. It served their hatred of Jesus.

But rising to a yet more dangerous charge the accusers alleged that he claimed "to be Christ, as king!" In the just preceding Jewish court the term "Christ" was taken to mean "son of God."(22:67,70) Yet here before Gentile Romans the same "Christ" is given the content, "king." By any means the enemies of truth employ any method to accomplish preplanned results. Truth is not the goal; only foregone determinations.

The term "king" piqued Pilate. His position required that he protect the political power of Rome. So he privately examined Jesus: "Are you the king of the Jews?" As Luke reports, it suggests a summary examination. Jesus answered: "You are saying!" This admits the charge but makes clear that Pilate perceived that his kingdom was "not of this world." It could not mean that he, Jesus, was a threat to Rome's power. His was a kingdom of spirits! The kingdom of God! As interpreted by hate he was guilty; as understood by Pilate Jesus was "not guilty." And he so rendered his verdict before the Jews. To repeat: the judge, after thorough examination, pronouced Jesus: "Not guilty."

This verdict from Rome's high court in Judea infuriated the enemies of Christ. Already at white heat their hatred boiled over: "They kept laying out their strength insisting, 'He arouses the people, teaching throughout Judea, beginning from Galilee even unto here.'"

Christ before Herod!

The mention of Galilee offered Pilate, the politician, a two-fold opportunity. It could free him from presiding over a distasteful judicial murder of a man he had already declared innocent. It also was a step toward easing a nagging conflict with Herod. Herod's domain included Galilee. So Herod ought be respected as Tetrarch and as such entitled to preside at the court judging Jesus! So "Pilate, having gotten knowledge that he (Jesus) was of the authority of Herod, sent him to Herod, being in Jerusalem during these days."

Jesus before Herod is only chronicled in Luke. This episode must have contributed something special to Luke's theme. The leading fact of the scene lies in the lack of any semblance of judicial sentence on Jesus, guilt or innocent. In fact, Herod's whole interest lay in his personal curiosity to see and exploit Jesus much as though he were a court jester.(9:9) He wished to probe the reported "signs" of the man, whether slight of hand magic or was he in league with evil powers? "He was hoping to see some sign being done by him!" To add to the excitement "the highpriests and scribes stood by vigorously pressing their accusations." In response to this sordid, base view of such a serious circumstance Jesus maintained a profound silence. Such silence impresses Luke's reader of Christ's complete control of himself and the situation. Jesus sensed the basic issue of life and death. It was no time for trifling!

Though Herod did not pass any official judgment on Jesus he did yield to contempt. No man would ignore a Herod and escape insulting, caustic abuse. "But Herod with his soldiers, having set him at naught, mocked him. Having wrapped him in shining garments, he sent him back to Pilate." Though an attempt at ridicule, the "shining garments" were, not royal purple, but those worn by noble grandees at gala affairs. They signaled "innocence," a subtlety accenting Pilate's verdict, "not guilty!"

Verse 12 inserts another signal detail. "But both Herod and Pilate became friends with one another on that day. For previously they were being enemies with one another." What contribution does this make to Luke's thesis? Christ's presence on earth was a ministry of reconciliation. How remarkable that two enemies, both of whom sat in judgment on him, were reconciled, even on the political level, because of their role as judges of Christ! Herod a half-Jew, Pilate a weak vacillating Roman became "friends" as a result of Christ's humanity! Symbolic, to say the least, of the purpose of the presence of the Christ on earth!

The Final Sentencing!

Upon the return of Jesus to Pilate's court the governor was saddled once again with an unwanted decision. As judge he recognized that for "envy" the Jews were pressing for the death sentence. Justice called for release of this innocent man. Conscience demanded it! But as a politician, a human subject to selfish concerns, Pilate wavered, temporizing with fair play. "Having summoned the highpriests and the rulers" he reviewed the legal procedures already settled. He recalled his conclusion: "And I, having judged before you, found nothing in this man worthy of the things of which you are accusing against him." To support his own judgment he added, "But not even Herod (found anything), for he sent him back to us. Behold, nothing worthy of death has been practiced by him; so, having chastised, I will release him."

Pilate's downfall was his attempt to compromise justice by attempting to placate the clearly unjust will of the accusers. To trifle, accommodate, or delay justice is to invite defeat. To trample truth is to lose one's soul under the guise of being crafty. If the moral universe is ruled by truth then truth will triumph and he who tampers with it will sink into the darkness of oblivion.

The thought of "release" inflamed the accusers. They demanded the release of the notable prisoner Barabbas in keeping with the Roman custom at Passover. Here again is Luke's weaving of a thread in his theme. The name "Barabbas" means "son of the father." He who was imprisoned for a "certain revolt" was released. But Jesus the "son of the Father" was to be crucified that the sons of the Father might be set free from sin!

"But again Pilate called to them, wishing to release Jesus." Pilate's judicial sense as well as his deep human feeling was to set the innocent free. But with shocking force the Jews with loathing shouted, "Crucify, crucify him!" To which raw justice appallingly cried, "Why? What evil did this man do? Not one cause for death did I find in him? Having chastised I will release him." With vivid lines Luke sketches the persistence with which Pilate tried to maneuver the release of Jesus. Nothing is clearer than that Jesus did "nothing worthy of death."

Why, then, did he die? If it was the "will of God" the question remains, Why? One clear reason lies in Luke's theme: God as man must identify with and taste the pain, the loneliness, the "passing" of the soul. Man is mortal! He who is immortal must "know" what it is to be mortal. He must absorb all that death can devise!

Less clear is another reason! At the transfiguration (9:28-36) this mystery was probed by Moses and Elijah. They spoke of "his decease which he was about to accomplish!" For Christ death was to be "achieved," "accomplished!" A victory was to be found in Christ's crucifixion! Just what that victorious achievement was is not directly developed

381

though Luke begins to prepare the reader's mind for an answer as to why! The darkness over "all the earth," the tearing of the temple veil, the Roman centurion's opinion about the dying Christ, the offering of a newly hewn tomb by one of the counselmen, the women carrying spices to the tomb, the encounter with two disciples on the Emmaus road followed by the "upper room" all contribute to a perception of why Jesus died.

But the full answer comes in the letters of Paul, Peter and John to which must be added Luke's second volume, the Acts of the Apostles. The struggle of the churches in their attempts to deal with the human problems of its people produces the answer Why?

The abuse of justice by Jewish and Gentile authorities was devastating to faith! But the open, empty tomb followed so soon by selected appearances of the risen Christ gave light as of the rising sun on a new dawn! At the synagogue in Antioch of Pisidia Paul summarized the gospel: In telling of Jesus before Pilate, he said, "Though they found no cause of death, yet asked they of Pilate that he should be slain...they took him down from the tree, and laid him in a tomb. But God raised him from the dead ... he whom God raised saw no corruption ... through this man is proclaimed remission of sins: and by him everyone who believes is justified (declared 'not guilty') from all things." (Acts 13:28-39) This depicts why Jesus "must die," that is, "that every man might be justified!" Jesus died and rose that God might fulfill his eternal intent of having a people "in his own image."

It is for this reason that Luke details with care the conflict between himself and the Jewish authorities as whether to release or crucify Jesus.(13-25) So far as legal and moral justice was concerned Pilate is on record for time and eternity in declaring "I find no crime in this man." Pilate's personal tragedy was that he failed to follow his instincts as a judge. His weakness as a human being led him to compromise truth and justice. The awesome miscarriage of justice is recorded in, "Their voices prevailed!" "Jesus he delivered up unto their will!" Such is the triumph of evil in human experience.

What is Luke telling Theophilus in this episode? From Peter's denials, through the abuse and beatings of men, to the official betrayal of the innocent son of man by every kind of human court, God in Christ encountered every kind of indignation to which man is subject in this sinful world order. No pain to which men are vulnerable was left out of God's experience while in "flesh" on this earth! How much more human can God get? And he tolerated it for "all" men!

AN OUTLINE OF LUKE 23:26-32
On the Way to Golgotha!
Judgments of human courts are matters of record. Pilate
had "delivered Jesus to their will." And "they led him off"
to do their will, that is, to crucifixion. On the way to
the place of the Skull three matters of import occurred.
I. SIMON, THE CYRENIAN. 23:26
   1. The ancient world and crucifixion!
   2. Simon of Jerusalem community of Cyrenians.
      (a)He was "coming from the field."
      (b)They "laid on him the cross."
      (c)He carried it "after Jesus."
II. THE GREEN TREE AND THE DRY! 23:27-31
   1. The crowd and the mourning women. 20a
   2. A Word of Warning! 28b-31
      (a)For whom to mourn?
      (b)Why? The "green" and the "dry."
      (c)Judgment to come.
III. TWO EVIL-DOERS! 23:32
   1. Two "different kinds" of evil-doers! 32a
   2. For the purpose of being crucified with him. 32b
   Three kinds of humanity surfaced on the way to the cross,
all of whom were affected by, involved in, and blessed by
what happend on Calvary! He who helped carry the cross, the
wailing women, the wretched outlaws, all were affected by
the events of that day!

* * * * * * *

ON THE WAY TO GOLGOTHA!
   When death by crucifixion was pronounced, the condemned
must bear his cross to the place of execution. Moreover,
the crime which the victim committed was placarded about
his neck or carried before him. As the initial act of
execution, a brutal, bloody beating was inflicted before
the quarry was settled onto the cross. Though he was aware
of Pilate's chastisement in trying to get Jesus released,
Luke avoided describing the beginning of the execution by
beating. But with dramatic power Luke recounts how Jesus
toiled under the load of the cross. In fact, as Luke tells
it, the first event on the way to Golgotha was Simon's
being forced to share Christ's cross.
The Cross and Simon the Cyrenian!
   Among numerous peoples of the ancient world, including
Greeks, Romans and Jews, capital punishment often was
imposed by crucifixion. The Romans reserved it for slaves
and flagrant criminals; brigands, assassins, rebels.
   The position of the victim on the cross assured the
utmost pain. About midway on the upright wood the prisoner
was placed (literally saddled) onto a seat of wood lest his
weight rip body from the nails in hands and feet. Legs,
bent unnaturally, were held rigid by the nails in the feet.

Arms, extended by the cross bar, were held aloft by nails in the hands! Normally the crucified would live twelve hours although some lived even into the third day. "The fever which soon set in produced a burning thirst. The increasing inflammation of the wounds in the back, hands, and feet; the congestion of blood in the head, lungs, and heart; the swelling of veins, an indescribable oppression, racking pains in the head; the stiffness of the limbs, caused by the unnatural position of the body" (Godet, The Gospel of Luke, pg.490) all combined to make the pain dreadful beyond bearable. Can deity be subject to such suffering? Yes! Because this was deity in human nature!

Because Jesus knew such suffering lay ahead Gethsemane's prayer was offered: "Father, remove this cup from me!" Man's abuse of man cannot surpass this agent of misery. The guillotine was swift like light! Not so the cross! It's promise of death was designed to prolong life in as intolerable pain as human imagination could envision.

Why would the good God allow his "only begotten" son to be subject to such gruesome grief? The Jews' hate-driven venom used the Roman government to impose this shameful suffering. Yet God allowed them to inflict this their will on this innocent godly man. Why? The most succinct answer comes from Paul, himself a Jew, "...whom God set forth...in his blood, to show his righteousness because of the passing over of the sins done aforetime...that he might himself be just, and the justifier of him who has faith in Jesus." (Rom.3:25-26) God, in the person of his Christ, assumed the consequences of unrighteousness that he might be righteous in redeeming the unrighteous.

Somewhere in the opening stages of this, the Christ's ordeal, Simon the Cyrenian was compelled to share the burden of the cross of Christ. He was "coming in from the country" where his "field" of labor yielded his livelihood. He would share in the festivities of Passover. But the city even at this early hour was thronged with surging mobs of excited people. Why Simon was picked to bear Christ's cross is not stated. Jesus was fainting under his heavy load. Maybe he was pressed into service to prevent the victim's death before the appointed execution. It's possible Simon was a believer who voiced his protest too vigorously. It could be the soldiers merely gratified their sense of power over another human. The fact is Simon was not allowed to escape from sharing the weight of the cross. Symbolic indeed! No man, particularly a believer, can escape sharing the cross of Christ, it's power and meaning! However insignificant or remote, no flower, blade of grass, bird or animal in God's creation can escape the influence of creation, be it sun, shadow, rain, wind or snow! We are bound, whether or no, in this creation under the sovereign will of God! We, each of us, at some point in time, must feel the burden of the cross of Christ!

384

Christ "suffered without the gate" as did each condemned man. It suggests exile from the society of the city! Thus Jesus was classed as unworthy of human kind! And Simon was forced to identify with him whom man ejected.

The Green Tree and the Dry!

"But a great multitude of the people were following him and of women who were beating their brests and bewailing him." Jesus addresses these wailing women as "Daughters of Jerusalem." They represent "Jerusalem" as that historic city represents Israel. These women voice the popular feeling for Jesus. Only a few days before Jesus had ridden the crest of popular acclaim as "Blessed the one coming, the king, in the name of the Lord...glory in the highest." (19:38) Yet now these "daughters" were bemoaning his fate as a common criminal! How sad! How tragic that one so genuinely good could be so demeaned by an unkind fate! But, sincere as they were, these women could not see below the surface event. They saw only man's unjust cruelty to man. They were unable to see the hand of God justifying Himself and His moral ways with men. Nor could they envision God's hand in justifying his coming judgment on Jerusalem in which they, these women, would be inundated!

"Jesus, having turned, said, 'Daughters of Jerusalem, quit weeping over me. But be weeping over yourselves and over your children!'" In other words, it is you and your children for whom you should mourn! This world is a moral unity whose sovereign God rules with unyielding honesty in moral matters. Every injustice is noted and corrected. Every crook from moral right is made straight. If I am unjustly executed, the moral redress of God will heap judgment in full measure on those who impose the injustice. Woe to those who fall under that judgment. They share the injustice of their moral order. This is more certain than that the sun rise!

As these "daughters" lifted the death-wail over Jesus, he in turn raises the death-wail over Jerusalem and them as residents of that doomed city. Jerusalem, and the women as inhabitants, may expect utter destruction as a result of the injustice wrought upon him.

Jesus pronounced a prophetic word about the coming judgment. "Behold! days are coming in which they will say, 'Blessed are the barren, and the wombs which never gave birth, and the breasts which did not give suck.'" So horrible is the judgment that the pride of motherhood will be reversed. Instead of being honored with children it is the childless women who are blessed.

At this point Jesus reflects the prophet Hosea's word to another generation, "They shall begin to say to the mountains, 'Fall on us' and to the hills, 'Cover us'" He then encased a prophetic word in a vivid metaphor, "If to the green tree they are doing these things, what shall happen to the dry?" When green wood is put on a fire it sizzles and pops but does not turn to ashes. But when dry wood is cast on a fire it flames up and is soon devoured by the fire. Even though exemplary in gentle virtues Jesus, the "green tree," is killed as a criminal. The Jewish people as represented in their leaders were "dry wood," ripe for burning. They bring promise of God's judgment through the sword of Rome. Justice is as inevitable as God is good! The more contrary to justice it is that Jesus should be crucified as a criminal the more it is in keeping with the justice of God that Israel perish for its immoral behaviour! It is contrary to righteous justice that Jesus die; it is contrary to the goodness of God's justice that the people and ecclesiastics of Judaism live! The roots of judgment were now taking hold. The fruit would be harvested in 70 A.D. when Rome leveled the city. The Jew has never since been deputized as "the people of God."

Two Evil-Doers!

On the road to the Calvary three kinds of humanity surfaced. Simon, who helped carry the cross of Christ was one. A second were the "wailing women" who bemoaned the unjust brutality of man against man. A third were the two malefactors. "But they were leading others, two evildoers, to be crucified with him." That which happened on the cross the next paragraph reports. But these two "evil doers" belong in this paragraph which describes that which happend on the way to Calvary.

In describing the "two others, malefactors" the word "others" is ἕτεροι. In the long history of this word the notion of "others of a different kind" was evident. It referred to more than a distinction between individuals. It also marked the idea of a difference in quality. Before the world three "evil-doers" became silhouetted against the sky. But two were of a "different kind." The evil of which the two were guilty was decidedly different in quality from that for which the one was executed! The "evil" of which God is accused is always different in quality from the "goodness" of man, even at his best! That these two of a "different kind" were crucified with the Christ testifies to the unity between the death of the one and that of the two. With the Christ humanity dies!

The Christ's death also testifies to the disparity between the death of the one and that of the two. He died because he was guiltless of wrong. They died because of the guilt of their wrong doing. Yet in his death lay their hope of redemption, for in his death they could live anew!

That which Luke relates to Theophilus in this scene on the way to the crucifixion draws back the veil on the moral darkness of representatives of all human kind. The universal depravity of man can only be cancelled by the universal redemption through the Christ.

386

AN OUTLINE OF LUKE 23:33-49
The Spectacle of the Cross!
What went on at Calvary? What happened on the cross?
What happened at the cross? And why did it happen?
  I. THREE WORDS OF JESUS EXPRESSING TRUST.
      1. "Father forgive them...!" 34
      2. "Today you shall be with me in Paradise!" 43
      3. "Father, into your hands I deposit my spirit!" 46
 II. THREE REBUKES EXPRESSING DISTRUST.
      1. The "rulers were sneering..." 35
      2. The "soldiers mocked..." 36-38
      3. A criminal's reproach! 39
III. THREE TESTIMONIES TO GOD'S PRESENCE!
      1. "Darkness came over the whole earth..." 44-45a
      2. "The veil of the sanctuary was divided..." 45b
      3. "Really, this (man) was righteous!" 47-48a
     If the scriptures truly report the presence of God in
history then no doubt the events on and at Calvary are the
most important of all time and eternity. If Jesus be God's
Christ, then he could not save himself if he was to "save
others."   But only the fact itself could make possible
salvation, much less any perception of why he died! The
man, the day, the event were awesome beyond description!

* * * * * * *

THE SPECTACLE OF THE CROSS!
     What happened on and at the cross? The simplest answer
is, Christ died! But that oversimplifies! Why did such
happen to him who, aside from being "Son of God" was a good
man, gentle, loving, kind, with powerful insight into moral
and religious truth! Is this the way human beings normally
treat a "good" man?
     All the details of Calvary, gathered in one list, tell
an astounding lot about divine and human nature. They say
a lot about the divine nature when it lived in human
nature. But no one of the four gospel narratives tells all
that happened.   Each selects facts that disclose his
particular point of view, his own thesis. Together the
four report seven statements Jesus makes from the cross.
Yet Luke notes only three, those which suit and sustain his
view of the Christ.
          Three Words of Jesus Expressing Trust!
     "And when they came to the place, the one being called,
Skull, there they crucified him." Such is the bare
statement of what happened at Calvary. "They crucified
him!" But not alone; "...and the criminals, one on the
right and one on the left."   Between the two Christ
occupied the middle cross, the one intended for Barabbas,
the "son of the father." This fact is an intimation of the
meaning of Christ's cross. He died on the cross on which
the worst of men were to die had he not endured it himself.

387

The first word of Jesus from the cross was a prayer for
others! "Father, forgive them, for they don't know(realize)
what they are doing." While the "they" might include the
"soldiers" it more pointedly refers to the "rulers" who had
engineered his death through both Jewish and Roman courts.
He had come "to seek and to save the lost." His mission
encompassed those who heaped physical, emotional, and
mental torture on him. Full knowledge or ignorance was not
the concern. In the hurt imposed by their ignorance his
first thought was their forgiveness. Such an idea governed
his ministry and such a longing dominated his death!
"Father, forgive them their guilt even in their ignorance
of the import of that which they do! This word sums up his
person, his point in coming, his purpose dying.

After months of public ministry and rejections by these
for whom he prayed what hope did he have that his prayer
would be answered? It must be noted that forgiveness
involves two, him who is offended and him who offends. I
may wish to forgive him who has wronged me. But until and
unless he who has wronged me accepts my forgiveness no
reconciliation can take place. God is the one offended and
to whom Christ appealed. The "rulers" must be led to the
point at which they are willing to be forgiven. The Jewish
rulers, even in the act of crucifying the Christ, are the
guilty for whom the Christ prayed. Could they be persuaded
to accept forgiveness?

Even before "this day" was over "all the crowds having
gathered at this spectacle, having beheld the things which
happened, were returning, beating their breasts."(vs.48)
They were shaken by what they saw. The "people" were
suffering pangs of conscience if not guilt. They were
shaken to the depths! The leaders, though callous, were
subject to the same things the crowds witnessed. We know
of two by name who were open to faith, Nicodemus and Joseph
of Arimathea. Not long after Christ's resurrection and the
gospel began its ministry of preaching Luke testifies that
a "large number of priests became obedient to the
faith."(Acts 6:7) And history testifies that forty years
was yet to pass before God's judgment on Isarel finally
fell. It is more than possible that "many (more) priests
became obedient to the faith." The gospel "is the power of
God to everyone who believes!" The prayer of Jesus to
"forgive them" was heard and well answered. An answer was
made possible by the very cross on which he was dying and
from which he prayed! It was Christ's confidence in his
Father-God that led him both to pray and to fulfill his
mission even in the process of dying. And that for those
who put him to death! What faith! What grace!

Christ's second word from the cross was none the less a
display of faith in God as well as a fulfillment of his
mission, another prayer for others. One of the criminals
appealed, "Remember me when you come in your kingdom!" Not

388

only for enemies but for a castaway on the garbage heap of humanity Jesus answered an appeal for redemption. God does "not wish that any should perish..." Without hesitation Jesus responded, "Verily to you I say, Today you shall be with me in the Paradise!" No depth of man's depravity nor height of man's defiance can outreach God's grace. It is not what a man does wrong nor the lurid stain with which he blemishes his spirit that bars him from grace. It's his refusal to ask God to receive him. God does not, nor will he, force his grace onto an unwilling man. The mind, heart, and spirit of a human being must be open to receive grace or it will not be given. But once a change of mind, emotions, and will, toward God takes place, then comes the word "Today you shall be with me..." God provides redemption! He waits for a man's appeal, "Remember me!"

Luke notes one more of the seven words from the cross. It expresses total trust in God! In his baptism at the Jordan Jesus committed himself to God's plan for human redemption. Through all the rejections, rebuffs, rebukes, and abuse Jesus kept faith with God in that commitment even unto death. Now, in the process of dying, he made the supreme dedication of trust, "into your hands I entrust my spirit." The word translated "entrust" is a banking term meaning "deposit." When one puts his money in a bank he "deposits" it for safe keeping. Death did not snare Jesus! The Lord was not "captured" by death! Jesus did not die involuntarily as other men. On the contrary, he offered himself. His life was a gift given on the cross in the act of death! He said, "Verily, into your hands I deposit my spirit (for safe keeping)"

We observe too that that which Jesus "deposited" was his spirit. In both Hebrew and Greek the word translated "spirit" contains also the idea of "breath." In his effort to communicate the essence of who or what he essentially is man resorts to "breath." "Breath" is the most ethereal of physical elements. At the same time it is the most spiritual constituent of the human being. It's that in the human that enables him to think, feel, and will. He whose "breath" has ceased is dead. And it isn't "breath" that is buried in a grave. The real human, the spirit, cannot be interred in a stone sepulcher. The essence of a man, his "spirit," is that in man which is created in "the image of God." It is that which is immortal, unquenchable, eternal. That is what Jesus "entrusted" to God! Having done so, "he breathed out!" As a mortal it was his final act of commitment!

Three Rebukes Expressing Distrust!

The cross displayed not only trust but distrust! Thrice Jesus felt the slur of disbelief! With sarcasm "the rulers were sneering, Others he saved, let him save himself if this is the Christ of God, the elect." To "sneer" literally means "to turn up the nose." It is an emotional,

389

not an evidential response. The content of their sneer, "He saved others" implied evidence. They accepted the premise, "he saved others." But their moral and mental dullness so blinded them that they did not follow the logic to its consequences! That he "saved others" should sufficiently testify that he was a degree higher than other men. But their emotions overrode their mental processes. They covered the logic with an outburst of sneers.

These rulers confessed "he saved others!" Based on their logic, "if this be the Christ of God, the elect (and we assume he is) then he ought to be able to save himself." Unknowingly these "rulers" were hovering around the truth of the gospel. His "saving others" did reveal his unusual powers. It did illuminate his unique Person! In terms of "saving himself" he could have come down from the cross. But only at the cost of not "saving others." Had the "rulers" pushed their logic a step further they might have asked, "When he could come down, why does he stay on the cross?" This question is the core and heart of the gospel. Christ did not suffer the cross because he was forced. He chose to stay there in order that he might "save others." But when emotions take over, logic loses its place in human thought.

World "rulers" ignore that Jesus "saved others." They go on sneering at the possibility that the Christ on his cross just might have the answer to the puzzle of how to "save others." And when we consider that Jesus actually was (is) "the Christ of God" what fearful blasphemy it was (is) to "sneer" at God's sacrificial approach to man! That men should deal with God in such a way is alarming!

"Soldiers" constituted a second group of mockers. "But coming to him, the soldiers also mocked, bringing him sour wine and saying, If you are the king of the Jews, save yourself." Professional soldiers not to say government bureaucrats, get immune to human suffering. At least to them it becomes the "usual" if not boring. They need to play games to block out the victim's pain. These soldiers "mocked." But the word for mock is different. These soldiers acted the part of "children" who play games in imitation of their elders. These soldiers "acted like children" in imitating the mockery of the "rulers."

Their "mockery" took the form of offering the drink of king or commoner. While it might sooth suffering, that was not the motive. The soldiers were "mocking" Jesus as "King." That Jesus was "Christ" could mean little to Roman soldiers. But that he was crucified as "King" was manifest by the inscription, "This is the king of the Jews." The soldiers were playing a game and thus degrading this Jesus.

The underlings of governments ever play their games imitating the patterns of persecution of "rulers" who mock and condemn the "king" of God's kingdom! They even imitate the logic of the rulers by saying, "If you are the king of the Jews, save yourself." These imitators, as are most mimics, were not very creative. In their mockery they just adopted the pattern of the prototypes around them. "Save yourself" was the identical demand of those who perpetrated this monstrous judicial murder. The soldiers only imaged that which their models depicted.

A comrade in crucifixion made a third rebuke! "One of the felons who was hanged blasphemed him, _You_ are the Christ aren't you? Save yourself and _us_!" This culprit was "in the same condemnation" as the other, not to mention the Christ. Yet his companion in crime observed, "...we indeed (are condemned) justly; for we are receiving that which our deeds deserve. But this man did nothing out of place!"

Both criminals had the same opportunity to observe the "rulers," the "soldiers," and the Christ in the present situation. All circumstances on and around the dying Jesus were equally available to both felons. Why the difference in the attitude and behaviour toward Jesus? Belief or disbelief, trust or distrust, turning to God or turning in on one's self is the reason for the difference. One opened his heart in faith toward God. The other felt no faith, displayed no repentance. He showed a self-serving spirit by his plea, "save yourself and _us_!" He had no interest in Christ's saving himself. If he was interested in anyone it was "_us_," himself in particular. Man looks on outward appearance; God looks on the heart!

Three Testimonies to God's Presence!

Three factors serve as a backdrop foil enhancing the importance of the crucifixion event in world history. "And it was now about the sixth hour and, the sun failing, darkness spread over the whole land until the ninth hour." Darkness at midday is astounding to say the least. But this unusual event holds a symbolic figurative meaning. It not only pressed onto Jesus the moral darkness which put him on the cross but also has left the lesson of the moral, spiritual darkness with which the world is enveloped both then and now. Since Eden the light of truth has been in perpetual eclipse. The death of Jesus is God's response to rid the "whole land" of this prodigious moral midnight. The death of Jesus spread a sinister moral spiritual effect "on the whole land."

A second symbolic phenomenon was: "The curtain of the sanctuary was torn in two!" At the very beginning, as Luke tells the story, the ancient Simeon prophesied: "This child is marked for the fall and rise of many...to be a _symbol_ that will be rejected..."(2:32) The tearing of the sanctuary veil is part of that symbolism. Only priests were allowed into the temple sanctuary; only highpriests into the Holy of Holies. But at the death of Jesus the temple veil was ripped in two. It signifies the free open access for _all_ men into the intimate personal presence of God. It says that _all_ are now "priests" to God.

commoner, I may talk to God on intimate terms about me and my personal problems, needs, and hopes "in Christ."

The word of the Roman centurion, though different, proves to be symbolic and typical of the human portion of creation. He stood at his post at the foot of the cross. The moment Jesus "breathed out" the text reports, "Having seen what happened, the centurion began glorifying God saying, Really, this man was righteous." This centurion had only the events surrounding the trials and crucifixion from which to form his opinion, "This man was righteous!" So far as we know he was present, at least privy to the facts of the trial before Pilate. He witnessed the poison venom of the Jewish authorities. He heard Pilate's verdict, "I find no fault in him." He noted the sneers of the "rulers" and himself may have shared in the mimicking of the soldiers, "Save yourself." He listened to the caustic rebuke of one thief and the penitent plea of the other, "Remember me." He heard, like rolling thunder, the hissing hatred of the crowds; and admired the stoic loyalty of the relatives, friends, and disciples of the victim. Above all he felt the silent power of the deportment of Jesus toward his persecutors. On such a basis this centurion drew his conclusion, "Really, this man was actually innocent." In the context in which the centurion spoke the word rendered "righteous" in many versions had reference to "innocence" of "this man" before the court of law. He really was not a criminal. He did not deserve this sentence, much less this kind of public humiliation. The centurion recognized a gross perversion of justice.

The typical or symbolic interest in all this is that he, the centurion, is a sample of untold millions world-wide and age-long who, upon honest, serious scrutiny of the death of Jesus come to the conclusion, "This man was really innocent" of wrong. The implications of such a conclusion is: His claim of being Son of God is true!

Thus comes to a close the "Spectacle of the Cross!" That which happened at Calvary is deeply human in its universal appeal. Miscarriage of justice instinctively arouses the most profound emotions in humankind. That a man suffers and how he suffers is equally of universal human interest. And that this man was the Son of God gives to this death a world-wide age-long universal meaning. In Pauls' terms of the gospel as being the "death, burial, and resurrection" (I Cor.15:3f) this spectacle stands first as "good news." Theophilus was an intelligent, well educated nobleman of good tastes. Hardly could he miss the significance of this scene! How human can God get? Death is the ultimate in mortality!

AN OUTLINE OF LUKE 23:50-56
The Burial!
In early apostolic preaching the burial of Jesus held a
prominent place. Paul recognized the "burial" as a link in
the "good news" which "we received."(I Cor.15:3f) How can
the burial of a body be "good news"?
I. JOSEPH OF ARIMATHEA! 23:50-53
    1. Who he was. 50
       (a)Councilor of Arimathea, a "city of the Jews."
       (b)A "good and just" man.
    2. His character. 51
       (a)Didn't agree to the "plan and deed" of Council.
       (b)Was "expecting the kingdom of God."
    3. What he did! 52-53
       (a)"Requested the body of Jesus."
       (b)"Wrapped...put it in rock-hewn tomb."
II. THE WOMEN OF GALILEE! 23:54-56
    1. They "followed after Joseph to the tomb." 55a
    2. They "had followed Jesus from Galilee." 55b
    3. What they saw and did! 55c
       (a)Where Jesus was buried and how he was buried.
       (b)"Returned" and "prepared" herbs & oils.
The burial helps to make the "news" of the death and
resurrection "good." It confirms that the body that was
crucified was the same that arose and was seen alive!

                    .. * * * * * *

                    THE BURIAL!
    Redemption was accomplished on the cross and in the
resurrection. In those events Christ did what God sent him
to do. In the burial he did nothing. Others did that!
Why then do the apostles speak of the "burial" as part of
the "good news" of their message? Paul declared, "...they
took him down from the tree and laid him in a tomb. But God
raised him..."(Acts 13:29f) Moreover, the burial became
symbol of the turning in conversion, "Having been buried
with him in baptism..." (Col.2:12) There are reasons why
the burial is part of the message of Christ.
                 Joseph of Arimathea!
    The Jewish Sanhedrin consisted largely of those who
badgered Jesus throughout his ministry. In the synagogues
of every city, town or village they heckled and harassed.
Yet among them were some choice souls who did not "agree in
the plan and deeds" of the Council. Such was Joseph of
Arimathea. He is known in the Gospel records only in
junction with the burial of the body of Jesus. Apparently
Joseph was now a resident of Jerusalem though his native
home was a Judean "city of the Jews." He was thoroughly
Jewish but not like his fellow Councilmen in their motives
in pursuit of Jesus. Nor did he approve of their methods
in seeking the death of Jesus.

                        393

Luke identifies Joseph as having two specific virtues, "good" and "just." "Good" (ἀγαθός) presents him as noble in heart. Such would possess a kindly spirit, benign disposition, gentle in relations with other men. As "just" (δίκαιος) Joseph would display a high degree of exactitude. "Just" does not deny the positive kindness of "good" but it does make more prominent the sense of justice. Such a man would embody "correctness" in every situation. These qualities suggest that Joseph was winsome but firm. As a member of the Council he was respected in Jerusalem.

The character of the man is further seen in an action he took as one of the Jewish leaders. "This (man) had not consented to their decision and deed." Subjecting "right" to personal and political maneuvering found no support from him in the deliberations of the Sanhedrin. His sense of justice, plus "goodness" of soul, led him to oppose the "decision and deed" against Jesus.

Moreover, Joseph was waiting for and "expecting the kingdom of God." This classes him with the spiritual disposition of Simeon (2:29-32) and Anna (2:38-39). He certainly qualified for those "looking for the redemption of Jerusalem." It is quite possible, even probable, that he sympathized with the teaching of Jesus and admired him personally. He may have become a disciple eventually. At least that he "was expecting the kingdom of God" marks him as deeply religious. He was a man of benign spirit, sound mind, practical justice, sensitive to spiritual impulses.

Joseph performed two deeds relating to the burial that exemplify his personality. "Having come to Pilate, he requested the body of Jesus." When we consider that normally crucified criminals were buried in a common grave this request shows Joseph's great respect for Jesus. He treated the body with dignity. Furthermore, having been granted the body, he dealt with it with reverence: "And having taken it down he wrapped it in linen and put it a rock-hewn tomb wherein no one had yet been laid." From the human viewpoint this treatment of the body reflected the gentility of Joseph. He thus revealed the best in human dignity toward a fellow man who had fallen under man's injustice. But much more is involved. Unbeknown to Joseph, these simple deeds of dignity played a significant role in fulfilling God's eternal plan for human redemption.

It's at this point that "burial" takes on the quality of "good news." During his ministry several times Jesus told the twelve that "he must suffer many things and be rejected of the...chief priests...and be killed, and the third day be raised." This was shocking, incredible, impossible to the disciples. Such skepticism of deity dying demanded that the resurrection be above doubt. The supporting evidence must be clear, decisive, reliable, irrefutable. Had Christ's body been rudely dumped into a mass grave how could his risen body be identified? Or even had he been

394

buried in a single grave, the body that arose must possess
untarnished proof that it was the same body. "Chance" did
not provide that a thoughtful, esteemed gentleman would ask
"for the body of Jesus" and supply the "linen" burial
cloths befitting an honorable man.

That Joseph could offer a particular type of tomb is of
special import. He placed the body in a "rock-hewn tomb
wherein no one had lain." Had the tomb possessed numerous
burial niches in which family members had already been
buried then an objection might always be lodged that the
risen body was not that of Jesus. It could have been one
of the others. By coming into the Christ story at this
point Joseph became an important tool in God's hand to give
good assurances as to the identity of the body of Jesus.
God does not guide human affairs by "chance." He lives and
moves on and in the hearts of human beings to accomplish
his purposes.

The Women of Galilee!

God threaded many strands to weave the fabric of his
divine plan. Women had been the financial support of
Jesus' ministry.(8:2f) Out of devoted love these same
women were present through the trying times of the final
week in Jerusalem. With heavy hearts they witnessed the
brutal death of their Lord. They stayed until they
witnessed Joseph take the body down, wrap it in linen, and
they "followed all the way to the tomb." They too played
an effective role, however meager, in the Christ event.
They were eyewitnesses to where Jesus was buried. They
observed how he was buried. Because "the Sabbath was
dawning" they, "returning, prepared aromatic spices and
perfumed ointments." It is of value to note that it was
these Galilean women who were the final witnesses to the
details of the burial of the body. They too proved to be
first to witness the risen Christ. But the point here is
that there were numerous, qualified witnesses to the burial
of the body of Jesus. The identical body that came out of
the tomb is the one that went into the tomb. Such careful
notations about the burial guarantees that the news is
"good."

Theophilus was a Greek familiar with the mythology of
the Greek gods. Such pagan deities were the "creation" of
the imaginations of men. And these gods fought wars,
imbibed in drunken revels, and otherwise imitated the vices
of men. They were killed, died, and went to the nether
worlds. Yet nothing is ever told about any of these gods
being buried. They did not "return to the dust" since they
did not come from the dust. Only Jesus, incarnation of the
"living" God who "became flesh" died and was buried. It's
"good news" to know that God entered into the total human
experience, lived as man, died as man, was buried as man,
and in his resurrection insured that man would "live" like
God intended when he created him "in his own image."

AN OUTLINE OF LUKE 23:56-24:12
Why Seek the Living With the Dead?
Disciples, "women" and "others" witnessed the death of
Jesus. The women witnessed where and how the body was
buried. But no one saw the resurrection!
I. FAITH PERPLEXED. 23:56b-24:1-8
  1. A duty to perform at the tomb. 23:56b-24:1
  2. What the "women" discovered at the tomb. 2-3
   (a)The stone rolled away.
   (b)Tomb empty of the body.
  3. "Perplexity" concerning this. 4a
  4. "Two men stood by them." 4b-8
   (a)Homage of the women.
   (b)Word of the "two men."
II. FAITH RESISTED! 24:9-12
  1. What the women did. 9-10
   (a)Told "these things" to the eleven and
    "all the rest."
   (b)Were "repeatedly telling the apostles."
  2. The apostles resisted believing the testimony. 11
   (a)Treated the report as "idle tales."
   (b)Repeatedly disbelieved "these words."
  3. Peter's investigation! 12
The death of Jesus redeemed. The burial certified who!
His resurrection documented life! Though no one witnessed
the point or process at which he "arose" many were those
who witnessed him alive after his death and burial!

* * * * * * *

WHY SEEK THE LIVING WITH THE DEAD?
In stating requisites for a successor to Judas Peter
included that such a one "become a witness with us of his
resurrection."(Acts 1:22) It is clear he did not mean that
anyone of them was present to view the first stirrings of
returning life to the body of Jesus while it lay in the
tomb. No one observed that! But he and many "others" did
witness the risen Christ after he appeared alive once
again.

Yet it must be remembered that the twelve were slow to
believe. They whose preaching became the standard by which
all preaching of the gospel has since been measured were
themselves hard to convince that he was alive. Three years
or more of personal presence, face to face teaching, plus
particular instructions about his impending death and
resurrection was not enough to shake them out of their
settled opinions. Their materialistic concept of the
kingdom of God was like a vice on their minds. They were
too much imprisoned by a structured political kingdom.
Resurrection was just too far out of the playing field even
to be a part of the game. Death was too normal and final
for resurrection to gain entrance to their thinking.

396

Faith Perplexed!

It was a mission of respect that called the women of Galilee to the tomb on Sunday morning. "On the one hand they rested on the Sabbath in keeping with the law but on the other hand at deep dawn on the first day of the week they came to the tomb bringing the spices which they had prepared." The crucifixion had wounded but not destroyed the faith of these women. To them he was still "Lord" though why this could have happened was baffling. But it did not dampen devotion. It was this dedication that incited them to see that his body was properly buried. The haste with which Joseph was compelled to bury the body left much to be done. Respect for Jesus prompted them to visit the tomb to complete the embalming.

In private family tombs such as Joseph's a large circular stone was set in a channel chisled across the front of the tomb. To secure the tomb the stone would be rolled along the channel. It's immense weight demanded several hands to manipulate. Luke omits how the stone was rolled back. He thus stresses the fact that the women "found the stone having been rolled back from the tomb, but having entered, they did not find the body of the Lord Jesus." Since the day Jesus' body was buried in Joseph's tomb no body has ever been found!

Their mission was thwarted! They came to anoint the body. When they arrived no body was to be found! A long tradition of Christian belief as to the risen Lord did not lay behind these women. To say the least, they were "perplexed." How were they to show respect for the body when there wasn't a body? Christ's crucifixion was not a figment of their imagination. They saw him die; they saw where and how he had been buried. But where was the body now? Had someone stolen it? How else account for the fact of no body? "And it came to pass while they were being perplexed about this, Behold! two men in glistening clothing stood by them." More bewildering than the puzzle about the body was the appearance and demeanor of such "two men." In frightened awe the women "bowed their faces toward the earth..." The grief of the past two days; the emotional build up of this early morning experience at the open, empty tomb was more than mortal hearts could carry without "being afraid," awe-struck, and "perplexed." "Women" were the first to face these facts!

The "two men" said three things to the frightened hearts of the women. First, "Why are you seeking the living with the dead?" From time immemorial people go to cemetaries to honor the memory of people now dead. Living people do not have fellowship with corpses. Fellowship with living people is not held in cemetaries. Living fellowship with living people is experienced in social groups. Family, religious, business, governmental, athletic institutions and arenas are for social activities.

Another observation of the two men was: "He is not here, but he is risen!" The substance of a human body consists of material molecules. The essential he is not the "he" that inhabits the body. Had the women found the body they would not have found him whom they loved and trusted! From "dust" the body is made and "to dust" the body returns. But the "he" simply moves from time to eternity. From the cross Jesus cried, "Into your hands I deposit my spirit!" It was the spirit not the body that Jesus committed to God. The essence of the real Jesus could not be kept in a tomb!

With the message, "He is not here" arises the question, "Where then is he? Is he dwelling in celestial abodes? And if he is "not here" where is his body?" Thus the "two men" added, "but he is risen!"

Had the men left the women with this information they would have remained startled and "perplexed." So the men stirred their memories. "Remember how he spoke to you while being with you in Galilee, saying that it was necessary that he be given over into the hands of sinful men and that he be crucified and on the third day rise?" When Jesus delivered this warning the disciples, including these women, were so preoccupied with visions of triumphant glory over Jewish power, not to say Roman, little could they comprehend the need for his dying. The soil of their souls was too unreceptive to the seed of this truth for his teaching to take root. It took the plowing of his actual rejection and crucifixion for them to accept the suffering of Jesus as fact! Even now the emotional upheaval blinded them to the memory of "on the third day rise!"

Thus this third word from the "two men" brought the women face to face with the reality of the Christ's rejection, death, burial, and now his resurrection! To the credit of the women, "they remembered his words." How thoroughly the women put together all the pieces of the gospel puzzle may be questioned. But it is true that the women were the first to hear and grasp the "good news" of God's gospel for humanity!

Faith Resisted!

What does one do with news, especially "good news"? The human instinct is to tell it to the nearest neighbor. There may be circumstances under which such news is to be kept to oneself. Jesus once told his disciples, "tell this to no one!"(9:21) But the fact Jesus exhorted them to "tell no one" shows how eager the human heart is to broadcast news. Here at the open empty tomb the fact announced by the two men was too good to be kept. So the women, "having returned from the tomb, declared all these things to the eleven and all the rest." Luke identifies these first female evangelists; "they were Mary Magdalene and Joanna and Mary the (mother) of James; and the other (women) with them were telling these things to the apostles."

398

Twice in three verses (9-11) Luke states that these women "declared all these things "to the <u>eleven</u> and all the rest."(9) After naming three he adds, "and the rest (of the women) with them...were telling these things to <u>the apostles</u>."(10) These women were the first evangels of the risen Christ. They sought to bring faith to the apostles. Luke accents this! We would expect the eleven be receptive to the news of the resurrection! Were they not privileged to the Christ's teaching for more than three years? They too should have remembered that "it was necessary that he be crucified and the third day rise!" So it is a surprise that the witness of the women, "appeared before them as idle words."

Once a wrong idea gets lodged in a human heart, fixed in "concrete" as it were, it takes efforts beyond normal to unlodge it. In fact, using the metaphor of <u>concrete</u>, it must be <u>blasted</u> to powdered dust before new ideas can invade the mind. The apostles resisted believing. Verse 10 says "they were <u>repeatedly</u> telling these things to the apostles." The verb form emphasizes "repeatedly." And in vs.11 Luke declares the apostles "<u>repeatedly</u> disbelieved." The eleven discounted each effort of the women to stir faith. With equal force the apostles ridiculed and rejected as idle tales what these highly strung, overly agitated, nervously confused women stated as fact. How hard it was (and is) for dedicated disciples to recognize the victory of Jesus over death.

Nestle's text resigns verse 12 to a secondary reading. But good evidence supports it as genuine. It surely shows that doubt can yield to faith. And it is a legitimate gospel tradition. "But Peter, having gotten up, ran to the tomb and having peered in sees the linen cloths apart; and he went off wondering to himself what happened." The apostolic resistance to faith must yield at some point. In keeping with his impetuous personality and his leadership of the group Peter decided to investigate for himself. It was the first break in the determined defiance to faith. Investigation is better than the stupidity of dull doubt. When Peter left the tomb, not having as yet seen his risen Lord, he was "marveling to himself at what had happened." But somewhere Jesus gave Peter a personal appearance. Where, when and how we do not know. But we do know that his investigative attitude paid dividends. Luke reports the detail, "The Lord has risen indeed and <u>has appeared</u> to Simon."(24:34)

As in his earthly life so in his risen appearances Jesus had difficulty getting his chosen to arrive at a trusting faith. But with the help of these loyal women faith finally came; first, Peter, then the Emmaus travelers, finally the upper room band of believers. So the risen Christ became safely installed in the hearts of the apostolic group from which the good news began its worldwide thrust.

AN OUTLINE OF LUKE 24:13-35
The Road of the Burning Heart!

Among the appearances of the risen Christ, including
John 21, only the journey with two Emmaus disciples shows
the Lord walking with disciples as before!

I. MEETING WITH TWO DISCIPLES. 24:13-15
1. Two disciples traveling home. 13
2. Joined by Jesus. 15
II. CONVERSATION WITH UNRECOGNIZED CHRIST. 24:16-27
1. Their "eyes were restrained." 16
2. A leading question by Jesus. 17a
3. "Sad, they stopped!" 17b-24
   (a)A question and response.
   (b)Hope frustrated!
   (c)Reports of the resurrection.
4. Jesus teaching from the Old Testament. 25-27
   (a)Rebuke: Failure "to believe...the prophets."
   (b)Christ must "suffer" and enter his "glory."
   (c)Explanation of "Moses and all the prophets."
III. MEAL IN THE EMMAUS HOME. 24:28-32
1. Invitation to stay. 28-29
2. Jesus hosts the meal. 30-31
   (a)At bread breaking their "eyes opened."
   (b)Jesus "vanished."
   (c)"Was not our heart burning within us..?
IV. RETURN TO JERUSALEM! 24:33-35
1. They returned "that very hour." 33
2. Mutual confirmation of resurrection. 34-35
   (a)The "eleven" and "those with them."
   (b)The Emmaus two.

Appearances of the risen Christ were essential for
identifying him as the one who had become incarnate as
Jesus. But now he appeared in his glory body! He partook
of physical food, had nail scars. Yet his "glory" body
appeared.

* * * * * * *

THE ROAD OF THE BURNING HEART!

After his resurrection Jesus was the same person as
before yet different from the incarnate Jesus. The same
body that was buried arose as a changed body. He had the
body scars inflicted on the cross, nail prints, sword
scars; he ate food to identify himself. Yet he appeared
through locked doors and "appeared" and "vanished" at will.
There was continuity between the Jesus of history and the
only begotten son of God. But the difference between this
mortal, earthy "flesh" and the other, heavenly life of
"glory" is part of that which he came to reveal. The link
between "this" world and "that" heavenly world is displayed
in the forty day period between the resurrection and the
ascension.

400

Meeting with Two Disciples!

Among the crowds of visitors in the city for Passover were two disciples from Emmaus, seven miles North West of Jerusalem. Crushed by the tragic events of the week they turned sad faces toward home. But the judicial murder of Jesus whom "they had hoped should redeem Israel" weighed heavily on their hearts. The whole week had become an incredible series of miscarriage of justice. Unbelievable that one good man could be subjected to such impossible pain! And on them personally the horrible ordeal fell like an unexpected earthquake. They were shaken to the depths! They "were conversing with one another about all these things that had happened."

For three years they had pursued a growing attachment to this Jesus, now dead. With his entombment their hope of redemption from Rome's tyranny lay buried. From his baptism in Jordan to the recent cleansing of the temple they reviewed his whole public life. Every miracle, move, sermon and parable they retraced in detail. The bitter opposition of the Jewish leaders they surveyed with critical insight from countryside through Jewish and Roman courts. A baffling puzzle! They could not decipher the Why! With absorption they were talking when, with scarce notice, Jesus joined them.

Conversation with the Unrecognized Christ!

"It happened that while they were conversing and questioning, Jesus himself was walking along with them." The intensity of their dialogue modified by their sombre mood blinded them to this traveling stranger. "Their eyes were restrained so they did not recognize him."

If Jesus were to accomplish his purpose he must break into the discussion. With characteristic shrewdness he asks a question. "What are these words which you are casting back and forth to one another as you walk?" That diverted the flow of thought from themselves. The force of their feeling turned to him. In amazed wonder Cleopas aired his emotions: "Are you a lone stranger in Jerusalem and don't know the things which happened there these days?" Impatient wonder sharpened his word! But with the calm dignity of a lawyer pursuing his point Jesus answered: "What sort of things!" Jesus asked that Cleopas specify the quality of "things" to which he was referring!

To Cleopas the all-consuming events were those surrounding the scheming of the Jews against Jesus. What other sort of things were important in such a week? So he detailed them: "The things about Jesus of Nazareth, a man, a prophet mighty in work and word before God and all the people. And how our highpriests and rulers delivered him to a verdict of death and they crucified him!" In view of their "hopes" in this Nazarene what other sort of events were there? "We were hoping that he was the one about to redeem Israel! But indeed added to all these things this

is the third day since these things happened." In spite of
"hopes" three days seem to declare that such hopes were
misplaced! The fact of death, the permanancy of death give
assurance of the folly of faith in him as promised redeemer
of Israel. Hope and fear fought for possession of the
hearts of these two who themselves were examples of the
struggle in all the disciples who shared the same "hopes."
The presence before death of a Christ who could be heard,
touched, and seen face to face now rested only in sad
memories. Moreover such a Christ now became subject to all
kinds of speculative rumors. "Yea, also certain women of
us amazed us, having been early at the tomb, and not having
found his body they came saying that they had seen a vision
of angels, who were saying that he lives." How can
credence be put on the testimony of emotionally-unstable,
highly-strung women whose desires have overcome better
judgment? Nevertheless, "certain of those with us went off
to the tomb and found thus just as the women said, but him
they did not see!"
The basic problem of the two disciples was reconciling
their deeply held notion of the nature of the expected king
and kingdom of promise to the reality of Jesus of Nazareth
"a man, a prophet mighty in word and work before God and
all the people..."
This seemingly irreconcilable matter Jesus immediately
assaulted. "O foolish and slow in heart so as to be
trusting upon all which the prophets spoke." From their
point of view it was just the fact that they did believe
"all the prophets" that created their dilemma. From the
point of view of Jesus their perplexity could only be
untangled by looking below the surface to the meaning of
Old Testament forshadows. How could it be possible for
"two disciples" with the grandeur of a conquering military
machine crushing Roman legions explain such prophetic words
as, "The wolf shall dwell with the lamb,...and a little
child shall lead them...the sucking child shall play on the
hole of the asp, and the weaned child shall put his hands
on the adder's den."(Is.11:6,8) And what flames engulfed
the "burning hearts" of the "two men" on that Emmaus road
when Jesus explained the meaning of "unto us a child is
given; and the government shall be upon his shoulder...and
of peace there shall be no end, upon the throne of David,
and upon his kingdom to establish it, and to uphold it with
justice and righteousness from henceforth and forever."
(Is.9:6,7) During that hour and half walk the word of all
the prophets took on new life, new insights never imagined
before in the minds and hearts of these two. With eyes not
yet fully "unrestrained" their firey glow of flaming hearts
stirred their sagging spirits. Eternal truth, seen through
so many material images, took on a rebirth, a new life of
the Spirit! And what smouldering embers of truth burst
into flame when this stranger quoted, "he has borne our

griefs, and carried our sorrows; yet we esteemed him stricken of God. But he was wounded for our transgressions, he was bruised for our iniquities...and Yahweh laid on him the iniquity of us all."(Is.53:4-6) A suffering Messiah! A kingdom based on moral, not political, power was different, new, unrivaled. In light of the _fact_ of Jesus' death "the prophets" enlightened their view of the recent suffering of Jesus! Joel heralded, "I will pour out my Spirit on all flesh"(2:28), while Micah added, "They shall beat their swords into plowshares...neither shall they learn war any more."(4:3) Nor did this stranger-teacher overlook the prophetic Psalms. "My God, my God, why have you forsaken me?...they pierced my hands and my feet"(22:1,16) pictures him _suffering_. Yet the same Psalm praises the triumph of that "forsaken" one by saying, "when he cried unto him he heard...All the ends of the earth shall remember and turn unto Yahweh..."(22:24,27) True, the repudiation, suffering and death of Messiah lay buried in the historical events of the Old Testament scriptures. But the events were the shell containing the kernel of Messiah. The rejection and crucifixion of Jesus was fulfillment, not denial, of the moral power of his kingdom. Jesus' death was the triumph of the Spirit of God over the sordid selfish corruption of human kind embodied in the leaders of Israel. Thus on the way to Emmaus the Stranger opened the minds of the two: "It was necessary, was it not, that the Christ suffer and _enter into his glory_?" It was "from Moses and _all_ the prophets he explained in _all_ _the_ _scriptures_ the things about himself." As the two listened, sadness turned to sunshine, doom to delight, grief to gladness. Their bitter barren road turned into a highway rising to an enlightened "burning heart."

The Meal in the Emmaus Home!

The eyes of these two were "restrained" so as not to recognize who this stranger might be. But by now it was time for _them_ to become evangels of the risen Christ. Jesus must reveal _who_ he was and _what_ he was in terms of his "glory." "And they drew near unto the village where they were going, and he made as though he would journey farther. And they pressed upon him: 'Stay with us! It is evening and the day is already far spent.' And he entered to stay with them." On the road to Emmaus the two had marvelled at this wayfarer's lack of knowledge of the "things that had happened." By now the two were marvelling at the depth of insight of this teacher as to the _meaning_ of that which happened in Jerusalem. The tables turned!

Yet another turning of tables was becoming clear. It was _their_ house and home. They were hosts; he was guest. But in the serving at meal time _he_ assumed the role of host; _they_ became his guests! "And it came to pass that when he sat down with them, having taken the loaf _he_ blessed and when he broke it _he_ _was_ _giving_ to them."

403

When Jesus "entered to stay with them" he took charge.
He was in position to direct the thought and in so doing
accomplish his purpose. His teaching had taken place over
the six mile, two hour walk. It remained now to confirm
that instruction by revealing who he was. That would not
only erase any trace of grief due to the crucifixion, it
would light a fire in them to tell any and all what they
had learned and sampled.

In Eastern lands among the Semites the table was the
institution that sealed friends and bound heart to heart.
To break bread together tied stranger to family as brother.
Thus "it happened when he sat down (in fellowship) with
them, having taken bread, he blessed and when he broke it
he was distributing to them." How could they miss the
meaning of what he was saying in this sharing his meal with
them? Too often before had they witnessed him do this to
fail to "see" now who he was and what he was declaring in
this act. Whatever scales, physical or figurative, had
blinded them now retreated: "Their eyes were opened, and
they recognized him." His glory broke through; they now
tasted for themselves what the angel announced to the
women: "He is risen!"

Luke testifies, "They knew him!" They not only
"recognized" him as the Jesus to whom they had attached
themselves as disciples but they now knew him as risen
Lord! He was more than Jesus who could save them from Rome
but the Christ whose rising spoke of a redemption other
than from Rome's tyranny. Such were the seed thoughts now
germinating in their hearts.

Scarcely did they "know" this risen Christ than "he
vanished from them!" That itself revealed even more about
this Jesus. They could identify him as the same one who
was crucified and buried and now risen. Yet he was
different! He "appeared" but he also "disappeared" at will.
It was the recognizable body; yet obviously with elements
that transcended physical barriers. They could no longer
deny, "he is risen." Nor could they explain his appearance
and disappearance. "To each other they said, 'Was not our
heart burning in us, as he was speaking to us on the way,
when he opened to us the scriptures?'"

The Return to Jerusalem!

Hardly more than two hours ago they were immersed in
sorrow over the death of their master. Now, with hearts
aflame, they could not rest until they shared their joy
with fellow disciples. Can flood waters be restrained
within a river's banks? No more than fired-up hearts can
be passively peaceful until they broadcast to others their
good news! Though "it was evening and the day far spent,"
that "very hour they returned to Jerusalem." There they
would share their new found knowledge and joy. "And they
found the eleven assembled and those with them." The news
borne by the two added to the growing evidence that "he is

risen." The eleven were saying, "The Lord really is risen and he appeared to Simon!" To that the two from Emmaus joined their experience of walking with Jesus. "They were recounting the things in the way and how he became known to them in the breaking of the bread."

Two factors threaded their way through all these various accounts. One, it was the identical Jesus that was seen after his death and burial. His form could be identified as that of Jesus. Yet his "appearances" left a new and different impression. There was something beyond the usual, the natural, the normal! Locked doors didn't hinder his entrance or exit. Food was optional but not essential for life. It was his body but glorified! His human nature came through as divine and his deity appeared as human. It was heaven's life piercing the realm of mortal yet with no more death to die! It became a foregleam of heavenly existence. His "appearances" were the real glorified Person, not the flesh and blood illusion of mortality of this material world. How does one communicate that which "eye has not seen nor ear heard" to those who only have "eyes" and "ears"?

In this narrative Luke introduces a new dimension of the Christ. He has revealed Jesus as "the Christ of God" who is truly human whose mission is universally available for all humanity. But now the risen Christ transcends the limits of sinful humanity. He lifts man into the realm of eternity with its divine dimension. He who has become truly human raises man to his divine destiny beyond flesh and blood.

AN OUTLINE OF LUKE 24:36-53
"<u>Thus It Is Written</u>!"
A tree casts a shadow, not a shadow the tree! There can
be no shadow until some physical object casts it. Prophecy
is the shadow; fulfillment is the reality. Fulfillment
gives <u>meaning</u> to prophecy. A different <u>meaning</u> was seen by
those who <u>first</u> <u>heard</u> a prophecy than by those who
experienced <u>its</u> fulfillment. Even the prophet did not
discern his own prophecy in terms of its final fulfillment!

I. THE RISEN CHRIST <u>IDENTIFIES</u> HIMSELF. 24:36-43
   1. Sudden appearance of the risen Christ. 36
   2. The believers' reaction. 37
   3. The Christ's challenge. 38-40
     (a)Why "troubled" and "thoughts arise?"
     (b)Empirical evidence: "Behold my hands..."
   4. Continuing disbelief "<u>for joy</u>!" 41-43
II. RISEN CHRIST <u>TEACHES</u>, "THUS IT IS WRITTEN."24:44-49
   1. Same facts taught before & after death. 44a
     (a)But now they are events of history!
     (b)Source: Moses, prophets, Psalms.
   2. Substance & content: "It is written." 44b-47
     (a)"The Christ should suffer."
     (b)"He should rise from dead on third day."
     (c)"Repentance...forgiveness to <u>all</u>..."
   3. You are witnesses of these things! 48-49
     (a)My representatives.
     (b)Your <u>need</u> for <u>power</u> supplied "from on high."
III. THE RISEN CHRIST <u>ASCENDS</u>! 24:50-53
   1. Atop Mount of Olives Christ "blesses" them. 50
   2. While blessing he "was carried into heaven." 51
   3. Their consequent conduct: 52-53
     (a)"Worshipped him."
     (b)"With <u>joy</u>" returned to Jerusalem."
     (c)Were "constantly praising God."

Before teaching is acceptable the identity and integrity
of the teacher must be established. The student's mind is
to be "thoroughly opened" so as to fit facts to <u>meaning</u>.
Then joy, worship and praise can follow!

* * * * * * *

"<u>THUS IT IS WRITTEN</u>!"
To believe the unbelievable is the triumph of faith!
Doubt drugs one into disbelief! The dulling depressant of
doubt can be conquered by the fullness of faith grounded in
objective incredible fact. To believe the unbelievable is
victory! That kind of faith nothing can quench!
A tree casts a shadow! The shadow does not create the
tree. There can be no shadow without first the tree. The
eternal Christ dwelt in the "bosom of the father." He was
eternal Word (λόγος) who "became flesh and tabernacled
among us and we beheld his glory." This <u>Word</u> cast numerous

406

shadows throughout the Old Testament. "God, having of old time spoken to the fathers in the prophets at many times and in various ways, at the end of these days has spoken to us in (one who is) Son..."(Heb.1:1) This "Son" drew all lines of prophecy unto himself. HE is the objective reality, the historical person, who cast all the shadows which the prophets spoke!

For his disciples the life of Jesus terminated in disappointment! The Emmaus two exclaimed, "We were hoping that he was the one about to redeem Israel!" The death made it an ill-founded fancy. And the report that his tomb was found empty aggravated a baseless hope. But as the excited two, breathlessly told their tale of "eyes opened," "hearts burning," and the "breaking of bread" and how "he opened the scriptures," "he stood in their midst!"

Were their senses deceiving them? Normal sight and sound seemed now unreliable. Death was so universal! They themselves had watched him die. They had seen the corpse, observed the place of burial. Eyes and ears were not now to be trusted in view of their personal perception of his death and burial. "Having become terrified, fear having overwhelmed them, they were supposing they saw a ghost!" Yet they could not explain the well-remembered voice and the familiar greeting, "Peace to you!" When reason abandons us feelings take control. Emotions override man's rational nature when events lie beyond explanation!

To undergird his word of "Peace" he reviewed their disturbed emotions. "Why are you troubled and for what reason are thoughts rising in your heart?" To calm them he added a challenge. "Behold! my hands and my feet, that I myself am he!" It was more than hands and feet he urged on them; it was the scars of nail prints that could identify him as the same person they had seen crucified. In fact when he urged them to use their sense of touch he insisted they "handle" with critical examination his hands and feet. "Examine me and see that a ghost does not have flesh and bones as you behold me having!" How do we verify the unusual, the impossible, the incredible? In this world man is left to determine facts by the physical senses of sight, sound, touch, smell and taste. These exhaust physical evidences.

Luke reports that "they were still unbelieving." But the source of unbelief was "from joy and marvelling." No longer could they plead lack of evidence. They had seen, heard, touched and examined. Rationally they were convinced; emotionally doubt prevailed. The "joy" and "marvel" of such an incredible person and event overwhelmed better judgment. Could they believe the unbelievable? As yet faith had not triumphed over doubt. Until then Jesus must persist in identifying himself as the object of faith, the ultimate reality that gave meaning to Hebrew history. He alone could shed light on the shadows of scripture!

Jesus makes the decisive appeal for faith: "Do you have here anything edible?" To which they "gave him a piece of broiled fish. And he ate it before them!" The risen Jesus appeared before them in his body of glory. He could be distinguised by marks of his crucified body. Yet he was not limited by walls or locked doors. Nor did he need food for nourishment. Nevertheless "he ate before them" to authenticate his person. It clinched their faith!

The Risen Christ Teaches!

Having established his identity Jesus began to explain the Old Testament in the light of the fact of his death. "He said to them, 'These are my words which I spoke to you, yet being with you.'" He taught nothing afterward that he had not explained before his death. But the difference lay in their inability before to accept the possibility of his dying. Now his death could not be denied. It was an event of the past, a reality however harsh and unjust. Now he could pry open their minds and inject into their hearts the meaning of the week-end events. Or more importantly, the meaning of scripture viewed from the facts, his death, burial and resurrection!

Everything in the Old Testament, Moses' law, the prophets, the Psalms opened with the light of truth, new truth when seen in perspective of his death, burial and resurrection. He plainly taught them, "It was necessary (logical, reasonable, sensible) that all things having been written in the law of Moses and the prophets, and the Psalms about me be fulfilled." When the OT was read aright, Messiah's death should have been anticipated. But until the fulfillment, that is, until Messiah died and thus fulfilled in reality the shadowed outlines, the OT remained vague, hidden, obscure.

To him who had eyes with which to see and heart to understand the old scriptures clearly claimed two divinely determined specifics. One, the substance of God's grace in redemptive facts, that "the Christ suffer and rise from the dead on the third day." And two, God's commission to selected instruments that they "herald in his name repentance and forgiveness to all the nations."

Consider Peter's dullness of mind when with oaths he rejected the possibility of Jesus' death before that death. Whence did that same Peter get such clear insight to the necessity and joy of that death? Just fifty days after Christ's death Peter proclaimed with such spiritual meaning the prophecy of Joel! Where did he learn that Jesus was "delivered up by the determinate counsel and foreknowledge of God." (Acts 2:23) And whence this salty fisherman's insight of Psalm 16, "My heart was glad, and my tongue rejoiced; moreover my flesh also shall dwell in hope: because you will not leave my soul unto Hades, neither will you give your Holy One to see corruption." (Acts 2:27) How did Peter change from a dull disciple to a brilliant interpreter of scripture?

When Peter and John were brought before the Jewish tribunal for healing a lame man at the Beautiful temple gate, in defense they said, "You killed the prince of life...But the things which God foreshowed by the mouth of all the prophets, that his Christ should suffer, he thus fulfilled." Little more than a month earlier Peter had denied ever knowing Christ. Where now did he, with John, get this idea about the death of Jesus? Cowardice had changed to courage, power replaced weakness, knowledge supplanted ignorance. How did this happen?

The change lay in that the risen Christ had "thoroughly opened their minds to understand the scriptures." Had it not been for his teaching after the death and resurrection there would have been no Pentecost, no gospel.

It is notable that, according to Luke, when the Emmaus two returned to the gathered disciples in the upper room they heard, "The Lord really is risen and has appeared to Simon." Apparently Jesus gave a personal private teaching session to Simon Peter, who had denied him! And that to reassure him of his being restored to his place in the disciple group. And also to "open his mind to understand the scriptures." Jesus rehearsed for Peter "all that stands written in the law of Moses, and the prophets and the Psalms about me." The resurrection is the key that unlocks the meaning of Christ's death, not to mention the Old Testament law, prophets and Psalms. It was the resurrection after his death that proved to be the lever with which Jesus could pry open the calloused mind. With distinct clarity Peter later wrote, "You were redeemed, not with corruptible things...but with precious blood, as of a lamb without blemish and without spot, of Christ: who was foreknown before the foundation of the world..." (I Peter 1:18-21) Peter learned this personally from Jesus during the period between the resurrection and ascension.

But Jesus taught something more than his death and resurrection. It was their same Old Testament scriptures that shadowed forth the spiritual nature of the world wide, age-long nature of the kingdom of God. At the fountainhead when God chose the Hebrews as his instrument for redemption he said to Abraham, "in you shall all the families of the earth be blessed." From the beginning it was God's purpose to reach all nations by choosing to reach them through one nation. That people was selected because God sought to save every nation.

Furthermore, the kingdom of God is determined in moral and spiritual terms, not political, economic, or racial. Thus Jesus taught: "it stands written that repentance and remission of sins should be preached in my name unto all nations, beginning at Jerusalem." No peace can come between man and man until peace prevails between God and man. Man repents; God forgives! Then peace comes!

But if that peace of redemption is to come on earth it must have someone to announce it. Hence Jesus said, "You are witnesses of these things." Those who testify to men with persuasion are fellow men, not angelic witnesses. Human beings who themselves have seen, heard, touched the facts can best bring others to experience the power of the gospel. Man is to witness to man the deeds of God's grace. But these witnesses are not to embark on a world task in their own strength. Awesome work demands awesome power. Jesus promised: "I send forth the promise of my father upon you. But you stay in the city until clothed with power from on high!" Be aware that you did not initiate this redemption. Nor can you execute it in your strength. It is God's project and only God's power can perform it. Therefore, wait for that promised power to invade you.

The Risen Christ Ascends!

In his second volume (Acts 1:3) Luke reveals that Jesus "presented himself after he suffered...appearing for forty days." So we learn that Jesus took time and trouble to teach with care "the things about the kingdom of God." However, in the story of the upper room Luke summarizes the forty-day teaching. Once having "thoroughly opened their mind to understand," his earthly task is over. The only essential left is to return visibly to the heaven that sent him. When his disciples are aware that his appearances have completed their purpose and that he has withdrawn, then they will sense their responsibility to "witness to these things." Thus he led them to Mount Olivet and there was "blessing them." And while blessing he was "carried into heaven" and disappeared from sight.

Three factors mark this as part of the gospel story. Luke says, "they worshipped him." For the first time before or after his death the disciples got Jesus in proper focus. Ingrained into their subconcious souls was: "Thou shalt have no other Gods before me." Without compromise they now "worshipped" Jesus for the deity that he is.

Moreover, "with joy they returned to Jerusalem." Gone was the morose, "we had hoped that it was he who should redeem!" Sadness at his death turned to "joy" in that death and the kingdom of which it was the basis.

Thirdly "they were constantly praising God." Life no longer was a series of mountaintops and low valleys. In knowledge of the daily presence of the living God and endued with power "from on high" valleys became high points of daily fellowship with God in Christ.

Thus Luke concludes his narrative of "the matters having been fulfilled among us." He has told of God as an unborn human "beginning" life as all humans do, an embryo in a woman's womb. He has traced him from boyhood through manhood. He has revealed how a truly good man fares in a world of evil. He followed the growth of a disciple group as well as growing opposition of Jewish leaders that finally fruited in crucifixion. The teaching of Jesus was

410

the expression of his personal life as God designed life to be lived by man. He embraced all life as moral stewardship. Above all two notes sounded forth from all that Jesus said and did. One, the spiritual nature of God's sovereign rule. Two, the universal extent of that kingdom. The narrative of the person of Jesus is complete. It remains for his second "treatise," the Acts, to continue telling how Jesus after his ascension worked out this universal kingdom through his chosen witnesses. That is another story!

BOOK II

DIAGRAMS WITH NOTES

THE DIAGRAM

The sentence is a unit of thought. When an author projects ideas in organized forms, he creates sentences. When a reader envisions the writer's thought, with instinct he analyzes the sentence and thereby reconstructs the idea of the author. The creation of a sentence followed by the analysis of that sentence by the reader is an important and necessary element in normal communication. Hence, one stone in the foundation of good exposition is sentence analysis.

The term "analysis" stems from the preposition ἀνά "up" joined to the verb λύειν "to loose." Analysis consists of reducing the sentence to its simplest parts (words, phrases and clauses), and critical scrutiny of each of these parts in its relationship to the whole. Analysis "loosens up" a sentence into its constitutional elements. It then puts the parts back together in a visual form.

When analysis is objectified in the form of a written diagram, it pictures relationships. A diagram images the sentence, meets the eye, stirs the imagination, objectifies the logic of the thought by means of visible impressions. Diagram dramatizes ideas, makes prominent what is prominent paints dependent that which is dependent. It even calls to the attention the obscurities, ambiguities, or confusions in an author's writing. In spite of certain limitations which diagramming has, it remains a very practical working tool for the expositor. If a student would trace a writer's thought, he must _retrace_ the author's thought. The discipline of diagramming offers one of the best maps available for guiding the student over the devious pathways of the thinker whose ideas have been put to paper.

* * * * * * *

A DIAGRAM OF LUKE 24:45

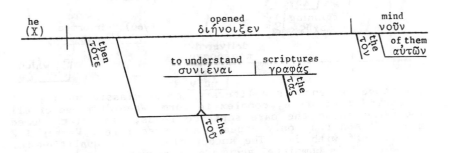

1

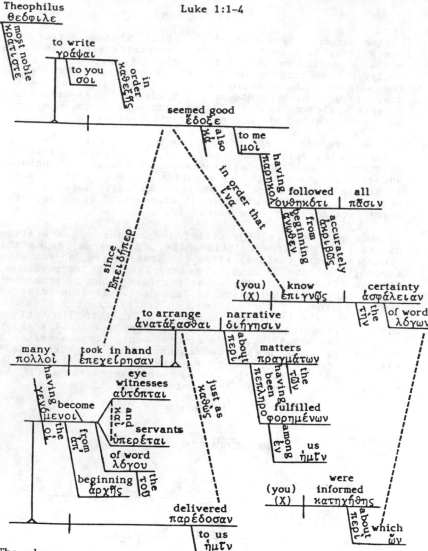

Luke 1:1-4

The above sentence is a literary gem of classic quality. It is periodic in style, complex in form. When disrobed of all modifying ideas the bare sentence reads, "To write seemed good..." And that only appears at verse three. Verses 1-2 balance off with 3-4. The author claims four qualities for his work. It's complete, accurate, thorough, orderly.

2

The independent clause says: "To write to you in an orderly arrangement seemed good to me also having traced all things accurately from the start." Adverb clause begun by ἐπειδήπερ gives a valid stimulus which prompted Luke to write. It asserts, "In as much as many took in hand to arrange an account..." διήγησιν is object of infinitive "to arrange" and means "connected account" carried through to its climax. "Account" is described by prepositional phrase "about matters." These are events (πραγμάτων) described by attr.pf.pas.ptc. "having been fulfilled" (πεπληρο-φορημένων). It means "bring to full measure." The tense suggests permanently fulfilled.

καθὼς ushers in a comparative adverb clause, "just as the ones from the start became eye-witnesses and servants of the word delivered..." By the article οἱ with participle plus "eye-witnesses" and "servants" Luke refers to one set of men with two functions. The eye-witnesses were servants. "From the start" (ἀπ' ἀρχῆς.) points to the beginning of Jesus' ministry. These witnesses were acquainted with the whole story. Luke made thorough preparation.

No doubt is left as to his purpose. The ἵνα adverb clause states, "that you may fully know the certainty..." "Certainty" indicates "assurance." But Luke's purpose is more than apologetic. He has positive information that Theophilus needs for a solid foundation to intelligent faith. He wants to give "assurance" from that which he learned from "eye-witnesses and ministers." ἀσφάλειαν "certainty" is quite emphatic by its position, last in the sentence. λόγων "words" indicates a "message," a connected group of words conveying an extended announcement.

The dependent clause introduced by ὧν is adjectival descriptive of λόγων "...certainty of the words about which you were informed..." To have some information about Christianity is one thing. But to have enough accurate and convincing information to bring conviction and conversion is another. The latter is precisely that which Luke set out to provide for his noble friend. Thus the Gospel supplies full, accurate, convincing explanation of the events of Jesus' life. It reveals what happened during those crucial years when Jesus walked, lived, died and arose.

καθεξῆς is an adverb. It is a word used only by Luke of the New Testament authors. It is compounded from preposition κατά "down" and adverb ἐξῆς = "successively" which in turn is derived from ἔχω "have," "hold." When κατά is used distributively "down along" a series of points successively appearing, the idea is that of "vital sequence," one event building on and springing from a previous one. Each prepares for and lays foundation for the next. Luke proposes a well-arranged, logical order of events. His story isn't chronological but psychological.

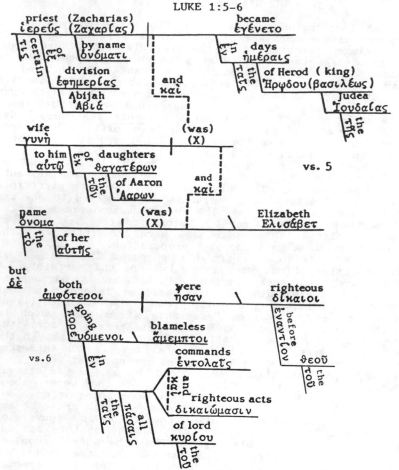

LUKE 1:5-6

vs. 5

vs. 6

The sentence of verse five above has three independent clauses. Thus it's compound in structure. The bare clauses assert: "priest became," "wife (was)," and "name (was..." In the third "Elizabeth" is predicate nominative referring back to subject "name."

The subject of the first clause is the agent noun ἱερεύς meaning "priest." All nouns ending in -ευς express "agent" who performs the action in words of the same root. Hence ἱερεύς is one who serves in sacred temple services. To identify this priest his name is given, Ζαχαρίας = Zacharias. It means "Yahweh has remembered."

4

THE DIAGRAM OF LUKE 1:5-6

Used with Zacharias is dative ὀνόματι = name. It is the possessive use of the dative, "Name to him, Zacharias." ἐφημερίας is compounded from ἐπί "upon" and ἡμέρα "day." It literally would be "day upon day," or daily. By usage it came to refer to the "divisions" or "courses" into which the sons of Aaron were organized based on I Chr.23:6 and 24:7-18. It indicated the "daily" duties performed by the priests in the temple. Preposition ἐξ with ablative denotes source or origin. Zacharias was "from" the division of Abia.

ἐν with locative ἡμέραις locates the general time within which. The particular Herod "king of Judea" is Herod "the great" who ruled from 37 B.C. until his death in 4 B.C.

ἐγένετο 2nd aorist of defective γίνομαι "become" is more than "be." It means "to arise," "come into being," "occur," "take place," "come to pass." That which Luke is reporting "came to pass." It arose like flowers bloom from seed. Providential circumstances brought this to pass.

The second clause of verse five says, "wife (was)." Once again the dative of possession appears in αὐτῷ; "wife to him." The diagram shows the ἐκ phrase as adjective describing "wife." She was "of the daughters of Aaron." The phrase might be treated as predicate after understood verb "was." In either case it's adjectival, attributive or predicate.

The third clause of the sentence of verse 5 identifies the wife by name. "Her name (was) Elizabeth." Note change from possessive dative to possessive genitive αὐτῆς "of her." The name "Elizabeth" means "My God is an oath" which seems to suggest that God is absolutely faithful, the one on whom one can count.

Verse six structures a simple sentence, "Both were right-eous..." Preposition ἐναντίον with genitive ushers in an adverbial phrase indicating where they were righteous, "before God." That is to say that "before God" they got a verdict of "righteousness." He dealt with them as righteous.

Circumstantial present participle πορευόμενοι "going" or "proceeding" in some translations is rendered "walking." As they moved through life men found them "without blame." The present tense indicates continuing, ongoing action. It testifies to a life of blamelessness. The sphere in which they were "going" is introduced in the ἐν phrase, "in all the commandments and righteous acts of the Lord." The word for "commands" ἐντολαῖς underlines the idea of surrender to moral authority. That for "righteous acts" is a -μα word indicating result of action in the verb of the same root. δικαίωμα "right act" is the result of "doing right," that is, the righteous deed done. They were the standards by which God acts. Zacharias and Elizabeth yielded to the moral authority of God's law. They imitated the deeds done by God himself. It was a life-long habit of conduct.

and
καί

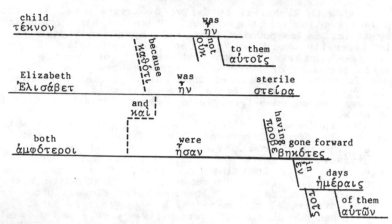

child
τέκνον

was
ἦν

not
οὐκ

to them
αὐτοῖς

Elizabeth
Ἐλισάβετ

because
καθότι

was
ἦν

sterile
στεῖρα

and
καί

both
ἀμφότεροι

were
ἦσαν

having
προβε

gone forward
βηκότες

days
ἡμέραις

of them
αὐτῶν

Verse seven constitutes a complex sentence of three clauses. The independent clause states the fact, "And a child was not to them." Subject τέκνον = "child" comes from the verb τίκτω = "to bring forth." The word signifies a child who comes by <u>natural</u> birth, hence inherits the nature of the parents as well as their legal heritage, that is, the <u>rights</u> of heir.

Personal pronoun αὐτοῖς "to them" is possessive dative used after strong negative οὐκ "not." All datives express personal interest but the context modifies the particular aspect to be emphasized. καθότι "because" is a "good Attic word" confined in the New Testament to Luke's writings. It is compounded of κατα, ὅ, τι, literally meaning "according to what." Here it introduces an adverbial dependent clause "because."

Two dependents support the fact stated in the independent clause. "Because the wife was sterile" is the first. The second is "...and both were well advanced in their days." Imperfect ἦσαν "were" couples with supplementary perfect participle προβεβηκότες "having advanced" to form a periphrastic past perfect, "had advanced far in their days." This form gives added emphasis to the permanent hopeless plight of the ancient pair. Any expectation of a child was permanently long gone.

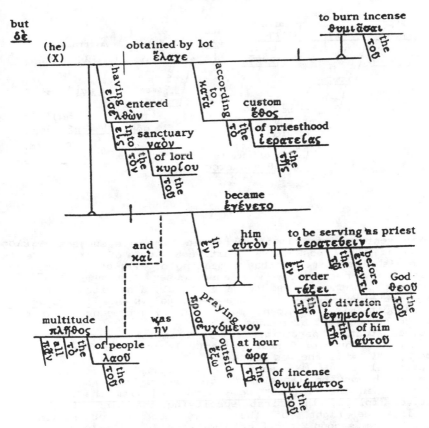

The sentence of 1:8-10 is compound-complex. The noun clause
"he obtained..." is subject of aorist verb ἐγένετο = "became"
literally, but it may be decoded as "happened," "came to pass."
Aorist infinitive θυμιᾶσαι = "to burn incense" is object of verb
"obtained." Circumstantial participle εἰσελθὼν "having entered"
is not temporal as if "he obtained _when_ he entered." It may be
classed as attendant circumstance or even purpose. The ἐν
infinitive phrase technically is not a clause. It is infinitive
with accusative of general reference. But practically it serves
as a clause, "...while he was serving as priest it happened..."
    The second independent clause states, "crowd...was praying."
The periphrastic imperfect ἦν προσευχόμενον "was praying" lends
importance to the linear action inherent in all imperfect tenses.
They persisted praying without ceasing. "At the hour of incense"
is adverbial telling _when_ they were praying. Adverb ἔξω indicates
where.

7

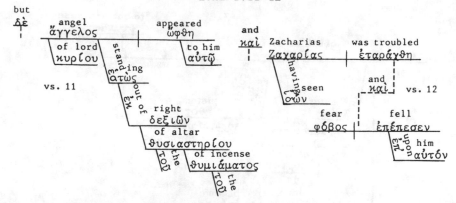

LUKE 1:11-12

The sentence of 1:11 is simple in form. Its subject ἄγγελος is identified by possessive genitive κυρίου "of Lord." He is the Lord's messenger. The basic meaning of ἄγγελος is <u>messenger</u>. It literally means "one who announces." It is used in the Septuagint "in the special sense of <u>angel</u>, a spiritual, heavenly being, attendent upon God and employed as his messenger to men."(Abbott-Smith, Lexicon, pg.4) But by no means is it confined to such spiritual beings.

Circumstantial participle ἑστὼς "standing" is perfect tense but with the force of linear present. It is to be classified as temporal, "...while he was standing..."

Literally ἐκ δεξιῶν means "out of rights" but it is a fixed idiom which may be translated "on the right." Ablative case suggests that the "rights" were separated from the altar. Two genitives follow, the first specifying the <u>kind</u> of "right," that is, the right "of the altar" not any other kind of "right." The second specifies the <u>kind</u> of altar; it was the "altar of <u>incense</u>, not any other kind. Genitives are descriptive. They describe more sharply than adjectives.

ὤφθη is aorist passive of ὁράω "see." "He was seen" is translated "appeared." The point action of aorist presents the action as fact rather than offering a description.

Verse 12 offers a compound sentence of two clauses. Without modifiers the bare sentence reads, "Zacharias...was troubled" and "fear fell." The verbs in both clauses are simple narrative aorists. There's no attempt on Luke's part to dress up the action by any linear descriptives.

Again, the participle ἰδών "having seen" is temporal circumstantial. But this time the aorist suggests "when he saw" not "while." That is, it's punctiliar, not linear

8

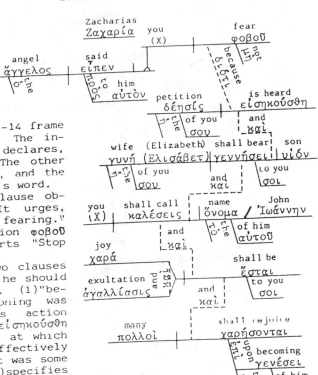

The 7 clauses of 13-14 frame a complex sentence. The independent clause declares, "The angel said." The other six tell what, why, and the effect of the angel's word.

First is noun clause object of "said." It urges, "Zacharias, quit fearing." Present linear action φοβοῦ with negative exhorts "Stop what you're doing."

διότι inserts two clauses giving reasons why he should quit being afraid. (1)"because your petitioning was heard." δέησις is action noun. Aor. pass. εἰσηκούσθη looks to the point at which the praying was effectively heard though now it was some years later; (2)specifies how their praying was about to be answered. "...your wife...shall bear son..." Delay in answering prayer does not mean that prayers are not answered. The answer is delayed to suit God's timing, not man's eager impatience. The final three clauses spell out in detail the fallout from the answered prayer. "You shall call his name John." Future καλέσεις is prophetic, not futuristic or deliberative. It addresses the will, hence is volitional. The name John, "God is gracious," indicates the child's work in the divine purpose. John is objective complement. Without it "You shall call his name..." would be incomplete.

The next dependent states what the meaning of this answered prayer will be to the elderly priest, "Joy and exultation shall be to you." The final clause reveals what it will mean to the "many" who shall be blessed because this couple were blessed with this child; "many shall rejoice."

γενέσει "becoming" is from γίνομαι "become." "Be" is static, expressing state. "Become" suggests more an entering into a state, a developing growth.

9

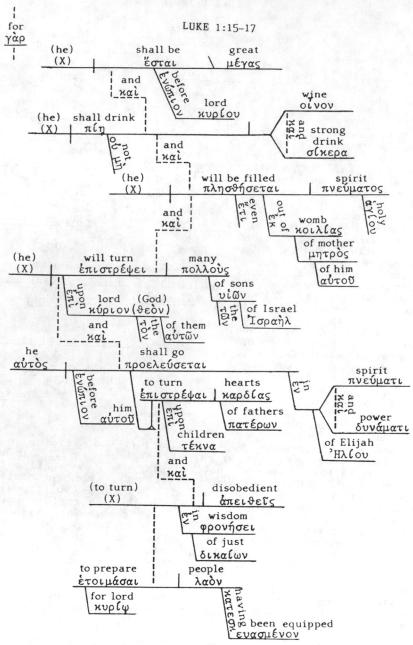

10

THE DIAGRAM OF LUKE 1:15-17

Since infinitive phrases are technically not clauses the sentence of 15-17 is a compound of five independente. They project the person and work of the son, John. The first three speak of his person; "he shall be great," "he shall not drink wine and strong drink," and "he shall be filled...with Holy Spirit." The other two denote what his work is to be. "He will turn many of the sons of Israel upon the Lord their God," and "he shall go before him in spirit and power of Elijah." From this fifth and last clause hang three infinitives of purpose: "to turn..." "(to turn)..." and "to prepare..." Though such are phrases, not clauses, because they have no subject to limit them, they perform the function of clauses. Each infinitive has an implied accusative of general reference "him" performing the verbal action. They may be translated, "that he may turn hearts...disobedient...and to prepare..."

In the first clause the adjective "great" is predicate. Prepositional phrase "before Lord" is adverbial and discloses where he is great. His greatness is not veneer, it's genuine.

The next two clauses trace the greatness negatively and positively. He shall not (οὐ μὴ is strong negative) get stimulent artificially by going to strong drink. Rather "He shall be filled from his mother's womb with the Holy Spirit." Verbs of filling regularly take the genitive, the case which expresses this and not that. Adverb ἔτι "even" with ἐκ "out from" suggests that even before birth God's Spirit was the intoxicating energy influencing behaviour.

The third clause reports, "he shall turn many of the sons..." πολλοὺς "many" is used substantively. He does not say, "he will turn many sons..." but, "he shall turn many of the sons..." υἱῶν "sons" is partitive genitive specifying the kind of "many" whom he will turn. ἐπὶ in the phrase "to the Lord" literally means "upon the Lord."

In clause five prepositional phrase "before him" is adverb in force expressing where. Note that the antecedent of αὐτοῦ "him" is "Lord(God)" of the preceding clause. The Lord God is the Messiah; the child of Zacharias is to "go before him." Prepositional ἐν phrase is adverbial in function indicating manner: "in spirit and power of Elijah." The angel gives the valid meaning of Malachi 4:5. John is the promised Elijah; he will work in the same spirit, having the same powerful results as the first Elijah in 9th century B.C.

ἐπιστρέψαι "to turn" is aorist active infinitive of ἐπιστρέφω meaning "I turn," a word used for conversion. It is a purpose infinitive. John's work was to prepare the people morally and spiritually for the appearance of the Christ who was to redeem his people from sin.

Another aorist infinitive "to prepare" (ἐτοιμάσαι) has λαὸν "people" for its direct object. κατεσκευασμένον "having been equipped" is perfect ptcp. indicating permament preparation.

11

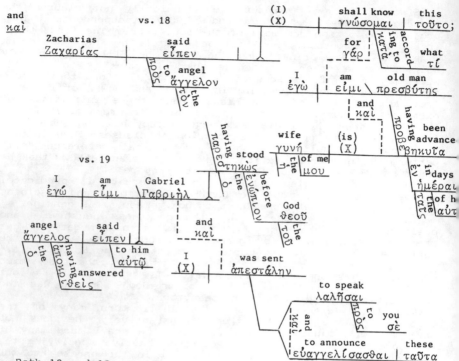

Both 18 and 19 are structured as complex sentences. Except subjects the independent clauses are identical, "Zacharias said" and "the angel said." The modifying phrases "to the angel" and "to him" differ in cases; accusative indicates direction toward; dative is more directly personal.

Object of "said" in 18 consists of three noun clauses, "How shall I know," "I am old," and "my wife is advanced..." κατὰ τί "according to what?" asks for standard of measurement. Abraham asked the same, (Gen.15:8) but because he believed; Zacharias because he doubted.

Emphatic ἐγώ of verse 18 matches the ἐγώ in verse 19. "I am old," versus "I am Gabriel." Age versus God's word is the issue. "My wife is advanced..."is the priest's next basis for doubt. Periphrastic perfect "is advanced" reminds that her age was permanent. She would always be beyond child-bearing.

Attr.,Pf.,Ptcp. παρεστηκώς "having stood," appositive to Gabriel, is to impress Zacharias that he doubts, not man but God.

The final dependent clause of 19 undercuts the doubt. "I was sent." Two infinitives tell why:"to speak" and "to announce."

LUKE 1:20-21

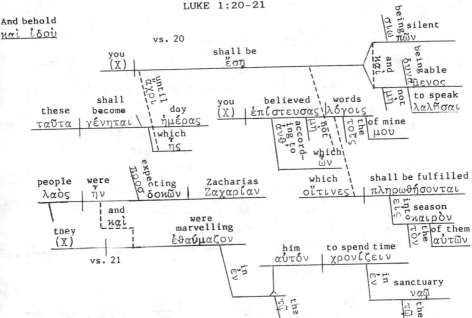

"And behold!" introduces the complex sentence of verse 20. ἰδού "behold" is imperative of ὁράω "see" but it has become a fixed form as interjection expressing emotion. The independent clause has a compound predicate. Two present participles supplement future ἔσῃ to say, "You shall be silent and not able to speak..." Future, normally point action, here is linear by virtue of the periphrasis: "You shall go on being silent and continue being unable to speak."

Two of the three dependents are temporal. ἄχρι ἧς "until which" inserts the idea of when, "until which day..." Another dependent is adverbial of cause, ἀνθ᾽ ὧν "according to which..." λόγοις "words" is dative after verb "believe." The case of personal interest blends with the verbal idea. οἵτινες "which" is qualitative relative pronoun introducing an adjective clause describing "words." "Which by their very nature shall be fulfilled..."

Verse 21 encompasses a compound sentence of two clauses. The supplementary present active participle προσδοκῶν combines with ἦν to form a periphrastic imperfect by which Luke emphasizes linear action. Regular imperfect ἐθαύμαζον cooperates with the periphrasis to stress the descriptive linear. "Expecting and marvelling" grew into bewilderment and anxiety. ἐν τῷ and infinitive literally says, "in the to spend time in the sanctuary in reference to him." The infinitive is linear present, "...while he was in the sanctuary."

13

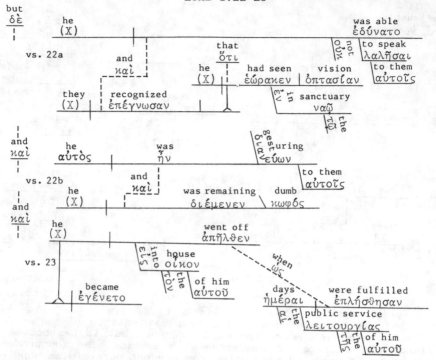

Verse 22a is compound-complex sentence with two independent and one dependent clause. The first independent says, "He was not being able to speak." Imperfect middle with οὐκ is conative. He repeatedly tried but failed. Punctiliar aorist of infinitive "to speak" completes the idea in the imperfect "not being able. "Speaking" was seen as a single act though the attempt was repeated. The second independent declares "they knew..." ἐπέγνωσαν is aorist. Preposition ἐπί with perfective force compounds with γίνωσκω and means "know thoroughly." There came a point at which the people "got to know." What they came to know is stated in declarative ὅτι noun clause, "that he had seen..." ἑώρακεν is perfect; what he saw became a fixed part of his experience.

The sentence of 22b is a two clause compound. Verbs in both clauses are linear imperfects but ἦν διανεύων is periphrastic giving special stress to linear action. Personal pronoun αὐτός "he" adds its own emphasis.

Verse 23 frames a complex sentence. "It came to pass" represents the independent idea. That which came to pass is in noun clause subject of the sentence, "He went off." The second dependent is adverbial telling when he went off.

14

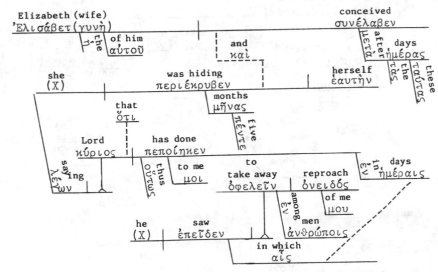

24-25 develop a compound-complex sentence of four clauses. Two independent ideas say, "Elizabeth conceived" and "she was hiding." In apposition to "Elizabeth" is "wife." συνέλαβεν is aorist of compound συλλαμβάνω "bring together" and often means "conceived." It's an old word in general use but appears only sixteen times in NT, eleven in Luke. When she conceived is set forth in adverbial phrase, "after these days."

περιέκρυβεν of the second independent clause may be aorist of περικρύπτω "conceal entirely" or imperfect of περικρύβω a later form. The preposition is perfective. Imperfect presents the picture vividly and suits the context. Elizabeth felt compelled to keep hiding herself until her pregnancy became manifest. Five months is accusative extent of time.

The first dependent clause is ὅτι noun clause object of circumstantial participle "saying." Perfect πεποίηκεν "has done" is extensive perfect detailing completed action with abiding results. Adverb οὕτως "thus" adds stress to "the Lord has done...to me." Elizabeth's frustrating years were included in the "thus." Nevertheless, the immediate meaning of the "thus" lies in prepositional phrase "in (the) days..." "Days" is expanded in adjective clause, "in which he saw to take away my reproach..." Infinitive phrase is object of verb, "he saw." ὀνειδός is accusative, object of infinitive. It means "censure," "reproach," "disgrace." Prepositional phrase "among men" is adverbial denoting where. In Hebrew culture to be childless was thought of as divine displeasure, but that was man's opinion. The shame of the reproach was "among men," not God.

15

but
δέ

angel (Gabriel)
ἄγγελος (Γαβριὴλ)
o- the

and
καί
πρός
to virgin
παρθένον

in month
ἐν
μηνι
the
σ̄ sixth
ἕκτῳ

from
ἀπό
God
θεοῦ
the
τοῦ

was sent
ἀπεστάλη

εἰς
unto city
πόλιν
of Galilee
Γαλιλαίας
the
τῆς

name (was)
ὄνομα (X)
o- the
of virgin
παρθένου
the
τῆς
Mary
Μαριάμ

having
ἐμνηστ-
been
betrothed
ευμένην
to man
ἀνδρί

name (was) Nazareth
ὄνομα (X) Ναζαρὲτ
to which
ᾗ

vss. 26-27

name (was)
ὄνομα (X)
to whom
ᾧ

Joseph
Ἰωσὴφ

of house
οἴκου
of David
Δαυίδ

and
καί

having been
μεχαρι-τωμένη
(you)
(X)
favored
rejoice
χαῖρε

vs. 28
he
(X)
said
εἶπεν

Lord
κύριος
(is)
(X)
with
μετά
you
σοῦ

having
entered
εἰσελθών
πρός
o- her
αὐτήν

but
δέ

that one
ἡ
was perplexed
διεταράχθη
ἐπί
upon word
λόγῳ
the
τῷ

and
καί

salutation
ἀσπασμός
the
o-
might be
εἴη
οὗτος
this
what
ποταπὸς

vs. 29
she
(X)
was reasoning
διελογίζετο
Mary
Μαριάμ

and
καί

vs. 30

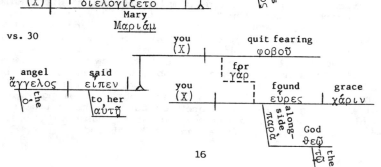

you
(X)
quit fearing
φοβοῦ

angel
ἄγγελος
o- the
said
εἶπεν
to her
αὐτῇ

for
γάρ
you
(X)
found
εὗρες
grace
χάριν
along-
side
παρά
God
θεῷ
the
τῷ

16

LUKE 1:26-30

The sentence encased in verses 26-27 involves four clauses. Two are independent and two dependent, hence it is classified as compound-complex. Stripped of modifiers, the main clauses state, "angel was sent" and "name (was) Mary." That these two clauses belong together is clear from the subordinate modifying elements in the rest of the sentence. Adverbial idea to whom he was sent appears in prepositional "to virgin..." "Virgin" is identified by circumstantial perfect participle ἐμνηστευμένην "having been betrothed." Dative ἀνδρί "to man" is adverbial which in turn is described by adjective clause, "name to whom (was) Joseph..." Another prepositional phrase, "in the sixth month" answers the question when the angel was sent. There follows two additional phrases answering from where and unto where he was sent; "from God" and "unto city of the Galilee." The noun πόλιν "city" is described by dependent adjective clause, "to which name (was) Nazareth."

The sentence of verse 28 is a complex of three clauses. The independent idea is, "He said." Circumstantial aorist participle εἰσελθὼν "having entered" is temporal, "when he entered." The two dependents are noun clauses objects of "said." Imperative χαῖρε "rejoice" has for its subject "you" which is amplified by the attributive perfect participle κεχαριτωμένη "having been favored." Verb χαῖρε "rejoice" is present, indicating continued action, "go on rejoicing." In the second dependent the prepositional adverbial μετά contains the idea of "fellowship with."

Verse 29 unveils a compound-complex arrangement. The initial independent states, "That one was perplexed." The diagram shows the subject as "that one." The text has the definite article ἡ which is the demonstrative use of the article, normal Greek use. The verb form translated "was perplexed" is punctiliar action aorist. This in contrast to linear of the imperfect in the next independent (διελογίζετο "was reasoning") looks at what was an ongoing "troubling" as a point. Mary "was reasoning" which is a description of a process going on. Yet her being "troubled" went on for the same period of time. Yet the author notes as a point her being troubled. But he describes her "reasoning." Dependent noun clause, "...what this salutation might be" is object of verb "was reasoning." The adjective ποταπός appears only six times in the New Testament. In "late writers" it = ποῖος "of what sort."

Verse 30 develops as a complex of three clauses. The single independent clause, "The angel said to her," supports two noun clauses, direct objects of "said." Present imperative φοβοῦ "quit fearing" implies that she is fearing. Linear action suggests that she "quit" what she is doing. The second dependent idea offers a reason why should quit; "for you found favor..." εὖρες is second aorist which indicates a point in the past at which she "found" favor. Prepositonal παρά phrase is adverbial and tells where she found favor, that is "alongside God."

17

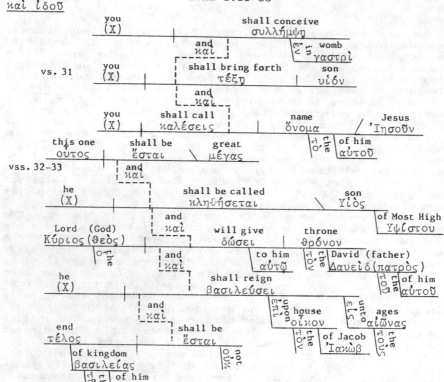

Verse 33 embodies a three-clause compound sentence. "You shall conceive" is first with adverbial "in womb" expressing <u>where</u>. Second comes, "You shall bring forth son." Then, "You shall call his name Jesus." In this third clause Ἰησοῦν "Jesus" is predicate complement.

The sentence of 32-33 is compound also but it employs five clauses. Subject of the first clause is demonstrative pronoun οὗτος used here as substantive, "this one." μέγας "great" is predicate adjective. In the next clause predicate nominative "Son" refers back to subject after passive verb. The third clause has θεὸς "God" in apposition to subject. Also πατρὸς "father" appositive to Δαυεὶδ "David."

The fourth clause has two adverb phrases mpdifying "shall reign." ἐπὶ "upon the house of Jacob" tells where. εἰς "unto the ages" expresses <u>how long</u>. The last clause makes a negative statement, "end shall not be." Genitive βασιλείας "of his kingdom" specifies which "end."

18

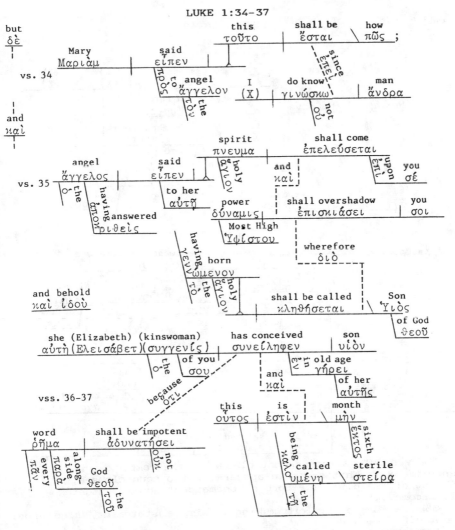

LUKE 1:34-37

Verse 34 involves a three-clause complex sentence. "Mary said" is independent, object of which is noun clause, "how shall this be," modified by causal ἐπεί "since" idea.

35 constitutes a four-clause complex. Three noun clauses serve as objects of verb "said" of the independent clause.

The sentence of 36-37 is compound-complex with two independent clauses and one dependent ὅτι causal clause.

19

LUKE 1:38-40

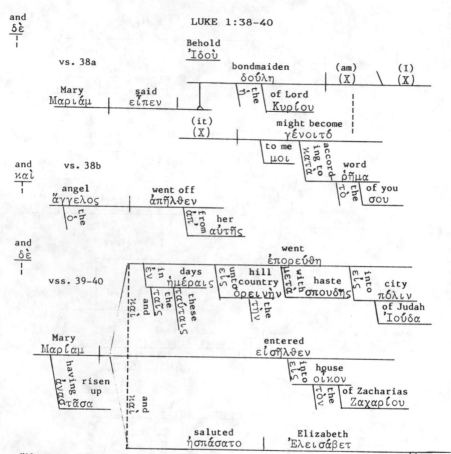

"Mary said" is independent clause in the complex sentence of 38a. What she said appears in two noun clauses, object of "said." "The Lord's bondmaiden" and "...might it become..."

38b is simple in form making a simple statement, "The angel went off from her."

The sentence of 39-40, as diagrammed, is a simple sentence. But it has a compound predicate. It might be treated as a compound sentence of three clauses. But with "Mary" as subject it appears best to view it as a three-pronged compound predicate. The four prepositional phrases modifying the initial verb ἐπορεύθη "went" are adverbial indicating when, where, how, and where. Similarly the phrase modifying the second predicate is adverbial answering the question where.

20

LUKE 1:41-42

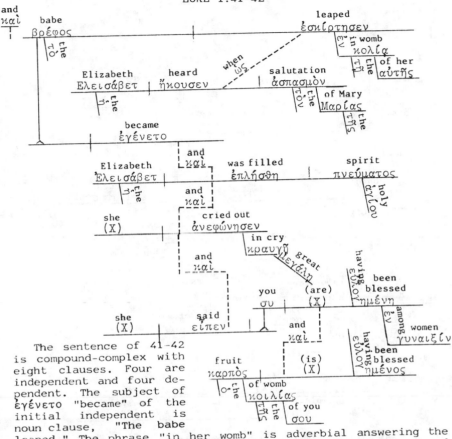

The sentence of 41-42 is compound-complex with eight clauses. Four are independent and four dependent. The subject of ἐγένετο "became" of the initial independent is noun clause, "The babe leaped." The phrase "in her womb" is adverbial answering the question where. A dependent adverbial temporal clause ushered in by ὡς "when" supports the subject-noun clause.

The second of the independents states, "Elizabeth was filled with (the) Holy Spirit." Genitive πνεύματος "spirit" as direct object after verb of filling is normal.

The third independent expresses the result of being filled with the Holy Spirit. "She cried in a great cry." κραυγῇ "in great cry" is adverb idea expressing manner.

That which Elizabeth cried appears in two dependents, objects of "said" of the fourth independent clasue. "You (are) having been blessed" and "the fruit of your womb (is) having been blessed." The two supplementary participles with understood forms of εἰμί form periphrastic perfects. They emphasize continuance of past action.

21

LUKE 1:43-45

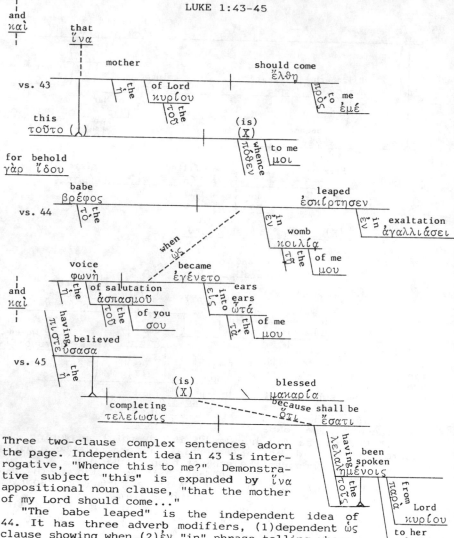

Three two-clause complex sentences adorn the page. Independent idea in 43 is interrogative, "Whence this to me?" Demonstrative subject "this" is expanded by ἵνα appositional noun clause, "that the mother of my Lord should come..."

"The babe leaped" is the independent idea of 44. It has three adverb modifiers, (1)dependent ὡς clause showing when, (2)ἐν "in" phrase telling where, "in my womb,"(3)a 2nd "in" phrase of manner, "in exaltation."

Subject of independent clause of 45 is aor.act.attr.ptcp. πιστεύσασα "the one having believed." ὅτι clause might be viewed as noun object of πιστεύσασα giving the content of what she believed. The diagram has it causal giving reason why she is "blessed."

22

LUKE 1:46-51

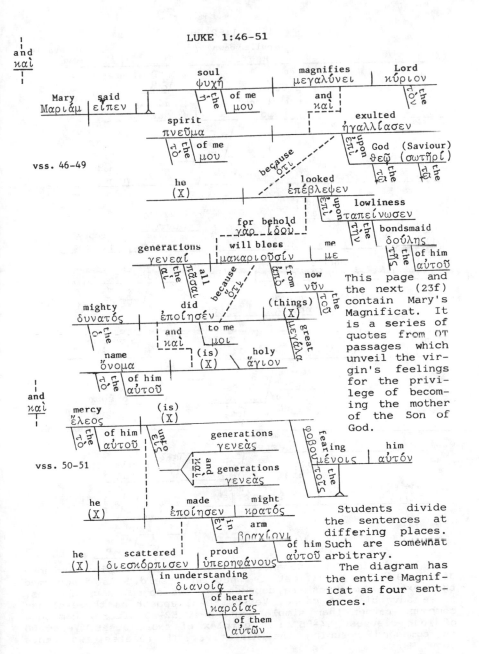

vss. 46-49

and καὶ

Mary Μαριάμ — said εἶπεν

soul ψυχή — magnifies μεγαλύνει — Lord κύριον τὸν

the of me μου

spirit πνεῦμα — the of me μου

and καὶ — exulted ἠγαλλίασεν

because ὅτι

he (X) — looked ἐπέβλεψεν — upon ἐπὶ — God (Saviour) θεῷ (σωτῆρί) the the

upon ἐπὶ — lowliness ταπείνωσεν — the bondsmaid δούλης — the of him αὐτοῦ

for behold γὰρ ἰδοὺ — will bless μακαριοῦσίν — me με — now νῦν — from ἀπὸ — the

generations γενεαί — the all because ὅτι

mighty δυνατός — the

did ἐποίησέν — and καὶ — to me μοι — (things) (X) the — great μεγάλα

name ὄνομα — (is) (X) — holy ἅγιον — the of him αὐτοῦ

and καὶ

vss. 50-51

mercy ἔλεος — the of him αὐτοῦ — (is) (X) — unto — generations γενεὰς — and generations γενεὰς — fearing φοβουμένοις the — him αὐτόν

he (X) — made ἐποίησεν — might κρατός — in arm βραχίονι — of him αὐτοῦ

he (X) — scattered διεσκόρπισεν — proud ὑπερηφάνους — in understanding διανοίᾳ — of heart καρδίας — of them αὐτῶν

This page and the next (23f) contain Mary's Magnificat. It is a series of quotes from OT passages which unveil the virgin's feelings for the privilege of becoming the mother of the Son of God.

Students divide the sentences at differing places. Such are somewhat arbitrary.

The diagram has the entire Magnificat as four sentences.

23

LUKE 1:52-56

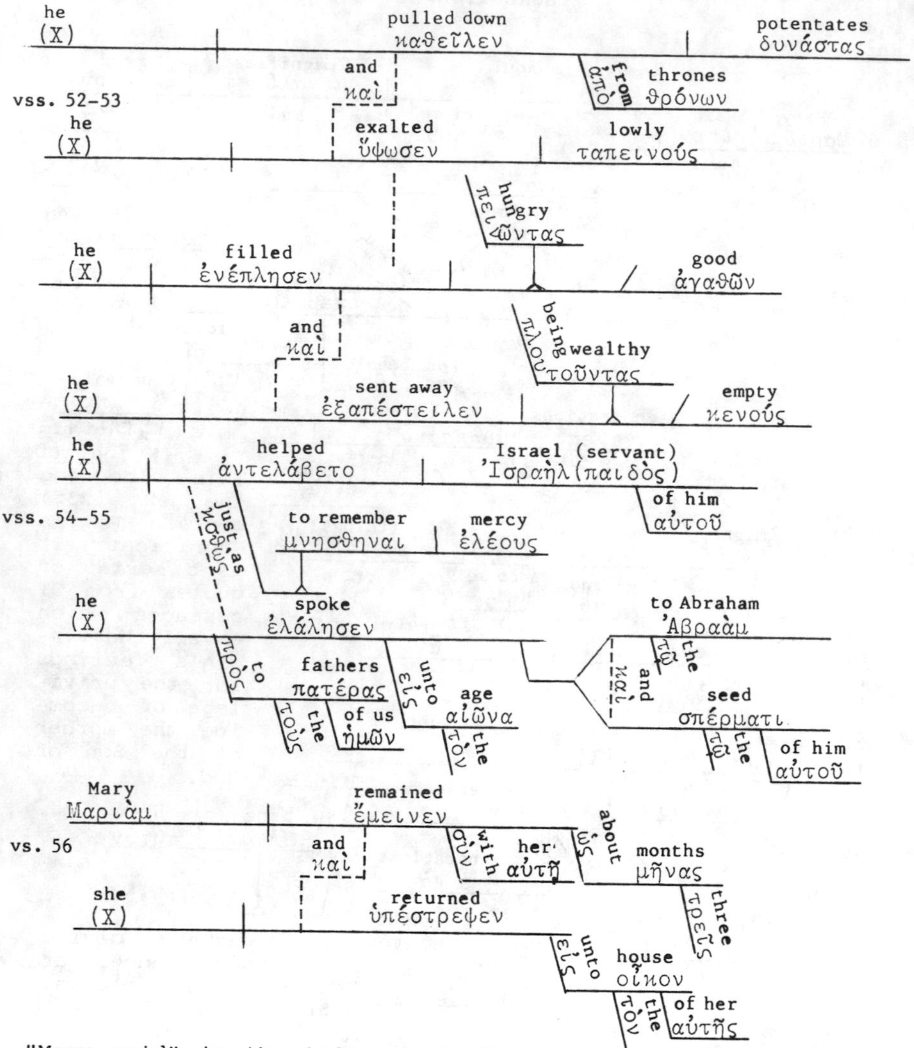

vss. 52-53

vss. 54-55

vs. 56

"Mary said" is the independent clause in the complex sentence of 46-49. The Magnificat is what she "said." As diagrammed the next six clauses are dependents, two object noun clauses, three adverbial of cause. Verses 50-51 appear as three-clause compound rather than simple sentences. 52-53 offer a compound of four clauses. 54-55 is a complex of two clauses. Verse 56 is compound resuming the narrative. It relates two facts about Mary.

24

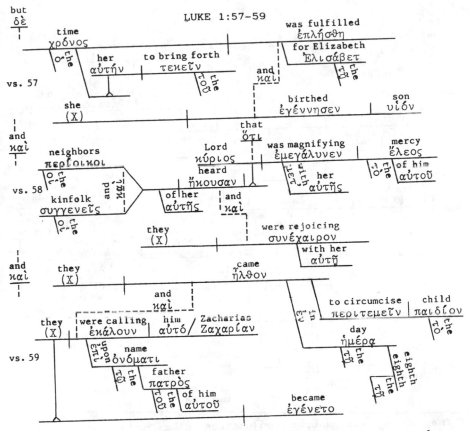

The sentence of 57 is compound of two clauses. χρόνος "time," subject of the first clause, is described by τοῦ and infinitive with accusative of general reference.

58 displays a compound-complex of three clauses. Subject of "heard" in the first clause is compound, "neighbors and kinfolk." Object of "heard" is dependent noun ὅτι clause, "that Lord was magnifying..." Imperfect "was magnifying" flashes a moving picture. Imperfect συνέχαιρον "was rejoicing" matches the imperfect action of "was magnifying." Each point of "magnifying" found human responses of "rejoicing."

ἐγένετο "became" is the verb in the independent clause of the complex sentence of 59. It's subject is compounded of two dependent noun clauses. "They came..." and "they were calling him..." The ἐν phrase indicates when, "in the eighth day." Aorist infinitive περιτεμεῖν gives purpose why they came, "to circumcise..." The ἐπὶ phrase explains why they were attempting to call his name Zacharias.

25

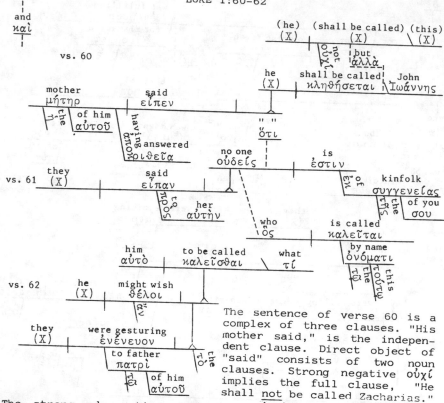

LUKE 1:60-62

The sentence of verse 60 is a complex of three clauses. "His mother said," is the independent clause. Direct object of "said" consists of two noun clauses. Strong negative οὐχί implies the full clause, "He shall <u>not</u> be called Zacharias." The strong adversative conjunction ἀλλά "but" sets off the contrast, "he shall be called John."

Another three-clause complex arises in verse 61. "They (the neighbors etc.) said" is independent. Direct object of "said" is noun clause, direct discourse, unveiled by ὅτι, "no one is there of your kin..." Subject, "no one" is described by adjective clause, "who is called by this name."

The sentence of 62 is complex. But it has only two clauses. Infinitive καλεῖσθαι "to be called" with accusative of general reference αὐτό technically isn't a clause, though in the English it translates as a clause, "what he should be called." Neighbors and kin repeatedly motioned to the father. ἐνένευον is iterative imperfect describing animated gestures. "They were nodding to the father the 'What he might wish it to be called.'" Neuter accusative article τὸ is used with indirect question as though the whole clause were a substantive. θέλοι is present optative.

26

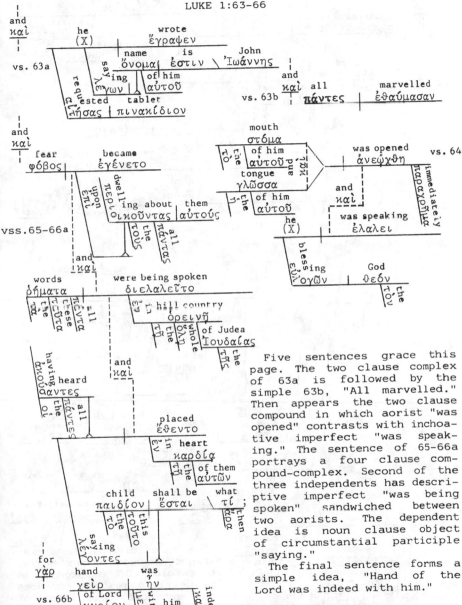

Five sentences grace this page. The two clause complex of 63a is followed by the simple 63b, "All marvelled." Then appears the two clause compound in which aorist "was opened" contrasts with inchoative imperfect "was speaking." The sentence of 65-66a portrays a four clause compound-complex. Second of the three independents has descriptive imperfect "was being spoken" sandwiched between two aorists. The dependent idea is noun clause object of circumstantial participle "saying."

The final sentence forms a simple idea, "Hand of the Lord was indeed with him."

27

LUKE 1:67-75

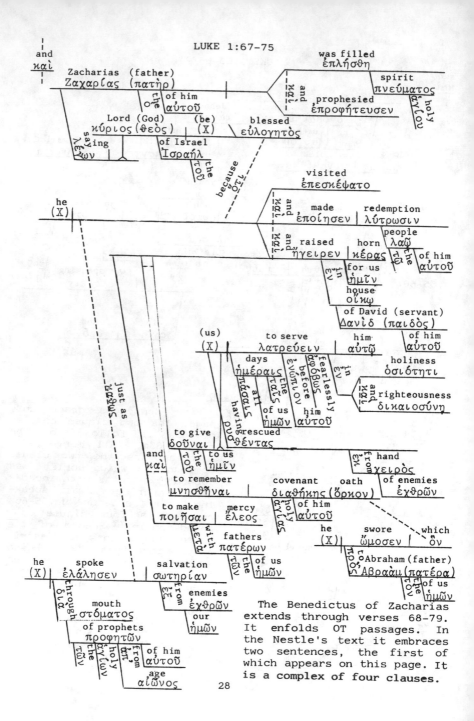

The Benedictus of Zacharias extends through verses 68-79. It enfolds OT passages. In the Nestle's text it embraces two sentences, the first of which appears on this page. It is a complex of four clauses.

28

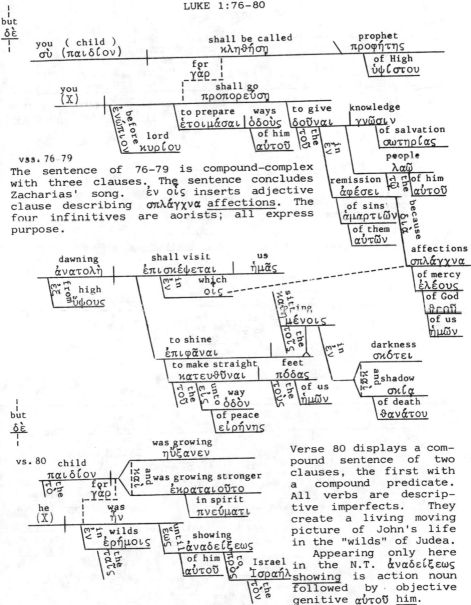

but
δέ

you (child)   shall be called   prophet
σύ (παιδίον)   κληθήσῃ   προφήτης
of High
ὑψίστου
for
γάρ

you   shall go
(X)   προπορεύσῃ

before   to prepare   ways   to give   knowledge
ἐνώπιον   ἑτοιμάσαι   ὁδούς   δοῦναι   γνῶσιν
lord   of him   of salvation
κυρίου   αὐτοῦ   σωτηρίας

people
λαῷ

vss. 76-79

The sentence of 76-79 is compound-complex
with three clauses. The sentence concludes
Zacharias' song. ἐν οἷς inserts adjective
clause describing σπλάγχνα affections. The
four infinitives are aorists; all express
purpose.

remission   of him
ἀφέσει   αὐτοῦ
of sins
ἁμαρτιῶν
of them
αὐτῶν
because

affections
σπλάγχνα

dawning   shall visit   us
ἀνατολή   ἐπισκέψεται   ἡμᾶς
from   high   which
ὕψους   οἷς

of mercy
ἐλέους
of God
θεοῦ
of us
ἡμῶν

sitting
καθημένοις

to shine
ἐπιφᾶναι
to make straight   feet
κατευθῦναι   πόδας
the   way   of us
ὁδόν   ἡμῶν

darkness
σκότει
and   shadow
σκιᾷ
of death
θανάτου

of peace
εἰρήνης

but
δέ

was growing
ηὔξανεν

vs. 80   child
παιδίον
for   was growing stronger
γάρ   ἐκραταιοῦτο
in spirit
πνεύματι
he   was
(X)   ἦν

in   wilds
ἐρήμοις

showing
ἀναδείξεως
of him   Israel
αὐτοῦ   Ἰσραήλ

Verse 80 displays a com-
pound sentence of two
clauses, the first with
a compound predicate.
All verbs are descrip-
tive imperfects. They
create a living moving
picture of John's life
in the "wilds" of Judea.
Appearing only here
in the N.T. ἀναδείξεως
showing is action noun
followed by objective
genitive αὐτοῦ him.

LUKE 2:1-5

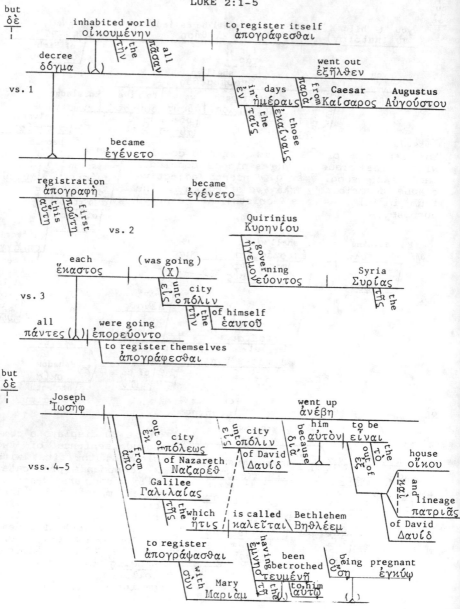

30

The facing page(30)contains four sentences. Verse one embraces a complex sentence of two clauses. The independent is a one-word clause, ἐγένετο, literally, "it became," commonly, "it came to pass" or "it happened." The "it" is made more concrete by δόγμα = "decree," which is the subject of the noun dependent clause, "decree...went out." The specific content of the decree is more fully amplified by the linear action present middle infinitive ἀπογράφεσθαι," to register." This present is most likely distributive, "all the inhabited world," each separate single human being. οἰκουμένην "inhabited world" is accusative of general reference defining who was involved in registering. The two prepositional phrases, "in those days" and "from Caesar Augustus" are adverb in function indicating when and whence.

Verse two is simple in structure announcing, "This first enrollment happened..." When it happened is mentioned in genitive absolute, "Quirinius being governor..." The term "absolute" indicates that there is not any formal grammatical agreement between the single clause and the idea in the present participle "governing." The linear action of the present tense is probably temporal and may be translated "while Quirinius was governing..."

The two clauses of verse three are so arranged as to create a complex sentence. The independent clause states, "All were going..." Present infinitive relates the purpose for which they were going, that is, "to register..." Linear action of the infinitive is distributive; each separate one of the "all" as a distinct individual was going to register.

Though it contains a number of adverbial modifying phrases the sentence of verses 4-5 involves but two full clauses. They are so arranged as to form a complex sentence. "Joseph went up" is the independent idea. "From Galilee" is adverbial expressing whence, as also does "out of city of Nazareth." The phrase "unto city of David" indicates to where. The διὰ with present infinitive εἶναι with accusative of general reference αὐτὸν answers the question why. Aorist infinitive rendered "to register" presents purpose. The one dependent clause is adjectival introduced by relative ἥτις "which is called Bethlehem." The clause describes "city."

Participles ἐμνηστευμένη and οὔσῃ, since they are participles, function as adjectives. However, they perform their descriptive role differently. The first is attributive, "the-one-having-been-betrothed-to-him Mary." On the other hand, οὔσῃ is an added circumstantial predicate, "Mary, being pregnant."

It is well also to note the difference in their tenses; perfect versus present. First, "having been betrothed," hence in a fixed relationship. The other, "being pregnant" describes a current but passing condition. It is a descriptive present.

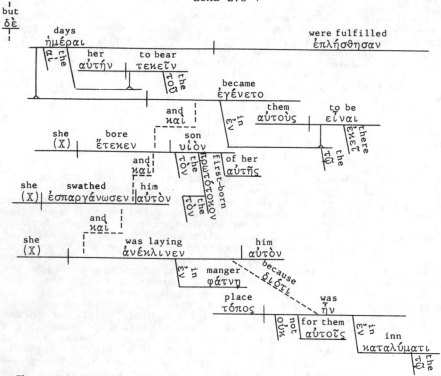

The sentence of vss.6-7 entails six clauses, four independent and two dependent. The initial independent consists of one word ἐγένετο "it became." As subject it has dependent noun clause, "days were fulfilled." ἐπλήσθησαν is effective aorist presenting all her pregnancy as a completed point. Aorist genitive infinitive τοῦ τεκεῖν with acc. of general reference αὐτήν specifies kind of days. The ἐν infinitive phrase is adverb, "in the-to-be in reference to them," familiarly, "while they were..."

The next three clauses are independents expressing what "she" (Mary) did, "she bore," "she swathed," and "she laid." "First born"(πρωτότοκον)is attributive adjective. It naturally suggests later children though that's not a necessary inference. No doubt Jesus had "brothers."(Lk.8:19ff) ἐσπαργάνωσεν "swaddled" is a narrative aorist. The verb comes from σπάργανον "swathing band" and appears in NT only here and verse 12.

The final clause is dependent causal introduced by διότι. The noun καταλύματι "lodge" or "guest room"(See Lk. 22:11). The word is compounded from κατά plus λύω and literally means a place where one can "let down," both himself and his baggage.

32

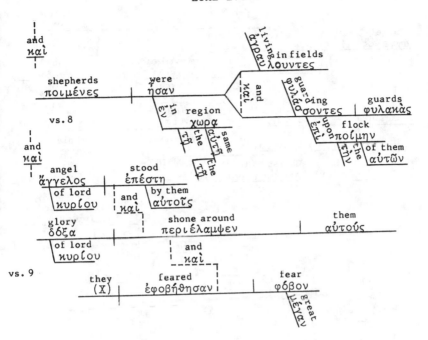

Verse eight structures a simple sentence. But its predicate is most striking. It is not only compound in form but both verbs are periphrastic imperfects. Present participles translated, "living in fields" and "guarding," combine with imperfect ἦσαν "were." In so doing they emphasize the linear action of the imperfect. It makes them even more vividly descriptive. The ἐν "in" phrase is adverbial telling where. ἐπὶ "upon" is also adverbial indicating the manner in which the "shepherds were guarding guards." φυλακὰς "guards" is cognate accusative.

Verse nine embodies a compound sentence of three clauses of equal rank. The clauses affirm, "The lord's angel stood..," "the lord's glory shone..," and "they feared great fear." All verbs are narrative aorists. Subjects "angel" and "glory" are definite by virtue of the genitives κυρίου "lord's." It specifies whose. Preposition περι has its local force "around" rather than perfective as used with verb "shone around."

In the third clause, "they feared a great fear," φόβον "fear" is cognate accusative.

LUKE 2:10-12

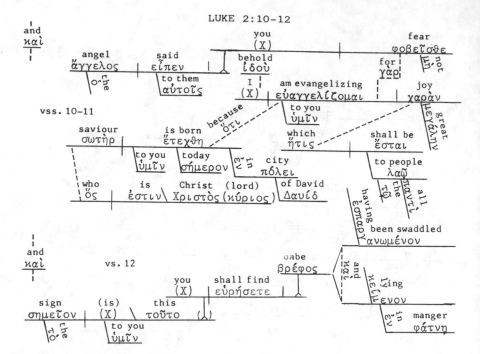

The two sentences above are both complex in form. But that of 10-11 has five dependent clauses; that of verse 12 has but one. Independent "the angel said" has as its object two noun clauses, "quit fearing" and "I am evangelizing." Linear action of negative present φοβεῖσθε signifies to "quit what you're doing." Obviously they were being afraid. The exhortation is to "stop being afraid." Present "I am evangelizing" is descriptive. The dependent introduced by relative ἥτις is adjective describing "joy." The ὅτι clause is adverbial causal explaining why. σήμερον "today" is adverbial accusative of time. The ἐν "in" phrase tells where. Relative ὅς clause is adjectival describing "saviour."

Verse 12 has two clauses. The independent avers, "The sign is this..." Appositional to "this" is noun clause, "you shall find..." The participles rendered "having been swaddled" and "lying" are predicate supplementary. They each complete the verb εὑρήσετε "shall find". Luke doesn't say, "You shall find a babe." He declares "You shall find a babe that has been swaddled...etc." This is a form of indirect discourse in which the participles carry the essential idea. "Having been swaddled is perfect; "lying" is present.

34

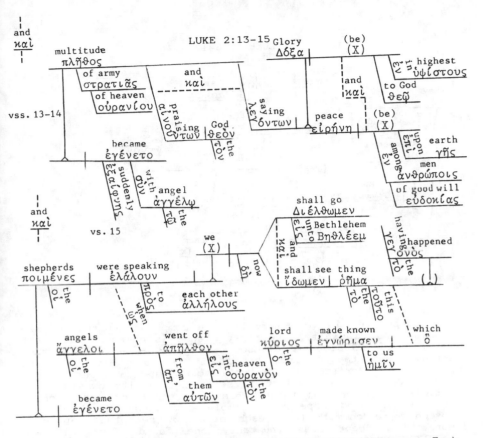

The above sentences are both complex in structure. Each has identical independent clauses, namely aorist ἐγένετο "became." In each of the sentences the subjects are noun clauses. The sentence in 13-14 has as its subject πλῆθος "multitude." This subject is modified by circumstantial present participles, "praising" and "saying..." πλῆθος is singular while αἰνούντων is plural; contruction according to sense. Direct objects of the verb aspect of "saying" are two noun clauses, "Glory (be)..." and "peace (be)..." It should be noted that εὐδοκίας "good will" is genitive specifying the kind of men.

The sentence of 15 is similar in form, having independent clause "became" whose subject is noun clause, "shepherds were speaking." When the shepherds were speaking is introduced by adverbial ὡς clause. Direct object of verb "speaking" is the compound noun clause, "we shall go" and "shall see." ῥῆμα "thing" is described by adjective clause inserted by relative pronoun ὅ, "which the Lord made known to us."

35

and
καί

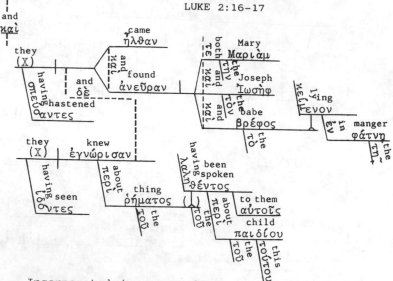

Incorporated in verses 16-17 is a compound sentence of two clauses. As diagrammed the first clause is compound. It might be seen as two separate clauses saying, "They came" and "they found." But the diagram treats it as one with compound predicate. Aorist verb ἀνεῦραν "found" has a three-pronged direct object. Each object is set apart by its own definite article. τε καί "both and" binds together by underscoring some inner bond more than simple καί would do. Mary and Joseph were committed to each other by betrothal. Furthermore, the "babe" was the only one found "lying in the manger." κείμενον is present supplementary predicate participle. It completes verb "found" as normal in indirect discourse. Luke does not say "they found the babe." He says, "they found the babe lying in the manger." That's the essential part of this portion of the predicate. The clause would lose its essential idea if it were only an incidental (circumstantial) participle.

Conjunction δέ which joins the clauses is often adversative but here it appears best to take it as simple "and."

Subjects "they" in both clauses are taken from the verb endings. They also both have circumstantial participles modifying: "having hastened" and "having seen." Both are temporal and might be translated as though a clause, "when they..." ἐγνώρισαν of the second clause is aorist indicative active from causitive verb γνωρίζω to make known. All words derived from root γνω- suggest knowledge of experience in contrast to οἶδα intuitive, absolute knowledge. λαληθέντος is aorist passive participle. It is attributive participle in apposition to ῥήματος "things."

36

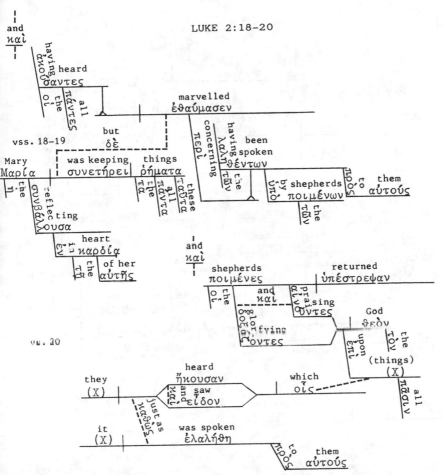

vss. 18-19

vu. 20

"All who heard marvelled" and "Mary was keeping..." are two independent clauses framing the compound sentence of 18-19. Aorist "marvelled" contrasts with descriptive imperfect "was keeping." The first clause has attributive participle "having heard" as subject and "ones having been spoken" as adverbial in prepositional phrase. Circumstantial ptcp. "reflecting" modifies subject "Mary" of the second clause.

Verse 20 encases a complex sentence of three clauses. The independent idea, "Shepherds returned" is embellished by two circumstantial ptcps. of manner, "glorifying and praising." οἷς "which" introduces an adjective clause describing understood "things." καθὼς adds adverbial clause of comparison.

37

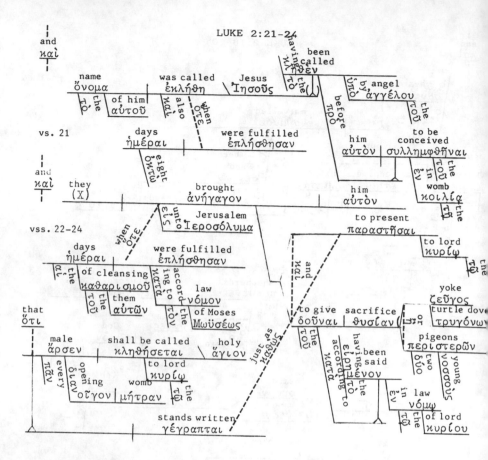

LUKE 2:21-24

The sentence of 21 is complex. The independent clause says, "name was called Jesus." Aorist passive ptcp. κληθὲν "having been called" is attributive and is in apposition to "Jesus." One dependent clause introduced by ὅτε is temporal, translated "when eight days were fulfilled."

Verses 22-24 are also complex but with four full clauses. The independent states: "they brought him." Dependent ὅτε clause indicates when they brought. The two infinitives "to present" and "to give" show the purpose for which they brought him. καθὼς introduces comparative adverbial clause, "just as...stands written." Subject of perfect γέγραπται is the ὅτι noun clause, "that every male opening..." Present participle διανοῖγον "opening" is temporal circumstantial, "when he opens." It's an iterative present, "each individual male opening..."

38

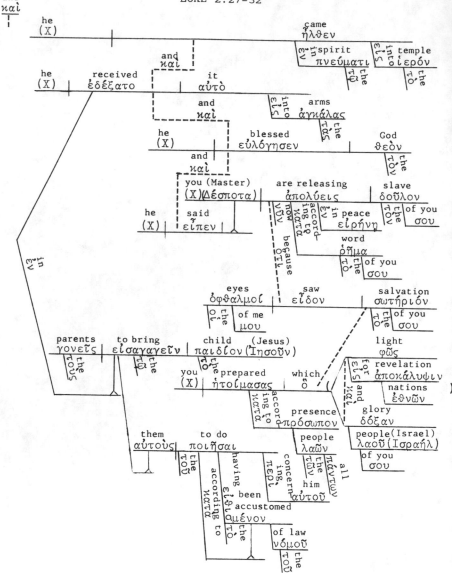

40

THE DIAGRAM OF LUKE 2:27-32

This sentence includes not only that which Simeon did but also what he said, much of which comes from Old Testament sources. It is a compound-complex arrangement. Four clauses of equal rank contribute the compound element. Three dependent clauses, a noun, adverb and adjective, provide the complex vein. In addition to such clauses two infinitive phrases appear. Each of them is used with accusative of general reference and thus, though technically not clauses, they perform similar functions. In English they appear as clauses.

"He came" constitutes the first independent idea. The ἐν "in" and εἰς "into" phrases tell how and where he came.

"He received it (the child) into his arms" represents the next independent clause. A third, "he blessed God" is closely yoked to the fourth, "he said." All four of these verbs are aorists, "he came...received...blessed...said..."

The three dependent clauses declare what he "said." First is noun clause, direct object of εἶπεν, "Now, Master, you are releasing your slave..." Linear action present ἀπολύεις "are releasing" is either descriptive of action in process or it is futuristic present, "you are going to release." Probably the former. "Master" is vocative, in apposition to subject "you." A second dependent idea is adverbial expressing cause inserted by ὅτι, "because my eyes saw your salvation." The aorist εἶδον "saw" is point action, not perfective as the English would prefer.

Relative pronoun ὅ "which" ushers in an adjective clause which describes σωτήριόν "salvation." Relative "which" is object of the aorist "prepared" and is expanded and clarified by compound apposition "light" and "glory." ἐθνῶν "nations" modifying ἀποκάλυψιν revelation" is objective genitive; revelation to nations (gentiles).

ἐν "in" with aorist infinitive εἰσαγαγεῖν "to bring" with the accusative of general reference γονεῖς "parents" offers a temporal expression. It may be rendered "when the parents brought the child Jesus..." The infinitive is aorist looking to the point at which they "brought."

Springing off of this infinitive "to bring" is a second infinitive construction. It too uses accusative of general reference to express the action. The infinitive ποιῆσαι "to do" expresses purpose. The parents brought the child Jesus "that they might do..." αὐτοὺς is accusative of third personal pronoun. English grammmers would call it "subject" even though the term "infinitive" implies it is not limited by a subject. Accusative with infinitive is an often used Greek idiom in which the accusative does show a limit to the action expressed in the infinitive.

κατὰ "according to" expresses the standard by which an idea is measured. εἰθισμένον "having been accustomed" is perfect passive participle. "Measured by the custom of law."

41

LUKE 2:33-35

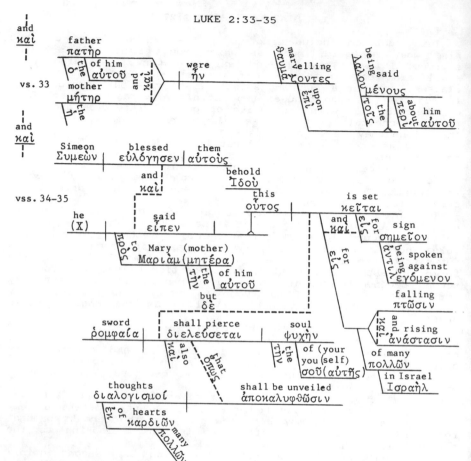

Verse 33 embraces a simple sentence. It has a compound subject, "His father and his mother..." The predicate consists of a periphrastic imperfect costructed by ἦν "were" and present participle θαυμάζοντες "marvelling." ἐπί with attributive perfect participle functions adverbially giving the basis on which (why) they were marvelling.

34-35 frames a compound-complex sentence of two independent clauses and three dependent. "Simeon blessed...and he said" comprise the compound elements. Object of εἶπεν "said" are two noun clauses, "this (one) is set" and "sword shall pierce..." ὅπως introduces adverbial purpose clause, "that thoughts shall be unveiled." In the adversities of Mary's mission in life God works his divine purpose.

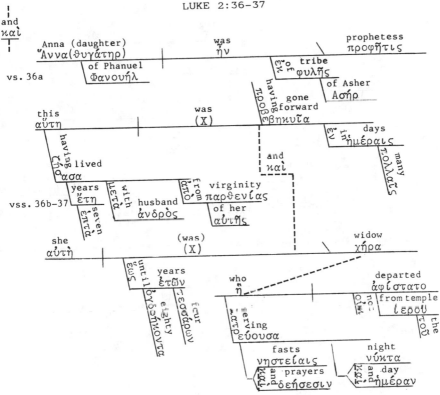

The diagram treats 36a as a simple sentence rather than as a first clause in a compound-complex of 36-37. It says, "Anna was prophetess." The adverbial ἐκ phrase tells <u>from where</u>.

Verses 36b-37 expose a compound-complex sentence. Of two independent clauses the first affirms, "This (one) had gone forward..." Perfect participle προβεβηκυῖα supplements understood imperfect "was" to form periphrastic pluperfect, "had gone forward." ἐν "in" phrase is adverbial explaining <u>how much</u>. Circumstantial participle ζήσασα "having lived" details her married experience of seven years. A second independent states the fact of her widowhood. "Until 84 years" shows how <u>long</u>. Relative dependent ἥ "who" is adjectival clause describing "widow." Circumstantial participle "serving" is temporal, "as she was serving." "Fasts and prayers" express means by <u>which</u>; "night and day" represents accusative extent of time. τοῦ ἱεροῦ "from the temple" is adverbial indicating from <u>whence</u>.

43

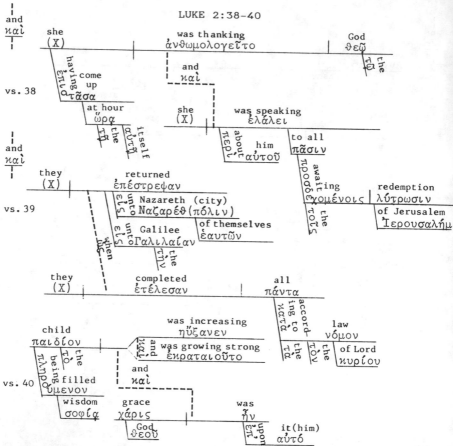

LUKE 2:38-40

Two clauses of verse 38 provide a compound scheme relating what Anna did. "She was thanking and she was speaking." The imperfect tenses are in turn descriptive and inchoative; "was speaking" and "began to speak."

Verse 39 is complex. "When they completed all" is adverbial temporal dependent. It supports the independent idea, "they returned." Both εἰς phrases are adverbial telling where. The κατὰ phrase expresses the measure or standard by which they "completed."

The sentence of verse 40 fashions a compound design of two clauses. The first has a compound predicate of imperfect tenses, "was increasing" and "was growing stronger." The 2nd states both the means and result of his growth. "God's grace was upon him." Present participle "being filled" is circumstantial and may be classed as causal.

44

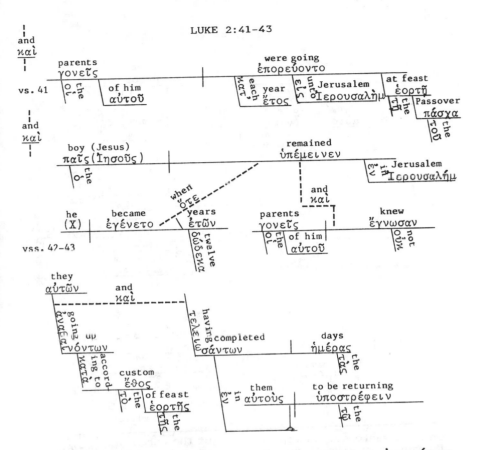

Verse 41 encases a simple sentence. Imperfect ἐπορεύοντο is iterative as guaranteed by distributive κατά "each." "Unto Jerusalem" indicates <u>where</u>. "At the Passover feast" suggests <u>when</u>.

42-43 forges a compound-complex and then adds two genitive absolutes to expand the sentence. Two independent clauses declare, "The boy Jesus remained...and his parents did not know." When this happened is set forth in ὅτε dependent adverbial clause. The absolutes use present ἀναβαινόντων "going up" and aorist τελειωσάντων "having completed." The "going up" is descriptive; the aorist is effective looking to the point of completion. ἐν τῷ and infinitive with accusative of general reference is typical of Luke's style. Here it may be translated, "while they were going." Though technically not a clause, a genitive absolute has the practical force of an additional clause.

45

LUKE 2:44-46

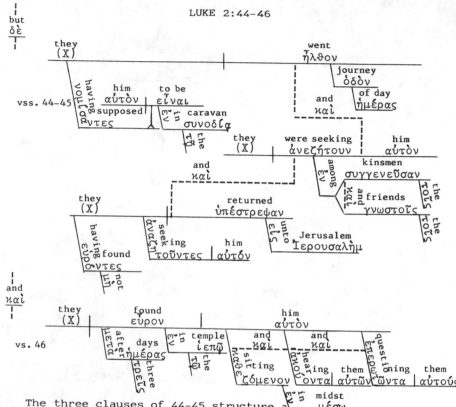

The three clauses of 44-45 structure a compound sentence. In reporting about the parents of Jesus they give three facts: "they went...they were seeking...they returned." "Journey of a day" tells how far." Infinitive phrase εἶναι is object of circumstantial participle "having supposed" and may be phrased, "that he was in the caravan." ἀνεζήτουν is imperfect, descriptive of their urgent search. The third clause, "they returned" is a narrative aorist reporting a fact as fact. An aorist plus present circumstantial, "not having found" and "seeking" show <u>time</u> and <u>purpose</u> respectively.

Verse 46 yields up a simple sentence. The μετὰ "after" and ἐν "in" phrases answer questions <u>when</u> and <u>where</u>. The three participles, "sitting," "hearing," "questioning," are treated as circumstantial, though they might be viewed as supplementary in indirect discourse. In either case they describe the <u>manner</u> of the son's behaviour when "they found him."

46

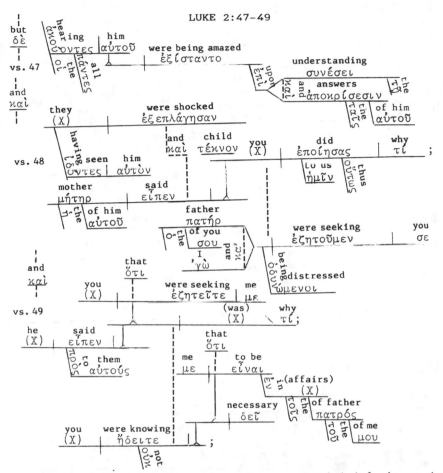

Verse 47 forms a simple sentence. Participial phrase is subject. Compound adverbial ἐπὶ phrase expresses why!

48 is a four-clause compound-complex sentence with independent, "mother said," having two object clauses; "Why did you do thus..? and "Your father and I were seeking..." Aorist ἐποίησας presses the search into a point. Imperfect ἐζητοῦμεν describes the anxious three day searching.

49 encases a complex sentence. Object of independent "he said" is the double-claused "Why (was it) that you were seeking me?" ὅτι clause appears as subject of implied "was." Another object clause has οὐκ expecting "yes" as an answer: "You were knowing were you not...?" Object of "were knowing" is the ὅτι noun clause.

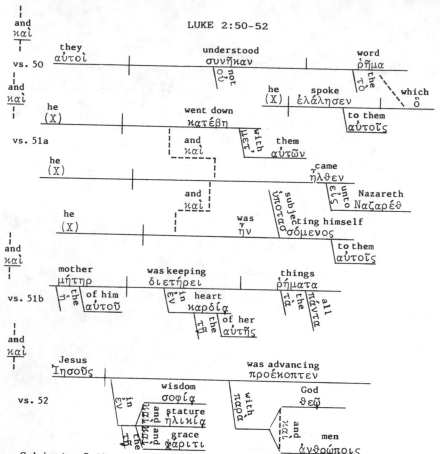

LUKE 2:50-52

Subject of the complex sentence of verse 50 is personal pronoun αὐτοί "they," emphatic by its very appearance. Dependent clause inserted by relative ὅ is adjective describing "word."

51a emerges as compound of three clauses. In the third the verb is periphrastic imperfect forged by ἦν and present middle participle ὑποτασσόμενος. The voice insists that he chose the "subjecting." Periphrastic stresses the continuing of his free obedience "to them."

By use of imperfect "was keeping" the simple sentence of verse 51b vividly describes the mother's reaction to what happened in Jerusalem. Besides "words" ῥήματα includes also other factors, "deeds" etc., hence the translation "things,"

52 is also simple whose verb is imperfect "was advancing." παρὰ literally means "alongside." In this context "with" is a suitable rendering.

but
δὲ

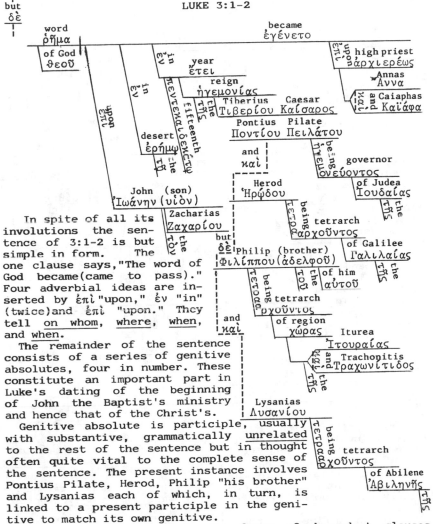

word
ῥῆμα
of God
θεοῦ

became
ἐγένετο

in
ἐν
year
ἔτει
reign
ἡγεμονίας
Tiberius   Caesar
Τιβερίου Καίσαρος
Pontius   Pilate
Ποντίου Πειλάτου

upon
ἐπι
high priest
ἀρχιερέως
Annas
Ἄννα
Caiaphas
Καϊάφα

in
ἐν

upon
ἐπι

desert
ἐρήμῳ

the fifteenth
πεντεκαιδεκάτῳ

John (son)
Ἰωάνην (υἱὸν)

Zacharias
Ζαχαρίου

and
καὶ

Herod
Ἡρῴδου

being governor
 governor
ονεύοντος
of Judea
Ἰουδαίας

In spite of all its involutions the sentence of 3:1-2 is but simple in form. The one clause says,"The word of God became(came to pass)." Four adverbial ideas are inserted by ἐπὶ "upon," ἐν "in" (twice)and ἐπὶ "upon." They tell on whom, where, when, and when.

but
δὲ
Philip (brother)
Φιλίππου(ἀδελφοῦ)

being tetrarch
tetrarch
ἀρχοῦντος
of Galilee
Γαλιλαίας

of him
αὐτοῦ

being tetrarch
tetrarch
ρχοῦντος
of region
χώρας   Iturea
Ἰτουραίας
and Trachonitis
Τραχωνίτιδος

and
καὶ

The remainder of the sentence consists of a series of genitive absolutes, four in number. These constitute an important part in Luke's dating of the beginning of John the Baptist's ministry and hence that of the Christ's.

Lysanias
Λυσανίου

Genitive absolute is participle, usually with substantive, grammatically unrelated to the rest of the sentence but in thought often quite vital to the complete sense of the sentence. The present instance involves Pontius Pilate, Herod, Philip "his brother" and Lysanias each of which, in turn, is linked to a present participle in the genitive to match its own genitive.

being tetrarch
tetrarch
χοῦντος
of Abilene
Ἀβιληνῆς

These constructions have the force of dependent clauses. Here one may be translated, "while Pontius Pilate was governing Judea..." Another, "when Herod was tetrarch of Galilee..." In the present instance all the participles are presents. They report that during their occupancy of those positions of ruling power, "God's word came to John..."

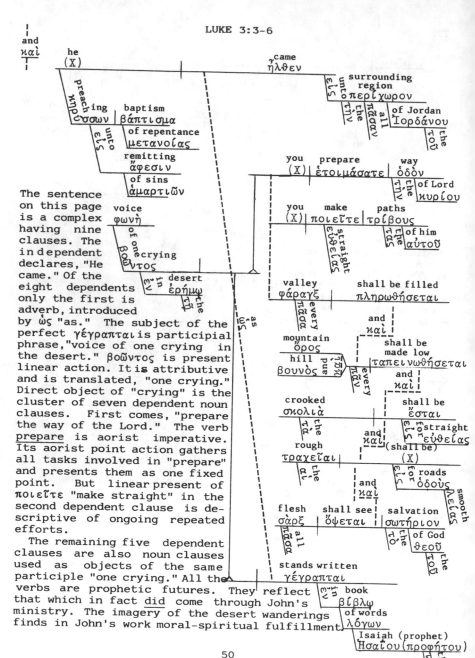

The sentence on this page is a complex having nine clauses. The independent declares, "He came." Of the eight dependents only the first is adverb, introduced by ὡς "as." The subject of the perfect γέγραπται is participial phrase, "voice of one crying in the desert." βοῶντος is present linear action. It is attributive and is translated, "one crying." Direct object of "crying" is the cluster of seven dependent noun clauses. First comes, "prepare the way of the Lord." The verb prepare is aorist imperative. Its aorist point action gathers all tasks involved in "prepare" and presents them as one fixed point. But linear present of ποιεῖτε "make straight" in the second dependent clause is descriptive of ongoing repeated efforts.

The remaining five dependent clauses are also noun clauses used as objects of the same participle "one crying." All the verbs are prophetic futures. They reflect that which in fact did come through John's ministry. The imagery of the desert wanderings finds in John's work moral-spiritual fulfillment.

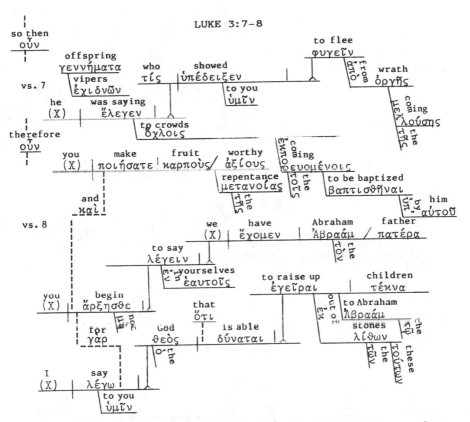

"He was saying" is the independent element for the complex sentence of verse seven. Noun clause,"who showed you to flee" is direct object of "was saying." Imperfect ἔλεγεν reflects repeated messages of John. Iterative action is also seen in present participle "the crowds coming..."(ἐκπορευο-μένοις)

Verse eight assembles a compound-complex sentence by means of three independent and two dependent clauses. The independents say, "You produce," "don't begin to say" and "I say to you..." In the first clause ἀξίους "worthy" is objective complement. Genitive "repentance" specifies the quality of the fruit's "worth." In the second clause, negative μὴ with aorist means, "Don't begin..." Noun clause "we are having Abraham..." is object of infinitive "to say"(itself object of ἄρξησθε "begin"). πατέρα "father" is objective complement.

The final clause of the sentence is dependent noun introduced by ὅτι "that" though the ὅτι might represent quotation marks of direct discourse.

51

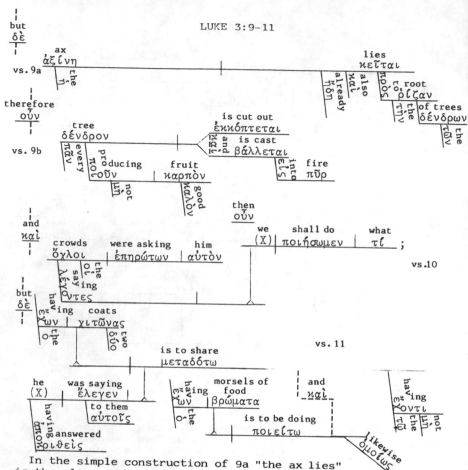

LUKE 3:9-11

In the simple construction of 9a "the ax lies" is the clause. The verb κεῖμαι "lies" is used as passive of τίθημι "to be laid" or as here "lie." <u>Where</u> the ax lies appears in adverbial πρὸς phrase.

9b is simple in form with compound predicate. Both verbs are furturistic present and state universal truths. ποιοῦν is circumstantial present participle of <u>cause</u>. The εἰς phrase is adverbial expressing <u>where</u>.

The complex sentence of vs.10 has two clauses. Imperfect ἐπωρώτων is both iterative as well as distributive; they kept on asking and they each asked. The dependent clause is noun, object of circumstantial participle "saying."

Verse 11 creates a complex sentence. ἔχων "the one having" is subject in both dependent clauses. All verbs are presents indicating repeated action.

52

LUKE 3:12-14

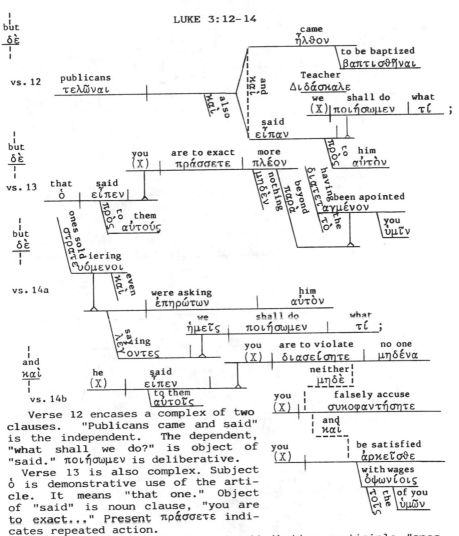

Verse 12 encases a complex of two clauses. "Publicans came and said" is the independent. The dependent, "what shall we do?" is object of "said." ποιήσωμεν is deliberative.

Verse 13 is also complex. Subject ὁ is demonstrative use of the article. It means "that one." Object of "said" is noun clause, "you are to exact..." Present πράσσετε indicates repeated action.

14a is complex too. Present attributive participle "ones soldiering" is subject of imperfect ἐπηρώτων in the independent clause. Object of circumstantial "saying" is dependent noun clause, "what shall we do?" ἡμεῖς "we" adds emphasis.

14b is complex. It has three dependent noun clauses, objects of "said." Aorists διασείσητε and συκοφαντήσητε say, "don't even begin to..." But present ἀρκεῖσθε suggests, "be satisfied as an ongoing matter."

53

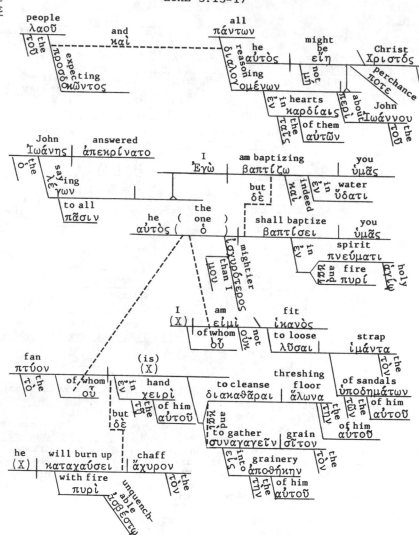

Verses 15-17 establish a complex sentence with seven clauses. Bared of all modifiers the sentence says: ""John answered." But preceding are two genitive absolutes. Object of διαλογομένων is negative noun clause "perchance he might not be the Christ." εἴη is present optative, indirect question altered from indicative in the direct.

THE DIAGRAM OF LUKE 3:15-17
(continued from page 54)

Genitive absolutes, though not clauses, often do function as clauses. In the present instance they may well be translated, "While the people were expecting and were reasoning in their hearts concerning John if perchance he might be the Christ..." The thought is related to the main part of the sentence although there is no formal grammatical connection.

The independent clause announces, "John answered..." Who or what did he answer? He answered the "reasonings" of the people about who he might be, the Christ or someone else!! John instinctively perceived what the crowds were speculating about him. He answered their conjectures. λέγων "saying" is circumstantial participle. The present tense suggests that he "kept on saying." That which he said appears in the noun clause, direct object of "saying," "I am baptizing you..." The phrase "in water" is adverbial indicating where.

A second noun object clause contrasts both the person performing the baptism and the element in which the baptism took place. Emphatic personal pronoun αὐτός "he" contrasts with equally emphatic ἐγώ "I" while "in Holy Spirit" is set over against "in water." The absence of the definite article with "spirit and fire" is suggestive of quality. The "mightier one" is to baptize "in" that which by its very nature is of the quality of "spirit" and "fire."

In apposition to subject "he" (αὐτός) is the demonstrative use of article ὁ. It may be translated "that one." It is expanded by the appositional comparative "mightier than I." It is further amplified by two adjective clauses both of which are introduced by οὗ "of whom." The first says, "of whom I am not fit..." Aorist infinitive λῦσαι expresses purpose, "to loose the strap..."

The second οὗ clause, also adjective, declares "whose fan is in his hand..." Here again aorist infinitives "to cleanse" and "to gather" express purpose. The εἰς phrase "into the grainery" is adverbial designating where.

The construction changes with the final clause of the sentence. John in his speaking (or Luke as he reports it) changes from the infinitive to a full clause with finite verb. Conjunction δὲ "but" introduces the contrast between the purpose of cleansing-gathering and the result (conceived purpose) to "burn up the chaff." καταχαύσει "will burn up" is a simple future indicative. "With fire" is adverbial indicating how. The full clause reads, "...but he will burn up the chaff with unquenchable fire."

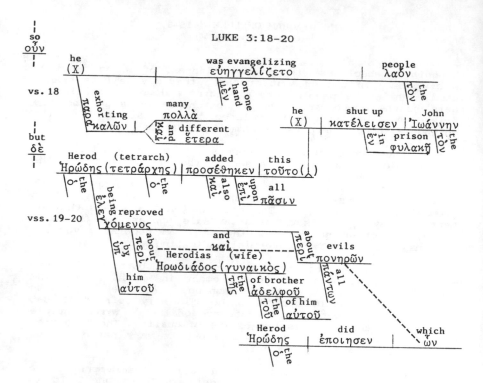

LUKE 3:18-20

Verse 18 encloses a simple sentence which declares, "He was evangelizing the people." Imperfect "was evangelizing" draws a moving picture of John's incessant activity. He never stopped. Present active participle παρακαλῶν "exhorting" portrays one aspect of the manner of his evangelizing; he used exhortation as a method of persuasion. Direct object of the participle is compound "much and many" apparently referring to "many" people and "different" ways and ideas. Note the μέν "on the one hand" modifying the verb "was evangelizing." It emphasizes the word with which it is used <u>and</u> contrasts with the δέ "but on the other hand" of the next clause or sentence. "John was evangelizing...but Herod added this evil..."

The sentence created in verses 19-20 represents a complex. It has three clauses. "Herod the tetrarch added this" is the independent idea. In apposition to τοῦτο "this" is noun clause "he shut up John in prison." Ushered in by relative ὧν "which" is an adjective clause describing "evils." ἐλεγχόμενος "being reproved" is present passive circumstantial participle. The two περί phrases are adverbial setting forth the causes which prompted John's reproving of Herod.

56

21-22 fashion a sentence embracing a rare array of word groups. It enfolds an independent clause, two dependents, four infinitives each with an accusative of general reference. Also a compound genitive absolute. ἐγένετο "became" is the verb of the independent. For subject three infinitive phrases appear. They are, "to be opened," "to come down," "to become." Each has its accusative of general reference limiting the action in the infinitive as a subject limits a finite verb. They are:"heaven,""spirit," and "voice." The translation may read: "That the heaven opened and that the spirit came down and that a voice came out of heaven became..."

In apposition to φωνὴν "voice" are noun clauses, "you are my beloved son," and"I thought well of you." Another infinitive phrase stems off ἐγένετο as an adverbial temporal idea, "while all the people were getting baptized..." The action denoted in the extended subject "came to pass" during the time when the people were being baptized. Sometime during this same period Jesus too was baptized and spent prolonged periods in prayer. These two ideas are stated by two genitive absolute participles. βαπτισθέντος "having been baptized"is aorist passive while προσευχομένου "praying" is a linear action present.

By definition a genitive absolute does not formally connect with the sentence. It is "absolute." However, in the present instance conjunction καὶ "and" tends to point to a connection to the infinitive phrase "to be baptized in reference to the people..."

heaven — οὐρανόν | to be opened — ἀνεωχθῆναι | but — δὲ
spirit — πνεῦμα | to come down — καταβῆναι
him — αὐτόν
appearance — εἴδει
dove — περιστερὰν
you — σὺ | are — εἰ | son — υἱός
of me — μου
I (X) | thought well — εὐδόκησα
you — σοὶ
voice — φωνὴν | to become — γενέσθαι
heaven — οὐρανοῦ
became — ἐγένετο
people — λαὸν | to be baptized — βαπτισθῆναι
Jesus — Ἰησοῦ
praying — προσευχομένου
having been baptized — βαπτισθέντος

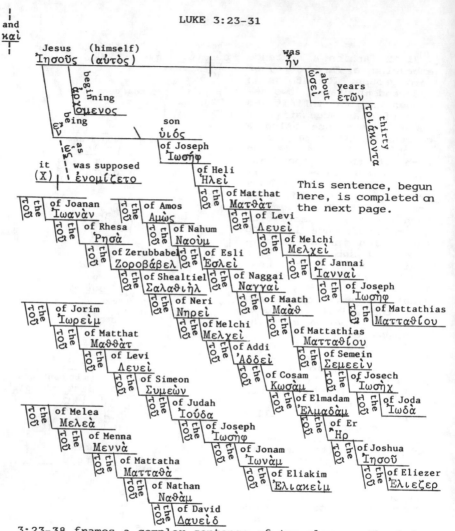

This sentence, begun here, is completed on the next page.

3:23-38 frames a complex sentence of two clauses. The independent states "Jesus was..." Use of intensive αὐτὸς "himself" gives emphasis to the person of Jesus. Circumstantial participle "beginning" is temporal, translated, "when he began." Obviously it refers to his public ministry. Dependent ὡς "as" clause makes clear Joseph was not the father of Jesus although the public "supposed" him to be. The rest of the sentence gives the genealogy of Jesus back to Adam, whose source was "of God."

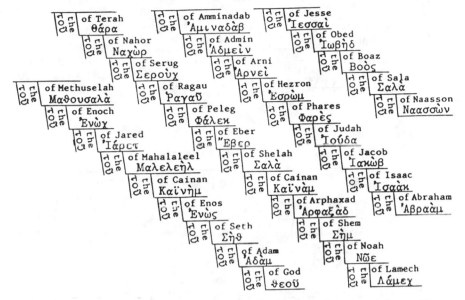

The sentence beginning at verse 23 (as diagrammed on the opposite page(58)concludes above, extending through verse 38.

A number of facts should be noted about this genealogy. No article appears with Ἰωσήφ above although the τοῦ is used with all of the rest of the names except θεοῦ "God." In the author's mind Joseph wasn't in the same relationship as those others so designated. In fact, with good cause, "of Joseph" might well be placed as modifying the verb "was supposed." So, "Jesus, being son of Jospeh, as was supposed," Thus the genealogy actually begins with Heli, not Joseph. Heli was the actual son of Jacob (Matt.1:16). He certainly did not have two fathers. Heli was Mary's father; Joseph was "son" of Heli in that he was married to Mary.

In chapters one and two Luke has made it clear that Joseph was not the father of Mary's baby. He had no need to give Joseph's genealogy. Luke writes for a different audience and purpose than Matthew. Luke wants to relate Jesus to the whole human race; Matthew only to the Jewish. Luke presents Jesus as a human being of universal connection to the divine nature through David, Abraham, Adam, and God. Joseph's genealogy in no way would serve that purpose. In Luke's genealogy Jesus is kin to all humanity while at the same time one with the divine nature.

If we leave the name "Joseph" out but include "God" the names in the genealogy totals

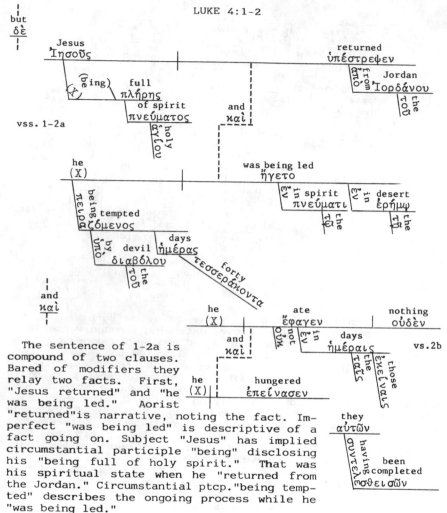

vss. 1-2a

The sentence of 1-2a is compound of two clauses. Bared of modifiers they relay two facts. First, "Jesus returned" and "he was being led." Aorist "returned"is narrative, noting the fact. Imperfect "was being led" is descriptive of a fact going on. Subject "Jesus" has implied circumstantial participle "being" disclosing his "being full of holy spirit." That was his spiritual state when he "returned from the Jordan." Circumstantial ptcp. "being tempted" describes the ongoing process while he "was being led."

Verse 2b is also a two clause compound, though it does have a genitive absolute which may be translated, "when they were completed." The Greek tolerates double negatives such as, "He did not eat nothing.." The aorists in both clauses state facts as facts. The phrase "in those days" is adverbial indicating when. ἡμέραις "days" locative denoting a point within which. The accusative ἡμέρας "days" in the sentence of 4:1-2a represents extent of time.

60

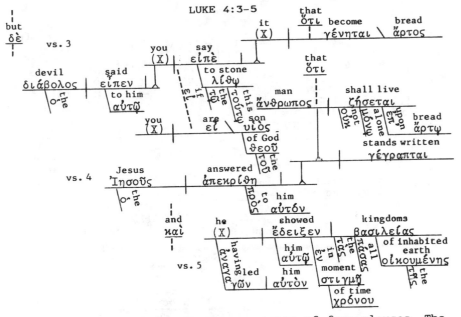

LUKE 4:3-5

Verse 3 chronicles a complex sentence of four clauses. The independent idea is: "the devil said..." The first dependent provides a noun clause object of εἶπεν "said." It has aorist imperative suggesting instant solution to the crisis facing Jesus. Another noun clause, object of the aorist, offers the crux of what he could say, "that it become bread." The third dependent is 3rd class conditional assumed to be true, "if you are (and you are) the son of God..." No temptation could be possible were he not God's son. The devil assumed that as true.

Verse four also emerges as complex but of three clauses. The independent is: "Jesus answered..." Subject of the noun-object clause "stands written" is another noun clause, "man shall not live by bread alone." The ἐπί phrase is adverbial and denotes how "man shall not live," that is, "not upon the basis of bread."

The sentence of verse five has but one clause hence in form is simple. It states, "he showed him..." The kingdoms which he showed Jesus are characterized in genitive as "of the inhabited earth." These were the kind of kingdoms offered as bait. Modifyingthe subject "he" is aorist circumstantial participle ἀναγαγών "having led." Jesus voluntarily subjected himself to all conditions in which mankind lived. Though he did not yield to the devil's suggested temptations, he was "led" by the devil into situations where temptations were present.

61

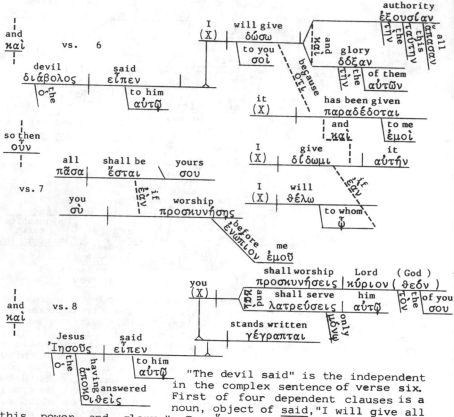

"The devil said" is the independent in the complex sentence of verse six. First of four dependent clauses is a noun, object of said, "I will give all this power and glory." Two ὅτι causal ideas brace the devil's promise of power. Perfect παραδέδοται advances the suggestion that the devil has a permanent hold on the world's power and glory. ἐὰν inserts a 3rd class condition with subjunctive leaving the condition undetermined though with some prospect of fulfillment.

Verse seven embodies a complex of two clauses. σου in the main clause is predicate genitive "yours." The 3rd class condition appears again. It's use here is quite significant. It is a striking contrast to the condition in verse three. The devil had no doubt about the sonship of Jesus to God. But here he is uncertain about his success in the temptation offered to Jesus. The result is left open.

The sentence in verse eight is complex. The two dependent clauses are both noun. Perfect "stands written" with its noun clause subject is the direct object of the independent "He said."

62

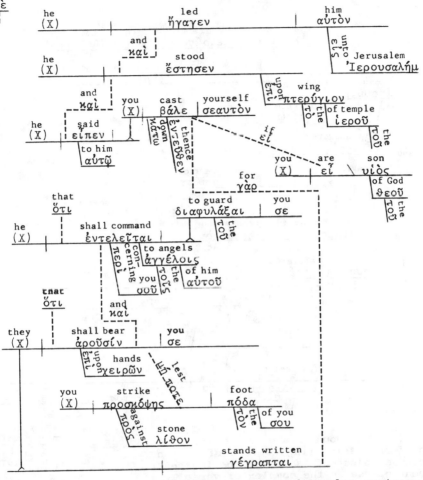

LUKE 4:9-11

The above diagram sets forth a compound-complex sentence. It has three independent clauses: "he led," "he stood," and "he said."

Six dependent clauses follow all of which the devil quotes from Psalm 91:11f. In other words they were not dependent ideas in their original context. The entire quote is what "he said." First, a noun clause object of "said." Then an "if"(εἰ) first class conditional determined as true. The γὰρ "for" inserts another noun object clause. And then two noun clauses, subject of γέγραπται. The μή ποτε "lest ever" inserts a purpose idea.

63

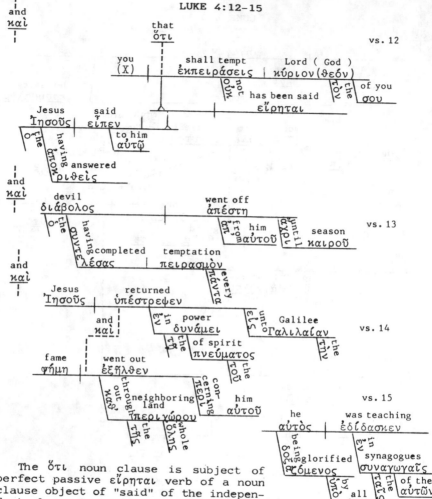

The ὅτι noun clause is subject of perfect passive εἴρηται verb of a noun clause object of "said" of the independent clause in the complex of verse 12. Remove all modifiers and the simple sentence of 13 says, "devil went off." Aorist circumstantial participle modifies subject "devil." Phrases ἀπ' and ἄχρι tell where and when.

The sentence of verse 14 embraces two independent clauses so is compound. "Jesus returned" and "fame went out" are the bare ideas. Phrases ἐν and εἰς tell how and where he "went out." καθ' and περί units are adverbial indicating where and about whom.

15 is simple in form. ἐδίδασκεν is inchoative imperfect with emphatic subject αὐτός. "He began teaching..."

64

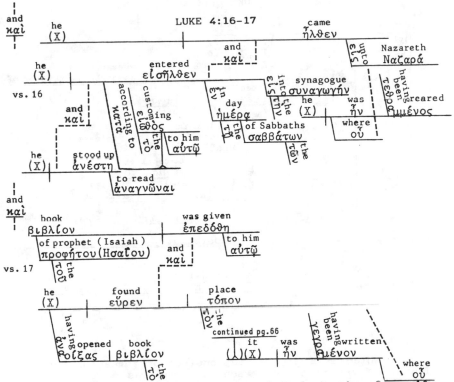

LUKE 4:16-17

continued pg.66

Three independent clauses plus one dependent make of vs. 16 a compound-complex. "He came unto Nazareth" is the first independent idea. "Unto Nazareth" is adverbial telling where. The dependent clause is adjective describing "Nazareth" as the place "where he had been reared." Imperfect ἦν coupled with perfect participle furnishes a periphrastic pluperfect.

The next independent states, "he entered." Attributive participle εἰωθός is perfect with force of present translated, "as was custom to him." αὐτῷ is dative of possession. A third independent affirms, "he stood up." Infinitive "to read" gives the purpose why he stood up.

Verse 17 introduces a compound-complex sentence which is completed on the next page. Two independent ideas appear above. They state, "book was given" and "he found the place." Noun dependent, "where it had been written" depicts "place" by use of a periphastic verb form. The diagram shows as subject the pronoun "it." The real subject is the full quotation from Isaiah as portrayed in the remainder of the sentence. It is in apposition to the "it," the diagram of which is continued on page 66.

65

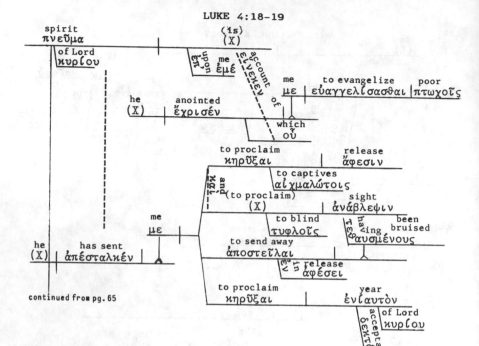

That which is framed above consists of three full clauses. Also are five infinitives each of which has an accusative of general reference. Though not technically clauses they serve in a practical way as clauses since the accusative limits the verbal action of the infinitives. Treating the entire group of clauses and phrases as a single unit it performs as subject of the adjective clause "it has been written" in the earlier part of the sentence on page 65. The entire group is a quotation from the scroll of Isaiah.

"Spirit (is) upon me" initiates the quotation. As it stands in this sentence it functions as a noun clause. An adverbial causal clause is seen in εἵνεκεν "on account of." Infinitive εὐαγγελίσασθαι(not με)is object of verb "anointed." The "me" is the one who performs the action in the infinitive. So, the other four infinitives above serve as direct objects of the perfect ἀπέσταλκεν "has sent." Perfect attributive participle τεθαυσμένους "ones having been bruised" is object of verbal action in infinitive "to send away."

The perfect ἀπέσταλκεν "has sent" signifies that Jesus' ministry "to proclaim" etc. has been permanently set. He came into this world on a predetermined ministry to the captives, blind, bruised, etc.

Compound labels the sentence of verse 20. Aorist "sat" makes sharp contrast to periphrastic imperfect "were looking intently." He sat; every eye "was intensely looking." Aorist participles of clause one are temporal circumstantial. But the present ptcp. of 2nd clause is supplementary.

Verse 21 is complex because it has two noun clauses as objects of "to say" infinitive object of "began" in the main clause. πεπλήρωται "has been fulfilled," perf. signifies scripture is permanent in its fulfillment.

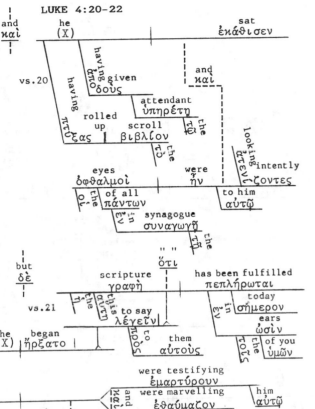

LUKE 4:20-22

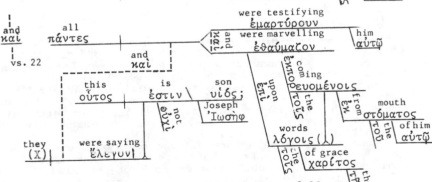

Verse 22 frames a compound-complex of three full clauses. "All" is subject of the first with compound predicate of two linear imperfects, probably distributive. Each separate one in the synagogue "was marvelling." Imperfect "were saying" in the 2nd clause has noun-object clause, "this is Joseph's son is it not?" Negative οὐχί expects "yes" for an answer.

67

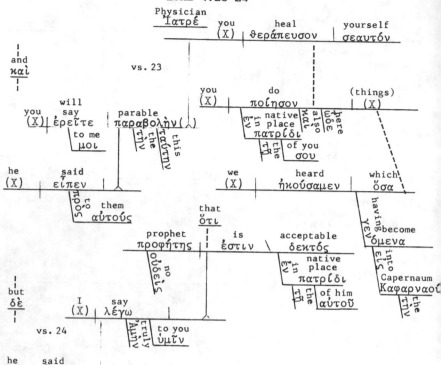

Five clauses yield a complex sentence in verse 23. The independent base notes: "he said." Object of "said" is noun clause, "you will say this parable." The rest of the sentence consists of two noun and one adjective clause all of which as a unit are in apposition to παραβολὴν "parable." ὅσα is quantitative relative pronoun, "however many." The diagram deals with the aorist participle γενόμενα as circumstantial describing ὅσα, "which became..." The εἰς expression suggests movement into.

Verse 24 fashions a three clause complex. Again, the basic idea is "he said." From this rises the noun-object clause, "Truly, I say to you." Another noun object clause completes the sentence, "no prophet is acceptable..." The adverbial phrase "in his native place" tells where.

πρὸς with accusative αὐτούς appears in verse 23; dative ὑμῖν in verse 24. No two idioms mean exactly the same. Though slight, meanings or emphases are to be noted. Dative stresses personal relations; accusative direction toward.

LUKE 4:25-27

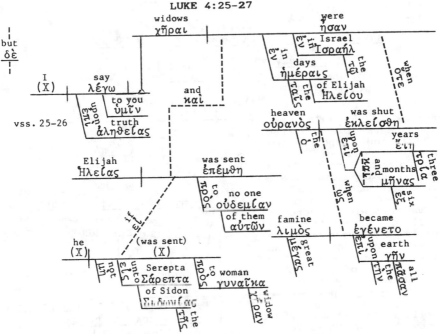

One independent and five dependent clauses shape the complex sentence of 25-26. Two noun dependents are the objects of "say" of the main clause: "widows were" and "Elijah was sent." Two adverb temporal clauses stem off of the first noun object clause and a 1st class conditional (negative) supports the 2nd of the noun-object clauses: "if he was not sent..." The first class assumes the condition as true. "If he was not sent (and he wasn't)..."

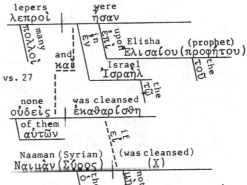

The two adverb clauses of time are introduced by ὅτε and ὡς both of which may be translated "when."

Verse 27 establishes a compound-complex sentence with three clauses. "Lepers were" and "no one was cleansed" disclose the two independent declarations. Another first class negative contional states: "if Naaman was not (cleansed)..."(assumed as true), then "no one was cleansed."

69

and
καί

LUKE 4:28-30

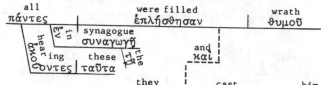

Following Nestle's text the diagram places verse 30 in the compound-complex sentence of 28-30. Thus four independents with one dependent frame this sentence. "Wrath" in the first clause is genitive following a verb of filling. Present Participle ἀκούαντες exposes vivid linear action, "as they all were hearing."

The fury of the anger is sketched by repeated ἐξ; once in perfective use on verb ἐξέβαλον as well as on strong ἔξω. They did more than "cast him." They cast him <u>out</u>.

The third independent declares, "they led him." ἕως "as far as" with genitive ὀφρύος "eye-brow," it came to mean a jutting prominence; here "ridge of the mountain." Infinitive with ὥστε indicates conceived result, which is very close to purpose.

ἐφ' οὖ brings a dependent adjective clause in to describe "mountain." ᾠκοδόμητο is pluperfect, "had been built." It emphasizes the fixed permanancy of their city, "it <u>stood</u> built."

Emphatic use of personal pronoun focuses attention on the person of Jesus; "he was going." Imperfect ἐπορεύετο offers a lucid brilliance to the force of Jesus' action "going" through this lynch mob. Such action is reinforced by διά appearing both in circumstantial participle διελθὼν (perfective use) to which again it appears in the phrase "through the midst..."

70

LUKE 4:31-34

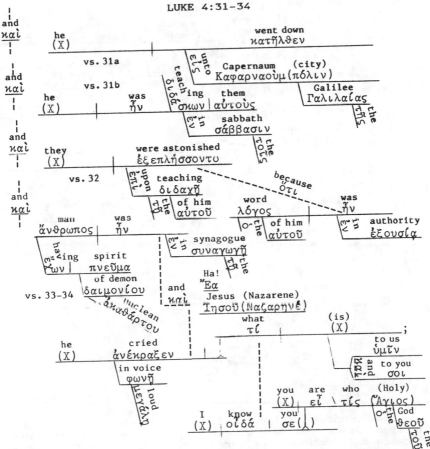

Of the four sentences above the first two are simple, the third is complex and that of 33-34 is compound-complex. The verb in 31b is periphrastic imperfect, "was teaching" giving striking proof of Jesus' ongoing habit on Sabbath days.

ἐξεπλήσσοντο of 32 is also imperfect; "were continuously being shocked." Dependent causal ὅτι clause gives reason why!

33-34 discloses a five-clause compound-complex sentence. "A man was..." initiates the sentence. The ἐν phrase tells where. Participle "having spirit of demon..." details the circumstances under which the man lived. The second independent, "he cried" has two noun clauses as objects of "cried." In apposition to "you," object of "cried" is noun clause, "Who you are, the Holy One of God."

71

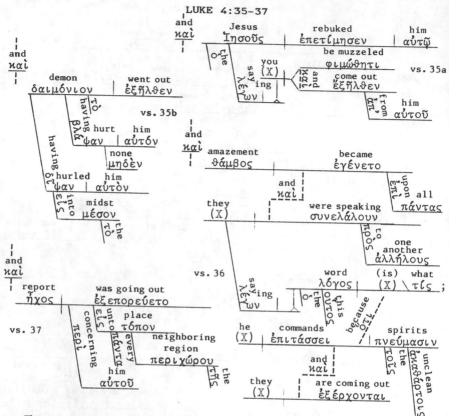

Three aorists in the complex of 35a dramatize the conflict between Jesus and the demon in the possessed man. In the independent "rebuked" is narrative. In the dependent, imperatives "be muzzled" and "come out" reveal authoritative power. "Demon went out" is the simple assertion of 35b. It has two circumstantial participles:(1)"having hurled" shows manner,(2)"having hurt none" suggests concession, "even though..."

The sentence of 36 is compound-complex. The two independent clauses display contrasting verbs. Aorist "became" reports a fact. Imperfect "were speaking" describes repetitive action on the part of the beholders of the fact. "This word is what" is a noun clause object of participle "saying." Two explanatory ὅτι causal clauses support the noun idea, "because he commands the spirits" and "they are coming out."

Verse 37 contains but one clause hence is simple. "Report was going out" is descriptive imperfect displaying a vivid picture of the inflamed talk unsettling the "neighboring region."

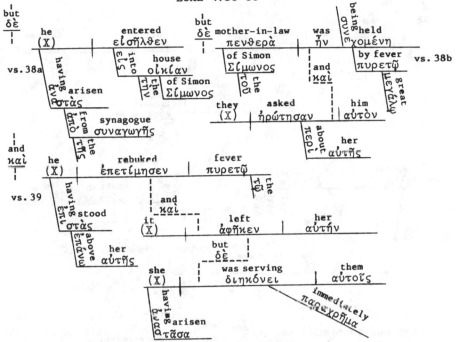

"He entered" is the naked clause of the simple sentence of verse 38a. The εἰς phrase is adverbial stating where; "into the house of Simon." Aorist circumstantial participle "having arisen" is temporal. The full phrase implies more than it says, "when he arose from his seat and left the synagogue."

38b admits to a compound arrangement. Periphrastic imperfect "was being held" sketches a graphic portrait of the severity of the fever. Aorist in the 2nd clause states the fact that they "asked" without describing repeated requests, even had there been any.

The sentence of verse 39 assembles three independent clauses into a compound category. Two aorists focus on facts as facts, "he rebuked fever" and "it left her." But the imperfect διηκόνει "was serving" of the 3rd clause is inchoative, "she began to be serving." Adverb παραχρῆμα "immediately" reminds the reader that no lingering weakness hung on as so often happens.

The circumstantial aorist participle ἀναστὰς "having stood" of the first clause adds an adverb idea "above her." This calls attention to a special aspect of this cure. Jesus stood "over her" with sympathetic feeling for the very human condition in her situation. A similer participle in clause three has no such modifying word.

73

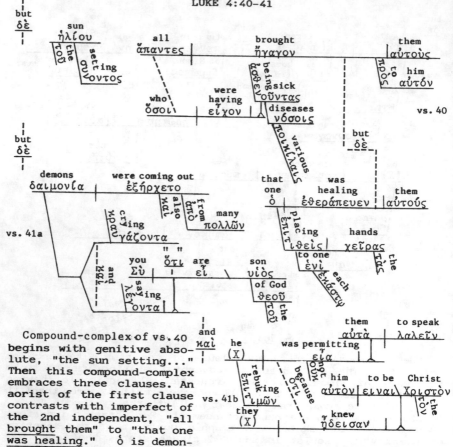

Compound-complex of vs. 40 begins with genitive absolute, "the sun setting..." Then this compound-complex embraces three clauses. An aorist of the first clause contrasts with imperfect of the 2nd independent, "all brought them" to "that one was healing." ὁ is demonstrative use of the article. Imperfect is descriptive and distributive. Supporting the distributive idea is present ptcp. "placing hands to each one." Quantitative relative ὅσοι "how-evermany" is subject of adjectival dependent describing "all." The imperfect εἶχον is also distributive. Present attributive ptcp. "the ones being sick" is object of εἶχον.

41a demonstrates a complex disposal of two clauses. Verb of the main clause is descriptive imperfect ἐξήρχετο "were coming out." Present circumstantial participles "crying and saying" add vivid descriptives to the action. What they said appears in noun-object clause, "you are the son of God."

41b presents a complex order of clauses. οὐκ with imperfect εἴα "was not permitting" describes Jesus' ongoing response to the demons' cryings. ὅτι is a causal clause telling why.

74

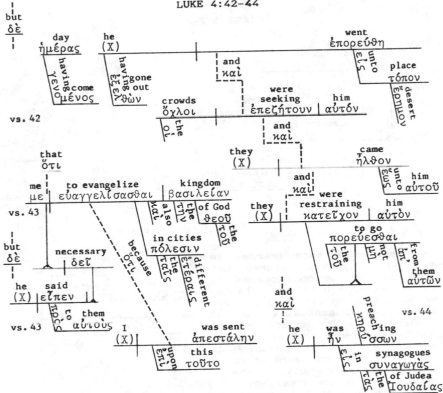

After beginning with a genitive absolute verse 42 shows four independent clauses, thus fashioning a compound sentence. The verbs appear in the following sequence; aorist "went," descriptive imperfect, "were seeking," aorist, "came," conative imperfect, "were restraining." τοῦ with negative μὴ and infinitive "to go" expresses result. They were trying to keep him from going away from them.

"He said" is the foundation of the complex of verse 43. As object of "said" is noun clause δεῖ. And it has for its subject the infinitive phrase introduced by ὅτι. Dependent adverb ὅτι causal clause stems off the infinitive. The ἐπὶ prepositional phrase modifying aorist "was sent" means, "upon the basis of."

In structure verse 44 embodies a simple sentence. The periphrastic imperfect enlivens the descriptive force of the verb. "He went on preaching" in the face of those who would restrain his reaching out to other cities. εἰς, though same root as ἐν, means more than "in." Here it suggests that Jesus was "gaining access into" synagogue after synagogue.

LUKE 5:1-3

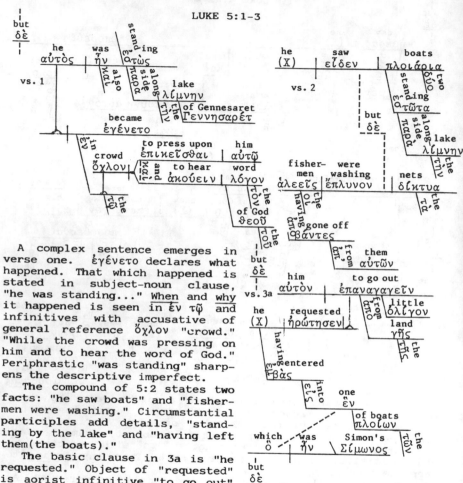

A complex sentence emerges in verse one. ἐγένετο declares what happened. That which happened is stated in subject-noun clause, "he was standing..." When and why it happened is seen in ἐν τῷ and infinitives with accusative of general reference ὄχλον "crowd." "While the crowd was pressing on him and to hear the word of God." Periphrastic "was standing" sharpens the descriptive imperfect.

The compound of 5:2 states two facts: "he saw boats" and "fishermen were washing." Circumstantial participles add details, "standing by the lake" and "having left them(the boats)."

The basic clause in 3a is "he requested." Object of "requested" is aorist infinitive "to go out" with its accusative of general reference αὐτὸν "him." Aorist participle ἐμβὰς "having entered" suggests time or even cause. Relative ὅ brings in an adjective clause describing "one."

Verse 3b displays a simple sentence. Stripped of modifiers it proposes: "he was teaching crowds..." Imperfect ἐδίδασκεν is inchoative, "he began to teach." Aorist circumstantial participle καθίσας "having sat" looks to the point when he sat. The ἐκ phrase is adverbial. He sat and spoke from "out of" the boat.

76

LUKE 5:4-6

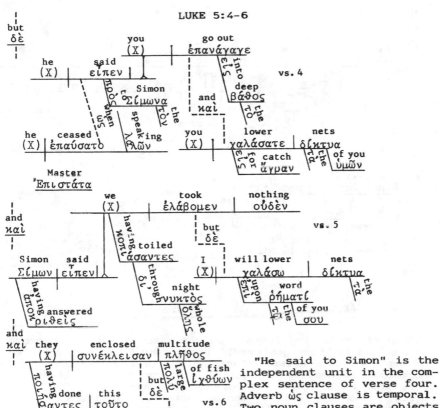

"He said to Simon" is the independent unit in the complex sentence of verse four. Adverb ὡς clause is temporal. Two noun clauses are objects of εἶπεν:"go out" and "lower your nets." The verbs are aorist imperatives suiting the decisive authority of Jesus. In the ὡς clause λαλῶν could be viewed as circumstantial but the diagram treats it as supplementing "ceased."

Verse five also is complex, independent being "Simon said." Two noun clauses serve as objects relating what he said. Circumstantial participle κοπιάσαντες "having toiled" may be seen as concessive, "even though..." Genitive case specifies, hence νυκτὸς is kind of time; it was night, not day. ἐπί with instrumental indicates "at your word."

Verse six is compound in structure. The clauses offer contrasting action. Aorist "enclosed" brings the action to sharp focus. Imperfect "were breaking" offers vivid description of action going on. Aorist circumstantial participle ποιήσαντες "having done" is temporal, "when they did this."

77

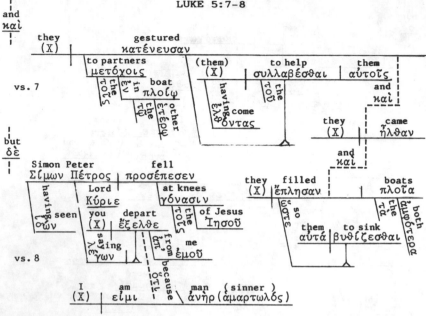

Strip all modifying items from verse seven, three independent clauses remain:"they gestured," "they came," and "they filled." The sentence is compound. Aorist infinitive συλλαβέσθαι has an understood accusative of general reference "them" indicating those who perform the action. It also has a "them"(αὐτοῖς)as object. So the entire phrase actually functions as if a clause, "having come, they might help them." The phrase "to partners" is adverbial signifying where. Also the ἐν "in the other boat" indicates where. κατένευσαν "they gestured" is used only here in the NT. Classical νεύω means "nod" or "bend the head." κατά intensifies the notion. Here it represents the excited motions of the fishermen to their companions.

Another infinitive phrase appears in the final clause. Here βυθίζεσθαι is present tense, linear action. Used with ὥστε it expresses result. "So they began to sink."(inchoative)

Verse eight establishes a complex arrangement of clauses. "Simon Peter fell" is the basic idea. Participles "having seen" and "saying" introduce the cause and effect on Peter of the large catch of fish. Object of "saying" is noun clause, "Depart from me Lord." The reason why is stated in adverb causal clause "because I am a man, a sinner." When Peter says, "I am a man" he makes a subtle suggestion that Jesus is something other than man. By adding appositional "sinner" he sharpens the idea of his sinfulness more than had he used simple adjective, "sinful man."

78

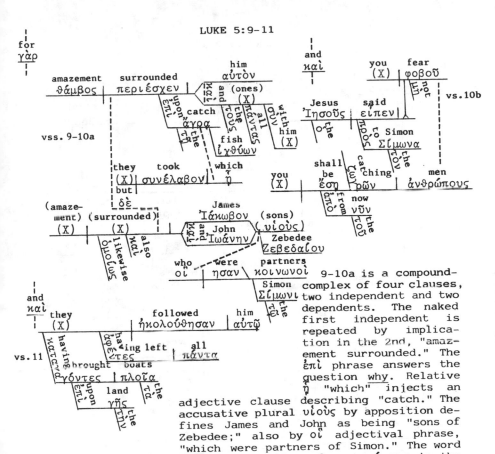

LUKE 5:9-11

9-10a is a compound-complex of four clauses, two independent and two dependents. The naked first independent is repeated by implication in the 2nd, "amazement surrounded." The ἐπί phrase answers the question why. Relative ἥ "which" injects an adjective clause describing "catch." The accusative plural υἱούς by apposition defines James and John as being "sons of Zebedee;" also by οἵ adjectival phrase, "which were partners of Simon." The word "partners" differs from μετόχοις in the 7th verse where the idea designates <u>participation</u> in objective blessings. Here κοινωνοί denotes personal inward <u>fellowship</u>, a similarity of views, tastes, ideas etc.

The complex of verse 10b enjoys two noun clauses, objects of εἶπεν "said" in the foundational independent clause. φοβοῦ with negative signifies, by its linear action, "stop fearing." ἔσῃ plus present supplementary participle ζωγρῶν accents continuous action. ζωγρέω comes from ζωός alive and ἀγρεύω <u>catch</u>. It means more than "catch." It indicates to "take <u>alive</u>."

Verse 11 emerges as a simple sentence with two circumstantial participles. "They followed him" is the basic thought. The aorist tense ἠκολούθησαν "followed" befits the decisiveness of the resolve made by the fishermen. Both participles are aorists also. κατάγω "to bring down" may be used as a nautical term and so here. Object of "having left" is "<u>all</u>." It suggests the finality of their choice to "follow him."

79

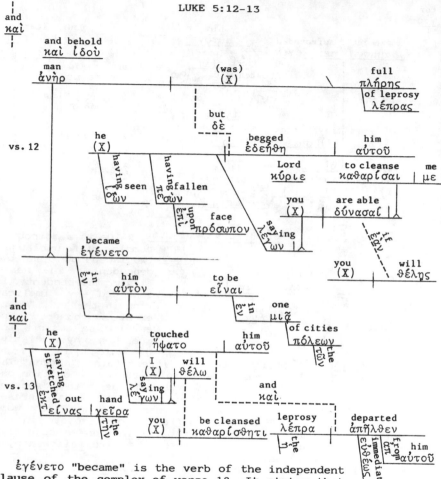

ἐγένετο "became" is the verb of the independent
clause of the complex of verse 12. It states that
something happend. What happened is in four dependents which, as a unit, form the subject.

"Man was full of leprosy" reports the problem. "He begged"
indicates what the man did. His plea appears in noun clause,
"you are able," object of participle, saying. The ἐάν "if"
clause is 3rd class condition, undetermined but with prospect
of determination. He never doubted the power; only the willingness of Jesus.

Verse 13 is compound-complex of four clauses. "He touched"
and "leprosy departed" are the independent facts. Noun clauses
"I will" and "be cleansed" relate how Jesus solved the problem.

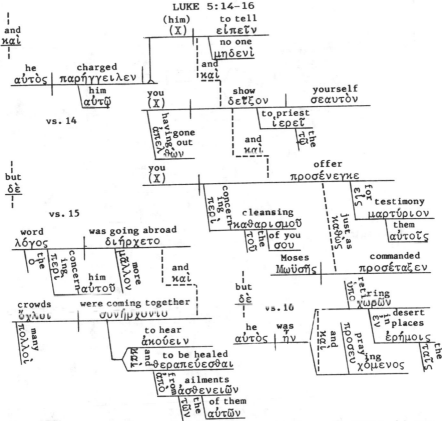

LUKE 5:14-16

Verbs in the four clauses of the complex of verse 14 are aorists. Subject of the independent is unmistakably emphatic by use of personal pronoun αὐτός "he charged." εἰπεῖν and two clauses are objects of παρήγγειλεν, "to tell," "show yourself," and "offer..." Their point action sharpens the urgency of the exhortations. καθώς instills adverb comparative clause, "just as Moses commanded."

The two verbs in the compound of verse 15 are descriptive imperfects, "kept on going abroad," and "many crowds kept on coming together." The infinitives "to hear" and "to be healed" also show continuing action by their present tenses.

Verse 16 frames a simple sentence though it has a compound predicate. The two periphrastic imperfects are quite descriptive. They give strong stress to their linear action: "was retiring(withdrawing)" and "was praying." Again personal pronoun αὐτός "he" gives striking emphasis to the subject.

81

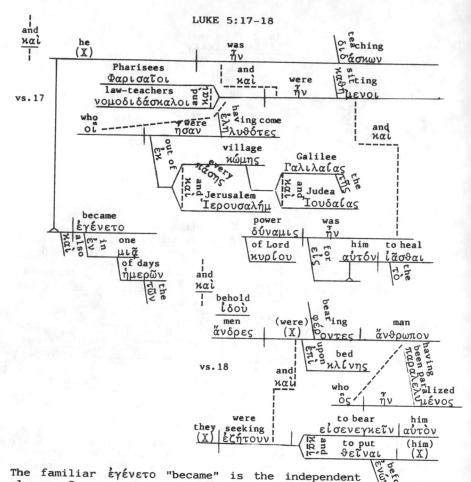

LUKE 5:17-18

The familiar ἐγένετο "became" is the independent clause of verse 18. What became appears in three subject noun clauses: "he was teaching," "Pharisees and law-teachers were sitting," and "power was for him to heal." Relative οἱ inserts adjective idea describing "Pharisees etc." When all this happened is set forth in an adverbial ἐν phrase, "in one of these days."

Verse 18 fashions a compound-complex of three clauses. Periphrastic "were bearing" enlivens the descriptive force of the imperfect in the initial independent. ὅς intrudes an adjectival dependent clause describing "man." In the second independent clause, imperfect ἐζήτουν is conative: in spite of hinderances "they kept on seeking..."

82

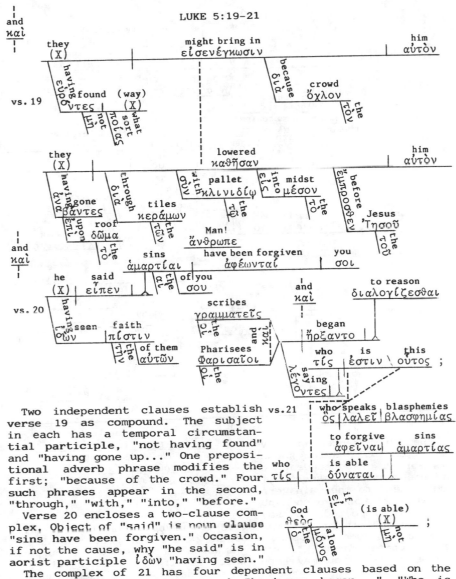

Two independent clauses establish verse 19 as compound. The subject in each has a temporal circumstantial participle, "not having found" and "having gone up..." One prepositional adverb phrase modifies the first; "because of the crowd." Four such phrases appear in the second, "through," "with," "into," "before."

Verse 20 encloses a two-clause complex, Object of "said" is noun clause "sins have been forgiven." Occasion, if not the cause, why "he said" is in aorist participle ἰδών "having seen."

The complex of 21 has four dependent clauses based on the independent, "The scribes and Pharisees began..." "Who is this" and "who is able to forgive sins..." are noun clauses, objects of participle "saying." ὅς inserts adjective clause; εἰ "if" an adverb first class conditional.

83

LUKE 5:22-24

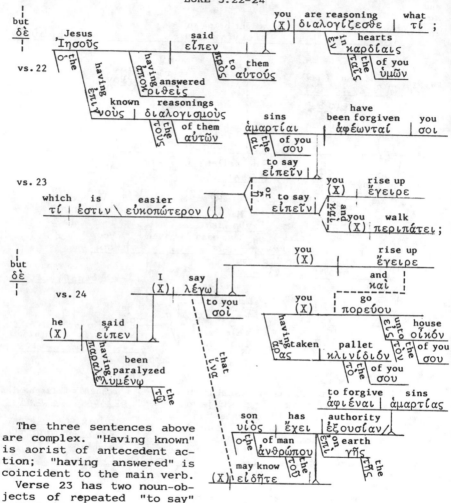

The three sentences above are complex. "Having known" is aorist of antecedent action; "having answered" is coincident to the main verb.

Verse 23 has two noun-objects of repeated "to say" both in apposition to comparative εὐκοπώτερον "easier."

Five dependent clauses arise in 24 stemming off "he said." First comes direct, "I say" to which is attached ἵνα purpose clause, "that you may know" which itself has noun-object "son has authority..." Object of λέγω "I say" are two noun clauses, "you rise up" and "you go..." The verbs are present imperative descriptive of the action commanded; "be rising and be going off..." Aorist cir.ptcp. is temporal, "having taken." εἰς is adverbial indicating **where**: "unto your house."

84

LUKE 5:25-26

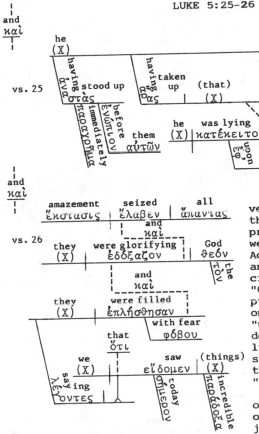

The complex sentence of verse 25 has two clauses, three circ. ptcps., three prepositional phrases. "He went off" is independent. Aorist "having stood up" and "having taken up" are circum. ptcps. of time. "Glorifying God" is descriptive present portraying ongoing action. The ἐφ᾽ ὅ "upon which" introduces a dependent clause, "he was lying," describing understood "pallet" or "that" the implied object of ἄρας "having taken up."

26 is compound-complex of three independent and one dependent clause. Subject of the first clause is "amazement" a compound word from ἐκ "outside" and ἵστημι "to stand." Our English word ecstacy reflects one who is "beside himself." "Amazement" is acceptable but tepid as a translation. ἐδόξαζον "were glorifying" is descriptive imperfect. The people "went on glorifying God." One may also detect a distributive idea, "Each separate individual kept on glorifying..."

The third independent declares, "they were filled with fear." Verbs of filling take genitive. Genitives specify this, not that.

The dependent idea is a noun clause, object of circ. ptcp. λέγοντες "saying." Introductory particle ὅτι might be thought of as representing direct quote. However, the diagram shows it as introducing indirect discourse, "that we saw..." σήμερον is adverbial accusative "today."

85

LUKE 5:27-29

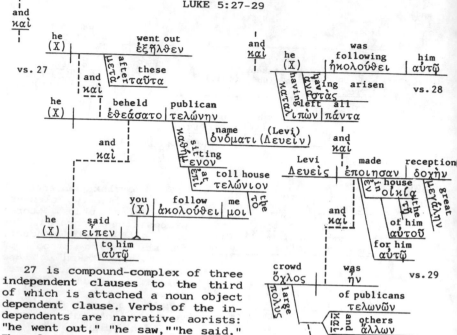

27 is compound-complex of three independent clauses to the third of which is attached a noun object dependent clause. Verbs of the independents are narrative aorists: "he went out," "he saw,""he said." They focus on facts as facts!

"After (μετά) these" indicates when thus is adverbial. The verb ἐθεάσατο "beheld" is more poetic, less prosaic than simple "saw." We get "theatre" from it, a place at which the imagination is stirred. Jesus "beheld" something that attracted him. ὀνόματι is dative of possession. In the noun clause ἀκολούθει is linear present, "be following."

Verse 28 structures a simple sentence. It has two aorist circumstantial participles. ἠκολούθει is inchoative imperfect, "he began to be following him." αὐτῷ is associative-instrumental case after the verb "following."

29 embraces a compound-complex of two independent clauses plus one dependent adjectival. "Levi made a great reception" initiates the sentence. Where is mentioned in the adverbial phrase, "in his house." Why, is in the "for him."

The second independent depicts a large crowd. Specifying the kind of crowd are genitives "publicans and others." Moving detail of the banquet is sketched in adjective clause injected by relative οἱ "who were reclining..." Periphrastic imperfect "were reclining" vivifies the bustle of the activity at the banquet. It empasizes the linear action.

86

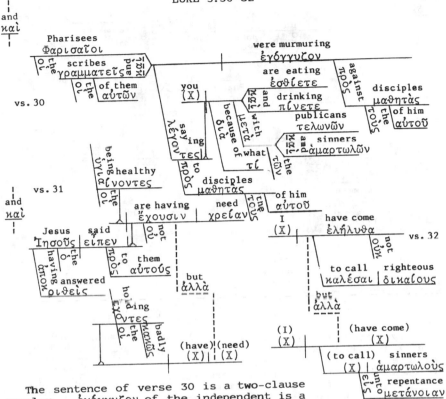

The sentence of verse 30 is a two-clause complex. ἐγόγγυζον of the independent is a descriptive imperfect, "were murmuring." It is onomatopoetic, a word which sounds like its meaning. The dependent clause is object of circumstantial λέγοντες "saying." Iterative presents inquire, "Why are you eating and drinking."

The three clauses of verse 31 are arranged as complex. Both subjects of the two subordinate clauses are attributive participles, "the ones being healthy" and "the ones holding badly." The predicate of the second is drawn from and implied by that of the first, "are having need."

Verse 32 provides a two-clause compound. Negative perfect of the first, "I have not come" appears by implication as verb (without negative) in the second. The perfect tense centers on the fixed purpose of his coming, that is, "to call sinners." The aorist infinitive καλέσαι "to call" expresses purpose in both clauses. μετάνοιαν "repentance" is a compound of two words meaning "change" and "mind." Basically repentance is a change of mind which indeed leads to a changed lifestyle.

87

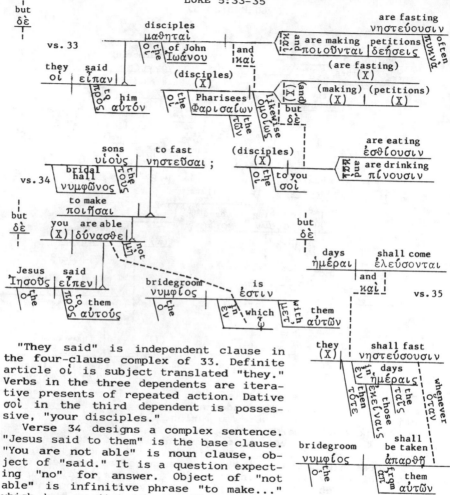

"They said" is independent clause in the four-clause complex of 33. Definite article οἱ is subject translated "they." Verbs in the three dependents are iterative presents of repeated action. Dative σοὶ in the third dependent is possessive, "your disciples."

Verse 34 designs a complex sentence. "Jesus said to them" is the base clause. "You are not able" is noun clause, object of "said." It is a question expecting "no" for answer. Object of "not able" is infinitive phrase "to make..." which has as its object infinitive with accusative of general reference, "the sons of bridal hall to fast." Another dependent clause(temporal adverb)appears in "while(ἐν ᾧ)the bridegroom is with them."

Verse 35 assembles a compound-complex with two independent and one dependent clause. It continues Jesus' answer to critics. Both verbs in the independents are point action futures, "days shall come" and "they shall fast." The ἐν phrase in the second is adverbial stating when. ὅταν "whenever" introduces an adverb phrase of indefinite time.

88

LUKE 5:36-39

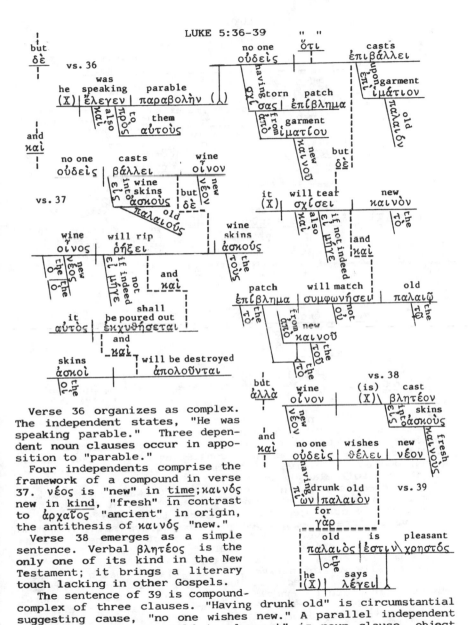

Verse 36 organizes as complex. The independent states, "He was speaking parable." Three dependent noun clauses occur in apposition to "parable."

Four independents comprise the framework of a compound in verse 37. νέος is "new" in time; καινός new in kind, "fresh" in contrast to ἀρχαῖος "ancient" in origin, the antithesis of καινός "new."

Verse 38 emerges as a simple sentence. Verbal βλητέος is the only one of its kind in the New Testament; it brings a literary touch lacking in other Gospels.

The sentence of 39 is compound-complex of three clauses. "Having drunk old" is circumstantial suggesting cause, "no one wishes new." A parallel independent supports the reason. "Old is pleasant" is noun clause, object of "says."

89

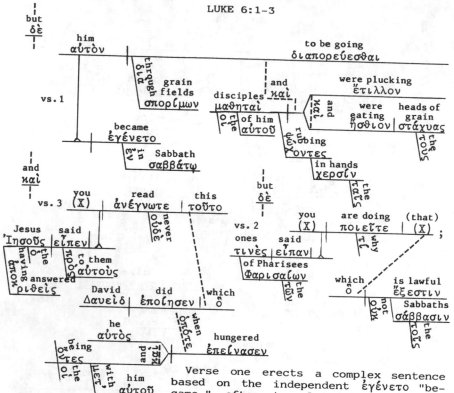

LUKE 6:1-3

Verse one erects a complex sentence based on the independent ἐγένετο "became," often translated "it came to pass." Subject is not the expletive "it" but that for which the "it" stands, usually a noun clause that follows. In this sentence, other than the adverb phrase "in Sabbath," the rest of the sentence is the subject consisting of two noun expressions, one an infinitive with accusative of general reference, the other a full clause.

Independent clause in verse two is: "Certain ones said..." "Why are you doing(that)" is noun clause object of "said." Relative ὅ introduces adjective clause describing implied "that."

In verse three the independent idea "Jesus said" has noun clause "did you never read this" as object. Another ὅ clause describes τοῦτο, "which David did..." Adverb ὁπότε clause completes the sentence, "when he and those with him..."

Technically an infinitive is not a clause. Being <u>infinite</u>, not limited by a subject, it doesn't have all the essentials. However, in actual usage the adverbial accusative(general reference)used to express the action of the infinitive serves in a <u>practical</u> way as though a subject. Verse one illustrates this.

90

LUKE 6:4-6

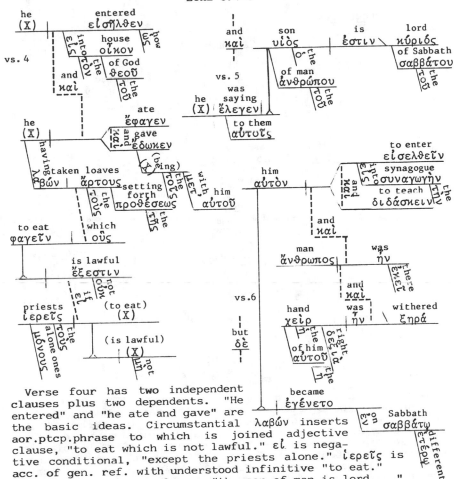

Verse four has two independent clauses plus two dependents. "He entered" and "he ate and gave" are the basic ideas. Circumstantial aor.ptcp.phrase to which is joined adjective clause, "to eat which is not lawful." εἰ is negative conditional, "except the priests alone." ἱερεῖς is acc. of gen. ref. with understood infinitive "to eat."

In verse five noun clause, "the son of man is lord...." is object of verb "was saying" of independent clause in this two-clause complex sentence.

The sentence of verse six has three full clauses plus an infinitive phrase with acc. of gen. ref. which when translated is equivalent to a clause. "It became" is the main clause. When it happened appears in adverbial, "on a different Sabbath." What "became" is disclosed in the tri-fold subject, "him to enter..." and "man was there" and "his right hand was withered." Repeated ἡ with δεξιὰ stresses "right hand."

91

LUKE 6:7-9

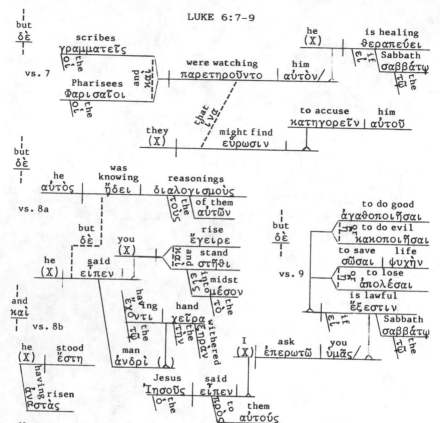

Verse seven exposes a complex sentence. "The scribes and the Pharisees were watching him" is the basic clause. εἰ "if" introduces an indirect question, "Whether he heals..." ἵνα involves an adverb purpose idea, "that they might accuse..."

Verse eight develops a compound-complex of three clauses. ἤδει is pluperfect with force of imperfect, "was knowing." The noun clause, object of "said," has a compound predicate; present "be rising up" and aorist "stand."

Verse 8b is treated as a distinct simple sentence, "he stood." "Having risen" is circumstantial participle of antecedent action describing the subject. "He, having gotten up, took his stand."

The sentence of verse nine is complex in form. Independent clause, "Jesus said," has for its object noun clause, "I ask you." An indirect question follows embodying a noun clause. Its subject consists of a four-infinitive compound, "to do good or to do evil etc..."

92

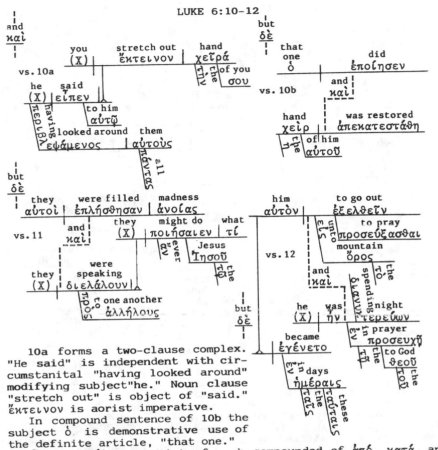

10a forms a two-clause complex. "He said" is independent with circumstanital "having looked around" modifying subject "he." Noun clause "stretch out" is object of "said." ἔκτεινον is aorist imperative.

In compound sentence of 10b the subject ὁ is demonstrative use of the definite article, "that one."

ἀπεκατεστάθη is aorist of verb compounded of ἀπό, κατά, and ἵστημι Aorist looks to the fact. Passive sees Jesus as agent. Jesus did nothing! He commanded; the man did the command.

Verse 11 frames a compound-complex sentence. Subject αὐτοὶ by virtue of being a separate word is emphatic. Object ἀνοίας is strong word "madness," α privative and νοῦς "mind." They went beserk, out of mind! The verb in the 2nd clause is descriptive imperfect, "were speaking." Object is noun clause, "whatever they might do to (objective genitive) Jesus."

Verse 12 combines two full clauses into a complex. But there is also an infinitive with accusative of general reference that serves as a practical dependent clause; "him to go out." The noun clause has periphrastic imperfect ἦν διανυκτερεύων "was spending night," emphasizing linear. He was praying all night long.

93

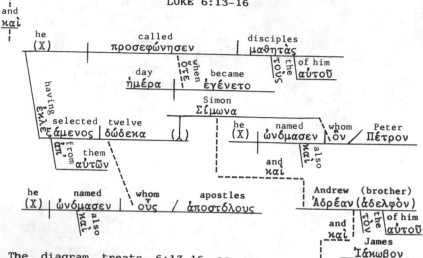

The diagram treats 6:13-16 as one sentence. It is complex in structure. "He called his disciples" is the independent concept. ὅτε inserts dependent temporal idea, "when day came." The sentence proceeds by aorist circumstantial participle "having selected twelve..." This object "twelve" is identified by descriptive adjective clause ushered in by relative οὕς "whom he named apostles." These "apostles" are distinct from "disciples" and "the people." They were to be his "ones sent out on a special mission (apostles)." Of the twelve named, two are amplified by adjectival descriptive clauses. First is "Simon, whom he named Peter." Last is "Judas Iscariot, who became (the) betrayer."

The verbs, including one participle, are matter of fact aorists. They give facts as facts without descriptive elaboration. The exception is attributive present participle, "one being called, Zealot."

In contrast to Mark, Luke "named" this group "apostles." Mark tells that Jesus "ordained" them to be "with him" and sent them "to preach" and "to cast out demons etc." In Matthew they are merely "twelve disciples" to whom he gave power "to cast out unclean spirits" and to "heal diseases." To Luke they were "emisaries," "ones sent out."

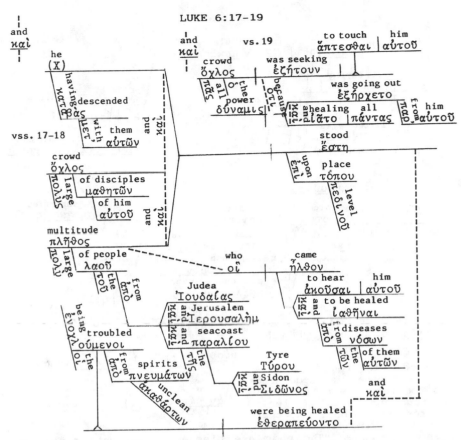

LUKE 6:17-19

The sentence of 6:17-18 has two independent clauses and one dependent. The first clause has a three-fold compound subject, "he," "crowd," and "multitude." Aorist "stood" affirms what they did. Adverb phrase, "upon level place" tells where. Relative οἵ inserts an adjective idea describing "multitude." Infinitives "to hear" and "to be healed" express purpose. The second independent has for its subject attributive participle "the ones being troubled." ἐθεραπεύοντο "were being healed" is descriptive imperfect but also suggests the distributive idea of each separate individual "was being healed."

In upper right is the complex sentence of verse 19. "All the crowd was seeking" is the basic independent idea. Descriptive imperfect ἐζήτουν vividly portrays the temper of the crowd. ὅτι inserts dependent causal idea. Both verbs are descriptive imperfects, "was going out" and "was healing."

95

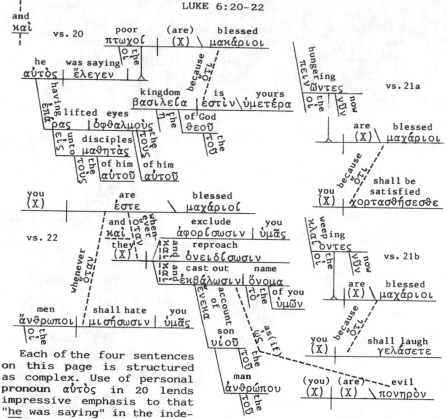

Each of the four sentences on this page is structured as complex. Use of personal pronoun αὐτὸς in 20 lends impressive emphasis to that "he was saying" in the independent clause. "The poor are blessed" dependent noun clause is object of "was saying." ὅτι inserts a causal clause telling why they are blessed. ἐπάρας is temporal circumstantial participle, "when he lifted his eyes..." Possessive pronoun ὑμετέρα shows that the "poor" are the "disciples."

The beatitudes of 21a and 21b are alike in pattern. Subject in each involves present attributive participle, then predicate "blessed." Each also enjoys a dependent ὅτι causal clause.

Supporting independent "blessed" of verse 22 are two ὅταν indefinite temporal clauses, "whenever men shall hate..." and the compound "whenever they shall exclude...reproach...cast out..." The ὡς clause is concessive, "as (though)...evil." The phrase begun by ἕνεκα "on account of" is adverbial telling why "they cast out..." ὄνομα "name" refers to one's person. To "cast out your name" is to cast out the person who wears the name.

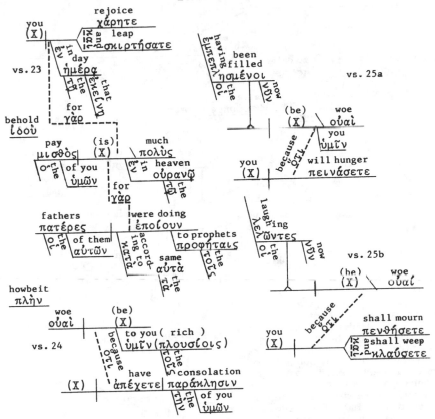

Verse 23 might be seen as three distinct simple sentences. But the ideas are closely related. The diagram treats the three clauses as compound sentence. The verbs "rejoice" and "leap" are aorists, sharp, pointed, energetic. Phrase "in that day" is adverbial expressing when. "In heaven" tells where. Imperfect "were doing" is repeated action.

Verse 24 provides a two-clause complex. Strong adversative πλήν "howbeit," contrasts the "rejoicing" of 23 with the "woes" of the rich. ὅτι is causal expressing why they may look forward to woe. Present ἀπέχετε means "paid in full," "receipted."

Verse 25 divides into two complex sentences the structure of which is alike. Attributive participle is subject; "woe" is predicate nominative. ὅτι clauses declare underlying cause.

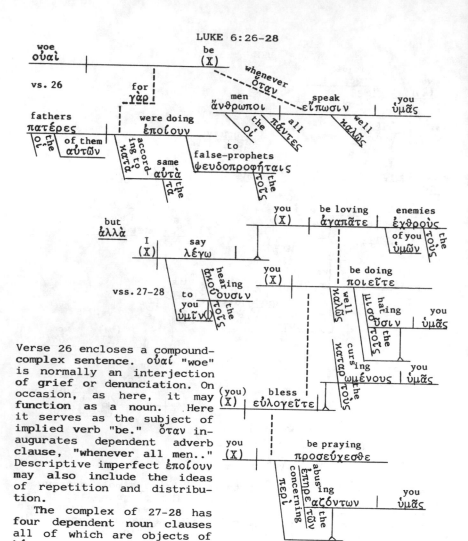

LUKE 6:26-28

Verse 26 encloses a compound-complex sentence. οὐαί "woe" is normally an interjection of grief or denunciation. On occasion, as here, it may function as a noun. Here it serves as the subject of implied verb "be." ὅταν inaugurates dependent adverb clause, "whenever all men.." Descriptive imperfect ἐποίουν may also include the ideas of repetition and distribution.

The complex of 27-28 has four dependent noun clauses all of which are objects of λέγω "say" of the independent clause. They are all exhortations which Jesus gives "to you, the ones hearing." Each has a linear action present: "be loving," "be doing," "be blessing," and "be praying." He exhorts to a practice, a life habit, not a single act. ἀγαπάω is the love of "intelligent good will." It doesn't spring of the emotions but of the will. Adverb καλῶς "well" is the same root as adjective καλός "good." It signifies "that which is appropriate," that which "befits" the need or occasion.

98

LUKE 6:29-31

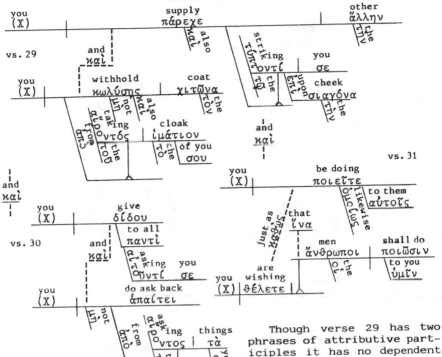

Though verse 29 has two phrases of attributive participles it has no dependent clauses. It is compound with two independent ideas. The present πάρεχε "offer" is in contrast to aorist κωλύσης "withhold." When anyone "strikes you on your cheek" and keeps on striking, in response you are "to keep on supplying to him your other cheek." The second independent clause urges the negative response. "Don't even start to withhold your coat from the one who keeps on taking your cloak." ἱμάτιον is "outer (cloak) garment." χιτών is "inner (coat) garment."

The sentence of verse 30 is another two-clause compound. The verbs are both present imperatives emphasizing continuous repetition, "go on giving" and "do not go on asking back." Two present participles also appear; αἰτοῦντί, circumstantial; but αἴροντος is attributive.

Verse 31 erects a complex of three clauses. The independent has another present imperative, "continue doing..." It's to be a habit, a life-style, an oft-repeated performance. καθὼς "just as" sets up the standard upon which one is to measure his life-style as urged by the independent. A third dependent is introduced by ἵνα. It is a noun clause, object of "wish."

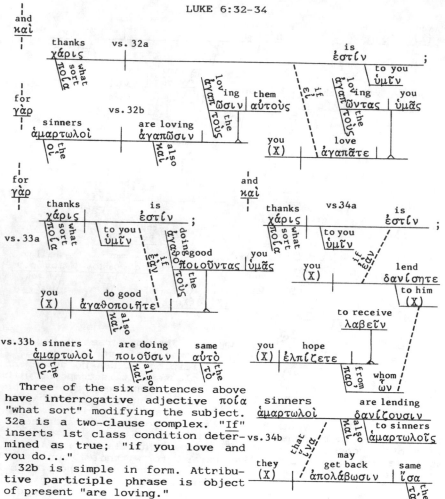

Three of the six sentences above have interrogative adjective ποία "what sort" modifying the subject. 32a is a two-clause complex. "If" inserts 1st class condition determined as true; "if you love and you do..."

32b is simple in form. Attributive participle phrase is object of present "are loving."

33a is complex but here the "if" initiates a 3rd class condition, undetermined but with prospect of determination; "if you do good and you probably do..."

33b is simple. The verb "are doing" is iterative present.

A three-clause complex develops in 34a. The 3rd class ἐάν "if you lend and you likely will..." appears. An adjective clause (ὧν) follows describing understood "him." Descriptive present "go on hoping" has aorist infinitive λαβεῖν "to get" as its object.

34b encases a two-clause complex. ἵνα installs adverb purpose clause, "that you may get back..."

Luke 6:35-37a

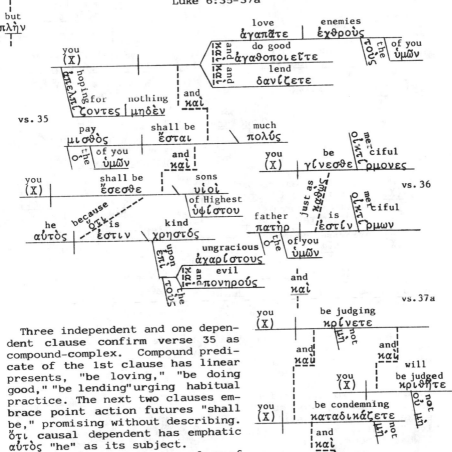

Three independent and one dependent clause confirm verse 35 as compound-complex. Compound predicate of the 1st clause has linear presents, "be loving," "be doing good," "be lending"urging habitual practice. The next two clauses embrace point action futures "shall be," promising without describing. ὅτι causal dependent has emphatic αὐτός "he" as its subject.

Both verbs in the complex of 36 are vivid periphrastics, "become merciful" and "is merciful." They give even more stress to the repetition of linear action.

The sentence of 37a is compound of four clauses each connected by coordinating καί. The two admonitions (negative) are put in present imperative. This gives emphasis to the adopting of life habits. The first and third clauses are contrasted by aorist passives in the second and fourth clauses. Adopt the habit of "not judging etc" and the fact of "being judged" will never even begin. Double negative οὐ μή is a most emphatic negative.

101

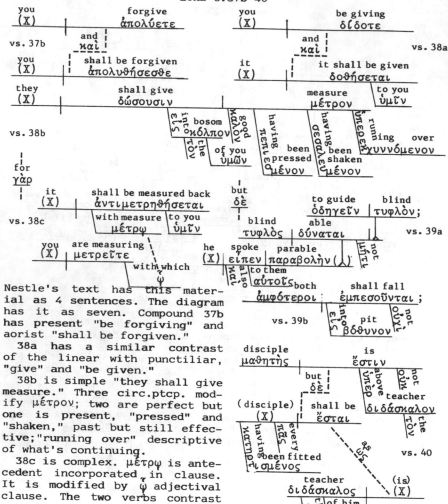

Nestle's text has this material as 4 sentences. The diagram has it as seven. Compound 37b has present "be forgiving" and aorist "shall be forgiven."

38a has a similar contrast of the linear with punctiliar, "give" and "be given."

38b is simple "they shall give measure." Three circ.ptcp. modify μέτρον; two are perfect but one is present, "pressed" and "shaken," past but still effective;"running over" descriptive of what's continuing.

38c is complex. μέτρῳ is antecedent incorporated in clause. It is modified by ᾧ adjectival clause. The two verbs contrast present to point-act.fut.pass.

Verse 39a is structured as complex. Dependent "blind is not able" is appositional to "parable" of the independent clause. Strong negative μήτι expects no for an answer. Close in idea is the simple of 39b. οὐχὶ expects yes as an answer.

Verse 40 is compound-complex. Two independents contrast "is" and "shall be." Pf.,circ.,ptcp. looks to a point when one became disciple and insists that "being fitted" is continuing process. ὡς inserts adverb clause, a goal to which a disciple aims.

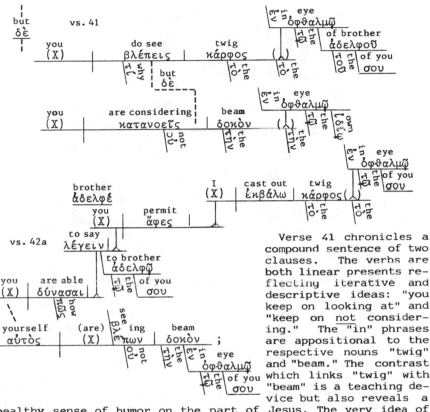

Verse 41 chronicles a compound sentence of two clauses. The verbs are both linear presents reflecting iterative and descriptive ideas: "you keep on looking at" and "keep on not considering." The "in" phrases are appositional to the respective nouns "twig" and "beam." The contrast which links "twig" with "beam" is a teaching device but also reveals a healthy sense of humor on the part of Jesus. The very idea of having an undressed log in one's eye is obviously impossible.

Verse 42a encompasses a complex sentence. Basic independent clause is the question, "How are you able to say?" The content of what is said is in the noun clause object of the infinitive λέγειν "to say." Furthermore, that clause has for its direct object another noun clause, "(that) I cast out..." Completing the sentence is another dependent, an adjectival describing subject "you" of the main clause: "you yourself (are) not seeing the beam..." The usual negative with a participle is μή but note here a rare appearance of οὐ with βλέπων. Maybe it is mere emphasis or it could be because the participle is supplementing an understood "are" thus becoming a form of a finite verb "are seeing." Periphrastic forms stress the continuing aspect of the action. Both the parabolic form plus the grammatical forms enliven the image.

103

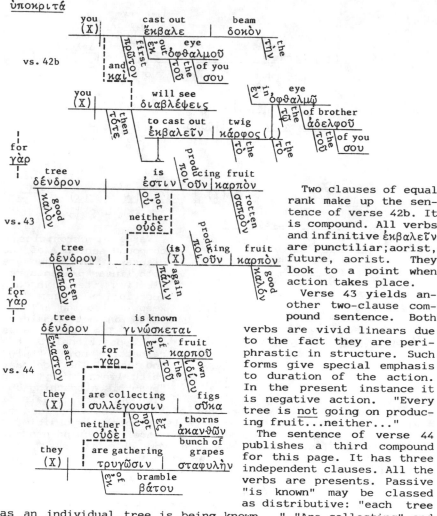

Two clauses of equal rank make up the sentence of verse 42b. It is compound. All verbs and infinitive ἐκβαλεῖν are punctiliar; aorist, future, aorist. They look to a point when action takes place.

Verse 43 yields another two-clause compound sentence. Both verbs are vivid linears due to the fact they are periphrastic in structure. Such forms give special emphasis to duration of the action. In the present instance it is negative action. "Every tree is <u>not</u> going on producing fruit...neither..."

The sentence of verse 44 publishes a third compound for this page. It has three independent clauses. All the verbs are presents. Passive "is known" may be classed as distributive: "each tree as an individual tree is being known..." "Are collecting" and "are gathering" are synonyms for <u>picking</u> or <u>gathering</u> fruit. λέγω, familiar for "say" in koine Greek, in classic times meant "pick out," "gather," "recount." Here, combined with σύν, it signifies to "gather" as in harvest, to "collect together." These last two verbs are in a negative expression. Singular σταφυλὴν signifies a <u>bunch</u> of grapes.

104

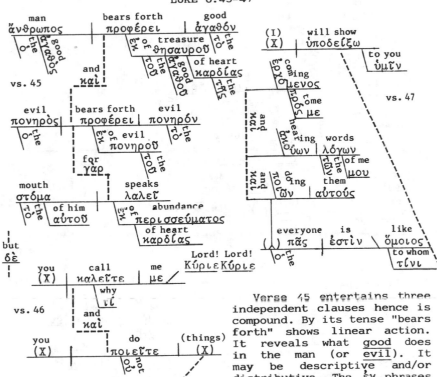

Verse 45 entertains three independent clauses hence is compound. By its tense "bears forth" shows linear action. It reveals what good does in the man (or evil). It may be descriptive and/or distributive. The ἐκ phrases incorporate ablative ideas showing source from which.

Verse 46 embraces a three-clause compound-complex. The presents again show animated description, positive and negative:"are calling...not doing." Relative ἅ inserts adjective clause modifying implied "things." Repetition of vocative "Lord, Lord" suggests the imperative nature of the relationship indicated by the term. "Doing" or "not doing" is a test of the vitality of the relationship.

The sentence of 47 is a complex of two clauses. Independent "I will show to you" proposes a promise. Interrogative τίνι is associative-instrumental after word of likeness. The three present participles "coming," "hearing," "doing" are all under the control of one definite article ὁ. This links them together in a unified progressive action. No use of "coming" if one isn't "hearing." Nor is there any use of "hearing" if one isn't "doing." And that includes "all"(πᾶς), in the singular, "everyone."

105

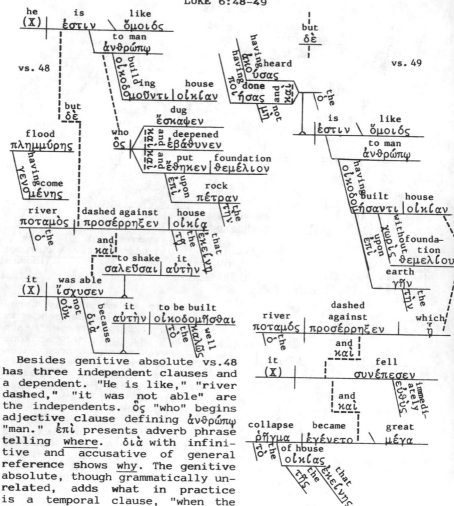

Besides genitive absolute vs.48 has three independent clauses and a dependent. "He is like," "river dashed," "it was not able" are the independents. ὅς "who" begins adjective clause defining ἀνθρώπῳ "man." ἐπὶ presents adverb phrase telling where. διὰ with infinitive and accusative of general reference shows why. The genitive absolute, though grammatically unrelated, adds what in practice is a temporal clause, "when the flood came."

49 embodies a four-clause complex sentence. Subject of the main clause is compound of two attributive participles, "the one having heard and did not do." Such a one "is like to a man..." This "man" is described by aorist circumstantial participle "having built." Where he built is noted by ἐπὶ "upon" phrase; how by the χωρὶς "without" phrase. Relative ἥ "which" inserts adjective clause describing "house" which the man built. The last two dependent clauses are also adjective.

106

LUKE 7:1-4

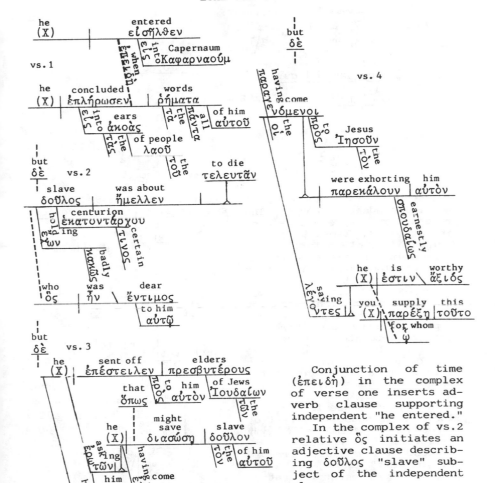

Conjunction of time (ἐπειδή) in the complex of verse one inserts adverb clause supporting independent "he entered."

In the complex of vs. 2 relative ὅς initiates an adjective clause describing δοῦλος "slave" subject of the independent clause.

In the complex of vs. 3 subject "he" is modified by two cir.ptcps., (1) temporal "having heard" (2) attendent circumstance "asking." ἐρωτῶν has two accusatives. αὐτόν is adverbial; ὅπως instills noun clause object of the participle, "that he might save his slave."

"Were exhorting him" is the independent in complex of vs. 4. The rest of the sentence is the subject including two ptcs. and the noun and adjective dependent clauses.

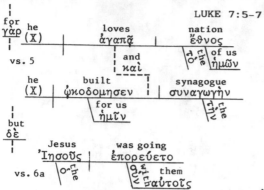

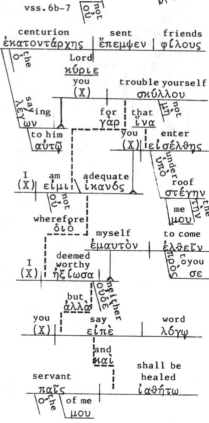

Verse five is a sentence of two independent clauses. The present ἀγαπᾷ represents a continuing state. Aorist "built" declares a single point.

6a forms a simple sentence. ἐπορεύετο, inchoative imperfect says, "he began to go..."

Verses 6b-7 might be viewed as more than one sentence. But the diagram treats it as one, complex in structure. First is genitive absolute. Though not grammatically attached to the rest of the sentence, it does offer an idea important to the thought: "he(Jesus)already being not far off..."

The basic clause is: "centurion sent friends." The rest of the sentence stems off λέγων participle of attendant circumstances. Noun clause, "trouble not yourself" is object. Negative μὴ with present imperative means "quit troubling..." The ἵνα clause stands in apposition to ἱκανός in sub-final use. Infinitive ἐλθεῖν completes "deemed worthy" as object and has acc. of general reference.

The centurion's servant is here addressed as παῖς "house boy." In verse two he's called δοῦλος "slave." He was a slave but one for whom the centurion had developed warm personal affection.

108

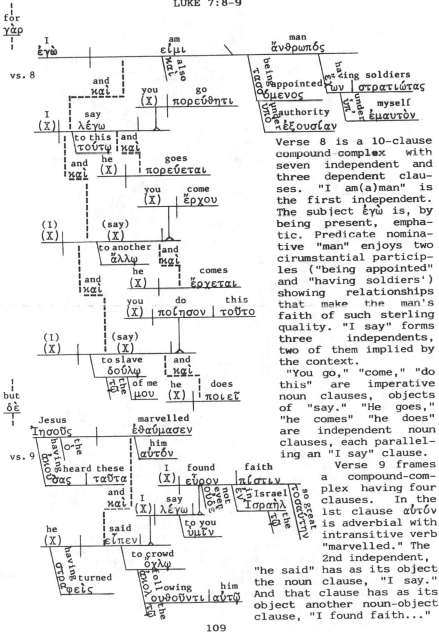

for
γὰρ

vs. 8

I
ἐγώ

am
εἰμι

man
ἄνθρωπός

and
καί

also
καί

you
(X)

go
πορεύθητι

being
appointed
ὁμενος

having
soldiers
ζῶν | στρατιώτας

under
myself
ἐμαυτόν

I
(X)

say
λέγω

authority
ἐξουσίαν

to this
τούτῳ

and
καί

and
καί

he
(X)

goes
πορεύεται

you
(X)

come
ἔρχου

(I)
(X)

(say)
(X)

to another
ἄλλῳ

and
καί

he
(X)

comes
ἔρχεται

you
(X)

do
ποίησον

this
τοῦτο

(I)
(X)

(say)
(X)

to slave
δούλῳ

and
καί

of me
μου

he
(X)

does
ποιεῖ

but
δέ

Jesus
Ἰησοῦς

marvelled
ἐθαύμασεν

him
αὐτόν

vs. 9

having heard these
ἀκούσας | ταῦτα

and
καί

I
(X)

found
εὗρον

faith
πίστιν

I
(X)

say
λέγω

not ever
in Israel
Ἰσραήλ

so great
τοσαύτην

he
(X)

said
εἶπεν

to you
ὑμῖν

to crowd
ὄχλῳ

having turned
στραφείς

following
ἀκολουθοῦντι

him
αὐτῷ

Verse 8 is a 10-clause compound-complex with seven independent and three dependent clauses. "I am(a)man" is the first independent. The subject ἐγώ is, by being present, emphatic. Predicate nominative "man" enjoys two cirumstantial participles ("being appointed" and "having soldiers') showing relationships that make the man's faith of such sterling quality. "I say" forms three independents, two of them implied by the context.

"You go," "come," "do this" are imperative noun clauses, objects of "say." "He goes," "he comes" "he does" are independent noun clauses, each paralleling an "I say" clause.

Verse 9 frames a compound-complex having four clauses. In the 1st clause αὐτόν is adverbial with intransitive verb "marvelled." The 2nd independent, "he said" has as its object the noun clause, "I say." And that clause has as its object another noun-object clause, "I found faith..."

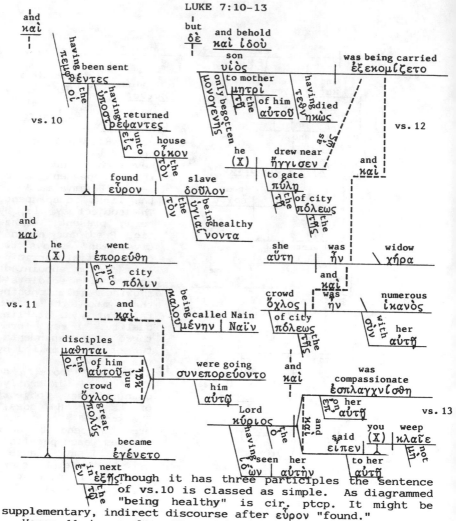

Though it has three participles the sentence of vs.10 is classed as simple. As diagrammed "being healthy" is cir. ptcp. It might be supplementary, indirect discourse after εὗρον "found."

Verse 11 is complex. Its subject is compounded of two noun clauses, the second of which has a compound subject. Adverbial ἐξῆς implies "day." συνεπορεύοντο is descriptive imperfect.

Verse 12 forges a compound-complex. Dependent ὡς "as he drew" is adverbial indicating when. The other three are independents. ἐξεκομίζετο is descriptive imperfect.

Verse 13 is complex but with a compound predicate. Dependent "weep not" is noun clause object of "said."

LUKE 7:14-17

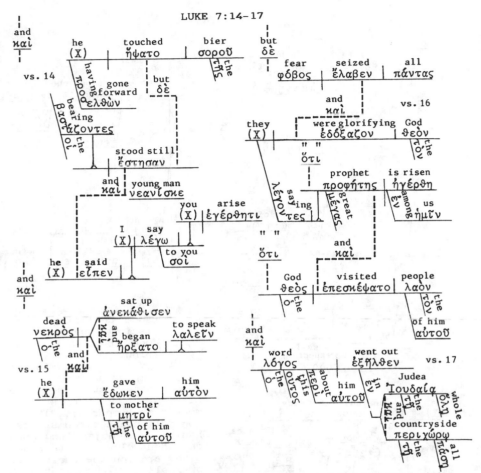

Verse 14 frames a compound-complex. The independents with narrative aorists state:"he touched..the ones bearing stood still..he said." Noun-object clauses report that "he said" and what he said.

Two independent clauses make 15 a compound. A compound predicate states(aorists):"sat up," "began to be speaking." Then a report of what Jesus did:"he gave..." Present infinitive denotes that the speech was more than momentary.

Verse 16 is compound-complex. The independent clauses state a fact "fear seized" and describe an effect "were glorifying." Two noun clauses recite what the people concluded: "prophet is arisen," "God visited."

Verse 17 recounts a simple sentence, "the word went out."

111

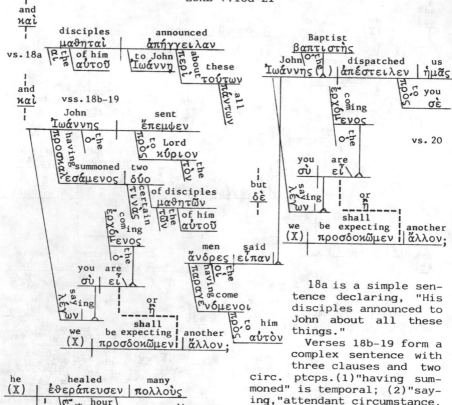

18a is a simple sentence declaring, "His disciples announced to John about all these things."

Verses 18b-19 form a complex sentence with three clauses and two circ. ptcps.(1)"having summoned" is temporal; (2)"saying,"attendant circumstance, has for its object two noun dependent clauses(interrogative)"are you the one coming or shall we expect another?" Present προσδοκῶμεν is deliberative subj., "shall we expect another?" ἄλλον is other of the same kind not another kind!

The same two noun clauses as objects of circ. ptcp. "saying" are in the complex sentence of verse 20. In the dependent "Baptist" is appositive to subject "John." The verb ἀποστέλλω suggests authoritative sending in contrast to πέμπω.

Verse 21 provides a compound sentence: "He healed...and he bestowed to see(sight)." The ἐν phrase tells when; ἀπὸ shows separation from.

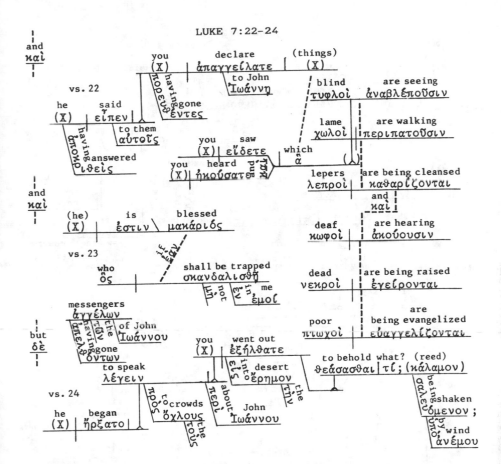

LUKE 7:22-24

Eight dependent after independent "he said" form a complex sentence of verse 22. "You declare" is noun clause object of "said" of the main clause. Relative ἅ inserts adjective clause describing understood "things." The other six are noun clauses in apposition to ἅ. Note dramatic effect of asyndeton.

Verse 23 is complex. Third class (ἐάν) conditional supports independent "If who shall not be trapped...(he) is blessed."

24 has two infinitive phrases and a genitive absolute but only two full clauses. λέγειν completes the main clause, "he began to speak..." Object of λέγειν is interrogative noun clause, "you went out..." Infinitive θεάσασθαι notes purpose as to why "you went out." Present circumstantial participle "being shaken" describes "reed" which in turn is in apposition to interrogative "what."

113

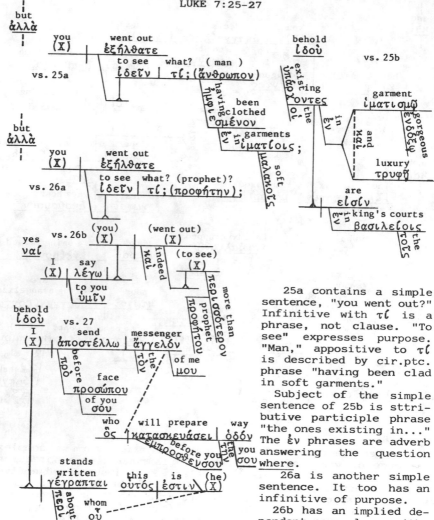

25a contains a simple sentence, "you went out?" Infinitive with τί is a phrase, not clause. "To see" expresses purpose. "Man," appositive to τί is described by cir.ptc. phrase "having been clad in soft garments."

Subject of the simple sentence of 25b is sttributive participle phrase "the ones existing in..." The ἐν phrases are adverb answering the question where.

26a is another simple sentence. It too has an infinitive of purpose.

26b has an implied dependent noun clause with understood purpose infinitive. This entire clause is object of λέγω of the independent clause.

Verse 27 forms a complex of four clauses. "This is (he)" is the independent idea. Prepositional phrase "concerning whom" introduces the first dependent idea, "stands written." Subject of "stands written" is the noun clause, "I send my messenger." Adjective clause inserted by relative οὖ describes "messenger."

114

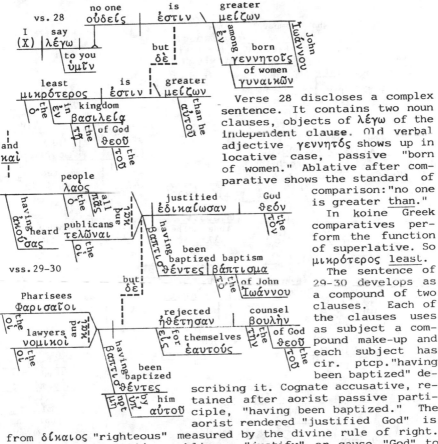

Verse 28 discloses a complex sentence. It contains two noun clauses, objects of λέγω of the independent clause. Old verbal adjective γεννητός shows up in locative case, passive "born of women." Ablative after comparative shows the standard of comparison:"no one is greater than."

In koine Greek comparatives perform the function of superlative. So μικρότερος least.

The sentence of 29-30 develops as a compound of two clauses. Each of the clauses uses as subject a compound make-up and each subject has cir. ptcp."having been baptized" describing it. Cognate accusative, retained after aorist passive participle, "having been baptized." The aorist rendered "justified God" is from δίκαιος "righteous" measured by the divine rule of right. How may people and/or publicans "justify" or cause "God" to be righteous? By obedience to divine commands a publican acknowledges God to be "right." By refusal one denies God as being righteous. Coordinating conjunction δέ "but" sets in contrast, by its adverse quality, the two clauses. The "people and publicans justified God but the Pharisees and lawyers rejected the counsel of God." ἠθέτησαν is first aorist active from ἀθετέω "reject" which in turn derives from the root of τίθημι combined with an alpha privative. It means to nullify. βουλή in classical Greek referred particularly to the purpose of the gods. In the NT it points to the divine purpose. "For themselves" (εἰς ἑαυτούς) equals the dative of disadvantage. Their rejection proved to be "for themselves."

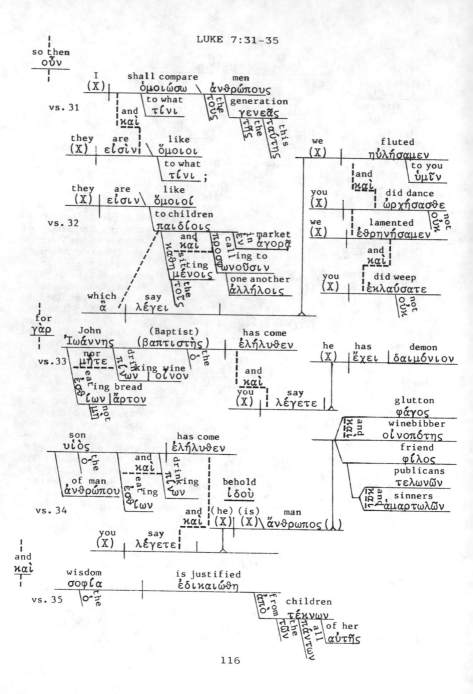

116

LUKE 7:31-35

Verse 31 develops a two-clause compound sentence. οὖν expresses consequence thus relates what follows to 29-30. Words of likeness take associative-instrumental case, hence τίνι.

The sentence of verse 32 is complex of six clauses. "They are like children" is the independent idea. Instrumental παιδίοις is described by adjective clause introduced by relative ἅ "which." Direct objects of λέγει "say" are four noun clauses: "we fluted and you didn't dance, we lamented and you didn't weep." The four tenses are narrative aorists presenting facts as facts without describing.

Two independent clauses give the compound flavor to verse 33. But one object-noun clauses insists on classifying it as compound-complex. Circumstantial participles "eating and drinking" describe the manner in which John "has come." Perfect "has come" pictures the permanent impression left by John's lifestyle.

Verse 34 also embodies a compound-complex. However, object of say is "(he is) man" subject and verb of which is implied in this context. ἄνθρωπος is expanded by descriptive appositions, "glutton etc..."

Verse 35 is a simple sentence: "Wisdom is justified..." The phrase "from all her children" is adverbial. The children are viewed as the source(ἀπὸ)from which wisdom "is justified.

LUKE 7:36

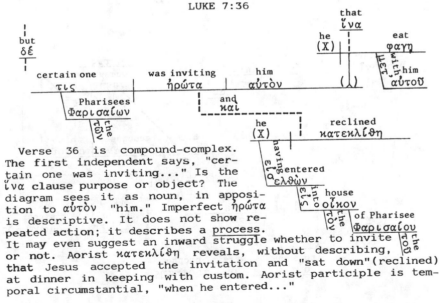

Verse 36 is compound-complex. The first independent says, "certain one was inviting..." Is the ἵνα clause purpose or object? The diagram sees it as noun, in apposition to αὐτὸν "him." Imperfect ἠρώτα is descriptive. It does not show repeated action; it describes a process. It may even suggest an inward struggle whether to invite or not. Aorist κατεκλίθη reveals, without describing, that Jesus accepted the invitation and "sat down"(reclined) at dinner in keeping with custom. Aorist participle is temporal circumstantial, "when he entered..."

117

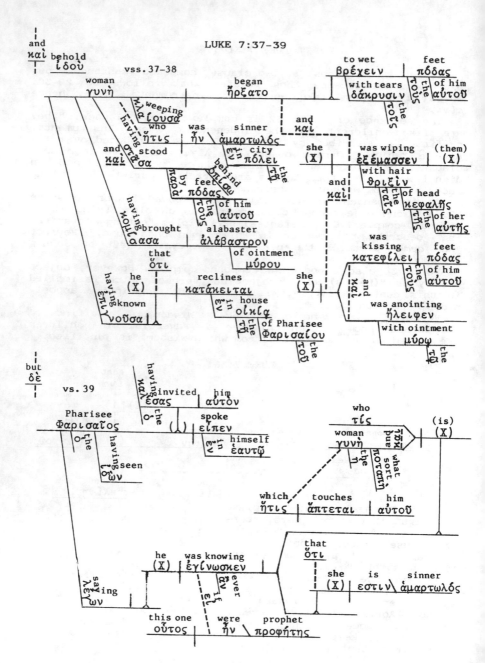

LUKE 7:37-39

118

The diagram of 37-38 shows three independent clauses and two dependents, plus four circumstantial participles. It is a compound-complex. The independents reveal the basic ideas: "woman began...was wiping...was kissing and anointing..." Aorist "began" combined with present infinitive "to wet" makes a vivid picture. Add the imperfects "wiping," "kissing," "anointing" and the total impression is an animated description. Three times the instrumental indicates the means by which the woman performs:"with tears," "with hair," "with ointment." The four participles describe "woman." The aorists fill out the facts, "having known,...brought,... stood..." Present "weeping" enlivens and complements the linear "to wet." Object of "having known" is noun ὅτι clause of indirect discourse, "that he was reclining..." Note adjective clause inserted by qualitative pronoun ἥτις "who by the quality of her life was sinner..."

Verse 39 has six clauses, five of which are dependents. It is complex. "The Pharisee spoke" is independent. Attributive participle "the one having invited" identifies the particular Pharisee. The "in himself" phrase tells where he "spoke." Why he "spoke" (as well as when) is set forth in ἰδών "having seen." What he spoke "in himself" appears in the five remaining clauses. First is noun clause, apodosis to 2nd class condition, determined as unfulfilled. "If this one were prophet (but he isn't) he would be knowing (but he doesn't)..." Conditions portray how facts are perceived not how they are. Direct objects of "was knowing" are two noun clauses one with and one without ὅτι. Qualitative relative ἥτις brings in a dependent adjective clause describing "woman."

Verse 40 discloses two sentences each with two clauses. Both are complex in structure. The independent clause of 40a "Jesus said" has aor.cir.ptcp. "having answered" modifying subject "Jesus." Object of verb "said" is the noun dependent "I have something to say to you." Note "to you" is dative σοί but in the independent clause "to him" represents πρός with accusative. Dative stresses the personal element; πρός and accusative signifies the more general idea of direction toward.

Subject of 40b is demonstrative use of definite article ὁ rendered "that one." Both sentences use vocative of address.

LUKE 7:40

LUKE 7:41-43

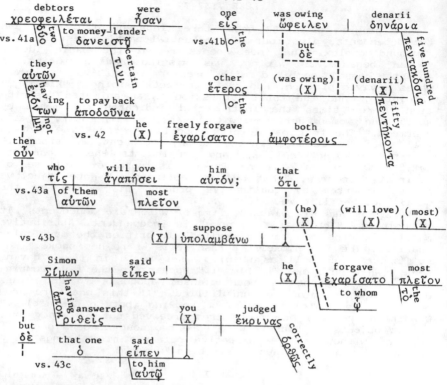

Verse 41a involves a simple sentence. δανειστῇ is dative of possession. First declension masculine nouns having nominatives in -της express <u>agent</u>. Thus χρεοφειλέτης is an agent noun.

41b is a two-clause compound. Linear action of imperfect ὤφειλεν indicates that both debts were remaining unpaid.

A genitive absolute occurs in the simple sentence of 42. Aorist ἐχαρίσατο states fact without descriptive elaboration.

43a presents a simple interrogative sentence. πλεῖον is comparative which in koine Greek often functions as superlative.

43b emerges as a complex with three dependent clauses. "I suppose," noun clause object of "said" of the main clause, has for its object a ὅτι clause which is entirely implied by the context; "that (he will love most)..." Relative ᾧ brings in an adjective clause describing understood "he" of the ὅτι clause.

The sentence of 43c is complex. Subject ὁ is demonstrative use of the definite article and is translated "that one." Object of "said" of the main clause is the noun clause "you judged correctly."

120

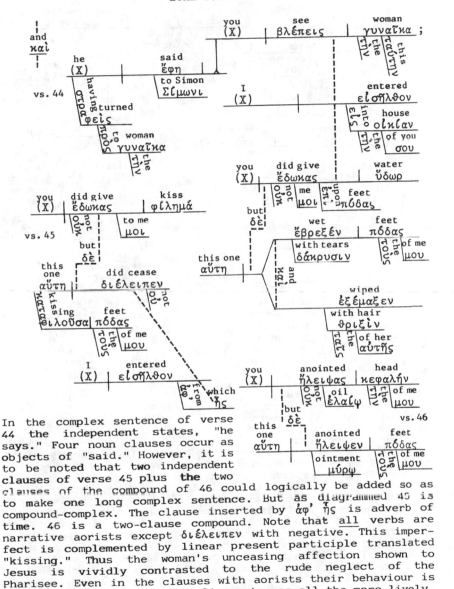

In the complex sentence of verse 44 the independent states, "he says." Four noun clauses occur as objects of "said." However, it is to be noted that two independent clauses of verse 45 plus the two clauses of the compound of 46 could logically be added so as to make one long complex sentence. But as diagrammed 45 is compound-complex. The clause inserted by ἀφ' ἧς is adverb of time. 46 is a two-clause compound. Note that all verbs are narrative aorists except διέλειπεν with negative. This imperfect is complemented by linear present participle translated "kissing." Thus the woman's unceasing affection shown to Jesus is vividly contrasted to the rude neglect of the Pharisee. Even in the clauses with aorists their behaviour is contrasted which makes these linear tenses all the more lively.

121

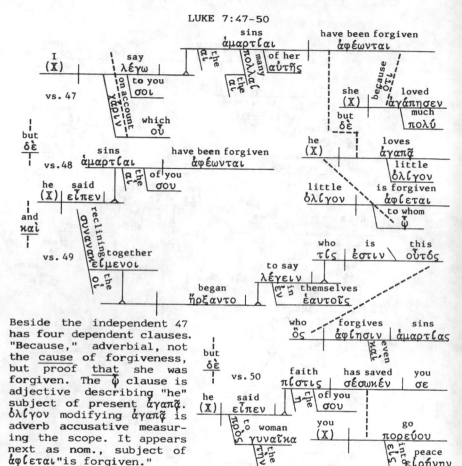

Beside the independent 47 has four dependent clauses. "Because," adverbial, not the cause of forgiveness, but proof that she was forgiven. The ᾧ clause is adjective describing "he" subject of present ἀγαπᾷ. ὀλίγον modifying ἀγαπᾷ is adverb accusative measuring the scope. It appears next as nom., subject of ἀφίεται "is forgiven."

As to form the sentence of 48 is complex. Independent "he said" has for its object noun clause, "your sins have been forgiven." Perfect ἀφέωνται accents the permanancy of her relief in forgiveness (as indeed also in the preceding sentence).

Subject of the complex sentence of 49 is attributive participle "the ones reclining together." The infinitive "to say" completes the idea in main verb "...began to say." ἐν ἑαυτοῖς is adverbial indicating where. Object clause, "who is this" tells what they began to say. Relative ὅς is adjectival describing demonstrative "this." καί is ascensive use "even."

Verse 50 displays another complex, a main clause, "he said" followed by two noun clauses, objects of "said." Present imperative plus εἰς show peace is a process "into" which the forgiven enter.

122

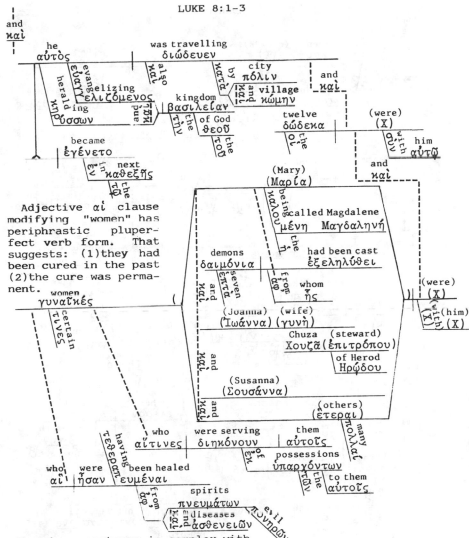

Adjective αἱ clause
modifying "women" has
periphrastic pluper-
fect verb form. That
suggests: (1)they had
been cured in the past
(2)the cure was perma-
nent.

The above sentence is complex with
seven clauses. ἐγένετο is the independent idea. It has three
noun clauses as subject: descriptive imperfect διώδευεν "he
was travelling" and "the twelve...certain women (were) with
him." ἀφ᾽ ἧς "from whom" inserts adjectival idea describing
"Mary." Relative αἱ and qualitative relative αἵτινες are
adjective clauses describing "women."

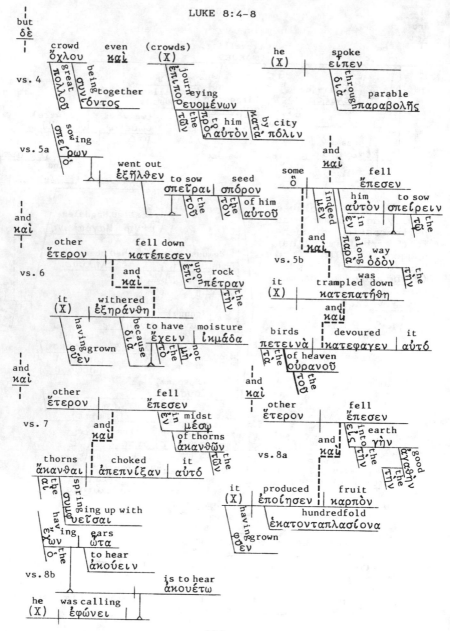

124

LUKE 8:4-8

Verse 4 admits of but one complete clause hence is classed as simple. Yet two genitive absolutes may be rendered as if clauses: "when a great crowd gathered, even the ones who were journeying with him..." κατά is distributive, "city by city." διά with genitive denotes agent. Without the article παραβολῆς shows that he taught by that which by nature was parable.

The simple sentence of 5a has as subject present attributive participle "the one having." Infinitive "to sow" states purpose. 8:5b embodies a compound. Demonstrative use of ὅ is subject in the first clause: "Some fell..." ἐν τῷ plus infinitive with accusative of general reference is temporal, "while he was sowing..." In the third clause κατά with the verb has perfective force, "birds ate it down." They thoroughly devoured."

Verse six is compound. Aorist passive circumstantial participle φυὲν indicates time, "when it sprouted..." διά with negative infinitive mentions why the seed withered. This is the only appearnce of ἱκμάδα in the New Testament.

Another two-pronged compound sentence arises in verse 7. The ἐν phrase is adverbial telling where. It's worth noting this ἐν compared with and in contrast to the ἐπί (upon) phrase in the previous sentence (vs.6) and the εἰς (into) in the sentence of verse 8a. The root idea in each preposition befits the kind of environment on, in or into which the seed was cast. The σύν in present participle συμφυεῖσαι has its local force, the thorns were "springing up with" the seed.

Verse 8a reveals another two-clause compound. Repetition of definite article, "into the earth, the good..." gives sharp emphasis to the adjective "good."

Verse 8b is a complex sentence with two clauses. Imperfect ἐφώνει means to "shout aloud." Jesus spoke in a strong voice! The dependent is a noun clause, object of ἐφώνει. Participial phrase "the one having ears" is subject. Verb ἀκουέτω is present imperative giving emphasis to linear action: "go on hearing."

LUKE 8:9

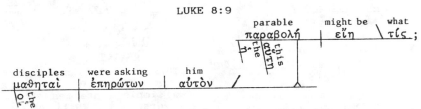

Verse nine combines two clauses into a complex arrangement. In the independent clause ἐπηρώτων is imperfect compounded from ἐπί and ἐρωτάω. Both preposition and tense combine to signify "eager and repeated" inquiries on the part of the disciples. The dependent is a noun clause serving as objective complement. It supplies the content of that which they were repeatedly asking. εἴη is present active optative of εἰμί. They wanted to know "what this parable might mean."

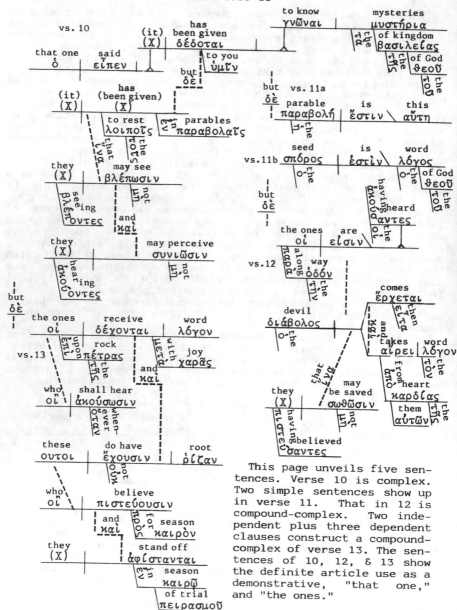

This page unveils five sentences. Verse 10 is complex. Two simple sentences show up in verse 11. That in 12 is compound-complex. Two independent plus three dependent clauses construct a compound-complex of verse 13. The sentences of 10, 12, & 13 show the definite article use as a demonstrative, "that one," and "the ones."

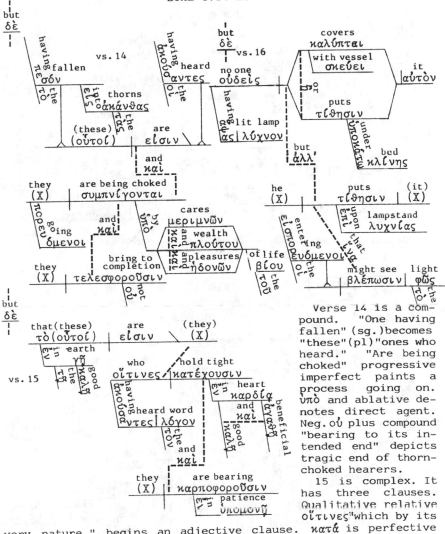

but
δέ

vs. 14

having
πεσόν fallen
τό the

thorns
ἀκάνθας
τάς the
εἰς into

(these)
(οὗτοί)

are
εἰσιν

and
καί

they
(X)

are being choked
συμπνίγονται

cares
μεριμνῶν
ὑπό by

and
καί

πορευόμενοι
going

wealth
πλούτου
καί and

they
(X)

bring to completion
τελεσφοροῦσιν

pleasures
ἡδονῶν
καί and

of life
βίου
τοῦ the

not
οὐ

but
δέ

having
ἀκούσαντες heard
οἱ the

but
δέ
vs. 16

no one
οὐδείς

lit lamp
λύχνον
ἅψας

but
ἀλλ'

he
(X)

puts
τίθησιν

enters in
εἰσπορευόμενοι
οἱ the

entering in

that
ἵνα

might see
βλέπωσιν

light
φῶς
τό the

covers
καλύπτει

with vessel
σκεύει

or

puts
τίθησιν
ὑποκάτω under

it
αὐτόν

bed
κλίνης

(it)
(X)

puts
τίθησιν

upon
ἐπί

lampstand
λυχνίας

but
δέ

that(these)
τό(οὗτοί)

are
εἰσιν

(they)
(X)

vs. 15

earth
γῇ
τῇ the
ἐν in
καλῇ good

who
οἵτινες

hold tight
κατέχουσιν

having heard word
ἀκούσαντες λόγον
τόν the
οἱ the

heart
καρδίᾳ
ἐν in
καί and
ἀγαθῇ beneficial

and
καί
καλῇ good
καί and

they
(X)

are bearing
καρποφοροῦσιν

patience
ὑπομονῇ
ἐν in

Verse 14 is a com-
pound. "One having
fallen" (sg.)becomes
"these"(pl)"ones who
heard." "Are being
choked" progressive
imperfect paints a
process going on.
ὑπό and ablative de-
notes direct agent.
Neg.οὐ plus compound
"bearing to its in-
tended end" depicts
tragic end of thorn-
choked hearers.

15 is complex. It
has three clauses.
Qualitative relative
οἵτινες"which by its

very nature," begins an adjective clause. κατά is perfective
on compound "hold tight." They "go on holding (linear) tight."
Synonyms καλῇ & ἀγαθῇ are difficult to translate; they display
good in form and good in moral quality.

The ἵνα purpose clause plus two independents turn 16 into
compound-complex. Verbs "covers" and "puts" are gnomic. They
show timeless, customary truth.

127

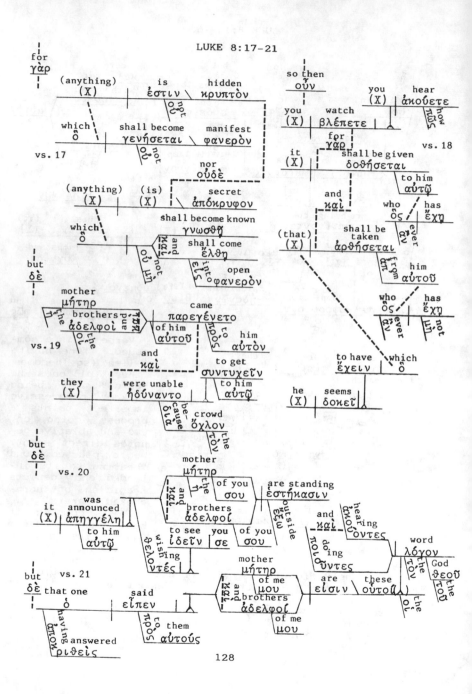

128

Two independent clauses and two adjective dependents form a compound-complex sentence of verse 17. Subjects "anything" are implicit in the context:"Anything is not hidden" says the same as "nothing is hidden." κρυπτὸν means "hidden." Add ἀπό to it and it means "hidden off," "secret." Double negative οὐ μὴ gives strong emphasis that absolutely everything shall "become known and...into the open."

Verse 18 entails a compound-complex. The first independent states: "Be watching how (manner) you hear..." It's important to be careful what we hear. But it's more important to watch the manner of listening. Attitude determines outcome. Positive and negative reasons follow:(1)"It shall be given" and (2)"it shall be taken away." Relative ὄς and ὄ introduce adjective clauses describing antecedents αὐτῷ and understood demonstrative "that."

Verse 19 fashions a compound sentence of two clauses. The compound παρεγένετο "came along side"(παρά)indicates that they actually arrived near(πρός)"to him." But the next clause with aorist and preposition with infinitive shows that they did not "get" to meet with him. Reason why is stated by διά with accusative: "because of the crowd."

In verse 20 a dependent noun clause is object of the verb of the main clause "was announced." The sentence is complex in structure. ἑστήκασιν is perfect with force of present. Circumstantial participle with infinitive expresses purpose, "wishing to see..."

The complex of verse 21 has demonstrative use of article ὁ as subject of its independdent clause, "that one." The rest of the sentence consists of noun clause, object of "said." Demonstrative οὗτοί "these" is predicate nominative pointing back to "my mother and my brothers." Attributive participles "the ones doing and teaching..." are in apposition to "these." They define more explicitly who the "these" are!

LUKE 8:22

Three independent clauses plus two dependent noun clauses make 22 compound-complex. διέλθωμεν is volitive subjunctive.The other verbs are narrative aorists.

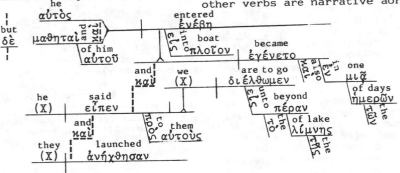

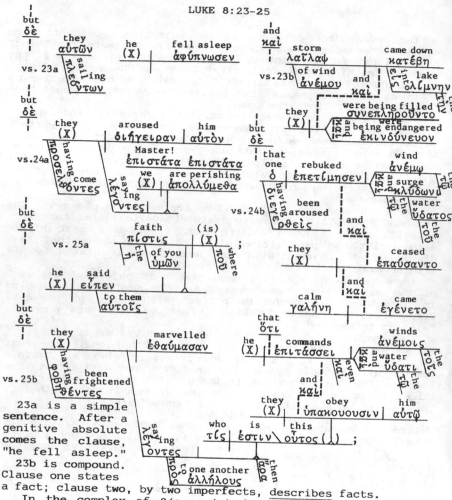

23a is a simple sentence. After a genitive absolute comes the clause, "he fell asleep." 23b is compound. Clause one states a fact; clause two, by two imperfects, describes facts.

In the complex of 24a aorist in the main clause depicts the fact, "they aroused him." Noun-object clause describes a process going on, "we are perishing."

The three verbs of compound 24b are aorists that focus on facts. Note demonstrative article as subject in clause one.

Complex 25a has noun clause, object of main verb, "said."

Verse 25b structures a complex sentence. After independent "they marvelled" are three noun dependents. Object of "saying" is noun clause "who is this?" In apposition to οὖτος are two noun clauses introduced by declarative ὅτι.

130

LUKE 8:26-28

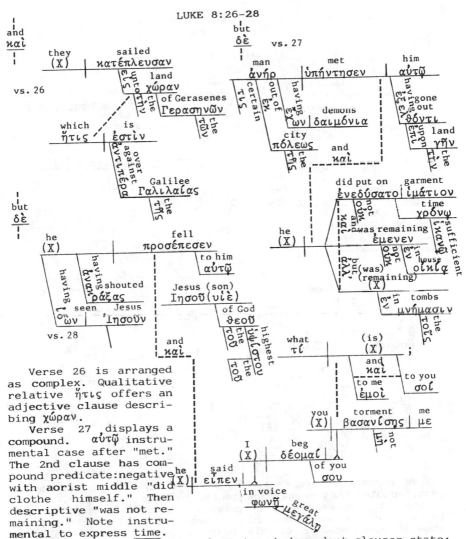

Verse 26 is arranged as complex. Qualitative relative ἥτις offers an adjective clause describing χώραν.

Verse 27 displays a compound. αὐτῷ instrumental case after "met." The 2nd clause has compound predicate: negative with aorist middle "did clothe himself." Then descriptive "was not remaining." Note instrumental to express time.

In the compound-complex of 28 two independent clauses state: "he fell...and...he said." Personal interest of dative befits verb "fell." Peter felt awe, reverence, fear. Three dependents follow: "I beg" is object of "said" of the independent idea. "What to you and me" and "don't torment me" are objects of δέομαι. Negative μὴ with aorist subjunctive signifies, "Don't begin to torment." Ethical datives ἐμοὶ and σοὶ mean, "What do we have in common?"

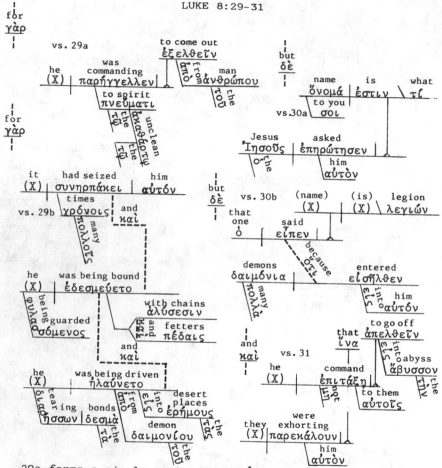

29a forms a simple sentence. παρήγγελλεν, inchoative imperfect, denotes that he was "beginning to command..."

29b is a three-clause compound. Plu-perfect "had seized" looks to a past when men "had seized by force." Two imperfects show ongoing results of his being seized. ἀπὸ with ablative "from the demon" in this context says, "by the demon."

Verse 30a sketches a complex with a noun clause object of "asked." The diagram treats αὐτὸν as adverbial accusative(also in 31). σοι is dative of possession, "name to you is what?"

30b is complex with object noun clause and adverbial ὅτι.

Also 31 unveils a complex. Imperfect "were exhorting"shows the nervous panic of repeated exhortations.

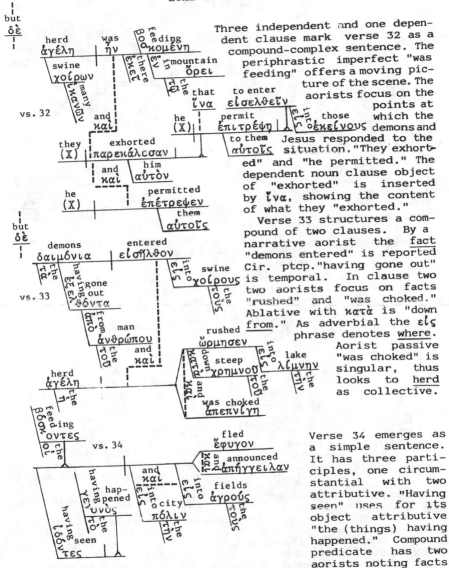

Three independent and one dependent clause mark verse 32 as a compound-complex sentence. The periphrastic imperfect "was feeding" offers a moving picture of the scene. The aorists focus on the points at which the demons and Jesus responded to the situation. "They exhorted" and "he permitted." The dependent noun clause object of "exhorted" is inserted by ἵνα, showing the content of what they "exhorted."

Verse 33 structures a compound of two clauses. By a narrative aorist the <u>fact</u> "demons entered" is reported Cir. ptcp. "having gone out" is temporal. In clause two two aorists focus on facts "rushed" and "was choked." Ablative with κατά is "down <u>from</u>." As adverbial the εἰς phrase denotes <u>where</u>. Aorist passive "was choked" is singular, thus looks to <u>herd</u> as collective.

Verse 34 emerges as a simple sentence. It has three participles, one circumstantial with two attributive. "Having seen" uses for its object attributive "the (things) having happened." Compound predicate has two aorists noting facts without describing.

The εἰς phrases indicate <u>where</u> they "fled" and "announced." Repeating preposition <u>and</u> article views each act as distinct.

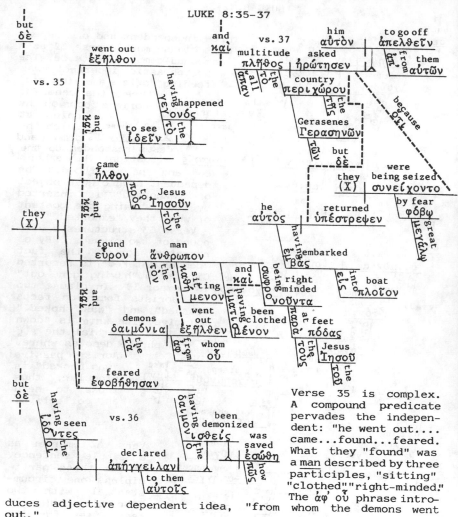

LUKE 8:35-37

Verse 35 is complex. A compound predicate pervades the independent: "he went out.... came...found...feared. What they "found" was a man described by three participles, "sitting" "clothed""right-minded." The ἀφ᾽ οὗ phrase introduces adjective dependent idea, "from whom the demons went out."

Verse 36 forms a two clause complex. Attributive participle "ones having seen" is subject of the independent "declared." Another attributive is subject of the dependent noun clause which itself is direct object of "declared."

37 embodies a compound-complex. The independents state: "multitude asked" and "he returned." Dependent adverbial ὅτι clause tells why they "asked." συνείχοντο imperfect passive depicts an ongoing emotional reaction of the Gerasenes.

134

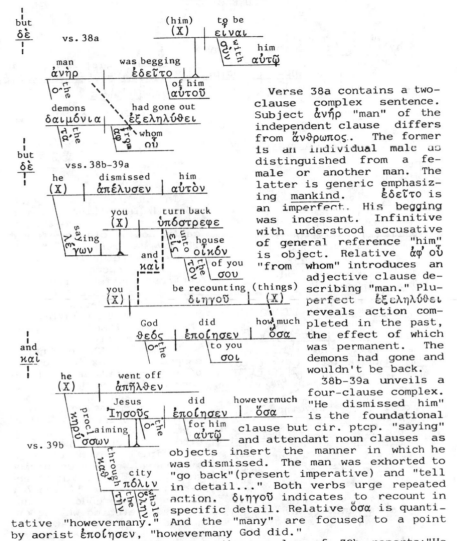

Verse 38a contains a two-clause complex sentence. Subject ἀνήρ "man" of the independent clause differs from ἄνθρωπος. The former is an individual male as distinguished from a female or another man. The latter is generic emphasizing mankind. ἐδεῖτο is an imperfect. His begging was incessant. Infinitive with understood accusative of general reference "him" is object. Relative ἀφ' οὗ "from whom" introduces an adjective clause describing "man." Pluperfect ἐξεληλύθει reveals action completed in the past, the effect of which was permanent. The demons had gone and wouldn't be back.

38b-39a unveils a four-clause complex. "He dismissed him" is the foundational clause but cir. ptcp. "saying" and attendant noun clauses as objects insert the manner in which he was dismissed. The man was exhorted to "go back"(present imperative) and "tell in detail..." Both verbs urge repeated action. διηγοῦ indicates to recount in specific detail. Relative ὅσα is quantitative "howevermany." And the "many" are focused to a point by aorist ἐποίησεν, "howevermany God did."

In its independent part the complex of 39b reports;"He went off" as exhorted. Object of cir. ptcp. "proclaiming" is noun clause, "howmuch Jesus did..." In reporting what the man proclaimed Luke uses "Jesus" rather than "God." This was a subtle suggestion to Theophilus that the man Jesus was God as man. Jesus as God in man does God's work in and as a human.

LUKE 8:40-42

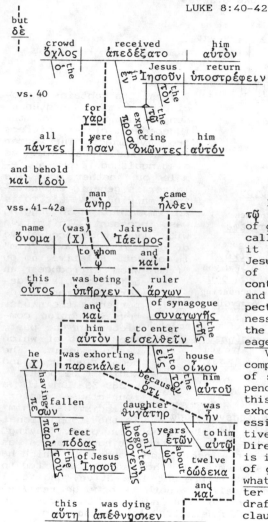

vs. 40

but
δὲ

crowd
ὄχλος | received ἀπεδέξατο | him αὐτὸν
the ... Jesus Ἰησοῦν | return ὑποστρέφειν
for γὰρ | were ἦσαν | expecting προσδοκῶντες | him αὐτόν
all πάντες

and behold
καὶ ἰδοὺ

vss. 41-42a

man ἀνὴρ | came ἦλθεν
name ὄνομα | (was) (X) | Jairus Ἰάειρος
to whom ᾧ and καὶ
this οὗτος | was being ὑπῆρχεν | ruler ἄρχων
and καὶ of synagogue συναγωγῆς
him αὐτὸν | to enter εἰσελθεῖν the
he (X) | was exhorting παρεκάλει | into house οἶκον | him αὐτοῦ
because ὅτι
having fallen πεσὼν | daughter θυγάτηρ | was ἦν
at feet πόδας | only begotten μονογενὴς | years ἐτῶν | to him αὐτῷ
of Jesus Ἰησοῦ about twelve δώδεκα
and καὶ
this αὕτη | was dying ἀπέθνῃσκεν

but
δὲ

crowds ὄχλοι | were pressing συνέπνιγον | him αὐτόν
the ... him αὐτὸν | to be going ὑπάγειν

vs. 42b

In the compound of vs. 40 τῷ with infinitive and acc. of general reference technically not a clause, though it may be translated "while Jesus was returning." Verbs of the independent clauses contrast aorist "received" and periphrastic "were expecting." Besides the vividness of the periphrastic the word itself suggests eager expectation.

Verses 41-42a portray a compound-complex collection of six clauses. Three independents affirm:"Man came.. this(one) was ruler..he was exhorting.." Dative of possession ᾧ brings in adjective clause describing man. Direct object of παρεκάλει is infin."to enter" and acc. of general reference giving what he exhorted:"him to enter into...house." The ὅτι drafts two dependent causal clauses sketching why he exhorted. αὐτῷ is dative of possession:"daughter was to him." ἀπέθνῃσκεν is imperfect. Death struggle was in process!

Verse 42b incorporates a simple sentence. Again we see ἐν τῷ with infinitive and accusative of general reference which, in English, turns into a subordinate "while he was going..." συνέπνιγον is imperfect, a moving picture of the jostling of the multitude of people pressing upon him in the way.

136

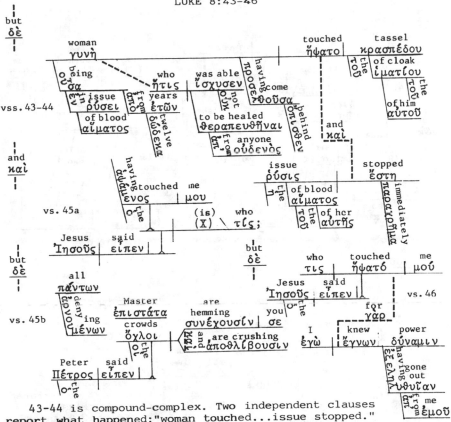

43-44 is compound-complex. Two independent clauses
report what happened:"woman touched...issue stopped."
ἥτις inaugurates adjective clause describing "woman."
Participial phrases "being" and "having come" modify "woman."
"Jesus said" is independent clause in 45a, object of which is
noun clause"one having touched me is who?" ἅπτω ="cling to."
Genitive absolute, "all denying" begins the complex of 45b.
Object of independent "said" is noun clause with compound
predicate, "are hemming you...are crushing." Both verbs are
presents stressing continuous pressure of the crowds.
   The sentence of verse 46 is complex with two noun clauses as
objects of independent "said." Note emphatic ἐγὼ as subject of
ἔγνων = "I knew." Jesus was conscious of power "having gone
out." This personal pronoun and perfect participle in indirect
discourse vividly insist on "the terrible nervous loss from
his healing work."(ATR-Grammar,pg.1041). "I on my part knew
(experienced) that power had gone out from me."

137

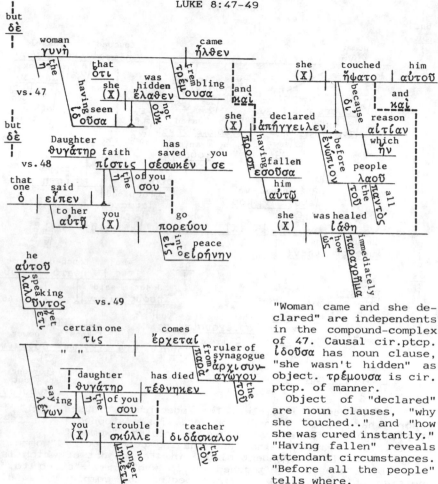

"Woman came and she declared" are independents in the compound-complex of 47. Causal cir.ptcp. ἰδοῦσα has noun clause, "she wasn't hidden" as object. τρέμουσα is cir. ptcp. of manner.

Object of "declared" are noun clauses, "why she touched.." and "how she was cured instantly." "Having fallen" reveals attendant circumstances. "Before all the people" tells where.

Verse 48 produces a complex with two noun clauses, objects of "That one said." "Faith has saved" is object. But faith is personal, hence, "faith of you." Pf. σέσωκέν indicates that faith is more than a point; it's a fixed relationship. Present "be going" plus preposition into peace (not in) confirms that faith is a continuing condition.

49 embraces a complex arrangement. First a genitive absolute, "he yet speaking..." Independent "certain one comes" states a fact. Adverb παρὰ phrase shows from where. Object of "saying" are noun clauses. Perfect "has died" suggests permancy of death. Negative with σκύλλε says, "quit troubling."

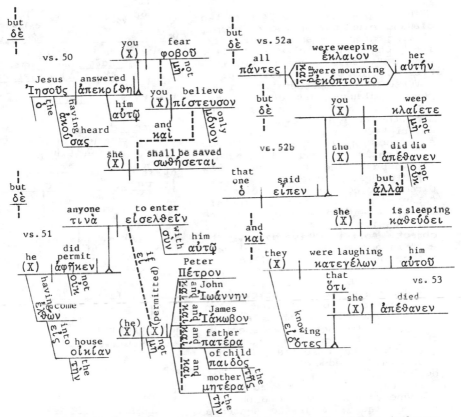

Three noun clauses are objects of "answered" of the independent in the complex sentence of verse 50. Negative with present φοβοῦ means "stop fearing." πίστευσον, ingressive aorist means "get faith." Future passive σωθήσεται is point action.

εἰσελθεῖν with accusative of general reference is object of "permit" in main clause of vs. 51. εἰ "if" instigates 1st class condition determined as true. The condition assumes he didn't, though in fact he did. "If he did not permit Peter etc..."

52a frames a simple sentence with compound predicate having two descriptive imperfects: "were weeping and were mourning." The complex of 52b has demonstrative article as subject of εἶπεν of the main clause. μὴ and pres. imper. says, "Stop weeping." Descriptive imperfect contrasts with aorist "didn't die."

53 is complex. Preposition on imperfect κατεγέλων is perfective use: "they laughed him down(scornfully)." "Knowing" is circumstantial participle of cause.

The complex of verse 54 uses two clauses plus temporal cir. ptcp., "having grasped" and manner "saying." Object-noun clause, "Child, rise up" makes verse 54 complex. Present ἔγειρε = "be rising up."

Verse 55 encompasses three independent clauses, hence is classed compound. Narrative aorists present the action as events without description: "spirit returned... she stood up..he charged." πνεῦμα may rightly be rendered "breath." παραχρῆμα "immediately" shows how rapidly Jesus' power took effect. Direct object of verb διέταξεν "charged" is a brace of infinitives:"to eat to be given..." Aorist passive δοθῆναι is the basic object. Aorist active φαγεῖν "to eat" is accusative of general reference used as the so-called subject of "to be given." In his WORD PICTURES, Vol.II, pg. 123 A.T.Robertson calls φαγεῖν an "epexegetic purpose." That which Jesus "ordered" was that "eating" be given to her. The specific food is left to those who would give it. The essential is that the normal needs of life not be neglected.

If infinitive with accusative of general reference be a phrase, not a clause, then the sentence of vs.56 is two-clause compound. Literally it says, "them to tell to noone." English makes it a noun-object clause, "that they tell no one." Two independents declare, "parents were amazed but that one ordered." Aor. ἐξέστησαν literally means to "stand outside oneself." The parents were "beside themselves," "in an ecstacy."

Note another demonstrative ὁ as subject. τὸ γεγονός is attributive participle, "the thing which happened." Why would Jesus order "to tell noone" when all knew "she died" and now saw her alive? He had said, "she was sleeping." So don't tell that HE raised her!

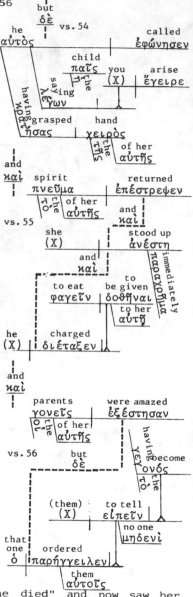

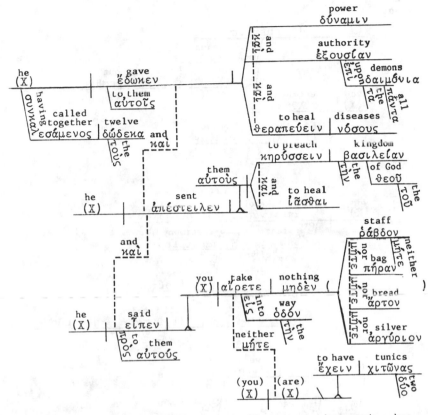

9:1-3 has three independent clauses,"he gave...he sent...he said..." Object of εἶπεν "said" are noun clauses, "take nothing" and "neither (are you) to have..." The sentence is compound-complex.

Verbs in the independent clauses are aorists. But in the dependents the ideas are linear presents.

Direct objects of ἔδωκεν in clause one consist of two nouns plus an infinitive, itself a verbal noun, present = "to be healing."

The second clause has as its object two present infinitives with accusative of general reference αὐτοὺς "them" to indicate who was to do the "preaching" and "healing." Present infinitive ἔχειν "to have" might be considered independent almost with the force of a finite verb paralleling αἴρετε "take." In apposition to μηδὲν "nothing" are four nouns, "staff," "bag," "bread," and "silver," with negatives μήτε "neither...nor."

141

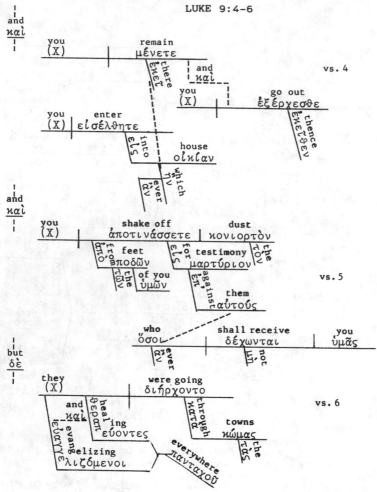

The two independent clauses of the compound-complex of vs.4 have present imperatives exhorting, "remain" and "go out." The dependent is adverbial further defining where they "remain" and from whence they "go out." It is introduced by relative ἥν "which" used as adjective modifying "house."

Verse five is complex. ἀποτινάσσετε "shake off" is present indicating repeated action as they leave each village which rejects them. ὅσοι is quantitative relative with indefinite ἄν "whoever" and introduces an adjective clause.

κατὰ in the simple sentence of vs.6 is distributive used indicating "to go down along town by town..."

142

LUKE 9:7-10ᵃ

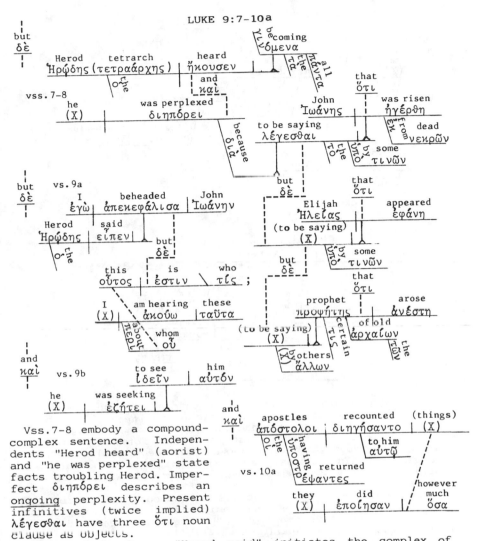

Vss.7-8 embody a compound-complex sentence. Independents "Herod heard" (aorist) and "he was perplexed" state facts troubling Herod. Imperfect διηπόρει describes an ongoing perplexity. Present infinitives (twice implied) λέγεσθαι have three ὅτι noun clause as objects.

Independent clause "Herod said" initiates the complex of 9a. There follows two object-noun clauses plus one adjectice clause inserted by περὶ οὗ describing οὗτος. ἐγὼ is emphatic subject, "I on my part beheaded..."

9b is simple in form with infinitive phrase "to see him" as object of iterative imperfect "was seeking."

10a is complex. Qunatitative relative ὅσα introduces an adjective clause desribing understood "things." Both verbs are narrative aorists.

143

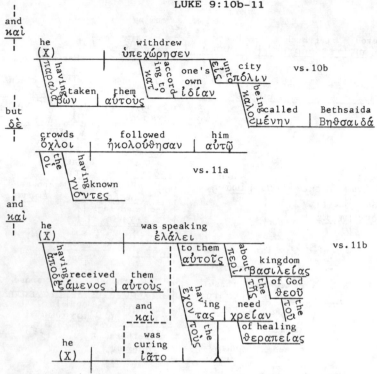

10b is a simple sentence, "he withdrew..." When he withdrew is set forth by circumstantial participle παραλαβὼν. Why and where are proposed by prepositional phrases κατ' and εἰς.

The sentence of 11a is also simple in form. Circumstantial participle γνόντες "having known" may be translated "having recognized." "The crowds, having recognized what he was doing, followed him." αὐτῷ is instrumental, normal with verb ἀκολουθέω "follow."

The sentence of 11b involves a compound combination. The two independent clauses are animated by imperfect tenses. ἐλάλει is inchoative imperfect, "he began to speak and went on speaking..." Middle imperfect ἰᾶτο reflects both iterative and distributive action. "he was repeatedly curing and thus from this one to that one to the next one etc. went on curing..." ἀποδεξάμενος is circumstantial participle, probably temporal, "when he received them..." αὐτοῖς "to them" is dative, case of personal interest. The περὶ phrase is adverbial indicating in a general way why he was speaking. Present participle ἔχοντας is attributive, "the ones having." It, with its phrase, serves as direct object of "was curing."

144

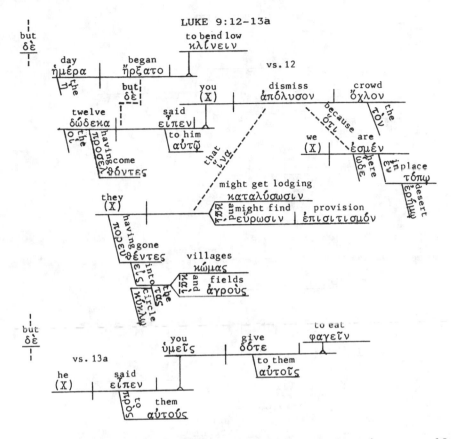

LUKE 9:12-13a

Two independent clauses with three dependents make verse 12 into a compound-complex sentence. Present infinitive κλίνειν coupled with aorist ἤρξατο describe the waning of the day. The second independent declares,"The twelve said." Object of εἶπεν is noun clause exhortation "You dismiss the crowd." The purpose for such a dismissing is in the adverb ἵνα clause. The reason why such seems logical is stated in the ὅτι clause, "because we are here in desert place."

Verse 13a develops as a complex arrangement of two clauses. The independent states: "He said..." Just what he said is found in the noun clause object of "said." The use of ὑμεῖς as subject is quite emphatic;"You give to eat to them." By thus heightening the "you" he challenges the twelve with the problem and thereby places in bold relief his own solution which he is about to supply. Even point action aorists (rather than linear presents) underscore the fact of the problem rather than any continuing solution.

145

LUKE 9:13b-15

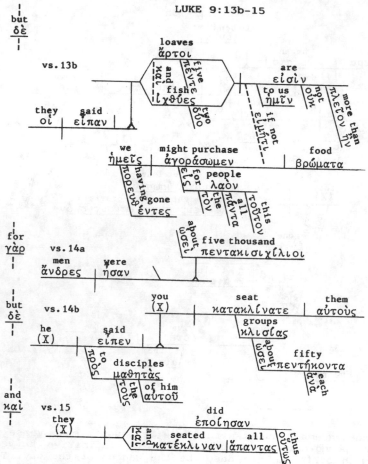

Introducing 3rd class condition with subjunctive is εἰμήτι instead of the usual ἐάν. It supports a noun clause, object of εἶπαν "said" of the main clause. The sentence is complex.

14a presents a simple sentence. The diagram has "about five-thousand" as predicate nominative pointing to subject "men."

The complex of 14b has as object of "said" noun clause exhortation "you seat them.." κλισίας is adverbial cognate accusative "in groups." Distributive use of ἀνὰ = "fifty by fifty..." ὡσεὶ indicates an approximate number.

As diagrammed the sentence of verse 15 is classed as simple in structure with compound predicate. "They did thus (as he instructed) and seated all." Thus seated it made for an easy, accurate count.

146

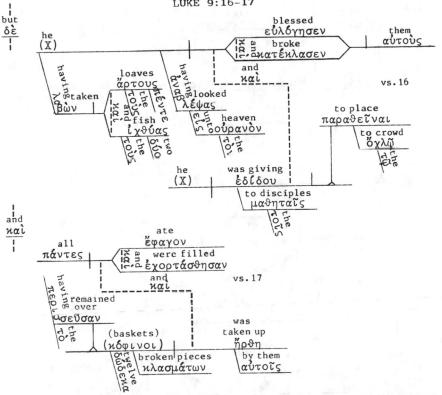

In the compound sentence of verse 16 the aorist participles are circumstantial. They both are temporal depicting incidents which describe the subject "he." They also relate to the action of the main verbs "blessed" and "broke." Imperfect ἐδίδου paints the action as repetitive contrasted to narrative aorists in the first clause. Aorist infinitive παραθεῖναι "to place" is accusative case object of "was giving." Preposition παρά "beside" compounded with τίθημι "place" is local in force: "place beside..."

The sentence of 17 is another two-clause compound. The πάντες "all" is subject of compound predicate (both verbs are narrative aorists) "ate and were filled." Subject of the second clause is the neuter singular attributive participle περισσεύσαν "having remained over." In apposition to this singular subject is plural κόφινοι "baskets" with its modifiers. Thus the aorist verb ἤρθη "was taken up" is singular in spite of the plural "baskets." αὐτοῖς is instrumental "by them."

147

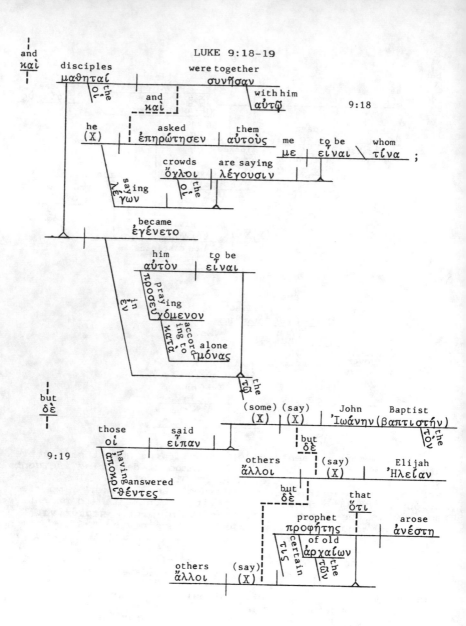

9:18

9:19

The sentence of 9:18 consists of one independent clause, three dependent noun clauses and two infinitive phrases. ἐγένετο "it came to pass" or "it happened" is the verb of the independent idea around which the remainder of the sentence gathers. It has a compound subject of two noun clauses: "the disciples gathered together" and "he asked them." What he asked is seen in noun clause, object of present circumstantial participle λέγων: "the crowds are saying me to be whom?" Infinitive εἶναι with its accusative of general reference is object of λέγουσιν. Another infinitive stems off of the main verb as adverbial modifier (ἐν τῷ and εἶναι...) "while he was praying alone." αὐτὸν another accusative of general reference has present circumstantial participle "praying" modifying it. Prepositional κατὰ phrase is adverbial modifying the participle. It displays manner, "alone."

One independent and four dependent noun clauses identify verse 19 as complex. The foundational clause is, "they, having answered, said..." As diagrammed aorist passive participle, "having answered" is circumstantial. It describes subject "they" which is demonstrative use of article οἱ. Yet it might be viewed as attributive with the article modifying the participle, "the ones having answered."

Three noun clauses, each of which has some ellipses in it, appear as objects of εἶπαν "said." A fourth noun clause introduced by declarative ὅτι "that" shows up as the object of understood "say" of the third noun clause, "...that a certain prophet of the old (ones) arose." Aorist ἀνέστην looks to the point when he alledgedly "arose."

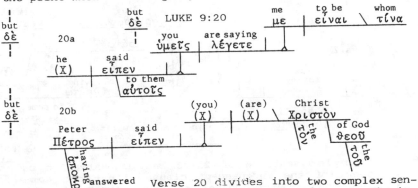

Verse 20 divides into two complex sentences, each with two clauses. The independent clauses are, "he said" and "Peter said." 20a has noun clause object of "said." It has emphatic ὑμεῖς as subject of λέγετε. Object of "are saying" is infinitive εἶναι with accusative of general reference. In 20b object of "said" is "the Christ of God." An implied subject and verb "you are" fill out the clause.

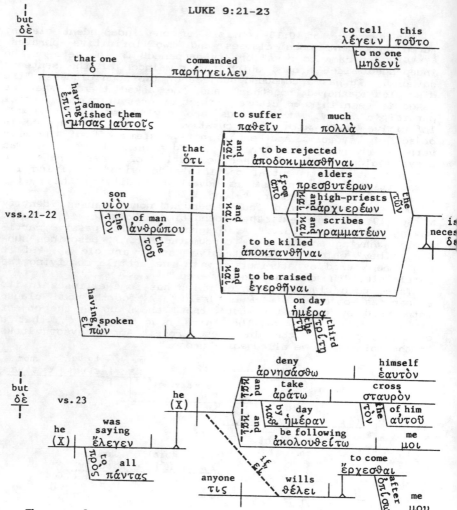

LUKE 9:21-23

The complex sentence of 21-22 has demonstrative use of ὁ as subject of the independent clause, "that one commanded." Dependent noun clause, object of ptcp. εἰπών, is introduced by ὅτι. The verb δεῖ has compound subject, four infinitives with accusative of general reference υἱόν.

Verse 23 begins with independent, "he was saying..." Object of ἔλεγεν is compound noun clause with three verbs all supported by first class dependent conditional, εἰ "if anyone wills to be coming..." Linear present ἀκολουθείτω "be following" after a pair of aorists is to be noted.

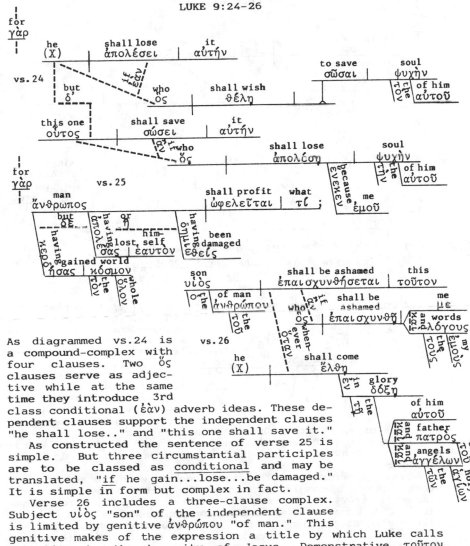

As diagrammed vs.24 is a compound-complex with four clauses. Two ὅς clauses serve as adjective while at the same time they introduce 3rd class conditional (ἐάν) adverb ideas. These dependent clauses support the independent clauses "he shall lose.." and "this one shall save it."

As constructed the sentence of verse 25 is simple. But three circumstantial participles are to be classed as conditional and may be translated, "if he gain...lose...be damaged." It is simple in form but complex in fact.

Verse 26 includes a three-clause complex. Subject υἱὸς "son" of the independent clause is limited by genitive ἀνθρώπου "of man." This genitive makes of the expression a title by which Luke calls attention to the humanity of Jesus. Demonstrative τοῦτον appears in the diagram as though a direct object. In fact it is more an adverbial accusative, "The son of man shall be ashamed as to this one." The ὅς clause is both adverbial conditional as well as adjective describing "this one." Indefinite ὅταν "whenever" inserts an adverbial temporal clause.

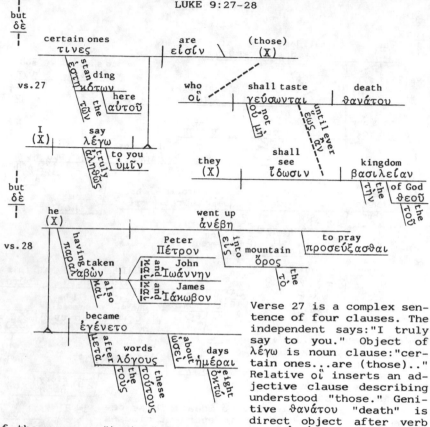

Verse 27 is a complex sentence of four clauses. The independent says:"I truly say to you." Object of λέγω is noun clause:"certain ones...are (those).." Relative οἳ inserts an adjective clause describing understood "those." Genitive θανάτου "death" is direct object after verb of the senses, "taste." Double negative οὐ μὴ is quite strong in its negation. Dependent adverbial clause of time is introduced by ἕως ἂν "until ever." ἂν inserts an indefinite note "whenever."

A new paragraph in the text begins with verse 28. The verse encases a complex sentence. The verb of the independent clause is ἐγένετο. "Became" is literal but it may be translated, "It came to pass..." Two prepositional adverb phrases tell when, "after these words" and "about eight days." Subject of ἐγένετο is noun clause "he went up..." εἰς introduces adverbial idea of where, "into the mountain." Aorist infinitive προσεύξασθαι "to pray" indicates why, that is, the purpose of his going up. Circumstantial aorist participle παραλαβὼν "having taken" may be classified as occasion or attendant circumstances.

152

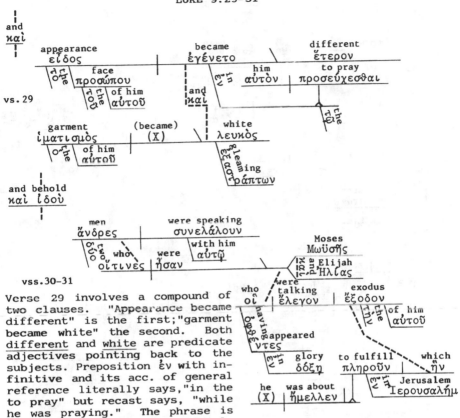

vs. 29

and behold
καὶ ἰδοὺ

vss. 30-31

Verse 29 involves a compound of two clauses. "Appearance became different" is the first;"garment became white" the second. Both different and white are predicate adjectives pointing back to the subjects. Preposition ἐν with infinitive and its acc. of general reference literally says,"in the to pray" but recast says, "while he was praying." The phrase is adverbial. Present participle ἐξαστράπτων "gleaming," though without article, is attributive.

Verses 30-31 have four clauses but only one independent. The sentence is complex. Verb συνελάλουν "were speaking" is imperfect displaying continuing action. It was a vigorous, lively conversation between three minds and hearts all of whom knew of the coming death of Jesus and discerned its necessity. Relative οἵτινες is qualitative "who by their nature." Moses and Elijah, in view of who they were, perceived the import of the cross. Hence the next clause informs that they were talking about "the exodus." It's an adjective clause describing the two Old Testament men. Another adjective clause, introduced by relative οἳ, describes even more clearly this "exodus" as something to be "fulfilled" in keeping with Old Testament anticipations. Imperfect ἤμελλεν and present infinitive πληροῦν underline continued action. It was a process already entering into its "being fulfilled."

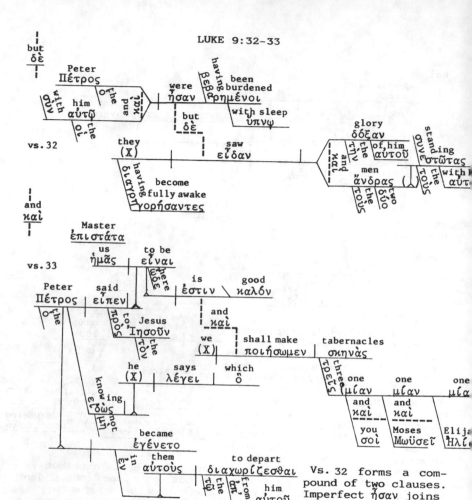

LUKE 9:32-33

Vs. 32 forms a compound of two clauses. Imperfect ἦσαν joins Pf. ptcp. βεβαρημένοι to form periphrastic pluperfect "had been burdened." Part of compound subject is article οἱ which treats phrase σὺν αὐτῷ as a substantive, "the ones with him." συνεστῶτας is attributive participle in apposition to ἄνδρας "men."

Verse 33 is a complex of five clauses. ἐγένετο is the independent. Its subject is noun clause, "Peter said." Object of "said" is noun clause, "us to be here is good," whose subject is infinitive εἶναι with acc. of general reference ἡμᾶς "us." "We shall make tabernacles" is a second clause, object of "said." Circ. ptcp. εἰδὼς "knowing" has as its object noun clause, "he says (that) which." Preposition ἐν "in" inserts temporal phrase, "as they were departing."

LUKE 9:34-36a

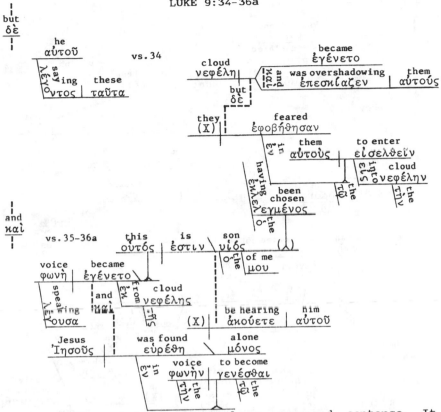

Verse 34 contains a two clause compound sentence. It starts with a genitive absolute, "He, saying these (things)" The first clause has a compound predicate one of which is aorist, ἐγένετο "became" (arose). The other is descriptive imperfect ἐπεσκίαζεν "was overshadowing." The "in" phrase of the second clause is temporal "when" or "after they entered..."

The sentence of 35-36a has a compound-complex arrangement. "Voice became" is the first independent idea. The diagram has λέγουσα as circumstantial participle modifying the subject φωνή "voice." It also displays two noun clauses as predicate nominative after verb "became" thus pointing back to the subject "voice" which was "speaking." However, they might be considered as direct objects of "speaking." The 2nd noun clause has genitive αὐτοῦ as object of verb of hearing.

The other independent clause has an "in" phrase indicating when "Jesus was found alone." That is, "in the to become in reference to the voice (when the voice came)."

155

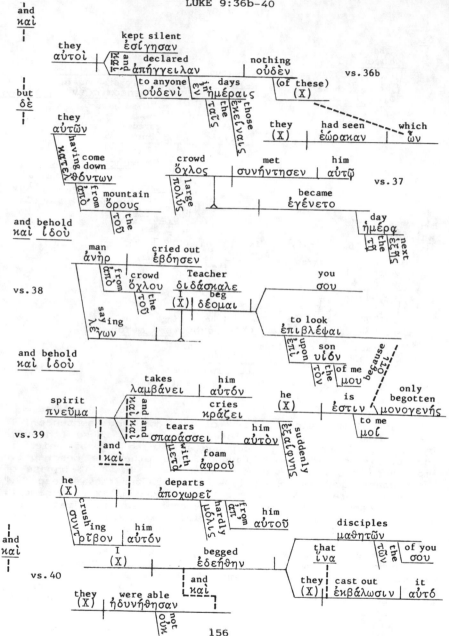

156

Verse 36b closes a paragraph. It is a complex sentence. The independent clause has emphatic third personal pronoun as subject of compound predicate, "kept silent" and "declared nothing." ἐσίγησαν is an ingressive aorist. Relative pronoun ὦν "which" in the dependent clause is genitive attracted from accusative α, object of perfect ἑώρακαν "had seen."

Verse 37 begins a new paragraph, another episode. Genitive absolute opens the sentence, "they, having come down,.." The remainder of the sentence is a complex of two clauses. The noun clause "large crowd met him" is subject of aorist ἐγένετο "became" of the independent clause. Locative "on the next day" is adverbial telling when.

The sentence of verse 38 entails three clauses so arranged as to form a complex. "Man cried" is the independent clause. ἀπὸ "from the crowd" might be viewed as adverb modifying predicate "cried out." However, the diagram deals with it as adjective describing the subject "man." λέγων "saying" is circumstantial, the object of which is noun clause stating that which the man "cried." Present δέομαι "beg" has a double object, genitive "you" plus aorist infinitive "to look." ὅτι ushers in adverb clause of cause. It states why he should "look upon my son." μοί "to me" is dative of possession.

Verses 39-40 are a part of that which the man "cried out saying..." However, the diagram presents them as two distinct sentences. The "and behold" seems to set them off.

39 is a two-clause compound sentence. The first clause has a three part compound predicate. It affirms three actions of the subject "spirit." It "takes," "cries," and "tears." Prepositional phrase "with foam" is adverbial depicting how he leaves the lad. The second independent idea uses present ἀποχωρεῖ "departs" as its verb. It not only is descriptive of the struggle involved when the spirit "departs" but also suggests repeated action. Present participle συντρῖβον refers to the circumstances in which the boy is left. It is both adjectival describing subject "he" and is loosely attached adverbially to the main verb.

Verse 40 is another two-clause compound arrangement. Again the verb "begged" takes a double object. The genitive "disciples" refers to them and no other." The ἵνα introduces a purport (object) noun clause. It gives the content of what he "begged." The second clause is negative. It states that which the disciples were "not" able to be.

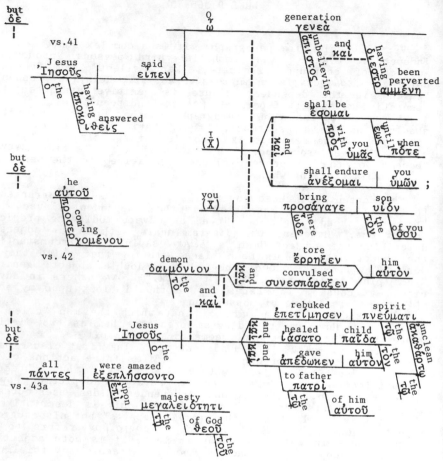

Verse 41 involves a complex sentence. "Jesus said" is the independent clause. "0 unbelieving generation..." is not a clause, it is vocative introducing the two noun clauses objects of "said." ὑμῶν after direct middle ἀνέξομαι is ablative, "I shall hold myself from you." προσάγαγε is aorist active, "bring here..."

Verse 42 is a two-clause compound sentence. Each clause has a compound predicate. After genitive absolute, "As he (the boy) was coming," the clauses declare, "demon tore and convulsed" and "Jesus rebuked...healed...gave him back..."

ἐξεπλήσσοντο of simple sentence of 43a is descriptive imperfect, "were being amazed."

158

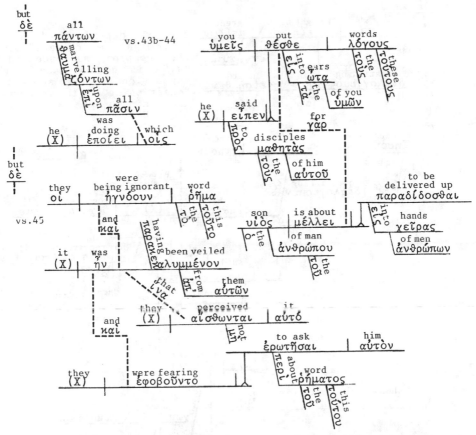

The complex sentence of 43b-44 begins with genitive absolute, "while all were marvelling." Enclosed in it is adjective οἷς clause, "which he was doing." Independent clause "he said" has two noun clauses, objects of "said." Emphatic ὑμεῖς is subject of the first one, "you put these words..." "Into your ears" is adverbial telling where.

Verse 45 embraces a compound complex combination; three independent and one dependent clause. In the first clause article οἱ appears as subject "they." Imperfect ἠγνόουν denotes that they "went on being ignorant." Imperfect ἦν joins with perfect participle to form periphrastic plu-perfect, "had been veiled and remained veiled." Adverbial dependent introduced by ἵνα seems to be result rather than purpose. The linear action of imperfect ἐφοβοῦντο describes their continuing reluctance to ask "about this matter."

159

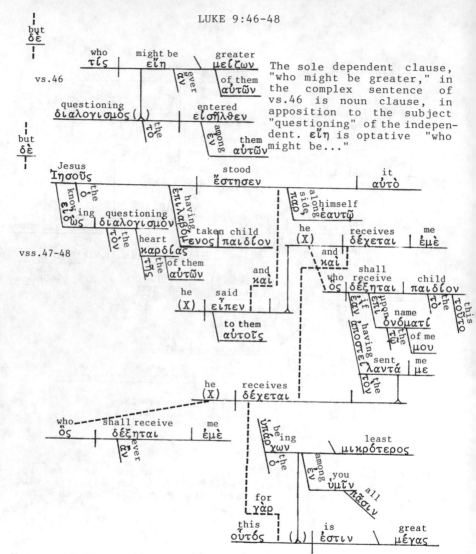

vs.46

The sole dependent clause, "who might be greater," in the complex sentence of vs.46 is noun clause, in apposition to the subject "questioning" of the independent. εἴη is optative "who might be..."

vss.47-48

Verses 47-48 comprise a compound-complex with two independent and five dependent clauses. The compound ideas are: "Jesus stood it" and "he said." Objects of "said"(εἶπεν) are two noun clauses, "he receives me" and "he receives the one having sent me." These noun clauses have relative (ὃς) adjective clauses describing subjects "he." γὰρ "for" inserts a 3rd object clause, "this one...is great." In apposition to demonstrative subject οὗτός "this" is participial phrase, "the one being...least."

160

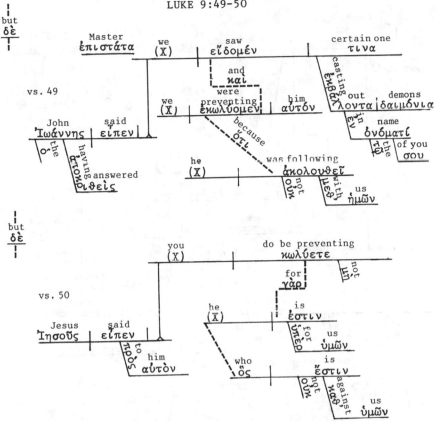

Two sentences adorn this page. They are structured similarly. Both are complex in form. The independent clauses are formed in the same way, "John said" and "Jesus said." Each has two noun clauses which serve as direct objects of εἶπεν "said." Although each has a third dependent idea the sentence of verse 49 has an adverbial ὅτι causal clause, "because he was not following with us." But the sentence of verse 50 has a ὅς adjective clause modifying subject "he who is not against us..." Luke uses linear verbs to vivify his narrative. ἐκωλύομεν is conative imperfect indicating repeated attempts, "we were trying to prevent..." ἀκολουθεῖ is emphatic descriptive present, "he does not follow..." In verse 50 present imperative κωλύετε with negative μή orders the disciples to "quit preventing." The two prepositional phrases ὑπὲρ and καθ' display a striking contrast "for us" versus "against us."

161

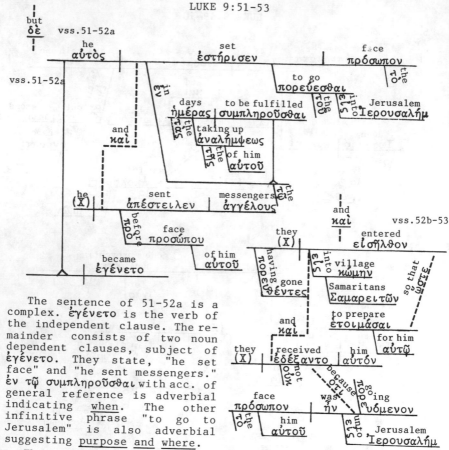

The sentence of 51-52a is a complex. ἐγένετο is the verb of the independent clause. The remainder consists of two noun dependent clauses, subject of ἐγένετο. They state, "he set face" and "he sent messengers." ἐν τῷ συμπληροῦσθαι with acc. of general reference is adverbial indicating <u>when</u>. The other infinitive phrase "to go to Jerusalem" is also adverbial suggesting <u>purpose</u> and <u>where</u>.

The verbs of both these noun-subject clauses are aorist. The point action befits the situation. It's the final journey of Jesus to Jerusalem with national rejection and the cross as his destination. "Set" and "sent" suit the crisis! πρὸ with ablative "before his face" expresses an adverbial idea.

The sentence of 52b-53 is compound-complex. Aorists appear in both independent clauses: "they(the messengers)entered" and "they(the villagers)did not receive..." The punctiliar action signals the decisiveness of the action, especially the negative reaction of the villagers. The reason <u>why</u> they would not "receive" is stated in the dependent ὅτι clause, "because his face was going unto..." ἦν joins with present participle πορευόμενον to form periphrastic imperfect "was going." It gives special added emphasis to the ongoing progress of the action.

162

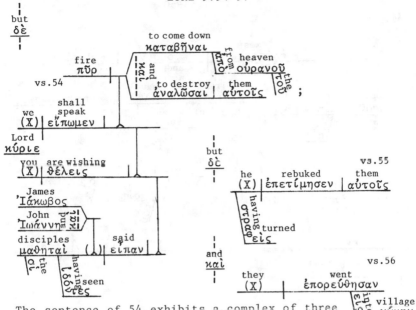

The sentence of 54 exhibits a complex of three
clauses. εἶπαν "said" is verb in the independent
clause. Its subject "disciples" has "James & John"
in apposition. Noun clause "do you wish" is object
of εἶπαν. It in turn has for object the volitive
subjunctive εἴπωμεν "we shall speak." That verb
has for its object the two infinitives "to come down" and "to
destroy" with accusative of general reference πῦρ "fire."

Verses 55 and 56 contain simple sentences. 55 reports that
"having turned, he rebuked." Cir. ptcp., "having turned" adds
force to the rebuke with which Jesus confronted the vengeful
disciples. εἰς phrase "into a different.." is adverbial _where_.
ἑτέραν is more than "another." It is "different."

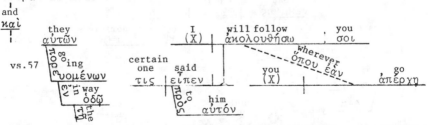

Genitive absolute begins the complex sentence of verse 57. The
object of "said" of the independent idea is noun clause, "I
will follow you." σοι is instrumental case after ἀκολουθήσω.
ἐὰν has the force of ἄν "ever" after adverb ὅπου "where."

163

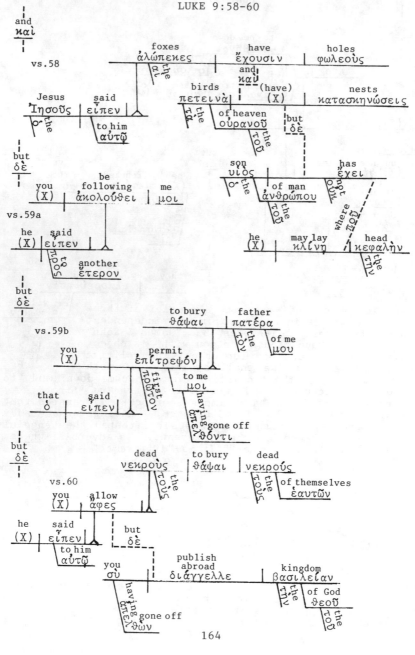

164

Four sentences decorate the preceding(164)page, all of which are patterened as complex. Though the subject of each is slightly altered they are uniform. "Jesus said" sets the pattern. The sentence of 59b uses demonstrative article ὁ ("that one") as its subject. The other two use "he" as subject.

In verse 58 three noun clauses emerge as direct objects of "said" of the main clause. First comes the gnomic present ἔχουσιν "the foxes have holes..." That's a universal truth! That gomic present is implied in the second noun-object clause "the birds (have) nests..." Present ἔχει of the third object noun clause is descriptive of one problem Jesus was experiencing; "the son of man is not having..." Adverb ποῦ "where" doubles as conjunction introducing adverb clause, "where he may lay the(his)head."κλίνῃ is present subjunctive, "may be laying..."

Verse 59a enjoys but one noun clause, again object of "said" of the main clause, "he said." ἀκολούθει is present imperative, "you be following..." It's an exhortation for continuing commitment, "full time service" so to speak. Associative-instrumental case μοι is used as object with that particular verb.

In the sentence of 59b a single object clause once again appears. Aorist imperative ἐπίτρεψόν contrasts with the present "be following" of the preceding sentence. It is a "permission" sought, not a repetition! "To bury" is object infinitive. Though in a fixed form it is accusative case.

In the sentence of verse 60 "he(Jesus)said" two things. (1)"You allow..." and (2)"publish abroad..." Object of aorist imperative ἄφες "allow" is infinitive θάψαι "to bury" with its accusative of general reference νεκροὺς "dead." A similar "dead" follows as direct object of the infinitive. διάγγελλε "publish abroad" is linear action present imperative suggesting continuous and repeated preaching. The subject "you, by virtue of its appearing as a separate word, is very emphatic.

Note that in the sentences of 58 and 60 dative αὐτῷ "to him" appears whereas in verse 59a πρὸς with accusative "to another" is used. Is there any discernable difference in these expressions? Just the difference between dative and accusative cases! Dative expresses personal interest "to him." Accusative measures an idea in "content, scope or direction." πρὸς and accusative is the more general; dative depicts a warmer more personal relationship.

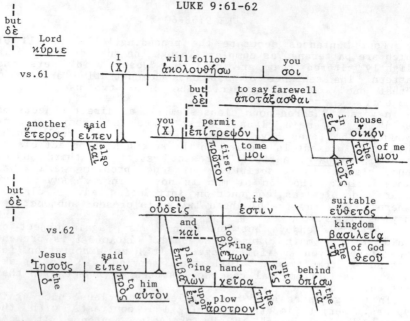

The two sentences on this page also present complex forms
with their independent clauses stating ἕτερος "said" and
Ἰησοῦς "said." ἕτερος means "another of a <u>different</u> kind.
ἀκολουθήσω is a volitive future expressing the man's
<u>determination</u> to give himself to Jesus as a disciple. Once
again we note the associative-instrumental case σοι after the
verb "follow." The clause is dependent noun, object of "said."

Another noun object clause is presented by the adversative
conjunction δὲ "but..." Aorist infinitive ἀποτάξασθαι "to say
farewell" is accusative, object of "permit." Dative article
τοῖς treats the εἰς prepositional phrase as a unit of thought,
"the ones-of-my-house." The man wanted "first" to say a fond
farewell to his family.

Jesus begins with the adversative "but" because his answer
would draw a contrast between the would-be disciple's wish and
the immediate total commitment demanded of one who understood
the meaning of discipleship. Direct object is the noun clause,
"no one is suitable..." εὔθετός is a compound of εὖ "good,"
"noble" "well" plus τίθημι "put" "place." He would follow
Jesus yet would place <u>anyone</u> "first" would not "fit in" with
the demands of dicipleship to God. The two participles
"placing hand" and "looking back" set forth in a simple figure
of common rural experience the necessity of concentrating on a
goal without distraction. By use of neuter article τὰ adverb
ὀπίσω "behind" is treated as substantive, "the things behind.

166

LUKE 10:1-2

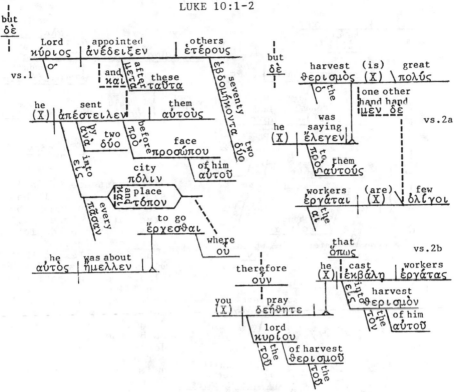

Two independent clauses plus one dependent gives to the sentence of verse one the compound-complex flavor. The independents state the facts: "The Lord appointed others..." and "he sent them..." Adverb phrase "after these" tells when he appointed. ἀνὰ δύο "two by two" indicates how he sent, hence is adverbial. εἰς & πρὸ "into" and "before" also insert adverb phrases showing where. Relative οὗ "where" establishes an adjective clause describing "city and place." By use of personal pronoun αὐτὸς "he" the subject is given particular emphasis.

Verse two could be considered a complex with four dependent clauses stemming off the independent "he was saying." But the diagram treats it as two distinct complex sentences. The two dependents of vs.2a are given strong contrast by μὲν δὲ "on the one hand but on the other hand."

In verse 2b the expression "the lord of the harvest" is probably ablative, "ask from the lord of the harvest..." ὅπως "that" injects a noun clause object of the verb "pray." The prepositional εἰς phrase is adverbial denoting where, "into his harvest."

167

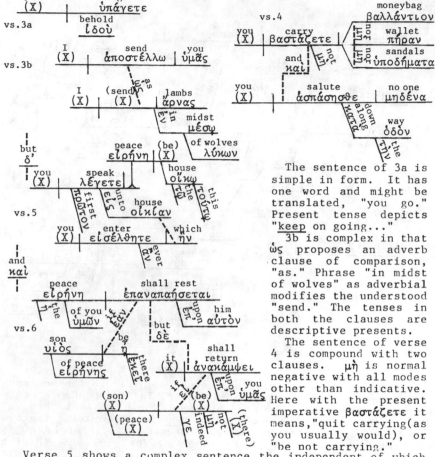

The sentence of 3a is simple in form. It has one word and might be translated, "you go." Present tense depicts "keep on going..."

3b is complex in that ὡς proposes an adverb clause of comparison, "as." Phrase "in midst of wolves" as adverbial modifies the understood "send." The tenses in both the clauses are descriptive presents.

The sentence of verse 4 is compound with two clauses. μὴ is normal negative with all modes other than indicative. Here with the present imperative βαστάζετε it means,"quit carrying(as you usually would), or "be not carrying."

Verse 5 shows a complex sentence the independent of which exhorts, "be speaking." εἰς οἰκίαν "unto house" tells where. Relative ἥν ushers in adjective clause describing house as "whichever you enter." Adverb πρῶτον, as diagrammed, suggests the "first" thing is to "speak..." It might modify "enter" of dependent clause, "unto which house you first enter."

Verse 6 admits of two independent and two dependent clauses. Adversative δὲ highlights the contrast between the independents, "your peace shall rest upon him but it shall return upon you." ἐὰν with subjunctive marks a 3rd class condition, undetermined with prospect, "if a son of peace be there and he may be..." εἰ with indicative is first class, "if he be not there and he isn't..."

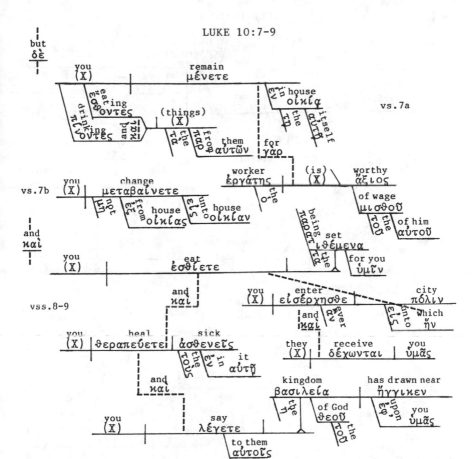

Besides circumstantial present participles the sentence of 7a has two independent clauses. So it frames a compound. Present imperative μένετε means "keep on staying." The ἐν phrase is adverbial specifying where. The αὐτῇ is intensive "itself." Note that αὐτῇ in verse 9 appears as personal pronoun "it."

Verse 7b is a simple sentence. Present imperative μεταβαίνετε with negative suggests, "do not make a practice of changing." ἐξ and εἰς phrases are adverbial, "from house to house."

From three independent and three dependent clauses verses 8-9 construct a compound-complex sentence. Verbs of the independents are all present imperatives, "...be eating...healing...saying..." They are to continue all three activities. Of the verbs of the dependents the first two are linear present subjunctives. But the third, a noun clause object of λέγετε "say," is perfect indicative, "has drawn near" representing a point in the past and the action still goes on.

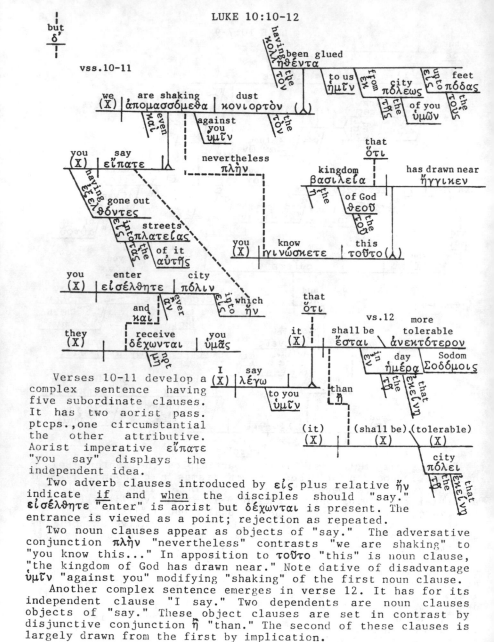

LUKE 10:10-12

Verses 10-11 develop a complex sentence having five subordinate clauses. It has two aorist pass. ptcps., one circumstantial the other attributive. Aorist imperative εἴπατε "you say" displays the independent idea.

Two adverb clauses introduced by εἰς plus relative ἥν indicate if and when the disciples should "say." εἰσέλθητε "enter" is aorist but δέχωνται is present. The entrance is viewed as a point; rejection as repeated.

Two noun clauses appear as objects of "say." The adversative conjunction πλὴν "nevertheless" contrasts "we are shaking" to "you know this..." In apposition to τοῦτο "this" is noun clause, "the kingdom of God has drawn near." Note dative of disadvantage ὑμῖν "against you" modifying "shaking" of the first noun clause.

Another complex sentence emerges in verse 12. It has for its independent clause "I say." Two dependents are noun clauses objects of "say." These object clauses are set in contrast by disjunctive conjunction ἢ "than." The second of these clauses is largely drawn from the first by implication.

170

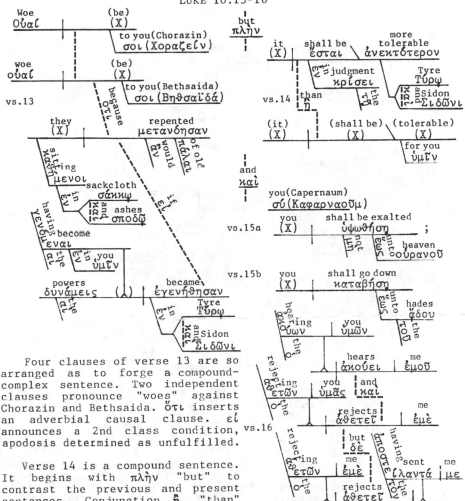

Four clauses of verse 13 are so arranged as to forge a compound-complex sentence. Two independent clauses pronounce "woes" against Chorazin and Bethsaida. ὅτι inserts an adverbial causal clause. εἰ announces a 2nd class condition, apodosis determined as unfulfilled.

Verse 14 is a compound sentence. It begins with πλήν "but" to contrast the previous and present sentences. Conjunction ἤ "than" joins with ἀνεκτότερον to form a comparison.

Verse 15 has two simple sentences. The first is a negative (μὴ) expecting "no" for an answer. The second is a strong affirmation, "You shall go down unto Hades."

Verse 16 exhibits a three-clause compound. Each clause has as its subject an attributive participle. ἀκούων(and ἀκούει)has genitive ὑμῶν (ἐμὲ) as object. Accusative accents what is heard; genitive stresses who is heard. Present tenses depict repeated action; participles too except aorist ἀποστείλαντα "the one having sent" which looks to the decisive act when he was "sent."

171

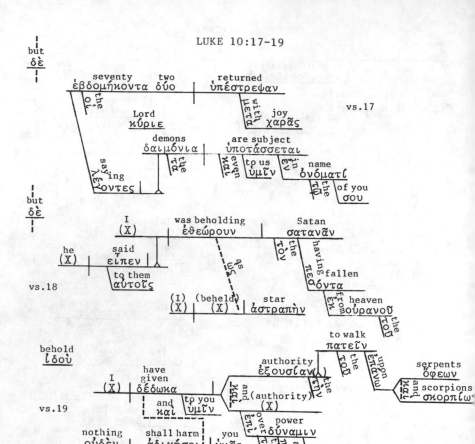

"The seventy two returned" is the independent clause of the complex sentence of verse 17. "With joy" tells how they returned. Noun clause "demons are subject..." is object of cir. ptcp. "saying." ὑποτάσσεται is iterative as well as distributive present. They were "subject" to each disciple and repeatedly so.

Verse 18 unveils a complex with "he said" as independent. ἐθεώρουν "was beholding" is descriptive imperfect. The difficulty of translating participles is noted in πεσόντα "having fallen." This is a timeless constative aorist "fall." ὡς implants a comparative clause, "like a star falls."

Verse 19 is compound. δέδωκα "have given" is perfect. It expresses a point in the past the effect of which still is operative. Greek uses double negative to emphasize, "nothing shall not harm..." Infinitive πατεῖν is appositional to ἐξουσίαν.

172

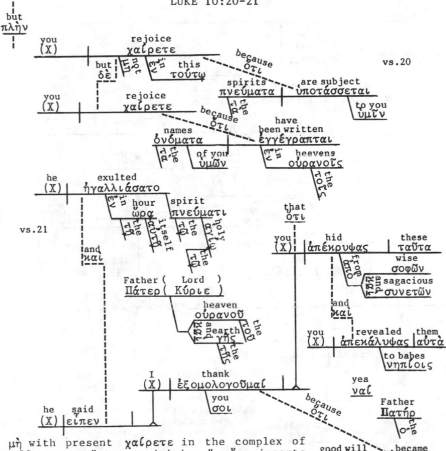

μὴ with present χαίρετε in the complex of
vs.20 means "stop rejoicing." ὅτι inserts
adverb of cause not declarative noun clauses.
Perfect ἐγγέγραπται marks permanancy of action, the
names "had been and still are written."
    Two independent clauses form the base structure of
the compound-complex of verse 21: "he exulted" and "he
said." "In the hour itself" designates when. "In the
holy spirit" may be locative sphere within which or instrumental, means by which.
    Present ἐξομολογοῦμαί describes his continuing thanks. Object
of "thanks" are declarative noun clauses prefaced by ὅτι, "that
you hid" and "that you revealed..." A second ὅτι establishes an
adverbial causal clause, "because thus (your) good will became
before you." One may note the use of vocatives in connection
with this sentence.

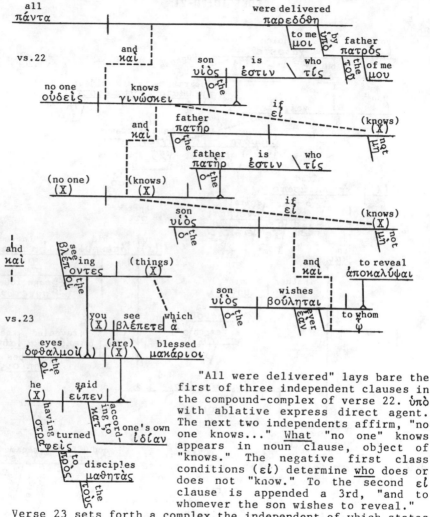

"All were delivered" lays bare the first of three independent clauses in the compound-complex of verse 22. ὑπὸ with ablative express direct agent. The next two independents affirm, "no one knows..." What "no one" knows appears in noun clause, object of "knows." The negative first class conditions (εἰ) determine who does or does not "know." To the second εἰ clause is appended a 3rd, "and to whomever the son wishes to reveal."

Verse 23 sets forth a complex the independent of which states "He said." Subject "he" has aorist circumstantial participle "having turned" describing it. Prepositional phrase κατ᾽ ἰδίαν literally "according to one's own" may be rendered "privately." Dependent noun clause "the eyes (are) blessed" is object of "said." In apposition to subject "eyes" is attributive present participle "ones seeing." An adjective clause injected by relative ἅ describes understood "things" object of the participle.

LUKE 10:24-25

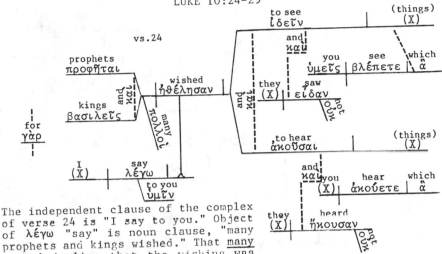

The independent clause of the complex of verse 24 is "I say to you." Object of λέγω "say" is noun clause, "many prophets and kings wished." That <u>many</u> wished implies that the wishing was done repeatedly and by numbers of persons. That is the temper inviting linear action. Yet ἠθέλησαν is aorist. Jesus focuses to a point all the "wishing" that the "prophets and kings" did. ἠθέλησαν has a compound object of two infinitives having understood objects("things"). Two adjective clauses (ἅ = which) describe "things." Coordinated to the object infinitives and connected by καί are the noun clauses "they saw not" and "they heard not." Note the emphasis gained by use of personal pronoun ὑμεῖς in the first relative ἅ clause. "Prophets and kings" could only "wish." But <u>you</u> see and hear!

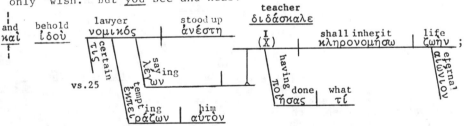

Verse 25 entails a complex sentence with three circumstantial participles and two full clauses. "Lawyer stood up" is the independent idea. His motive is mentioned by descriptive present participle "tempting." What he did when he stood is expressed by the second participle "saying." That which he "said" is seen in the noun clause, object of "saying," "having done what, shall I inherit eternal life." Aorist participle ποιήσας "having done" reveals the lawyer's philosophy of salvation, that is, it must be won by <u>doing</u> something worthy of such an inheritance!

175

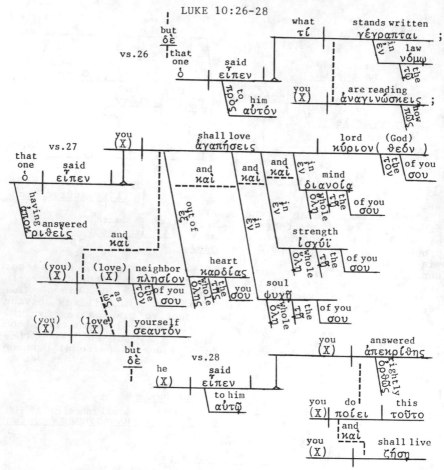

LUKE 10:26-28

All three sentences on this page are complex in structure. Demonstrative ὁ appears as subject in verses 26 and 27, "that one." In 26 object of the main verb "said" are two noun clauses, "what stands written" and "how are you reading."

The sentence of 27 also has two noun clauses as objects, then adds adverb clause of comparison,"(as you love)yourself." ἐξ and three ἐν phrases are adverbial defining how intense "you shall love your lord..." shall be. ἐκ with ablative defines source, ἐν with locative points to sphere within which.

In verse 28 the three dependent noun clauses are objects of main verb "said." Present ποίει insists on "keep doing this." Future indicative ζήσῃ is point action, "get life."

176

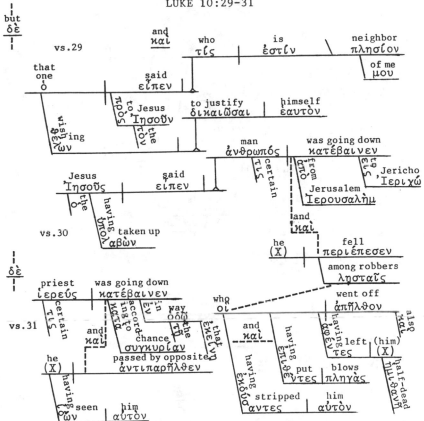

Verse 29 constitutes a sentence of two clauses so arranged as
to form a complex. Demonstrative ὁ is subject of the independent
clause, "that one said." Circumstantial participle of cause
θέλων "wishing" gives the reason for his "saying." Noun clause
"who is my neighbor" is object of "said" of the main clause.

Verse 30 develops as a complex with "Jesus said" as the main
clause. Literally ὑπολαβὼν means "taking under(hold)" the speech
of someone. Noun clause, "man was going down" is object of
"said." It uses descriptive imperfect κατέβαινεν. A second
object clause uses aorist "he fell" to depict what happened.
Locative "among robbers" is described by οἱ adjective clause,
"who also went off."

The two clauses of verse 31 are arranged as a compound. The
descriptive imperfect "was going down" reappears in the first
clause. Preposition ἀντι in aorist ἀντιπαρῆλθεν gives a snapshot
of the behaviour of the priest. He saw, as the participle
reports, but he passed by "against," that is, "opposite."

177

LUKE 10:32-34

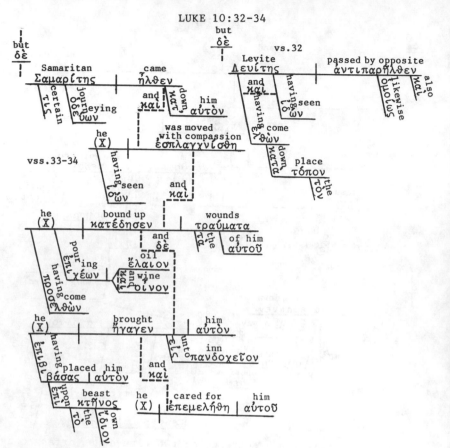

Verse 32 frames a simple sentence: "Levite passed by." The preposition ἀντί couples with παρά and aorist ἦλθεν to paint a graphic picture. This Levite "came" "alongside" and "opposite." He held a clear view but he wasn't about to contaminate himself by offering aid to this one in such a bloody unclean condition.

The sentence of 33-34 displays five independent clauses, all with narrative aorists. This compound thus relates five facts about the Samaritan. He "came," "was compassioned," "bound up" "brought," and "cared for." Present circumstantial participle ὁδεύων is temporal, "as he was journeying." Also ἰδών "when he saw." In the compound aorist κατέδησεν the preposition literally means down. He "bound down." But the English uses "bound up." The verb ἐπιμελέομαι prefers genitive as object. It's a medical term used in reference to the sick or injured. Compound word πανδοχεῖον derives from verb δέχομαι "receive" and πᾶς "all." Caravanserai provided a "home away from home" for all.

178

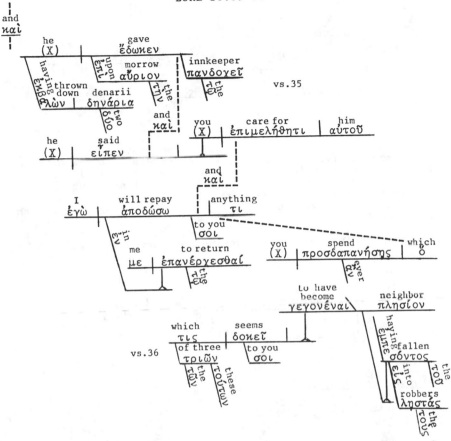

Verse 35 deploys five clauses so alined as to form a compound complex sentence. "He gave" and "he said" record the independent clauses. Circumstantial ἐκβαλών not only describes subject "he" but also "loosely" relates to the verb "gave." It tells both the manner and what he gave.

Direct objects of "said" are two noun clauses, "you care for" and "1 will repay..." ὅ introduces adjectival clause describing τι "anything." ἐν τῷ and infinitive "to return" with its accusative of general reference με, while not technically a clause, has the practical force of one: "when I return."

Infinitive phrases aren't clauses. Thus verse 36 is simple in form: "Which of the three seems to you..." "To have become" is object. Perfect tense suggests permanency. εἰς here would mean "among the robbers."

179

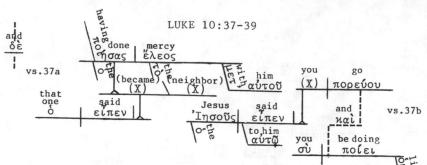

LUKE 10:37-39

Verse 37 divides into two complex sentences. Subjects are demonstrative ὁ and Ἰησοῦς in independent clauses but the verbs are identical. 37a has a largely eliptical noun clause as object of "said." The subject of that clause is attributive participle with its object, "the one having mercy." Note the phrase "with him"(μετ') not "to him." Mercy is something shared not bestowed.

37a has two noun clauses as objects of "said." Both verbs are linear presents. πορεύου is urging "be on your way..." Emphatic σὺ with ποίει insists on "be doing likewise" as a life pattern.

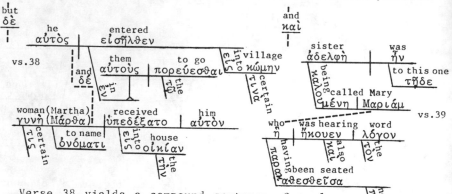

Verse 38 yields a compound sentence. One clause states, "he entered." When appears in ἐν τῷ and infinitive with accusative of general reference αὐτοὺς. The εἰς phrase tells where, "into certain village." The second clause says, "certain woman... received him." ὀνόματι is dative of possession.

Verse 39 generates a complex sentence. The independent clause states, "Sister was to this one..." τῇδε is an old demonstrative pronoun ἥδε indicating that which is present, seen, pointed out, person just named, etc. Circumstantial participle καλουμένη identifies the "sister." Relative ἥ introduces adjective clause describing Μαριάμ. Imperfect ἤκουεν describes Mary's intensive and continuing behaviour.

180

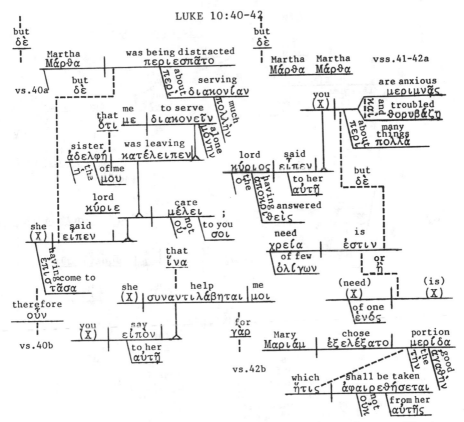

LUKE 10:40-42

Two sentences above left depict Martha's disturbance. First is a compound-complex portraying why she was distressed. περιεσπᾶτο is imperfect passive. She was "drawn around" with anxiety. "Having stopped over(ἐπιστᾶσα)she said..." What she said is the remainder of the sentence, μέλει with noun clause(ὅτι)subject, "that my sister was leaving me to serve alone is a care to you is it not?" οὐ in a question expects yes for an answer.

40b is complex. It has ἵνα noun clause as object of εἰπὸν. Verb "help" is compounded of σύν "with" and ἀντί "opposite" and middle of λαμβάνω "take." "Take your end of the load!"

Above right are two complex sentences displaying Jesus' answer. After independent, "the lord said" three noun clauses state what he said. Compound predicate "are anxious" and "are troubled" represent descriptive presents. The complex of 42b uses aorist ἐξελέξατο to show a deliberate, conscious choice on Mary's part.

181

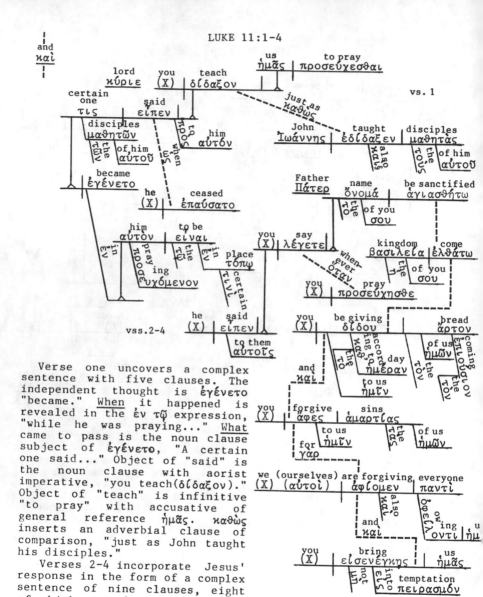

LUKE 11:1-4

vs. 1

Verse one uncovers a complex sentence with five clauses. The independent thought is ἐγένετο "became." When it happened is revealed in the ἐν τῷ expression, "while he was praying..." What came to pass is the noun clause subject of ἐγένετο, "A certain one said..." Object of "said" is the noun clause with aorist imperative, "you teach(δίδαξον)." Object of "teach" is infinitive "to pray" with accusative of general reference ἡμᾶς. καθὼς inserts an adverbial clause of comparison, "just as John taught his disciples."

Verses 2-4 incorporate Jesus' response in the form of a complex sentence of nine clauses, eight of which stem from independent "he said to them." First comes imperative noun clause, "you say," object of εἶπεν "said." ὅταν inaugurates indefinite adverbial clause indicating whenever. Six noun clauses follow each of which depicts a petition in a model prayer. The tenses are suggestive: four aorists; two presents.

182

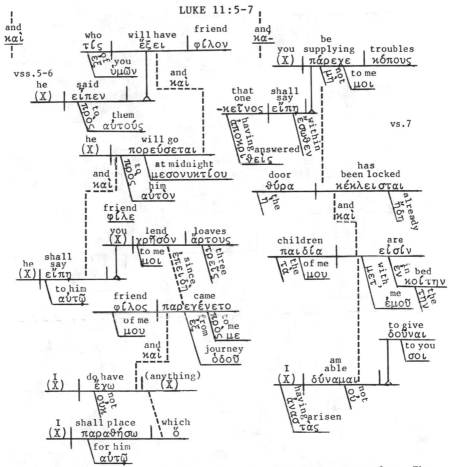

LUKE 11:5-7

Both of the above sentences are to be classed as complex. The independent clauses are identical except subjects: "he(that one)said..." In verses 5-6 five noun-object and two adverb clauses plus an adjectival fill out the sentence. "Who will have ," "he will go..." and "he shall say" are all noun, objects of εἶπεν. Object of εἴπῃ is "lend me three loaves" to which is appended two causal clauses, "since my friend came..." and "I do not have..." Relative ὅ brings in an adjectival idea describing understood "anything."

The sentence of verse 7 is similarly constructed with four noun clauses as objects of εἴπῃ. Present πάρεχε with negative means "quit supplying..." Perfect κέκλεισται indicates that the doors "have been locked and remain locked."

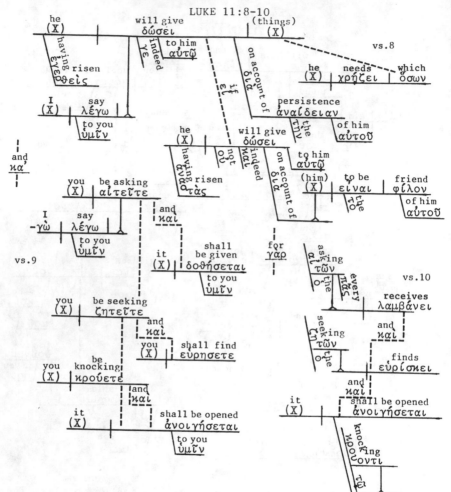

LUKE 11:8-10

In the complex sentence of vs.8 the independent idea is "I say." Noun clause, object of "say" is "he will give(things)..." That clause is supported by 1st class conditional εἰ "if he will not give..." ὅσων initiates an adjective clause. The two διά phrases give reasons why he will or will not "give."

Subject of independent clause of the complex of vs.9 also is "I" but here emphatic ἐγώ is used. Six noun-object clauses complete the sentence. Three present imperatives are followed by point action futures:"be asking...it shall be given, be seeking...you shall find, "be knocking...shall be opened."

Verse 10 is a three clause compound sentence. Attributive participles are subjects in the first two clauses.

184

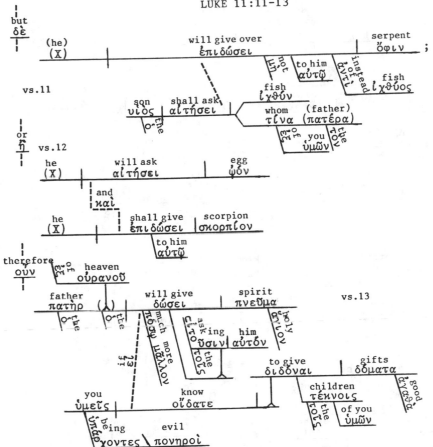

The sentence of verse 11 is complex. The text deserves the term anacoluthon for it "fails to follow" the usual rules of grammatical agreement. The accusative τίνα is object of αἰτήσει with πατέρα in apposition. But "he" (nom.case) alludes to (acc.) father. A question with μὴ expects "no" for an answer: "...he will not give will he?"

The compound of verse 12 is also a question. Though no μή is expressed yet it is implied: "Or he will ask an egg, and shall he give him a scorpion?" The answer expected would be: "no."

Verse 13 is a two-clause complex sentence. It has a 1st class conditional supporting independent, "how much more will the father...give..?" Personal pronoun ὑμεῖς you is quite emphatic. ὑπάρχοντες "being evil" is a present concessive circumstantial participle. "...you, even though you being evil, know..." Present infinitive διδόναι is iterative. Even an evil parent repeatedly gives.

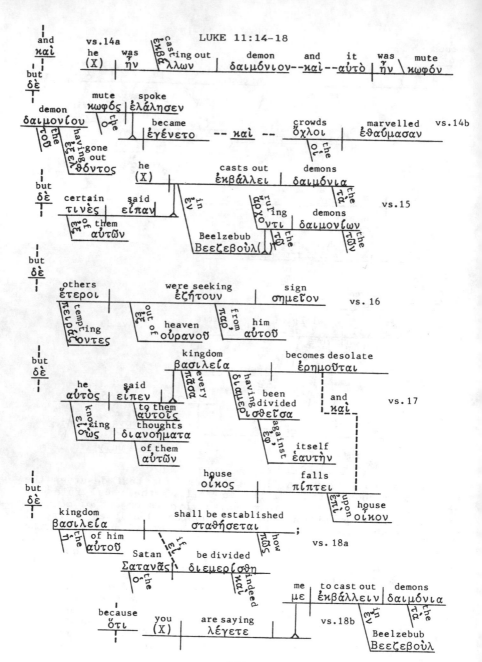

186

As diagrammed 14a is a compound of two clauses. Periphrastic "was casting out" animates the descriptive force of imperfect tense.

Two independent clauses plus one dependent constitute verse 14b a compound-complex sentence. It contains also a genitive absolute indicating when the demon spoke. Dependent "The mute spoke" is subject of ἐγένετο of the first independent. All verbs are aorists.

The sentence of verse 15 embraces two full clauses. After independent "Certain of them said" comes the noun-object clause "he casts out the demons..." Present ἐκβάλλει is iterative. It acknowledges not only that he did cast them out but that he also did so regularly and repeatedly. The "in Beelzebub"(ἐν)phrase with appositional attributive present participle "the one ruling the demons" is what some grammarians call the "instrumental use of locative case." The entire phrase is adverbial alledging how he managed to cast them out.

Verse 16 concerns but one clause hence the sentence is simple in structure. Imperfect ἐζήτουν implies that they "were seeking" repeatedly a sign. The present circumstantial participle πειράζοντες "tempting" is purpose; as present it matches the linear action of imperfect ἐζήτουν. The prepositional phrases ἐξ and παρ' are both adverbial in function answering the questions where from. ἐξ says "out from a point" (source) whereas παρά means "from the side of."

Verse 17 engages three clauses to construct a complex arrangement. "He said" is the independent idea. Circumstantial εἰδώς "knowing" is probably causal. Two dependent clauses are both objects of the verb of the main clause, "said." ἐρημοῦται "is being desolated" and πίπτει "falls" are both gnomic presents. This is what happens universally under such a situation.

The sentence of 18a is a question, complex in form, which envelops a first class condition. The condition is assumed to be true, "if Satan be divided and he is..." On such a protasis the apodosis concludes, "how shall the kingdom be established?" The obvious answer is, "It can't!"

Since infinitive with accusative of general reference technically is not a clause 18b represents a simple sentence. Introduced by causal ὅτι "because" Jesus picks up the accusation made against him in verse 15, "Because you are saying..." Object of "saying" is the infinitive phrase, "that I am casting out demons." In the infinitive Jesus repeats the linear action of the accusation of verse 15, ἐκβάλλειν "to be casting out."

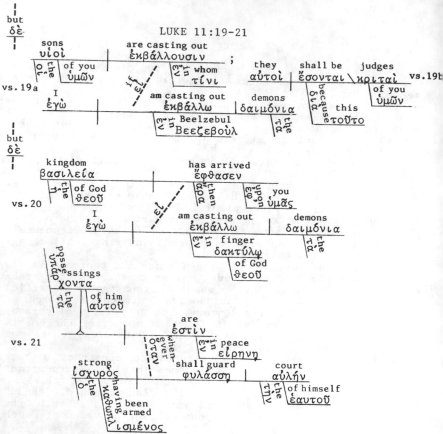

LUKE 11:19-21

The two clauses of 19a are arranged so as to put together a complex sentence. εἰ introduces a first class condition determined as true. The "if" deals only with the statement of fact not the fact. The personal pronoun subject ἐγὼ is decidedly emphatic. "If I cast out...in whom do the sons of you..."

19b brings in a simple sentence, "They shall be your judges." διὰ with accusative "because of this" is adverbial stating why.

Verse 20 embodies another two-clause complex first class contional. ἔφθασεν is a timeless aorist from φθάνω "come" "arrive."

Another complex appears in verse 21. This time an indefinite temporal adverb clause launched by ὅταν "whenever" supports the independent clause, "his possessions are in peace." Note perfect passive participle καθωπλισμένος "having been fully armed." This is an example of perfective use of preposition κατά in composition with ὁπλίζω. Neuter plural present active participle ὑπάρχοντα is used here as substantive with genitive "his possessions."

188

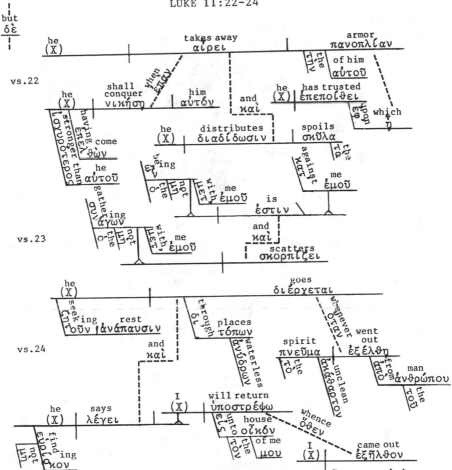

Verse 22 is a four-clause compound-complex sentence. ἐπὰν is an adverb clause relating when whereas relative ᾗ is adjectival describing armor. Perfect ἐπεποίθει stresses permanant trust.

23 displays a compound of two clauses. Subjects are attributive participles "being" and "gathering." μετά and genitive denotes "fellowship with." All verbs and verbals are linear presents animating the action.

Verse 24 presents a compound-complex with two independent and three dependent clauses. Indefinite ὅταν inserts adverb clause of time. ὅθεν ushers in adverbial clause indicating from where! Object of λέγει is noun clause "I will return..."

189

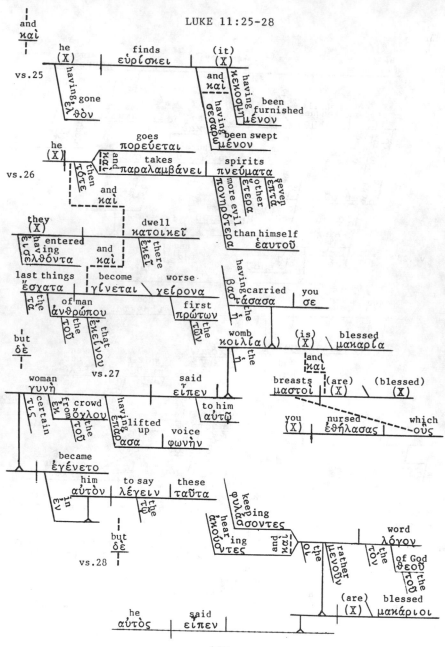

190

The sentence of verse 25 is to be classified as simple since it has but the one clause, "he finds (it)." Three circumstantial participles complete the sentence. The aorist ἐλθὸν "having come" is temporal, "after he came (back)..." The perfects, "having been furnished" and "having been swept" focus on the endurance of the condition of "having been furnished" etc.

Verse 26 mirrors a compound sentence having three clauses. The first clause itself has a compound predicate, "he goes and takes..." The action of the entire sentence is vividly dramatic because all four verbs are linear presents, "goes and takes...dwells...become." In the first and third clauses comparative adjectives with ablatives offer comparisons: "more evil than himself" and "worse than the first." The presence of ἑπτά "seven" and ἕτερα "other" add distinct brilliance to the picture of "more evil." "Seven" is symbolic of full perfection. The word translated "other" indicates "other of a different kind" rather than "other of the same kind." That's the reason the "last things became worse."

Verse 27 displays a complex sentence of five clauses. The independent clause has ἐγένετο "became" or "happened" for its verb the subject of which is noun clause "certain woman said." This "certain" woman is further described by the adjective phrase as one "out of the crowd." Without question, though she was more vocal, she reflected the feeling of many. She was the one from the "many" who "lifted up her voice." The substance of what she said is depicted by the noun clause object of "said," "blessed (is) the womb." In apposition to subject "womb" is aorist attributive participle "the one having carried you." A second noun-object clause is added, "blessed (are) breasts." And "breasts" are described by adjective clause introduced by relative οὓς "which you nursed."

The infinitive phrase ἐν τῷ λέγειν and its accusative of general reference αὐτὸν is adverb in function,"while he was saying these." The present tense of the infinitive indicates "while." Had it been aorist we would translate: "when he said." So her crying out was an interruption, "while he was speaking."

The response of Jesus to this woman's outburst of praise corrects her idea of what is "blessed" in life. The sentence of verse 28 is complex in structure. It enjoys two clauses the independent of which is "he said." Direct object of "said" is the noun clause "the ones hearing and keeping...are blessed." The compound attributive participial phrase forms the subject of that dependent noun-object clause. Linear action of the present participles implies continuous and repeated "hearing and keeping." In other words, obedience to the moral authority of the word of God is of more vital value than physical, parental relationship.

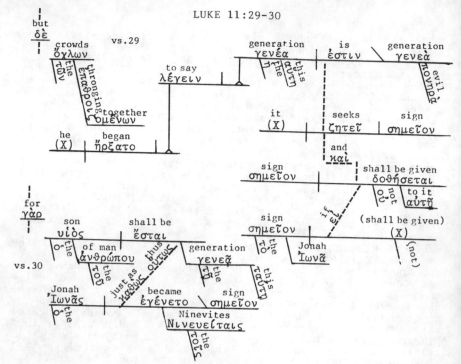

LUKE 11:29-30

A genitive absolute inaugurates the sentence of verse 29. Plural "crowds" is described by present middle participle ἐπαθροιζομένων "thronging together." It's a vivid picture of masses mingling together. Multitudes were surrounding, cramming, jamming upon Jesus. Then "he began to be saying..." This expression is more weighty than simple "he said." "Began" is aorist; "to be saying" is linear present. Following this independent clause are four dependents. Three are noun clauses, objects of infinitive "to say." One is adverb first class conditional, "if the sign of Jonah(shall not be given)and it won't, then a "sign shall not be given...."

The first noun-object clause has demonstrative αὕτη "this" to point with emphasis to this generation. Adjective πονηρὰ is actively evil, evil which is not content until it is corrupts others; agressively evil!

In the second noun-object clause ζητεῖ is present, that is, "repeatedly seeking." The sentence is complex in form.

The sentence of verse 30 has two clauses so arranged as to construct a complex sentence. Adverbial dependent is comparative (καθὼς), "Just as Jonah became sign to the Ninevites." On that standard of comparison "thus (οὕτως) the son of man shall be to this generation."

192

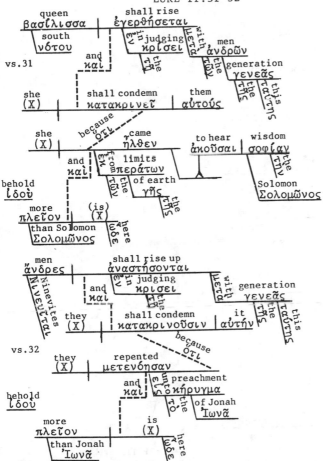

LUKE 11:31-32

The two sentences on this page are both compound-complex. They each have two independent clauses supported by two causal (ὅτι) dependents. Locative phrase of article with action noun τῇ κρίσει appears in each sentence. κρίσις, often translated "judgment," really is "judging," a process rather than verdict. God's judgment is not an attempt to sift evidence. It's a procedure that develops and reveals character of the one being judged by his making moral choices! In the sentence of 31 ἀκοῦσαι is infinitive of purpose. In verse 32 κήρυγμα is a result noun. In accusative with εἰς it suggests, "in view of the thing preached." Each sentence uses πλεῖον as a substantive with ablative to express comparison.

LUKE 11:33-36

vs.33

no one / οὐδεὶς
puts / τίθησιν
but / ἀλλ'
neither / οὐδὲ
having / lit / lamp / ἅψας λύχνον
under / into / ὑπὸ
bushel / μόδιον / the / τὸν
cellar / κρύπτην / the / ocellar
he (X)
(puts) (X)
upon / lampstand / ἐπὶ λυχνίαν / the / τὴν
entering / ering / εἰσπορευόμενοι / the / οἱ
that / ἵνα
may see / βλέπωσιν
ray / φέγγος / the / τὸ

vs.34a

lamp / λύχνος / the / of body / σώματος / the / τοῦ
is / ἐστιν
eye / ὀφθαλμός / the / of you / σου

vs.34b

body / σῶμά / the / whole / you / σου
is / ἐστιν
brilliant / φωτεινόν
whenever / ὅταν
be / ῇ
but / δὲ
single / ἁπλοῦς
eye / ὀφθαλμός / the / of you / σου
body / σῶμα / the / you / σου
(is) (X)
dark / σκοτεινόν
whenever / ὅταν
it (X)
be / ῇ
also / καὶ
evil / πονηρὸς

therefore / οὖν
you (X)
be watching / σκόπει
lest / μὴ
vs.35
light / φῶς / the / in / ἐν / you / σοι / the / τὸ
is / ἐστίν
darkness / σκότος

vs.36

it (X)
shall be / ἔσται
brilliant / φωτεινὸν / wholly / ὅλον
if then / εἰ οὖν
body / σῶμά / the / τὸ / of you / σου
(be) (X)
brilliant / φωτεινὸν
as whenever / ὡς ὅταν
having / ἔχον / not / μὴ
part / μέρος / any / τι
dark / σκοτεινόν
lamp / λύχνος / the / illuminates / φωτίζῃ
you / σε
with flash / ἀστραπῇ / the / τῇ

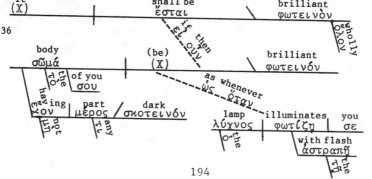

194

The diagram of verse 33 unveils a compound-complex sentence. It employs two independent clauses the second of which must be inferred from the context. "No one puts" is the basic idea. Adverbial phrases εἰς and ὑπό indicate <u>where</u>; "into cellar" and "under the bushel." Subject and verb of the 2nd clause are "(he puts)" modified by adverbial "upon the lampstand." ἵνα launches an adverbial purpose clause indicating <u>why</u>. Present participle "the ones entering" serves as subject of the ἵνα clause.

The single clause of the simple sentence of 34a states, "The lamp of the body is your eye." When both subject and predicate nominative have the article, as here, they are "equal and interchangeable." "Your eye" is "the lamp..." is as good as "the lamp is the eye..." as a translation.

Verse 34b employs four clauses to form a compound-complex arrangement. The independents make the affirmations, "Your whole body is brilliant(light)" and "your body (is) dark." ὅταν is a temporal particle which literally means "when if." "Whenever" is normal as a translation. Thus the time and condition upon which "the whole body is brilliant" is set forth in the ὅταν clauses. δέ is a coordinating conjunction, usually adversative "but" as it here joins as it contrasts the independent clauses.

Verse 35 develops as a complex sentence. The introductory particle οὖν is inferential "therefore." Linear action of present imperative σκόπει is an exhortation to "<u>be</u> watching," that is, "keep alert, always be on the lookout!" μή proposes a negative purpose idea, "lest"(in order that not...). Since the subject of this sentence has the article and the predicate does not, then subject and predicate are not "equal and interchangeable" as they were in 34a. Here the clause makes an unalterable statement, "the light in you <u>is darkness</u>."

Verse 36 encloses three clauses so disposed as to structure a complex sentence. Present circumstantial participial phrase ἔχον "not having any part dark," while not a clause, plays a significant role in the sentence. It <u>might</u> have been stated as a clause. As it is the participle is conditional, "if (it) does not have any part dark." σκοτεινόν is predicate adjective used as objective complement.

The main clause affirms, "it shall be wholly brilliant." The condition upon which that affirmation rests is, "if then your body is brilliant(light)." A second dependent clause contains a comparative idea (ὡς = as) as well as temporal condition ὅταν = whenever. φωτίζῃ is <u>present</u> subjunctive = "keeps on illuminating..." ἀστραπῇ is instrumental, "with its flash."

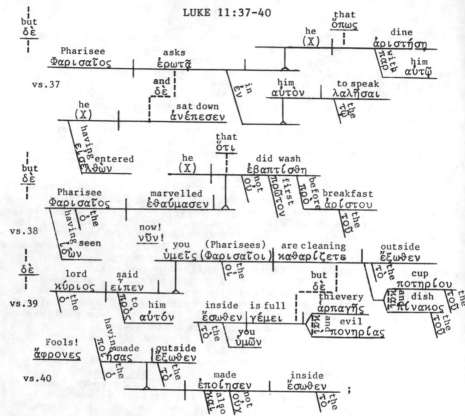

LUKE 11:37-40

The sentence of 37 is compound-complex. ἐρωτᾷ is a historical present, "he invites." When is in ἐν τῷ and infinitive "as he spoke." The content of his invitation is seen in ὅπως noun clause, "that he dine..." The second independent clause says, "he, having entered, sat down(fell onto the sofa)."

Verse 38 structures a two-clause complex. "The Pharisee marvelled" is the independent idea. Circumstantial participle ἰδὼν reveals when, "having seen." As diagrammed ὅτι is noun clause object of "marvelled" rather than adverbial causal.

Verse 39 unveils a complex with two noun clauses as objects of main verb "said." Emphatic ὑμεῖς is subject. In apposition is "Pharisees." Present καθαρίζετε is iterative as well as distributive; "repeatedly cleaning" and "each of you." Verb of fullness γέμει takes genitive as object.

Verse 4 is a simple sentence. Vocative ἄφρονες "Fools" is a pointed address. Subject is attributive participle ποιήσας "having made." οὐχ in a question expects "yes" for an answer.

196

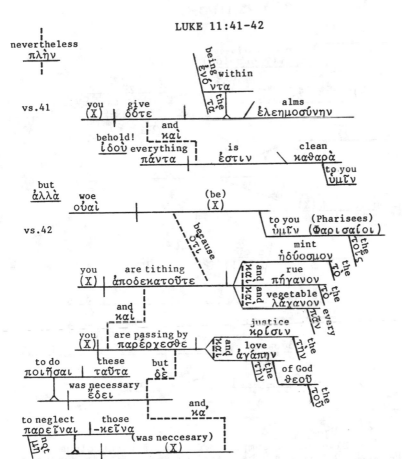

Verse 41 forges a compound sentence. Aorist imperative δότε "you give," without denying the necessity of repeatedly giving, focuses on the urgency to give. Attributive present participle "the things being within" serves as direct object. It centers on what forms <u>real</u> giving. "Alms" are more than just objective <u>things</u>. They include inner resources of the spirit. In fact, it's the inward that makes the outward "alms." The second clause explains the first. The inward matters of the spirit determine what is genuine almsgiving. They make "everything" <u>clean</u>.

Verse 42 erects a complex sentence. The independent lays down the proposition, "Woe (be) to you the Pharisees." Four adverbial ὅτι causal clauses support the "woe" by giving reasons <u>why</u>! All verbs in these subordinate clauses are linear action tenses, either present or imperfect.

197

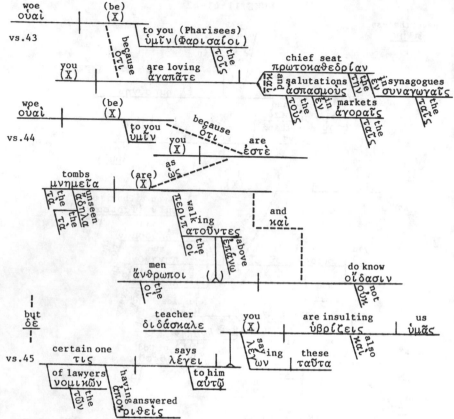

Verse 43 evolves as a complex with independent clause being "woe (be)..." Dative is the case of personal interest; it reveals something done **to**, **for** or **against**. Here ὑμῖν is dative with "Pharisees" in apposition. ὅτι inaugurates an adverbial dependent clause of cause. ἀγαπᾶτε is iterative present; it also includes the distributive idea.

Verse 44 develops as a complex sentence. It too has a supporting ὅτι clause of cause. It is amplified by adverb ὡς "as the unseen tombs..." A third dependent clause is added paralleling the ὡς. Attributive present participle "the ones walking above" is appositional to subject "men."

The two clauses in verse 45 are arranged as complex. "A certain one says" is the independent. τις is specified by genitive "of the lawyers." Dative αὐτῷ underlines the personal pique of this τις. Circumstantial participle λέγων is probably temporal, "when you say..." It could be conditional.

198

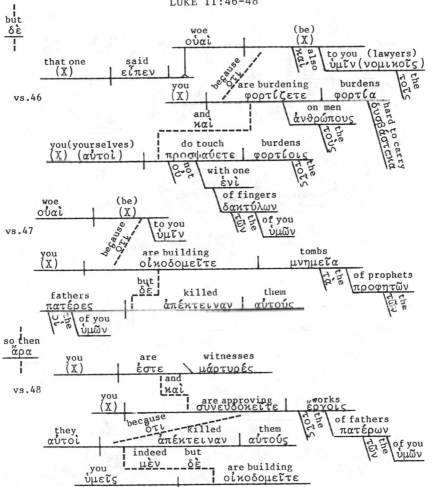

Three sentences adorn this page. Verse 46 involves a complex with a noun-object clause supported by two ὅτι causal clauses.

The sentence of 47 is complex. Here too the ὅτι causals give reasons independent "woe (be) to you" had to be pronounced.

The four clauses of 48 establish a compound-complex. The current activity of these "lawyers" is shown by linear present in the two independent clauses and the second dependent. In the 1st dependent an historical aorist collects into one point all the "religious" murders of their fathers. μὲν - δὲ contrast past and present behaviour.

199

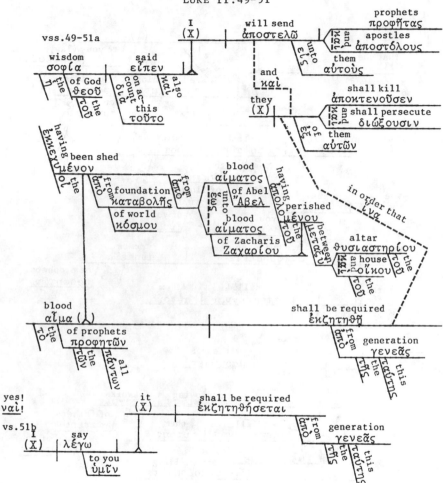

49-51a embrace a complex sentence. διὰ τοῦτο "on account of this" ties this pronouncement to the previous sentence. Two noun clauses, objects of εἶπεν of the independent, give the sequence of providential counsels: first, God sends "prophets...apostles" and then they are "killed...persecuted." The ἵνα clause states the purpose or consequent result. After all, purpose is nothing but conceived result. The guilt of <u>all</u> generations is shared by <u>each</u> generation. The history of man is the history of guilt.

51b is a two-clause complex. It summarizes what has been said in the previous sentence.

200

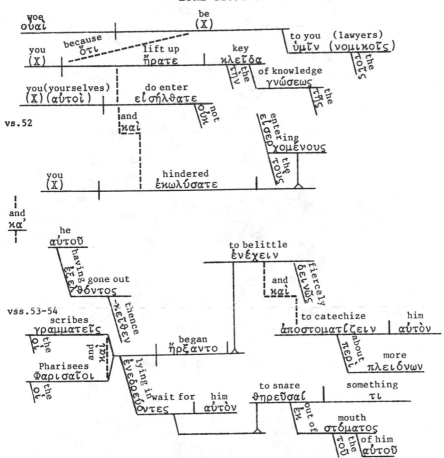

vs.52

vss.53-54

Again Jesus assaults the lawyers, "Woe(be)to you..." In this complex sentence the "Woe" is verified by three ὅτι causal clauses. Each of these subordinates gives a reason why these hypocritical lawyers merit such a woe. κλεῖδα "key" is described by genitive γνώσεως "of knowledge." It's the knowledge kind of key. In apposition to subject you of the 2nd dependent is intensive pronoun αὐτοί "yourselves." It's quite emphatic.

Verse 53 has but one full clause hence is simple. After genitive absolute, "he having gone out," the bare sentence is "scribes and Pharisees began..." Object of and supplementing "began" are two infinitives, "to belittle" and "to catechize." Linear action of present "lying in wait for" indicates repeated persistence "to snare(aorist)something out of his mouth."

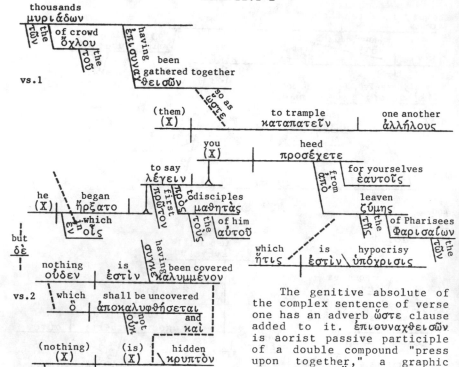

The genitive absolute of
the complex sentence of verse
one has an adverb ὥστε clause
added to it. ἐπισυναχθεισῶν
is aorist passive participle
of a double compound "press
upon together," a graphic
description. ὥστε and present
infinitive "to be trampling"
add color to the portrait. To
commence a sentence with a
relative as ἐν οἷς is classic Greek. The only antecedent would
be the affairs of 11:53f, "in which matters." The independent
clause, "he began," takes its cue from these "matters" as he
"first"(πρῶτον) "began to say to his disciples." The content of
what he said is noun clause object of λέγειν. Present προσέχετε
is "be taking heed" continuous action. ἀπὸ with ablative says to
"separate yourself from..." Qualitative relative ἥτις initiates
adjective clause, "which by its very nature is hypocrisy." A
ὑποκριτής is a "stage player," an actor. Actors in ancient plays
wore masks, they pretended to be something other than
themselves. Thus the hypocrite is a "pretender."

The sentence of verse two enfolds a compound-complex of four
clauses. Perfect participle συγκεκαλυμμένον joins present ἐστὶν
to form the vivid periphrastic "has been covered." It contrasts
with punctilar future passive "shall not be uncovered" of the
first of two adjective ὃ clauses. κρυπτὸν is predicate adjective
affirming a fact about implied subject "nothing."

202

Compound-complex is the category in which the sentence of vs.3 falls. "It shall be heard" and "it shall be heralded" are independent clauses. Where this publicity shall take place appears in adverb units "in the light" and "on the roofs." Precisely what was to be so openly announced emerges in the adjective clause inserted by quantitative relative ὅσα, "howevermuch you said in the dark." A simple singular relative initiates the next relative "which you spoke..." πρὸς "to the ear" alludes to a whisper in secrecy. The "inner chamber" adds emphasis to the secrecy. This is where the secret whisper takes place.

Verse 4 may be classed as complex. The personal force of dative ὑμῖν is intensified by apposition φίλοις "my friends." The noun clause object of the independent "I say" is ingressive aorist, "Do not begin to fear..." The one article with both participles "killing...having" join the actions as one. They are both ablative of separation with ἀπό.

One independent clause forms the basis for the complex sentence in verse five. But whether both noun clauses which follow are objects of ὑποδείξω or not is a matter of judgment. In the diagram the second is viewed as a separate simple sentence.

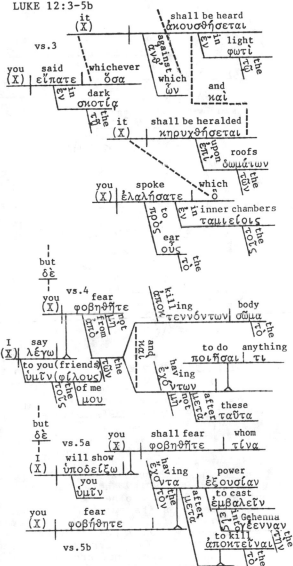

LUKE 12:3-5b

In 5a φοβηθῆτε is aorist subjunctive. φοβήθητε is imperative in 5b. One is statement; the other exhortation. Present participle ἔχοντα is attributive, object of φοβήθητε. Infinitive with μετὰ is adverbial indicating when.

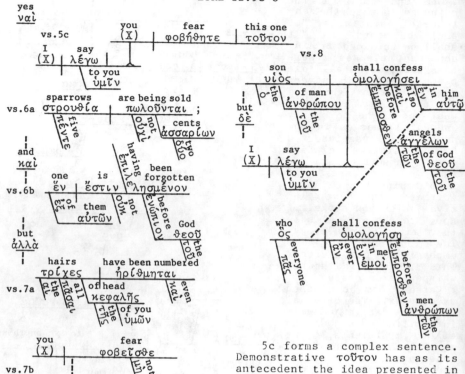

5c forms a complex sentence. Demonstrative τοῦτον has as its antecedent the idea presented in 5a-b. The term "Yes!" picks up that idea and reaffirms the one to be feared.

The sentence of 6a is simple in form. οὐχί in the question expects yes for an answer. ἀσσαρίων is genitive of price.

6b is also classed as simple. But its verb is a periphrastic built of present ἔστιν and perfect participle ἐπιλελησμένον. The sentence of 7a is another simple. ἀλλά often adversative "but" yet here retains its original "another." The idea is carried on by ἀλλά. Here it may be translated "Yea!" The fact that each hair has been counted shows God's concern for details of human life.

Two clauses of 7b construct a compound; asyndeton avoids a conjunction and thereby increases emotional power. Both verbs are presents: "quit fearing" and descriptive "are excelling."

The complex of 8 has three clauses. Noun clause "son shall confess" is object of main verb "say." Relative ὅς begins adjective clause describing αὐτῷ "him."

LUKE 12:9-10

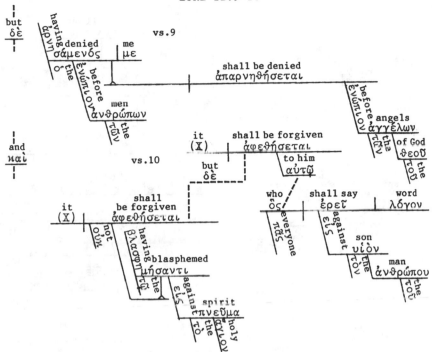

Verse eight develops as a simple sentence. Its subject is the aorist attributive participial phrase, "the one having denied me before men." ἐνώπιον "in the sight of" is an improper preposition with genitive. Genitive is the specifying case. It specifies this not that. "Before men" balances with "before angels." The verb ἀπαρνηθήσεται, future passive of compound ἀπό and ἀρνέομαι, intensifies the simple "deny." The preposition strengthens. The denial (the verb appears twice in the sentence) is a thorough rejection of acquaintance with the person under question. It's a genuine denial; a vigorous repudiation!

Verse ten assembles a compound-complex sentence having three clauses. The independents offer a sharp contrast, "it shall be forgiven" and "it shall not be forgiven." Both future tenses are volitive involving the will of him who does the forgiving, that is, God. Relative ὅς clause is adjectival describing dative personal pronoun αὐτῷ "to him." εἰς, the root meaning of which is "in" or "into," in this context has the resultant meaning of "against." To "blaspheme" signifies "to hurl a slander against." In the expression "son of man" ἀνθρώπου is genitive specifying the kind of "son." It's the mankind, human kind of "son." It identifies Jesus with humanity.

205

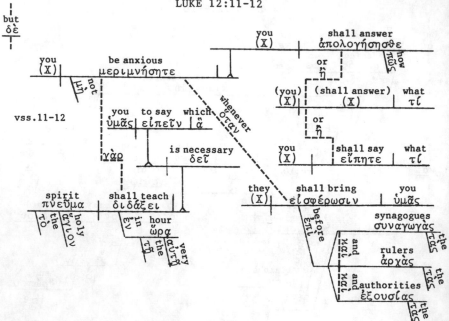

Verses 11-12 fashion a compound-complex combination. The first independent clause contains aorist active subjunctive with μὴ in prohibition, "don't become anxious..." μεριμνήσητε "be anxious" is compounded from μερίς "part" and νοῦς "mind." To be anxious is to have a "half a mind," "to be divided in mind." What could create anxiety is set forth in three noun-object clauses: "how you shall answer," "what (you shall answer)," and "what you shall say." These are indirect questions which retain deliberative subjunctive of the direct. ὅταν establishes an indefinite temporal clause indicating when anxiety is to be shunned. εἰσφέρωσιν is present subjunctive active suggesting iterative action, "whenever they are bringing..." Definite article τὰς repeated with "the synagogues," "the rulers," "the authorities," sets forth each substantive as sharply distinct. ἐπί literally means "upon." The translation of a preposition depends of three factors:(1)root idea (2)case with which it appears (3)context in which it is used. Here ἐπὶ means "before."

The second independent idea promises, "the Holy Spirit shall teach..." διδάξει is volitive future. Direct object is the noun δεῖ clause, "the things which it is necessary that you say." The subject of δεῖ is infinitive εἰπεῖν with accusative of general reference ὑμᾶς. Relative ἃ is neuter plural object of the infinitive, "which things."

206

LUKE 12:13-15

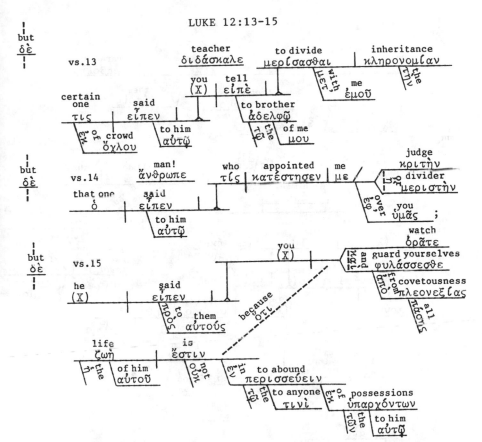

Indefinite pronoun τις used as a substantive is subject in the complex sentence of verse 13. This "certain one" is identified as "out of (ἐκ) the crowd." Object of main verb "said" is aorist imperative εἰπὲ of noun clause "Say to my brother." Infinitive phrase μερίσασθαι is object of this imperative "tell."

In the complex of verse 14 demonstrative use of article is subject of independent clause, "that one said..." Noun-object clause has for its subject interrogative τίς "who?" "Judge and divider" is objective complement after με "me."

In the complex of verse 15 Jesus warns the multitudes. Object of main verb "said" is noun clause exhortation, "be watching and guard yourselves." φυλάσσεσθε is middle voice. Both verbs are present, "keep on watching...guarding." The adverb causal clause gives the philosophical reason (ὅτι) lying as foundation why. τινὶ and αὐτῷ are dative of possession. ἐν τῷ and infinitive is a characteristic idiom of Luke's.

207

but
δέ

vs.16

he
(X)
spoke
εἶπεν
parable
παραβολὴν
πρὸς them
αὐτοὺς

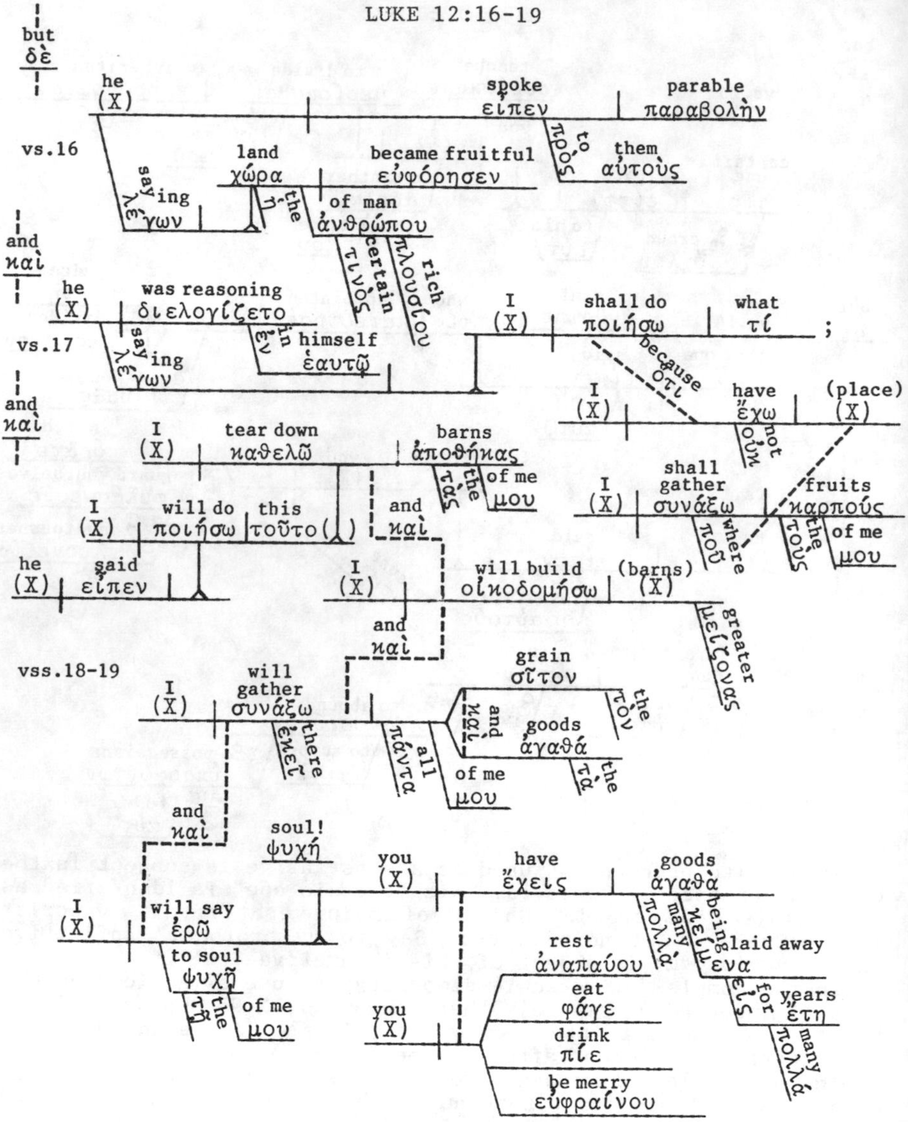

say ing
λέγων
land
χώρα
became fruitful
εὐφόρησεν
the
of man
ἀνθρώπου
rich
πλουσίου
certain
τινὸς

and
καὶ

vs.17

he
(X)
was reasoning
διελογίζετο
ἐν himself
ἑαυτῷ
say ing
λέγων

I
(X)
shall do
ποιήσω
what
τί
;
because ὅτι

I
(X)
have
ἔχω
οὐκ not
(place)
(X)

and
καὶ

I
(X)
tear down
καθελῶ
barns
ἀποθήκας
the
τὰς
of me
μου
and
καὶ

shall gather
συνάξω
where
ποῦ
fruits
καρπούς
the
τοὺς
of me
μου

I
(X)
will do
ποιήσω
this
τοῦτο( )

he
(X)
said
εἶπεν

I
(X)
will build
οἰκοδομήσω
(barns)
(X)
greater
μείζονας

and
καὶ

vss.18-19

I
(X)
will gather
συνάξω
there
ἐκεῖ
all
πάντα
grain
σῖτον
the
τὸν
and
καὶ
goods
ἀγαθά
the
τὰ
of me
μου

and
καὶ
soul!
ψυχή

I
(X)
will say
ἐρῶ
to soul
ψυχῇ
the
τῇ
of me
μου

you
(X)
have
ἔχεις
goods
ἀγαθά
many
πολλά
being κείμενα laid away
for years
ἔτη
many
πολλά

you
(X)
rest
ἀναπαύου
eat
φάγε
drink
πίε
be merry
εὐφραίνου

208

LUKE 12:16-19

The sentence of verse 16 is a two-clause complex. Independent clause certifies that he "spoke parable to them." αὐτοὺς "them" refers primarily to the disciples although the "multitudes" were in the background. πρὸς with accusative is less personal than the dative would have been. He spoke "facing" or "toward." The parable was steered in their direction; it was for their benefit. Object of the present circumstantial participle λέγων is noun clause, "land became fruitful..." εὐφόρησεν is compounded of εὖ "well" and φέρω "bear" meaning it "bore well." Hence ingressive aorist "became fruitful" is acceptable translation.

The sentence of verse 17 displays three dependent clauses besides the independent. The verb διελογίζετο of the independent is imperfect, "was reasoning." It describes the continuing perplexity with which this "certain rich man" struggled. ἐν ἑαυτῷ "in himself" is an adverbial phrase indicating <u>where</u> the tussle took place. The dependent clauses detail his problem. First, the noun clause, "what shall I do?" It is object of present participle λέγων "saying." That is followed by adverb ὅτι causal clause, "because I do not have..." ποῦ "where" is an adverb although it also initiates an adjective clause describing understood "place."

Eight clauses constitute the building blocks of the complex sentence of verses 18-19. "He said" is the independent element. "I will do this" is noun clause object of "said." In apposition to τοῦτο "this" are four noun clauses all of which have volitive futures: "I will tear down...will build...will gather...will say." To this are added two more noun clauses objects of ἐρῶ "say." Circumstantial participle κείμενα is present tense the linear action of which vividly describes the illusionary feeling of this rich man. He has, so he envisions, "lying," that is, continuously present to his daily demands. The final clause is attached without any formal connection. Such asyndeton adds stylistic effect. In fact this last clause uses asyndeton within itself. It has four imperatives forming a compound predicate. Two are present imperatives, "be resting..." and "be making merry..." Also two aorist imperatives, "eat...drink..." Asyndeton is the method of joining these exhortations together. It demonstrates the dramatic emotional effect which this "fool" has about his anticipated future.

Of the futures referred to above two are liquid futures. κείμενα "will tear down." Of this form A. T. Robertson states, "Future active of καθαιρέω, an old verb, the usual future being καθαιρήσω. This second form from the second aorist καθεῖλον (from obsolete ἕλω)." (Word Pictures, Vol II, Luke, pg.175)

ἐρῶ is the usual liquid future of εἶπον which in turn appears as second aorist of λέγω "say."

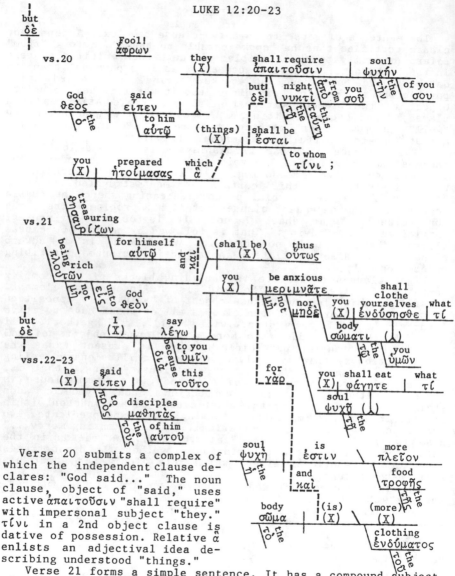

Verse 20 submits a complex of which the independent clause declares: "God said..." The noun clause, object of "said," uses active ἀπαιτοῦσιν "shall require" with impersonal subject "they." τίνι in a 2nd object clause is dative of possession. Relative ἃ enlists an adjectival idea describing understood "things."

Verse 21 forms a simple sentence. It has a compound subject of two attributive participles. They are presents intimating continuing practice of "treasuring" and "not enriching." αὐτῷ is dative of advantage "for himself." Frequently οὕτως appears as adverb but here it is predicate adjective "thus."

210

LUKE 12:22-23
(continued from page 210)

One independent and six dependent clauses make verses 22-23 complex sentence. "He said" is the independent idea. Of the first noun-object clause διὰ τοῦτο is adverbial explaining why "I say to you." Antecedent of τοῦτο is the preceding parable and its application. Negative μὴ with present imperative urges "stop being anxious." ἐνδύσησθε as well as φάγητε are deliberative subjunctives retained in these indirect questions. Comparative πλεῖον followed by ablative is a normal way of expressing comparison.

LUKE 12:24

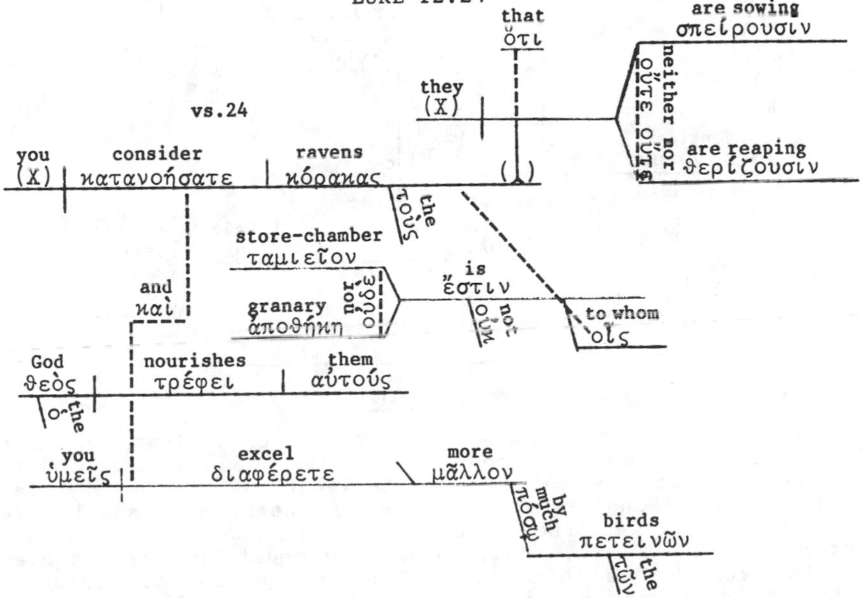

The sentence of 24 is compound-complex. Two subordinate clauses stem from the first clause. ὅτι inserts a noun idea, in apposition to κόρακας. It is a second object giving the content of that which is to be considered. The present tenses of its compound predicate "are sowing...are reaping" describe habits of ravens. Aorist κατανοήσατε literally is "hold your minds down to..." Possessive dative οἷς initiates an adjective clause describing "ravens."

"God nourishes them" is the second independent clause. τρέφει is present tense portraying God's constant care.

Subject of the third independent is emphatic ὑμεῖς. Present διαφέρετε represents a continuing state. πετεινῶν is ablative after comparative, "more, by much, than the birds." "Excel" is compounded from διά plus φέρω "to bear between," "to differ."

211

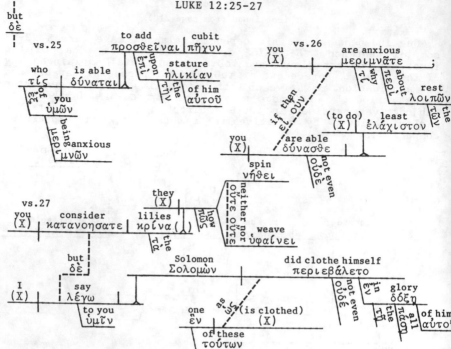

Verse 25 indulges a simple sentence. Its bare clause inquires "Who is able..?" The verb needs infinitive "to add" to complete the idea. ἡλικίαν may refer either to length of life or physical size of body. Scholars divide which is nothing unusual! Note that " τρίπηχυς was the Greek equivalent for a short, and τετράπηχυς for a tall, man...nobody can modify his height even to the extent of a third of the average quantum of stature." (Field as quoted in New Int. Com., Luke, pg.360) Circumstantial participle μεριμνῶν is either cause or manner.

The εἰ "if" clause in verse 26 inaugurates first class condition assumed to be true: "since you are not able even (to do) least, and you aren't." τί appears in independent clause as adverb. Present μεριμνᾶτε raises the point, "why go on being anxious about the rest?"

27 unveils a compound-complex sentence. "Consider the lilies" is independent. In apposition to "lilies" is compound noun clause, "they neither are spinning nor weaving." The adverb ὡς clause sets up a standard of comparison on which Solomon's royal wardrobe is compared. In the noun clause, object of "say" aorist περιεβάλετο is middle, "clothed himself."

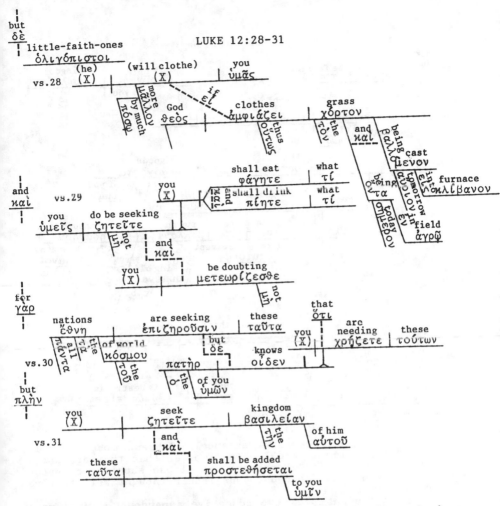

LUKE 12:28-31

The complex of 28 has a first class condition determined as true supporting independent "(he will clothe) you."

Two present imperatives with μὴ give 29 the compound flavor: "quit seeking" and "quit doubting." μετεωρίζω literally means "up in midair." Quit being tossed like a balloon out of control. There is also a noun-object clause, "what you shall eat..." It is a compound-complex sentence.

30 embodies a compound-complex. It has two independent and one dependent noun-object clause. The verbs are descriptive presents. Perfect οἶδεν has the force of a present.

Verse 31 is a compound of two clauses. Present imperative ζητεῖτε urges to <u>continue</u> to seek.

213

LUKE 12:32-34

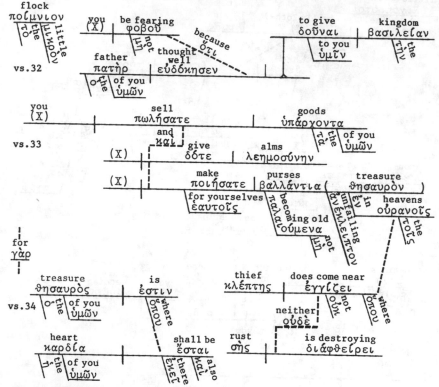

Verse 32 traces a complex sentence. Present φοβοῦ with μὴ exhorts: "stop being afraid," which implies that they are doing just that. So "quit it!" Dependent ὅτι clause supplies a reason why they should quit, "because your father thought well to give you the kingdom."

Three independent plus two adjective dependent clauses make verse 33 a compound-complex sentence. Three aorist imperatives express sharp, pointed, decisive, and fixed charges to "sell...give...make..." Doing the first two makes possible the third, that is, the making "purses not becoming old..." "Purses" are defined by apposition "treasure" located "in heavens" and characterized as "unfailing." Linear presents enliven dependent clauses, "does not come near" and "neither destroys." They are adjective clauses describing "the heavens."

Verse 34 might be considered part of the sentence of vs.33. It gives a reason why one should "sell...give...make." But the diagram treats it as a separate complex sentence. It still gives the reason why. It is more distinct when standing alone.

214

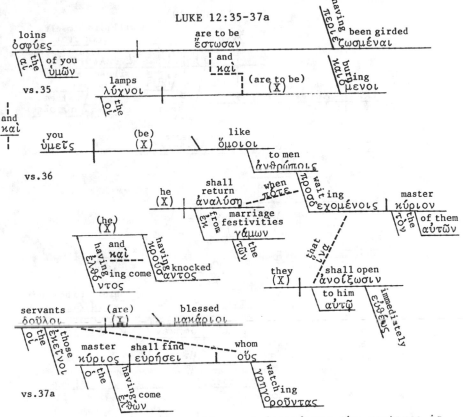

LUKE 12:35-37a

The two clauses of verse 35 are independent; the sentence is compound. Present imperative ἔστωσαν combines with perfect ptcp. περιεζωσμέναι to form periphrastic "be girded." It's an emphatic way of saying, "keep yourself constantly girded." Also the verb of the second clause is periphrastic. The participle is present, "Your lamps are to be kept burning."

Verse 36 entails a complex sentence. The use of pronoun ὑμεῖς "you" headlines the subject. ὅμοιοι is predicate adjective. Words of "likeness" use instrumental "men." That is described by present circumstantial participle "waiting." When appears in adverbial πότε clause. Plural γάμων = "wedding festivities." ἵνα inserts adverb result clause. Genitive absolute completes the sentence, "having come...having knocked."

37a occasions a two-clause complex sentence. Subject of the independent idea is δοῦλοι "bondslaves." They are described by adjective clause initiated by relative οὕς. They are further described by present participle "watching." ἐλθών is temporal circumstantial participle, "when he comes."

215

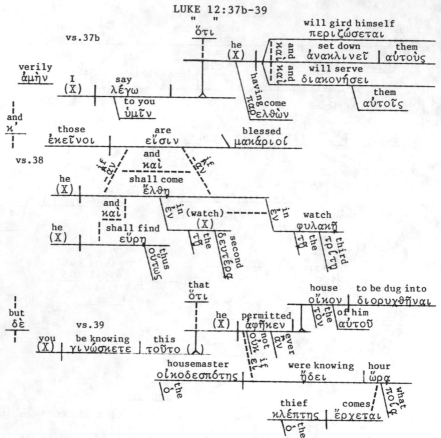

LUKE 12:37b-39

In 37b ὅτι sets up a noun clause with a compound predicate of three futures. The clause is object of independent "I say..." περιζώσεται is future middle.

As diagrammed verse 38 represents a three-clause complex. ἄν in the "if" clauses are what's left after crasis of καί ἐάν. It inserts 3rd class conditionals, undetermined with prospect of determination. Asyndeton which prevails between the two ἐν phrases does not debar an "or" being implied.

In the complex sentence of 39 present imperative γινώσκετε denotes "keep on knowing." In apposition to "this" is noun ὅτι clause "he did not ever permit..." This is supported by the 2nd class (εἰ) condition determined as unfulfilled, "if the master of the house were knowing and he wasn't..." ποία is qualitative interrogative pronoun used as adjective "what sort of." The final clause "the thief comes" is adjectival modifying "hour."

216

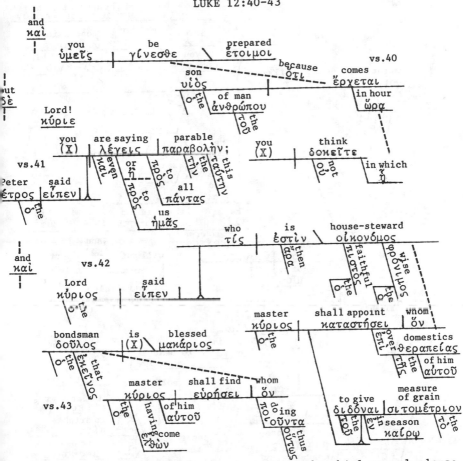

In verse 40. ὅτι brings in a dependent adverbial causal clause showing why "be prepared." ἥ injects adjective clause describing instrumental ὥρᾳ. Subject ὑμεῖς of independent clause is very emphatic. The sentence is complex.

41 is also complex. Noun clause, "Are you speaking this..." is object of verb of independent clause, "Peter said."

After independent "The Lord said" vs.42 has two dependent clauses. Object of "said," is "who is the faithful, the wise steward." Repetition of article gives sharp weight to each adjective. ὅν inserts adjective clause characterizing "steward." Present infinitive δίδοναι expresses purpose.

43 is complex. Relative ὅν inaugurates adjectival clause that describes δοῦλος "bondsman" subject of main idea.

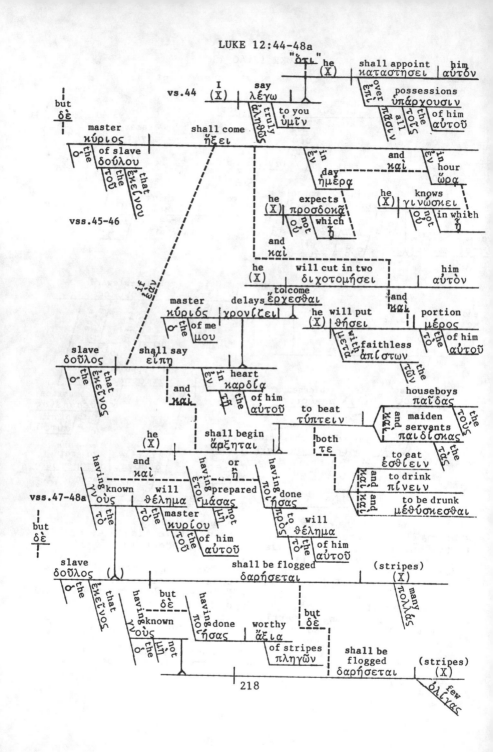

LUKE 12:44-48a

218

Verse 44 entails two clauses. An independent states, "I say." Adverb ἀληθῶς reinforces "say" by adding the idea of "really," "truly." Dative "to you" makes it even more intensely personal. Dependent noun ὅτι clause is object of "say." Prepositional ἐπὶ phrase functions adverbially indicating why "he shall appoint." Verses 45-46 have eight clauses. With three independent and five dependent it classifies as compound-complex. It opens with two ἐὰν 3rd class conditions undertermined but with prospect of being true: "if that slave shall say" and "shall begin..." Though he may not, he might! Object of "shall say" is noun clause, "my master delays to come." χρονίζει and object infinitive are both presents; the delay to come goes on and on. Adverbial ἐν καρδίᾳ appears to designate where the slave "might say," that is, "in his heart." Doubt begins within before it looms up outside. The second "if" clause shows what happens when inner doubt appears without: "if he shall begin to beat..." τύπτειν is present, "be beating." The beating is repeated; it becomes habitual. His repeated abuse of young "men and maidens" is accompanied by periods of carousings as his pattern of behaviour.

"If" that slave should do all this three consequences follow as voiced in the independent clauses. "The master shall come..," "he will cut him in two..." and he "will put his part (destiny) with the faithless." The future tenses are volitive. The ἐν phrases "in day" and "in hour" are adverbial reporting when the master will come. Moreover, "day" is described by relative adjective clause ᾗ "in which he does not expect." And "hour" is described by adjectival "in which he knows not." ἀπίστων may mean "unbelievers." But in this context "faithless" seems preferable. He was a servant whose trust in his master proved weak, faulty. He got to the point in which the master deposited him among those whose faith became less than trust.

47-48a embrace two independent clauses. It is compound in form. "That slave" is still the subject in view. However, the "slave" is defined by three attributive participles in apposition to the subject. γνοὺς is ingressive aorist, "having gotten to know." Its object is θέλημα, a result word hence "the thing willed." This slave got knowledge of that which his master willed. But his knowledge was countered by failure to respond, "not having prepared or done..." When he faced (πρὸς) that will he didn't do it. What happens to such a slave? "He shall be flogged "much"(πολλάς). He is held to greater accountability than the one of the second clause. This one did not do but he lacked knowledge, "not having known." Such lack placed him in the unenvious position of "having done (things) worthy of stripes." But because of that lack of knowledge, though punished, he "shall be flogged with few (stripes)."

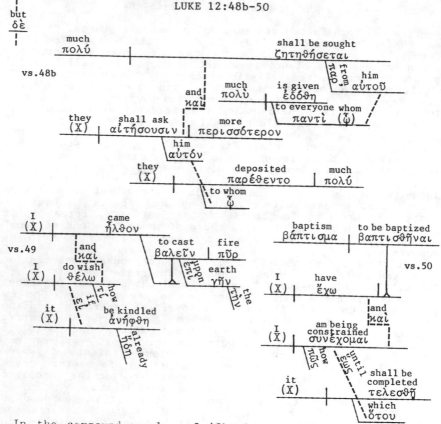

In the compound-complex of 48b the two dependent adjective clauses describe "him" who, in differing degrees, is held accountable. Ablative αὐτοῦ "from him" indicates source. αὐτόν is adverbial accusative, "as to him." παρέθεντο is aorist of a banking term, "deposit," "commit."

Verse 49 is interrogative, compound-complex in form. Aorist infinitive βαλεῖν is purpose. The εἰ clause is technically the protasis of 1st class conditional. Practically it may be translated as though a declarative ὅτι noun clause "that."

Verse 50 is compound-complex. Object of ἔχω "have" is aorist passive infinitive "to be baptized" and acc. of general reference βάπτισμα. Qualitative relative ὅτου "which by its very nature" implies "time." ἕως ushers in an adverbial clause.

On the facing page (221) the complex sentence of 51b answers the question posed in the complex of 51a. Present δοκεῖτε is the most subjective word for "think." It may be mean "suppose." οὐχὶ is the strongest possible negative.

220

LUKE 12:51-53

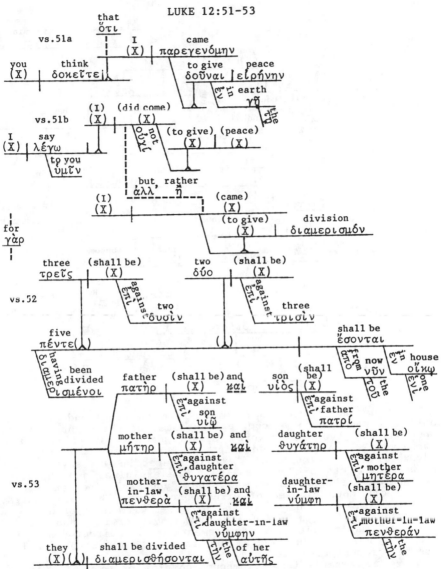

52 & 53 may be <u>one</u> sentence with its two independent clauses related by asyndeton. The iagram shows them as two complex sentences with all eight dependents being noun clauses in apposition to subjects "five" and "they." ἐπί in <u>this</u> context means "against."

221

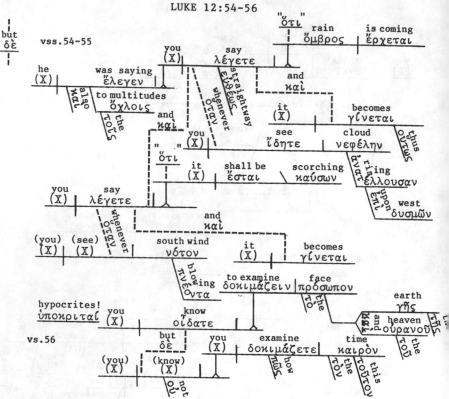

Eight dependent clauses stemming from one independent create out of verses 54-55 a complex sentence. Of the eight, six are noun-object; two are adverb, established by indefinite ὅταν "whenever." ἔλεγεν is descriptive imperfect, "was saying." Adverbial "to the multitudes" tells <u>where</u> "he was saying." Two clauses, objects of "were saying," are explained and supported by the temporal ὅταν insertions. <u>What</u> "you say" finds expression in the ὅτι noun clauses of direct quotation. The two clauses, "it becomes," are joined to and parallel with noun object "you say" clauses. The participles ἀνατέλλουσαν "rising" and πνέοντα "blowing" may be viewed as supplementary in indirect discourse. They may be! But the diagram has them as circumstantial. They are both descriptive presents.

Verse 57 exemplifies a compound-complex pattern. The second of the two independents is elliptical except for negative οὐ, "you know but (you do)not(know)." Object of οἴδατε is present infinitive phrase "to be examining." But object of implied "know" is noun clause, "how you examine this(present)time."

222

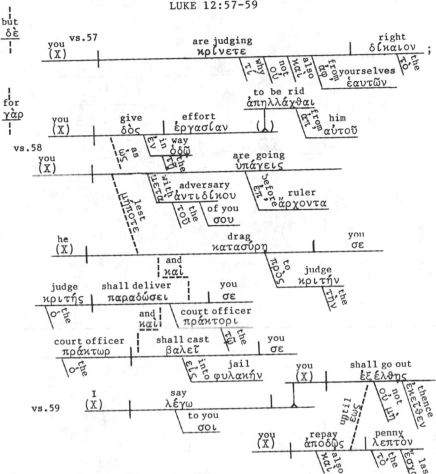

57 frames a simple sentence:"Why do you not also judge
the right?" ἀφ' ἐαυτῶν denotes that each person has moral
responsibility for judging "the right."

The complex sentence of verse 58 has three negative purpose
clauses heralded by μήποτε "lest." They reveal progressive steps
of deterioration in human conflicts. δός of the independent
clause is aorist. It insists on decisive immediate action:
"Give!" Perfect infinitive ἀπηλλάχθαι signifies to "get rid
permanently." By apposition it defines specifically what the
"effort" is. ὡς is temporal, "as you are going..."

Verse 59 adopts the complex form. Independent, "I say to you"
is pointed(σοι dative). Double negative οὐ μὴ is insistent. ἕως
brings in an adverbial dependent indicating when.

223

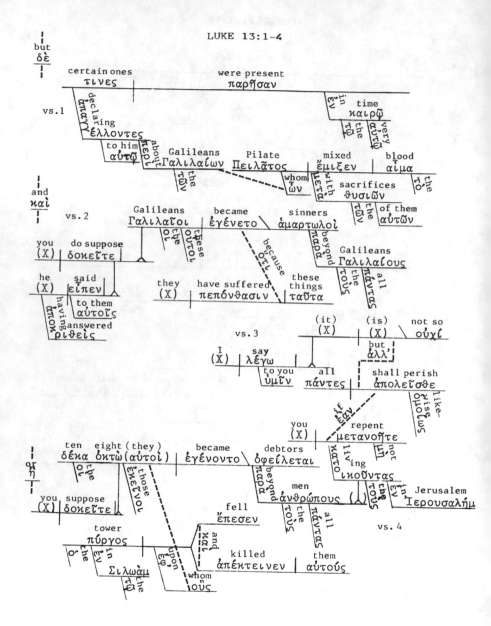

224

THE DIAGRAM OF LUKE 13:1-4

The two clauses in verse one are arranged as a complex sentence. Subject of the independent clause is indefinite pronoun τινες "certain ones." παρῆσαν is built by παρά "alongside" plus imperfect of εἰμί. Here it indicates, "certain ones came to." Present circumstantial participle ἀπαγγέλλοντες suggests purpose. These "certain ones" came to announce to Jesus about this stark tragedy imposed by the Roman governor on "the Galileans of whom Pilate mixed their blood with..." Aorist ἔμιξεν "mixed" points to the event without describing; its a narrative aorist. μετά with Genitive implies a sharing, a mingling, a mutual participation. It is appropriate to the idea in the verb "mixed." Relative ὧν introduces an adjective clause modifying "Galileans."

Verse two envelops a complex arrangement of four clauses. "Having answered he said to them" is the independent clause. ἀποκριθείς is temporal circumstantial participle of coincident action = "when he answered..." Object of "said" is interrogative noun clause, "Do you suppose..?" As object of "suppose" is noun clause, "these Galileans became..." ἁμαρτωλοί is predicate nominative pointing back to subject "Galileans." The expression παρά...Γαλιλαίους literally means, "alongside all the Galileans." It compares without using comparative forms. ὅτι signals a dependent causal clause: "because they have suffered these things?" πεπόνθασιν is perfect indicative active of πάσχω. It calls attention to the permanent results of that which they suffered.

Another complex sentence arises in verse three beginning with the solemn independent clause, "I say to you." Object of "say" is the noun clause, "(it is) not so!" Except for predicate "not so" the clause is entirely elliptical. οὐχί is strong negative: "No! Not so!" Heavy adversitive conjunction ἀλλ' "but" throws the next noun-object clause into contrast, "but all shall likewise perish..." This clause is supported and explained by 3rd class conditional (ἐάν) clause: "if you do not repent." The condition is undetermined but with some prospect of determination: "if you don't and you might not though the possibility is still open."

Verse four reveals another interrogative complex sentence. "Do you suppose..." is the independent element. For its object is the noun clause, "those eighteen...became..." Third personal pronoun αὐτοί "they" is in apposition to the subject δέκα ὀκτώ. And then it is described by adjective clause announced by ἐφ' οὓς "upon whom." Prepositional phrase "in Saloam" might be conceived as an adverbial idea modifying the verb "fell." The diagram prefers to view it as adjectival describing "tower."

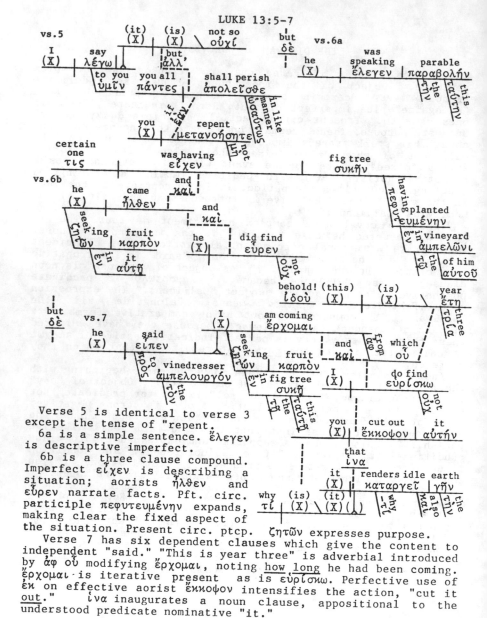

LUKE 13:5-7

Verse 5 is identical to verse 3
except the tense of "repent.
6a is a simple sentence. ἔλεγεν
is descriptive imperfect.
6b is a three clause compound.
Imperfect εἶχεν is describing a
situation; aorists ἦλθεν and
εὖρεν narrate facts. Pft. circ.
participle πεφυτευμένην expands,
making clear the fixed aspect of
the situation. Present circ. ptcp.
ζητῶν expresses purpose.
    Verse 7 has six dependent clauses which give the content to
independent "said." "This is year three" is adverbial introduced
by ἀφ οὗ modifying ἔρχομαι, noting how long he had been coming.
ἔρχομαι is iterative present as is εὑρίσκω. Perfective use of
ἐκ on effective aorist ἔκκοφον intensifies the action, "cut it
out." ἵνα inaugurates a noun clause, appositional to the
understood predicate nominative "it."

226

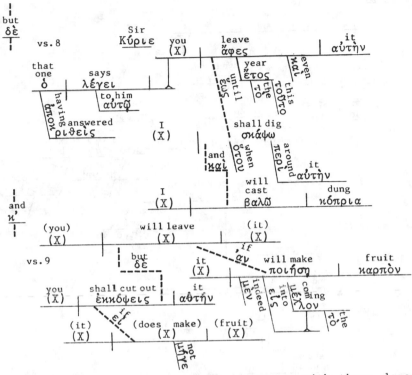

Verse 8 structures a complex sentence with three dependent clauses. Subject of the independent "says" is demonstrative use of the article ὁ = "that one." Verb in the noun clause, object of "says," is aorist imperative ἄφες "permit" expressing concerned urgency. ἔτος is accusative, extent of time. ἕως "until" brings forward two adverbial clauses of time. σκάψω and βαλῶ are volitive futures. κόπρια is accusative plural.

Verse nine combines four clauses in a compound-complex arrangement. Two of the clauses are entirely (or almost) elliptical, their content being implied from the context. As practical as a diagram is for picturing the grammatical logic of a sentence such ellipses reveal some limitations of a diagram. Good grammar is good logic. But to communicate emotion of speaker or writer is difficult if not impossible. Verse nine is an example. Tone of voice, shrug of shoulder, gestures are hard to include in the logical flow of grammatical structures. ἄν (ἐάν) introduces a third class condition, undetermined but with prospect of determination. εἰ brings in first class, determined as fact. Conditions deal with assumtions not realities.

227

LUKE 13:10-13

Verse 10 is a simple sentence with periphrastic imperfect ἦν
διδάσκων "was teaching." Two "in" phrases tell where and where.
Verse 11 is compound. The second clause has two periphrastic
imperfects. Present circumstantial participle ἔχουσα pictures
the woman's plight. ἔτη is accusative, extent of time. εἰς
phrase "unto the whole" means "perpetually twisted."
12-13 is compound-complex. The one dependent is noun clause
object of εἶπεν. Perfect "have been released"(ἀπολέλυσαι)notes
the entrenched nature of her affliction. Of the three
independents two have compound predicates. When Jesus made note
of her (aorist circumstantial ἰδὼν) he "called and said."
Second, he offered a visible clue of what he was about to do;
"he placed his hands on her." The third independent clause gives
two results: "She was straightened." ἐδόξαζεν is inchoative
imperfect, "she began glorifying..."

228

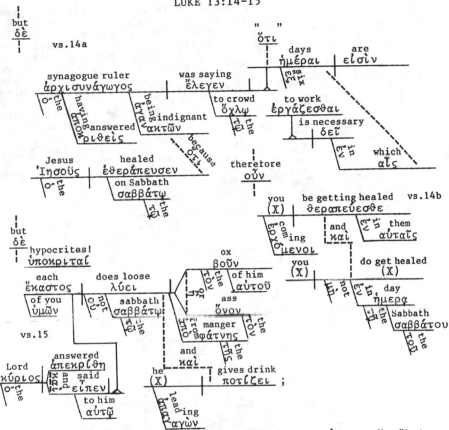

Verse 14a displays a complex sentence. ἀγανακτῶν "being indignant" is present circumstantial participle presenting a reason why the ruler "was saying." The ὅτι clause that stems off the participle is adverbial of cause indicating why he became indignant. Another ὅτι introduces noun clause object of "was saying." ἐν αἷς, as diagrammed, is adjective describing "days." It might be conceived of as adverb indicating when.

14b represents a two-clause compound. All verbal actions are linear presents, "when coming...be getting healed" and "stop getting healed..."

Verse six is interrogative, complex in form. Object of the independent "answered and said" is noun clause, "each of you looses does he not?" οὐ in a question expects "yes" for answer. Key issue in both 14a and 15 is not that "Jesus healed" or "each looses." Rather it is when they so acted.

229

LUKE 13:16-17

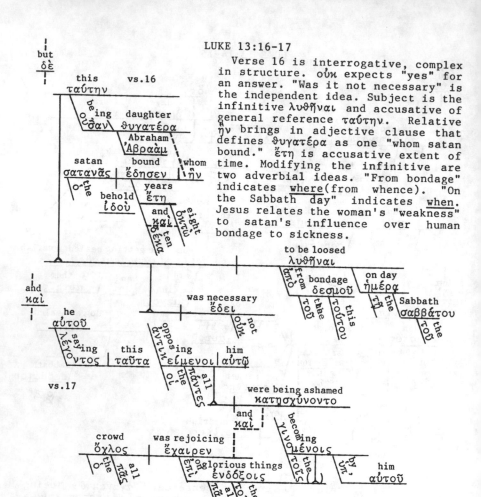

Verse 16 is interrogative, complex in structure. οὐκ expects "yes" for an answer. "Was it not necessary" is the independent idea. Subject is the infinitive λυθῆναι and accusative of general reference ταύτην. Relative ἣν brings in adjective clause that defines θυγατέρα as one "whom satan bound." ἔτη is accusative extent of time. Modifying the infinitive are two adverbial ideas. "From bondage" indicates where(from whence). "On the Sabbath day" indicates when. Jesus relates the woman's "weakness" to satan's influence over human bondage to sickness.

Verse 17 begins with genitive absolute, "he saying this." Two independent clauses follow making it a compound sentence. Each verb and verbal is linear action enlivening the total picture. The two main verbs are imperfects. κατῃσχύνοντο pictures the reaction of "the ones opposing" him. It is descriptive and distributive. They all "were keeping on being ashamed" as well as each single one of them. On the other hand, the crowd ἔχαιρεν "kept on rejoicing." Attributive participles "the ones opposing" and the "ones becoming" are linear presents. The first is descriptive; the other is distributive, each single separate "glorious thing" which kept on "becoming" (appearing) by him." ὑπ' with ablative expresses direct agent.

230

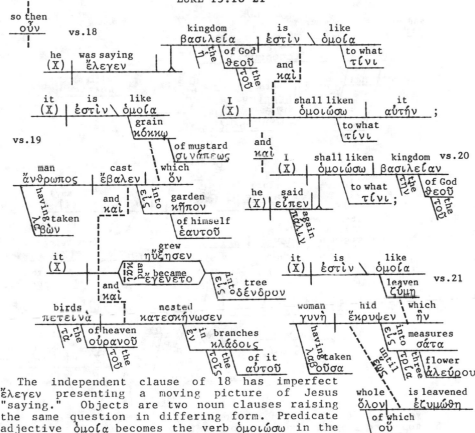

The independent clause of 18 has imperfect
ἔλεγεν presenting a moving picture of Jesus
"saying." Objects are two noun clauses raising
the same question in differing form. Predicate
adjective ὁμοία becomes the verb ὁμοιώσω in the
2nd clause. τίνι is interrogative.

The complex sentence of verse 19 answers the questions of 18.
κόκκῳ is associative-instrumental with words of likeness. Genitive σινάπεως specifies the kind of grain. Relative ὅν initiates
three adjective clauses describing "grain." It was one "which a
man cast..," "it grew and became..," and "the birds nested..."
The verbs are narrative aorists stating what happened without description. Yet each reports a distinct action in the total.

Verse 20 involves another interrogative complex sentence. It
repeats the question of 18 (πάλιν) "again."

The complex of 21 answers the question of 20: "It is like..."
Relative ἥν brings in adjective clause describing instrumental
ζύμη "leaven." σάτα is accusative extent of space. ἕως asserts an
adverb clause of time, "until."

231

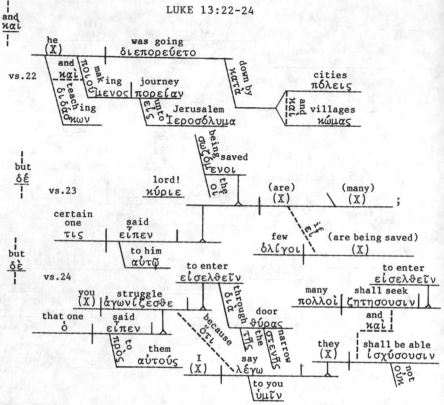

Verse 22 reveals a simple sentence: "he was going." Imperfect διεπορεύετο lingers over the movement to Jerusalem. Two present circumstantial participles add descriptive power. Distributive κατὰ and accusative means "city by city...village by village."

Verse 23 exemplifies the failure of the mind to follow grammatical stereotypes. It is difficult to diagram emotions. This sentence, as diagrammed, is highly elliptical. εἰ is treated as protasis of 1st class condition. The apodosis, noun clause object of "said," asks, "(are) the ones being saved (many)?"

24 is a five-clause complex sentence. Demonstrative use of article ὁ is subject of independent, "that one said..." Noun clause, "struggle to enter" is object of εἶπεν. Present imperative ἀγωνίζεσθε urges ongoing, persistent effort. Aorist infinitive εἰσελθεῖν reflects point of entrance. ὅτι brings in emphatic adverb causal clause, "I say to you..." What he says appears in two noun clauses objects of "say."

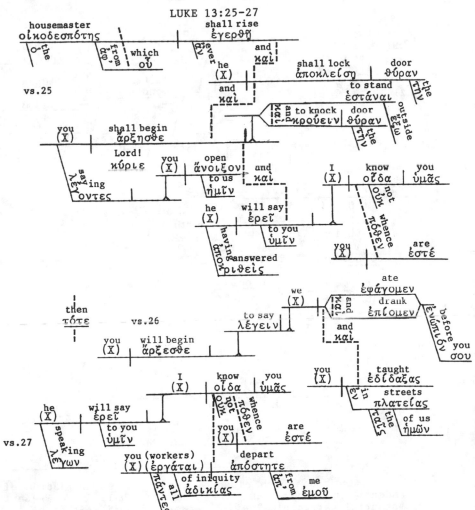

LUKE 13:25-27

Four independent and three dependent clauses label the sentence of verse 25 as compound-complex. πόθεν is adverbial "whence." Two noun clauses objects of infinitive λέγειν designate 26 as complex. ἄρξεσθε is future indicative; λέγειν is present. Verse 27 contains four clauses so arranged as to be complex. Asyndeton prevails between the two noun-object clauses. πόθεν involves an adverb clause indicating where. ἀπόστητε literally means "stand off." ἀπ' with ablative ἐμοῦ "from me" is adverbial phrase indicating from where they should "depart."

233

LUKE 13:28-30

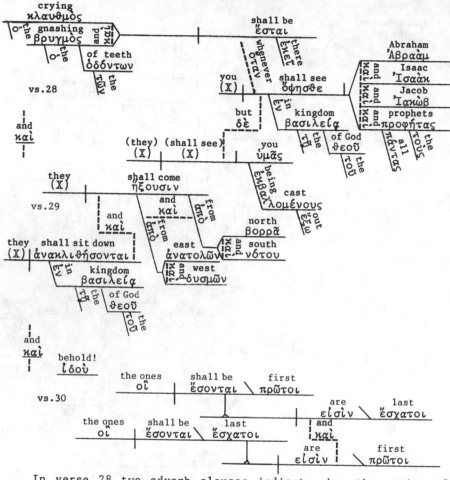

In verse 28 two adverb clauses indicate when the action of independent "the crying and the gnashing shall be." Present circumstantial participle "being cast out" describes the action; ἐν presents "Abraham, Isaac, etc." at rest "in the kingdom."

Verse 29 embraces two independent clauses hence is compound. All three prepositional phrases are adverb indicating where. The compound verb ἀνακλιθήσονται literally means "to recline up" as at a meal.

As diagrammed verse 30 offers a compound-complex sentence. Subjects are the relative οἵ clauses, "the ones who shall be first(last)..." The ones that are "last" now shall be the ones who shall be first.

234

LUKE 13:31-33

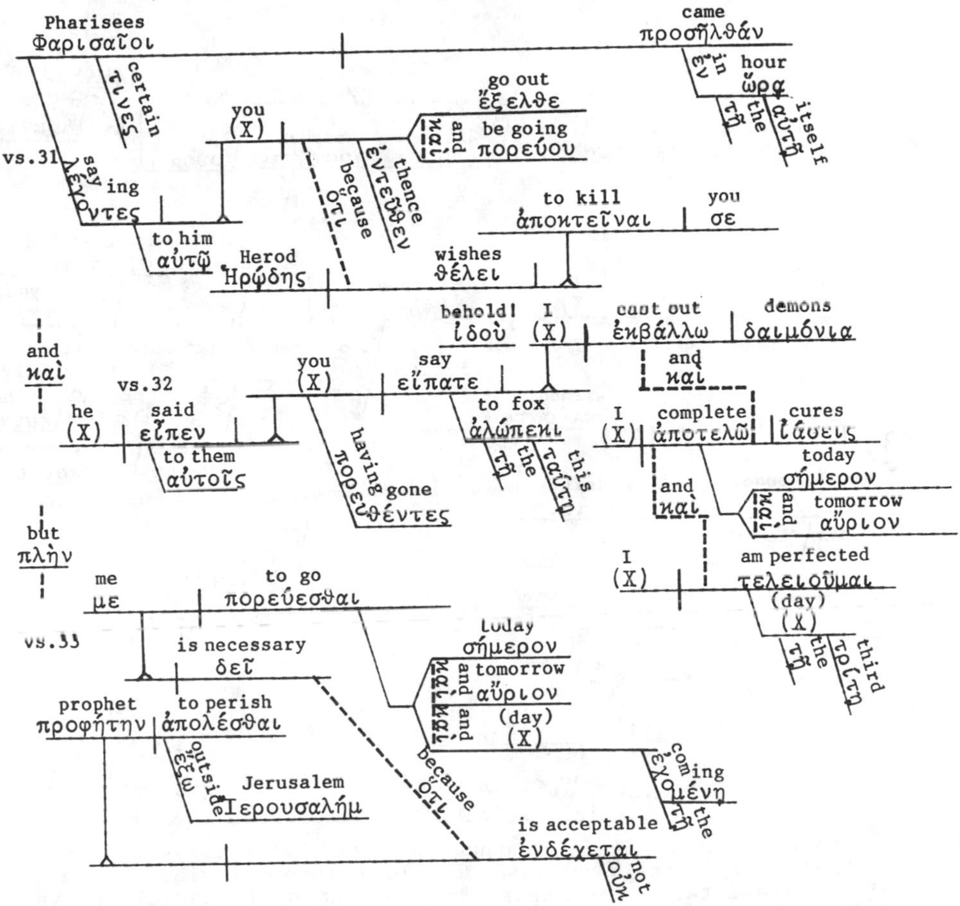

Pharisees / Φαρισαῖοι — certain / τινες — you (X) — say / λέγοντες — to him / αὐτῷ — Herod / Ἡρῴδης — go out / ἔξελθε — and be going / πορεύου — thence / ἐντεῦθεν — because / ὅτι — came / προσῆλθάν — in the hour itself / ἐν τῇ ὥρᾳ αὐτῇ — wishes / θέλει — to kill / ἀποκτεῖναι — you / σε

vs.31

and / καὶ — he (X) — said / εἶπεν — to them / αὐτοῖς — you (X) — say / εἴπατε — behold! / ἰδοὺ — I (X) — cast out / ἐκβάλλω — demons / δαιμόνια — and / καὶ — having gone / πορευθέντες — to fox / ἀλώπεκι — this / ταύτῃ — I (X) — complete / ἀποτελῶ — cures / ἰάσεις — and / καὶ — today / σήμερον — tomorrow / αὔριον — I (X) — am perfected / τελειοῦμαι — (day) / (X)

vs.32

but / πλὴν — me / με — to go / πορεύεσθαι — is necessary / δεῖ — prophet / προφήτην — to perish / ἀπολέσθαι — outside / ἔξω — Jerusalem / Ἱερουσαλήμ — today / σήμερον — tomorrow / αὔριον — (day) / (X) — because / ὅτι — third / τῇ τρίτῃ — is acceptable / ἐνδέχεται — not / οὐκ — coming / ἐχομένη

vs.33

The complex of 31 has its two dependent clauses rooted in the circumstantial participle λέγοντες. Noun-object clause has compound predicate, aorist imperative "go out" coupled to present "be going." The warning was: "go" and "keep going." In an adverbial clause ὅτι inserts the reason why.

The complex of 32 has three noun clauses, objects of εἴπατε itself a noun-object clause. τελειοῦμαι is prophetic present, a present looking to the future, "I am going to be perfected."

Verse 33 contains only two clauses but has two infinitive phrases each of which is subject of its clause. ὅτι brings in an adverb clause of cause. ἔξω is adverb phrase indicating where. με and προφήτην are accusatives of general reference. They designate the action involved in the infinitives.

235

LUKE 13:34-35

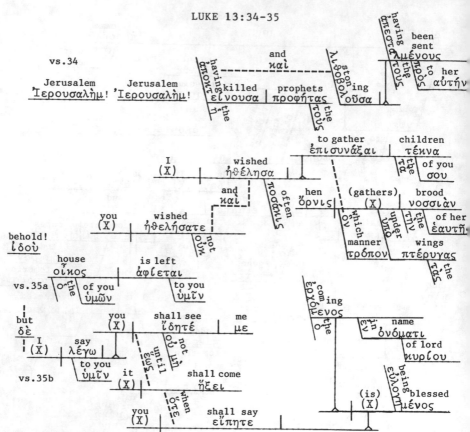

The sentence of 34 is compound-complex. It begins with strong double interjection Ἰερουσαλήμ to which three attributive participles are attached by apposition. Object of ἠθέλησα is aorist infinitive phrase, "to gather our children." Prepositional phrase "in which manner" introduces adverb clause stating the manner in which he would like to have gathered. Accusative τρόπον has been attracted from locative to accusative, an instance of antecedent being attracted into the relative clause.

Verse 35a represents a simple sentence. Linear action of present ἀφίεται = "is being left." It's a process going on.

35b is complex. "I say to you" is the independent idea. Noun clause, object of "say" has strong double negative οὐ μή. Two temporal adverb clauses define when: "until" and "when." The final dependent is a noun clause. By virtue of its definite article ἐρχόμενος is subject. εὐλογημένος supplements implied "is" to form periphrastic "is being blessed."

236

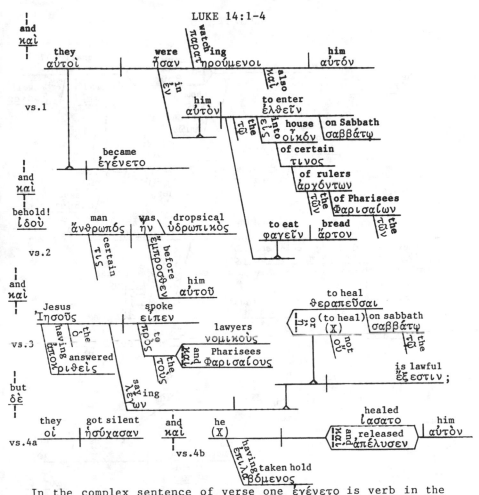

LUKE 14:1-4

In the complex sentence of verse one ἐγένετο is verb in the independent clause. Noun clause "they were watching" is subject. Periphrastic imperfect emphasizes continuous "watching." ἐν τῷ and infinitive is temporal, "when he entered." εἰς phrase = where. σαββάτῳ = when. Infinitive φαγεῖν expresses purpose.

Simple sentence (vs.2) has predicate adjective ὑδρωπικὸς, a medical term used only here in the New Testament.

Independent "Jesus spoke" of verse 3 is joined by noun clause "to heal on the sabbath or not..." to create a complex sentence. The clause is object of circumstantial participle λέγων.

Verse 4 has two simple sentences. Demonstrative use of οἱ is subject of ingressive aorist ἡσύχασαν. Three aorists of 4b give snapshots of distinct acts: "hold," "healed," "sent off."

237

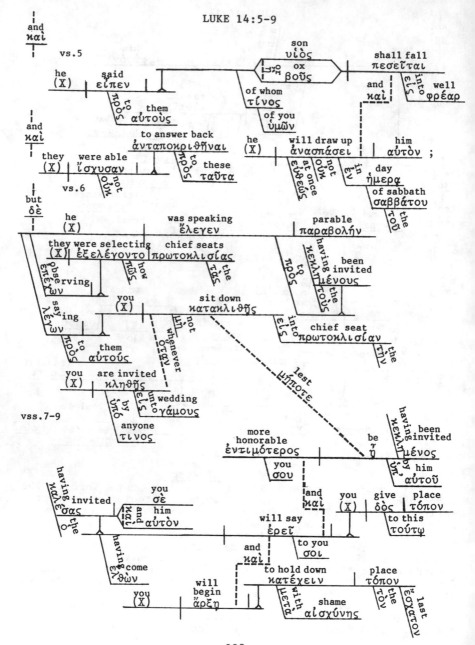

238

Verse five produces a complex sentence of three clauses. "He said to them" is the independent idea. Two noun clauses follow, objects of "said" of the main clause. πεσεῖται "shall fall" has a compound subject, "son or ox." The εἰς phrase is adverbial in dicating <u>where</u>. In the 2nd object clause οὐκ involves a question expecting "yes" for answer, "will he not draw him up." ἐν phrase is adverbial indicating <u>when</u>.

In form verse six is simple. ἴσχυσαν is ingressive aorist, "they got not able..." In other words, "they became unable." The ἀντί on compound infinitive gives the sense of "back" or "in return" to the basic idea of "answer" in ἀποκρίνομαι. They were stymied, jolted, unable to return answer.

Verses 7-9 create a long involved sentence, complex in pattern. ἔλεγεν of the independent clause is descriptive imperfect. Present active circumstantial participle ἐπέχων is compounded of ἐπί + ἔχω. It literally means "hold (the mind) upon." Serving as object is the noun clause, "how they were selecting..." In the diagram πῶς is adverb; in practical use it is like declarative ὅτι "that." The middle voice of imperfect ἐξελέγοντο is to be noted, "they were selecting <u>for themselves</u>." Its imperfect is distributive <u>and</u> descriptive; each "was selecting." A vivid scene! The perfect attributive participle κεκλημένους suggests "the ones having been invited" had had invitations for quite a while.

Another circumstantial participle λέγων introduces what Jesus said as he "observed" their self-centered grabbing of seats. The prohibition, "don't sit down" reflects negative μὴ with aorist, "do not even begin to sit..." This noun-object clause is supported by indefinite adverbial ὅταν "whenever you are invited." Plural γάμους = "weddings" or "wedding festivities." μήποτε brings in negative purpose clause, "lest (one) more honorable than you be invited..." Comparative ἐντιμότερος with ablative σου, in the diagram, appears as subject of subjunctive perfect periphrastic ᾖ κεκλημένος "may have been invited." ὑπό with ablative αὐτοῦ expresses direct agent as in ὑπό τινες in the ὅταν clause above. To the negative purpose idea is added a kindred purpose idea. Subject is attributive aorist participial phrase, "the one having invited you and him." Liquid future ἐρεῖ has for its object noun clause, "give place to this (one)." Aorist δός is peremptory, decisive, admitting of no debate.

Yet another negative purpose clause appears: "you will begin to occupy..." Aorist subjunctive ἄρξῃ looks to the <u>point</u> of beginning. Present infinitive pictures the continuos "holding down" (sitting) in "the last place." Literally κατέχειν means "to hold down." The manner (adverb) with which he must be holding down the "last place" is seen in the μετὰ expression, "with shame."

LUKE 14:10-11

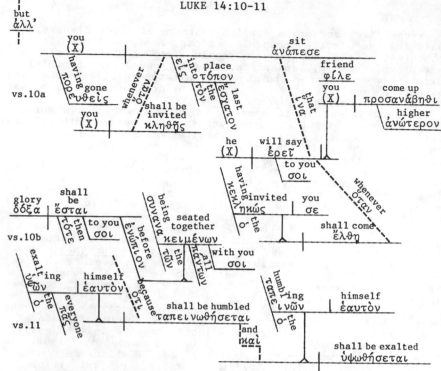

Four dependent clauses and one independent structure 10a as complex. Aorist imperative exhorts "you sit." ὅταν introduces indefinite temporal adverb clause "whenever you be invited." ἵνα brings in adverb clause of purpose, "that he will say..." Object of "will say" is noun clause, "friend, come up higher." The purpose is explained and sustained by another ὅταν temporal adverbial clause. Perfect tense κεκληκώς suggests that the invitation had been given and was still in effect.

Verse 10b displays a simple sentence. "Glory shall be" is the basic idea. τότε expresses time and conclusion. σοι is dative of possession. ἐνώπιον inserts an adverbial phrase indicating where. A second σοι is associative-instrumental.

Causal ὅτι begins the compound sentence of verse 11. In thought it relates to verses 7-10. It states a principle embedded in the nature of things. Subjects in both clauses are attributive participials. ὑψῶν and ταπεινῶν are presents indicating ongoing patterns of behaviour. Results of such regular behaviour are expressed in point action futures, "shall be humbled" and "shall be exalted." Habitual actions become a part of basic character. At some given point they reap a harvest of open display, that is, "they shall be..."

240

LUKE 14:12-14

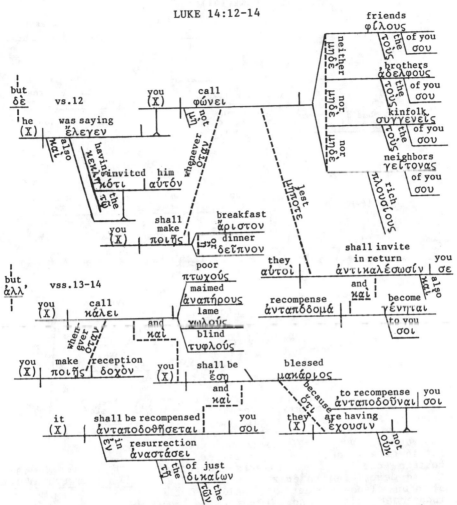

The sentence of verse 12 is complex. Object of independent ἔλεγεν is noun clause having four substantives each with its own article. That makes each group named stand out with sharp distinction. μή with present φώνει means "quit inviting," "do not have the habit of inviting." ὅταν displays temporal adverb clause. μήποτε introduces two negative purpose clauses.

Three independent clauses plus dependent temporal ὅταν adverb and causal ὅτι clause structure the sentence of 13-14 as compound-complex. Four substantives, objects of κάλει "call" by being anarthrous, speak of the nature of the items involved.

241

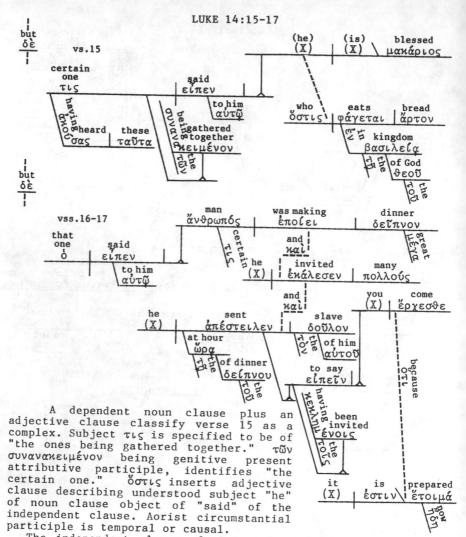

A dependent noun clause plus an adjective clause classify verse 15 as a complex. Subject τις is specified to be of "the ones being gathered together." τῶν συνανακειμένον being genitive present attributive participle, identifies "the certain one." ὅστις inserts adjective clause describing understood subject "he" of noun clause object of "said" of the independent clause. Aorist circumstantial participle is temporal or causal.

The independent clause of the complex of 16-17 states, "he said to him." Subject is demonstrative use of ὁ = "that one." Three noun clauses, objects of main verb "said," announce: "man was making dinner," "he invited many," and "he sent slave..." Imperfect ἐποίει "was making" is descriptive. Narrative aorists ἐκάλεσεν and ἀπέστειλεν report without describing. εἰπεῖν is aorist infinitve of purpose. It has as its object noun clause, "you come!" ἔρχεσθε is present imperative, "be coming," "be on your way." The reason is given in ὅτι causal clause, "because it is already prepared."

242

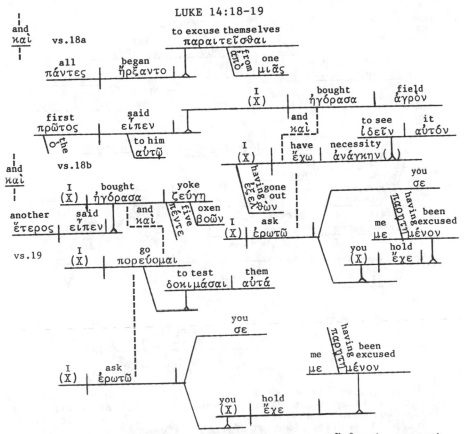

Verse 18a produces a simple sentence. παραιτεῖσθαι is present middle epexegetic infinitive. It explains the content of what "all began." ἀπὸ with ablative cardinal μιᾶς suggests "from one opinion." The source of their excuses sprang from "one origin."

Both 18b and 19 are complex. They are of "one source" and they follow identical sentence patterns. "The first said" is independent to which three noun-object clauses are attached: "I bought..." "I have need..." and "I ask..." Aorist infinitive ἰδεῖν is appositional to ἀνάγκην. In both sentences ἐρωτῶ "ask" has double objects: σε "you" and clause "you hold me having been excused." Perfect participle παρῃτημένον might be viewed as circumstantial modifying object με but the diagram treats it as supplementing ἔχε with με as adverbial accusative. The perfect tense indicates that the excuse was determined, permanent, fixed, unalterable. In verse 19 aorist infinitive δοκιμάσαι expresses purpose.

243

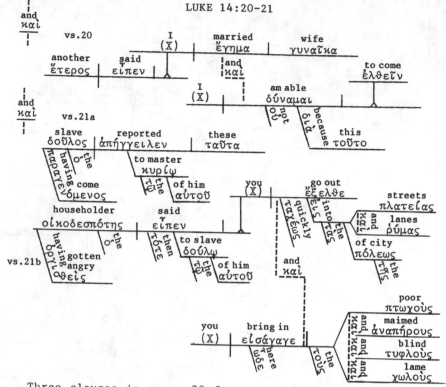

Three clauses in verse 20 form a complex sentence. ἕτερος, subject of independent clause, means "another" of a different kind. Two noun clauses, objects of "said," declare quite bluntly, "I married (aorist ἔγημα) wife and am not (strong negative) able to come." The διά phrase is adverbial giving the reason why.

Verse 21a is shaped as a simple sentence. Temporal circumstantial participle in conjunction with aorist predicate verb says, "when he came the slave reported..." He divulged without describing.

21b is a complex of three clauses. The -της ending indicates that compound οἰκοδεσπότης is an agent word "householder." Aorist circumstantial participle, "having gotten angry" does not exhibit irate, explosive, impulsive anger but rather the wrath that responds on settled principle of the reaction of purity to wrong. The two noun-object clauses each has aorist imperative verb: "go out" and "bring in." These are sharp, pointed, peremptory commands. The one article τοὺς lumps all people into one general group even though they represent differing kinds of underprivileged. τὰς with "streets and lanes" is similar in use.

244

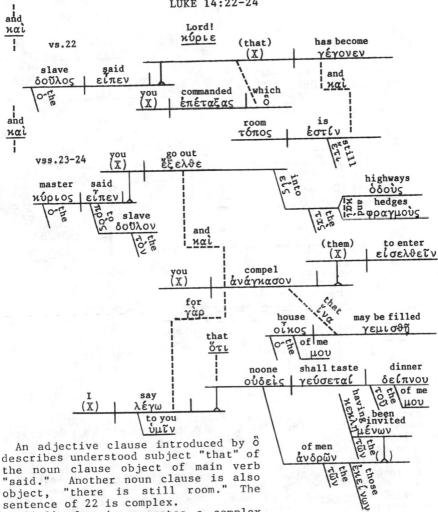

An adjective clause introduced by ὅ describes understood subject "that" of the noun clause object of main verb "said." Another noun clause is also object, "there is still room." The sentence of 22 is complex.

23-24 also incorporates a complex sentence. "Go out" and "compel" represent aorist imperatives. They reflect urgency! Object of ἀνάγκασον is infinitive εἰσελθεῖν with implied accusative of general reference "them." ἵνα and subjunctive "may be filled" is adverb purpose clause. As diagrammed γάρ brings in another object clause. It has ὅτι noun clause as its object in indirect discourse. Genitive δείπνου is object after verb of sensation "taste." Perfect attributive participle κεκλημένων is appositional to ἀνδρῶν "those men."

245

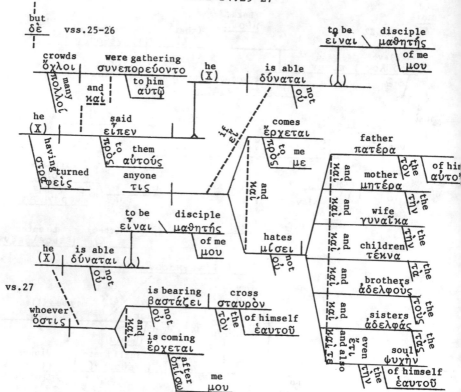

Two independent plus two dependent clauses constitute a compound-complex sentence of 25-26. "Many crowds" as subject of descriptive imperfect συνεπορεύοντο pictures diverse crowds converging on Jesus. This independent is followed by, "He, having turned, said..." εἰ, the protasis of the first class conditional adverb clause, supports the apodosis noun clause, object of "said" of the independent. "If anyone comes and does not hate" is _assumed_ to be true. The inevitable conclusion is: "he is not able..." Infinitive εἶναι is epexegetic defining "is not able." Seven objects of μίσει cover the range of closest human relationships. Loyalty to Christ must surpass the dearest human ties.

Verse 27 is a two-clause complex sentence. Indefinite relative begins adjective clause describing subject "he." οὐ in the dependent goes only with βαστάζει in the compound predicate. Both presents stress linear action:"...is _not_ regularly bearing his cross and is coming after me..."

246

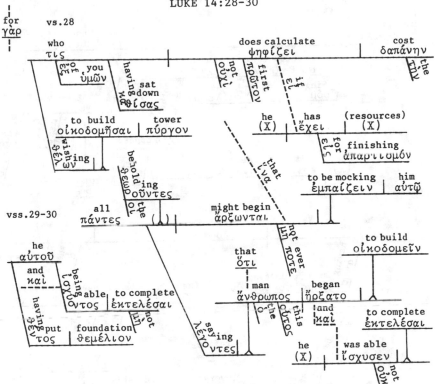

Turn to the diagram of 13:9, page 227; also 13:23, page 232 for diagram of 13:23. What is said there applies here at 14:28 and 29-30. As diagrammed the εἰ "if" clause of vs.28 is protasis of 1st class condition. Yet this strains the logic of grammar. In reality the "if" has the force of ὅτι = "that" and demands that something be supplied such as "to see if (whether)..." If it is protasis of 1st class then the apodosis is implied: the conditional becomes elliptical. The sentence as diagrammed is complex of two clauses.

As diagrammed, verses 29-30 do not form a complete sentence for there is no independent clause. ἵνα is a purpose clause implying something such as, "he does this..." or it may require a repetition of the independent clause of verse 28, "who of you does not...in order that all the ones beholding might not ever begin..." If such be true, the sentence becomes complex with ἵνα being purpose and ὅτι introducing two noun clauses objects of participle λέγοντες. αὐτοῦ with aorist and present participles θέντος and ἰσχύοντος is genitive absolute.

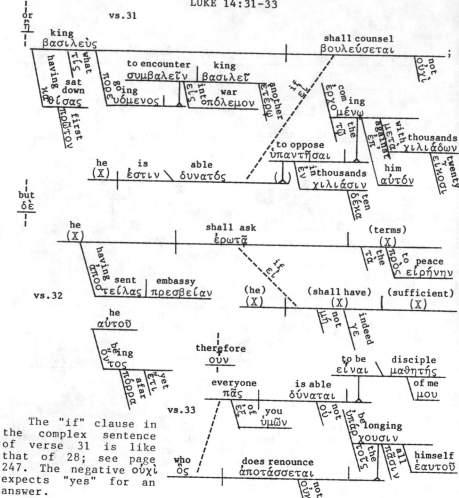

The "if" clause in the complex sentence of verse 31 is like that of 28; see page 247. The negative οὐχί expects "yes" for an answer.

Verse 32 forms another complex sentence. It has a first class conditional with the "if" similar to that of verse 28, page 247. Not only is the apodosis implied, the protasis itself is almost entirely elliptical.

Another complex appears in 33. Relative ὅς clause brings in an adjective clause limiting subject (πᾶς) of the independent. Object of ἀποτάσσεται is present attributive participial phrase "all the ones belonging..." Though ὑπάρχουσιν is a verbal it may be rendered "possessions."

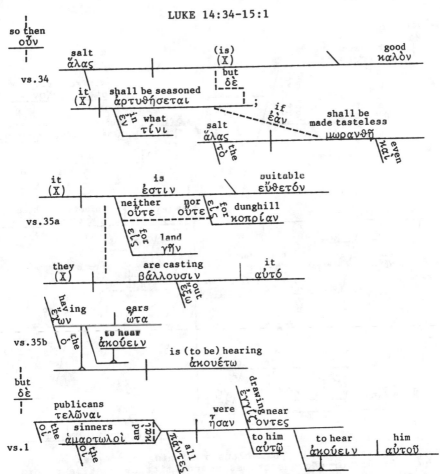

Two independent clauses plus a 3rd class condition determine verse 34 to be compound-complex. ἐάν with subjunctive is the condition of expectancy. One might become "insipid" as a disciple.

Verse 35a is compound with asyndeton joining the two clauses. Predicate adjective εὔθετόν is compounded from εὖ and τίθημι. βάλλουσιν is gnomic present; this the universal practice.

35b is simple in form. ἀκουέτω is present imperative. It's an admonition that "the one having ears "be hearing.""

The simple sentence of 15:1 has periphrastic present "were drawing near" describing with unusual vividness the gathering of "the publicans and the scribes." Repeated οἱ distinguishes two particular groups. Infinitive ἀκούειν expresses purpose. αὐτοῦ is genitive after verb of the senses.

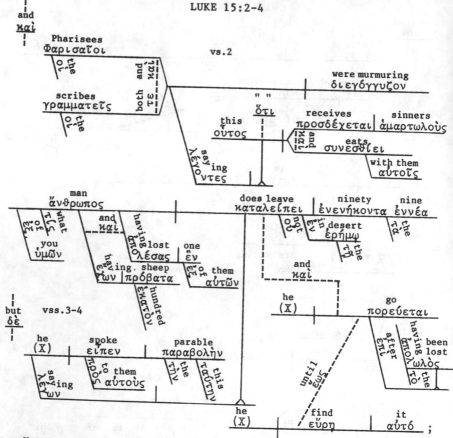

Verse two contains two clauses forming a complex sentence. Imperfect διεγόγγυζον describes an unremitting hostile carping. The repetition of article οἱ sets off both "<u>the</u> Pharisees" and "<u>the</u> scribes" as distinct groups. ὅτι symbolizes direct quotation marks introducing a noun clause, direct object of present circumstantial participle

In the complex sentence of verse 3-4 the independent clause informs, "he spoke(εἶπεν)this parable..." In apposition to "parable" are two noun clauses. They pose a negative question with οὐ that expects "yes" for an answer. Interrogative τίς coupled with ἐξ ὑμῶν isolates each man as one who would act as here described. Both verbs in the noun clauses are gnomic presents. They represent universal behaviour. The context suggests that ἐπὶ expresses the <u>goal</u> hence, "<u>after</u> the one lost." ἕως ushers in a temporal adverb clause, "until..."

250

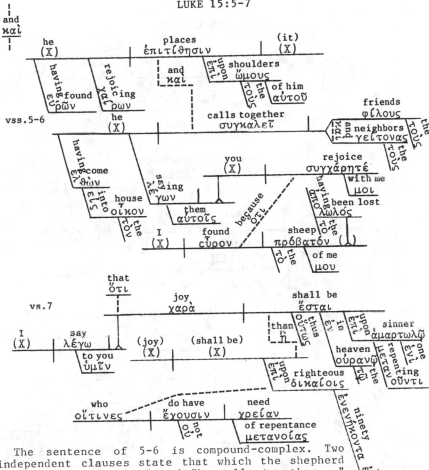

The sentence of 5-6 is compound-complex. Two independent clauses state that which the shepherd does:"he places it..." and "he calls together..." Both clauses display participles depicting the circumstances environing the verbs of their clauses: "having found," and "rejoicing;" then, "having come into" and "saying." Object of "saying" is the noun clause which urges, "you rejoice..." To that is appended an adverb causal clause giving a reason for rejoicing. Attributive participle ἀπολωλός is in apposition to "sheep" further defining the lostness. Its perfect tense suggests how desperate was the lost condition.

After independent, "I say to you" in the complex of verse 7 three dependent clauses appear. Two are noun clauses objects of λέγω. Qualitative relative οἵτινες means, "who by their nature." It inserts an adjective clause modifying "righteous."

251

LUKE 15:8-10

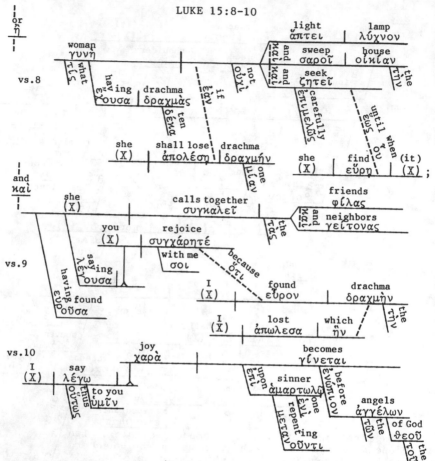

Verse 8 is complex. ἐὰν instigates 3rd class conditional undetermined but with prospect. ἕως is adverb temporal clause, "until she find..." οὐχὶ expects "yes" as answer. Predicate in main clause is compound of three vivid presents.

Verse 9 is a four-clause complex. The independent affirms: "She calls together..." Circ. part. "saying" suggests why, that is, "that she might say." Noun-object clause states what she exhorted: "rejoice with me." ὅτι brings in a causal adverb clause. ἦν is adjectival describing "drachma."

The complex of verse 10 has one noun clause object of λέγω of the independent idea. Circ. part. μετανοοῦντι is present tense intimating that repenting is a process as much as an event.

252

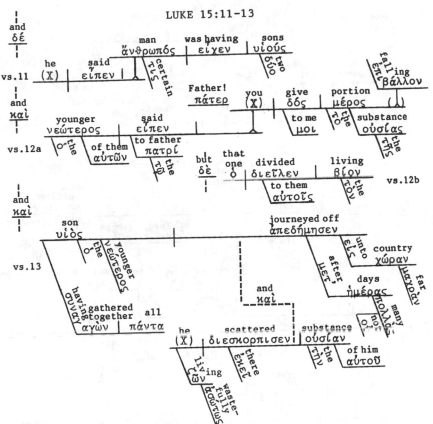

The sentence of verse 11 is complex. "A certain man was having two sons" is a noun clause object of "said." Imperfect εἶχεν signifies continuing responsibility. The father did more than "have" sons, they were his constant care.

12a is also complex. It too has noun clause, object of "said" of independent clause. Aorist imper. δός is demanding; it suggests impatience. οὐσία derives from present participle of εἰμί = being. Present participle ἐπιβάλλον is attributive, "the falling to me portion."

12b reflects a simple sentence. διεῖλεν is second aorist of διαιρέω "cut asunder" "divide." βίος is life in the sense of "livihood" rather than the essence, the life principle.

Verse 13 is a two-clause compound sentence. The son "journeyed" and "scattered." The verbs "journey" and "scatter" are compounded with σύν and διά. The prepositions are perfective. They intensify the action. Note contrast between "gathered together" and "scattered thoroughly."

253

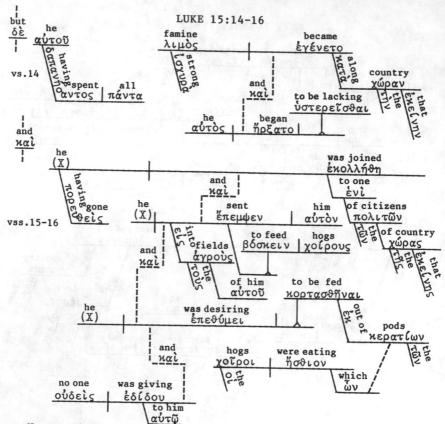

LUKE 15:14-16

Verse 14 develops a compound sentence. Genitive absolute
begins the sentence, unrelated grammatically. Two independent
clauses form the basic sentence. 2nd aorist ἐγένετο = "became"
may be translated, "came to pass" or "arose." The root of κατὰ
is "down." With accusative, "down along." In this context,
"throughout." Use of αὐτός as subject intensifies "he."
Present ὑστερεῖσθαι advances the idea of ever increasing lack.

Five independent clauses and one dependent make a complex
of 15-16. κολλάω = "glued." He was desperately "stuck" with
the "citizen." The 2nd clause shows how he was forced into an
odious job: present βόσκειν is continuous action. χοίρους
without article indicates the nature of the job. The 3rd
clause uses descriptive imperfect ἐπεθύμει with infinitive
phrase to envision desperate hunger. Relative ὧν inserts
adjectival clause descriptive of "pods." They were the regular
(imperfect ἤσθιον) diet of hogs. In the final clause imperfect
continues the description of his lonely, isolation from human
fellowship. "No one was giving to him."

254

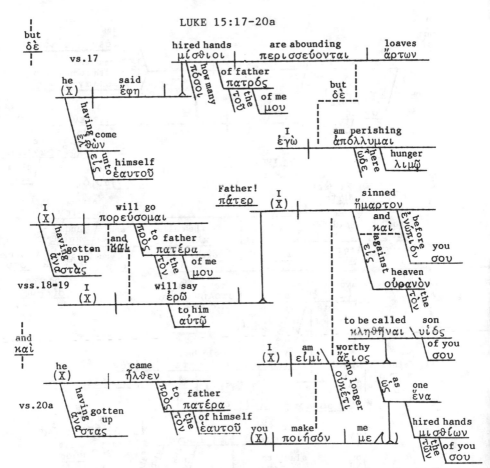

Two dependent noun clauses serve as objects of ἔφη "said," of the independent in the complex sentence of verse 17. Present περισσεύονται etches a moving sketch of the father's "hired hands" with full stomachs amidst bursting graneries. In contrast the present ἀπόλλυμαι charts his ever worsening condition of perishing by starvation.

18-19 embraces a 5-clause compound-complex. Aorist ἀναστὰς and future indicative "I will go" record his resolution. After "I will say" the sentence terminates in three noun clauses, objects of ἐρῶ. The ὡς phrase is objective complement after με.

Verse 20a forms a simple sentence. It reports that he executed his resolution:"Having gotten up he came to his father."

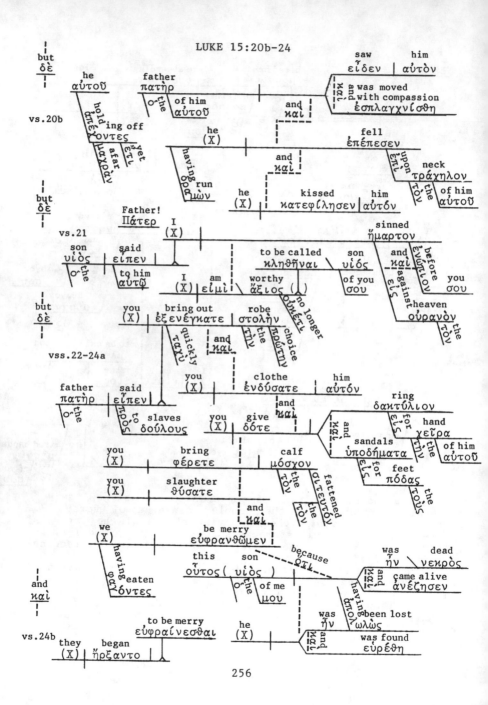

256

Genitive absolute plus three independent clauses form the structure of a compound sentence in verse 20b. The absolute displays, "he (the son) holding off (being) yet afar..." Then the clauses declare (1)how the father felt ("moved with compassion") (2)that is followed immediately by two things which the father did, ("...fell upon his neck") and ("kissed him.") All the verbs are narrative aorists. The actions are immediate, pointed, factual, human. Aorist δραμὼν expresses a temporal circumstance surrounding the verb "fell." The clauses reflect the feelings of the father. ἐσπλαγχνίσθη is formed from σπλάγχνον "inward parts," seat of feelings. κατεφιλήσεν is compounded of κατά and φιλέω affectionate love. Here κατά becomes adverbial intensifying the action. He really loved, kissing him again and again.

Verse 21 reveals a complex sentence. It has two noun clauses, objects of "said" of the independent clause. The son attempts to state his prepared speech of repentance. Aorist ἥμαρτον gathers the whole fiasco and shows it as a single factual point. εἰς and ἐνώπιον phrases are adverbial: sin is "against" the moral universe not to mention "before you" the person immediately offended. The next noun clause states the shattered filial relationship which sin disrupted. Though forgiven, received, welcomed his actual state of affairs is, "I am no longer worthy..." The infinitive phrase "to be called your son" is appositional defining more specifically his lack of worth.

Manuscripts differ as to whether the father allowed the son to finish his speech. Aleph, B and D include, "Make me as one of your hired hands." But Nestle's text shows the father interrupting. Turning to the household slaves the father orders immediate preparations for joyful festivities. In rapid fire succession six clauses portray the excited joy of the father. Two descriptive presents injected among four aorists flash before the reader the emotional upheavel of the happy father. "Bring out the first(choice)robe...clothe him...give ring...sandals...be bearing the calf, the fattened one...slaughter, and "let's be merry..." The sentence ascends to a dramatic climax with two adverbial ὅτι clauses giving the underlying reasons why "be merry." Both of these clauses have compound predicates each of which pictures a positive issue of a past negative predicament: "he was dead...became alive." Preposition ἀνα compounded with ζάω has the force of "again," "he lived again." "He was having been lost and was found." Perfect participle ἀπολωλὼς is supplementary. It combines with imperfect ἦν to form a periphrastic pluperfect, "had been lost." The fixed permanancy of the pluperfect is dispelled by the aoristic point at which he "was found." It may be that he was "no longer worthy" but from the father's point of view he "was found" because he had "come alive again."

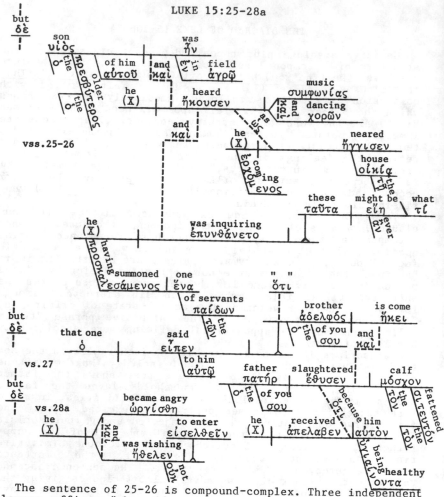

vss.25-26

vs.27

vs.28a

The sentence of 25-26 is compound-complex. Three independent clauses affirm: "the older son was in the field," that "he heard music and dancing," and "he was inquiring..." The ὡς clause tells when he heard, "as he neared the house." Imperfect ἐπυνθάνετο describes his rising ire. Noun clause "whatever these might be" is object of ἐπυνθάνετο, "was inquiring."

Demonstrative article ὁ "that one" is subject of independent clause of the complex of verse 27. Two noun clauses, objects of "said," and ὅτι causal clause complete the sentence. Present ἥκει has force of a perfect. ὑγιαίνοντα is circumstantial.

28a is simple sentence in form with compound predicate. The aorist ὠργίσθη is ingressive; ἤθελεν imperfect with negative.

258

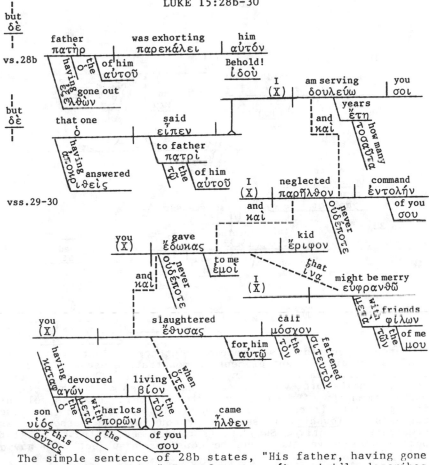

The simple sentence of 28b states, "His father, having gone out, was exhorting him." Imperfect παρεκάλει vividly describes the concerned father reiterating his appeal.

29-30 structure a complex sentence. Demonstrative ὁ is subject of independent, "that one said." Four noun clauses serve as objects of "said." δουλεύω is progressive present. It reaches into the past and describes continuous and repeated action through the years, "I am serving..." The verbs of the next three clauses are appropriately point action aorists:"I never neglected," you never gave," "you slaughtered." ἵνα involves an adverb purpose clause. ὅτε inaugurates an adverb temporal idea. οὗτος is <u>very</u> emphatic, even sarcastic. It gains additional force by appositional attributive participle "the one having devoured." We can feel the sneer "with harlots!"

LUKE 15:31-32

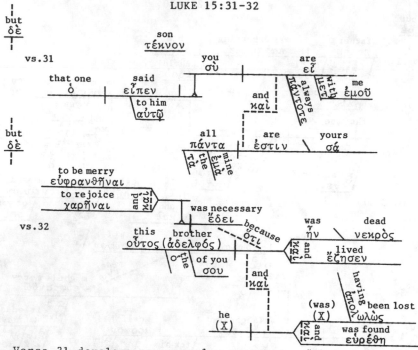

Verse 31 develops as a complex sentence. "That one said to him" is the independent element. Demonstrative use of article ὁ is subject. Vocative τέκνον is from τίκτω "beget," "bring forth." Unlike υἱός which accents privileges of sonship τέκνον marks community of nature. By virtue of being used as well as its position (first) σύ is emphatic. μετά with genitive suggests fellowship. Possessive pronoun of 2nd person σά is predicate nominative. Subject, as diagrammed, is πάντα but 1st person possessive ἐμά might be considered subject with πάντα modifying it.

Verse 32 proposes a three-clause complex. Imperfect ἔδει reflects continuing logical necessity. The subject of ἔδει is a compound of two aorist infinitives, "to be merry" and "to rejoice." ὅτι advances two adverb clauses of cause. In apposition to subject "this" is "your brother" which plays on the family relationship as an appeal: "your brother." Both noun-object clauses have compound predicates each of which contrasts the prodigal's "dead" and "lost" condition versus his present "live" and "found" state. ἔζησεν is ingressive aorist, "he became alive." Perfect participle ἀπολωλὼς supplements understood ἦν "was" to form pluperfect, "had been lost." In contrast to such permanent lostness he is now "found." εὑρέθη marks the fact and point at which he "was found."

260

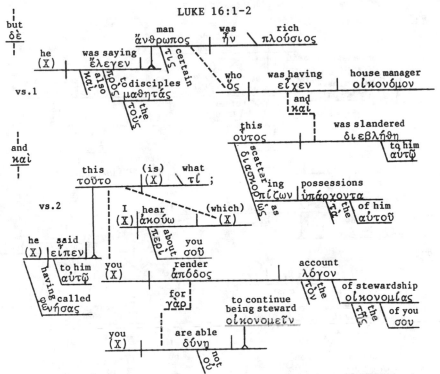

Verse one forms a complex sentence. The καί of independent "he <u>also</u> was saying" hints that this parable is "to the disciples" in contrast to the preceding to Pharisees. ὅς injects an adjective clause describing "man" of the noun-object clause. εἶχεν is imperfect indicating this "steward" had occupied this place over an extended period. Demonstrative οὗτος is emphatic pointer, "this one." διεβλήθη aorist compounded from διά + βάλλω = throw through, to slander. ὡς with circumstantial participle "is a fine Greek idiom for giving the alleged ground of a charge."(ATR, Word Pictures, Vol.II,pg.215) Participles are verbal adjectives. In the diagrams they appear under substantives they modify. But it must not be forgotten that they are also "loosely attached" to the main verb. Diagrams fail to display this double connection. Participle ὑπαρχοντα here is used as substantive.

Verse two is also complex but with four dependent clauses. "This is what" is noun clause object of "said." Implied "which" introduces adjective clause modifying "this." Asyndeton joins a 2nd object clause: "render the account..." A 3rd object clause gives consequences of his alledged abuse; "you are not able to continue (present) being steward."

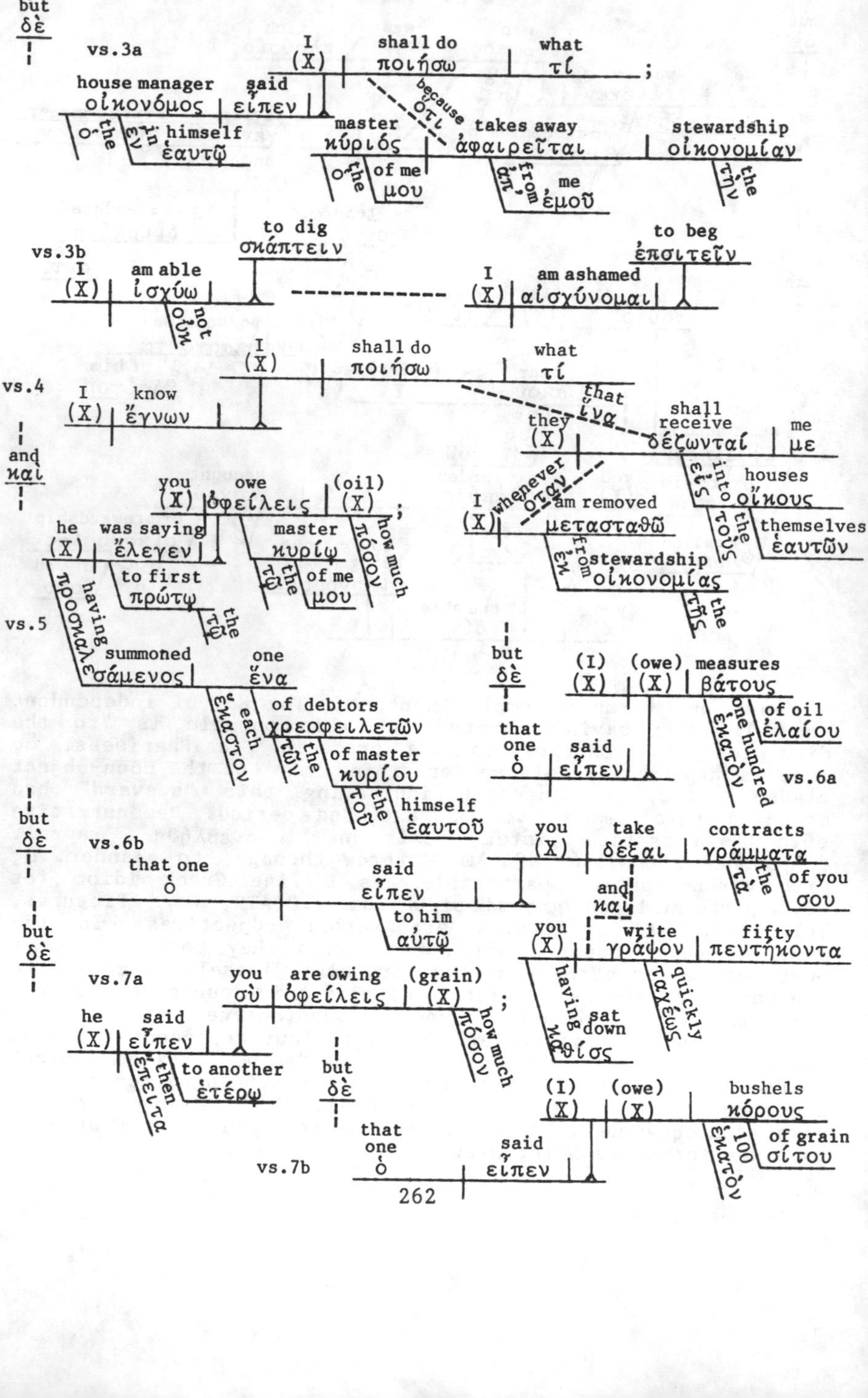

LUKE 16:3-7

but
δὲ

vs.3a

house manager | said | I (X) | shall do ποιήσω | what τί ;
οἰκονόμος | εἶπεν
the o- ἐν himself ἐαυτῷ

because ὅτι | master κύριός | takes away ἀφαιρεῖται | stewardship οἰκονομίαν
the o- of me μου | from ἀπ' me ἐμοῦ | the τὴν

vs.3b

to dig σκάπτειν
I (X) | am able ἰσχύω — — — — — I (X) | am ashamed αἰσχύνομαι | to beg ἐπαιτεῖν
not οὐκ

vs.4

I (X) | shall do ποιήσω | what τί
I (X) | know ἔγνων

and καί

that ἵνα
they (X) | shall receive δέξωνται | me με
whenever ὅταν | into εἰς houses οἴκους
I (X) | am removed μετασταθῶ | the τοὺς themselves ἑαυτῶν
from ἐκ stewardship οἰκονομίας | the τῆς

vs.5

you (X) | owe ὀφείλεις | (oil) (X) ;
he was saying (X) | ἔλεγεν | master κυρίῳ | how much πόσον
to first πρώτῳ | the τῷ of me μου | the τὸ

having summoned προσκαλεσάμενος | one ἕνα
each ἑνὸς | of debtors χρεοφειλετῶν | of master κυρίου
the τῶν | the τοῦ himself ἑαυτοῦ

but δὲ
that one ὁ | said εἶπεν | (I) (X) | (owe) (X) | measures βάτους
one hundred ἑκατόν | of oil ἐλαίου

vs.6a

vs.6b

that one ὁ | said εἶπεν | you (X) | take δέξαι | contracts γράμματα
to him αὐτῷ | the τὰ of you σου
and καί

but δὲ

vs.7a

he said (X) | εἶπεν | you σύ | are owing ὀφείλεις | (X) ;
then ἔπειτα | to another ἑτέρῳ | but δὲ | how much πόσον
you (X) | write γράφον | fifty πεντήκοντα
having sat down καθίσας | quickly ταχέως

vs.7b

that one ὁ | said εἶπεν | (I) (X) | (owe) (X) | bushels κόρους
100 ἑκατόν | of grain σίτου

262

THE DIAGRAM OF LUKE 16:3-7

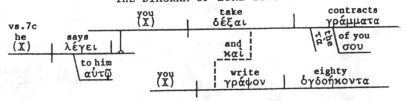

Of the nine sentences of 16:3-7 one (3b) is compound. The others are various arrangements of complex. The independent clause of 3a says, "The house manager said." Adverb phrase "in himself" displays where; a pensive reflection. That on which he meditated is a question, noun clause, object of "said," "What shall I do?" A reason why it was a problem is in ὅτι causal clause. ἀφαιρεῖται is futuristic present, "is going to take away..."

The sentence of 3b might be viewed as two simple sentences but more probably a compound, as diagrammed, with asyndeton. The two infinitives, "to dig" and "to beg" are presents. As infinitives they indicate that the steward was envisioning the action rather than experiencing it. Had he used participles, "digging, I am not able" or "begging, I am ashamed" he would be reporting that which even then he was actually experiencing.

In verse 4 the ἔγνων is hard to translate. The dawning of a plan bursts with explosive effect: "I got it!" Noun clause "what I shall do" is object of ἔγνων. The ἵνα is purpose clause. ὅταν brings in a temporal idea. Aorist passive μετασταθῶ looks to the point of removal.

The remaining six complex sentences use ἔλεγεν or εἶπεν as verb in their independent clause followed by a noun clause as object. ἔλεγεν describes how the steward implements his plan. The noun clause is a question, "How much oil do you owe...?" The circumstantial participle, "having summoned" depicts a real experience, not a hypothetical situation as in the infinitives of 3b. "Each one of the debtors" shows this is a pattern followed with every debtor.

The answer of the debtor appears in 6a. Demonstrative use of article ὁ is emphatic subject, "That one said..." (see also 6b and 7b) βάτους is accusative; it measures the amount.

In the context of 6b "letters" γράμματα means "written documents." Accusative πεντήκοντα "fifty" in reality is an adjective as ἑκατὸν "one hundred" just above in 6a. In the diagram it appears as a substantive, object of "write."

In the noun-object clause of verse 7a οὺ is emphatic: "How much are you owing?" It singles him out from the others.

The noun-object clause in 7b has both subject and verb implied. In such rapid speech ellipsis is not only normal but quite potent. It heightens the emotional effect.

Verse 7c follows the pattern of 6b. It uses familiar "he" as subject instead of the more dramatic demonstrative use of the article "that one."

LUKE 16:8-9

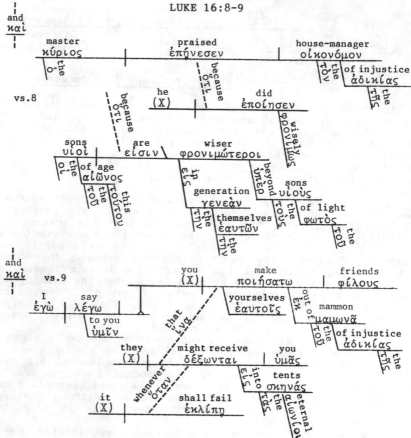

Verse 8 conceivably could contain two sentences. If so the second ὅτι would introduce the second sentence as simple. It is best to view the sentence as a three-clause complex. The first ὅτι brings in a causal clause giving the reason why "the master praised..." The second ὅτι doesn't relate so much to the independent clause as to "the moral of the whole parable." The genitive is the case of specification; it characterizes that which it modifies. ἀδικίας is the house manager characterized by "injustice." He's this kind, not that kind!

Verse 9 is complex having three dependent clauses. Noun clause, "make friends," is object of "say." ἵνα initiates a purpose clause stating why "make friends." ὅταν brings in an indefinite temporal clause, "whenever it shall fail." The verbs in dependent clauses are aorists.

264

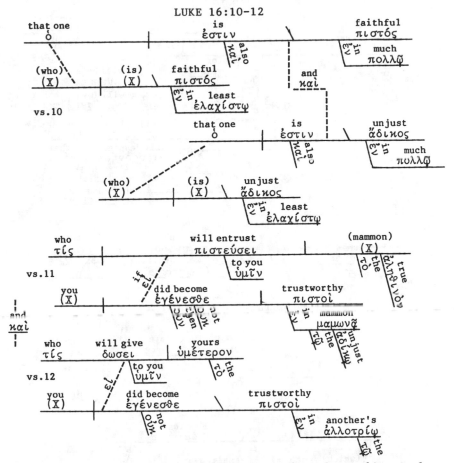

LUKE 16:10-12

Verse 10 has two independent and two dependent adjectival clauses. It is compound-complex! Demonstrative ὁ is subject in the independents. The adjective clauses are elliptical in subjects(who)and verbs(is). The idea of the clauses is seen in predicate adjectives, "faithful" and "unjust."

Verse 11 is a two-clause complex. εἰ inserts a first class condition assumed as true. πιστεύω = "faith" but here has the idea of "trust." Faith is more than belief. It involves trust as an essential element. Note adjective πιστοὶ is more than "faithful." It signifies "trustworthy."

The sentence of 12 has the same structure as verse 11, a two-clause complex with first class condition supporting independent, "who will give yours to you?"

265

LUKE 16:13-16

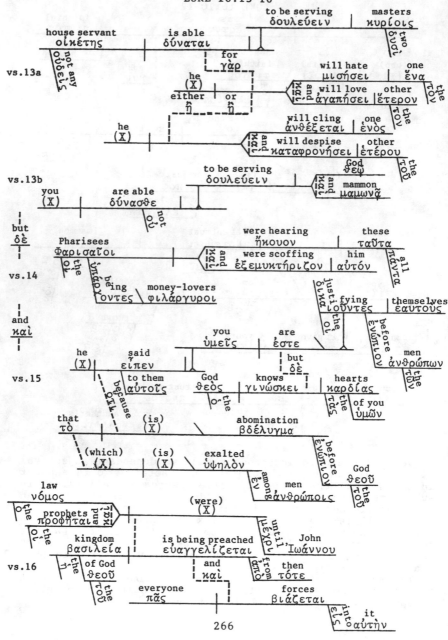

266

THE DIAGRAM OF LUKE 16:13-16

The sentence of 13a is a three-clause compound. Words that end in -της express agent; οἰκέτης is a "house-servant." The present infinitive dramatizes his <u>continuous</u> inability to be serving two masters. γὰρ is a coordinating conjunction which adds a clause making clear the impossibility of being loyal to two masters. That is joined by ἢ...ἢ "either...or" which brings in a clause confirming the impossiblity. ἀγαπάω is a moral choice of the intellect. It's opposite is "hate." In compound verbs of the final clause ἀντί "to hold oneself against face to face" contrasts with κατά "think down on someone."

Verse 13b displays a simple sentence. The "two masters" alluded to in 13a are clearly identified in vs.13b; "God and mammon." Dative is the case of personal interest and appears as object of δουλεύειν "serve" as slave. One will be the slave's <u>real</u> master; the other a counterfeit.

Though it employs a compound predicate the sentence of 14 is simple in structure. Modifying "Pharisees" circumstantial participle ὑπάρχοντες = "existing" or "being." The participle is <u>causal</u>. φιλάργυροι in its root means "lovers of silver." Both verbs are descriptive imperfects. They paint vivid pictures of ongoing and repeated "hearing" and "mocking."

The sentence of verse 15 has five clauses. Only one is an independent so the sentence is complex. "He said to them" is the independent. Two noun clauses are objects of "said." The presence of ὑμεῖς "you" as subject makes it very emphatic. The attributive present participle δικαιοῦντες "the ones justifying" is predicate nominative. <u>Where</u> they "justify" is in adverbial phrase "before men." The second noun-object clause contrasts with the first: "God knows your hearts."

The ὅτι clause, in spite of its position, is best taken as adverbial of cause modifying "said." It expresses why "he said," not why "God knows hearts..!" In the diagram, definite article τὸ appears as demonstrative. However, conceivably it might be adjectival modifying understood "thing." It is described by an adjective clause, "(which is) exalted..." "Before God" and "among men," are contrasting adverbial phrases, indicating <u>where</u>.

Verse 16 forms a three-clause compound sentence. Asyndeton connects the first two clauses. The third is joined by conjunction καί "and." The articles with each member of the compound subject "<u>the law</u>" and "<u>the prophets</u>" make each stand out as distinct. Present εὐαγγελίζεται "is being preached" is both descriptive and distributive. The preaching is both continuous and widespread.

βιάζεται is linear action present, direct middle voice: "everyone is forcing <u>himself</u>..."

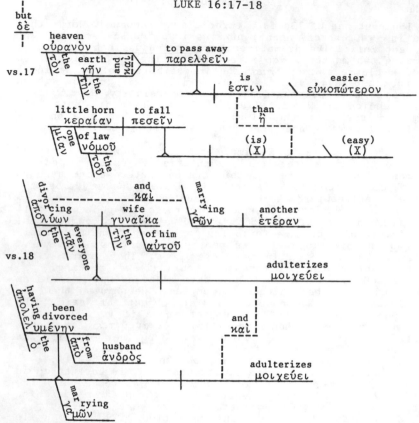

Verse 17 shows a two-clause compound sentence. Except for subject the second clause is elliptical. Subjects in both clauses are infinitives each with accusative of general reference. When an infinitive appears, that which does the action is put in accusative; it performs the function of subject of a finite verb. "Heaven," "earth" and "horn" are examples. κεραίαν = "least projection" of a Hebrew letter. Jesus says that "right" and "wrong" are structured into the universe; they reflect the moral nature of God, hence are inherently authoritative, unalterable, ever-present.

Verse 18 also forms a two-clause compound. Each clause has as its subject an attributive participial phrase. ἀπολύω literally means "loose off" or "release." "Adulterize" as translation for μοιχεύει is an attempt to retain the verb action in the word.

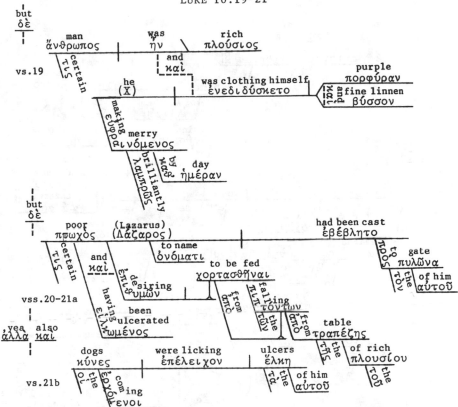

The two clauses of verse 19 form a compound sentence. They depict two distinctive conditions of one of two characters. "A man was rich" and he "was clothing himself..." Predicate adjective πλούσιος displays his economic status. Linear imperfect ἐνεδιδύσκετο shows how he flaunted his wealth. Accusative after verb of clothing is normal. Present circumstantial participle adds a feature as to how he used or abused his wealth. κατά with accusative is distributive, "day by day." Adverb λαμπρῶς throws in another colorful description, "brilliantly."

20-21a involve a simple sentence; "a certain poor...had been cast." Pluperfect suggests he "had been cast" and left there permanently. Circumstantial participles depict the state of his health and his ongoing hunger (perfect and present). πιπτόντων is attributive, "the (crumbs) falling."

21b is another simple sentence. The only medical help came from dogs. They "were licking..." is descriptive imperfect.

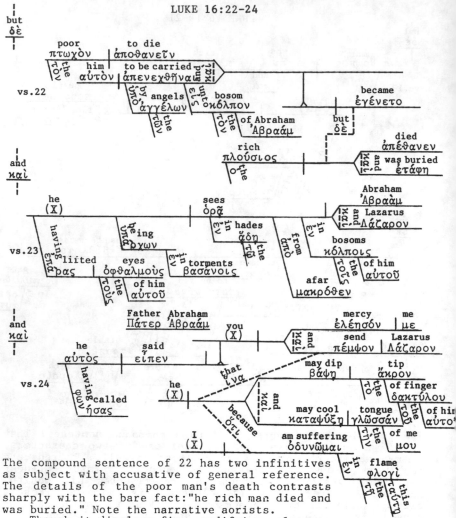

The compound sentence of 22 has two infinitives
as subject with accusative of general reference.
The details of the poor man's death contrasts
sharply with the bare fact:"he rich man died and
was buried." Note the narrative aorists.

Though it displays five modifying elements
verse 23 is simple in form. Two participles describe the man's
condition. Adverbial "in hades" tells where. Adverbial ἀπὸ
phrase relates to Abraham; ἐν "in bosoms" to Lazarus.

Four clauses of 24 form a complex sentence. Emphatic αὐτὸς
"he" is subject of the independent. Object of "said" is noun
clause "mercy me...send Lazarus." Aorists ἐλέησόν and πέμψον
are imperious, peremptory. His character hadn't changed. ἵνα
introduces purpose and ὅτι a causal clause. Aorists "dip" and
"cool" contrast to present "am agonizing..."

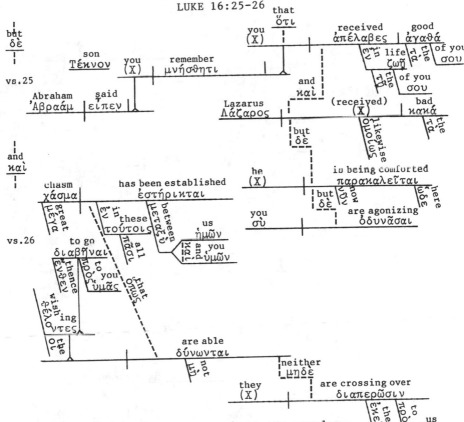

LUKE 16:25-26

As diagrammed both sentences above are complex.
But that of 26 is continuation of what "Abraham
said." Hence it might be treated as three more
clauses of one long complex sentence.

"You remember" is noun clause object of independent "said."
ὅτι governs four noun-object clauses of indirect discourse.
The first two have aorists gathering into a point all the
past life of the men. The second two clauses have presents
describing their current contrasting conditions.

In verse 26 ἐν πᾶσι τούτοις = "among all these things"
which is to say, "besides all this." Perfect ἐστήρικται declares the <u>permanent</u> rigidly <u>fixed</u> condition of the "chasm."
ὅπως inserts a purpose idea. Infinitive διαβῆναι is object of
the attributive present participle θέλοντες "wishing." πρὸς
appears two times. It suggests direction toward with
accusative. μεταξὺ "between" is an improper preposition used
with ablative. It indicates separation.

271

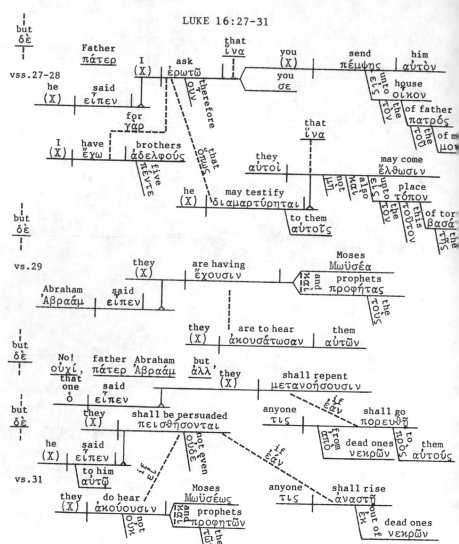

All four sentences above are complex in form. Independent "he said" has two noun clauses as direct objects; ὅπως is adverb of purpose. The ἵνα clauses are sub-final(objects).

Verse 29 displays two clauses joined by asyndeton. They are objects of independent, "Abraham said."

Verse 30 offers ἐάν and subjunctive, 3rd class condition, supporting independent "they shall repent."

272

LUKE 16:31

Verse 31 (preceding page 272) continues the conversation: "He (Abraham) said to him (Lazarus)" is the independent clause. Noun clause, object of "said" is "they shall not even be persuaded." This finds support in two conditional clauses; εἰ begins first class, "if they do not hear" and they don't. Then ἐάν with subjunctive, "if anyone shall arise..." and it's possible someone might.

LUKE 17:1-3a

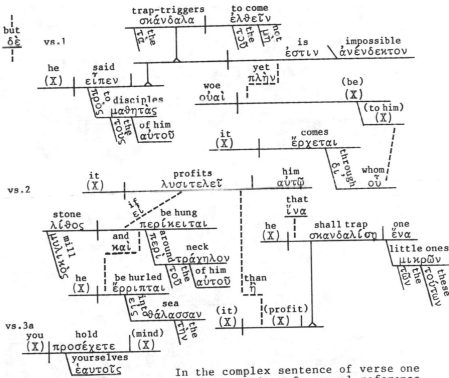

In the complex sentence of verse one infinitive τοῦ ἐλθεῖν with its accusative of general reference is subject of noun clause object of "said" of independent "he said..." "Woe" serves as subject of another noun-object idea. οὗ introduces adjective idea modifying understood "him."

In the compound-complex of vs. 2 two 1st class conditions endorse independent apodosis, "it profits him." Noun clause ἵνα is object of elliptical independent ("it profit").

Verse 3a is simple in structure. Dative adverbial ἑαυτοῖς tells where, "on yourselves."

273

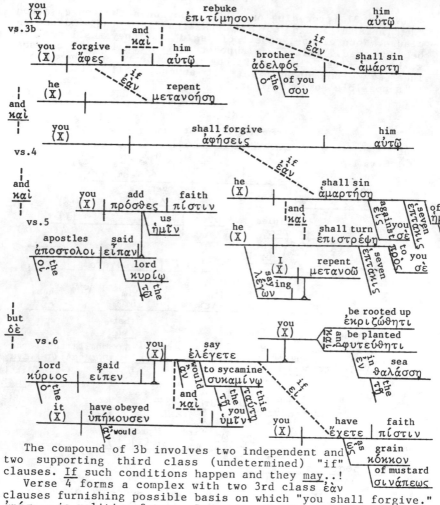

The compound of 3b involves two independent and two supporting third class (undetermined) "if" clauses. If such conditions happen and they may..!

Verse 4 forms a complex with two 3rd class ἐὰν clauses furnishing possible basis on which "you shall forgive." ἀφήσεις is volitive future. Present μετανοῶ is repeated action.

Ten words of verse 5 form a two-clause complex. πρόσθες is aorist of banking term, "deposit."

In three-clause complex of vs. 6 εἰ begins 1st class condition but imperfect ἐλέγετε with ἄν is apodosis of a 2nd class. This is a "mixed" condition. "If you are having and you do have...you should be saying..." The idea is that, faith, by its very nature, will root up and replant a firmly fixed object such as a tree!

274

LUKE 17:7

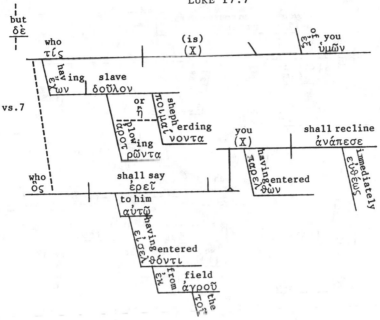

Verse seven, as diagrammed, forges a complex sentence of three clauses. The sentence begins with interrogative pronoun τίς as subject. But before any finite verb emerges the relative ὅς appears and <u>it</u> exacts the verb ἐρεῖ "shall say" with its modifiers that we would have expected in the independent clause. As a result τίς of the independent clause is left hanging without any expressed predicate verb. So the copula "is" fills in for the lack. Had the clause been fully developed the phrase ἐξ ὑμῶν "of you" normally would have modified τίς. Even as is it might be placed under τίς. But the diagram prefers to consider it as a predicate adjective: "But who is there of you..."

The subject "who" is described by circumstantial participle ἔχων "having slave." In turn the <u>slave</u> is described by two present participles, "plowing or shepherding." All participles reflect durative action.

Though relative ὅς is redundant, it <u>does</u> appear hence we must consider its function. It introduces an adjective idea and is subject in its clause. αὐτῷ is indirect object "to him." And this "him" is described by aorist circumstantial participle of time, "having entered" or "when he entered." Direct object of ἐρεῖ is noun clause, "you shall recline (sit down)." Adverb "immediately" sharpens the unsuitable action of a servant who would so behave.

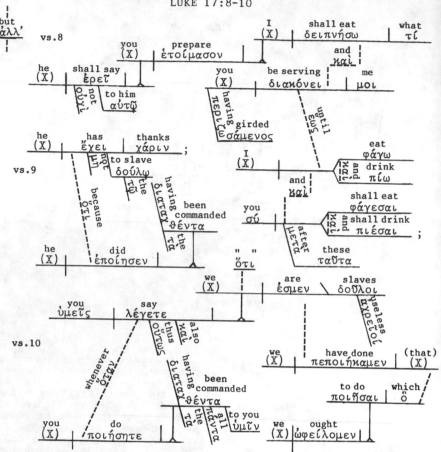

Verse eight shows a negative complex question expecting "yes"(οὐχί)for answer. Three noun clauses follow, objects of ἐρεῖ. Then two temporal (ἕως) adverb clauses appear. σύ is very emphatic as subject of the last temporal clause.

The sentence of verse 9 is complex, a question expecting "no" (μὴ) for answer. ὅτι brings in adverbial causal clause.

In the complex sentence of verse 10 subject of independent clause is emphatic ὑμεῖς "you." ὅταν inserts indefinite clause of time "whenever" with the subjunctive ποιήσατε "shall do." Attributive participle διαταχθέντα is object (as also in 9) but here with πάντα "all" which underscores the "useless" state of any "slave" even though he be flawless in his obedience. Two noun-object clauses, introduced by ὅτι, are direct discourse. An adjective clause inserted by ὅ completes the sentence.

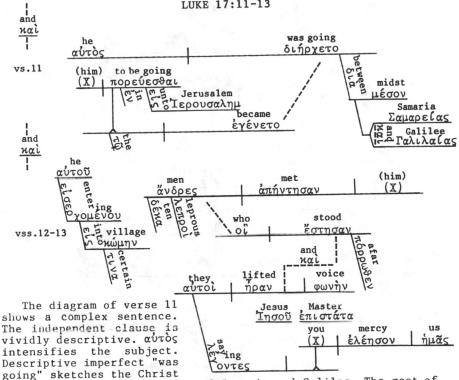

The diagram of verse 11 shows a complex sentence. The independent clause is vividly descriptive. αὐτὸς intensifies the subject. Descriptive imperfect "was going" sketches the Christ moving "between" the borders of Samaria and Galilee. The root of διά = "by twos" hence with accusative (case of extension) it tells us that he was travelling along the borders.

At bottom the dependent clause is a temporal adverb idea, "it came to pass while he was journeying..." A literal rendering makes awkward English: "in the to be journeying in reference to him came to pass..." The infinitive phrase is subject of ἐγένετο "came to pass." The infinitive identifies what "came to pass."

Verses 12-13 furnish a complex sentence. It begins with a genitive absolute, "while he was entering into a certain village..." The subject of the independent idea is ἄνδρες "men." The remainder of the sentence stems from and modifies this "men." First are two adjectives, "ten" and "leprous." Then an adjective clause ushered in by pronoun οἱ describes the relative position of these "men." A second adjective clause adds the descriptive, "they (emphatic αὐτοὶ) lifted (their) voice." Though ten were involved φωνὴν is singular. Common misery led to one voiced plea. Present circumstantial participle λέγοντες introduces a noun-object clause reporting the content of what they were "saying." Aorist imperative ἐλέησον implores "Mercy us" which is to say, "have mercy on us."

277

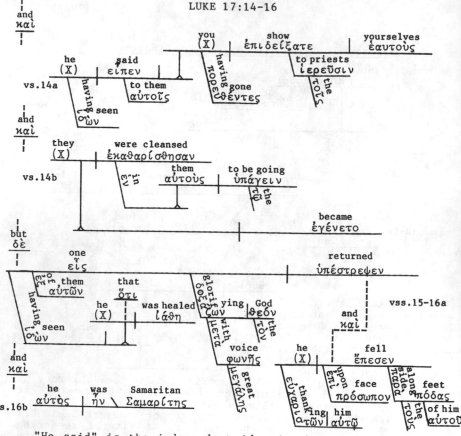

"He said" is the independent idea in the complex sentence of 14a. Aorist imperative with reflexive ἑαυτοὺς dominates the noun clause, object of "said." ἱερεῦσιν is indirect object.

Subject of independent clause ἐγένετο in 14b is noun clause "they were cleansed..." The ἐν infinitive phrase is temporal. Literally it says: "in the to go in reference to them." It may be translated, "while they were going." The sentence displays a complex structure.

Verses 15-16a incorporates two independent clauses: "one returned" and "he fell..." It gains a complex element by the ὅτι noun clause, object of circumstantial ἰδών. Circumstantial δοξάζων shows the manner in which he returned. In form it is a compound-complex sentence.

The diagram treats verse 16b as a separate simple sentence. Presence of αὐτὸς as subject is <u>very</u> emphatic. No article with "Samaritan" indicates quality. "<u>He</u> was Samaritan!" Not "the" Samaritan.

278

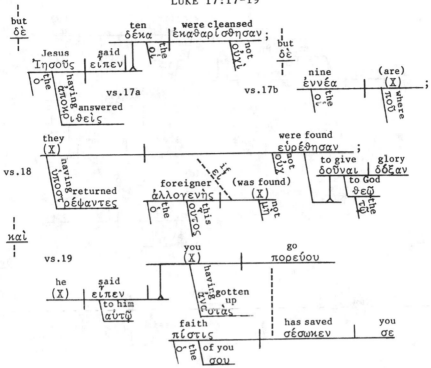

The sentence of 17a appears as a two-clause complex. "Jesus said" is the independent clause. Noun clause, object of "said" is a question expecting "yes" (οὐχὶ) for an answer: "ten were cleansed were there not?" 17b is simple in form but continues the wonder suggested by 17a: "But where are the nine?"

Verse 18 embraces a two-clause complex. The independent also is a question which, by using negative οὐχ, indicates it expects "yes" for answer: "They were found were they not?" The dependent clause is a negative first class conditional, "...if not (except) this foreigner." Aorist infinitive phrase δοῦναι is probably best viewed as purpose. Circumstantial participle ὑποστρέψαντες is best classed as temporal, "when they returned they were not found except...were they?"

Verse 19 embodies a complex arrangement with three clauses. After independent "he said to him" two noun clauses appear, both as objects of "said." The two are related to each other by asyndeton. πορεύου "you go" is present imperative insisting "you keep on going..." σέσωκεν is perfect indicating that the cure is permanent. "Your faith saved you at a point in the past and your salvation reaches to your present experience."

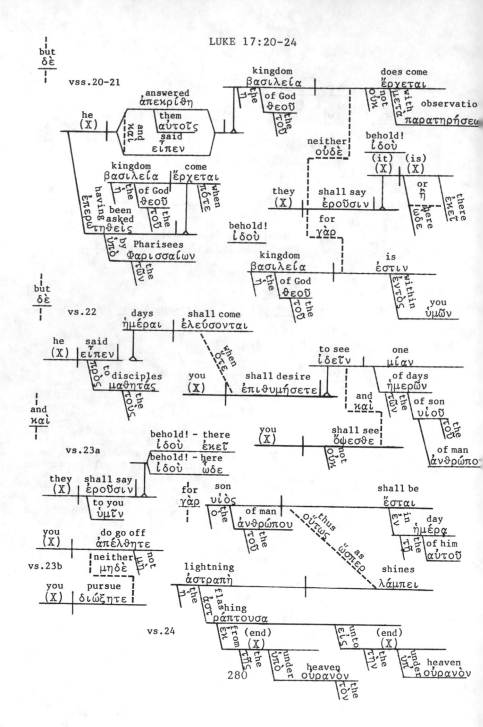

280

THE DIAGRAM OF LUKE 17:20-24

Verses 20-21 structure a six-clause complex sentence. The independent clause is compound, "But he answered them and said." Circumstantial participle "having been asked" may be temporal although it could be considered causal. ἐπερωτηθείς "having been asked" is modified by the ὑπό phrase "by the Pharisees." ὑπό with ablative expresses direct agent. Noun clause "when the kingdom...comes" is object of the participle. Another noun object clause follows, "the kingdom...does not come with observation." The noun παρατηρήσεως is compounded of παρά "alongside" and τηρέω "to guard" "watch" "preserve." It's an action word whose nominative ends in -σις; this suggests "observing." The next noun-object clause "they shall say" itself has as its object an elliptical clause, "behold, (it is) here or there." A final noun-object clause declares, "the kingdom of God is within you." ἐντός can mean "among." But here the context seems to demand "within."

Verse 22 entails four clauses framed as a complex sentence. The independent "he said" has as its object noun clause "days shall come." Absence of definite article with ἡμέραι stresses the quality or nature of the days to which he alludes. Adverb ὅτε inserts temporal idea, "when you shall desire." Infinitive ἰδεῖν is accusative, object of verb "desire." Its object μίαν is characterized by a series of qualitative descriptive genitives "the days of the son of man." Another noun-object clause completes the sentence: "you shall not see (it)."

If the exclamations, "Behold, there! Behold, here!" are to be viewed as objects of ἐροῦσιν, the sentence of verse 23a is to be classified as simple in form.

Is there any difference between "to you" of 23a and "to the disciples" of verse 22? It would be the difference between dative ὑμῖν and πρός with accustaive. That is to say, ὑμῖν emphasizes personal interest; πρός with accusative suggests "direction toward."

Verse 23b is a two-clause negative compound sentence. Both verbs are aorists (punctiliar) suggesting, "Don't even start to go...neither pursue (follow.)"

Verse 24 brings in a complex sentence. The dependent clause is adverbial of comparison, "as the lightning shines, so the son of man shall be..." The prepositional ἐν phrase indicates when, "in the day of the him." ἀστράπτουσα "flashing" is circumstantial participle of manner. Its present tense reveals descriptive linear action. "The lightning, flashing back and forth, shines..." The phrases ἐκ and εἰς "from the (end) to the (end)" means "from horizon to horizon."

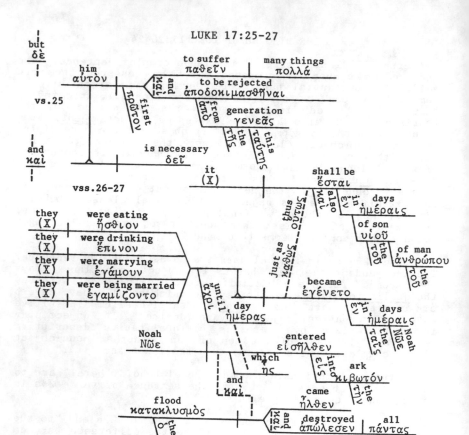

Since infinitive with accusative of general reference isn't deemed a clause the sentence of vs.25 is classed as simple. The compound infinitive phrase is subject of δεῖ. That verb indicates "logical necessity." ἀπὸ with ablative in this context suggests "origin."

The sentence of vss.26-27 has eight clauses only one of which is independent. Hence it is complex in structure.

καθὼς "just as" introduces an adverb clause of comparison. That clause has <u>four</u> noun clauses which form a compound subject: "they were eating...drinking...marrying...were being married." These verbs are to be classed as descriptive imperfects. The aorist verb ἐγένετο may be translated "happened." <u>When</u> it "happened" finds expression in adverbial phrase "in the days of Noah." "Until day" is also adverbial phrase. Two adjective (ἧς) clauses describing ἡμέρας "day" complete the sentence. Verbs in the last clauses are narrative aorists.

282

LUKE 17:28-30

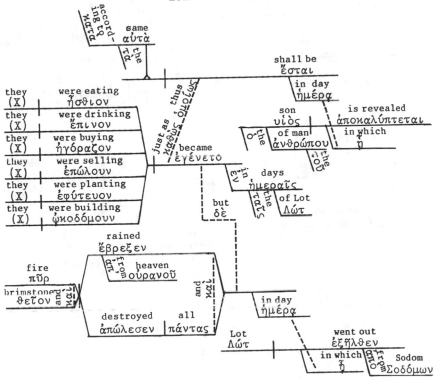

The diagram presents 17:28-30 as a complex sentence of 11 clauses. Subject of the independent clause is prepositional phrase, "the according to the same." The article τὰ treats the phrase as substantive. When these "same things" "shall be" is expressed by locative ἡμέρᾳ "in day" which in turn is defined by adjective clause "in which the son of man is being revealed". ἀποκαλύπτεται is linear present. Definite article τοῦ with ἀνθρώπου lifts the noun to the general idea of "humanity."

Comparative adverb clause is inserted by καθὼς "just as." Its verb ἐγένετο "became" has for its subject the compound consisting of six noun clauses. Each of these has a vividly descriptive imperfect tense:"were eating,..etc." δὲ "but" adds a parallel comparative adverbial clause though in this one the tenses are narrative aorists, "rained...destroyed." The subject is compound "fire and brimstone."

Again, when it "rained etc..." is revealed by ἡμέρᾳ "day" which itself is described by adjectival clause, "in which Lot went out..."

283

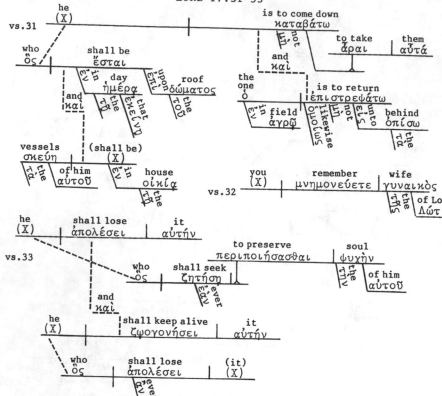

The sentence of vs.31 is classed as compound-complex. The independent ideas are: "He is to come down" and "the one in the field is to return." The verbs are aorist. Article ὁ is demonstrative: "the in the field one." ὅς is subject of an adjective clause describing "he." Another adjective clause is appended: "his vessels (shall be) in the house." Aorist infinitive ἆραι expresses purpose. Both verbs with the main clauses are aorist with negative μή: "don't even begin to..."

The exhortation of verse 32, in form, is simple: "Remember the wife of Lot." Its verb displays linear action (present) "Go on remembering..." "Ever keep in mind." The past produces lessons for present living!

Verse 33 reveals a four clause compound-complex sentence. Two relative adjective clauses describe the subject "he" of the two independents. The indefinite ἐάν(ἄν)"ever" suggests "whoever if..." Aorist infinitive περιποιήσασθαι is formed from περί "around" and ποιέω "make." περί is "perfective" hence "to make to remain over" "to preserve."

284

LUKE 17:34-37

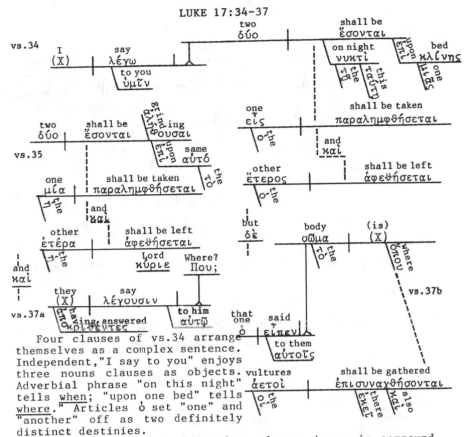

Four clauses of vs.34 arrange
themselves as a complex sentence.
Independent,"I say to you" enjoys
three nouns clauses as objects.
Adverbial phrase "on this night"
tells when; "upon one bed" tells
where." Articles ὁ set "one" and
"another" off as two definitely
distinct destinies.

Verse 35 has three independent clauses hence is compound.
It continues the "I say..." of verse 34 though it forms a new
sentence. Nominative present participle ἀλήθουσαι supplements
future ἔσονται. Together they form future active "shall be
grinding." Futures are normally point action but here the
periphrastic accents linear, repeated action. The resultant
idea of ἐπὶ τὸ αὐτό is "together."

Verse 36 is omitted by the best manuscripts.

If adverb ποῦ "where" of verse 37a implies a full clause
then the sentence is complex. Otherwise it may be classed as
simple in structure.

The sentence of 37b is a three-clause complex. Article ὁ is
demonstrative use "that one," subject of independent clause,
"that one said to them." As direct object is noun clause,
"where the body (is)." Adverb clause indicating where supports
the noun clause; "there the vultures shall be gathered."

285

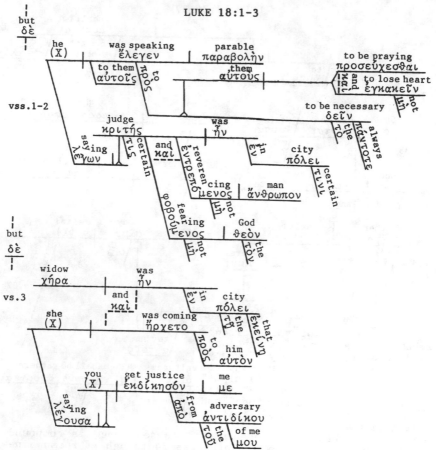

Verses 1-2 present a complex sentence. "He was speaking to them parable" is the independent idea. Technically πρὸς τὸ δεῖν is prepositional phrase. But practically it serves as a dependent clause, "that they be praying and not lose heart be always necessary." Object of circumstantial participle λέγων is noun clause, "certain judge was..." Describing "judge" are two negative circumstantial participles "not fearing God and not reverencing man."

Verse three displays a compound-complex arrangement. The initial independent states: "Widow was..." The ἐν phrase indicates <u>where</u>. Imperfect ἤρχετο is iterative; she kept on coming. Noun clause, object of participle λέγουσα, has aorist ἐκδίκησον "avenge" me. Ablative with ἀπὸ designates <u>from whence</u>.

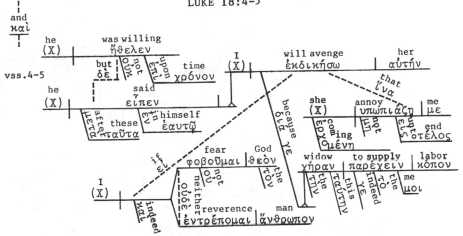

Verses 4-5 develop a compound-complex sentence. It exhibits two independent and three dependent clauses. It also has διά with τό and infinitive παρέχειν which is technically a phrase but it has the practical force of a dependent clause.

ἤθελεν with negative οὐκ is iterative imperfect. It clearly reveals the judge's repeated conscious refusals to render justice to the widow. The adverbial "upon time" is accsative extent of time. It means "over prolonged period of time."

The second independent, "he said," has two adverbial ideas, "after these (things)" indicating when; "in himself" signals where. Though he "was not willing" the widow's constant and repeated pressure was having its effect "in himself."

The dependent ideas reveal the practical effects. "I will avenge her" is noun clause object of εἶπεν. ἐκδικήσω is volitive future; it involves the will. The ἵνα clause is purpose with negative μή, "that she not annoy me." ὑπωπιάζῃ is present suggesting repeated annoyances" even unto the τέλος = "end." The word literally means "unto the intended goal. It was the widow's "goal" to break down the will of the judge. The ultimate brow-beating on the part of the widow reached its intended goal.

εἰ introduces a negative first class condition, "even if I do not fear...neither reverence" and I don't.

The introduction of διά and infinitive τό παρέχειν with accusative of general reference χήραν gives variety to the sentence structure. In practical force it serves in place of a dependent clause, "because this widow is furnishing labor to me." παρέχειν is present infinitive denoting repeated action.

Note how the verbs throughout this parable vivify the action.

287

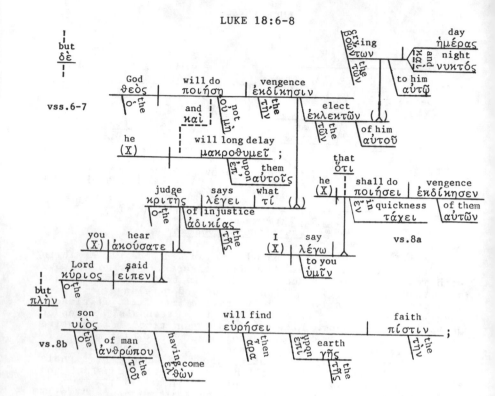

vss.6-7

vs.8a

vs.8b

The complex sentence of vss.6-7 seems more perplexing than it is. Object of independent "The Lord said," is noun clause aorist imperative ἀκούσατε "you hear." Aorist suggests that they pay attention so it won't need repetition. What they are to hear is stated in noun clause, "what the unjust judge says." In apposition to τί are two interrogative noun clauses, "will not God do vengence?" expecting "yes" for answer. A second noun clause asks, "will he long delay..?" ἐκλεκτῶν is objective genitive. Attributive participle βοώντων is in apposition to elect. ἡμέρας "day" and νυκτός "night" are genitives indicating kind of time, not accusatives, extent of time.

The ὅτι clause introduces noun clause object of λέγω in the complex sentence of vs.8a. ἐν τάχει is adverbial = "quickly." αὐτῶν "of them" is objective genitive.

8b is a simple sentence in form. Circumstantial participle ἐλθών is temporal "when he has come." Its aorist tense looks to the point of his coming. ἐπὶ "upon" is adverbial denoting where, "upon the earth."

288

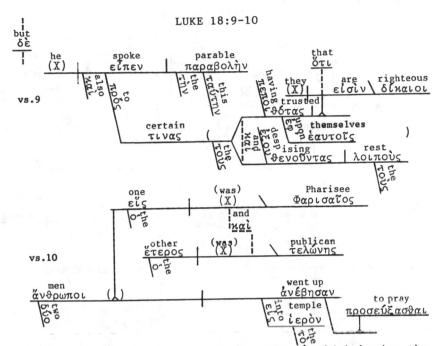

Verse 9 is a two-clause sentence. The δέ which begins the sentence is a coordinating conjunction, somewhat adversative "but." The preceeding paragraph closed with, "Will he find faith..?" He may or may not, "but" that which he finds will be genuine, not rooted in self-righteousness.

Independent clause, "he spoke this parable" has πρός phrase modifying as an adverb idea; it indicates why he so spoke. καί is also adverb in function.

The dependent idea comes in the pair of participles in apposition to τινας. Article τούς governs both participles. ὅτι introduces noun clause object of πεποιθότας "the ones having trusted." Its perfect tense implies that they not only trusted but the trust was a fixed, permanent disposition. The other participle ἐξουθενοῦντας is present emphasizing the ongoing continuous "despising." These viewed the "rest" as valued at zero. The ἐκ is perfective, prefixed to οὐθενέω.

Verse 10 is a three-clause complex. "Two men went up" is independent. εἰς brings in adverb phrase signifying where. Aorist infinitive προσεύξασθαι expresses purpose. The tense is not so much descriptive as it merely states the purpose as fact. Two noun clauses are appositional to subject "men." Definite articles ὁ used with "one" and "other" set these subjects off as distinctly different personalities.

289

LUKE 18:11-14

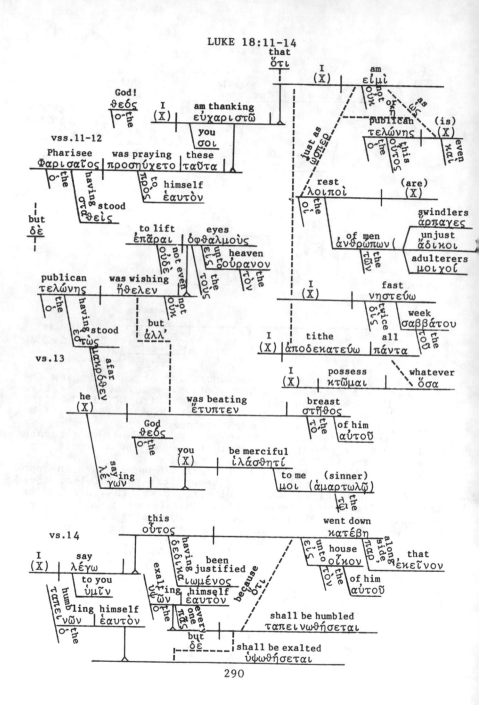

290

THE DIAGRAM OF LUKE 18:11-14

Verses 11-12 entertain eight clauses. They appear as complex in form. The independent clause animates the action by descriptive imperfect προσηύχετο "was praying." By adverb πρὸς phrase, "to himself" adds dramatic effect. Posturing himself (aorist σταθεὶς "having stood") in traditional form for prayer he was reciting his own virtues "to himself."

The initial dependent is a noun clause, also with imperfect "am thanking," describing prolonged praying. ὅτι brings in a second noun-object clause, this one negative, "that I am not..." Two adverb clauses of comparison spring out of the idea of the negative, "just as the rest of men..." and "even as this publican." The Pharisee does not generalize. He specifies three kinds of men whom he is not like; "swindlers," "unjust," "adulterers." Asyndeton adds stress to these ideas. Verb ἁρπάζω "plunder" gave birth to ἅρπαξ "robber."

After this array of negatives the Pharisee cites his virtues in two noun clauses joined by asyndeton to the first ὅτι noun clause. "I am fasting twice weekly." νηστεύω is iterative present. The δὶς "twice" confirms that his fasts were repetitive. τοῦ σαββάτου is idiomatic for "week." "I am tithing..." represents repeated action as his income permitted. This iterative idea is enforced by the adjective ὅσα clause, "whatever I possess." ὅσα is quantitative relative, "how ever much." κτῶμαι is present tense.

The sentence of 13 has two independent clauses and two dependents; it's compound-complex. The verbs are imperfects in the independents. ἤθελεν with negative may be rendered "was not willing." Aorist participle ἑστὼς "having stood" is enhanced by adverb μακρόθεν "afar." It represents how the publican consciously felt separated from the Pharisee, if not other men. Imperfect ἔτυπτεν enlivens the picture by portraying the publican flogging his breast like a drummer battering his instrument. In the dependent object noun clauses aorist tense appears. They report facts without describing.

It is worthy of note that definite article τῷ "the" appears with ἁμαρτωλῷ "sinner" in Nestle's text. External evidence supports it; internal evidence demands it. When one becomes convinced of his desperate need due to his own sin, then "the" sin, his own, is the one coming within the horizon of his consciousness. So is the prayer of anyone under conviction of his own guilt. He's not, one among many; he's the sinner!

Verse 14 embodies a complex sentence of four clauses. Object of independent "I say" is noun clause "this (man) went down..." The εἰς phrase tells where he went. παρά literally means "alongside of." When the publican's prayer is "laid alongside of" the Pharisee's, the publican, is "having been justified" more than. ὅτι brings in two adverb causal clauses gving reasons why. The subjects are attributive participial phrases, "everyone exalting himself" and "the one humbling himself."

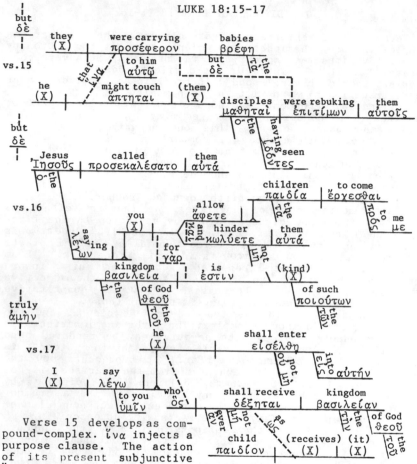

Verse 15 develops as compound-complex. ἵνα injects a purpose clause. The action of its present subjunctive ἅπτηται matches that of independent προσέφερον. Parents "were continuously carrying babies" that Jesus might "touch each." Imperfect ἐπετίμων displays repeated action of the disciples.

Independent clause in the complex of vs. 16 states, "Jesus called(aorist)them(disciples)..." What he "called" appears in two noun clauses, objects of λέγων. Aorist imperative ἄφετε "be permitting" contrasts with present negative μὴ κωλύετε "quit hindering." Accusative of general reference with infinitive is object of ἄφετε. ποιούτων is qualitative, "of such (kind of people)."

In the complex of verse 17 ὅς announces an adjective clause descrbing subject "he" of the preceding noun clause object of "say." ὡς brings in adverb clause of comparison. The ἂν is difficult to translate adequately. It suggests contingency!

LUKE 18:18-21

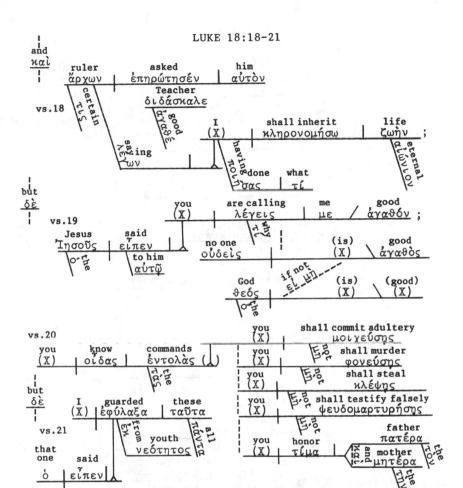

Aorist temporal circ.ptcp. ποιήσας also suggests cause. The entire clause is noun, object of λέγων and is translated: "I, having done what, shall inherit..?" Verse 18 is complex.

Verse 19a is interrogative complex. But because the next two clauses are part of what "Jesus said" the diagram embodies them in the one sentence. εἰ μὴ here may be rendered,"except."

In the complex of vs.20 "you know the commands" five appositional noun clauses names them. They link to each other by asyndeton. τίμα is imperative., linear present.

In the complex of 21 subject ὁ is demonstrative use of the definite article. Aorist ἐφύλαξα "guarded" gathers the whole boyhood of the young man into a single point. ἐκ indicates origin rather than separation.

LUKE 18:22-26

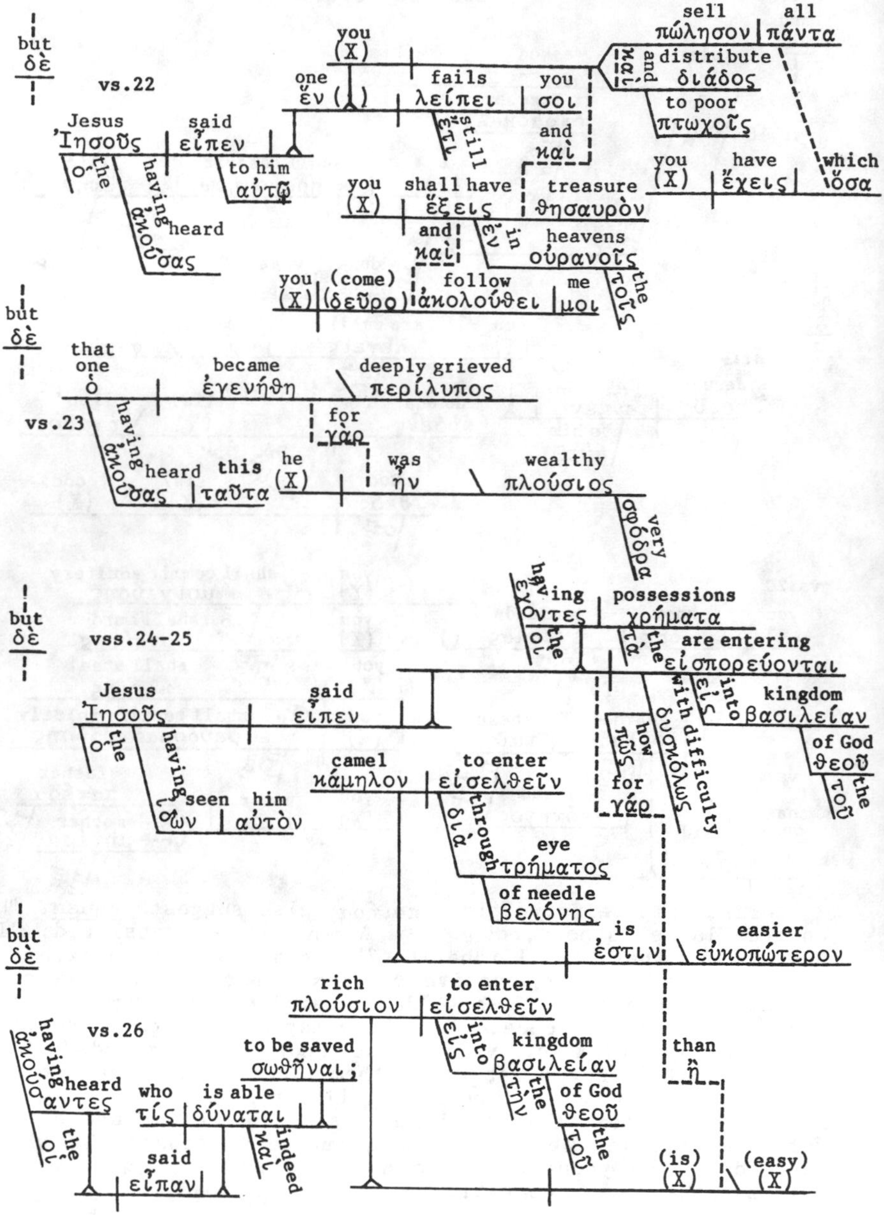

but
δὲ

vs.22

Jesus said
Ἰησοῦς εἶπεν

the

having heard
ἀκούσας

to him
αὐτῷ

you
(X)

one
ἓν (↓)

still
ἔτι

fails
λείπει

you
σοι

sell all
πώλησον πάντα

and distribute
διάδος

to poor
πτωχοῖς

and
καὶ

you shall have
(X) ἔξεις

and
καὶ

treasure
θησαυρὸν

in the
ἐν τοῖς

heavens
οὐρανοῖς

you have which
(X) ἔχεις ὅσα

you (come) follow me
(X) (δεῦρο) ἀκολούθει μοι

but
δὲ

vs.23

that one
ὁ

having heard
ἀκούσας

became deeply grieved
ἐγενήθη περίλυπος

for
γὰρ

this he was wealthy
ταῦτα (X) ἦν πλούσιος

very
σφόδρα

but
δὲ

vss.24-25

Jesus said
Ἰησοῦς εἶπεν

the

having seen him
ἰδὼν αὐτὸν

having
ἔχοντες

possessions
χρήματα

the
τὰ

are entering
εἰσπορεύονται

into
εἰς

kingdom
βασιλείαν

of God the
θεοῦ τοῦ

with difficulty
δυσκόλως

how
πῶς

for
γὰρ

camel
κάμηλον

to enter
εἰσελθεῖν

through
διὰ

eye
τρήματος

of needle
βελόνης

is easier
ἐστιν εὐκοπώτερον

but
δὲ

vs.26

having heard
ἀκούσαντες

the
οἱ

who is able
τίς δύναται

to be saved
σωθῆναι;

indeed
καὶ

said
εἶπαν

rich
πλούσιον

to enter
εἰσελθεῖν

into
εἰς

kingdom
βασιλείαν

the
τὴν

of God the
θεοῦ τοῦ

than
ἢ

(is) (easy)
(X) (X)

294

THE DIAGRAM OF LUKE 18:22-26

Verse 22 incorporates a complex sentence. The independent begins with aorist temporal circumstantial "when he heard, Jesus said..." First of dependents is noun clause object of εἶπεν, "one (thing) fails you still." Transitive λείπει takes personal interest dative σοι as object. In apposition to ἕν is noun clause "you sell...and distribute..." The verbs are both aorists. διάδος = "give to various poor." Luke's style, purpose, and personality lead him to use this compound "distribute" rather than Matthew and Mark's simple δός "give." Note also abscence of article with πτωχοῖς = those who in nature are "poor." This is Luke's human touch.

ὅσα is quantitative relative thrusting in an adjective clause modifying πάντα "all how-ever-much..."

The two remaining dependents are noun clauses. The consequence of selling and distributing is, "you shall have treasure..." ἕξεις is simple futuristic future. Literally ἐν τοῖς οὐρανοῖς = "in the heavens."

The final noun clause presents a challenge, "come, be following me." Present imperative ἀκολούθει = "be following" is an exhortation to cut loose from the past and commit to perpetual discipleship. Object μοι is dative emphasizing personal interest. Adverb δεῦρο may mean "hither." Here it approaches an imperative idea.

Verse 23 unites two clauses in a compound category. As subject ὁ is demonstrative use of article. Preposition περί has perfective force in περίλυπον signifying that grief completely surrounded him. The second clause declares the ground for his great grief, "he was exceedingly wealthy."

The sentence of 24-25 is complex. ἰδὼν is temporal with a bit of causal suggested: "when and because he saw, Jesus said..." All three of the subjects in the dependent clauses are phrases. First comes noun clause object of independent "said." Subject is participlial phrase, "the ones having possessions." ἔχοντες is present emphasizing, not the getting, but the having of possessions. Present εἰσπορεύονται is gnomic idea; anyone and everyone who has possessions "enters with difficulty." The combination of πῶς δυσκόλως means, "with how much difficulty."

Subjects in the next two clauses consist of aorist infinitives with accusatives of general reference. "Camel to enter" may be translated, "that a camel enter." Also "that a rich (man) enter..." διὰ with genitive denotes the means through which. The εἰς expression is adverbial indicating where.

Verse 26 displays a complex sentence. Subject of the independent "said" is attributive participle, οἱ ἀκούσαντες "the ones who heard." Object of "said" is noun clause, "who indeed is able..." Aorist passive infinitive σωθῆναι in the diagram is presented as object. It is adverbial accusative by nature.

295

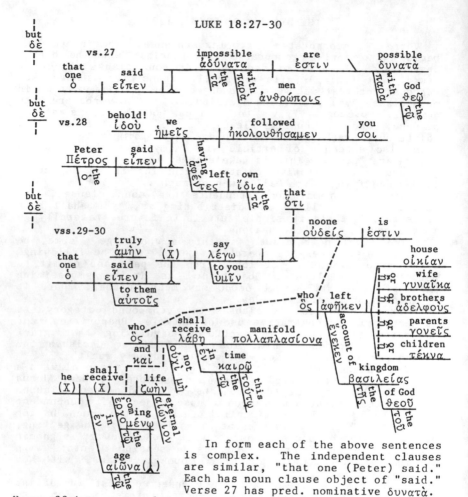

In form each of the above sentences is complex. The independent clauses are similar, "that one (Peter) said." Each has noun clause object of "said." Verse 27 has pred. nominative δυνατὰ. Verse 28 has personal interest dative as object. Use of ἡμεῖς intensifies the subject; it contrasts him who didn't "follow."

The ὅτι of vss.29-30 brings in another noun-object clause, "there is noone..." Three ὅς adjective clauses follow each of which contributes some idea descriptive of οὐδείς. The first ὅς clause points out the sacrifice of him who "left" something precious "on account of the kingdom." The second promises that which he λάβῃ "shall receive" ἐν "in this time." Even greater is the promise of what is the finest reward, "eternal life" in "the age, the one coming." ἐρχομένῳ is diagrammed in apposition though it may be as attributive adjective, "in the coming age."

296

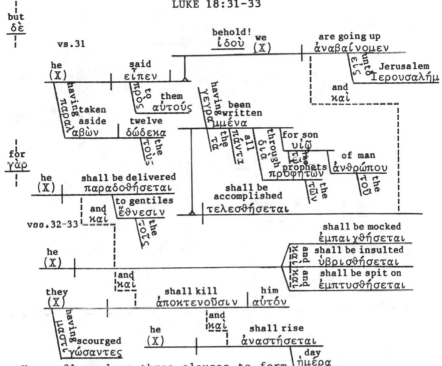

Verse 31 employs three clauses to form a complex sentence. Aorist cir. participle παραλαβὼν suggests privacy for that which "he said." Futuristic present ἀναβαίνομεν announces the private revelation. Subject of a 2nd noun object clause is attributive participle phrase γεγραμμένα. The perfect tense says that "all things stand written." διὰ with Genitive indicates agent through which. Dative υἱῷ expresses advantage and disadvantage. The root of future passive τελεσθήσεται has the idea of "intended goal." From the time they were written those "things written" were goal oriented.

Verses 32-33 unite four independent clauses in a compound sentence. Their ideas represent the goal of that which had "been written." The four clauses present six events. The clauses include six verbs depicting prospective facts. There are four future passives, one future active and one direct future middle. The direct middle indicates, "he shall raise himself." Life is inherent in the son of God by his very nature as divine. The fulfillment was far different than the disciples expected. Their Messiah didn't fit this brutal picture.

297

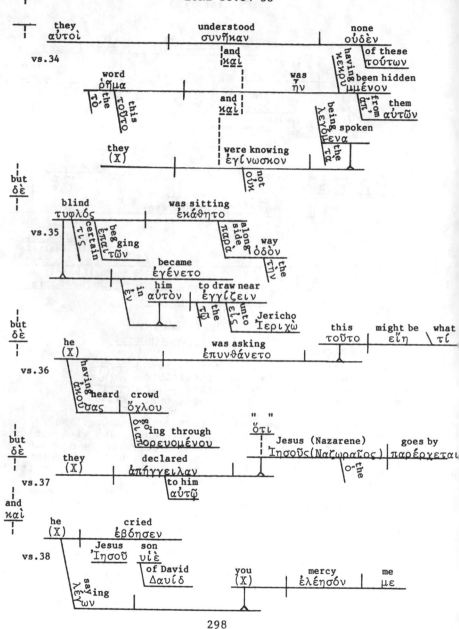

vs.34

vs.35

vs.36

vs.37

vs.38

298

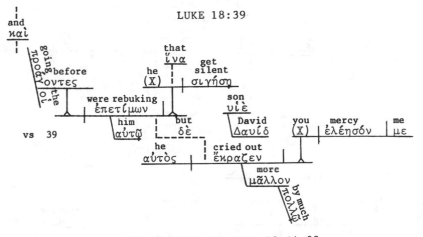

LUKE 18:39

THE DIAGRAM OF LUKE 18:34-39

The sentence of 18:34 is a three-clause compound. Personal pronoun αὐτοί gives prominence to the subject of clause one. Aorist συνῆκαν summarizes in a point their dulness. Plu-perfect in 2nd clause, "was having been hidden" focuses on the fixedness of their sluggish minds. Negative with iterative imperfect ἐγίνωσκον dramatizes their continuous density.

Dependent noun clause, "blind was sitting," molds the subject of ἐγένετο of the complex of verse 35. ἐκάθητο is descriptive imperfect. ἐν τῷ and present infinitive with accusative of general reference forms temporal idea, "while he was drawing near..."

In the complex of 36 imperfect ἐπυνθάνετο calls attention to his incessant questioning. Noun clause, object of the repeated inquiries, asks (present optative) "what this might be."

Verse 37 is a complex that reports the crowd's, "they declared..." The ὅτι inserts noun clause, direct object, a quote of the answer. παρέρχεται is descriptive present.

The independent idea of the complex of 38 has aorist ἐβόησεν "cried" which collects to a point what must have been oft repeated, almost panicky series of "cries." Dependent noun clause is object of λέγων. Aorist imperative ἐλέησόν is transitive with με its object.

Verse 39 (see above) involves a compound-complex sentence. Imperfect ἐπετίμων reflects iterative action on the part of participial phrase subject "the ones going before." ἵνα introduces object clause, "that he get silent." σιγήσῃ is ingressive aorist.

The second independent uses emphatice personal pronoun αὐτὸς for subject. The author keeps the imperfect ἔκραζεν to make vivid the excited outcries of the blind man, even adding double adverb idea "by much more."

299

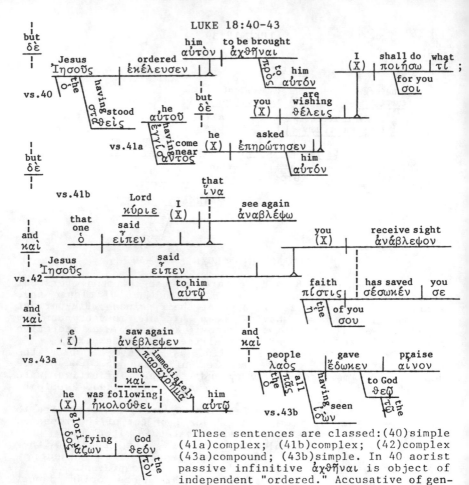

LUKE 18:40-43

These sentences are classed:(40)simple
(41a)complex; (41b)complex; (42)complex
(43a)compound; (43b)simple. In 40 aorist
passive infinitive ἀχθῆναι is object of
independent "ordered." Accusative of general reference tells who is "to be brought."

Genitive absolute in 42a refers to the blind, "he having
come." The main clause "he asked him" refers to Jesus. αὐτόν is
adverbial accusative. Two noun clauses follow, each an object
of the preceding verb. θέλεις = continuing wishing.

In 41b ἵνα injects noun clause object of main verb "said."
Subject ὁ is demonstrative use of definite article.

42 shows two noun object clauses joined by asyndeton.
Perfect σέσωκέν suggests permanency of the recovery.

In 43a aorist ἀνέβλεψεν looks to the immediacy of recovery;
whereas imperfect ἠκολούθει describes ongoing behaviour.
is associative instrumental after verb of following.

43b reports (aorists) the reaction of "the people."

300

LUKE 19:1-4

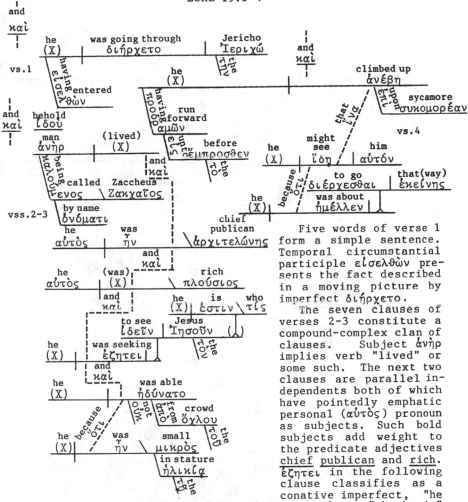

Five words of verse 1 form a simple sentence. Temporal circumstantial participle εἰσελθών presents the fact described in a moving picture by imperfect διήρχετο.

The seven clauses of verses 2-3 constitute a compound-complex clan of clauses. Subject ἀνήρ implies verb "lived" or some such. The next two clauses are parallel independents both of which have pointedly emphatic personal (αὐτός) pronoun as subjects. Such bold subjects add weight to the predicate adjectives chief <u>publican</u> and <u>rich</u>. ἐζήτει in the following clause classifies as a conative imperfect, "he was attempting to see Jesus." Dependent noun clause,"who he is" is in apposition to the entire infinitive phrase, "to see..." Again a conative imperfect appears in the final independent clause, "he was not able" even though he repeatedly tried. ἀπό with ablative ὄχλου indicates that the crowd kept him "from" accomplishing his desire to see Jesus. The context suggests the <u>cause</u> why he was not able.

ὅτι brings in an adverb clause giving another reason that hindered his getting a view of Jesus: "because he was small in stature."

301

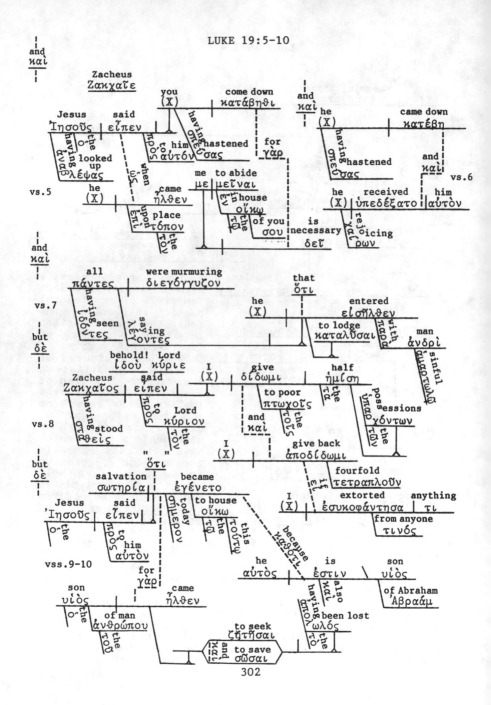

302

THE DIAGRAM OF LUKE 19:5-10

On opposite page 302 left top, verse 5 appears as a complex sentence. Besides the independent clause it displays three dependents. Circumstantial participle ἀναβλέψας is descriptive of Jesus as he lifted his eyes to Zachaeus. ὡς in this context suggests "when he arrived at(upon)the place." Two noun clauses emerge as direct objects of εἶπεν "said" of the independent clause. The aorist imperative κατάβηθι is appropriate to the temper of the occasion. Even aorist circumstantial participle adds urgency; σπεύσας hints at manner. There's no time for delaying. The second of the noun object clauses has δεῖ "is necessary" as its verb. δεῖ implies logical necessity. Its subject is aorist infinitive μεῖναι with accusative of general reference με. No doubt is left as to where he plans to "abide." The ἐν adverbial phrase determines that: "in your house."

Verse 6 appears at top right on the page. It is a two-clause compound sentence. "He came down" and "he received him" present the basic ideas. Aorist participle is repeated from the earlier sentence expressing manner. Manner is also reflected in participle χαίρων but this time the present tense demonstrates continuing and repeated "rejoicing."

Verse 7 is a complex of two clauses. Subject of independent is πάντες "all" which suggests that what Jesus had said and done was "seen"(ἰδόντες)by the crowd. Furthermore, they "all were murmuring..." διεγόγγυζον is a descriptive imperfect. There was a continuous buzzing of voiced disapproval of the behaviour of Jesus and Zachaeus. ὅτι, as diagrammed, introduces an indirect quotation. It may actually be a direct quote of what many of the crowd were "saying." Aorist infinitive καταλῦσαι is expressing purpose. παρά literally means "at the side of." The context here results in "with" as its meaning.

Verse 8 manifests three dependent ideas attached to independent "Zachaeus said." Aorist circumstantial σταθείς hints that Zachaeus "took a firm public stand" to make his confession. In the initial noun object clause δίδωμι is futuristic present. It was a pledge of what he was going to do. In the next object clause he uses the compound ἀποδίδωμι in which the preposition adds the idea of "back." He intends to restore whatever may have been taken by blackmail. Conditional εἰ clause is first class, determined as true. It says that in fact he had "extorted." It was a clear promise to repay "fourfold."

The sentence of 9-10 also presents a complex arrangement. "Jesus said to him" is the independent thought. ὅτι inaugurates a direct quotation of Jesus' actual words, "salvation came..." Adverb "today" expresses when; "to this house" exhibits where. γάρ brings in another noun object clause which states the basic philosophical reason why such a salvation experience could be possible. καθότι inserts a dependent clause giving a more immediate reason why such salvation should come to this particular person. Emphatic personal pronominal subject αὐτός "he" makes this man's salvation even more significant, "he also is son of Abraham."

303

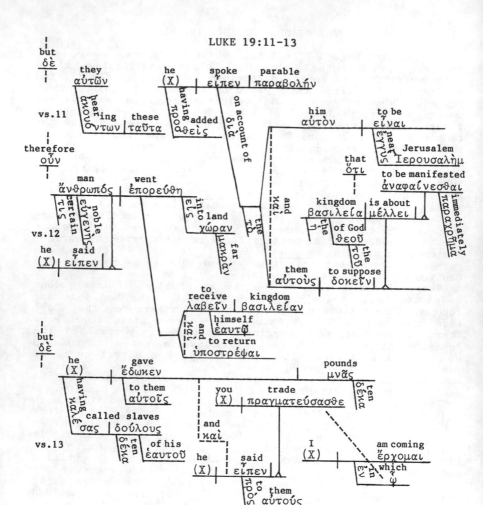

Verse 11 is complex. Other than two clauses it has genitive absolute; also τὸ with two infinitives. Each infinitive has its own accusative of general reference. ὅτι displays indirect discourse, noun clause object of δοκεῖν.

"Certain noble man went" is noun clause object of main verb "said" of the complex of verse 12. λαβεῖν and ὑποστρέψαι are aorist infinitives expressing purpose.

The sentence of verse 13 is a four-clause compound-complex. πραγματεύσασθε of noun-object clause is aorist imperative. ἐν ᾧ = "while" and involves an adverb clause. "He gave" and "he said" are the independent clauses.

304

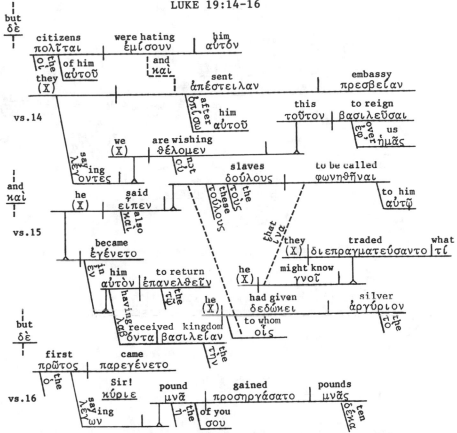

Verse 14 develops as compound-complex. Descriptive imperfect
ἐμίσουν graphically chronicles ongoing hate. Aorist ἀπέστειλαν
reports the fact without description. The one dependent clause
is noun, object of λέγοντες.

The sentence of 15 is formally and really complex. ἐγένετο
is verb of the independent clause. Its subject is noun clause,
"he also said." Object of εἶπεν is aorist passive infinitive
φωνηθῆναι with its accusative general reference "slaves." ἵνα
brings in purpose idea. Object of γνοῖ is noun clause, "they
traded what." οἷς registers an adjective clause modifying
δούλους. τῷ and infinitive ἐπανελθεῖν is temporal "when he
returned."

Verse 16 reflects a two-clause complex. The preposition on
παρεγένετο adds "along side." On προσηργάσατο the preposition
means "in addition," "besides," "more." It "wrought ten more."

305

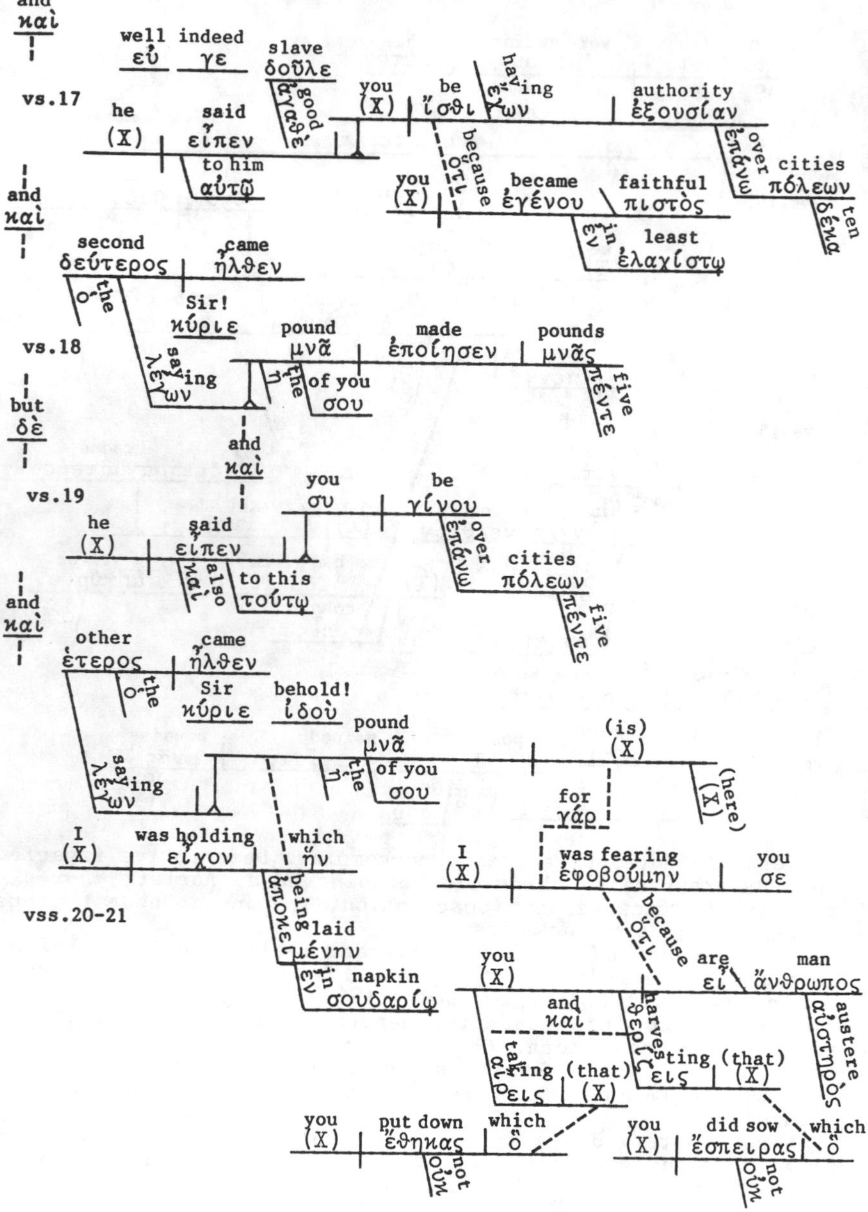

and
καί

well indeed
εὖ γε
slave
δοῦλε
good
ἀγαθέ

vs.17

he
(X)
said
εἶπεν
to him
αὐτῷ

you
(X)
be
ἴσθι
having
ἔχων
authority
ἐξουσίαν
over
ἐπάνω
cities
πόλεων
ten
δέκα

because
ὅτι

you
(X)
became
ἐγένου
faithful
πιστὸς
in
ἐν
least
ἐλαχίστῳ

and
καί

second
δεύτερος
the
o-
came
ἦλθεν

vs.18

Sir!
κύριε

saying
λέγων
the
η-
pound
μνᾶ
of you
σου
made
ἐποίησεν
pounds
μνᾶς
five
πέντε

but
δέ

and
καί

vs.19

you
σύ
be
γίνου
over
ἐπάνω
cities
πόλεων
five
πέντε

he
(X)
said
εἶπεν
also
καί
to this
τούτῳ

and
καί

other
ἕτερος
the
o-
came
ἦλθεν

saying
λέγων

Sir
κύριε
behold!
ἰδοὺ

the
η-
pound
μνᾶ
of you
σου
for
γάρ
(is)
(X)
(here)
(X)

I
(X)
was holding
εἶχον
which
ἥν
I
(X)
was fearing
ἐφοβούμην
you
σε

vss.20-21

being
ἀποκει-
laid
μένην
in
ἐν
napkin
σουδαρίῳ

because
ὅτι

you
(X)
harvesting
θερί-
ζεις
are
εἶ
man
ἄνθρωπος
austere
αὐστηρός

and
καί

taking
αἴρεις
(that)
(X)
harvesting
ζεις
(that)
(X)

you
(X)
put down
ἔθηκας
which
ὅ
not
οὐκ
you
(X)
did sow
ἔσπειρας
which
ὅ
not
οὐκ

306

LUKE 19:22a

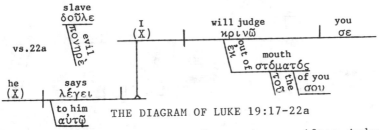

THE DIAGRAM OF LUKE 19:17-22a

Verse 17 embraces a complex sentence. After independent clause "he said" two dependents follow, one a noun, then adverbial ὅτι of cause. The subordinate clauses represent direct quote. They begin with an emotional interjection εὖ γε "well indeed!" γε is an enclitic postpositive and is often untranslatable into English. It stresses the word with which it is used. ἴσθι ἔχων is periphrastic present giving particular prominence to linear action.

Verse 18 fashions a complex sentence of two clauses. Numeral adjective δεύτερος implies "slave" but with article constitutes a practical noun, hence appears as subject. Verb ἐποίησεν is more prosaic, less imaginative than προσηργάσατο of the "first" slave as reported in verse 16. It seems more suitable to one who made only five with the same opportunity as he who gained ten.

In 19 the complex has one dependent noun clause, object of main verb "said." Personal pronominal subject σύ is very emphatic. This time linear idea in present imperative γίνου stresses continuing authority but with less animation than the periphrastic as in verse 17.

Six dependent clauses involve themselves in structuring the complex of 20-21. "The other (slave) came" is independent idea. All the dependents stem from present participle λέγων "saying." First, noun object clause, "(here is) your pound." Describing μνᾶ is adjective clause ushered in by relative ἥν. The present participle ἀποκειμένην by its linear action stresses the fact that he was keeping the μνᾶ safe. A second noun object clause states, "I was fearing (note linear imperfect ἐφοβούμην) you." It is supported by an adverbial ὅτι causal clause. It gives the presumed reason why he "was fearing." The adjective ὁ clauses amplify the reason for such fear. They modify implied demonstrative pronouns "that."

The sentence of 22a (above) has the Master begin his judgmental statement on the "evil" slave: "He says to him" is the independent clause. λέγει "is saying" is descriptive present. πονηρός is actively evil. It will not rest until it has made others evil. κρινῶ is volitive future; the will is involved. The ἐκ phrase is adverbial in function; it identifies the source from whence the judgment.

307

LUKE 19:22b-24

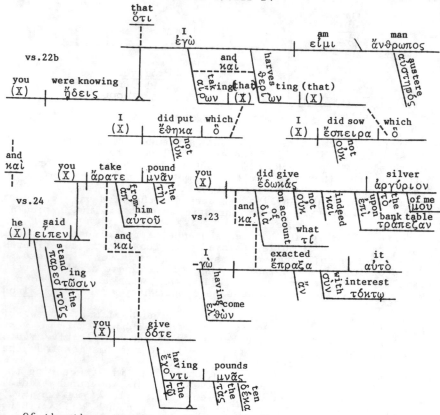

Of the three sentences above both 22b and 23 are questions.
To read otherwise is to misread them. In fact, 22b has a bite
of sarcasm that the diagram fails to show unless read aloud.
Its form is complex. The main verb ᾔδεις is pluperfect with
force of imperfect. ὅτι is noun clause object of "were
knowing." Adjective ὅ clauses reflect those of 20-21.(pgs.306f)

Verse 23 is compound of two clauses. The tenses are all
aorists. Subject -γὼ is emphatic. ἄν, often untranslatable,
introduces contingency. Here the context helps circumstantial
participle ἐλθὼν imply an apodosis of second class condition.
So ἄν would be, "I would have exacted..."

The sentence of 24 appears as complex with independent "he
said" having two object clauses, "you take" and "you give." The
two participles of the sentence are both attributive. Perfect
παρεστῶσιν "the ones standing" and present ἔχοντι "the one
having..."

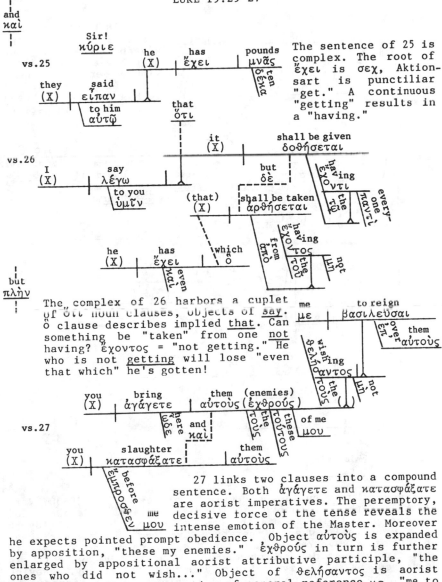

The sentence of 25 is complex. The root of ἔχει is σεχ, Aktionsart is punctiliar "get." A continuous "getting" results in a "having."

The complex of 26 harbors a cuplet of ὅτι noun clauses, objects of say. ὅ clause describes implied that. Can something be "taken" from one not having? ἔχοντος = "not getting." He who is not getting will lose "even that which" he's gotten!

27 links two clauses into a compound sentence. Both ἀγάγετε and κατασφάξατε are aorist imperatives. The peremptory, decisive force of the tense reveals the decisive force of the tense reveals the intense emotion of the Master. Moreover he expects pointed prompt obedience. Object αὐτοὺς is expanded by apposition, "these my enemies." ἐχθρούς in turn is further enlarged by appositional aorist attributive participle, "the ones who did not wish..." Object of θελήσαντος is aorist βασιλεῦσαι with its accusative of general reference με, "me to reign over them."

309

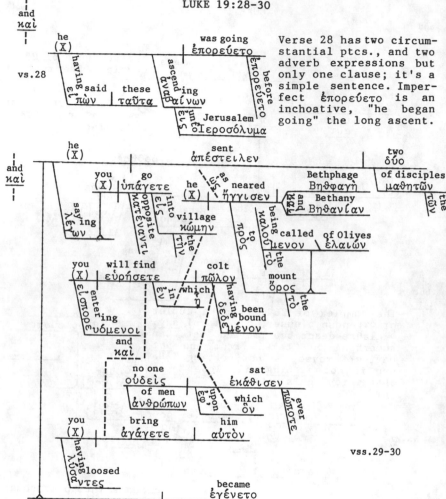

vs.28

Verse 28 has two circumstantial ptcs., and two adverb expressions but only one clause; it's a simple sentence. Imperfect ἐπορεύετο is an inchoative, "he began going" the long ascent.

vss.29-30

Seven clauses build the complex sentence of vss.29-30. Verb of the independent is ἐγένετο "it came to pass." "He sent two" is noun object clause stating basically what "became." Adverb ὡς clause tells when. Imperative "you go" is noun clause, object of λέγων urging what the "two" were to do. ἐν ᾗ is adjective clause describing κώμην "village." πῶλον "colt" is described by adjective clause launched by ἐφ᾽ ὅν. "Having loosed, bring him" could be a separate simple sentence. The diagram displays it as paralleling the ἐν ᾗ adjective clause. And it is definitely adjectival modifying πῶλον.

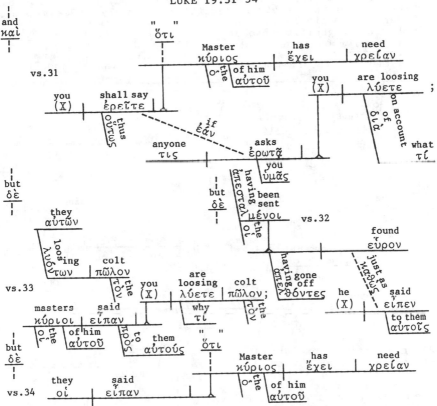

In the complex of 31 ἐὰν with present subjunctive ἐρωτᾷ inaugurates 3rd class condition, undetermined with prospect of determination, "if any should ask and one may..." ὅτι begins noun clause, object of ἐρεῖτε. "On account of what...?" is another noun clause object of ἐρωτᾷ.

Subject of independent clause in the complex of 32 is attributive perfect passive participle ἀπεσταλμένοι. Adverbial comparative clause is introduced by καθὼς.

The complex of 33 begins with genitive absolute following which comes independent clause, "his masters said..." Object of εἶπαν is interrogative noun clause, "Why are you loosing the colt?" λύετε is descriptive present.

In the complex sentence of 34 demonstrative use of article οἱ appears as subject "they." The use of personal pronoun αὐτοῦ (cf.also vs.31) is subtle reminder that Jesus is the ultimate, real <u>Master</u> of that to which human beings hold legal title. For the Master to have need (χρεῖαν) is tantamount to an order.

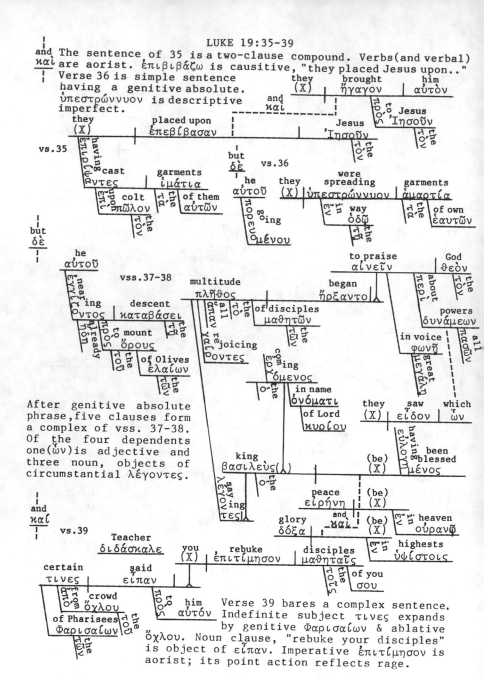

LUKE 19:35-39

and **The** sentence of 35 is a two-clause compound. Verbs(and verbal)
καί are aorist. ἐπιβιβάζω is causitive, "they placed Jesus upon.."
Verse 36 is simple sentence
having a genitive absolute.
ὑπεστρώννυον is descriptive
imperfect.

they — placed upon — ἐπεβίβασαν

vs.35

having — cast — ὄντες — ἐπιβαλόντες — upon colt — ἐπί πῶλον τόν — garments ἱμάτια τά — of them αὐτῶν

they (X) — brought — ἤγαγον — him αὐτόν — πρός to Jesus Ἰησοῦν τόν the

Jesus Ἰησοῦν τόν the

but δέ

but δέ **vs.36**

he αὐτοῦ — πορευομένου going — they (X) — were spreading — ὑπεστρώννυον — ἐν in way ὁδῷ τῇ the — garments ἁμαρτία τά the — of own ἑαυτῶν

vss.37-38

he αὐτοῦ — ἐγγίζοντος nearing — already — descent καταβάσει τῇ the — mount ὄρους τοῦ the — of Olives ἐλαιῶν τῶν the

multitude πλῆθος — ἅπαν all τό the — of disciples μαθητῶν τῶν the — χαίροντες rejoicing

began ἤρξαντο — to praise αἰνεῖν — περί about — God θεόν τόν the — in voice φωνῇ μεγάλῃ great — powers δυνάμεων — πασῶν all

ἐρχόμενος coming — ἐν in name ὀνόματι — of Lord κυρίου

they (X) — saw εἶδον — which ὧν — having been blessed εὐλογημένος (be) (X)

After genitive absolute
phrase, five clauses form
a complex of vss. 37-38.
Of the four dependents
one(ὧν)is adjective and
three noun, objects of
circumstantial λέγοντες.

king βασιλεύς(Λ) ὁ the — λέγοντες saying

peace εἰρήνη — (be) (X)

glory δόξα — and καί — (be) (X) — ἐν in heaven οὐρανῷ τῷ

and καί **vs.39**

Teacher διδάσκαλε — you (X) — rebuke ἐπιτίμησον — disciples μαθηταῖς τοῖς the — of you σου

highests ὑψίστοις τοῖς the

certain τινες — said εἶπαν — crowd ὄχλου τοῦ the — ἀπό from — of Pharisees Φαρισαίων τῶν the — πρός him αὐτόν

Verse 39 bares a complex sentence.
Indefinite subject τινες expands
by genitive Φαρισαίων & ablative
ὄχλου. Noun clause, "rebuke your disciples"
is object of εἶπαν. Imperative ἐπιτίμησον is
aorist; its point action reflects rage.

312

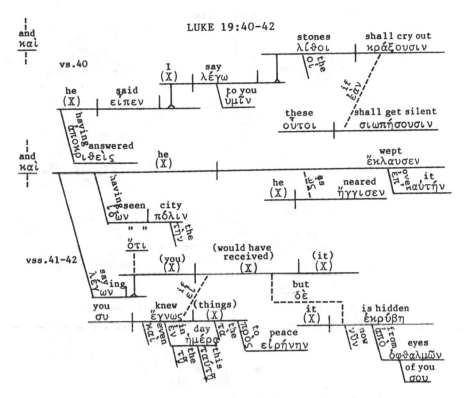

LUKE 19:40-42

Verse 40 has four clauses arranged as a complex sentence. Temporal aorist circumstantial participle ἀποκριθεὶς "having answered" may be translated, "when he answered." Noun clause, "I say" is object of εἶπεν. That which "I say" appears in noun-object clause, "the stones will cry out." ἐὰν intrudes a 3rd class condition determined as fulfilled. Though ἐὰν is used, because of indicative the condition is <u>first</u> class.

Verb in the independent clause of the complex of vss.41-42 is ingressive aorist ἔκλαυσεν "wept." Apparently, "when he saw(ἰδὼν)the city" he "burst(audibly)into tears." ὡς inserts a temporal adverbial idea, "as he neared."

Objects of present circumstantial participle λέγων are two(ὅτι)noun clauses, direct quotes. The first is implied by context,("you would have received"). By suppressing it in the spoken version it is more effective. The εἰ clause is 2nd class condition determined as unfulfilled, "if you knew (had known) these (things) but you didn't!" Subject "it" of the second noun object clause has for its antecedent εἰρήνην "peace." καὶ in "if" clause is ascensive = "even." Subject συ is unusually emphatic.

313

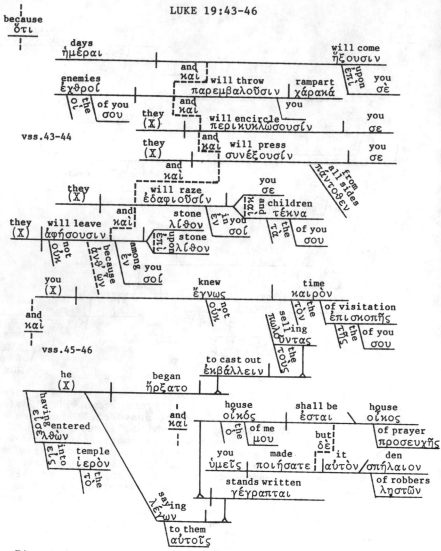

Five independent clauses bring a compound quality into the compound-complex sentence of 43-44. ἀνθ᾽ ὧν literally says "opposite which" or "in return for which." It here inserts an adverbial causal clause. The independent verbs are futuristic merely stating what will come. ἐδαφίζω = "beat level" "dash down" built off ἔδαφος "bottom" "base" "ground."

314

THE DIAGRAM OF LUKE 19:45-46

On page 314 preceding, verses 45-46 disclose a complex sentence. "He began to cast out" is the independent idea. Object of present ἐκβάλλειν is present attributive ptcp. πωλοῦντας. Linear action of the tenses is to be noted. There are three dependent clauses. Object of λέγων is perfect indicative γέγραπται. Its tense emphasizes that it stands as a permanent matter of record; this word is fixed! Its subject is compound, consisting of two noun clauses, "house shall be" etc. Appearance of personal pronoun ὑμεῖς makes the subject distinctly emphatic. σπήλαιον is objective complement.

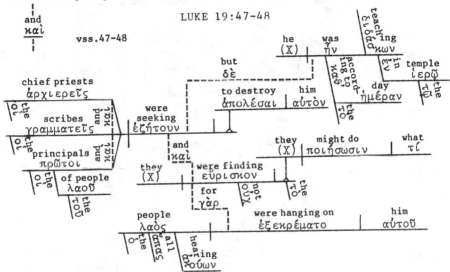

Four independent clauses and one dependent constitute the sentence of 47-48 as compound-complex. The dependent is noun clause, "what they might do." ποιήσωσιν is deliberative aorist subjunctive. It is object of imperfect εὕρισκον. All four verbs in the independent clauses are vividly descriptive imperfects. In fact periphrastic imperfect ἦν διδάσκων gives even greater emphasis to linear action, "he was teaching in the temple." Definite article τὸ with prepositional phrase "the according to day" makes awkward English but vivid Greek. It's a distributive idea meaning, "day by day" or "daily." That suits the linear idea of the periphrastic.

Both ἐζήτουν and εὕρισκον are conative imperfects. That is, "they were attempting to destroy..." and "they were not finding..." They tried repeatedly but failed. Imperfect middle ἐξεκρέματο = "to hang from." It's a vivid picture of "all the people" hanging with suspense on every word of Jesus as they were "hearing" him.

315

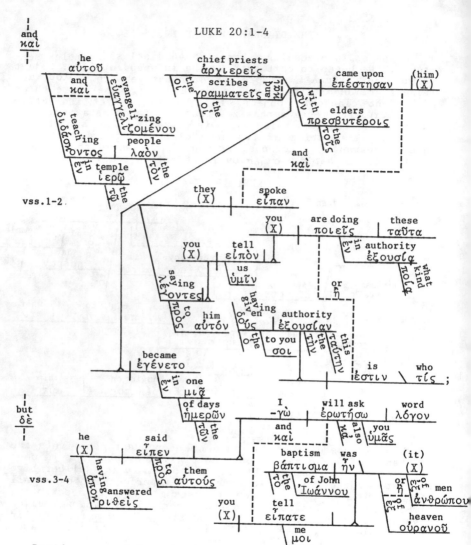

Besides a genitive absolute the sentence of vss.1-2 shows a complex of five dependent clauses. Two combine to form the subject of independent ἐγένετο. Three are noun clauses that stem off circumstantial λέγοντες.

Verses 3-4 contain four clauses formed as complex. The sentence reports what "he said." ₇Emphatic ἐγὼ is subject of a first noun clause, object of εἶπεν. A 2nd object clause urges, "you tell me." A 3rd gives the content of Jesus' challenge.

316

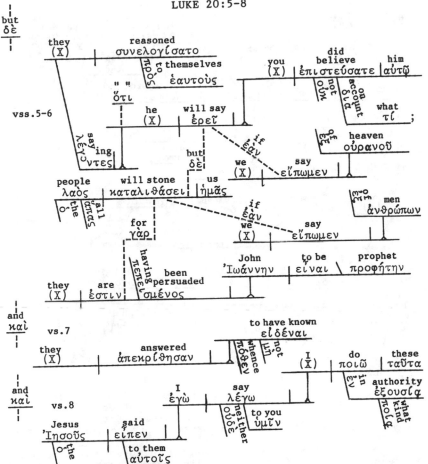

The six dependent clauses of the complex sentence of verses 5-6 stem directly or indirectly off circumstantial λέγοντες. They represent direct quote (ὅτι) of what "they reasoned..." Perfect periphrastic ἐστιν πεπεισμένος makes prominent the permanent fixed firmness of the people's view that "John was a prophet." The two ἐάν clauses are protases of 3rd class conditions, undertermined, "if we should say!" The ἐξ expressions are compressed, almost elliptical, of full clauses, "it is from heaven (men)."

Verse 7 forms a simple sentence with infinitive as object.

Verse 8 involves a three-clause complex. Adjective ποίᾳ is qualitative interrogative, "what kind."

317

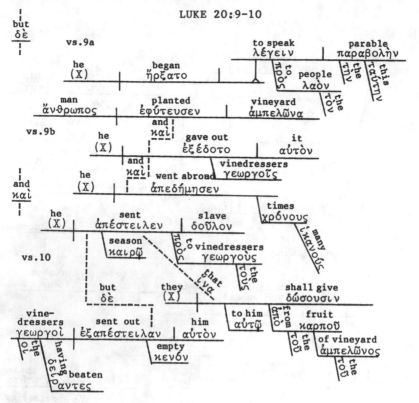

The sentence of 9a is simple in form. Present infinitive phrase "to speak this parable" is direct object of main verb ἤρξατο. παρά = "along side" plus βάλλω = "cast." A parable is a story "cast alongside" a truth so as to throw light on the truth.

9b incorporates three independent clauses in a compound sentence. The subject, man, discharged three deeds: he "planted," "gave out," and "went abroad." The verbs are all narrative aorists. They report without describing. γεωργός is compounded of γῆ and ἔργον = "worker in earth." In this context, "vinedresser." Plural ἱκανούς χρόνους in English = "a long time."

Verse 10 embodies a compound-complex sentence. ἵνα purpose clause here has indicative rather than usual subjunctive. It is obvious that in this situation the master clung to no misgivings but that the vinedressers would honor their obligation. Aorist circumstantial δείραντες is a strong word, "flay," "thrash," "beat." They really insulted and mistreated the master's messenger!

318

LUKE 20:11-13

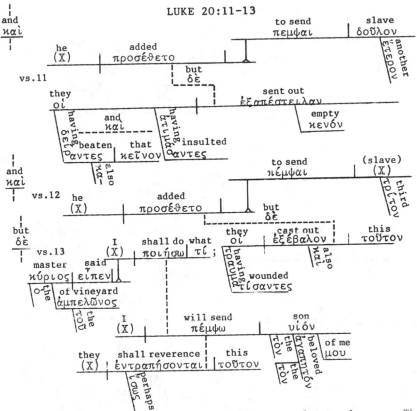

Verse 11 produces a compound sentence of two clauses. The aorist "added" is composed of πρός "to" plus τίθημι "place" resulting in "to add." Aorist infinitive "to send" is object of προσέθετο; ετερον is "another" in the sense of different. οἱ is demonstrative use of the article. Circumstantial participle "having insulted" derives from α privative and τιμή "honor." Hence to "dishonor." κενόν is adverbial accusative showing how.

The two clauses of verse 12 form a compound sentence. "He added but (δέ) they cast out" are independent ideas. δέ as adversative contrasts what the husbandmen expected with what the vinedressers did. They didn't welcome the "third slave" but "cast him out." Aorist circumstantial participle "having wounded" reports conditions besetting the "casting out."

Verse 13 exposes a three-clause complex sentence. Noun clause, "what shall I do" is object of εἶπεν. ποιήσω is deliberative future. The next clauses answer the question. Absence of formal conjunctions adds drama. The tenses are volitional futures.

319

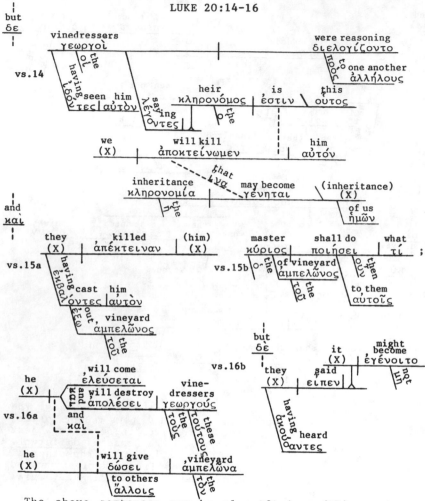

The above sentences may be classified as:(14) complex,
(15a)simple; (15b)simple; (16a)compound; (16b)complex.

In 14 διελογίζοντο is descriptive imperfect. ἀποκτείνωμεν
is futuristic present, "let us kill." ἵνα is purpose clause.

In 15a circumstantial "having cast" is coincident action
with that of the main verb "they killed him."

15b entertains deliberative future, "What shall I do?"

The futures of 16a are prophetic. The indicative mode
guarantees the <u>certainty</u> that "he will come,..destroy,..etc.

16b has optative of wish about the future with μὴ "may it
not become."

320

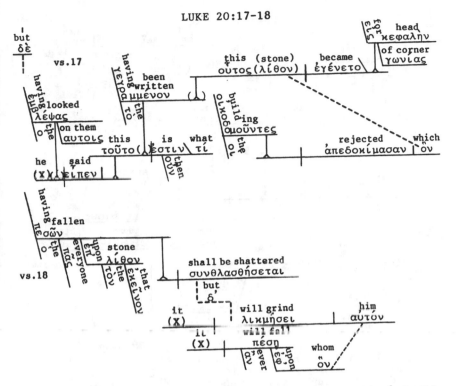

The sentence of verse 17 is complex. In practical terms it is an intricately complex arrangement of words and clauses. Independent "he said" is the foundation upon which the superstructure rests. Subject "he" is expanded by appositional participial phrase, "the one having looked." Interrogative noun clause "what is this" is object of ειπεν. In apposition to τοῦτο is perfect participle "that which stands written." The tense insists on the <u>fixed</u> <u>perpetuity</u> of that which had been and still is "written." Noun clause "this (stone) became for head..." is in apposition to the participle. Prepositional εἰς phrase, as a unit of thought, is predicate nominative. λίθον, in apposition to nominative οὑτος, is accusative case attracted out of nominative to case of relative ὁν.

Verse 18 exhibits a compound-complex sentence. Aorist attributive participle πεσὼν "every one having fallen" is subject of future passive, "shall be shattered." λικμάω literally means "winnow" hence to scatter to the winds. If this stone falls on anyone "it will utterly smash it to bits." Relative ὁν brings in an adjective clause which describes αὑτόν. ἁν introduces indefinite idea "whomever."

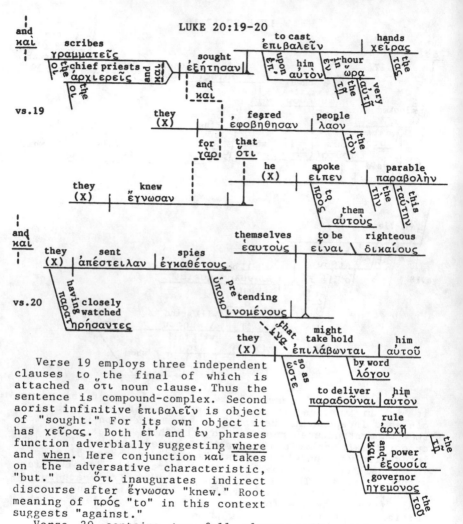

LUKE 20:19-20

Verse 19 employs three independent clauses to the final of which is attached a ὅτι noun clause. Thus the sentence is compound-complex. Second aorist infinitive ἐπιβαλεῖν is object of "sought." For its own object it has χεῖρας. Both ἐπ' and ἐν phrases function adverbially suggesting <u>where</u> and <u>when</u>. Here conjunction καὶ takes on the adversative characteristic, "but." ὅτι inaugurates indirect discourse after ἔγνωσαν "knew." Root meaning of πρός "to" in this context suggests "against."

Verse 20 contains two full clauses. The sentence is complex. παρατηρέω is "to watch <u>insiduously</u>" with evil intent. Its aorist participle here reveals the motive of the heart. The word for "spies" is compounded of ἐν "in" κατά "down" and τίθημι "put." He who was "put-down-in" some situation became one who was "hired to trap." εἶναι "to be" is object of circumstantial "pretending." ἑαυτοὺς is accusative of general reference with infinitve. ἵνα inserts a purpose clause. Here ὥστε with infinitive introduces a purpose idea. Genitive αὐτοῦ is normal object with verb of taking hold.

322

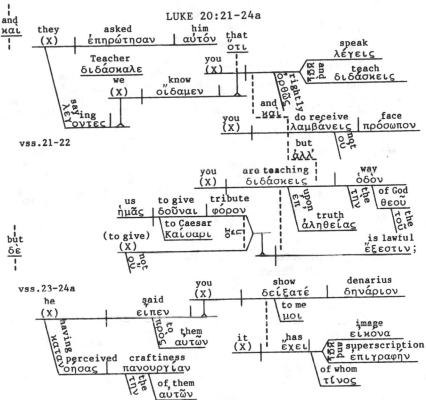

LUKE 20:21-24a

The sentence of 21-22 exhibits one independent clause and five dependents. It is complex in structure. Object of the circumstantial λέγοντες is noun clause, "we know." Object of οἴδαμεν are four noun clauses introduced by ὅτι. Both λέγεις and διδάσκεις are present tense depicting interative action, "to say repeatedly" and "to teach repeatedly." To "say" declares something; to "teach" makes clear the basis for what one "says." λαμβάνεις πρόσωπον, a babarism to Greeks, appears only in Luke. It means "to accept the face" which is to say, "accept the person." The ὁδὸν θεοῦ refers to the unswerving line defined by the law independent of human political consequences. The ἐπ' ἀληθείας is adverb in force: he teaches "on the basis of truth, reality, facts."

Verses 23-24a give rise to a complex sentence of three clauses. The circumstantial participle "having perceived" is causal implying a reason why. Object of εἶπεν are the two noun clauses, "show me denarius" and "whose image and superscription..." πανουργία literally meant "ready to do anything, good or bad." But usually, in actual use, in a bad sense = "craftiness."

323

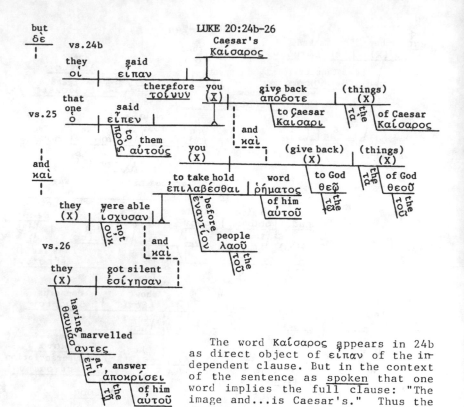

The word Καίσαρος appears in 24b as direct object of εἶπαν of the independent clause. But in the context of the sentence as <u>spoken</u> that one word implies the full clause: "The image and...is Caesar's." Thus the sentence may be classed as complex. οἱ represents the demonstrative use of the article. It is subject of the independent clause.

Verse 25 has a compound object of the independent verb εἶπεν. It consists of two clauses one of which is mostly suppressed, implied by the context. Aorist imperative ἀπόδοτε="give <u>back</u>." That which one gets in service from government demands equal moral obligation from those who receive the service. Καίσαρι and θεῷ are datives, the case of <u>personal</u> interest.

Verse 26 entails a compound sentence of two clauses, one negative and one positive. ἴσχυσαν with οὐκ, being point action aorist, draws to a focus the many efforts of these evil pretenders to "take hold of his word before the people." The aorist reports it without drawing the details of the picture. ἐσίγησαν is an ingressive aorist, "they <u>got</u> silent," "they <u>became</u> silent." Circumstantial "having marvelled" seems to suggest cause. ἀποκρίσει is an action (-σις) word. It was not only the content of his answer that overwhelmed them, it was also the process and the manner in which he answered.

324

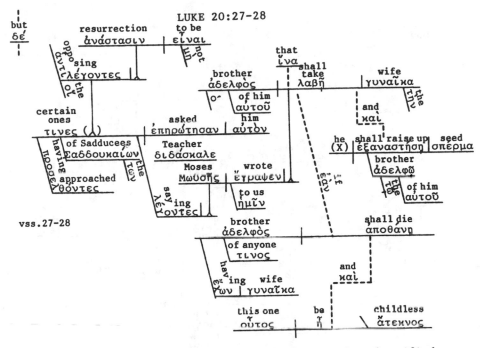

LUKE 20:27-28

vss. 27-28

The sentence contained in verses 27-28 is to be classified as complex. Besides the independent there are five dependent clauses. "Certain ones asked him" is the independent. Genitive Σαδδουκαίων specifies who these "certain ones" were. In apposition to τινες is the attributive participial phrase, "the ones opposing..." Infinitive εἶναι is object of the participle. The idea is: They were speaking against(ἀντί)there being resurrection. The doctrine of resurrection is what they "opposed."

The dependent clauses represent in one way or another that which they "asked, saying." Participle "saying" is coincident in action with that of the main verb "asked."

Object of λέγοντες is noun clause "Moses wrote." ἵνα brings in a pair of subfinal (object) clauses. They give the content of that which "Moses wrote." The first object clause is: "his brother shall take his wife." Article τήν, modifying γυναῖκα is used in place of and as pronoun "his." The second of these noun object clauses is: "he shall raise up seed." Dative, the case of personal interest, ἀδελφῷ = "for his brother."

ἐάν with subjunctive puts forward two conditions upon which the brother shall exercise the duty of levirate marriage. These are 3rd class conditions, undetermined but with prospect of determination: "if anyone's brother, having wife, shall die..." It may or may not happen! Demonstrative pronoun οὗτος is here used as substantive subject "this one."

325

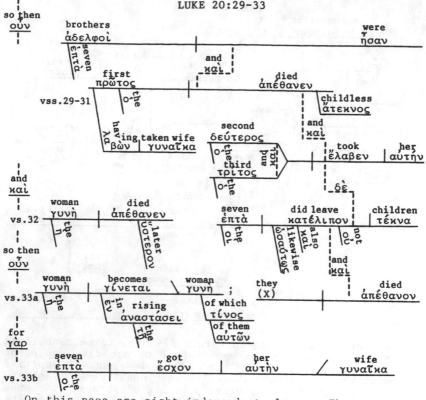

On this page are eight independent clauses. They emerge in four sentences. Verses 29-31 constitute a compound sentence of five clauses. They present a stock story in the arsenal of arguments with which the Sadducees advanced their denial of resurrection. The first clause furnishes the basic fact: "Seven brothers were." Next, a report of what occured in the marriage of the first. Circumstantial λαβὼν "having taken wife" gives the factual setting; then the main verb, "the first died childless." Each clause advances the story through seven marriages. Then the ultimate end: "they died."

Verse 32 forms a simple sentence. Coupled with narrative aorist ἀπέθανεν "died" is adverb ὕστερον "later" showing when.

Another simple sentence appears in 33a. The verb changes to present γίνεται "becomes." ἀνάστασις is an action word giving more attention to the process of rising though the end result of resurrection is certainly included.

In the simple sentence of 33b γυναῖκα in the diagram shows up as objective complement, "the seven got her as wife." It might be viewed as in apposition to object αὐτὴν "her."

326

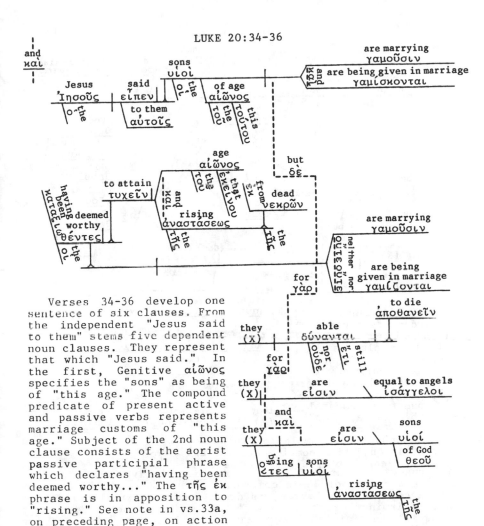

Verses 34-36 develop one sentence of six clauses. From the independent "Jesus said to them" stems five dependent noun clauses. They represent that which "Jesus said." In the first, Genitive αἰῶνος specifies the "sons" as being of "this age." The compound predicate of present active and passive verbs represents marriage customs of "this age." Subject of the 2nd noun clause consists of the aorist passive participial phrase which declares "having been deemed worthy..." The τῆς ἐκ phrase is in apposition to "rising." See note in vs.33a, on preceding page, on action noun ἀνάστασις. The next clause publishes the absence of death in "that age" to come. Adverb ἔτι "any more" underscores the lack of death.

In the next clause ἰσάγγελοι "equal to angels" is predicate adjective describing "they" of "that age." The word is made by joining ἴσος "equal" to ἄγγελος "angel." It means "equal to angels" and appears only here in the New Testament.

The final clause helps define the natives of "that age" as "sons of God." Circumstantial ὄντες adds to the description, "being sons of the rising."

327

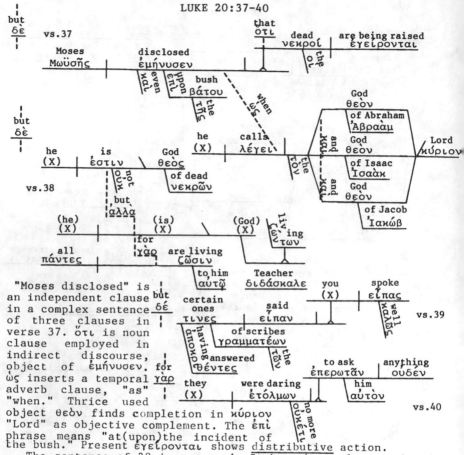

"Moses disclosed" is an independent clause in a complex sentence of three clauses in verse 37. ὅτι is noun clause employed in indirect discourse, object of ἐμήνυσεν. ὡς inserts a temporal adverb clause, "as" "when." Thrice used object θεὸν finds completion in κύριον "Lord" as objective complement. The ἐπί phrase means "at(upon)the incident of the bush." Present ἐγείρονται shows distributive action.

The sentence of 38 is compound. It has three clauses though the second, except ζώντων, is drawn from context. The first is not affirming "He is not God;" rather "he is not God of dead (ones)." Participle ζώντων similarly has the vital "living ones." Strong adversitive ἀλλὰ sharpens the contrast. The third clause states a fact of revelation as a basis for Jesus' argument. Personal interest of the dative αὐτῷ is especially fitting: "To him all are living," or "All are living to him."

The sentence of 39 is complex. Indefinite τινες "certain ones" is specified by Genitive "of scribes." That which they "said" is in noun object, "you spoke well." καλῶς is adverb meaning "beautifully." It was a sharp answer!

In the simple sentence of 40 ἐτόλμων is conative imperfect. They might wish but they didn't dare!

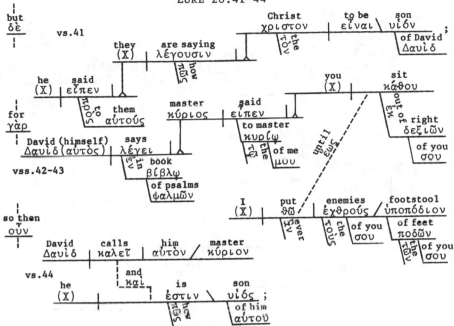

Verse 41 includes two full clauses, so related as to form a complex sentence. Infinitive εἶναι is technically a phrase, yet in translation it has the force of a clause: "that the Christ is son of David." Since an infinitive by definition is <u>infinite</u> not limited by a subject he who does the action depicted by the infinitive is in accusative and given the name "accusative of general reference." Here εἶναι is object of λέγουσιν.

In Luke's narrative the expression "He said <u>to him</u>" or "<u>to them</u>" frequently appears. The reader will note that sometimes that expression is depicted by a πρός with accusative <u>or</u> by a simple dative without a preposition. The terms are similar but not <u>exactly</u> the same. The difference lies in the cases. πρός with accusative entails "to" or "towards." He speaks "toward" someone, that is, in the direction of someone. Dative suggests <u>personal</u> involvement. Observe a <u>for</u> or <u>against</u> with dative.

The sentence of 42-43 registers four clauses, three of which are dependent. Intensive pronoun αὐτός expands and enforces the subject Δαυίδ. Noun clause, object of λέγει is "Master says to my <u>master</u>(dative κυρίῳ). A 2nd noun object clause has present imperative κάθου, linear action, "be sitting." ἕως inaugurates temporal adverb clause. ὑποπόδιον is objective complement.

Verse 44 involves an interrogative compound sentence of two clauses. οὖν implies a logical inference to be drawn.

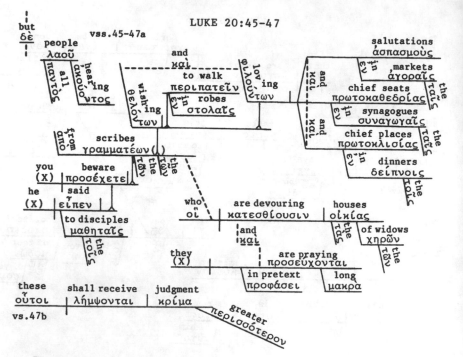

Present active participle as Genitive absolute begins the complex sentence of vss. 45-47a: "while all (the) people were listening." The independent clause states: "he said to (dative μαθηταῖς for the sake of) the disciples." The linear action of προσέχετε urges, "have the habit of being aware." The ἀπὸ phrase is treated as a single unit of thought, object of "beware." The two present participles, "wishing" and "loving" governed by one article τῶν, show the attitude and reason lying back of such a warning. The word for love is φιλέω which gives emphasis to emotional, affectionate love.

Relative οἱ is subject in an adjective clause which further describes the "scribes." Present indicative κατεσθίουσιν is both descriptive and iterative. κατα prefixed to ἐσθίω is perfective. It calls attention to the aggressive thoroughness of the action; they "eat up" (literally down). "Are praying represents another discriptive-iterative present. μακρὰ is adverbial accusative, extent of time. προφάσει is adverbial idea indicating how.

Even though verse 47b is part of what "he said to the disciples" it seems appropriate to deal with it as a separate sentence. κρίμα, being a -μα word, signifies result. This is not a process of judging; it is a "verdict" pronounced. "These shall receive greater sentence.

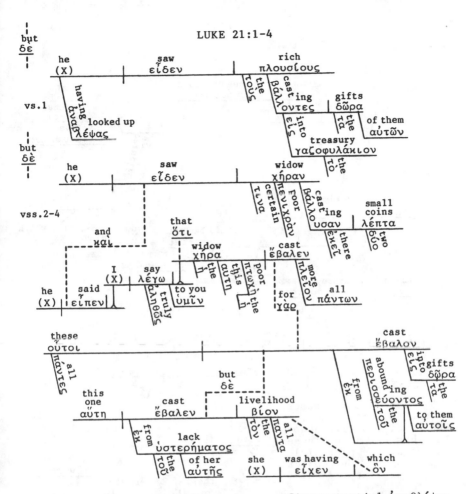

LUKE 21:1-4

Verse one forms a simple sentence. Circumstantial ἀναβλέψας is temporal aorist, "when he looked up." βάλλοντες is present in indirect discourse, "he saw that the rich were casting..."

Verses 2-4 develop as a compound-complex sentence. Two independents verify the facts: "he saw" and "he said." Noun clause "truly I say to you" is object of εἰπεν. Adverb ἀληθῶς plus dative ὑμῖν add a solemnity to that which he is about to "say." Three noun object ὅτι clauses give the content of that which Jesus so solemnly had to say. How much "this poor widow cast" is defined by πάντων after comparative: "more than all." The basis for such an evaluation of her gift is expressed in the contrast of the γὰρ and δὲ clauses. Relative ὃν inserts an adjective clause describing βίον "livelihood."

331

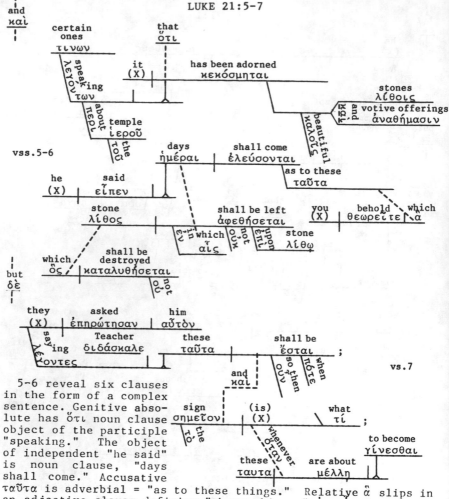

5-6 reveal six clauses in the form of a complex sentence. Genitive absolute has ὅτι noun clause object of the participle "speaking." The object of independent "he said" is noun clause, "days shall come." Accusative ταῦτα is adverbial = "as to these things." Relative ἅ slips in an adjective clause defining "these things." ἐν αἷς intrudes a second adjective clause sketching more precisely "days." ὅς inserts a third adjective clause, this time limiting λίθος. These dependents give the content of what "he said."

The independent clause of verse 7 relates a fact by aorist ἐπηρώτησαν "asked." No doubt they "asked" repeatedly, yet the aorist condenses the action into a point. It reports without describing. As to structure the sentence is complex. The three dependent clauses stem from circumstantial λέγοντες. Two are noun clauses, objects of the participle, asking, "when" and "what?" Indefinite ὅταν is adverb of time, "whenever."

332

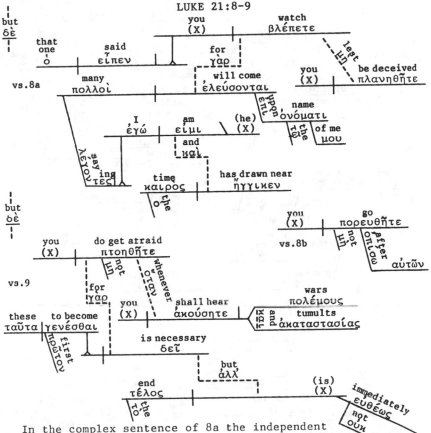

LUKE 21:8-9

In the complex sentence of 8a the independent
"that one said" supports five dependent clauses.
Present βλέπετε = "keep alert" "be watching." μὴ thrusts in a
negative purpose idea, "lest you be deceived." "Many will come"
is a 2nd noun clause object of εἶπεν. The claims of the "many"
are displayed in two noun clauses objects of "saying." Emphatic
ἐγώ deals with the Person of Christ; perfect ἤγγικεν claims the
time "has" at a past point and now still is "near at hand."

8b forms a simple sentence. Aorist πορευθῆτε suggests "don't
even begin to go after them."

The diagram pictures verse 9 as compound-complex. Indefinite
ὅταν is temporal "whenever." μὴ with aorist πτοηθῆτε = "do not
become terrified." δεῖ is logical necessity. Its subject is the
infinitive phrase, "these to become first." τέλος includes not
only "end" but a "goal" as the end. It's more than termination,
its a designed aim.

333

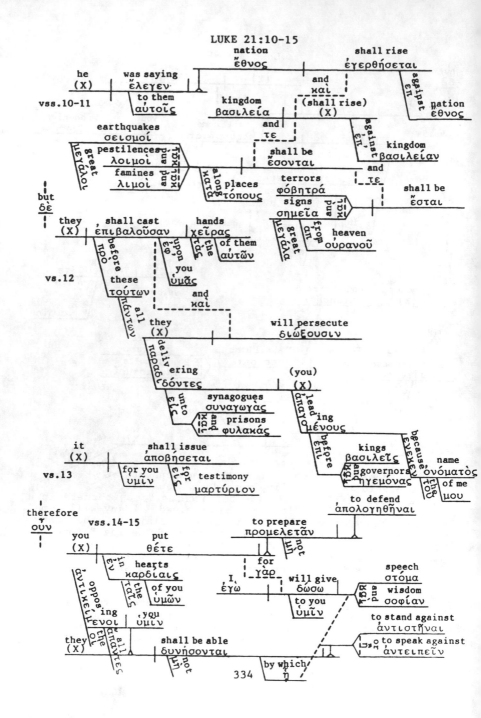

LUKE 21:10-15

334

The diagram of verses 10-11 shows four noun clauses of equal rank as objects of ἔλεγεν "was saying" of the independent element. It is a complex sentence. Imperfect "was saying" is more vividly graphic than aorist would be. Dative αὐτοῖς makes his "saying" directly personal. The tenses in the four object clauses are prophetic futures. Preposition ἐπί literally means "upon." In this context it becomes "against nation...against kingdom." κατά is used in the distributive sense here in "down along places," that is, place after place after place. τε appears twice along with καί once to join these clauses. τε denotes a closer union between words, phrases, clauses or sentences than καί. There is a close and intimate connection between "terrors and signs from heaven" and "earthquakes, pestilences and famines." Note the stylistic play on words that sound similar, λοιμοί and λιμοί. These along with φόβητρά (only used here in the NT) grab the reader's attention as well as paint a powerful portrait of coming persecutions. Good in a bad world may expect harsh treatment. So the people identified with the righteousness of God in Christ may expect such kind of response from this kind of a wicked world.

The sentence of verse 12 is compound; it employs two independent clauses: "they shall cast" and "they shall persecute." The πρὸ and ἐφ' phrases are adverbial. The first reveals <u>when</u> "they shall cast" and the second, <u>where</u>. The manner in which "they will persecute" is expressed by present participle, "delivering (you)." Its tense suggests iterative and/or distributive action. It will be a repetitious persecution; and it will extend to each of you, one after the other after the other. The parallel participle "leading" instead of present nominative appears in accusative agreeing with understood "<u>you</u>." The major concern is not their appearance "in synagogues and prisons" or "before kings and governors." The vital point is in the prepositional phrase ἔνεκεν "because of my name."

Verse 13 admits to a simple sentence of just four words. Middle of the future ἀποβήσεται is to be noted. "It shall turn out (issue) for you (ὑμῖν) for testimony." Middle voice emphasizes the <u>self</u> in some way or other as demanded by the context.

Verses 14-15 enclose a compound-complex sentence. The initial clause has present imperative θέτε with object infinitives "put not to prepare to defend." The present tenses imply "quit preparing..." The idea is enlivended by adverbial phrase "in your hearts." The second clause extends a promise with emphatic ἐγώ, "I on my part will give..." The relative ᾗ inserts an adjective idea describing "speech and wisdom." Subject of this clause is "they" which is expanded by appositional attributive participle, "all the ones who are opposing you." The preposition ἀντί on the participle indicates "opposite" "against" and pictures those present in some governing authority standing face to face against one another!

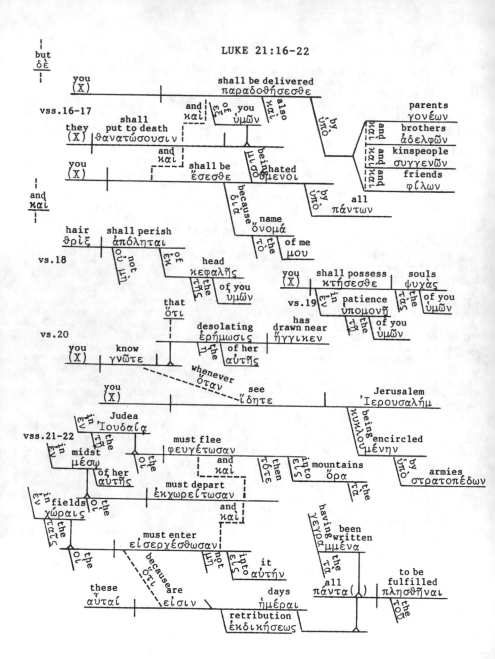

336

THE DIAGRAM OF LUKE 21:16-22

The three clauses of verses 16-17 are independent. The sentence is classed as compound. Future passive "shall be delivered" in the first clause is prophetic of a diverse source of persecution, people of warm personal relationships. ὑπό with ablative expresses direct agent, "parents, friends, etc." θανατώσουσιν is future active of a causative verb, "to make to die." The prepositional ἐξ expression is a unit of thought, object of "shall put to death." It implies, "some of you." ἔσεσθε and present participle μισούμενοι form a periphrastic future. In its nature future is usually point action. Periphrastic insists on durative action. The idea in "shall be hating" is an emphasis on the ongoing nature of this hatred. The very nature of the believer's relationship to the Person of Christ implies a repetitive hatred. The basis of such hatred is διά "because of my name."(See John 15:18-20) ὄνομα means more than an epithet that distinguishes one from another. It inculdes the total person, his character, personality, convictions, cause, etc. In form verse 18 is simple. Double οὐ μὴ is more drastic; "not even", none at all, hair..." In view of his preceding prediction, "they shall put some of you to death," what does he mean? It obviously does not mean that believers won't suffer martyrdom. So it must mean that through any suffering believers shall be strengthened to bear and survive even through death. Not even hair shall be destroyed. God protects here and hereafter.

Verse 19 is a simple sentence. κτήσεσθε is future of defective verb κτάομαι "procure for oneself, gain, acquire." Jesus is promising: "You shall gain for yourselves your souls..." How? The adverbial phrase answers, "in patience" through persecution. ὑπομονή is a compound of ὑπό "under" and μένω "remain." He who "remains" faithful "under" persecution shall acquire his soul's true life. This explains verse 18.

Verse 20 exposes noun and adverb clauses attached to independent, "know." γνῶτε is second aorist imperative; it's an exhortation. ὅτι denotes noun clause object of "know." ἐρήμωσις is an action word, "desolating." It designates a process. "Has drawn near" represents perfect tense, "has drawn near and still is near." ὅταν brings in adverb clause of time, "whenever."

Three independent clauses of vss.21-22 have one limiting dependent clause. ὅτι introduces a basic cause for the urgency of the independent ideas: "because these are days of retribution. ἐκδικήσεως is often translated "vengeance" "vindication." The root idea is "that which comes out of a judicial hearing." Punishment that comes to humans from the hand of Providence is not arbitrary or personal. It is the inevitable return of the fruit of human behaviour. The arrival of Roman armies at Jerusalem was as "natural" as any "law" of divine providence. Ignoring moral law brings moral retribution. It's built into the moral universe.

Subjects of the independent clauses are three prepositional phrases made attributive by definite article οἱ, "the ones in Judea" etc. The verbs are imperative: "must flee...must depart...must eneter."

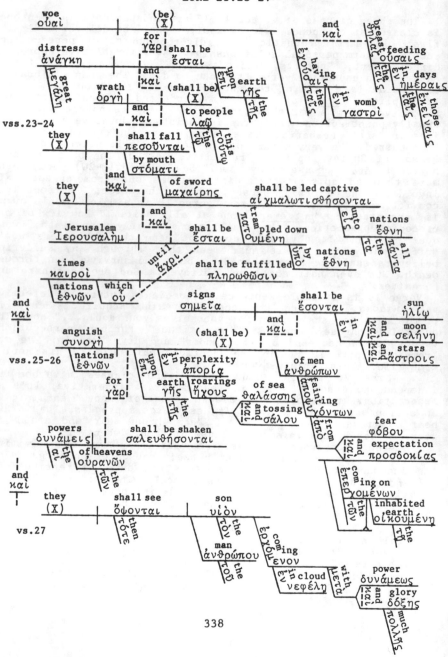

338

LUKE 21:28

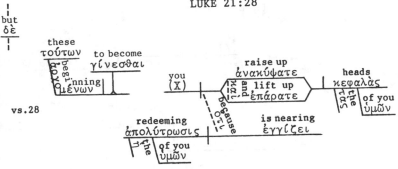

THE DIAGRAM OF LUKE 21:23-28

The sentence of 23-24 develops five independent and a dependent clause. It frames a compound-complex. οὐαί is usually interjection of grief or denunication. Here it is used as substantive, subject of independent "Woe (be) to the ones having in womb..." The linear present participles are dative, case of personal interest.

In the 2nd clause the ἐπί expression is adverbial where, "great stress shall be." In the 3rd, dative λαῷ is again appropriate, "to (against) the people." In the 4th στόματι is instrumental, "by the mouth (edge) of sword." αἰχμαλωτίζω "take captive" is used figuratively by Paul but this future passive is its sole literal use in the NT; "they shall be led captive..." To the Jew ἔθνος = "Gentile" and may be so translated where context demands.

The sixth independent has a periphrastic future passive ἔσται πατουμένη "shall be being trampled down." It thus emphasizes durative repetitive tramping.

The ἄχρι clause is dependent, adverbial of time "until when times of nations (Gentiles) shall be fulfilled..."

In creating a compound sentence verses 25-26 display three independent clauses: "signs shall be," "anguish (shall be)," "powers shall be shaken." ἐν "in sun and moon and stars" is adverb where.

In the second clause subject συνοχή is from σύν and ἔχω "to have(hold)with(together) "in the sense of "press together" hence "distress" "anguish" "violence." ἐπί "upon the earth" is adverbial where. ἐν "in perplexity" is adverbial manner. ἤχους is adverbial accusative (where genitive might have been expected).

Verse 27 involves a simple sentence. Present circumstantial participle is temporal "as" or "while."

The complex of 28 has genitive absolute, an independent and a dependent clause. "These beginning to become" is temporal genitive absolute, "as these..." The independent has a compound predicate of aorists; "raise up and lift up..." ὅτι is adverb of cause. ἀπολύτρωσις, an action noun, suggests a process "redeeming," which suits descriptive present, "is drawing near."

339

LUKE 21:29-33

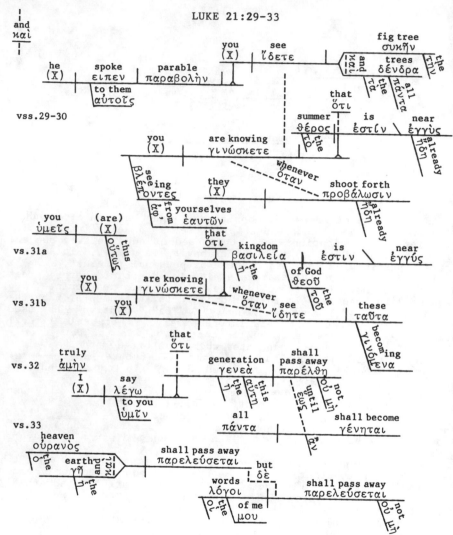

The sentences above are to be classed: (23-30) 5-clause complex, (31a) simple, (31b) 3-clause complex, (32) 3-clause complex, (33) two clause compound. 31a and 31b may be combined as one sentence with 31b appositional to οὕτως "thus." The two ὅτι clauses insert noun clauses used as objects. Two ὅταν and ἕως insert temporal adverb clauses, "whenever" and "until." ἄν is often untranslatable into English. It carries a note of contingency, "ever" etc.

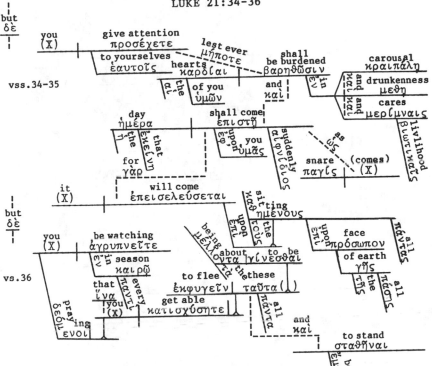

Vss.34-35, besides an independent clause, embrace four dependents. μήποτε introduces two negative purpose clauses. The γάρ clause confirms and supports the two purpose clauses. ὡς slips in an adverb clause of comparison, "just as..." The verb of the independent is present imperative προσέχετε communicating continuous repetitive action, "ever giving attention."

In the list with which "your hearts shall be burdened" is "βιωτικαῖς cares." ικος words mean "pertaining to." The "cares" are those pertaining to biological (physical) well being. These too distract; persons, not things, are vital.

A present imperative initiates the complex sentence of 38, "be ever watching." To underscore the linear action the adverbial "in every season" is added. The manner in which we must "be watching" is seen in participle δεόμενοι "praying." The ἵνα object clause states the content of the prayer, "that you get able..." Two infinitives detail that which we must "get able" to do: Aorists ἐκφυγεῖν "to flee.." and σταθῆναι to stand before..." The aorists' point action say: "get going" and "take a firm stand." They indicate specific points.

LUKE 21:37-38

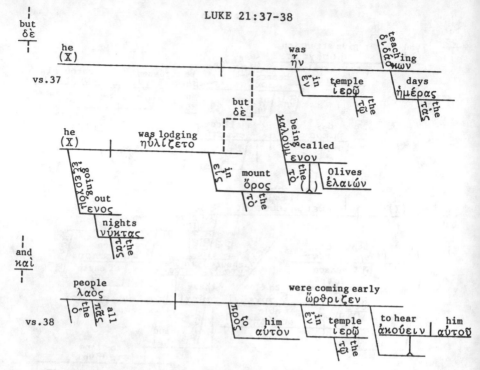

Three finite verbs appear in the two sentences above. They are all imperfects which express linear action. Two participles also come into the picture, both linear presents. The sentence of verse 37 is a two-clause compound. Though all imperfects are durative action, periphrastic imperfects are more strikingly dramatic than ordinary. So ἦν διδάσκων paints the picture with more vivid color. The appearance of ἡμέρας, accusative extent of time, underscores the durative action. "He was teaching day after day after day..." Adverbial phrase ἐν ἱερῷ states <u>where</u>.

Imperfect ηὐλίζετο "was lodging" matches "was teaching" but without periphrastic force. "Was lodging" is enforced by present circumstantial ἐξερχόμενος. Linear is stressed by accusative extent of time νύκτας "nights." εἰς with verbs of motion means "into" but sometimes "in" suits the context. In apposition to ὄρος is present articular participle "being called." Genitive "of Olives" specifies the name of the mount.

Verse 38, having but one clause, is simple in form. Imperfect ὤρθριζεν "were coming early" reports repeated action. It was a daily routine for "all the people." πρὸς and accusative implies movement <u>toward</u>, not neccesarily discipleship. They weren't yet personally attached to him. Adverbial "in the temple" indicates <u>where</u>. Present infinitive ἀκούειν "to hear" expresses purpose.

342

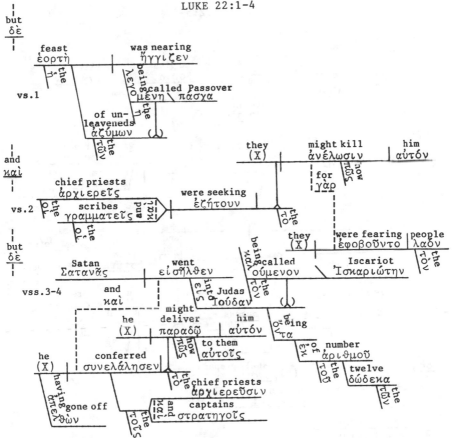

Verse one boasts of a single clause hence is simple in form. Genitive plural ἀζύμων "unleaveneds" specifies <u>kind</u> of "feast." It means "the Paschal feast" as appositional participle "the one being called" confirms. ἥγγιζεν is descriptive imperfect.

Verse two unveils a three-clause complex. ἐζήτουν is iterative imperfect. Article τὸ with indirect question and deliberative aorist subjunctive deals with the noun object clause as a substantized unit: "the how they might kill him." This idiom appears again in verses 3-4.

The sentence of 3-4 betrays two independent and a dependent clause hence it is compound-complex. In the first independent εἰσῆλθεν is ingressive aorist, "entered in." <u>Judas</u> is enlarged by participles, an attributive, "the one being called," and circumstantial "being of the number..." συν, prefix of aorist συνελάλησεν, determines the instrumental case with "chief priests and captains."

343

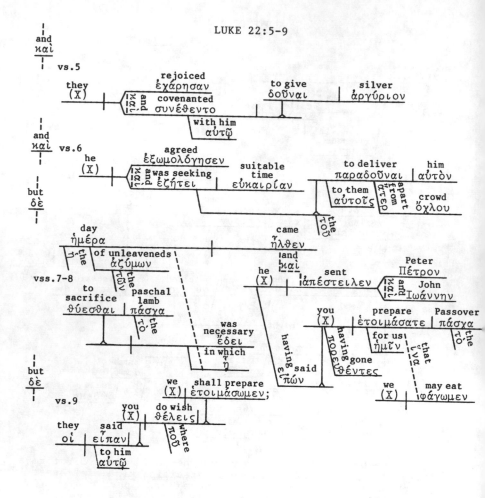

Each sentence in 5 and 6 is simple; each has compound predicate and each enjoys infinitive phrase attached to the second member of the predicate. δοῦναι is object; παραδοῦναι purpose.

Verses 7-8 employ two independent and three dependent clauses to create a compound-complex sentence. ῇ inserts an adjective clause modifying "day." Subject of imperfect ἔδει is present infinitive "to sacrifice." Noun clause, object of circumstantial εἰπών has ἵνα purpose clause stemming off it.

Verse 9 displays a complex of three clauses. "Where do you wish..." is noun clause object of εἰπαν. In turn θέλεις takes a noun object clause, "we shall prepare?"

344

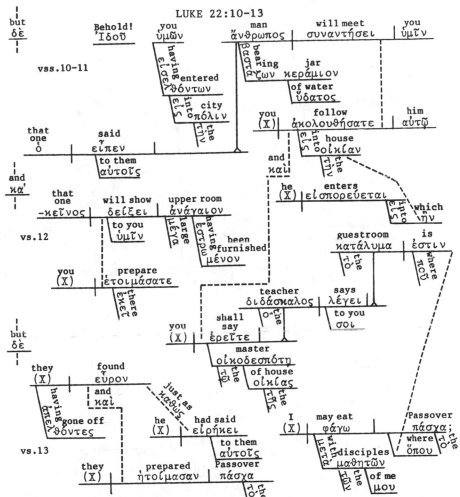

LUKE 22:10-13

After the independent clause the complex of 10-11, besides Genitive absolute, includes seven dependent clauses; three noun, objects of εἶπεν, one adjective describing οἰκίαν, a noun, object of ἐρεῖτε, noun object of λέγει and adverbial, inserted by ὅπου "where."

Verse 12 is a two-clause compound sentence with punctiliar future δείξει and aorist imperative ἑτοιμάσατε "you prepare." Participle ἐστρωμένον displays perfective action, "having been(and still is)furnished."

Verse 13 is compound-complex with καθὼς injecting dependent adverb clause of comparison.

345

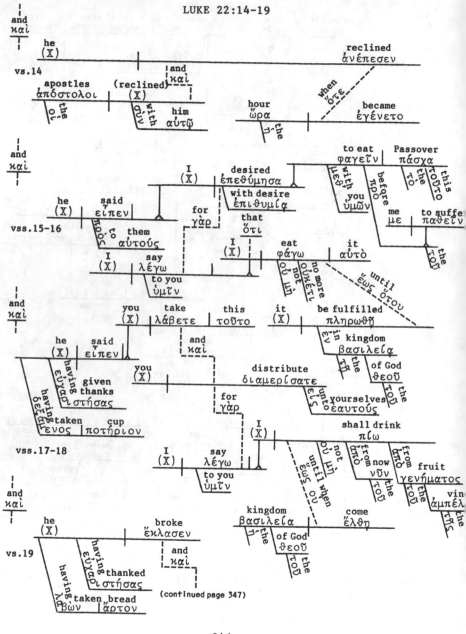

vs.14

vss.15-16

vss.17-18

vs.19

(continued page 347)

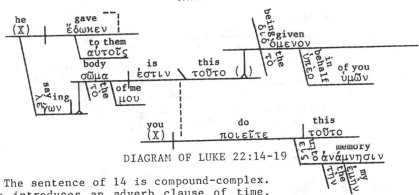

DIAGRAM OF LUKE 22:14-19

The sentence of 14 is compound-complex.
ὅτε introduces an adverb clause of time,
"when the hour came." ἀνέπεσεν literally
says, "he fell up" alluding to the custom
of recling around the banquet table.

Verses 15-16 incorporate five clauses to produce a complex
sentence. εἶπεν has two noun clauses as direct objects. ἐπιθυμίᾳ
is instrumental cognate idea with verb of same root, "I desired
with desire." Object of ἐπιθύμησα is infinitive phrase, "to eat
this Passover..." πρὸ τοῦ and infinitive with accusative of
general reference is adverbial, "before I suffer." Prepositional
phrase "with you" indicates manner, "in fellowship with you." ὅτι
brings in a noun clause object of λέγω. Note strong double
negative to which is added οὐκέτι giving triple force to the
negation. ἕως ὅτου "until when" is an adverb clause of time,
"until when."

Verses 17-18 display another complex having "he said" as the
independent idea. But the two aorist circumstantial participles,
"having given thanks" and "having taken cup,"set the the stage
on which Jesus makes point action aorist exhortation,
"take...distribute." These two object clauses are supported by
the γὰρ noun-object "for I say to you..." This is followed by
another noun object clause "I shall drink." πίω is aorist
subjunctive with strong double negative οὐ μή. "Until when" (ἕως
οὗ) indicates the limit of the negation.

The diagram of verse 19 begins on page 346 and concludes on
this page(347). It is compound-complex in structure. Again two
circumstantial participles give background for the action of the
two independent verbs "he broke" and he gave..." The two
dependent noun clauses are object of present circumstantial
λέγων. First comes "this is my body." Because σῶμα has the
definite article it is the subject. τοῦτο "this" is predicate
nominative, defined and described by present attributive
participle "the one having been given..." In the second noun
object clause present ποιεῖτε expresses the durative idea of "be
doing" repeatedly, regularly, continuously.

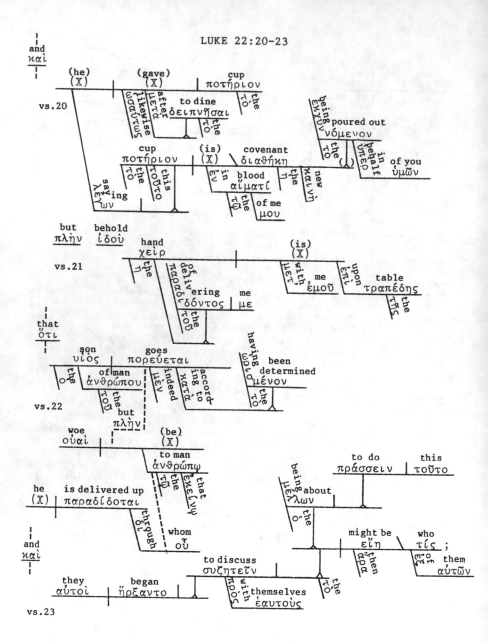

LUKE 22:20-23

348

Verse 20 frames a complex sentence. Independent clause gets
its subject and verb from vs.19, "he gave." Aorist infinitive
δειπνῆσαι, a verbal noun, is accusative with μετὰ "after the to
dine" which means, "after dinner." The dependent is noun clause,
object of circumstantial λέγων, "this cup (is) the new
covenant..." καινὴ signifies "new" in <u>kind</u> more than <u>time</u>.
Phrase "in my blood" is adverbial denoting <u>where</u>. The term
"covenant" has present attributive participial phrase in
apposition, "the one being poured out..." ὑπὲρ with ablative
literally = "over you." Context bespeaks "in behalf of."
   The sentence of 21 is simple in form. Implied by context the
verb "is" has adverbial expressions "with me" and "upon the
table," limiting it. Present genitive participle παραδιδόντος,
"of the one delivering me" describes a process. Its case
specifies the <u>kind</u> of hand.
   Verse 22 evolves into a compound-complex sentence of three
clauses. "The son goes but woe (be)..." represents the compound
elements. κατὰ "according to" presents the <u>standard</u> by which a
matter is judged. Perfect passive participle "having been determined" is accusative. The tense suggests permanent fixity of
what had "been determined." The dependent clause is inserted by
διά with relative "through whom." It is adjectival describing
ἀνθρώπῳ "man." The verb παραδίδοται is linear describing action
in progress, "is being delivered up."
   Verse 23 enjoys a complex arrangement. The independent
states, "they began to discuss..." Present infinitive συζητεῖν
is compounded from σύν "with" and ζητέω "search." Present tense
involves durative action; in cooperation "with" each other they
were "searching" an answer to the puzzle. πρὸς with reflexive
"themselves" underscores the idea of mutual "searching." The
resultant idea is: "they were discussing among themselves."
   The object (content) of what they were discussing is seen in
noun clause object of the infinitive. It has article τὸ with
indirect question with optative εἴη "might be." Subject is
present attributive participial phrase "the one being about..."

LUKE 22:24

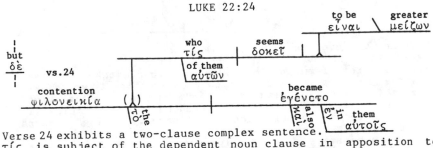

Verse 24 exhibits a two-clause complex sentence.
τίς is subject of the dependent noun clause in apposition to
φιλονεικία subject of the independent. The word translated
"contention" is compounded of φιλέω "love" and νεῖκος "strife."
Article τὸ makes the dependent clause a single substantive idea.
The ἐν phrase in this context means "among them."

LUKE 22:25-27

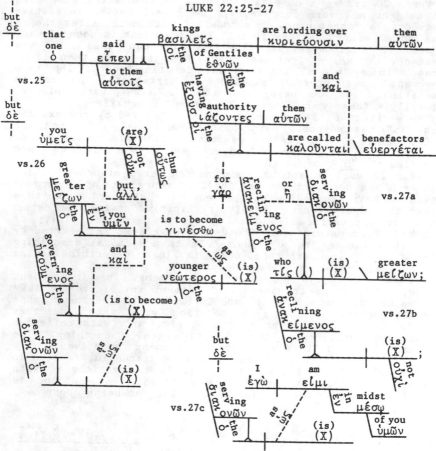

Verse 25 develops a three clause complex. Demonstrative use of ὁ is subject of independent followed by two object clauses. Verbs of ruling (κυρεύω and ἐξουσιάζω)take Genitive.

Verse 26 is a five clause compound-complex. Two ὡς are comparative dependent clauses. γινέσθω is present imperative.

Verse 27 displays two simple sentences and one complex. In 27a two present participles "reclining...serving" expand subject "who" by apposition.

27b is negative interrogative expecting "yes" as answer: "It's the one reclining is it not?"

The independent of 27c has emphatic ἐγὼ as subject, I on my part..." ὡς inserts comparative adverb clause,"as the one who serves..."

350

but
δὲ

vss.28-30

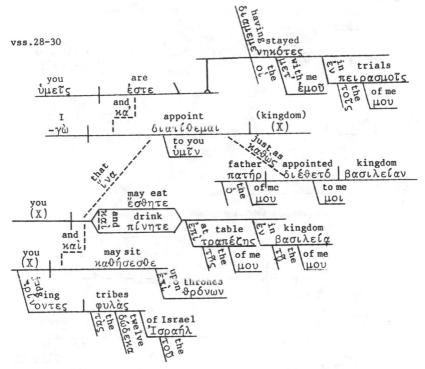

Verses 28-30 contain five clauses so arranged as to form a compound-complex sentence. The two independent clauses employ an emphatic personal pronoun as subject and thereby give special stress: "You are..." and "I appoint..." Perfect tense plus διά in composition gives to attributive participle διαμεμενηκότες the idea of "resolutely remained with me." διατίθεμαι is present middle of which Abbott-Smith lexicon comments, "with dative of person to assign..."(pg.112)

καθὼς inserts adverbial clause of comparison, "just as my father assigned to me..." ἵνα inaugurates two adverb purpose clauses, "in order that you may eat and drink..." Both "eat" and "drink" are aorist (punctiliar) action. They propose without describing. The ἐπὶ phrase is adverbial indicating where. The root meaning of ἐπὶ is "upon" but here the context suggests "at." ἐν brings in another adverb idea.

A second purpose appears in "that you may sit..." The ἐπὶ is adverbial telling where they "may sit." Circumstantial participle also suggests purpose, "judging the 12 tribes..."

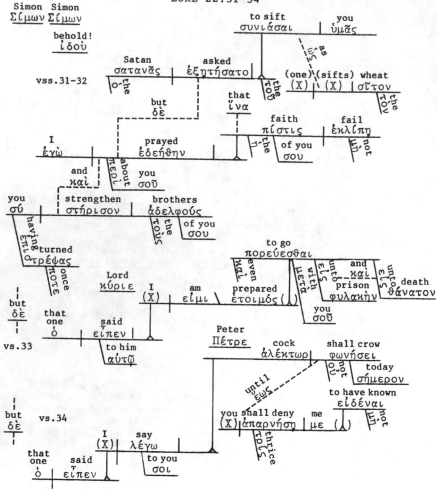

Of the sentences above 31-32 is compound-complex of five clauses. That of verse 33 is a two clause complex. The one of verse 34 is a complex of four clauses.

In 31-32 ὡς and ἵνα insert comparative and object clauses. Circumstantial ἐπιστρέψας is temporal "when once you turned." It has the <u>practical</u> force of a clause.

In verse 33 πορεύεσθαι is diagrammed in apposition to the adjective ἕτοιμός. It might rather be viewed as purpose.

Verse 34 entertains two noun object clauses. ἕως is adverb temporal, "until...

352

LUKE 22:35-36

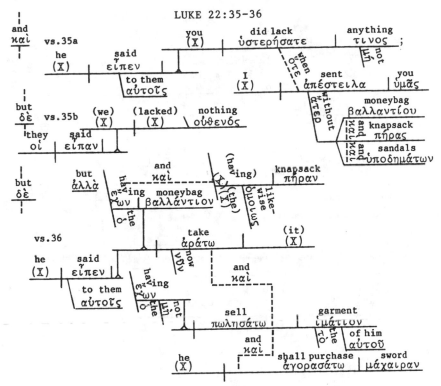

The three clauses of verse 35a form a complex sentence. "He said to them" is the independent clause. Dative αὐτοῖς signals that what he had to say was personal. Question, "Did you lack anything?" is noun clause object of "said." Ablative τινος, case of separation, follows ὑστερέω. Improper preposition ἄτερ "without" goes with ablatives, "moneybag and knapsack and sandals."

Verse 35b is the response to that which "he said to them." In structure it is a complex sentence. Subject οἱ of the independent clause is the demonstrative use of the article, "those (they) said..." οὐθενός is ablative after implied "lacked."

The sentence of verse 36 is complex with four clauses. Again, the independent clause is, "He said." To that are attached three noun clauses, all direct objects of "said." Subject of aorist imperative ἀράτω is compounded of two attributive participial phrases, "the one having moneybag and likewise (the one having) knapsack." Subject of the remaining clauses is represented by negative attributive participle, "the one not having...he..."

353

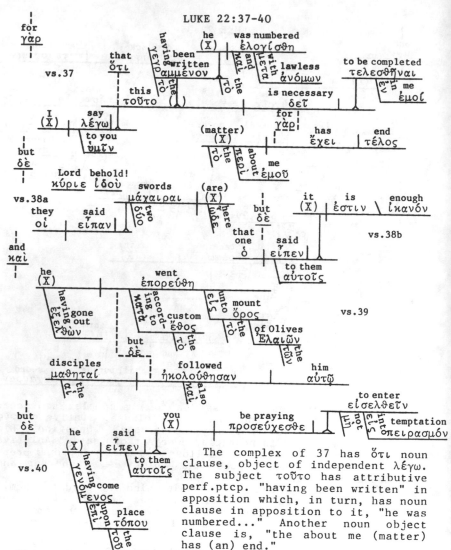

The complex of 37 has ὅτι noun clause, object of independent λέγω. The subject τοῦτο has attributive perf.ptcp. "having been written" in apposition which, in turn, has noun clause in apposition to it, "he was numbered..." Another noun object clause is, "the about me (matter) has (an) end."

The sentences of 38a and 38b are both complex each with two clauses, an independent followed by a noun clause object of the verb of the independent "said." In 38a οἱ is demonstrative use of the definite article. So also is ὁ of 38b. ὧδε in 38a is an adverb, "Here are two swords." Apparently the disciples took Jesus' words about buying a sword literally. Christ's response closes the conversation. Events will clarify his meaning!

The diagram of 22:39 (page 354 opposite) reveals a compound sentence of two clauses:"he went" and "the disciples followed." Aorist ἐξελθὼν is circumstantial temporal participle, "after he went out..." The κατὰ phrase is adverbial, probably best seen as answering the question why; "he went out because it was his custom." The εἰς phrase tells where. Direct object αὐτῷ of the second clause is associative instrumental case after the verb ἀκολουθέω which normally takes that case.

The sentence of verse 40 is complex in form. Circumstantial γενόμενος is temporal,"when he came..." Dative αὐτοῖς "to them" always adds a personal touch in contrast to πρός with acc. The noun object clause has present (linear) indicative "keep on praying..." The content of their prayer is seen in ingressive aorist infinitive, "that you don't enter into temptation."

LUKE 22:41-42

and	
καὶ	

he
αὐτὸς   was withdrawn
                         ἀπεσπάσθη

and
καὶ

he   was praying   them   about
(X)   προσηύχετο   from   αὐτῶν   throw
                                         ἀπ'   βολήν

having   Father   of stone
              πάτερ   you   remove   cup   λίθου
put   knees   (X)   παρένεγκε   ποτήριον
εἰς   γόνατα saying
              ων   nevertheless
                       πλήν   from
                                          ἀπ'
                                          ἐμοῦ   this
will   τοῦτο
θέλημά   is to become   you   will
              γινέσθω   (X)   βούλει
of me
μου   but
         ἀλλὰ   not

yours   (is to become)
σὸν   (X)

22:41-42 has two independent and four dependent clauses hence is compound-complex. Subject of the first independent is αὐτὸς, emphatic personal pronoun "he." Aorist "was withdrawn" presents the fact without describing. Imperfect "was praying" describes the fact of his praying: "he kept on praying..." Circumstantial participle θεὶς may express both manner and time. Object of λέγων are three noun clauses:"remove this cup" "not my will become" and "yours (is to become)." The εἰ clause is first class condition determined as true. Note that Jesus assumed that God in fact would will to remove the cup. This is another testimony to his real struggle as a human; "he learned obedience by the things which he suffered."(Heb.5:8)

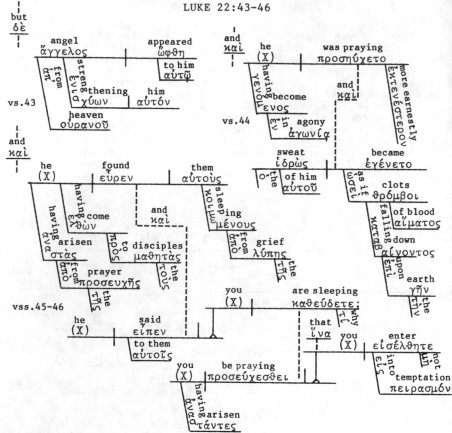

Verse 43 is a simple sentence. The word order suggests that the ἀπ' phrase is adjectival, not adverbial. Circumstantial participle ἐνισχύων suggests purpose.

Verse 44 evolves as compound sentence. Imperfect προσηύχετο is descriptive, "kept on praying." The words translated agony, sweat, and clots appear only here in the New Testament. Luke, a physician, was sensitive to the human in man.

45-46 involves a compound-complex of five clauses. "He found them" and "he said to them" are the independents. Three circumstantial participles attach themselves to the first clause, two to subject "he" and one to the object "them."

In the second, two noun clauses, objects of "said," appear. Verbs καθεύδετε and ποοσεύχεσθαι are linear presents. ἵνα inserts a noun clause object of "be praying." Ingressive aorist εἰσέλθητε = "not even begin to enter..."

356

LUKE 22:47-53

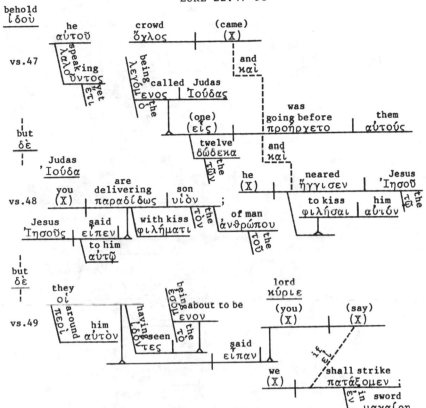

Besides Genitive Absolute, "he yet speaking" vs.47 has three independent clauses, hence is compound. "Crowd (gathered) [came] is the initial clause. Subject of the 2nd is attributive participial phrase "the one being called Judas." εἰς is in apposition defines him as "one of the 12." προῆρχετο is descriptive imperfect. Aorist infinitive of purpose φιλῆσαι follows constative aorist ἤγγισεν.

Verse 48 embodies a two clause complex sentence, "With kiss" is instrumental with deliberative present παραδίδως.

Verse 49   clause complex. Demonstrative article οἱ is subject. It, with amplifying phrase reads, "they, the ones around him." Aorist circumstantial participle "having seen" may be viewed as both causal and temporal. Its object is future attributive participle ἐσόμενον. With εἰ in indirect question is instrumental use of ἐν "(say) if we shall strike in (with) sword."

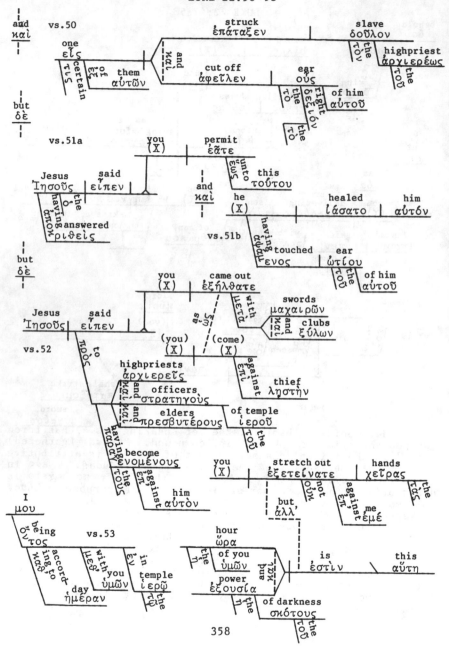

358

THE DIAGRAM OF LUKE 22:50-53

As diagrammed verse 50 embraces a simple sentence but with a compound predicate. Subject is cardinal εἷς modified by indefinite τις plus phrase "of them." Narrative aorists appear as the verbs of the predicate, "struck" and "cut off."

The sentence of 51a develops as a two-clause complex. In the independent "Jesus said" ἀποκριθεὶς is circ.ptcp. of coincident action. The linear action of present imperative ἐᾶτε should be noted: "go on permitting (even) unto this."

Verse 51b entails a simple sentence. Again a circumstantial participle, "having touched" expresses action coincident to the main verb "healed." ὠτίου "ear" is genitive after verb of sense ἁψάμενος "having touched."

Verses 52-53 could be viewed as one complex sentence with "he said" as the independent idea. But the diagram treats these verses as two separate sentences. Verse 52 as complex; verse 53 as compound with two independent clauses and genitive absolute.

In 52 the object of εἷπεν is noun clause "you came out." ὡς introduces a comparative idea "as " with context implying "you come." The preposition πρὸς introduces three classes of authorities "to" whom Jesus spoke. παραγενομένους is attributive participle with article, "the ones having come against him."

μου ὄντος "I(me) being..." is genitive absolute of verse 53. καθ᾽ ἡμέραν is idiomatic for "day by day." The remainder of the sentence consists of two independent clauses, one negative and one positive. "You did not stretch out your hands against me" indicates that their opposition was not openly public. <u>Their</u> "hour" was that which needed the "darkness" for its "power."

LUKE 22:54

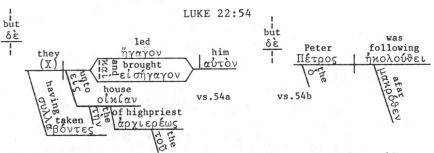

53a encloses a simple sentence with a compound predicate, "they led and brought him..." Aorist participle συλλαβόντες is circumstantial and is best viewed as <u>manner</u>, "having seized (arrested)..." The prepositional εἷς phrase is adverbial indicating <u>where</u>, "unto the house of..." Note the appearance of εἷς in both predicate verb and prepositional phrase.

The simple sentence of 54b has only five words, "But the Peter <u>was following</u> afar." Imperfect ἠκολούθει is descriptive. Like a magnet the events had a compelling effect on Peter but adverb μακρόθεν shows how Peter tried to keep his distance: "was following <u>from</u> afar."

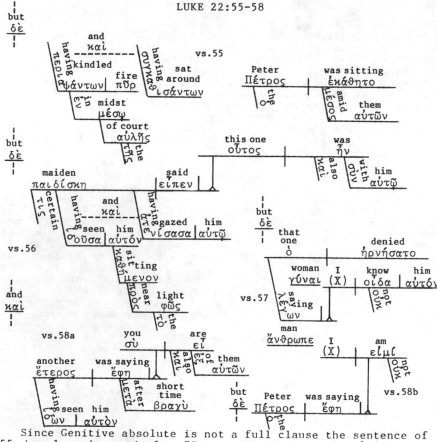

Since Genitive absolute is not a full clause the sentence of 55 is classed as simple: "Peter was sitting..." ἐκάθητο is descriptive imperfect. Adverbial μέσος reveals where. Genitive absolute is compound: "having kindled and having sat around..."

Verse 56 displays a two-clause complex, "maiden said, 'this one was also with him.'" Circumstantials ἰδοῦσα and ἀτενίσασα are temporal and causal showing when and what prompted her to speak up and identify Peter.

In the complex of verse 57 demonstrative use of ὁ is subject of the independent, "that one denied." Noun clause, "I do not know him" is object of circumstantial "saying."

58a is also complex of two clauses. Masculine subject ἕτερος is "another of a different kind," a male, not "woman." Subject σύ of noun-object clause is very emphatic "you."

The answer to the accusation, 58b, also two-clause complex, repeats descriptive imperfect ἔφη "was saying" as its verb.

360

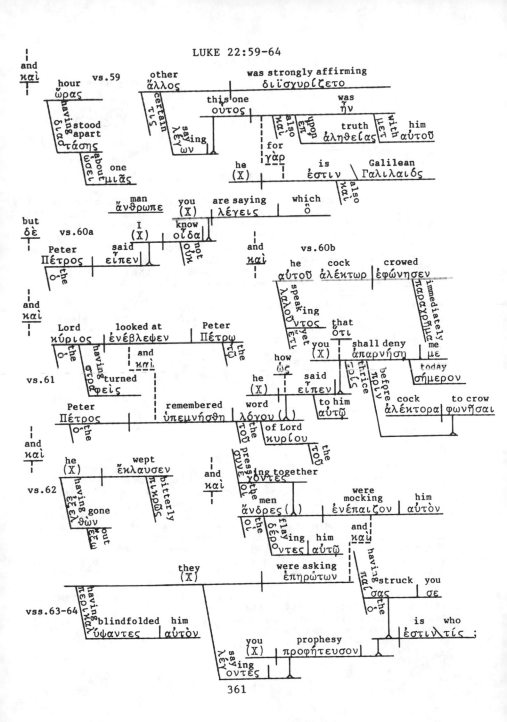

361

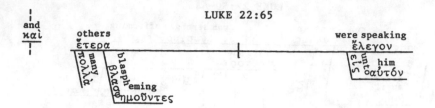

THE DIAGRAM OF LUKE 22:59-65

Verse 59 involves a Genitive absolute plus three clauses. It forms a complex sentence. "Was strongly affirming" is imperfect middle, "he repeatedly affirmed." The two dependents are both noun clauses objects of circumstantial "saying." Demonstrative οὗτος acts as a pointer, "this one." Peter's speech betrayed him for "he was Galilean."

"Peter said" is an independent clause in the complex of 60. "I do not know" is noun clause object of εἶπεν. Object of οἶδα is noun clause, "that which you say." λέγεις is linear iterative present, "are repeatedly saying."

Verse 60b forms a simple sentence with Genitive absolute and one clause: "while yet speaking, the cock crowed immediately."

Verse 61 appears as compound-complex. The compound elements reflect the Lord's action, "...looked at Peter..." and Peter's reaction, "...remembered the word..." λόγου is Genitive after word of remembering. ὡς introduces noun clause appositional to word. ὅτι may introduce direct discourse; the diagram shows it as in direct. πρὶν with ablative infinitive, here one of 11 times in the New Testament, a "literary touch" of Luke's.

The consequence of the picture developed in verse 61 appears in a simple sentence of 62, "Having gone out he wept bitterly."

Verses 63-64 entertain four full clauses forming a compound complex arrangement. Subject of the initial independent clause is the articular attributive συνέχοντες "the ones pressing(him) together." ἐνέπαιζον "were mocking" is both distributive, iterative and vividly descriptive. Present δέροντες adds radiance. Imperfect ἐπηρώτων in the other independent adds descriptive power. Two object noun clauses are hinged to circumstantial "saying." Aorist imperative προφήτευσον has for its object the noun clause, "the one having struck you is who?"

The sentence of verse 65 (this page above) is simple in form. ἕτερα signifies "others of a different sort." The opposition ran the gauntlet of all sorts and classes of people. Imperfect ἔλεγον suggests distribution as well as repetition. εἰς "unto" in this context intimates "against him." Circumstantial participle βλασφημοῦντες casts its shadow over the whole sentence. This is that in the context which specifically flavors the whole thought.

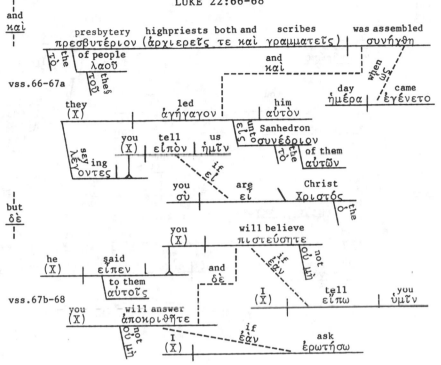

Two of the five clauses of verses 66-67a are independent while three are dependent. The sentence is compound-complex. Subject πρεσβυτέριον refers to a "body of elders." In this instance the particular "body" is defined by appositionals "highpriests" and "scribes." Both the verbs translated "was assembled" and "led" are narrative aorists. ὡς introduces an adverbial dependent clause, "as" or "when." Object of present circumstantial participle "saying" is noun clause "tell us." It is apodosis of 1st class conditional introduced by εἰ "if you are the Christ." The condition assumes that he is "the Christ." Personal pronoun σὺ gives special emphasis to "you."

In the complex sentence of verses 67b-68, "he said" is the independent element. It has a compound object consisting of two negative noun clauses, "you will not believe" and "you will not answer..." Each of these is apodosis for 3rd class conditions, undetermined but with prospect of determination, "if I tell..." and "if I should ask (you) and I may or I may not."

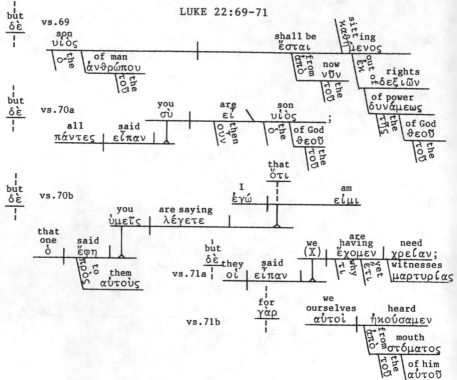

LUKE 22:69-71

Verse 69 reveals a simple sentence. Its verb is periphrastic future ἔσται and present participle καθήμενος. It emphasizes ongoing action. Adverbial "from the now" by use of article uses νῦν as substantive. Plural Ablative δεξιῶν "rights" alludes to the "right hand" or "right side."

Verse 70a is a two-clause complex. Subject "all" refers to "highpriests" and "scribes" of vs.66. Personal pronoun σὺ is emphatic, "Are you then the son of God?" This key issue is the only one that drew a response from Jesus. It's the sole reason why Christ submitted to the humilation of death.

70b is a complex of three clauses. "He said" is independent to which is attached the noun clause "You are saying..." Object of verb "are saying" is the ὅτι noun clause, "I am!" Jesus maneuvered them into stating the fact.

The diagram shows 71a as complex of two clauses. οἱ is the demonstrative use of plural article, "those said..." "Why are we yet having need" is noun clause object of "said."

71b might be viewed as noun clause object of εἶπαν of verse 71a. The diagram presents it as a separate simple sentence, "we ourselves (αὐτοὶ) heard." Phrase "from his mouth" is adverbial indicating from whence.

364

LUKE 23:1-3

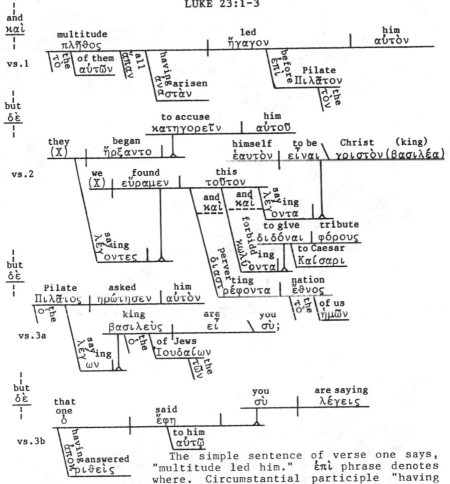

The simple sentence of verse one says, "multitude led him." ἐπὶ phrase denotes where. Circumstantial participle "having arisen" suggests antecedent action.

In the complex sentence of vs.2 present inf. κατηγορεῖν is object of independent ἤρξαντο "began." "We found this (one)" is noun clause object of circumstantial λέγοντες "saying." Three charges against Jesus appear in the participial phrases rooted in demonstrative τοῦτον "this (one)."

Two clauses in 3a frame a complex sentence. The noun object clause, "Are you king..." uses emphatic pronoun σύ.

The independent clause of the complex of verse 3b has demonstrative use of ὁ "that one" as subject. In dependent noun object clause "you are saying" σύ adds its intensive stress.

365

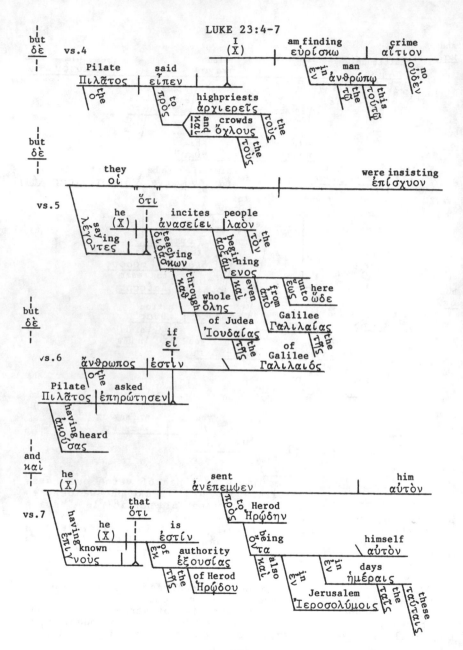

LUKE 23:4-7

THE DIAGRAM OF LUKE 23:4-9a

Verse 4 includes two clauses forming a complex sentence. The dependent noun clause is object of verb "said." Linear action of the present εὑρίσκω suggests repeated searching and no finding of any αἴτιον "cause" which in this context means "crime."
Another two-clause complex appears in verse five. Subject is demonstrative use of οἱ "those." Imperfect ἐπίσχυον is a vivid description, "they repeatedly used their strength." ὅτι brings in a noun clause, object of "saying," a direct quote. Present ἀνασείει confirms to the reader that Jesus repeatedly "shook up" the people by his teaching. Where? "Through the whole of Judea." More specifically, "beginning from Galilee even unto here." Thus ἀρξάμενος is viewed adverbially although it may be seen as circumstantial describing subject "he."
In the two-clause complex of verse six dependent εἰ "if" injects noun clause in indirect discourse; it is object of "asked." εἰ may be translated "whether."
Verse 7 presents another complex of two full clauses. ἐπιγνοὺς is temporal circumstantial participle, "when he knew." ὅτι inserts noun clause object of "having known." The πρὸς phrase is adverbial indicating where. ὄντα is circumstantial describing "Herod." The ἐν phrases are adverbial suggesting where "in Jerusalem" and when "in these days."
Verse 8 (below) forms a three-clause compound. Aorist ἐχάρη reports a fact, "Herod rejoiced." Periphrastic ἦν θέλων "was wishing" underscores an ongoing desire, a continuing attitude. Though not periphrastic ἤλπιζέν is descriptive imperfect of Herod's continuing secret fancy.
The simple sentence of 9a retains iterative imperfect. He asked question after question.

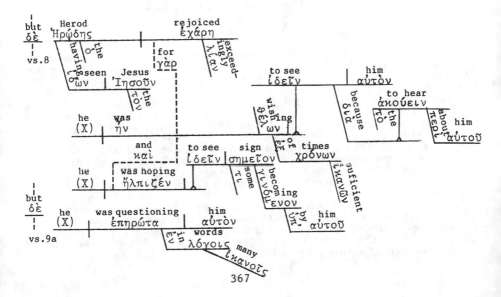

367

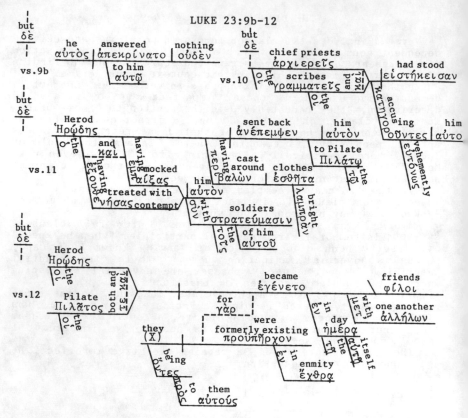

The simple sentence of 9b has but five words. Adversative δὲ sets the thought in opposition to the preceding. The pronoun αὐτὸς is very emphatic as subject. Aorist is point action fact.

The simple sentence of 10 has compound subject. Pluperfect εἱστήκεισαν indicates they "had taken a stand and persisted in it." Theirs had been a fixed attitude! As adjective present participle "accusing" describes the subject; as verb it shows what they did as they "stood."

Verse 11 forms a simple sentence, "Herod sent him back." But the circumstances preceding and surrounding such action is dramatized by three aorist circumstantial participles and their modifiers:"having dealt with contempt...mocked...thrown clothes around..."

Verse 12 structures a two-clause compound sentence. The conjunction τε combined with καὶ strengthens the intensity of the newly-found bond of friendship. The imperfect προϋπῆρχον contrasts the continuous former "enmity" to the fresh friendship displayed by point action aorist ἐγένετο.

368

LUKE 23:13-16

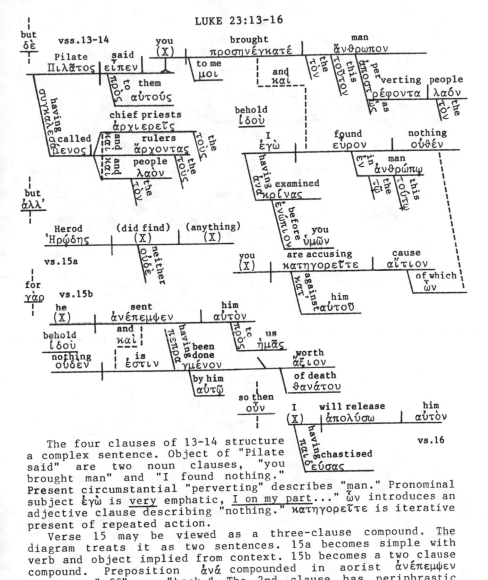

The four clauses of 13-14 structure
a complex sentence. Object of "Pilate
said" are two noun clauses, "you
brought man" and "I found nothing."
Present circumstantial "perverting" describes "man." Pronominal
subject ἐγὼ is _very_ emphatic, I on my part..." ὧν introduces an
adjective clause describing "nothing." κατηγορεῖτε is iterative
present of repeated action.

Verse 15 may be viewed as a three-clause compound. The
diagram treats it as two sentences. 15a becomes simple with
verb and object implied from context. 15b becomes a two clause
compound. Preposition ἀνά compounded in aorist ἀνέπεμψεν
suggests "off" or "back." The 2nd clause has periphrastic
perfect, "having been done..." "Worth" is predicate adjective.

Verse 16 appears as a simple sentence: "So then, having
chastised I will release him." παιδεύσας is temporal
circumstantial, "having chastised..."

369

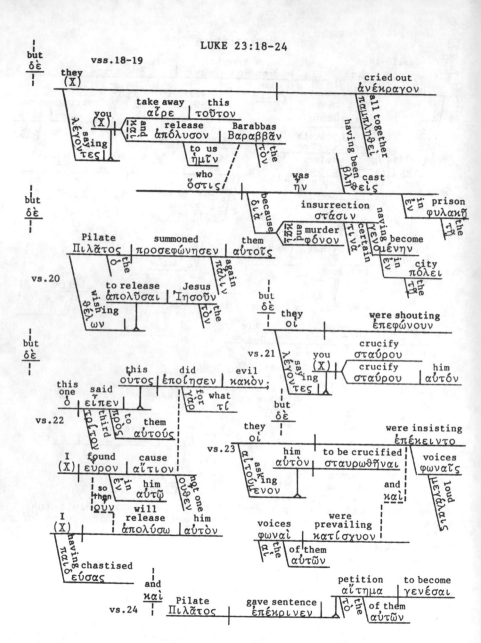

370

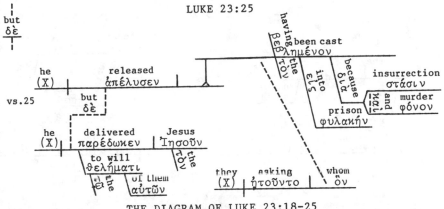

LUKE 23:25

THE DIAGRAM OF LUKE 23:18-25

Verses 18-19 give rise to a complex sentence. Point action aorist prevails in the independent clause. It is effective aorist, "they cried out." Note contrast of present αἴρε versus aorist ἀπόλυσον in the compound predicate of the noun clause object of saying, "be taking away" and "release now, immediately, on the spot..." ὅστις adjective clause has periphrastic pluperfect, "having been cast." Aorist circumstantial participle γενομένην portrays a point at which the "certain insurrection took place.

Verse 20 forms a simple sentence. Present participle θέλων infers purpose. Dative αὐτοῖς is direct object of "summoned."

In the complex of vs. 21 subject οἱ is demonstrative use of article. Direct object of present "saying" is noun clause with compound predicate imperative. σταύρου is present imperative: "go on be crucifying him..." "

As diagrammed 22 involves a complex with three noun clauses objects of independent "said." γὰρ in "for what" appears as if a preposition in the adverbial, "for what reason?" οὐθεν is emphatic "not one." The aorist εὗρον sums up his extended investigation into a point. Adverbial "in him" indicates where. ἀπολύσω is volitional future, "I will..."

Besides two independent clauses verse 23 has aorist passive infinitive "to be crucified" with accusative of general reference αὐτὸν object of participle "asking." Imperfect ἐπέκειντο is distributive and iterative. Imperfect "were prevailing" is descriptive.

In the simple sentence of verse 24 independent verb "gave sentence" is point action aorist with aorist infinitive and accusative of general reference as object.

Verse 25 unveils a compound-complex sentence. "He released ...but he delivered over..." constitute the compound elements. Object of "released" is attributive perfect participle "the one having been cast" with its modifiers. Modifying "Barabbas" is ὃν which inserts adjective clause "whom they were asking." Imperfect ἠτοῦντο "were asking" is iterative of repeated action.

371

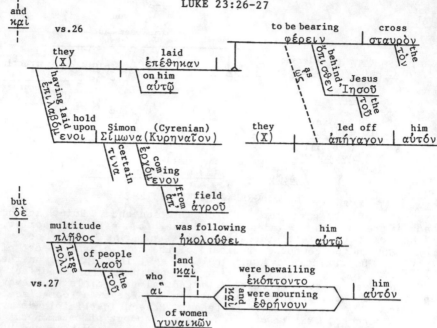

Verse 26 includes infinitive and participial phrases. It also has two clauses so arranged as to create a complex sentence. Present infinitive φέρειν underscores linear action "be bearing..." It is object of the verb of independent aorist ἐπέθηκαν. An infinitive, as noun, may <u>be</u> an object as here; as verb it may <u>take</u> an object as "cross" here. It also may be modified by adverbial expressions such as "behind Jesus." ὡς introduces adverbial clause of time = "as," or "when." "Having grabbed hold"(ἐπιλαβόμενοι)..." is circumstantial participle of time "when" though an element of purpose is also suggested. The present ἐρχόμενον is surely temporal, "as" or "while coming."

The sentence of 27 is compounded of two independent clauses. Imperfect ἠκολούθει "was following" is descriptive. Object αὐτῷ is associative instrumental, normal with verb ἀκολουθέω.

The second clause has a compound predicate of two imperfects "were bewailing" and "were mourning." They give vivid portrayal of some "of women" publicly demonstrating at the impending execution.

What to do with αἵ is a problem not to mention how to deal with genitive γυναικῶν. Some manuscripts have nominative γυναικές. The diagram has αἵ as relative used demonstratively as "they who of women" and places it as subject. The student is to decide for himself the solution to this odd mixture of words.

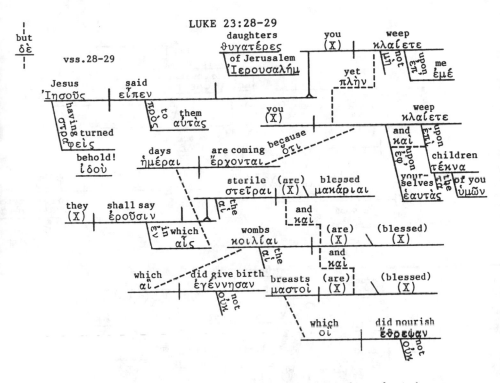

LUKE 23:28-29

Of the ten clauses in verses 28-29 nine are dependent hence the sentence is complex. "Jesus said" is the bare independent. Second aorist passive στραφείς is temporal circumstatial "when he was turned." Two noun clauses as objects of "said" tell <u>what</u> he said "to them," these "daughters of Jerusalem." Negative μὴ with the linear action of present imperative κλαίετε indicate "quit weeping." The conjunction πλὴν presents an opposite, <u>but</u>, <u>yet</u>, <u>nevertheless</u>: "<u>Yet</u> you are to <u>keep on</u> weeping..."

ὅτι introduces an adverb clause of cause giving the underlying reason why they should be weeping. Present ἔρχονται is futuristic, "days shall come." Relative phrase ἐν αἶς inserts an adjective phrase defining "days." Three noun clauses follow as direct objects of ἐροῦσιν "shall say." In the last two of the three noun-object clauses the predicate adjective "blessed" is implied from the context. The relative αἳ is subject of an adjective clause modifying "wombs." A second relative οἳ appears as subject of another adjective clause describing "breasts." The verbs ἐγέννησαν and ἔφρεψαν are both aorists with negatives. "Did not at any point give birth" and "did not nourish."

373

LUKE 23:30-33

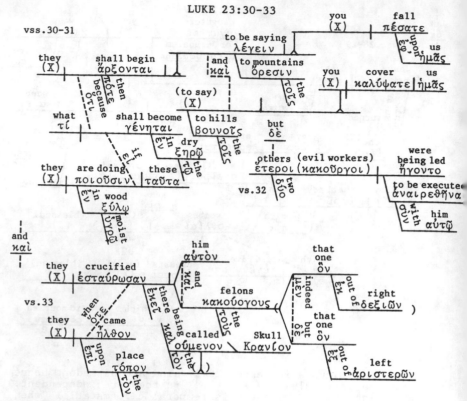

Independent clause "they shall begin to say" in the complex of 30-31 is followed by four dependents. Present infinitive "to be saying" (implied a 2nd time) takes as its objects the noun clauses, "fall upon us" and "cover us." ὅτι adverbial causal clause gives a reason why they "shall begin to say..." And that reason is based on a 1st class condition assumed as true, "if they do these..."

Verse 32 exhibits a simple sentence. ἕτεροι means "others" of a different kind. κακοῦργοι is compounded of terms for bad and worker and may be rendered "felon." Imperfect "were being led" is descriptive.

Verse 33 sets forth a two-clause complex. The aorist verb "crucified" of the independent clause has two objects, "him" and "felons." In apposition to "felons" are two relatives (ὃν) used demonstratively "that one." With ἐκ and ablative plurals δεξιῶν and ἀριστερῶν may equal, "one on the right...one on the left." ὅτε produces an adverb clause of time, "when they came." The adverbial ἐπί phrase declares where.

374

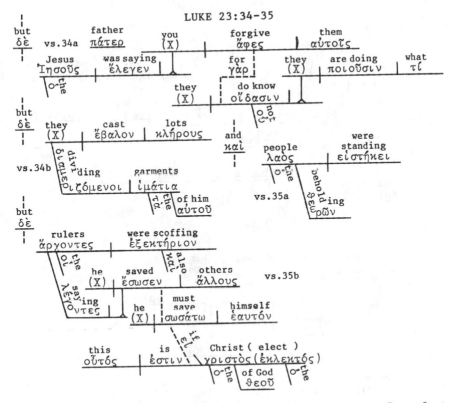

LUKE 23:34-35

The arrangement of 34a reveals a complex sentence. Imperfect ἔλεγεν "was saying" appears in the independent clause rather the usual aorist "said." It pictures Jesus in the process. What he was saying appears in the three noun object clauses, two of which are objects of ἔλεγεν. Perfect οἴδασιν has the force of linear present and supplies a contrast to aorist ἄφες. While forgiveness may be repeated, in its nature each forgiveness extended is a momentary _event_ not a process. Present ποιοῦσιν is a process going on.

34b represents a simple sentence. Circumstantial "dividing" gives a descriptive touch as to _how_ they "cast" loto.

35a also displays a simple sentence with a descriptive present participle.

35b enjoys descriptive imperfect in its independent clause, "were scoffing." Two noun clauses, objects of "saying", have aorists, indicative ἔσωσεν and σωσάτω is an imperative. εἰ introduces 1st class conditional, assumed to be true. Note the contemptuous use of demonstrative οὗτός.

375

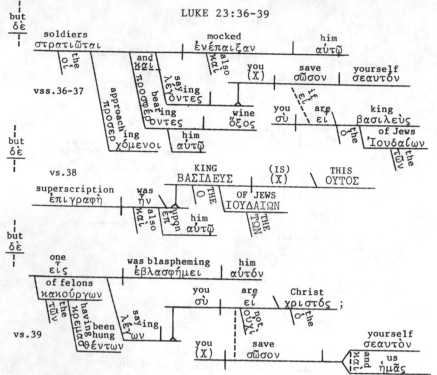

The sentence of 36-37 is complex. It has three full clauses and three circumstantial participles modifying the subject of the independent, "<u>soldiers</u> mocked him..." The present ptcps. describe the soldiers "approaching...bearing...saying..." That which they were saying is in the noun clause object of <u>saying</u>: "save yourself." σῶσον is aorist the point action of which suits the situation, that is, "get off the cross and out of this death experience." εἰ introduces a 1st class condition assumed as true. "Assuming you are king, to save yourself should logically follow!!

Verse 38 pictures a two-clause complex sentence. The ἐπ' αὐτῷ phrase is adverbial. ἐπ' literally, "upon" but here = "over." "The king of the Jews is this (one)" is noun clause serving as predicate nominative after ἦν.

Verse 39 displays a complex sentence. The subject "one" is identified by Genitive "felons" and as "having been hung." The imperfect ἐβλασφήμει "was blaspheming" paints a picture of the repeated revilings of the "one" felon. Object of participle, "saying" are two noun clauses. The 1st is a question expecting "yes" for an answer: "You are the Christ are you not?" The conclusion is stated in the 2nd object clause: "save yourself..."

376

LUKE 23:40-43

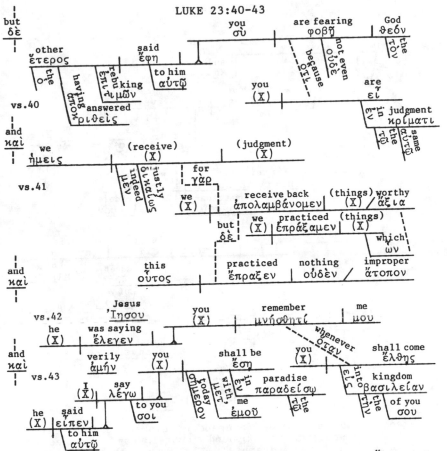

Verse 40 involves a three-clause complex sentence. ἕτερος is "other" of a different kind. Subject σὺ of noun object clause is emphatic. ὅτι brings in adverbial causal clause.

Three independent clauses and one dependent make 41 complex. Subject ἡμεῖς is very emphatic. μὲν "indeed" balances with δὲ "but." ἄξια "worthy" and ἄτοπον "improper" are objective complements. ὧν brings in an adjective clause.

Verse 42 encloses a complex of three clauses. Imperfect "was saying" is descriptive. Aorist imperative μνήσθητί has Genitive μου as object. The point action suits the urgent situation. ὅταν is indefinite adverbial conjunction of time "whenever."

Verse 43 presents a three clause complex. Heightened emphasis is gained by object clause: "Verily, I say to you" followed by its object clause declaring, "Today you shall be..."

377

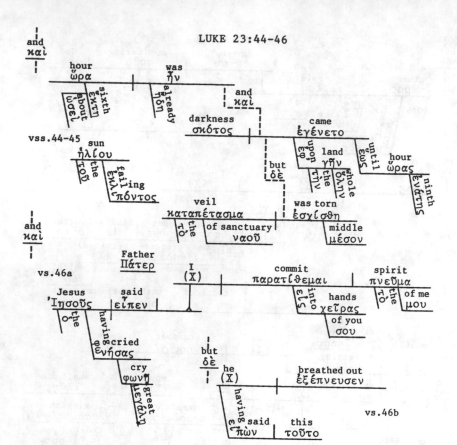

Verses 44-45 have three independent clauses and a Genitive absolute. The sentence is compound. ἕκτη is used as adjective, hence ὡσεί "about" is adverbial. The imperfect ἦν is aoristic and thus matches the point action of ἐγένετο and ἐσχίσθη in the next clauses. Prepositional phrases ἐφ' and ἕως are adverbs of place and time telling where and when the "darkness became." ναός is the inner sanctuary of the temple building and its facilities. μέσον is adverbial accusative = "in the midst."

Verse 46a comprises a complex sentence of two clauses. "Jesus said" is the independent idea. In the noun clause, object of "said" παρατίθεμαι is present describing action going on, "I am committing." It is a banking term = "deposit." Modifying Jesus of the main clause is circumstantial φωνήσας which in turn is modified by cognate instrumental, "with (φωνῇ) great cry."

With but four words 46b is a simple sentence. The aorist ἐξέπνευσεν "breathed out" may be translated "expired."

378

but
δέ

vs.47

centurion — ἑκατοντάρχης — the — ὁ
having happened — γενόμενον — the — τό
having seen — ἰδὼν — the — τό
was glorifying — ἐδόξαζεν
saying — λέγων
God — θεόν — the — τόν
man — ἄνθρωπος — the — ὁ
this — οὗτος
was — ἦν
righteous — δίκαιος
truly — ὄντως

and
καί

vs.48

crowds — ὄχλοι — all — πάντες — the — οἱ
having assembled — συμπαραγενόμενοι — upon — ἐπί
having happened — γενόμενα — the — τά
having beheld — θεωρήσαντες — the — τά
spectacle — θεωρίαν — the — τήν — this — ταύτην
were returning — ὑπέστρεφον
beating — τύπτοντες
breasts — στήθη — the — τά

but
δέ

vs.49

acquaintances — γνωστοί — all — πάντες — the — οἱ
to him — αὐτῷ
women — γυναῖκες — the — αἱ
following — συνακολουθοῦσαι — the — αἱ
him — αὐτῷ
from Galilee — Γαλιλαίας — the — τῆς
and — καί
seeing — ὁρῶσαι
these — ταῦτα
were standing — εἱστήκεισαν
afar — μακρόθεν — from — ἀπό

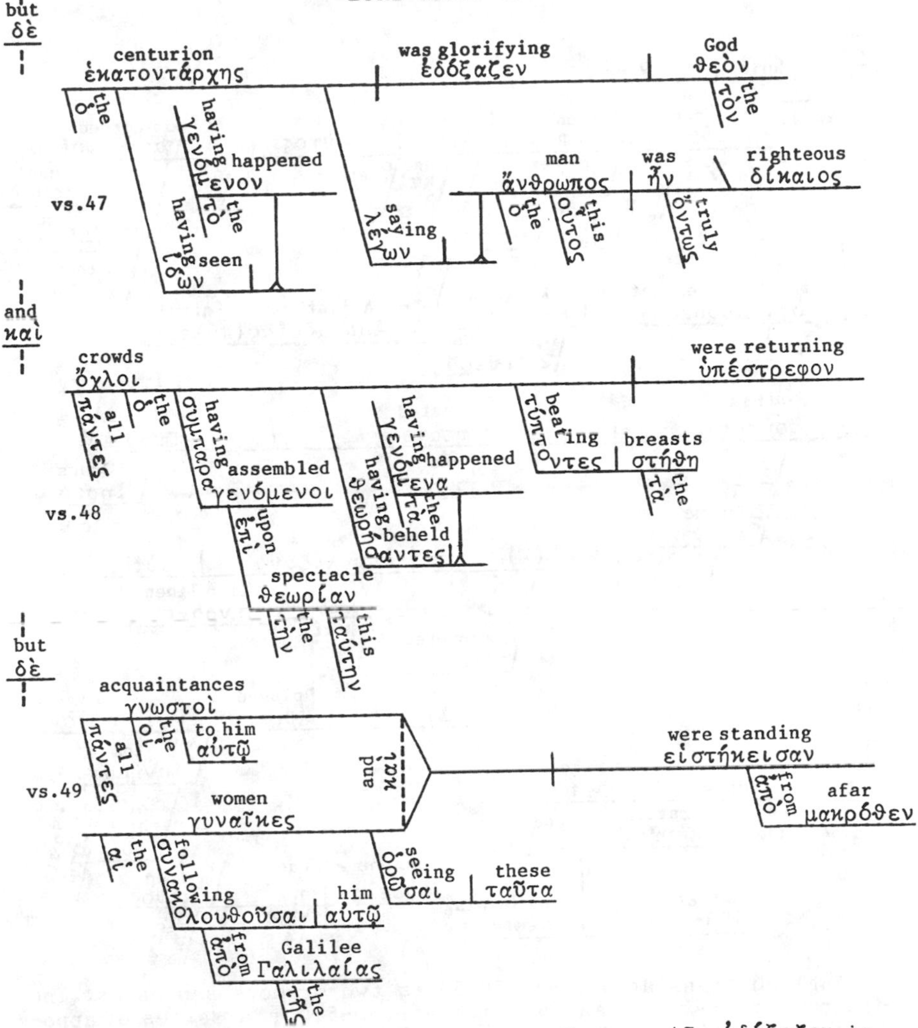

Two clauses form a complex sentence of verse 47. ἐδόξαζεν is imperfect describing continuing "glorifying" by the centurion.

"Crowds...were returning" is the simple sentence of 48 being stripped of all modifiers including three participial phrases. ὑπέστρεφον is descriptive imperfect.

49 forms a simple sentence. It has a compound subject. Pluperfect εἱστήκεισαν has the force of imperfect. αὐτῷ is instrumental after "to follow."

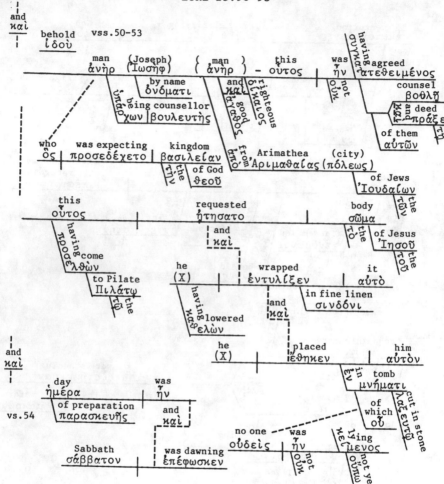

English translations see 50-53 as two or more sentences. The diagram treats them as one with vss.50-51 as a series of appositions plus independent "this (man) had not agreed..." Also a relative adjective clause describing ἀνήρ. Beginning at verse 52 three independent clauses combine to give a compound flavor to the sentence. Relative adjectival οὗ "of which" clause adds a complex notion. Subject οὗτος of vs.52 has as antecedent all of verses 50-51. Note periphrastics in 50 and 53.

Verse 54 is a two-clause compound. ἐπέφωσκεν is inchoative imperfect, "began to dawn."

380

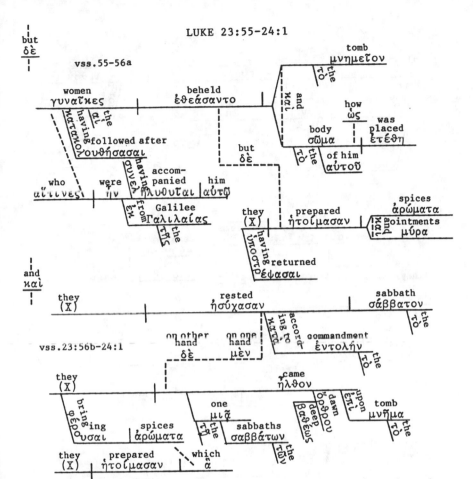

The sentence of 55-56a is compound-complex. Two independent clauses say: "women beheld...they prepared..." That which they beheld appears in a compound object one part of which is noun clause "how his body was placed." Qualitative relative αἵτινες ushers in adjective clause describing "women." Pf.ptcp."having accompanied" joins with ἦν as periphrastic pluperfect "had accompanied." Adverbial ἐκ with ablative shows <u>from whence</u>.

23:56b-24:1 forms a compound-complex of three clauses. μὲν δὲ balance the independent ideas, "on the one hand they rested but on the other hand they came..." ἅ adds an adjective clause describing "spices." The μιᾷ idea "the one(1st)of the sabbaths" is normal way of saying, "the first day of the week." The two Genitives "deep dawn" refer to time. It was dark when they started for the tomb!

381

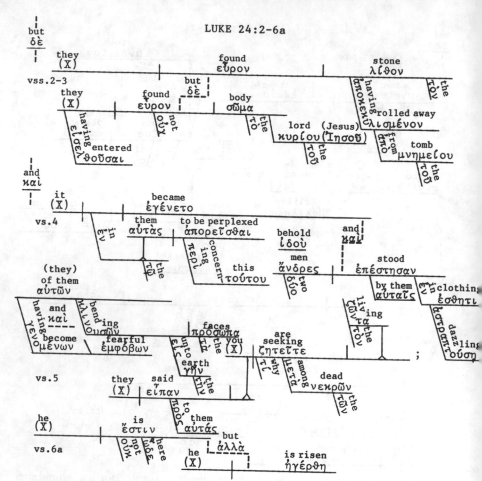

Verses 2-3 form a compound sentence. Adversative δὲ makes
the contrast, "they found...but they did not find..."

Verse 4 involves a two-clause compound: "it became...two men
stood..." ἐν τῷ with infinitive technically isn't a clause. But
in English it may appear as a dependent, "while they were perplexed about this..." αὐτὰς is accusative of general reference.

Verses 5-6a may be viewed as one complex sentence. But the
diagram treats them as separate. Independent "he said" has for
its object interrogative noun clause, "Why are you seeking..."
Attributive ζῶντα is object. μετὰ literally = "amidst."

As diagrammed verse 6a has negative and positive independent
clauses, "He is not here but he is risen." ἀλλὰ is strong adversative. Aorist ἠγέρθη focuses on the <u>fact</u>, not the process.

382

LUKE 24:6b-9

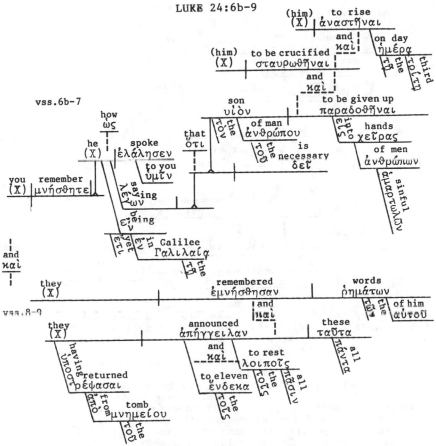

Aorist imperative μνήσθητε creates the independent clause in
the complex of 6b-7. Here ὡς is declarative how, much like ὅτι
which introduces noun clause object of λέγων "saying." Present
δεῖ has for its subject three infinitives each with accusative
of general reference which are stated or implied: "son to be
given up," "(him) to be crucified," and "(him)to rise..."
Present participial phrase ὢν ἐν is temporal, "while he was in
Galilee..."
     Verses 8-9 exemplify a two-clause compound. Genitive ῥημάτων
as object follows word of remembering. Aorist circumstantial
participle ὑποστρέψασαι is temporal "when they returned." The
action of both finite verbs, being aorist, presents factual
points though, no doubt, they probably were repeated. Luke
focuses on the facts, not the repetition.

383

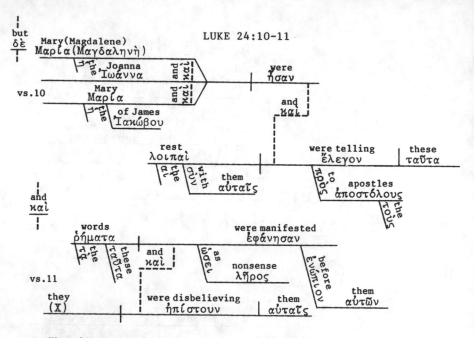

LUKE 24:10-11

The diagram of verse 10 demonstrates a compound sentence of two clauses. The adversative δὲ with which the sentence begins sets the following women apart as the ones of verse nine who "told these to the eleven and all the rest." Subject of the first clause identifies three women by name. The second clause with less specifics completes the group as "the rest...." Prepositional phrase "with them" may be conceived as adverbial modifying the verb; the diagram prefers to look on it as adjectival describing "the rest." Imperfect ἔλεγον captures the excitement by calling attention to the <u>repetition</u> of their experience. Prepositional phrase πρὸς is adverbial in function. It shows <u>where</u> they "were telling" ταῦτα "these things."

The diagram presents verse 11 as a two-clause compound. The adverb phrase introduced by ὡσεὶ might be considered as a truncated subordinate clause, "as if nonsense (is manifested.)" The word λῆρος "nonsense" appears only here in the New Testament. "Medical writers used it for the wild talk of those in delirium or hysteria."(A. T. Robertson, Word Pictures, Vol.II,pg.291)

The imperfect ἠπίστουν describes how that those who heard these women were repeatedly distrusting their report. The early disciples were not of such who "wanted" to believe such an impossible tale. They came by their faith only by persistent and stubborn evidence. αὐταῖς is direct object in dative after word for disbelief.

384

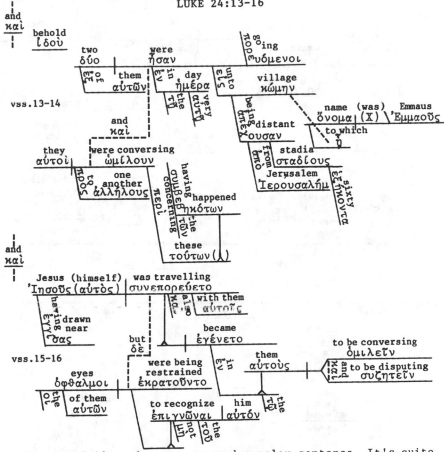

Verses 13-14 enclose a compound-complex sentence. It's quite animated due to the imperfects of the two independent clauses, periphrastic ἦσαν πορευόμενοι and ὡμίλουν. Relative ᾗ brings in adjective clause describing "village." Subject of second clause αὐτοί is emphatic, they were carrying on a spirited discussion.

ἐγένετο "became" of the complex of 15-16 enjoys a compound subject of two noun clauses. ἐγένετο literally means "became" but often is rendered "it came to pass." In this sentence what "came to pass" is stated in the compound subject. Both verbs are imperfects giving vigorous descriptions, "was travelling" and "were being restrained." τοῦ and infinitive "to recognize" are ablative, "...eyes were restrained from..." ἐν τῷ and present linear infinitives "to be conversing...disputing" express temporal idea, "while they were..."

LUKE 24:17a-20

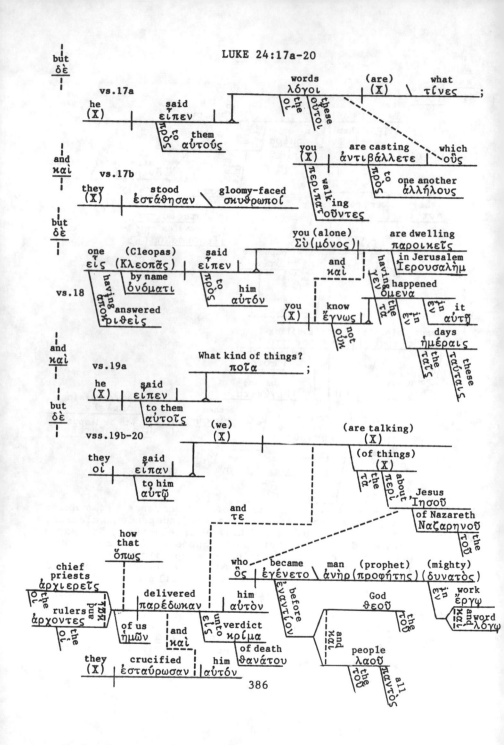

386

LUKE 24:21

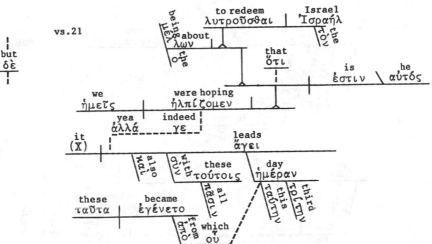

17a develops as complex. Noun clause, "what are these words" is object of independent, "he said." οὓς instills an adjective clause describing "words." Present ἀντιβάλλετε enlivens action by its repeated, "casting back and forth..."

The aorist of the simple 17b halts the action on a point, "they stood..." "Gloomy-faced" is predicate nominative.

Verse 18 displays a complex. Two noun clauses form object of independent εἶπεν. In the diagram μόνος appears in apposition to subject σύ. It could be viewed as predicate adjective. Aorist ἔγνως contrasts with linear "are dwelling."

Since qualitative interrogative ποῖα is what Jesus said in reply to the startled query of the two it infers a full clause. As such it is object of "said." Hence verse 19a is complex.

19b-20 form a complex sentence. Demonstrative use of οἱ is the subject of independent εἶπαν. Object clause, "we are talking..." comes from the context. Relative ὃς is an adjective clause describing "Jesus." Two other object clauses are added by τε which denotes a closer connection than καί. Aorists "delivered" and "crucified" offer facts without describing. As a -μα word κρίμα shows verdict, not a process.

Verse 21 involves a compound-complex sentence. Emphatic ἡμεῖς is subject of imperfect ἐλπίζομεν: "we on our part were hoping continuously..." Declarative ὅτι introduces noun clause object of "were hoping." Though present ἐστιν may be translated "was" following imperfect. Subject of ἐστιν is attributive participle phrase μέλλων, "the one being about to..."

Here ἀλλά "yea" is not adversative. Along with γε and καί it adds emotional effect. The rest of the sentence is difficult to put in acceptable English. The diagram has impersonal subject "it." The idea is clear but the Greek makes rough English. Relative οὗ depicts an adjective clause descriptive of "day."

387

LUKE 24:22-24

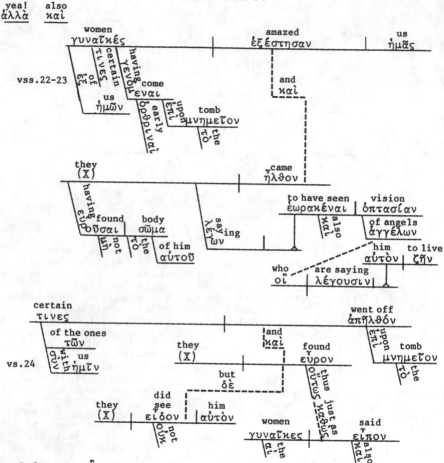

Relative οἵ in 22-23 is subject of adjectival clause which describes "angels." Two infinitive phrases though strictly not clauses are indirect discourse with the force of clauses. Two independent clauses report: "...women amazed us" & "they came." The sentence is structered as compound-complex.

Verse 24 is compound-complex of four clauses. καθὼς adds to οὕτως to introduce adverial comparative clause, "thus just as." Three narrative aorists supply verbs for independent clauses, "went off" "found" and "did not see." Literally ἐπί = "upon." It may mean, as here, "to" the tomb. τῶν modifying τινες offers an ellipsis for "of the ones." The entire phrase including σὺν reads, "of the ones with us," describing τινες.

388

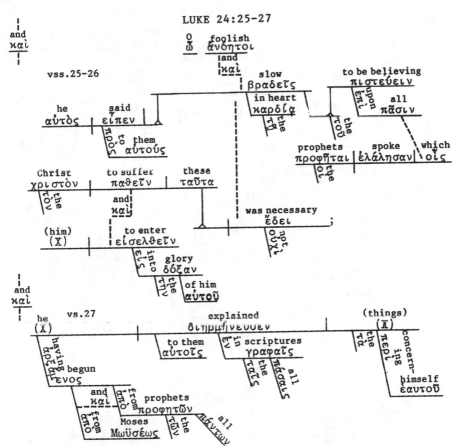

In the complex of vss.25-26 two full noun clauses follow the independent "he said." But the vocative adjectives ἀνόητοι and βραδεῖς serve as an elliptical clause, object of "said" of the independent. By its presence αὐτός gives distinct prominence to what "he" said. As an adjective clause οἷς expands and limits the "all" to that "which the prophets spoke." The full object clause, with ἔδει as verb, has a compound subject of two infinitive phrases each with accusative of general reference. ἔδει is imperfect of δεῖ indicating <u>logical</u> necessity.

Verse 27 structures a simple sentence: "he explained..." The "explaining" obviously continued over a lengthy period yet Luke uses aorist. He thus condenses the action to a focused point. It is the <u>fact</u>, not the movement, that Luke wants his reader to envision. Circumstantial participle ἀρξάμενος reveals point of departure. ἀπό with ablatives suggest the source from which!

389

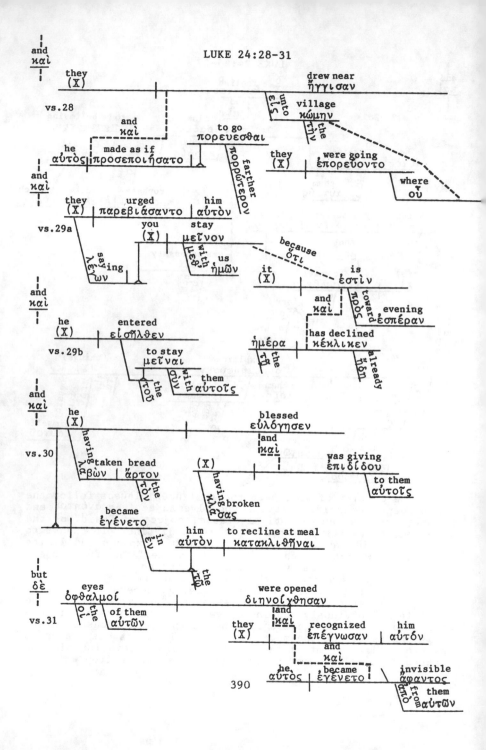

LUKE 24:28-31

390

LUKE 24:32

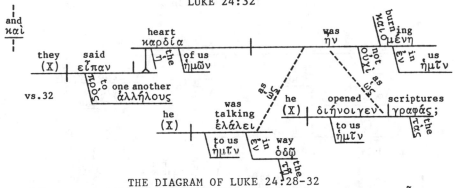

THE DIAGRAM OF LUKE 24:28-32

Verse 28 exhibits a compound-complex sentence. Adverb οὗ is modifying ἐπορεύοντο denoting where. Yet it inserts adjectival clause identifying "village." Incisive αὐτὸς adds distinctive force to the subject of the aorist of προσποιέω "to act as though," "to pretend." In verse 29a "you stay" is object of present participle "saying." μένω in its Actionsart is linear. Yet here in aorist imperative μεῖνον the action is focused to a point. ὅτι signals two adverb causal clauses: "because it is toward evening and the day has already declined." Perfect κέκλικεν signifies a fixed result.

29b unfolds a simple sentence, "he entered..." τοῦ with infinitive expresses purpose.

In the complex sentence of verse 30 aorist ἐγένετο "became" is sole verb of the independent clause. Yet a compound subject of two noun clauses demonstrates what "came to pass." Contrast between the aorist "blessed" and distributive imperfect "was giving" is to be noted, a single act versus repeated acts.

The result of his breaking bread is stated in three clauses of the compound sentence of verse 31. All verbs are aorists. The aorist passive διηνοίχθησαν is the same word as in vs. 32, "he opened the scriptures" and in vs. 45, "he opened their minds..." See below for force of preposition in composition.

Four clauses furnish the building material which structures the complex sentence of verse 32. "They said" forms the independent element. The noun-object clause, using periphrastic imperfect, bursts with excited feeling, "our heart was burning in us, wasn't it?" This negative expects "yes" for an answer. Both ὡς clauses are adverbial of time "while." Note contrasting verbs, aorist "opened" to show the fact; imperfect ἐλάλει tells of the ongoing discourse. Perfective use of preposition διά on verb "opened" means that he "thoroughly opened." Whenever a preposition in composition performs with "perfective" function it intensifies the action in the simple verb root. Whatever made their eyes "holden" was no longer present. Their eyes were completely clear in vision now.

391

LUKE 24:33-36

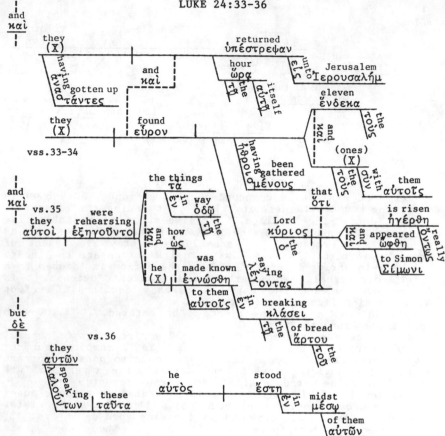

The sentence of 33-34 is compound-complex. Two independent ideas state: what the "two" <u>did</u> and what they <u>found</u>: "they returned" and "they found the eleven..." <u>When</u> they did it was that "very hour." They found the "eleven and the ones with them assembled." The growing conviction of Christ's rising is in the ὅτι noun clause, object of "saying." He "really" has risen.

The complex sentence of 35 has intensive subject αὐτοι. Imperfect ἐξηγοῦντο graphically sketches the drama of the "two" meeting with the Christ on "the way" and his "breaking of bread." ὡς displays dependent noun clause. It is one prong of the compound object of the main verb "were rehearsing."

The simple sentence of 36 is sudden and dramatic in effect. After genitive absolute, "they saying..." "<u>he</u> stood in their midst." Personal demonstration is the way to remove doubt. That which <u>they</u> were explaining <u>he</u> evidenced.

LUKE 24:37-39

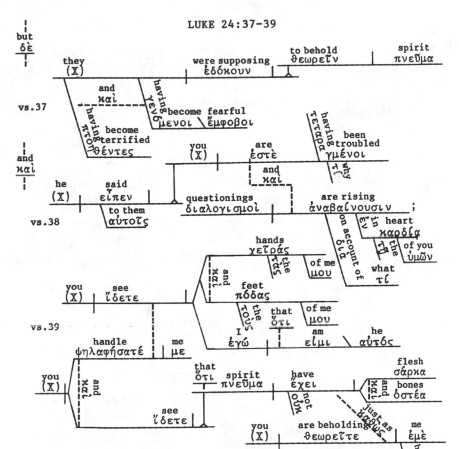

The above sentences are classified as: (37)simple,
(38)complex of three clauses, and (39)five-clause compound-complex. In 37 the aorist participles reckon the
point at which emotions displaced reason. Thus "they were
supposing..." δοκέω is subjective! They "seemed" to see.
Emotion is vital to motivate; less so for thought.

After independent "he said" Jesus, in 38, gives two ongoing
questions each prompted by their fear. ἀναβαίνουσιν is linear
action present thus enlivening the descriptive effect.

Imperative ἴδετε is in both independent clauses of verse 39
along with "handle." ψηλαφάω suggests a "touch" that involves
critical investigating. Object of the first ἴδετε is the
couplet "hands and feet" plus ὅτι noun clause, "I am he." A
2nd ὅτι clause is another object. And from it stems "just
as" adverbial clause of comparison. No article with πνεῦμα in
37 and 39 suggests quality.

393

LUKE 24:41-45

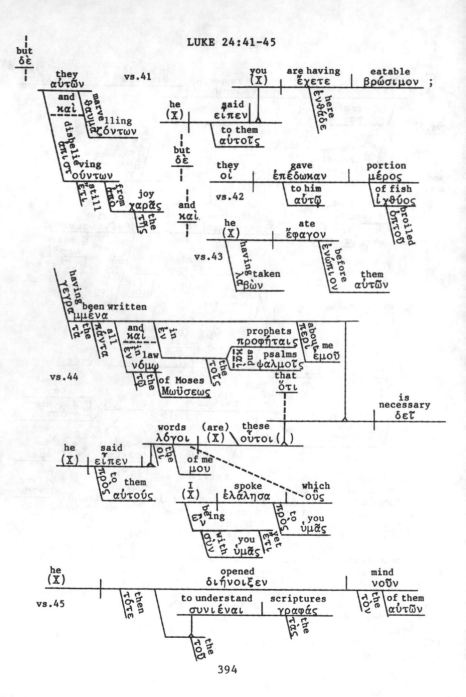

THE DIAGRAM OF LUKE 24:41-45

The sentence of verse 41 shapes itself as complex. Genitive absolute begins the thought of the sentence. The term absolute expresses the fact of its grammatical gap from the rest of the sentence. Yet its thought is suffiently connected that it still is part of the sentence. It is psychologically united if not grammatically. In the diagram its physical placement separates the two parts. Present participles "disbelieving and marvelling" make known the resolving of two ever-present contradictory factors, faith and doubt. ἀπὸ with ablative "from joy" discloses the emotion from which sprang their "disbelieving." Yet even in disbelief they were "marvelling" which suggests the presence of belief. Present tenses suggest continuous believing and continuous marvelling.

In the two full clauses Jesus implies a test by which doubt may be removed. Object of independent "said" is noun clause inquiring, "Are you having here anything eatable?"

The simple sentence of verse 42 answers his query. Subject is demonstrative use of article οἱ. Narrative aorist ἐπέδωκαν reports a fact with no description.

Another simple sentence demonstrates his response to their answer, "Having taken, he ate (it) before them." ἔφαγον is narrative aorist of fact. Irregular preposition ἐνώπιον means "in the sight of." He offers empirical experiential evidence.

Verse 44 engenders a rather involved complex sentence. It contains four full clauses plus a lengthy participial phrase. Upon independent "he said" route the dependent parts. Article οἱ assures that λόγοι is subject of noun clause, "the words are these." οὓς begins adjective clause identifying "words" as those "which I spoke..." When he spoke them is seen in present participle phrase "being yet with you."

In apposition to predicate nominative "these" is ὅτι noun clause whose verb is δεῖ "is necessary." It means logical necessity. Attributive perfect participle "having been written" is subject of δεῖ. Its tense insists on "stands written." The "things having been written" stand fixed, permanent. πάντα insures that "all" stands written. ἐν with locatives guarantees the places where it is written.

Only one complete clause appears in verse 45. Thus it is a simple sentence. Perfective use of διά on διήνοιξεν is quite significant. Not only did he get their minds open but he got them thoroughly open. Before his death they rejected even the possibility of Messiah dying. Before his death their addiction to a political, economic, social kingdom put an insurmountable barrier to the necessity of a redemptive death for sin. But now with his death a matter of record they could not deny the fact. He had died! Yet in the face of his manifest resurrection their minds were more flexible to "new" views of the kind of kingdom to which he was calling them. His resurrection unhinged their mind set. Now he was able to open their minds thoroughly.

LUKE 24:46-49

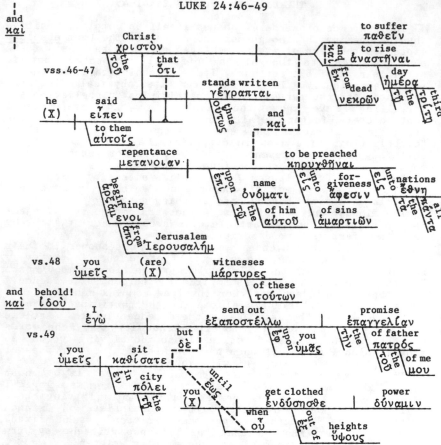

Distinctive features of the complex sentence of 46f include the aorist participial phrase, "beginning from Jerusalem." It is grammatically unrelated but similar to Genitive absolute though Nominative. In thought it connects with infinitive "to be preached." Note three infinitives with suitable accusatives of general reference. They're phrases, not clauses.

The simple sentence of 48 has a distinctive subject ὑμεῖς.

Three clauses in verse 49 form a compound-complex sentence. The independent clauses use emphatic subjects ἐγώ and ὑμεῖς. In the verb καθίσατε "sit" the idea suggests less initiative than "to remain." This is to be a time of "sitting." That is, they are to make themselves dormant, quietly receptive to the "promise of the father."

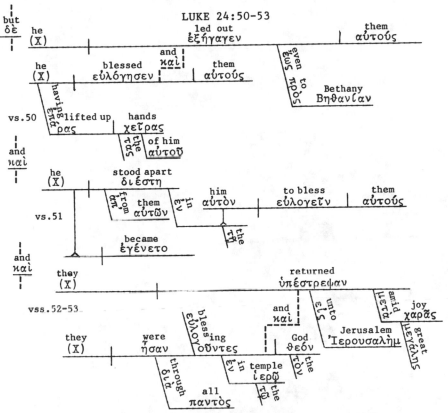

LUKE 24:50-53

The two clauses of verse 50 are both independent hence the
sentence classifies as compound. The use of relative particle
ἕως with preposition πρὸς is rare. When used of _place_ as here
ἕως means "as far as" or "even." Here the phrase is adverb in
function telling _where_ and _how far_ he led them.

Verse 51 structures a complex sentence of two clauses. The
verb ἐγένετο of the independent means "became" or "it came to
pass." Just _what_ came to pass is expressed by the subject,
noun clause, "he stood apart." Aorist διέστη here means "he
departed from them." ἐν τῷ with present infinitive εὐλογεῖν is
temporal, adverbial in function: "while he was blessing them."
This is the familiar infinitive with accusative of general
reference.

The final sentence of Luke appears as a two-clause
compound. Narrative aorist ὑπέστρεψαν reports a fact, they
returned." Periphrastic imperfect ἦσαν εὐλογοῦντες describes
what they went on doing. The διὰ expression "through all" is
adverbial in function. It coneys the idea of "always."

397